THE AUTOB

OF

JAMGÖN KONG ᴜʟ

THE TSADRA FOUNDATION SERIES

published by Snow Lion, an imprint of Shambhala Publications

Tsadra Foundation is a US-based nonprofit organization that contributes to the ongoing development of wisdom and compassion in Western minds by advancing the combined study and practice of Tibetan Buddhism.

Taking its inspiration from the nineteenth-century nonsectarian Tibetan Buddhist scholar and meditation master Jamgön Kongtrul Lodrö Tayé, Tsadra Foundation is named after his hermitage in eastern Tibet, Tsadra Rinchen Drak. The Foundation's various program areas reflect his values of excellence in both scholarship and contemplative practice, and the recognition of their mutual complementarity.

Tsadra Foundation envisions a flourishing community of Western contemplatives and scholar-practitioners who are fully trained in the traditions of Tibetan Buddhism. It is our conviction that, grounded in wisdom and compassion, these individuals will actively enrich the world through their openness and excellence. This publication is a part of Tsadra Foundation's Translation Program, which aims to make authentic and authoritative texts from the Tibetan traditions available in English. The Foundation is honored to present the work of its fellows and grantees, individuals of confirmed contemplative and intellectual integrity; however, their views do not necessarily reflect those of the Foundation.

Tsadra Foundation is delighted to collaborate with Shambhala Publications in making these important texts available in the English language.

THE AUTOBIOGRAPHY
OF
JAMGÖN KONGTRUL

A Gem of Many Colors

Jamgön Kongtrul Lodrö Thayé

Translated by
Richard Barron (Chökyi Nyima)

SNOW LION

Snow Lion
An imprint of Shambhala Publications, Inc.
2129 13th Street
Boulder, Colorado 80302
www.shambhala.com

Original cover design by Rafael Ortet

9 8 7 6 5 4 3 2 1

First Paperback Edition
Printed in United States of America

Shambhala Publications makes every effort to print on acid-free, recycled paper. Snow Lion is distributed worldwide by Penguin Random House, Inc., and its subsidiaries.

The Library of Congress catalogues the hardcover edition as follows:
Koṅ-sprul Blo-gros-mtha'-yas, 1813–1899.
Uniform title: Phyogs med ris med kyi bstan pa la 'dun siṅ dge sbyoṅ gi gzugs. English
Main title: The autobiography of Jamgön Kongtrul: a gem of many colors / Jamgön Kongtrul Lodrö Thay'e; translated by Richard Barron (Chökyi Nyima).

Published/Created: Ithaca, N.Y.: Snow Lion Publications, 2003.
Description: xxii, 549 p. : ill.; 24 cm.
xxii, 549 p.: ill.; 24 cm.
BQ968.O57 A3 2003
ISBN: 978-1-55939-184-9 (hardcover)
ISBN: 978-1-64547-315-2 (paperback; 2023 ed.)

Table of Contents

Acknowledgments

Given the role that Jamgön Kongtrul has played in my life, I feel as though I ought to remember the first time I heard his name mentioned with crystal clarity. But it was certainly very shortly after I became involved in the study and practice of the Tibetan tradition of Buddhism that I began hearing of the accomplishments of this great figure. Until a grant from the Tsadra Foundation permitted me to devote myself to translating these texts concerning Kongtrul's life on a regular basis for the last two years, the work proceeded in fits and starts over a period of more than fifteen years, during which time I have been guided and helped by many people.

First and foremost were my first two gurus—Kalu Rinpoché of the Kagyü School and Dezhung Rinpoché of the Sakya. Although I understood Kalu Rinpoché to be an incarnation of Jamgön Kongtrul even before I developed a personal relationship with him as my teacher, it was a long time before I had any real idea of what that fact signified. In the late 1970s I began studying and practicing Buddhism at Kalu Rinpoché's center in Vancouver, Canada, where I was enormously fortunate to receive teachings from the Sakya master Dezhung Rinpoché, Lungtok Tenpai Nyima. On many of those occasions, Dezhung Rinpoché shared with us his enthusiasm for Kongtrul's work and his boundless respect for the *ri-mé* ideals for which Kongtrul stood. Later on, when Kalu Rinpoché returned to Vancouver, I was able to establish a relationship with him that continues to sustain and inspire me. The most formative influences on me as a young student of the Tibetan tradition of Buddhism were the models of practice and study that Kalu Rinpoché and Dezhung Rinpoché embodied.

From 1976 to 1980, I participated in the first three-year retreat that Kalu Rinpoché conducted for Western students, which took place at his center of Kagyu Ling in the Morvan region of central France. During the retreat, I was impressed again and again with the amount of material we used—*sadhana*s, rituals, instruction manuals, prayers—that had been authored, or at least collected, by Jamgön Kongtrul. I was filled with admiration for his writing style in these works, inspiring when it came to practice and lucid and informative when it came to explanation. Jamgön Kongtrul became something of a personal hero of mine.

During that retreat, we were visited by the Sixteenth Karmapa, Rangjung Rigpai Dorjé, who brought with him the young incarnation of Jamgön Kongtrul—or rather, the incarnation of the incarnation. Following the passing of Jamgön Kongtrul Lodrö Thayé in early 1900, a number of rebirths, or *tulku*s, were recognized in the next few years. The fact that a great master can take rebirth in more than one form at the same time, or that such rebirths can take place not simultaneously, but over a period of years, does not faze the Tibetan Buddhist mind. One of the great Kongtrul's incarnations was Jamgön Kongtrul of Zhechen Monastery, Pema Drimé Lekpai Lodrö (d. 1960), a teacher of Chögyam Trungpa Rinpoché. Another, forever "unofficial" in that he was never formally enthroned, was Kalu Rinpoché (1905-1989). And yet another *tulku*, known as the "form" incarnation (in the Vajrayana schema of the various facets of enlightened being—form, speech, mind, qualities, and activity) was Jamgön Kongtrul of Palpung Monastery, Khyentsé Özer (1904-1953). Khyentsé Özer was the son of the Fifteenth Karmapa, Khakhyap Dorjé, the only Karmapa to marry and have children. The teacher we met in our retreat that day was the Third Jamgön Kongtrul, the rebirth of Palpung Kongtrul Khyentsé Özer.

This was my first meeting with the Third Jamgön Kongtrul, Karma Lodrö Chökyi Seng-gé. Following my retreat, I met him on several occasions during my travels as Kalu Rinpoché's interpreter. Back in Canada, in 1983 I received an unexpected telephone call from Kongtrul Rinpoché. He was visiting Seattle, Washington, a guest at the home of Mrs. Grace McLeod, a staunch patron and student of the Kagyü School of Tibetan Buddhism. Even before my surprise at hearing his voice at the other end of the line had subsided, Rinpoché got straight to the point with characteristic directness. He insisted that I translate the autobiography of his illustrious nineteenth-century predecessor, Jamgön Kongtrul Lodrö Thayé. Aside from his obvious affinity with the master of whom he was a recognized incarnation, Rinpoché felt that the story of this master's life would be of great interest and value to Western students of Tibetan Buddhism. Kongtrul did not gloss over problems or conflicts he encountered during his life, but tended toward a more "warts and all" treatment, more than is the case in many traditional biographies, and Rinpoché felt would make his autobiography more accessible for a modern Western audience. Little realizing at the time just how long a commitment I was making, I agreed to undertake the project. Kongtrul Rinpoché's tragic and untimely death in an automobile accident in India in 1992 deprived the Kagyü School of one of its finest flowers, and the world of a truly spiritual being. I had the honor of receiving teachings from Jamgön Kongtrul Rinpoché and serving as his translator on a number of occasions, and I am always touched to recall the great kindness he showed me at each of our meetings. Although this telephone conversation was not our last contact, for me it remains one of the most significant of our meetings, so I feel a real sense of accomplishment in seeing this translation finally come out in print.

I wish to acknowledge the Tsadra Foundation and its directors, Eric Colombel and Anthony S. Chapman (Lama Drupgyu Tenzin), for their generous support, which has made it possible to see this translation through to completion after so many years. Their vision for the future of the Buddhist teachings in the West has made it a pleasure and an inspiration to work under the Foundation's auspices.

Mr. E. Gene Smith has been another source of help and support. I first read his Introduction to Dr. Lokesh Chandra's edition, *Kongtrul's Encyclopedia of Indo-Tibetan Culture*, in the early days of my involvement with Buddhism. I still find it enormously informative and highly recommend it to anyone interested in Kongtrul and the *ri-mé* movement; the recent publication of Gene's essays (*Among Tibetan Texts: History and Literature of the Himalayan Plateau*) has made this Introduction and some of his other extraordinary contributions widely available, and we are all the richer for that. In addition, Gene's website at www.tbrc.org has proved a gold mine of information, one which I delved into for many hours in the preparation of this book. Although I have yet to meet Gene in person, I am very grateful to him for his help.

All of my teachers have contributed in some way to the project, but I am especially grateful to the Venerable Ringu Tulku, and his remarkable uncle, Döndrup Dorjé, for their help with many of the more difficult or elusive parts of the text. Their help is noted in the endnotes with the notations RT and DD. They not only provided me with much valuable information and insight, but gave me the confidence that I was on the right track in many of the more obscure passages. I can only hope that my efforts have done justice to their time and patience.

Lastly, I want to express my thanks to Sidney Piburn and the staff of Snow

Lion Publications, to my editor Steve Rhodes for his patience with a neophyte in the strange land of book publishing, and to my wife Jeanne for all her support and encouragement.

Foreword

If one wants to get a complete picture of Tibetan Buddhism as a whole, especially from an inner perspective, I think there is no book more important to read than *The Autobiography of Jamgön Kongtrul the Great.* This is the autobiography of a yogi who studied, practiced, and found the essence of each and every spiritual path in Tibet. Jamgön Kongtrul was a true saint, a great scholar, an exemplary teacher, a renowned physician, a peacemaker, and one of the most prolific writers of Tibet. The Five Great Treasuries of Kongtrul, which comprise over one hundred volumes of a thousand pages each, enshrine all the wisdom of Tibet. It is so very easy to see that if he did not compile, transmit, and publish these teachings, most of them would have been lost during the recent turmoil in Tibet.

Jamgön Kongtrul's greatest contribution, though, is seen as being the *Ri-mé* movement that he and Jamyang Khyentsé Wangpo revived, a movement that is actually the essence of the Buddhist approach. The *Ri-mé* movement did not mean the introduction of another school or lineage, but an approach where one followed one's own tradition, while at the same time showing respect toward other traditions and trying to learn from them.

I am overjoyed that Richard Barron has been able to complete his translation of this autobiography. I have no doubt that Richard's mastery of Tibetan language and his deep and vast knowledge (as well as his experience) of Tibetan Buddhism will make this translation an authentic source of information and inspiration.

Ringu Tulku
Gangtok, Sikkim
November 1, 2002

Translator's Note

Every translation brings its own set of problems and compromises. Works such as Kongtrul's accounts of his life and lives were written for people of his time and his cultural background, so there is the implicit assumption that an educated readership among his peers would understand the implications of the statements and observations he made. The same assumption cannot be made about an educated English-speaking readership. Jamgön Kongtrul's writing style is one that makes demands on his readership, for ideally it requires both a shared cultural heritage and a broad education in all aspects of Tibetan religious culture. I have tried to make the text accessible, hopefully without oversimplifying it. If a particular idiom or expression is used many times over, or would sound too strange if translated literally, I have taken the liberty that all translators take, and aimed for readability. Nevertheless, I have tried to preserve some of the flavor of the honorific forms found in the Tibetan language. If some of my endnotes seem too simplistic, it is because I feel it is still too early for me to assume that all readers will know what the author assumed they would. But while some translations (and translators) are more accurate, other less—and some may even surpass the original—a translation is never "spot on," but always and forever what, in the final analysis, is one person's aesthetic call (a sobering thought).

On this note, I have chosen to translate the titles of works into English, in the hope that this will give the reader unfamiliar with the Sanskrit or Tibetan titles of many standard works at least some idea as to the significance of the texts Kongtrul cites or mentions. Faced with the possibility of overburdening the text with too much detail, I have perhaps erred in the other direction and provided too little, but my primary intent has always been to help Kongtrul tell his story. At the same time, I have kept certain key terms in Sanskrit or Tibetan; perhaps I am more timid than some in this respect, in not attempting to render these terms in English, but I have great confidence in the English language to absorb new concepts and feel that English-speaking readers will develop associations over time and in context. My personal preference is to use the Tibetan version of a term only if there is no demonstrable equivalent in Sanskrit; I personally find the latter language easier to phoneticize and there is some merit to the argument that if a term was originally Indian in origin, using the Sanskrit places it closer to its roots. Personal names are in the languages their owners would have used, despite the fact that the Tibetans almost always translated Sanskrit names. I am not yet ready to make the leap to translating names from Sanskrit or Tibetan into English, any more than I am to translate my given names, Richard John (which are, respectively, Teutonic and Hebrew in origin), to Stern King-Grace of God. But the whole issue remains one of amiable contention among scholars and translators.

There are as many systems of phoneticization as there are translators, and I have yet to find a system that is entirely satisfactory, including my own. Aside from entries in the Bibliography, I have tried to render Sanskrit and Tibetan words in forms that allow most readers to approximate the sound of the words in the original languages as closely as is required for a work of this nature, where the emphasis is on the story line, rather than on precise academic details. Anything more precise or academic would overcomplicate the issue. Having said that, I would note that I have decided (largely in deference to established usage in other English translations) to retain the aspirate letters *th* and *ph*, which are pronounced in both Sanskrit and Tibetan as "hard" letters (as in boat*h*ouse or cup*h*ook), not as soft fricatives (as in wea*th*er or tele*ph*one).

Two editions of the texts were consulted in the preparation of this translation. The original draft was based on the Palpung woodblock prints, published in a large Western-style book format by Kandro of Bir, India, in 1973. All the folio numbers in the three texts refer to this edition. I discovered the second source quite serendipitously in 1999, in a bookstore on the Barkhor, the circumambulation road surrounding the Jokhang temple in Lhasa. Among the wealth of newly published material, a bibliophile's delight, was a paperback edition of a book published as *Kong sprul Yon tan rgya mtsho'i rnam thar*, that is, *The Biography of Kongtrul Yönten Gyatso*. It includes the three texts translated in this volume, as well as Nesar Tashi Chöphel's index of Kongtrul's collected works. Although there are a number of typographical errors in this new edition, it proved useful in more than a few places, where the original woodblock was unclear or corrupt.

Translator's Introduction

When there is such an overwhelming range of actual teachings that those who are interested in practicing (or simply interested in) the Buddhist path might study, why read a biographical account? Throughout history, Buddhist masters and other practitioners have devoted much time and energy to recording the deeds of former generations. The great pioneer Tibetologist, Professor Giuseppe Tucci, wrote, "Tibetans show a particular interest, if not precisely a great accuracy, in recording facts."[1] The standard reason the Tibetan tradition gives for reading biographies is that these accounts of the lives lived, and examples set, by figures in the past inspire our own faith. In the case of Jamgön Kongtrul, we have the life example of someone who rose from very humble origins to change the course of his country's history, not through the wielding of political power (although he came to have such power), but by his staunch and uncompromising adherence to the values of tolerance, understanding, and personal integrity in a world that, like our own, was often trying to undermine those qualities.

The approach of Westerners to traditional biographies can fall into either of two pitfalls. On the one hand, some may see these accounts as highly idealized and almost too good to be true; on the other hand, others may have rather too naïve a view of traditional Tibetan religious culture. Kongtrul describes the case of Kuntrul, a Kagyü *tulku* (albeit a minor one), who took his grudge against Kongtrul's guru Situ Rinpoché, Pema Nyinjé Wangpo, to such lengths that he tried to have Kongtrul killed in retaliation. We have only to read of such events to realize that, like people everywhere, Tibetans were and are only human after all. Rather than presenting a rosy vision of everything, Kongtrul takes as his theme that of "dignity in the face of adversity." His life and writings are full of hope and inspiration, but he does not gloss over the hard times.

Jamgön Kongtrul is famous as one of the principal figures in the nineteenth-century revival known as the *ri-mé*, or nonsectarian, movement. The term has gained some currency among followers of Tibetan traditions of Buddhism in Western countries, but an accurate understanding of what the *ri-mé* masters themselves envisaged is still a bit elusive. I have often felt that people use the term as a lofty-sounding title for their own specific approach, or attempt to mix all kinds of spiritual paths and techniques together in the name of so-called ecumenicism. My first teacher, Kalu Rinpoché, was himself by training a product of the *ri-mé* approach and someone respected by all lineages. Rinpoché was a rebirth of Kongtrul, although he was never formally recognized as such; in his autobiography (*The Chariot for Traveling the Path to Freedom: The Life Story of Kalu Rinpoché*), he recounts how his father elected to educate Rinpoché himself, instead of sending him to Palpung Monastery to be trained. In his teens, Rinpoché undertook a three-year retreat in the center founded by his illustrious predecessor, and following the program that the previous Kongtrul had developed. During the time I had the honor to serve as his interpreter (from 1980 to 1983), Kalu Rinpoché often addressed the *ri-mé* model, either in the context of a lecture or in response to a question from someone in the audience. He would use the metaphor of people mixing all kinds of foods inappropriately and at random on their plate. His point was that too simplistic an approach to the *ri-mé* ideal would result in a similarly unappetizing result.

In the mid 1980s, I had the opportunity to interpret a public talk given by the late Jamgön Kongtrul Rinpoché in Victoria, British Columbia, Canada. During that evening, Rinpoché spoke of the *ri-mé* approach. He defined this quite succinctly: "To adopt the *ri-mé* approach means to follow your own chosen path with dedication, while maintaining respect and tolerance for all other valid choices." The operative word here is "valid"; what is meant is not a blanket acceptance of anyone's doctrines. A *khenpo* of the Nyingma School recently remarked to me, "We are to maintain a pure outlook toward all other beings, but not necessarily toward their opinions." This is anything but a sloppy approach. In insisting on the freedom for everyone to choose a spiritual path, and on the validity of all authentic alternatives, the *ri-mé* approach is broadminded, avoiding the all-too-common pitfall of exclusivism, but does not promote simplistic beliefs. Our prejudices concerning spiritual matters may come from issues that are personal, ideological, or cultural, but regardless of their origin, these prejudices can place severe limits on our own ability to grow spiritually. Jamgön Kongtrul also stressed, in that evening talk, that it is important for the values of Buddhism to imbue a culture, not for those of a culture to imbue Buddhism. The *ri-mé* approach was not intended to serve some other agenda, but to provide a context for honoring the contemplative life in all of its manifestations.

Jamgön Kongtrul Lodrö Thayé was born into a culture that had been host to the Buddhist teachings for a millennium. Throughout its long history, the Tibetan tradition of Buddhism has seen many periods of mutual tolerance, particularly in the early stages of its development, when there was much interaction between the schools. We find accounts of many individuals who studied with masters of all schools and who in turn taught students from all schools. But there have been just as many times when political rivalries and power struggles led to sectarian polemic and even outright hostility. In a few cases, entire schools were suppressed. It would be bad enough if the grounds in such cases were (as claimed) doctrinal, in the name of keeping the teachings pure, but all too often a more mundane purpose was bring served. For people interested in more details on this subject, I can highly recommend Chapter 17 ("'Jam mgon Kong sprul and the Nonsectarian Movement") in Gene Smith's excellent book, *Among Tibetan Texts: History and Literature of the Himalayan Plateau*. The extent to which Buddhism imbued Tibetan culture over the centuries is nothing short of remarkable, but the extent to which that culture imbued the Buddhist teachings often resulted in unfortunate consequences.

An ongoing issue in a tradition like that of Tibetan Buddhism is the role of study *vis-à-vis* practice. There is a well-known saying that someone who tries to practice without first studying is like a blind person wandering on a vast plain, unsure of his or her direction, while someone who studies but never practices is like someone without arms, who can see the top of the cliff but is unable to climb up to it. These are obviously extreme cases, but the fact that they require mention demonstrates that tendencies toward such extremes exist in us to some degree. Without the balancing element of authentic contemplative practice, intellectual knowledge of the teachings in itself does not free the mind in the way the teachings intend that it be. In the century preceding the rise of Kongtrul and his fellow *ri-mé* masters, there had been a growing tendency in Tibet toward codification of the teachings of various schools, and this had led to rigidity of thinking and religious controversy almost for it own sake. Relations between the schools were often strained.

Kongtrul himself encountered intolerance in various forms throughout his life. After a childhood spent mastering the teachings of the pre-Buddhist tradition of Bön, he began his Buddhist training at the age of sixteen, when he entered the Nyingma monastery of Zhechen. There he came under the guidance of the Öntrul incarnation of that institution, Jamgön Gyurmé Thutop Namgyal, who also taught the famous Dza Paltrul Rinpoché. The devotion that the young man had for this master is evident in his descriptions of their relationship. Once he had reached his majority, the future Kongtrul received full monastic ordination from Zhechen Öntrul. "On that occasion," he writes, "I had an appropriate understanding of the symbolic meaning of what was going on, and a feeling of certainty that I had really received it, and all of it seemed very appropriate." [*Autobiography*, fol. 16.a.5] It was also at Zhechen that he had experienced his first glimpse of the nature of his mind—an enormously significant event for someone committed to the life of a contemplative.

Just over a year after his ordination, Kongtrul was conscripted by the more powerful Palpung administration and forced to move to that monastery. It was deemed necessary for him to formally change his affiliation, to the point that he was required to take his ordination again, this time from the Ninth Situ Rinpoché, Pema Nyinjé Wangpo, the ruling incarnation of Palpung Monastery. His distress at this heavy-handed treatment was compounded when he was recognized as a *tulku* officially aligned with Palpung, further ensuring that he would remain with this institution. Perhaps the newly-appointed Kongtrul could hear the advice of his first Buddhist master, Jamgön Gyurmé Thutop Namgyal, ringing in his ears:

> When I went to say goodbye to my spiritual master, . . . [h]e gave me very instructive advice, saying, "Always focus your mind, rely on your mindfulness and alertness, and don't be sectarian." [*Autobiography*, fol. 17.a.5-6]

We cannot overestimate the impact of such events on a sensitive and insightful mind like Kongtrul's. While he carried out his duties and responsibilities at Palpung faithfully, in less than ten years Kongtrul had obtained Situ Rinpoché's reluctant permission to establish Kunzang Dechen Ösel Ling, the hermitage near Palpung that would serve as Kongtrul's personal residence and the center for his activities for the rest of his life. It was when he met Jamyang Khyentsé Wangpo in 1840 that Kongtrul found the kindred spirit who, more than any other mentor, would foster in him a profound respect for all the spiritual traditions available in Tibet, including the Bön tradition that had been his birthright. Throughout his life Kongtrul managed to balance his commitments to a specific school and structure with his love for all manifestations of the spiritual life that existed in his culture, and his desire to preserve and promote these methods.

Kongtrul and his contemporaries did not so much invent the *ri-mé* ideal as rediscover it. Indeed, Kongtrul saw himself as the inheritor of a legacy that went back centuries. In his accounts of his past lives, the themes that emerge are those of tolerance, intelligent investigation, and a commitment to the authentic principles of spiritual development. As a writer and a compiler of large collections of texts, Kongtrul was a synthesist, always trying to emphasize the common ground shared by various traditions and interpretations. In these endeavors he was not unique. Again and again in Tibetan history, there have been great masters who have risen above dogmatic limitations and emphasized the fundamental principles underlying all truly authentic spiritual traditions. Such "*ri-mé* masters," if we may call them this, have always emphasized the need for study as a necessary basis for practice, but their approach to study was one of returning to the basics, rather than becoming ensnared in abstruse nit-picking over the finer points of logic and sophistry. Kongtrul and his associates were entirely in agreement with this approach. As Gene Smith writes:

> The nonsectarian tradition emphasized a different aspect of religious education . . . The trend was toward simplification. . . . [which] it was felt, would eliminate many controversies that arose through variant expositions of the same texts by different Tibetan exegetes. There was a parallel tendency to reject that theory that to identify and name the opponent [in philosophical debate] is paramount to defeating him. In other words, many of the great nonsectarian teachers rejected labels. [*Among Tibetan Texts: History and Literature of the Himalayan Plateau*, p. 246] [square brackets mine].

The legacy left by Jamgön Kongtrul is still with us. His Five Treasuries constitute an extraordinary body of literature; in compiling these collections, Jamgön Kongtrul ensured that teachings that might otherwise have died out have been brought back "into the mainstream." As well, Kongtrul's incarnations continue to manifest among us. I feel fortunate to have lived to see two of my teachers reborn to carry the *ri-mé* ideals on into the future—Chökyi Nyima, the rebirth of the Third Jamgön Kongtrul recognized in 1996 by the Seventeenth Karmapa, Urgyen Thrinlé Dorjé; and Kalu Yangsi, the rebirth of Kalu Rinpoché and another "Third Jamgön Kongtrul," who was born in 1990. They are tangible expressions of the aspiration and vision of this great master. It is my hope that this account of the life of one who, perhaps more than any other, defined this vision will contribute to an increase of mutual understanding and open-mindedness between the various schools of spiritual thought and practice (Buddhist and otherwise) that are emerging in the West.

Richard Barron
Weaverville, CA
November 27, 2002

1. *Tibetan Painted Scrolls,* vol. 1, p. 139.

A Gem of Many Colors

The Autobiography of Jamgön Kongtrul the Great,
an account of the origins of Lodrö Thayé,
the mere reflection of a virtuous practitioner,
who has unbiased and nonsectarian respect
for all teachings

Jamgön Kongtrul Lodrö Thayé

(1813-1900)

Introductory Verses of Homage

[1b] With great devotion, I pay homage and take refuge at the feet of you, my glorious and holy spiritual masters, who are imbued with unconditional and innate compassion and are indistinguishable from my special chosen deities. [2a] I pray that in all lifetimes you care for me out of your great compassion, and that you grant your blessings so that all my thoughts, words, and deeds may be perfected as a vast array of noble conduct.

[2b]   In the vault of the sky that is the peace of complete freedom, the orb
        of the sun of timeless awareness radiates,
            so that the rays of innate compassion shine everywhere in the world,
            felt in accordance with one's devoted intent.
[3a]   For one such as I, darkness is instantly dispelled and the lotus of my
            mind blossoms to embrace the two kinds of knowledge.[1]

I bow at the feet of my glorious spiritual master, powerful
    Vajradhara,[2] the actual embodiment of all buddhas.

[3b]   Caring for me to the utmost with your innate compassion in all my
        lifetimes,
you are truly Dorjé Thöthreng Tsal,[3] and the lord of the hundred
    buddha families.
O Pema Wangchen,[4] through the influence of your three secrets[5]
grant your blessings that this work of mine be to good purpose.

The hoped-for result of my prayers is the cloud banks of the golden
    age,
yielding whatever is desired without hindrance.
O most sublime of my special deities, as I pray to you,
grant me the power to benefit others in a consummate way.

The spiritual master, who is a buddha, manifests in forms that guide
    under any means necessary—
as you, Lord Vajra Mahakala,[6] and your lady.
In annihilating obstructive forces with the force of your innate
    compassion,
act as my allies to ensure that my altruism expresses itself fully.

Under the influence of confusion imposed by afflictive emotions,
I, an ordinary mortal being, have experienced the relentless and
    deceptive perceptions of samsara.
I am left without anything worthwhile to say, for I have exhausted
    any hope
that my life example might be associated with even the faintest
    positive hint of that of a holy person.

Having reinforced my ingrained habit patterns for such a long time—
from time without beginning—and being deficient in powerful
    antidotes,
I find my body, speech, and mind enmeshed in a web of confusion
and am unable to provide any marvelous and dramatic account of
    myself.

Nevertheless, my vajra guru said that there would be some purpose
for future generations in my setting down a record
recounting the traces of my one-pointed focus on spiritual practice,
which is due to my previous karma and incidental circumstances.
With his permission, and in response to insistent requests from my
    learned, kind, and devoted students,
[4a]   I have set down what I arrogantly presume to be a gem that can free
        one from bondage,
although its many colors may only provoke amusement in the wise.

INTRODUCTION

In general, the word in Tibetan for "biography" is *namthar*, while in Sanskrit it
is *vimoksha*; these translate as "complete liberation," or "complete freedom."
These terms refer to accounts of individuals who have become completely
liberated in one of several ways. At the very least, such individuals are completely liberated from lower states of rebirth through their totally pure faith.
Those of a middling degree are completely liberated from the ocean of samsara
through their totally pure renunciation. And in the best of cases, due to their
totally pure motivation, individuals become completely free of the two extremes of conditioned existence and peace.[7] In brief, the term applies to any
remarkable story that recounts how someone becomes completely freed from
suffering and its causes, and thus is able to free another's mindstream from
bondage. For those who read or hear of them, the purpose of relating these
kinds of stories is to cause any or all of the three kinds of faith[8] to arise in
their mindstreams. Once faith has arisen, the energy of their particular spiritual potential is awakened. *The Discourse on Planting the Seeds of Liberation* states:

Faith is the doorway that illuminates all the Buddhist teachings.

and

Ananda, apply yourself to faith. This is the request of the Tathagatha.

It is difficult for those who lack good fortune just to hear of the biographies
of buddhas, [4b] bodhisattvas, *shravakas*, and the hosts of spiritually advanced

beings and authentic scholars, accomplished masters, and spiritual mentors who have appeared in India and Tibet. But if they do hear of them, they experience unsurpassable benefit and happiness, in both the short and long term. Therefore, the holy ones of the past were accustomed to explain *The Garland of Rebirths*— the previous lifetimes of the Buddha[9]—as the main text of their public talks. The omniscient Taranatha[10] said, "If people are holy, it follows that wherever they go they leave in their wake an increase of faith and compassion, a diminishing of sectarianism and emotionalism, and people who are more gentle and relaxed by nature. When faith, respect, and compassion diminish; when sectarianism, factionalism, and negative emotions increase; and when people therefore become coarser by nature, given to argumentation and tale-telling and strife—these are signs that someone has been an anti-spiritual influence."

If you contemplate even a small portion of the biographies of holy ones and are able to explain it in a way to make it understandable to others, so that they have at that point even a slight feeling of faith and respect, then you have very definitely achieved a great purpose through planting this positive seed. People who have this meaningful connection are influenced by the compassionate attitude and aspirations of those who are the subjects of these biographies. [5a] The spiritual qualities of such individuals form the actual subject matter that is capable of inspiring that kind of faith. As qualities go, things such as family power and position, political influence, charisma, wealth, or fame have nothing to do with the teachings of the Sage.[11] These are worldly pursuits, which one is encouraged to discard. Instead, the most excellent qualities of the followers of the Victorious One[12] are the discrimination of erudite persons, the experiences and realizations of accomplished masters, and activities that promote the teachings and benefit beings. In these degenerate times, however, these qualities appear to be quite rare. Garwang Chökyi Wangchuk[13] referred to examples from scripture when he said:

> To my way of thinking, while there are many people who claim to be practitioners, I place no faith in their claims if there is no integration of inward practice, outward deportment, and the qualities which arise from these. Nowadays, people claim to be erudite and are full of convincing arguments; they say that they are venerable and have carried the rules of discipline to the limit; and they say that through meditation they are humble and have grown old in mountain retreats.

But they are nothing more than people who have barely put an end to conditioned existence.

There are many who claim that their accomplishment allows them to engage in uncontrived tantric conduct. The Buddha said, "Only I, and those like me, can gauge the measure of an individual," so for all who make such claims I maintain only an appreciation of the sacredness of the circumstances, and I will not [5b] offer any criticism. It is said, "At a certain point, through engaging in uncontrived tantric conduct, one is said to traverse the path of application and come to the path of seeing."[14] A tantric practitioner who is still on the path of application engages in uncontrived conduct in order to make the leap to the path of seeing. Having never had the good fortune to accomplish this, I have had to rely on practice which accords with my appraisal of my own capacity. If one misrepresents oneself as a total renunciant, or a greatly accomplished master, or someone with psychic powers, it is conceivable that there may be some small merit to be gained in the eyes of worldly fools, but it is best when both merit and true qualities can arise together. As long as they haven't arisen together, it is important to apply oneself to developing these qualities.

Therefore, if people have the qualities which are spoken of in the Buddhist teachings, they are worthy of respect and of being considered a spiritual master, regardless of how good or bad they appear to the world. As Avalokiteshvara[15] said:

> Wise people respect qualities, not buddhas or mighty lords and such like. To have respect where there is an absence of qualities is folly, and arises from nonvirtuous karma.

In this way, the victorious ones and their spiritual heirs[16] have strongly emphasized reliance not on individuals, but on the Buddhist teachings or enlightened qualities.

In my case, I have no personal acquaintance with, or experience of, any qualities worthy of praise, in either a spiritual or secular context; [6a] so there are no events to recount which would justify the cost of writing this book. The spiritual and mundane pursuits of those who are mere shadows of practitioners in these degenerate times are so many vague and confused actions, like the shimmering haze seen in the heat of summer. And in the end, the aims accomplished in their activities to benefit themselves and others disappear as a matter of course, like the mists at the beginning of autumn. But if you bring such things to mind even once and assess them, these genuine traces, which form the basis of my account, are at least like the seed of a lotus.

In speaking about my life in part, we can begin with my attainment of the working basis of an unflawed human existence, a well-favored state of leisure. We can then discuss my quite natural encounter with supportive circumstances in the four spheres of activity;[17] my involvement, to the best of my ability, in hearing, contemplating, and meditating on the Buddhist teachings in a proper manner; and the results of these activities, represented by the three spheres of renunciation, erudition, and activity.

BIRTH AND CHILDHOOD

TO BEGIN WITH, the region where I came into existence in this physical body was the middle province of Greater Tibet[18] known as Lingtri, in the middle one of its three departments. This area of Tibet is divided by four great rivers into the famous "six ridges."[19] My birthplace was on the slopes in front of a place called Pema Lhatsé, on the one known as the Zalmogang Ridge, between the two river valleys of the Drichu[20] and the Sharda.[21] One of some twenty-five major regions of eastern Tibet, Pema Lhatsé is known as an environment associated with the principle of the lotus family,[22] as one method of guiding beings. It is one of eight places in which emanations appear to guide beings.

I was born in a place called Rongyap,[23] a small secluded valley, into a household of moderate means. [6b] My nominal father was a lay Bön[24] priest named Sönam Phel, a skilled artisan and a very honest man with real faith and a virtuous mind, who had completed all the preliminary practices (which purify one and develop positive qualities), and who understood very well how to experience the nature of mind through meditation. He was also extremely energetic in the recitation of texts. My mother, Tashi Tso,[25] was a very gentle and patient person by nature, who had very great faith and sacred outlook, and who loved giving away whatever she had. During her lifetime she recited the six-syllable mantra *Om mani padme hum* one hundred and fifty million times.

These two, though they lived together as husband and wife, were without any issue.

My actual clan was said to be the Khyungpo. According to the legendary origins of this clan, an enormous *garuda*[26] emanated from the heart of the teacher of the zenith, Samantabhadra,[27] the King of the Radiant Illumination of Awareness, in order to guide beings. This *garuda* landed on the six-peaked mountain of Gyimshö. This event was witnessed by all the people of the region, and the report spread that a *garuda* had nested on the mountain peak. When the bird flew away, it left in its nest a clutch of four eggs—white, yellow, green, and black. In time these hatched and out came four youths. They went to the top of a high mountain in Puwo,[28] and each one with his prescience discerned his destiny in guiding beings. Three of them settled in the area of Gyimshö and established the white, black, and gold divisions of the Khyungpo clan. The other, Khyungpak Thramo, mounted a turquoise dragon [7a] and journeyed to Gyalrong;[29] from him came those of the primary lineage of Gyalkhyung. The mountain from which the children of the *garuda* went their various ways became known as Khyung Tor La.[30]

From the lineage of these brothers arose the secondary clans of Lhakhyung, Mukhyung, and Khyung Götok; many in these lines in fact attained the pure realm of Khechara.[31] A blood lineage arose, like an unbroken string of jewels, including Gyernam Zutsé and others; and there appeared many masters of awareness, such as Khyungpak Thramo and Dampa Khyung-gom, who attained the various levels of realization. Well-known figures such as Milarepa[32] and Khyungpo Naljor[33] appeared, in accordance with a prophecy that eighty accomplished masters would appear in the "family of the bird."[34] The clan also produced such holders of the secret treasury of profound *terma*s[35] as Tulku Loden Nyingpo,[36] Tokden Tashi Gyaltsen, and others. And there were also many who directed monastic communities with tens of thousand of students, like Rangdrol Lama Lodrö Gyaltsen and the greatly accomplished Shawa Rangdrol. Among all of these, the Gyalkhyung clan produced a branch family line in Rongyap, which descended from a nephew of Nangchen Drakpa Gyaltsen, a great figure who was acclaimed as a lama in Ling.[37] In this erudite and accomplished lineage appeared figures in successive generations such as Khyungpo Lama Namkha Özer, Rinchen Lhundrup, Tenpa Namgyal, Tsulthrim Choklek, and Nyima Tendzin. [7b] However, in later days this lineage has almost exhausted itself due to degenerating times. The successor of this lineage, Khyungpo Lama Yungdrung Tendzin, was reputed to be my actual father.[38]

The following are the circumstances of my birth. In the Female Water Bird Year of the fourteenth sexagesimal cycle [1813-1814],[39] my mother had several excellent dreams, though their import was not clear to her. For instance, she recalled dreaming that a vulture came from the northwest and roosted in her chapel room, and on another occasion that a very large person presented her with silk cloth and a mala of conch shell. Her body was very light, without her feeling the effects of her pregnancy at all, and her complexion was very healthy. I was born easily and without complication at sunrise on the tenth day of the tenth month. For about seven days I would not nurse, and was nourished with melted butter.

For some time in that region, frost, hail, and bad harvests had followed in close succession, so that grain was very scarce and people were going hungry. But that year, by scrounging what grain they could from the storage pots and planting it, the people enjoyed a most excellent harvest, and for the next twelve years there were abundant crops and excellent harvests.

By the time I could crawl, I was very scrupulous about hygiene, and I am told that I controlled my urination. As soon as I knew how to speak, it was said that I uttered many fine figures of speech: some of these I seem to remember myself. At about four years of age, I found a small booklet containing a meditation liturgy of White Manjushri,[40] [8a] and was able to recite it by repeating when someone else recited aloud, pointing at the syllables with my finger. From the time I was able to walk, I would wear a monk's shawl of raw silk, saying that I needed to tie it in a style that I called "Samantabhadra's offering,"[41] which no one else could imitate, wearing this constantly except when I was sleeping. At a certain point I wouldn't wear anything at all made with light colored cloth, but wore what pieces or strips of red material I could find.[42] In my childhood games, I would spend my entire time playing at bestowing empowerments, erecting miniature temples and ancient castles,[43] making *tormas*[44] out of earth, and performing *torma* rituals and *lhasang* ceremonies.[45] When I saw such ritual implements as vajras and bells, I was extremely delighted. So there were many very excellent signs of my connection with and propensity toward the Buddhist teachings. In late spring of the year I turned five, my foster father taught me the alphabet. While I knew the letters merely upon seeing them, I wasn't particularly interested in this, being a child without a long attention span. My sixth and seventh years were both spent in studying how to read, and because I practiced spelling and reading and had at least some motivation, from my eighth year onward I was able to surpass much older readers.

During my third year, the abbot of Menri Monastery in Tsang province,[46] Sönam Lodrö, had come to our region and my mother and father requested him to perform the tonsure ceremony for me. He gave me the name Tendzin Yungdrung,[47] and that became the name by which I was known in my youth. [8b] At this time, one day at sunrise, while I was sitting in a relative's lap, I saw someone coming from a corner of the fields, moving in an easterly direction. He seemed to be a wandering mendicant, carrying in his hands a victory banner encircled by streams of fire above, around, and below it. When I asked, "Who is that over there?," I was told that there was no one there at all. I remembered many previous existences without being able to put a name on them, and many circumstances and situations about which it was difficult to say anything at all with certainty—many joys and sorrows which came to mind both in waking consciousness and in visions. Some of those situations seem actually to have occurred to me later in life, exactly as I had seen them before. Later on, because I and other people were inattentive to things such as food and clothing, which can cause defilement and contamination, these visionary memories were arrested. My intelligence and sharpness of mind also became dulled.[48]

Yungdrung Phuntsok, a *tokden*[49] from the Tardé meditation center,[50] was a person very scrupulous in morals and very skilled at the practices of subtle energy and mind,[51] so that he possessed a degree of prescience. He prophesied to my grandfather and others, "This is a child of a bodhisattva family. He is one who has been touched by the radiance of Orgyen Pema.[52] In the future he will become famous, but at the age of about thirty he will encounter a great obstacle."

My memory is one of having great faith in Orgyen Pema alone and delighting in knowing how to recite the Seven-Line Prayer and in reciting the Vajra Guru mantra.[53] It gave me a great sense of faith to wonder, "When will I be able to meet the lamas who are said to be emanations of Orgyen Pema, masters such as Situ Pema Nyinjé,[54] Dzogchen Pema Rigdzin,[55] [9a] and Möngyal Pema Gyalpo?"[56] Among my childhood friends, I rather arrogantly proclaimed myself to be an emanation of Orgyen Pema as well. From time to time, I would look to the southwest with a strong yearning, wishing to myself that I might come to meet Orgyen Pema. I had very strong fears about the hells, and had waking nightmares about them.

One evening I dreamed that a very radiant lama came in the sky from the northwest toward the northeast, coming to earth in the village where I lived.

He spoke several words of prophecy, and having given me something pretty as a gift, he departed again. In another dream, there appeared someone I was told was Moma Kunshé Thikpo.[57] He cast divinations by knotting some colored threads three times,[58] and by way of interpretation said things such as, "Because the divination fell three times in a very positive manner, it is called a 'great lion'; it is a white lion with a turquoise mane,"[59] and so on in this manner. Finally he said, "From the east, where the sun rises, there will come a friend bearing red flowers." I think at this point that these dreams might have been directing me toward the monasteries of Zhechen and Palpung,[60] which lay to the east of my home.

One evening I dreamed of my grandfather, Ata,[61] and me finding ourselves in one of the hells. We were led through a gateway by a small black-and-white child, around a sort of circular pathway to the right and left, and finally inside a building, where we encountered a very radiant spiritual master who it seemed was Dharmaraja, the Lord of Death. [9b] We had an audience with him, and since my grandfather was reciting prayers, Dharmaraja said, "You are allowed to go on the path to liberation." From the window in front of him a shaft of white light like a rainbow lanced up toward the east, and placing his foot on it, my grandfather turned into a small sphere of white light about the size of my thumb, marked with the syllable A. This shot off out of sight, spinning as it went. I myself remained there, frightened, and following that I dreamed of a number of scenes of hell. On another occasion, I dreamed of going to the holy place of Tsari.[62] At first, my journey was very pleasant, but at a certain point I entered a narrow dark defile from which I eventually emerged into an open space, again quite pleasant. It seems in retrospect that my life turned out much like that.

By the time I had reached ten years of age, I had over a period of time copied out three or four volumes of ritual texts and liturgies as part of my study of calligraphy. Among these, I was especially delighted to find references to recognizing the nature of mind. I used to yearn like a thirsty man longing for water, thinking, "Will I ever meet a spiritual master who will give me instructions on the nature of mind?" Feeling myself poor and weak, I felt unable to offer any kind of thanks to such a spiritual master.

In general, my foster father was very strict. He would not tolerate from me anything but just sitting quietly when I practiced my reading or writing, or when I was sitting in formal ceremonies. At the slightest childish behavior, he would beat and discipline me. I had no freedom to go even out the door unless so ordered. [10a] He would recount many examples of other people who were reckless or greedy, or who drank a lot or stole or lied, and who were finally cast out from the ranks of their fellow men. Then he would scold us children constantly, saying, "When you grow up to be young men, you'll all end up like that." At such times, I would be very hurt, upset, and discouraged, but as I reflect on it later, the fact that I am now at least acceptable in the ranks of human beings is due to the kindness of that old father of mine, and I see him as extremely caring. I also feel that such an honest and wise man is very hard to find nowadays. As for Khyungpo Lama, he was very loving and affectionate toward me, and I on my part was always very glad to see him. Daily he would explain to me how to recognize various deities and so forth. But he passed away during the summer of my seventh year.

In that region there was a small Bön monastery, and everyone followed the Bönpo tradition. From the age of eight or nine, I began performing rituals, reading texts, and reciting liturgies from the Bön tradition. I would automatically memorize passages after reciting them just a few times, and I could perform rituals, make *torma*s, arrange offerings, play the drums and cymbals, and so forth, merely upon seeing these done once. I not only assisted at rituals performed by others, but also went many times to set up and perform them myself. While I had little interest in anything but the popular Bön liturgies, I became very interested in Mishik Dorjé's oral lineage practice focusing on the peaceful and wrathful forms of the Guru.[63] Because of my recitation and performance of this practice, [10b] people would tease me and say, "You're a Buddhist monk!"

The *tokden* lama of Tardé said that I needed to rely on the deity Shridevi,[64] and bestowed an oral transmission for this practice on me. After I performed the longer ritual, the shorter daily recitation, and several other related rituals, I experienced signs in dreams which agreed with those described in the texts of the practice. Once I dreamed that a woman gave me four or five knives without sheaths, and later on it seemed as though this was an indication of some small wisdom developing in me. Around that time, my dreams were very precise and clear. For example, I would know the evening before when a traveler would be arriving the next day.

On one occasion, people were talking of a certain Lama Nyima Özer of eastern Tibet, who was said to be able to recognize and control the dream state, and were considering this quite marvelous. So one evening when going to sleep, I focused my will to bring about this recognition, and it happened that

I did recognize the dream state for what it was. I knew my dream to be a dream, and in that realization the dream faded with me passing off into the east on a white cloud. Although even after that I could recognize my dreams whenever I focused my intent, I did not refine this ability, and these random occurrences did not really seem to serve any purpose.

Several people were requesting instruction from a certain lama on the transference of consciousness[65] found in The Secret Dakini Treasury, so I joined the group. After several practice sessions over about three days, lymph oozed from an eruption on the crown of my head and a stalk of grass could be inserted into it.[66] For some time after this, I repeatedly dreamed of sitting in a cross-legged posture and rising unhampered into the sky. Later on in my life, such excellent dreams and visions [11a] have all faded away like clouds in the sky; this is certainly due to the influence of contaminated or misappropriated offerings. I once fell into a faint outside the shrine of the protective deities belonging to the clan of the administrator of Rongyap, and dreamed of a gathering of many people, muttering among themselves. The year following this dream, the children of the administrator's family, who were brothers, had a falling out and the estate had to be divided.

About this time the administrator of Denchö, Amgön by name, came in the company of the envoy of the Dergé government.[67] As he had a family connection with my old father, he gave me a shawl made of raw silk, saying, "Now you're a lama!," which delighted me. This family with which my father was connected was a very exalted clan of noble lineage, and had produced lamas and monastic administrators generation after generation. For three generations afterward, it became even more prosperous, erecting various religious structures and doing good works in many ways. Nowadays, however, the bloodline has run out and the family fortunes have been taken over by others, so that only the name remains. And this is not an isolated occurrence. In fact, when I reflect on what has happened up until now in this country, and think of the rising and falling and change and reversal which are in the nature of things, these events are just like autumn haze. These events have been natural teachers for me. They have pointed out that there is no substance whatsoever to the happiness and wealth of conditioned existence, that all of it is illusory by nature, that there is only continual change and impermanence without an instant's stability, and that all the activities and concerns we have in our state of confusion are only causes of suffering in samsara. I feel that reflection on these things gave me a very uncontrived attitude of disenchantment and renunciation. [11b]

During the spring of my fourteenth year, my grandfather Ata died. He had recited about two hundred million mantras during his life and was very skilled at maintaining the experience of the nature of his mind. On the day of his cremation ceremony, there was a very clear sky with a whitish rainbow light spreading from east to west. I thought to myself that he had obtained liberation, just as it had occurred in my dream earlier. Before his death, he had hoped very much to complete one hundred repetitions of a particular ritual,[68] but was very discouraged that he could not complete more than eighty. I undertook to make up the remaining twenty, but I was unable to accomplish this, because not long afterward I had to go elsewhere.

From an early age I was extremely interested in painting as well as medicine, and with a very skilled hand I drew pictures of Vairochana[69] and the eight aspects of the Guru.[70] Upon merely hearing of the protective deity Bernakchen,[71] I was delighted. Since the figure was familiar to those of Namgyal Ling,[72] I asked some of them what the attributes of that figure were, and drew Bernakchen in that style. I memorized roughly texts such as *The Discourse on Pulse Diagnosis and Urinalysis,* from the so-called later tantra of the medical sciences.[73] I studied with a doctor named Karma Phuntsok and learned to identify the majority of medicinal herbs that were available.

In a dream one night in my fifteenth year (I'm not certain of the date), I dreamed that Orgyen Rinpoché[74] appeared in the sky, dressed as the king of Sahora,[75] surrounded by a mandala of orange light, the radiance of which was like the rays of the sun. [12a] From him emerged a small ball of light about the size of a hand mirror, and as it touched me I fell into a faint momentarily. When I regained consciousness in my dream, there were several women who said, "Now look up into the sky! The queen of the universe, with a hundred heads and a thousand arms, has come." Thinking that there was no force I could not withstand now, I looked upward to see the sky filled with rainbows, in the midst of which was a somewhat vague form. With that I awoke.

During these times, Tsewang Dorjé Rigdzin[76] was the ruler of Dergé, and the influence of the administrators from the riverbanks was on the rise.[77] Those in control imposed very heavy burdens on their subjects and the nomadic settlements, in the form of various needless punitive measures, so that about one-third of the administrative centers were brought to the point of destitution and the populace was completely impoverished. My own maternal uncle, having enough wealth to stand out in the area, was therefore in a position where others were only trying to steal from and dispute with him. Due to his connection with a third party, he entered into a dispute with the messenger from the house of the chamberlain who was the representative of the Dergé government, and all the districts around suffered great loss because of this. Due to the bad feelings in the wake of these events, the following year when the *gutor* ceremonies[78] were being performed at the local monasteries, the monks and laymen as one body killed all of those who had fallen on them the year before like Mongol hordes.[79] [12b] The following year, the relatives of the slain people inflicted far greater retribution and harsher measures than the envoy had previously in the wake of the original dispute. All families, high and low, without regard for status, were brought to ruin, and even my old father was thrown into prison. The suffering just went on and on. The general situation being so bad, with the heavy taxation and confiscation, my old mother said, "You needn't stay even one more day. You should leave in the face of such bad circumstances, and go to a monastery." She assured me that she would be able to get by somehow. But at that point in time, there was no monastery in our immediate vicinity that really appealed to me.

In the spring of my sixteenth year. I was sent to the place where my old father was imprisoned at Chödé Palace.[80] There, during both the spring and summer, I copied texts and recited prayers. With a chant master from Chamdo,[81] who was a caster of images, I studied the proportions for both drawn and cast images according to the Menri tradition.[82] For a brief time I also studied painting in a rough way.

So this old mother of mine, who was initially and fundamentally kind in giving birth to me in this body, also became the spiritual friend who freed me from entrapment in the life of a householder in samsara and caused me to enter the door of Buddhism. This sort of kindness is very difficult to repay.

Upbringing and Training

FROM A VERY EARLY AGE, I was quite humble and gentle by nature. No matter who ordered me to do something I was very accommodating, whether I could do it or not and whether their ordering me was appropriate or not. Therefore, both the weak and the powerful found me very personable and treated me only with kind affection. At this time in particular, [13a] Tsephel of the Khangsar clan, the chieftain of Chödé, was impressed with me. Toward the end of the summer, he told me that he needed a secretary and accordingly took me with him in the late summer. Traveling through Obshi Ruthok, we passed through the summer encampment of the Dergé government[83] and then continued on to Lhalung Khü and Rudam.[84] There, a lama named Jigmé Losel arrived from Zhechen Monastery. He asked me to explain the history of the Bönpo religion to him, and in response to this request I spoke for some time about the various liturgies and stories I had studied in the Bön tradition. The lama said, "You have a very clear intellect and a very skilled tongue," whereupon the old chieftain[85] added, "Because this fellow has very sharp intelligence, I am thinking of encouraging him to specialize in some field. Which would be most suitable?" The Zhechen lama said that it would be most appropriate to consult with the Öntrul[86] incarnation of Zhechen Monastery to decide which fields of study would be best for me. He arranged a list of texts to be printed for the study of the secular sciences and, after they had been printed up, made a present of them to me. When the Dergé encampment broke up, I was taken in the company of the supervisor who was traveling to Denkhok.[87]

In the ninth month I went out traveling again in the company of Pema from the Khangsar clan. We came to Obshi Ruthok and the supervisor provided me with an introductory letter to the Öntrul incarnation, together with three gifts (including a horse), provisions for several months, and two sets of clothing. With an escort, I then set out from Obshi Ruthok for the meditation center of Zhechen Monastery. On that day there was a great snowfall, which was a very good sign for the journey. [13b] The next day I met the incarnate master, Jamgön[88] Lama Gyurmé Thutop Namgyal,[89] and received his blessing. He sent the envoy back, and placed me under the care of an old lama from the meditation center whose name was Orgyen Paljor. Next, in order to awaken my interest initially, he taught me a system of astrology dealing with the interaction of the five elements,[90] and since I understood it after a single review, he remarked that I had excellent intelligence and then started me on a course of instruction based on *The Mirror of Poetics*.[91]

In all cases such as these, Jamgön Rinpoché would teach a moderately long section during the day, and during the evening I would memorize the source text and review the commentaries. He would examine me the next morning. This was extremely demanding, but by exerting myself as much as I could I impressed him a great deal. While I had to submit to his examination, at that time I had not the slightest knowledge of Buddhism, and so was often at a loss for words. Giving me a copy of the text *The Ocean of Enumerations*,[92] he told me to memorize it and also taught me something about etymology and no-menclature.[93] Other than the lists of technical terms in the text, I didn't actually understand the meaning of all this, and so from time to time I would request instruction from that lord among scholars, the extremely erudite Gyurmé Tendzin,[94] to help me make sense of it all. It was very hard going at the beginning, but I passed my examinations on all three sections of *The Mirror of Poetics*.[95] Following that I memorized the source texts of Tibetan grammar[96] and Jamgön Rinpoché bestowed on me an explanation, based on commentaries, of the histories of Buddhism. [14a] I also would offer my exercises for his inspection.

AT THE BEGINNING of the first month in the Iron Tiger Year [1830-1831], Jamgön Rinpoché bestowed on me the formal authorization[97] for White Manjushri according to the tradition of Mati, and the oral transmission for *Reciting the Names of Manjushri*.[98] After that I performed a meditation and mantra recitation daily without break, and chanted the text *Reciting the Names of Manjushri* once a day. The evening of the transmission I dreamed that a full moon rose directly up into the middle of the sky. The next day we began study of Chandragomin's system of Sanskrit grammar.[99] I memorized the source text and had examinations every morning without interruption on the commentary, as well as drawing exercises. Throughout the summer I was afflicted with illness, and he very kindly bestowed on me the blessing of Black Hayagriva[100] and performed a hundred repetitions of a ritual of purification focusing on the peaceful and wrathful deities.[101]

IN THE SPRING OF the Iron Hare Year [1831-1832], Jamgön Rinpoché received an invitation from the head of Dzong-go Monastery in Ling.[102] He was gone for more than two months, during which time I remained in the monastery. From a lama named Gyurmé Tenphel, who was devoting his life to remaining in retreat and who was deeply realized, I requested a spiritual connection in the form of the empowerments for Supreme Compassion: The Gathering of All Sugatas from the tradition of Mindroling,[103] and The Union of All Rare and Precious Jewels.[104] During the fourth empowerment of Supreme Compassion: The Gathering of All Sugatas, he introduced me to the nature of mind in great detail, using a mirror as a prop, and I gained a very excellent understanding of this. He also gave me the oral transmission and the practical techniques and training for the alchemical techniques[105] from the

Northern Treasures cycle,[106] and I practiced this technique for seven days. During this time, one day at midday I had a vision of a tree of enormous dimensions, [14b] the top and branches fading from sight, and around this tree flew a wonderful bird like a phoenix, spiraling upward.

This particular year, it was reported that in Seng-gé Namdzong,[107] there was a concentration of spiritual energy, making it a holy place where spiritual acts were one hundred thousand times more powerful than elsewhere. And so Kunzang Sang-ngak, a lama from the temple of the protective deities, said to me, "Let's also go on a pilgrimage there."[108] We went on a circumambulation of the mountaintop, and the going was very difficult, due to the north slope being blocked with snow and ice. One day, without having eaten any food, we were going in the afternoon up a small valley leading to a col. We were very exhausted and stopped to rest in the shelter of a large boulder. The lama remarked, "When you're extremely exhausted and fatigued due to hunger and thirst like this, if you rest your mind in the essence of this present moment of awareness, that's all there is to the nature of mind." He sat in the correct posture and began resting his mind in equipoise, and I also began sitting in meditation posture and recognized my awareness as having a lucid quality involving no conceptualization—something I could experience, but did not know how to talk about. I became so certain of this that I did not have to discuss whether or not it was so. In this way, it occurred to me that discussion of the nature, or essence, of the mind, and techniques of focusing the mind, resting in a nonconceptual state, and so forth were meaningless, just empty words; and that it was sufficient simply to guard this direct awareness of utter relaxation, complete and natural. Afterward, my experience of that essence never wavered or changed from this first glimpse.

From this teacher, the tantric scholar Kunzang Sang-ngak, I received instruction on the three vows, and from Gyurmé Tendzin [15a] I received a general explanation of the Seven Treasuries of Longchenpa.[109] At about this time, I became extremely attracted to The Union of All Rare and Precious Jewels, and so putting aside my previous practice of the peaceful and wrathful forms of the Guru, I now recited the *sadhana*[110] from The Union of All Rare and Precious Jewels. Now, whether it was the blessing of this practice or not, one evening in a dream I had the very clear impression and firm sense of identification that I was the Wrathful Guru[111] in the "lone hero" aspect,[112] holding a vajra in my right hand and a ritual *kila* dagger[113] in my left, and that I struck my *kila* into the head of a woman dressed in rags and annihilated her. Whereas previously there had often been signs that I was afflicted by the influences of demons and demonesses, following this dream such signs did not arise again.

On the evening following a feast offering in the temple of Khandro Tsokhang, I dreamed that in the mountains around there were several new spontaneously arisen images of Orgyen Rinpoché and others, and that there were many signs of *terma*s and of doorways to these.[114] Immediately upon Jamgön Rinpoché's return, we completed the instruction on Chandragomin's grammar, and he kindly instructed me in metrics;[115] I even composed several verses. When it came to the two grammar texts entitled *Kalapa* and *The Discourse of Sarasvata*,[116] I received only the basic outlines and standard instructions; since I had previously studied Chandragomin's *Discourse on Grammar*, I understood these two merely by looking at them and did not encounter any real difficulty in comprehending them. I also studied arithmetic, since it was essential for the study of metrics. He also very kindly bestowed on me an overview of the different schools of Buddhist philosophy.

In the eighth month of this year, [15b] I made a very brief visit to the Dergé encampment in Rudam, and in the early morning of the fifteenth day of that month I dreamed of many women saying that Orgyen[117] had come and reciting the prayer called *The Spontaneous Accomplishment of Goals*.[118] Looking into the distance, I saw a canopy of light revolving slowly, its shimmering radiance bathing the surrounding mountainsides. I joined the women in fervent prayer, and we beheld Orgyen dressed as the king of Sahora, and on his head was a white figure—the master of his buddha family.[119] He then faded completely away, from his crossed legs upward, whereupon I awoke.

The next day at the encampment, I requested a spiritual connection—the oral transmission for *The Prayer in Seven Chapters*[120]—from Palden Chögyal, a lama from Jamgön Rinpoché's monastic residence.[121] Then I came back to the meditation center for the completion of my studies, and also practiced for about three weeks using the longevity *sadhana* of the Mindroling tradition, known as *The Innermost Heart of Immortality*. The time that I was staying at this place was also the time during which the venerable Jamgön Lama himself was completing one hundred million recitations of the essence mantra of Supreme Compassion: The Gathering of All Sugatas. I went often as a servant or attendant to various ceremonies, such as the offering ritual for the protective deities and so forth. I learned some of the melodies and chants according to the tradition of Mindroling Monastery, and the venerable lama bestowed a partial instruction for two decorative styles of calligraphy, the *lancha* and *vartu* scripts.[122] He said, "Lama Pema Kalzang is a very excellent calligrapher, so you should study in great detail with him." [16a] Accordingly, I studied calligraphy in the Mindroling tradition, which he said was based on a form of script from eastern India.

With the chant master Gyurmé Chödar I studied the memorization of proportions for painting, and also studied an elegant style of ancient script known as *zabdri*. While I carried none of these things that I started with him through to completion, I did not waste my time uselessly or let myself get distracted, but exerted myself as much as possible in the training.

In the evenings, whenever I could find something with which to fuel a lamp, I would study and reflect on the Seven Treasuries of Longchenpa and other works, and write many outlines to these, until the lamp was exhausted.

DURING THE NEW YEAR'S season of the Water Dragon Year [1832-1833], Jamgön Rinpoché went to his monastic residence[123] at the monastery. That day he said, "I want to conduct a ceremony to confer the complete monastic ordination, and it would be very significant for you to request these vows and follow this lifestyle. If it is necessary for you to take the ordination again from someone else in the future, it would be all right to offer this ordination back."[124] And so he performed the complete ordination of "successfully hearing the three words"[125] for a group of three of us who were spiritual companions. On that occasion, I had an appropriate understanding of the symbolic meaning of what was going on, and a feeling of certainty that I had really received it, and all of it seemed very appropriate. The lineage of the precepts was the tradition of the Early Translation School.[126]

Following this, he gave a very detailed explanation on the practice of the "three bases" in accordance with a manual that he himself had written.[127] Beginning on the eighth day of that month, the Gyaltsap[128] incarnation, his teacher [16b] Pema Kalzang, and I received the oral transmission of the precious Kangyur[129] collection that Rinpoché bestowed on the three of us. And at the very beginning of this transmission, on the day that he was starting *The Discourse of the Fortunate Eon*,[130] the ground was lightly powdered with snowflakes in the forms of flowers. Finishing the Kangyur in about fifty days, he also bestowed the oral transmission for about ten volumes of the Tengyur.[131] He then returned to the meditation center.

When the Gyaltsap incarnation and his teacher also came to the monastic residence, Jamgön Rinpoché spent a long time bestowing the oral transmis-

sions for The Collected Tantras of the Nyingma Tradition;[132] the Seven Treasuries and the Trilogy of Being at Ease by Longchenpa, as well as his miscellaneous works; the retreat manual known as *The Ocean of Certain Meaning* by
Dolpopa;[133] *The Profound Inner Meaning* with autocommentary by Rangjung
Dorjé;[134] the thirteen volumes of The United Intent of the Gurus;[135] the two
volumes of *The Testament of the King;*[136] *The Record of Padma;*[137] the five
chronicles of ancient history;[138] the nine volumes of the collected works of
Jigmé Lingpa;[139] and commentaries on *The Definitive Explanation of the Three
Levels of Ordination.*[140]

We also received, through his kindness, the basic empowerments for the
Eight Commands,[141] as well as for the cycle of peaceful and wrathful deities
from the tradition of Karma Lingpa.[142] He also bestowed the complete ripening empowerments for the collection known as The Noble Wish-Granting
Vase[143] from the Mindroling tradition, and the oral transmissions for the volumes of *sadhana* texts, as well as detailed instructions on those he was familiar
with. He said things such as, "Don't ever forget these. Who knows which one
of you might make a beneficial contribution to the Buddhist teachings?" All of
the advice and words [17a] that he made a point of giving to people, turned out
afterward to be entirely prophetic.

During our stay here, I met a realized lama named Kunzang Sönam, who
had completed one hundred million recitations of each of the essential mantras
for Black Hayagriva of the tradition of Nyang;[144] Vajrasattva;[145] the Mindroling
tradition of Supreme Compassion: The Gathering of All Sugatas; Gartsé; and
Amitabha.[146] From him I received the empowerments for Vajrasattva and *The
Innermost Heart of Immortality*, as well as a "conferral of life force"[147] for
Black Hayagriva. As well, there was a retreatant named Samten who had
completed one billion, five hundred million recitations of the six-syllable
mantra[148] while practicing the *sadhana* of The Gathering of the Innermost
Heart Essence; I also requested the empowerment for this practice. At this
point, because I didn't own anything really valuable, I couldn't find anything to offer for these teachings other than the symbolic support of the
mandala offering.[149]

DURING THE SECOND MONTH of the Water Serpent Year [1833-1834], the
old chieftain said to me, "I'm preparing to depart for Palpung, to build a dor-
mitory for the monks. You should also go to Palpung, so get ready."[150] When
I went to say goodbye to my spiritual master,[151] my mind was filled with deep

affection and attachment to him and my place of residence. As I prostrated to him and was about to take my leave, Jamgön Lama Rinpoché gave me a monk's outer robe made of satin which he himself had worn, a pair of ritual vases, and a text of benediction prayers containing the phrase "an ocean of qualities."[152] These were auspicious signs that he was investing me as a spiritual teacher. He gave me very instructive advice, saying, "Always focus your mind, rely on your mindfulness and alertness, and don't be sectarian." [17b] I went to the seat of the Khangsar clan, where the old chieftain was staying, and immediately afterward we departed for Palpung. The day we arrived at the monastery, snow fell suddenly on the path, and afterward a very warm spring sun shone. These seemed to be omens of a very excellent journey. At the monastery, I offered prostrations to the Öngen[153] incarnation who was staying there. He seemed extremely delighted to see me. The work on building the monastic residence began, and on my part, I requested instruction from a lord among scholars, Lama Tashi Gyal, on calculating astrological charts according to *The Complete Collection of Essentials*.[154] After that, I drew out enough charts to provide a calendar for one year.

The king of Dergé had gone to Lhasa the year before and was now returning, accompanied by Thartsé Rinpoché[155] and his attendants and servants. In the later summer, it was necessary for the old chieftain to go to meet and escort them.[156] I also went along, hoping to make myself useful, if only as a scribe. The old chieftain traveled through Denkhok to Tsikhok. Most of the king's party had arrived safely, but we received much bad news from them. Pema of the Khangsar clan and five others had died in Lhasa of smallpox, and there were some fifty large lumps of silver[157] unaccounted for. But because the old chieftain's mind was extremely spacious, he did not indulge in the slightest sorrow, regret, or loss of faith in the deities. He merely carried out positive acts with whatever he had in hand, by way of inviting and receiving those great lamas who came to that place and arranging for their journeys, and arranging for the reception ceremonies in the various monastic centers. He traveled in the company of the monastic encampment as far as Thra-o Plain.[158] [18a] Then, stopping briefly at his palace at Chödé, he continued on to Dergé Gönchen.[159] Lama Palden Chögyal, who lived in the monastic residence, told me to compose several prayers of praise. He himself made a kind of prophecy to me, saying, "I also was meant to go to Palpung, but went to Palyul[160] first and never made it to Palpung afterward.[161] It would be for the best if you stayed at Palpung."

Immediately after that, the old chieftain returned after having traveled very briefly to Palpung Monastery. I myself was wondering just what use my understanding of all that I had trained in and learned would be at Palpung. Öngen, however, explained to me that it was necessary for me to stay there for some time into the future, and that when the Refuge Lord[162] returned, it was very important for me to request the vows of a fully ordained monk. With this, Öngen bestowed on me a complete set of monastic robes. Although I explained to him the way in which I had received the vows already when I stayed at Zhechen, he spoke very disparagingly of this and said, "It is essential that you request the vows from the Kagyü hierarchs."[163] Öngen went to act as an escort, to receive his refuge lord, Kuzhap Rinpoché,[164] for Situ had journeyed to central Tibet the previous year and was returning this year with another Öntrul incarnation, who had been born in the Lhasa area.

When Öngen first had an audience with Kuzhap Rinpoché at Kyodrak, he offered for his inspection one of my devotional works, an encomium written in a grid-like pattern,[165] which Öngen had told me to write previously. While I had not been capable of doing justice to this, [18b] I had written it simply that the order not be ignored. Öngen also told Kuzhap Rinpoché of my background. Kuzhap Rinpoché listened with great joy, saying, "Yesterday evening, I dreamed of the sun shining; that must have been connected with this. The Khangsar clan has from times past been an exceptional source of patronage, and as the head of the house, Tsephel[166] has sincere altruistic intent and vast faith. Yet again he has made a beneficial contribution to promote the Buddhist teachings."

Shortly thereafter, on the first day of the tenth month Situ Rinpoché and his retinue arrived at Palpung Monastery. I had the very good fortune of meeting his golden visage for the first time. On the sixth day of that month, because there were several people requesting the full ordination, Öngen said to me, "You must take the vows too." Although I repeated that I had previously requested the vows and that they had been bestowed on me by the Öntrul of Zhechen Monastery,[167] he said to me, "You absolutely must request this ordination now. It will suffice for you to offer back the residue of the previous ordination and for me to accept it." But the ceremony of my offering back my former vows never took place.[168] Since in the future it would be a matter of some importance who my fellow participants were, there were several important lamas and *tulkus* who would join me in requesting ordination; so it became impossible for me to avoid being included in the ranks of those receiving the ordination.

Such was the manner in which I received the transmission of the vows according to the tradition of the Great Scholar, which is known as the "tradition of upper Tibet."[169] It was in the great meeting hall of Tashi Temple [19a] at Palpung Thupten Chökhorling Monastery. The offices of abbot and preceptor were carried out simultaneously by that true manifestation of the protector Maitreya, Palden Tendzin Nyinjé Thrinlé Rabgyé Choklé Namdrol Pema Nyinjé Wangpoi Dé.[170] The private preceptor was Öngen Karma Thekchok Tenphel. The one marking the time of the ceremony was the doctor Karma Tsepal. The chant leader, who also explained the symbolism of the ceremony to us, was Karma Khetsün. The one who ensured that a quorum was convened was Lord Karma Thogmé, another of Situ Rinpoché's relatives. These five as a group performed the complete ordination through the successive transmission of the three stages.[171] I was given the ordination name of Karma Ngawang Yönten Gyatso Thrinlé Kunkhyap Pal Zangpo.[172] On this occasion, due to the impression I had that my previous ordination was blocking the experience, I did not feel that I had truly received the ordination.

One day shortly after this, I was given tea and advice in the holy presence.[173] He insistently pointed out to me a Chinese scroll that was hanging there, saying, "Look at that over there! It's the man of long life."[174] I think he was blessing me by setting up auspicious circumstances. He bestowed gifts of a vajra, a bell, and a monk's cassock on me.

During that winter, I memorized all that was immediately necessary for someone practicing in the Karma Kagyü tradition. Because Öngen had a great deal of affection and great hopes for me, he was afraid of losing me to others, and so he explained the situation to Kyabjé Rinpoché,[175] saying, "The Dergé government [19b] may suddenly requisition him as a secretary, or some other such mishap may occur. It's impossible to predict what might happen at any point, so it is important that he be given the title of a *tulku* belonging to our bloc."[176] The suggestion was a timely one, and so it was necessary to give me the title of an incarnation of one of the students from my lord's previous lifetime. However, Pawo Tsuklak Gawa,[177] Karmapa,[178] and Drukchen[179] had already advised Situ Rinpoché against recognizing any of three incarnations—Alo Kunkhyen, Tsewang Kunkhyap,[180] or Tamdrin Gönpo[181]—and if I were given any of these titles, Palpung Monastery would never be able to uphold its claim on me, and official reprisals would result.[182] As a case in point, during the settling of the dispute with the house of Khamba, it had been necessary for Kuntrul to be named suddenly by the steward while in the tribunal, and great obstacles had arisen afterward.[183] In this instance, then, Situ Rinpoché debated what would be the most appropriate course of action. He decided that bestowing the title of a student and attendant during the later part of the previous Situ's life, who had been known as Kongpo Bamteng Tulku, would ensure me sufficient connection. This being the case, his retinue was informed, and from that time forth this title of "Kongtrul" was applied to me.[184]

DURING THE SECOND MONTH of the Wood Horse Year [1834-1835], I was included in the ranks of about seven people who gathered when Situ Rinpoché bestowed the collection called The Precious Source of Sadhanas,[185] and through his grace received the formal authorizations in their entirety. When Öngen said, "It is important for this promising scholar to have a long life," Situ Rinpoché bestowed upon me in detail the empowerment for Ratna Lingpa's[186] Supreme Compassion: The Gathering of Secrets, and [20a] the formal authorization for White Tara in the tradition of Lord Atisha,[187] together with the instruction on the longevity *sadhana*. Henceforth, I practiced these on a daily basis without interruption.

During the third month my refuge lord journeyed with his relatives[188] to Karma Gön Monastery.[189] There he bestowed the oral transmission of the Kangyur to an assembly of many lamas and *tulku*s of all the affiliate branches of Karma Gön. The principal participants were the incarnation of Karma Chagmé[190] and Dzigar Choktrul.[191] He began with *The Discourse of the Fortunate Eon* on the fifteenth day of the fourth month.[192] By the end of the eighth month he had finished everything but the tantra section. During the summer, Öngen had been ill for a long time and during the many intervals when he was indisposed, from Karma Chagmé Tulku I received the empowerment for the peaceful and wrathful aspects (Ratna Lingpa's *sadhana* of enlightened mind), the oral transmissions for the main texts of these two practices, and those for Hayagriva: The Gathering of Secrets and Kila: The Innermost Secret from the "unsurpassable" class.[193] He also bestowed the oral transmissions for the original Karma Chagmé's *Manual for Mountain Retreats* and his definitive instruction on Mahakarunika;[194] for the liturgies of Ratna Lingpa's *sadhana* of enlightened mind, Vajrakila,[195] and other practices; for the *Kingkang* and *Molten Metal*[196] and for two volumes of essential *torma* rituals. From Dzigar Choktrul I received the oral transmissions for the collected works of the Jonang School (the Takten Phuntsoling[197] edition) and the four medical tantras. As well, the incarnation of Pema Karpo[198] [20b] bestowed the transmission for The One

Hundred Instructions of the Jonang School[199] as a triple transmission.[200] In all the morning and evening breaks, from Lhalung Khewang Tenphel I received extensive instructions based on the treatises of Rangjung Dorjé—*The Profound Inner Meaning, The Treatise Distinguishing Ordinary Consciousness from Timeless Awareness,*[201] and *The Treatise on Buddha Nature*[202]—as well as the "Single Intent" teachings of the Drigung Kagyü School. I studied the tables of Chandragomin's *Discourse on Grammar* with several very intelligent people.

In the first days of the ninth month, Situ Rinpoché led the ritual based on the Padmavajra cycle as a memorial for Karma Chagmé Tulku, who had passed away suddenly. One evening (I think it was one week after his death), I dreamed of a room with red doors in which there was a golden throne. Karma Chagmé Tulku came in front of this, looking very robust and radiant. I placed my head against his heart in a gesture of respect. Smiling, he placed both hands on my shoulders, and a very intense warmth pervaded my body, accompanied by some small sense of well-being.

After this, we broke camp at Karma Gön Monastery and returned to Palpung. My refuge lord, having spent several days in his monastic residence, went to the meditation center and bestowed the oral transmission for the tantra section of the Kangyur to Öngen and others. From this time onward until he passed away, some twenty years later, he remained in a very long retreat.

During the winter of this year and both the spring and summer of the next year, I received instruction from the doctor Karma Tsepal, a lord among scholars, [21a] on texts of the medical sciences, including the source tantra, the explanatory tantra, and the tantra of specific instructions. I maintained a daily practice of the source tantra and the *guru sadhana* of Yuthok.[203] In the first part of the winter, I memorized the rituals for the protective deities and later attended the year-end *gutor* ceremonies.

DURING THE FIRST MONTH of the Wood Sheep Year [1835-1836], I undertook a personal retreat[204] focusing on White Manjushri. While the signs in my dreams and so forth were not extremely clear, from this time forth my skill in composition improved. During the second month I received from Öngen the oral transmissions for the tantras of the secret mantra approach[205] and the series of peaceful and wrathful deity practices compiled by the Ninth Karmapa, as well as the empowerment for The Heart Drop of Yuthok.[206]

About this time, in accordance with the usual custom, I presented myself to my refuge lord and asked for some clear indication as to which deity practice would be best for me. He replied that it would be excellent if I took White Tara as my special deity, and undertake to do a personal retreat on this practice. Following his advice, I did a retreat on White Tara according to the tradition of Lord Atisha. During this, I dreamed of sunrises and very excellent harvests, of flying from the rooftops of five or six temples filled with countless *tsa-tsas*,[207] of hearing a voice predict the length of my life span, although I did forget the number of years! On another occasion, trying to recall that number, I dreamed of three stupas[208] of mountainous proportions. The first of these became as big as a mountain, with a white stream flowing down its face. To-gether with some friends, I washed my head and my body and drank the water. [21b] Looking across at the third stupa, I dreamed that half of it had become like sapphire or indigo in color, and that the far side of it simply disappeared far off into space so that the eye couldn't define it.

On another occasion, I dreamed that my refuge lord Vajradhara was seated in the back of a small room, while in the courtyard outside, a woman with great charisma (who seemed to be my lord's secret consort[209]) was sitting in the manner of Maitreya on a small throne.[210] With deep devotion, I touched my head to her feet saying many prayers such as, "I pray to the mother Yeshé Tsogyal."[211]

On another occasion I dreamed I was in my own room, looking just as I did in waking consciousness, and Öngen was saying to me, "I have brought some-thing to give to you." Someone gave me a reliquary box, and opening it I found it filled with many relics. The principal objects seemed to be three skull cups wrapped up in red silk. One, I was told, was from the skull of the great Indian Buddhist scholar Abhayakara.[212] Another was said to be that of a greatly learned and accomplished master, although I was unable to remember clearly who this was the next morning. And I was told that the other was the skull of Sok-ön Rigpai Raldri.[213] Looking inside it, I saw a form of the venerable Tara that had formed naturally in the bone of the skull; her right arm was in the gesture of generosity, but the forearm was slightly unclear, and the thought occurred to me, "This is mine."

In the summer and the autumn, I was poor and had few possessions that I could use as offerings. [22a] Nevertheless, encouraged by directives from my venerable refuge lord, Öngen Choktrul Rinpoché[214] showed his great affection and concern for both the newly arrived Öntrul and me. He bestowed on us the empowerments for the five deity mandalas of Vajravarahi and Chakrasamvara, for the nine deity mandala of Jinasagara, for the Sarvavid form of Vairochana, for Akshobhya,[215] for the nine deity mandala of Amitayus,[216] and for the *guru sadhana* of Karma Pakshi.[217] He also bestowed the oral transmissions for all the available editions published of the major and minor mandalas of the Karma Kagyü tradition, the book of standard Kagyü prayers and liturgies, the rituals focusing on the protective deities, and so forth. He also bestowed the empowerments and instructions for the Zurmang lineage of the Severance teachings.[218] In private, he graciously bestowed on me the detailed instructions for doing retreats on these practices; the extensive, intermediate, and abridged manuals on Mahamudra;[219] and instructions on the Six Yogas.[220]

In the ninth month, on the holy day commemorating the Buddha's descent from the gods' realm,[221] we were performing the *nyung-né* fasting ritual according to the tradition of Shri.[222] On the evening of the day of the main part of the ritual, I dreamed of a large and elegant pleasure grove, within which was the Teacher, the Lord of Sages.[223] His body was the color of gold, blazing with light, and his hair was a deep dark blue, like jet. The lower part of his body was not really visible, seated as he was in the pleasure grove, but his body was the height of a two-story building. I dreamed that I and many other people came into his presence and bowed to him with faith.

Following that, one evening I dreamed of an enormous building, seemingly limitless in size. I circled it in a counterclockwise direction, and found an extremely large stupa made of gold and copper. Mounting the steps to this stupa, I began circumambulating it in a clockwise direction. When I reached the alcove in the spherical body of the stupa, I beheld an image of Guhyapati,[224] with a form of Rechungpa crowning his head. [22b] When I circled around to the left side of this, the stupa seemed as though it were made of clay, with a cavity bored into the center of the spherical body. I put my hand into this and pulled out many manuscripts, such as *The Secret of Timeless Awareness*, which were written on yellow scrolls.[225] Next, I went to a hillside where there were many black yurts, large and small. I said to myself, "Since this is a dream, this must be a sign of some kind of negative influence affecting me." I had a very strong impression, from the very depths of my heart, that I was Yön-gé Ternyön,[226] and began stamping and leaping on top of these tents. I actually seemed to become Dorjé Drollö[227] at that point. As I brandished my dagger and danced, these black tents sank down into the earth. I then went to a narrow gully, where there was a malevolent being armed with a knife, and at first I was a bit frightened; but, immediately arousing the pride of my being Mingyur

Dorjé, I snatched the weapon from that being and broke it. I then pushed the being down off the path and hurled many stones at it, until only half of its corpse was to be seen. Continuing on, I came to a place which resembled Uchétem[228] and saw my own home, whereupon I awoke. The following morning, Karma Nyima Özer from Hor,[229] a student of Damden Dorjé, came and gave me a volume concerned with Dorjé Drollö, and before very long I received the complete empowerments and oral transmissions for this practice from Öngen. It occurred to me at that time that these were excellent auspicious circumstances, and indications of my good fortune.

During the tenth month [23a] I went to the main meditation center of Palpung Monastery and began completing one hundred thousand repetitions of each of the four preliminary practices of the Mahamudra tradition.[230] My health was good and I experienced many excellent signs in my dreams. One morning when I was practicing the *guruyoga* meditation, I drifted off slightly and seemed to find myself in a place that I had never seen before. It was very agreeable, filled with flowers, most of which were the orange color of marigolds, with leaves of an unrivalled green. Just as I came upon this place, I awoke.

DURING THE THIRD MONTH of the Fire Monkey Year, [1836-1837] I undertook a personal retreat focusing on the five deity mandala of Chakrasamvara. One evening during the fourth month, after I had finished the concluding ceremonies of the retreat, I dreamed that I entered a very finely appointed room (in the dream it seemed to be a kind of treasure chamber) and there saw Öntrul carrying what looked like several yellow scrolls of texts, wrapped up in brocade and giving off a fragrance like that of camphor. Realizing that this was a dream, I turned around and went to look outside. There was a kind of fenced-in yard in which there were many people, like children in form, of various sizes, and dressed in various ornaments and garments. I took them to be *mahasiddha*s of India, with Lavapa, Krishnapada, and Ghantapada[231] foremost among them. At a certain point they vanished from sight, while I remained, simply maintaining an awareness of the essence of my mind.

On the tenth day of the Monkey Month,[232] I began a week-long personal retreat focusing on The Union of All Rare and Precious Jewels, following this with one hundred feast offerings, and using the time as well to compose some new prayers. On the first evening of this undertaking, I dreamed that I was carrying a golden image of the Guru, about one span in height, [23b] and giving others blessing with it; in my dream, three or four young men showed no faith, but several women demonstrated faith.

Another time, I dreamed that I went to the top of a large mountain, and realizing that this was a dream I thought, "I will go to Chamara."[233] Flying through the air, I journeyed to a range of many mountains set in a circle. Within this was a mountain, a dark brownish-red color like carnelian, rising about half its height above this surrounding wall. The slopes were vaguely visible, but its peak was swathed in mist. As I thought to continue, still praying, from within the near side of the mountain there flowed an inconceivably enormous river. At that point, forgetting that I had previously recognized this to be a dream, I began to get frightened and awoke. I was sure that this showed a karmic block, because during that period, due to my thinking of myself as a Kagyü practitioner, I had allowed my interest in the Nyingma teachings to diminish somewhat. In the wake of this dream, I simply regretted the fact and confessed it.

During the summer and the autumn, I trained in a small way in Mahamudra and the Six Yogas. In connection with a *drupchö* ritual[234] he was performing, Vajradhara Pema[235] graciously bestowed on me the empowerment for the Padmavajra cycle of Yön-gé Mingyur Dorjé and the longevity practice entitled *The Integration of Means and Wisdom*. As well, Öngen received the empowerment for the nine deity mandala of Hevajra[236] according to the tradition of Saroruhavajra[237] from the collection *The One Hundred Transmissions of Mitra*, saying that he needed this in order to perform a *drupchö* ritual in the future, and I also received the empowerment at this time.

Zhechen Rabjam had formerly bestowed on me a treasured image of Mindroling Monastery—a statue of their great *tertön*[238] [24a] made by the *tertön*'s own hand. I offered this to Situ Rinpoché along with a bolt of printed gauze[239] I had. I requested the empowerment for the nine deity mandala of Jinasagara, and he very graciously bestowed this.

In response to a request from Dabzang Tulku,[240] Situ Rinpoché bestowed the empowerment of The Combined Practice of the Three Roots[241] discovered by Chöjé Lingpa,[242] and bestowed on me the secret name of Pema Gargyi Wangchuk Thrinlé Drodul Tsal. I received the oral transmission for the liturgies of this practice. As a follow-up to this, Kam Lama Tsewang Pema Norbu Tashi bestowed on me the instructions for this practice in some detail. I carried out the preliminary practices very briefly and practiced the *sadhana* and mantra recitation enough to establish some connection with this practice.

About this time, one evening, I dreamed that I had died, whereupon I thought that I should go to the Realm of Bliss.[243] Flying through the air, I arrived at a huge temple where there were the forms of deities and landscapes of pure realms carved in wood and molded in clay. I began to hide myself in one of the lotuses. Immediately after that, I recognized the dream state for what it was, and flying off in a westerly direction, I came to a flat-topped mountain peak. Seeing the realm of Sukhavati from a distance, I saw there a bodhi tree, vaguely visible but then obscured by gloom. Praying, I entered the realm and saw a white stone which I took to be the throne of Amitabha. It was covered with Sanskrit letters—mantras of Shakyamuni, Tara, Avalokiteshvara, and White Manjushri.[244] Some of the letters were right side up, some upside down. [24b] I prayed here and continued on, thinking, "I must meet Avalokiteshvara." In an elegant mansion I beheld the one-faced, four-armed form of Avalokiteshvara called "Tamer of Beings," and this turned into the form of a spiritual master. Taking this to be Karmapa, I requested his blessing and he replied, "You must return to your own land." So I returned, and on the way I encountered some significant omens.

One evening (I think it was while I was practicing The Combined Practice of the Three Roots) I dreamed of a region, which was one of three regions—either Dakpo, Kongpo, or Nyangpo[245]—although it was not clear to me which. There was a mountain in the background, covered with forests of juniper trees with their tops bending to the west, and at the foot of the mountain were many long prayer banners attached to poles. There was a house in a hollow on the mountainside; I had a very clear impression of a household of very moderate means, made up of three people, myself and a brother and sister (even afterward, I could recall this as though it had actually been so, though it was never clear whether this was some holdover from a previous existence or a premonition of what was yet to come). Then that impression faded and I found myself looking at a very fine monastic college, which I took to be Mindroling. Looking up, I saw a temple with golden eaves and I went there, having heard that the entombed remains of Terdak Lingpa were preserved there. There was an extremely beautiful stupa, with thick ropes winding around it on all sides.[246] I circumambulated it once, moving under these ropes. I dreamed that there I vaguely remembered some events from the past. [25a]

Again I flew to the top of a very tall snow mountain, and looking below, I saw the first light of the rising sun, the radiance of its glow making everything extremely beautiful. On another occasion, I had the clear impression of meeting the bodhisattva Shantideva.[247] On another occasion, a radiant lama (whom I took to be Bamteng Tulku), wearing a silk shawl the color of silver, said to me, "You are the rebirth of so-and-so," but by the next morning I had forgotten the name. Then again, on one occasion in Karmapai Tsengyé Temple in Ogmin Tsurphu,[248] on a high throne was my lord Pema Nyinjé,[249] and immediately there appeared a lama I took to be Zhamar Yeshé Nyingpo,[250] whose face had a very large nose and many pockmarks, and who was clothed in felt garments and approaching fifty years of age. And I dreamed that he bestowed several blessings and private words of advice.

Around this time, I felt some signs that I was afflicted by demons, yet I also felt the presence of the goddesses,[251] as well as signs indicating the presence of *terma*s. On this occasion, Lama Norbu bestowed on me some of the empowerments and oral transmissions for *The Lucid Expanse*, the Sky Teachings,[252] and the cycle of Rolpai Dorjé's *terma*s, as well as many other oral transmissions that were useful to me. He also gave instruction on the nature of mind to the retreatants as a group. All of them discussed their experiences with him personally, and although I had nothing to discuss, [25b] I explained my situation briefly to him. He responded, "You understand very well how to maintain an awareness of the nature of mind."

One night I dreamed of heading in a westerly direction and arriving in a large town, which seemed to be in Nepal. Going up the main thoroughfare, I came to a large temple, inside which there were many piled-up books with brocade tabs on their ends.[253] I examined the table of contents on the end flap of one of these volumes; the list included the title of a previously unknown tantra of the Guhyasamaja cycle.[254] I continued on from there. It seemed to be late spring or early summer, and I came upon a pleasant place, with blossoms showering down like snowflakes. There was a large temple, which I took to be the one at Nalanda, and off to the left of this stood an elegant white building with five tiered roofs. I knew that a certain great scholar had live there, but later forgot his name. I also dreamed that the Precious Fifth[255] had lived there.

When I read a bit from the biography and collected works of Karma Chagmé Rinpoché, I was filled with an extraordinary faith in him. One night I dreamed of a somewhat dilapidated temple that must have been Nedo,[256] with tattered banners of yellow brocade hanging on the pillars. Seated inside on a high throne was the incarnate master Mingyur Dorjé, and on another Karma Chagmé himself, and I felt that I had once been a student of Karma Chagmé in a former lifetime.

During that year Gyalwang[257] Karmapa Thekchok Dorjé[258] moved his monastic encampment to the eastern Tibetan provinces and settled at Karma Gön Monastery. [26a] A letter came from Karmapa to Situ Rinpoché requiring Situ to send me to instruct Karmapa in those aspects of Sanskrit grammar which he wished to study. It was imperative that I go, and after receiving my spiritual master's permission I left my retreat. When I was about to set out, I asked for advice and incidentally the oral transmission for *The Prayer in Seven Chapters*. As he recited the lines "In this way, all that appears in the field of vision . . . ," he remarked by way of explanation that this was the vajra speech of Orgyen Rinpoché himself, and the distillation of the meaning of hundreds and thousands of instructions on the nature of mind. Lord Chökyi Jungné[259] had in fact passed on his transmission to Gyalwang Duddul Dorjé[260] by offering him these very lines as an instruction to introduce that Karmapa directly to the nature of mind. In turn, the Thirteenth Lord Karmapa had also used this same quotation to pass his transmission on to my spiritual master. So it seemed very appropriate indeed.

Starting out with two companions, I journeyed to Lhokhok, where I first had an audience with Gyalwang Rinpoché[261] at a place called Tergar [Tertön's Encampment]. There I also established a spiritual connection with Karma Namgyal, a Dzogchen practitioner, who impressed me as having completely realized the stage of "the enrichment of meditative experience." When I was previously at Zhechen, I had practiced *tögal* techniques briefly and undergone numerous experiences of varying degrees of usefulness. During the refuge lord Karmapa's stay at the encampment, I developed a stable and direct experience of the true nature of reality.[262]

Later on, a series of invitations came to Karmapa from Kagyü monasteries in the region, and most especially an invitation from the three branches of the Zurmang complex,[263] [26b] to witness the sacred dances at the festival of Chakrasamvara. Accompanying Karmapa's party, I had a fine time seeing everything. On the road to Karma Gön Monastery, on a cliff face dedicated to a local protective spirit, from a long way off I saw very clearly an image of Lord Düsum Khyenpa[264] with a pale complexion, wearing the black crown of the Karmapas. I thought, "This must be a naturally occurring image," but when I got to the spot, it was no longer visible.[265] Continuing on, we reached the monastic seat itself, where I took up residence in Tsengyé Temple.

BEGINNING IN THE FIRST MONTH of the Fire Bird Year [1837-1838], I offered Karmapa a comprehensive teaching and review of the Sanskrit grammar entitled *Kalapa*. He insisted that he needed further notes to explain the basic text, so I composed these as well. He spent the fourth lunar month visiting members of his family, during which time I also gave him instructions on the grammar entitled *The Discourse of Sarasvata* and the work *Poetics: The Source of Riches*,[266] and he in turn bestowed on me several of his calligraphy exercises.[267]

In the fifth month, on his way to a region in upper Ga[268] to guide beings there, Karmapa witnessed sacred dances at Nangchen Camp. Having performed various rituals and the vajra crown ceremony,[269] he continued through Kyodrak to Jorna in Rongpo. On that occasion, the camp's chief steward incurred his displeasure, and from that point on my duties included, among other things, an explanation of the crown ceremony to those who witnessed it. Circumambulating Jowo Mountain in upper Ga, Karmapa continually fulfilled the requests of an unending stream of supplicants, who came requesting empowerments, performances of the vajra crown ceremony, and private audiences. He visited Thraben and other monasteries, as well as satisfying the requests of patrons both great and small, such as Buchen. [27a] On the way to Lao Monastery, we were met by a woman carrying the corpse of her small dead son. She pleaded with Karmapa to pray for the boy, wailing loudly in her distress. Taking pity on her, I performed the visualization for the transference of consciousness repeatedly, and that evening wrote down some amazing observations of what was likely to befall the child's consciousness for three or four lifetimes to come.

At Zurmang Dütsi Thil, Karmapa performed the enthronement of Trungpa Tulku.[270] For my part, I requested from Pema Tenphel, an emanation of the *tertön* Rolpai Dorjé, several empowerments and oral transmissions from that lineage.

BY STAGES WE RETURNED to Karma Gön Monastery, where Karmapa presided over the New Year celebrations for the Earth Dog Year [1838-1839] and began preparations for the ceremonies surrounding the manufacture of the precious black pills.[271] Karma Tsepal, who was the director of Palpung Monastery's pharmacy,[272] arrived and prepared the medicinal powders of eight metals and eight elements. The elaborate ceremony for refining the mercury went very well indeed. Performing the feast offering for the sambhogakaya aspect of Bhaishajyaguru,[273] the participants inaugurated a continuous recitation of the mantra of Bhaishajyaguru, and so completed the ceremony for the manufacture of the precious black pills. Although Karmapa had planned to journey back to Palpung during the fourth month, he was somewhat delayed by the illness of the Jé-ön Chenmo.[274] Since he needed explanatory notes to the Indian commentary on *The Discourse of Sarasvata*, I offered him these.

In the fifth month Karmapa struck camp and returned to the seat at Palpung. Father and son[275] were delighted to be reunited, and took turns requesting longevity rituals and empowerments from one another. They viewed, and even took part in, the sacred dances on the tenth day of the lunar month. On my part, I offered them prayers for their longevity, which I had composed based upon the grammatical construction of their names, [27b] as well as symbols of enlightened form, speech, and mind.[276] I also received kind gifts of thanks from them.

During the seventh month, when Karmapa moved his encampment to the steppes of Dza, I went in the escort party and travelled as far as Zhechen Monastery. At the meditation center, I had an audience with Jamgön Öntrul Rinpoché, who was extremely delighted to see me. I offered him a thanksgiving ceremony that included a hundred offering rituals focusing on the protective deities, and requested the empowerment of Gartsé. In return, he stated that he needed the empowerment for the five deity mandala of Chakrasamvara, and so I offered this to him.

At the same time, I made a special visit to meet with my teacher, Gyurmé Tendzin. He said, "This morning, when I got up, I saw the thousand-armed, thousand-eyed form of Avalokiteshvara, but the arms in back of the figure were somewhat unclear. This was a sign that I would meet you today, but it would seem from this that there is an obstacle to your longevity." This lama was someone who was continually experiencing the consummate degree of "the full expression of awareness."[277]

Next, I returned to my home region to visit my old mother. One evening, while I was practicing a ritual of Palchenma[278] for the purpose of being granted prosperity, I dreamed of my home valley being enormous, while on the surrounding slopes to the east and south there were huge beds of yellow flowers as large as houses. This was the first time that I personally had performed a prosperity ritual, but since that time I have devoted much preparation and effort to such techniques, which I feel have been of some small benefit. Another night, I dreamed of being in a large fine house, when I heard that Yeshé Palmo, the Queen of Existence, [28a] had arrived out in front. Going out to look at her, I found that the upper half of her body reached up to the vault of the sky, while the lower half was covered all round with a skirt of brilliantly shimmering peacock feathers. While I had made no offerings and offered no praises of any kind in connection with such deities previously, nor did I later on, this is a sign of her being a deity associated with the lineage of the Khyungpo clan.

I went to see the realized lama of Thardé,[279] for he had sent someone to fetch me. He received an empowerment for the peaceful and wrathful deities from me. In accordance with my refuge lord's instructions, I made brief trips to both Threnthang and Tsedrum.

One night about this time, I dreamed of a cave, next to which was a mansion with a large enclosed courtyard. One by one, the five Achi sisters[280] came out of the house and began performing a ritual dance. The "three goddesses of timeless awareness and commitment" were dressed like beautiful queens, the "goddess of power" was dressed unlike any of the others, while the "flesh-eating *dakini*" had the body of an ugly old woman.[281] Together they stamped their feet in the dance, and one by one left the yard and went into another building, until the extremely terrifying flesh-eating *dakini* was left dancing once the others had left. Feeling quite nervous, I sat watching her from a high vantage point, meditating myself to be a wrathful deity. Previously, around the time I was in the region of upper Ga,[282] I had had a marvelous dream of the five Achi sisters, each with her mount and style of dancing and garments; it had seemed to me that there was also a name for each of the styles of dance. At this time I had not performed any rituals specifically to develop a connection with these deities, [28b] so it occurred to me that this was a sign that they inhabited the environs of those monastic seats. Returning homeward, I spent the winter at Palpung Monastery in very fruitful pursuit of my practice, and was able effortlessly to recognize my dreams, and experienced many excellent signs of progress.

IN THE EARTH PIG YEAR [1839-1840], during the month commemorating the Buddha's spiritual miracles[283] I practiced as energetically as possible. I offered my lord Pema all the gold I had been given while serving Gyalwang Karmapa, and requested that he perform the formal ritual for arousing bodhichitta.[284] He bestowed an extensive transmission of the bodhisattva vow, and gave me the ordination name of Jangchub Sempa Lodrö Thayé.[285] One night on this occasion, I dreamed that I had died, and that my remains were cremated. They burned in an instant and the bones broke into fragments, which contained naturally formed images.[286] As well, two *sharira* relics fell out of the flames.[287] While I was reciting the source tantra of *Blazing Timeless Awareness*, I had the kinds of dreams mentioned in the text itself. And while I was engaged in proofreading the woodblocks for the ritual of Four-Armed Mahakala by Karma Chagmé Rinpoché, I dreamed of special signs indicating that protective deity's presence, which I was certain was a sign of receiving blessings.

During the fourth month I took part in eight sets of the fasting ritual.[288] On the night we began, I dreamed that I met a shining monk, whom I took to be Nivaranaviskambhin.[289] He had a small moustache, bloodshot eyes, and a ruddy complexion. Although he didn't say a word to me, with his two hands he sketched on the ground an outline of the thousand-armed, thousand-eyed form of Avalokiteshvara, [29a] adding a cushioned throne to the design.

Around this time, I had many obscure dreams, such as the one in which I met the great translator of Zhalu, Chökyong Zangpo.[290] He was staying in a certain house, where he gave me the Indian manuscripts of some three tantras, as well as the formal authorizations for them. While I was receiving the empowerments and oral transmissions for the cycle of Jatsön Nyingpo's[291] teachings from Öngen, I had many good dreams. In particular, the night he bestowed the transmission for the longevity *sadhana* called *The Vajra of Meteoric Iron*, I dreamed that the sun and the moon rose together, and that when I directed my gaze in meditation toward them, I experienced great progress in my experience of the visions of *tögal*.

Up to this point, I had not been reciting many texts on a daily basis, other than the Mahamudra preliminary practices, the *sadhana*s of Chakrasamvara and Vajravarahi, offering prayers to the protective deities, and a water offering ritual. From this time onward, I began a regular practice, on an uninterrupted daily basis, of texts from the six volumes of Jatsön Nyingpo's works—all the various *sadhana*s when I had the leisure, or just the meditations on the three forms of Padmakara[292] (the peaceful form, the wrathful form, and the *dakini* form known as Simhamukha[293]) and the daily *sadhana* text when I was pressed for time. Later on, as the empowerments and oral transmissions I received and the retreat practices I undertook got more and more numerous, my obligations for recitation of practices both of the old and new schools[294] grew correspondingly more numerous. Nowadays, with such high numbers, as it happens I am unable to maintain more than a devoted interest in most of these practices.

During these times, I developed stable and clear visualization in my practice of the stage of development[295] and mantra repetition, which influenced my dreams. I once dreamed that I was Dorjé Drollö, riding on a tigress, over-whelming everyone with my brilliant radiance. I dreamed of being the Wrathful Guru, holding in my hand a scorpion [29b] that was devouring demons. Appearing as Seng-gé Dradrok, I drove puny demons away with the flames blazing from the tip of my pointing left forefinger. Becoming Black Hayagriva, I tamed demonic *nagas*. I dreamed of a large lake, and on the meadows above it were sitting three *siddhas*, one of whom was Marpa the Translator.[296] As I requested their blessings, a fearsome demon appeared on the opposite bank of the lake; meditating myself as the Wrathful Guru, I drove the menace far away, with flames shooting out of the vajra I was holding in my right hand. There were many other positive signs occurring constantly in my dreams. As well, when I received new empowerments and oral transmissions, and practiced any daily recitations, whether long or short, I would continually experience some of the signs and indications of success connected with these practices.

During the middle of the summer that year, I trained with both Karma Tsepal, the director of the monastery's pharmacy, and the doctor Karma Tsewang Rabten. I studied the outer medical tantra in detail, and received clinical instruction in the manufacture and administration of medicines. I also trained in the identification of most herbs and plants. Beginning this year, and all during the next three years or so, I followed the instructions of Kyabjé Rinpoché and studied with Öngen Tulku, Karma Chöwang of Gulok, the doctor Karma Tsewang Rabten, the steward Tashi Chöphel,[297] and several of the monks.

I studied the entire text of Chandragomin's grammar, using the commentary by the omniscient Dharmakara;[298] the whole Kalapa system of Sanskrit grammar, using the commentary by Sazang;[299] [30a] and *Poetics: The Source of Riches*. From Ön Chimé Tulku[300] and others I learned the astrological system of *The Collection of Essentials*.[301] From several people, I learned poetics and the basic texts on Tibetan grammar, while I studied things such as calligraphy with many more teachers. But although I was constantly engaged in study and training, I didn't really accomplish much of anything. When I studied with Öngen, I found I understood a great deal, and showed myself a promising student at composition and the like, but following that he was unable to stay on. I began studying *The Profound Inner Meaning* and the two smaller related treatises[302] with two individuals, Karma Nyima Özer of Hor and Sherab Gyaltsen of Nyarong.[303] I studied these texts constantly from that point on and into the following year, when with the help of Lama Karma Ngédön[304] of Pangphuk in Lithang[305] I was able to gain an adequate certainty as to their meaning.

Around this time, I dreamed one night that I was dead, and thinking, "Now I must go to the Realm of Bliss," I traveled until I came to a temple, where I very clearly saw Amitabha. I had the impression that there were figures surrounding us, as I hid myself inside a lotus. Suddenly, Öngen appeared and said, "It is not time for you to stay here just now. After this lifetime, you will be reborn as three lamas, and following that in Nom as someone named Dorjé, who was prophesied by Ratna Lingpa and who must open the doorway to many *terma*s." I have forgotten the names of the three lamas he referred to in my dream. In another dream, the *tertön* Rolpai Dorjé, whose form was indistinct, [30b] said to me, "You are that person named 'A' who was prophesied to be the custodian of my teachings,[306] and who would spread the teachings of Jatsön Nyingpo widely." In yet another dream, a woman whose skin and garments were both green showed symbolic hand gestures to me, and I dreamed that on many occasions soon after and later on I saw signs of *terma*s and doorways to them, and also discovered such teachings.

On the evening of the eighth day of the ninth month, I had a dream in which I experienced something very much like actually dying, which saddened me greatly. In the dream I thought to myself, "In times when I was happy, I went through the motions of reciting and meditating, but somehow none of this ever sank home,[307] and so nothing was there to help me when I died. Not only was I not liberated in the first stage of the intermediate state after death, I was unable to find freedom in the second stage. Since what I now perceive is the stage of taking rebirth, it will not do for me to be distracted!" Though I stamped my feet on the ground, they left no impression, convincing me that this was in fact the intermediate state after death.

Thereupon, I found myself in a place I took to be Chamara. Here I also thought it inappropriate to be distracted, so I prayed one-pointedly to Pema Nyinjé. His form appeared clearly three times, only to fade again each time but the last, when he appeared to me, seated cross-legged and smiling. Directing my attention to his heart center, I performed the transference of consciousness twice, but my mind and body would not separate. Reminding myself, "This is because you did not practice the stage of development," I performed the transference technique from the Sky Teachings and ejected my consciousness into his heart center, but it was inconclusive whether I succeeded at transferring my consciousness. He laid his hand on my head in blessing, and said, "That will have to do," [31a] whereupon my lord vanished.

At that point, I was approached by a youth of about fifteen years of age with a dark complexion. Taking him by the hand in a friendly manner I asked, "Who are you?" He replied that he had come here because he had not fulfilled the great Orgyen's command, and would still have to undergo one more rebirth in Sok Zamkha.[308] He stated that he prayed with the aspiration that we would encounter one another then, after we had both reached the age of six or seven; and that at that point we would be ordinary people without the titles of lamas or incarnations, but would recall our former lifetimes merely upon meeting one another and be able to benefit beings. Upon hearing this, I agreed to it. But with that, a woman whom I took to be Yeshé Tsogyal reminded me, "You are required to take rebirth in Lhokhok after this lifetime. The great Orgyen has already commanded it so!" At these and other such comments, I was extremely depressed. I thought of my previous training and the twenty-odd years I had lived thus far.

Several people appeared—perhaps friends of mine?—whom I took to be guides to escort me, and I felt that it would be best to go with them. But I said, "Wait a bit! I have something to ask of Orgyen Rinpoché. Then we can be on our way." When we went on, we came to a palace which I supposed was Lotus Light.[309] Inside there was sitting a radiant figure dressed as a lay tantric master. The woman I had encountered previously was also there. I performed three prostrations, and in a very grateful frame of mind [31b] I kneeled and petitioned him. I spoke of my life, beginning with my birth in Rongyap, and what I had done up to my present age, in the prime of my youth. I indicated that while I had wondered whether I would be of any benefit to others, I had encountered only obstacles to my longevity, and that he had not yet favored me personally with a compassionate prophecy.

At that point he stopped me, and a well-dressed woman said, "Take this rebirth! We will accomplish something great with this life. At the age of eight you will receive a prophecy, and by thirteen your mission will be clear.[310] From the age of twenty on, you will discover *termas*." She spoke of how I would gradually discover some twenty-five *termas* in all, and spoke a number of different prophecies. It became plain that I had to return to my world. After this I awoke, and found that it was dawn. Although I began my morning recitations, I had the ongoing impression that I had died. Although I was somewhat distracted during the day, there was the unique realization of thinking, "This is the intermediate state after death."

At the end of the year, when I attended the year-end *gutor* ceremonies dedicated to the protective deities, at one point I saw a young monk enter, dressed in Tartar garb and carrying a bow and arrow on his back; he then disappeared. When we were chanting the offerings to Tseringma,[311] I saw in front of me a woman whose back was covered entirely with turquoise ornaments, seated facing away from me. I wondered at the time whether this was a sign from the guardian deities.

IN THE NEW IRON RAT YEAR [1840-1841], during the month commemorating the Buddha's spiritual miracles I pursued my practice with great diligence [32a] and had many positive signs in dreams and indications of success. When I was practicing a longevity *sadhana* as a ritual to aid Öngen, who was ailing slightly, I dreamed once of a lunar eclipse in the eastern sky, and the moonlight was extremely bright even though the moon was only half visible. I asked, "Who could have guessed that there would be this much light when it was only half visible? What would it be like if it were fully visible?" Several women answered me, "If it were to be completely visible, there would be some means of telling, for sure; but now it will be difficult for it to become visible again." This was a foreshadowing of the fact that Öngen would not live long after that.

On another occasion, I dreamed that I placed a ritual crown[312] on my head and took what looked like a vajra made of gold in my hand, and performed many different dance movements as I descended a staircase. At the foot of it was Kam Lama Norbu, looking even finer and in better health than before. He was saying to me such things as, "Although you've seen the essence of your mind, that alone won't put a halt to your confusion. When you're moving around, rely on mindfulness and alertness; when you're sitting down, rely on mindfulness and alertness; in all four types of behavior, eating and drinking and so on, if you focus your mindfulness again and again, you'll be ready for both sleep and death."

The day after old Lama Norbu passed away into peace, I dreamed of entering a temple and seeing a mat with red and green flower patterns spread out. [32b] On a table in front of this, someone had placed a yellow vajra about a cubit in length and a book wrapped in red brocade. Öngen came in, and I asked him whose these were. He replied that they belonged to the *siddha* Nagabodhi.[313] Moved with faith, I touched my head to them to receive blessing. At dawn on the day of the cremation of Lama Norbu's remains, I dreamed of him wearing a white ritual crown on his head and white bone ornaments on his body,[314] riding side-saddle on a young white mule. He was escorted by many women in blouses and skirts made of white brocade, playing *gyaling* horns and leading him up into the sky.

On another evening, I dreamed of being chased by a man-eating wild animal, and of running for a temple where Gyalwang Karmapa sat and reaching it. Extremely terrified, I hid in a small cubbyhole. Gyalwang Rinpoché said to me, "With your hopes of being a learned and accomplished master of the five fields of knowledge, why are you so afraid of this little thing? Why, when I was formerly at Densa Thil, this hallucination came to me once; I meditated on it being Kuzhap Rinpoché himself and it subsided." I thought of how right he was, and since the beast had come in front of me, I meditated on it being Pema Nyinjé and awoke as I was praying to him.

On the twenty-ninth day of the third month, Öngen Rinpoché conferred on me the life force empowerment[315] for the "Poison-Faced Molten Metal" form of Yamantaka.[316] [33a] He then said that a sign came to him in a dream that if I recited the mantra of Yamantaka, it might invite harm due to sorcery that would impair my activities to benefit beings, but an eye disease that I had contracted prior to this cleared up at this point.

Also around this time, I met for the first time with Karma Norbu, a hidden yogi who was an emanation of the glorious Mokchokpa.[317] I requested from him a transmission of the Six Yogas of Niguma and he bestowed an abridged version, saying, "Practice is important. Nothing would be served by having many explanations and instruction manuals. Once you have practiced, it will be fine for me to give a more extensive treatment." I met him once more after that, and he gave me a slightly more extensive transmission than before.

In the fourth month I did a week of practice of the longevity *sadhana* called *The Integration of Means and Wisdom*. I had some remarkable indications, both disturbances due to interferences with my longevity and blessings (such as dreaming of meeting with several *siddha*s). On the evening of the ritual for accepting the accomplishments of the practice, I dreamed of an Indian mendicant whom I took to be Luhipa,[318] wearing a cloak made of a hair blanket and acting out many kinds of tantric deportment, destroying and then restoring stupas and so forth. Finally, I dreamed that he blessed me with a bound-up text, saying that it was a tantra of Tarayogini that he had revealed from its place of hiding.

At this time, a master of discipline[320] from Threnthang Monastery arrived and, having consulted with him, I planned to sponsor a day-long longevity ritual at Threnthang. The venerable Lord Pema,[321] [33b] too, was delighted, and sponsored a day-long ritual, donating a painted mandala and *tsakli* cards depicting the parasol and so forth.[322] Öngen Tsephel arranged to sponsor a day-long ritual and "one hundred offerings."[323] After that, there were several who agreed to sponsor this on a regular basis, and nowadays without fail there is an annual practice of about a week of day-long rituals at Threnthang Monastery.

One night I dreamed of two incredible caves, appointed like temples, in which there was a lama named Dorjé something-or-other, a rebirth of Bairotsana[324] whom I took to be the fifth or sixth in a series of incarnations; at times it felt as though he and I were inseparable, while at other times we were distinctly separate individuals.

That year, when the eighth Pawo incarnation, Tsuklak Chögyal, was staying at my monastery, I received the oral transmission for the two volumes of Mahamudra texts translated from Indian sources,[325] and many unconnected oral transmissions and empowerments from the "*terma*s of enlightened intent"[326] of the Mindroling tradition, Chöjé Lingpa, Ratna Lingpa, and Dzigar. In each case, a significant sign occurred in my dreams. In particular, during the oral transmissions for the Mahamudra texts, I dreamed of Pawo Rinpoché himself seated on a high throne. In front of him, many longevity pills and fruits had been placed, and he was scooping these up in both hands and passing them out to three lamas, myself and two others. He gave me the most of all, and gave me as well a piece of white silk. [34a] From Lama Ngawang Lodrö, a descendant of the Buddhist master Tenpa Dargyé who was serving as an attendant to Pawo Rinpoché, I requested the oral transmissions for the entire cycle of Jatsön Nyingpo's teachings, as well as for the biography of this master.

One night during the sixth month, I dreamed of a fine mansion, elegantly appointed and with many stories. Inside were the Sixteen Elders,[327] and someone had to serve them their midday meal each day; as well, it was necessary to serve something different each time. After three or four times, when they had been served rice porridge and so forth, the day it was my turn I had to serve rice porridge. Filling a huge silver basin with rice porridge sprinkled with saffron, I served it from the head of the line, where the elder Angiraja[328] was seated. I was told that the next day my turn came, I would have to serve the nectar of flowers. I had the impression that some three or four days passed during this dream.

Another evening, using the dream state, I was flying in space, reciting the lines, "From beginningless time until the present, my own mind has not recog-nized itself . . . ," and so on, down to "May I cut through the root of dualistic clinging!" This poem of some twenty-three and one-half quatrains on the mean-ing of the Chö teachings sprang to mind. When I came back to earth, more-over, I had someone write down these lines and [34b] took them to offer for Situ Rinpoché's inspection. In my dream, he gave his enthusiastic approval, and the permission that they were worthy of being published for others.

In the seventh month Öngen Rinpoché went to the meditation center. About seven of us who were devoted students of his (principally Dabzang Tulku) received the empowerments for The One Hundred Instructions of Mitra, which he graciously bestowed.

In the ninth month I revised the prayer to the lineage for the visionary transmission from Lhatsün Namkha Jigmé[329] entitled *Averting Untimely Death*, in which many names in the lineal transmission were absent. The evening that I had added several new names of key gurus and *siddha*s in the lineage, Vajradhara Pema Nyinjé was so delighted that he bestowed the entire empow-erment for a previously unknown transmission of Manjushri Yamantaka. He began with an image of the deity as the support for his meditation, and then I beheld him in the actual form of the deity Yamantaka, dark blue in color with five faces; the faces to the right and left were green, the central face was red, and the face above that was white. His eight hands held weapons, and his body was decorated with garlands of teeth. There were several evil-looking figures there, and I myself became Yamantaka, crushing them with the axe in my hand. Rigdzin Tamdrin Gönpo appeared, smiling and radiant, and it seemed to me that together we made the gods and demons of the phenomenal world our servants. In particular, [35a] Dogyal[330] was there, following whatever instruc-tion we gave. The sun rose, with white billowing clouds scudding gently along, from which a shining rain was falling. It occurred to me that these visions were signs to me, as a supplicant, that with this practice I would be victorious over obstacles.

The texts housed in Thongdröl Lhakhang Temple at Palpung were in disar-ray, with no division into old and new schools and no real order to them. Öngen Rinpoché said that I should clear up the mess, dividing them into old and new schools and arranging them in a proper order, and accordingly I went to work for many days. At that time, I dreamed of the great Manjushri statue of Tsurphu, looking quite old, sitting in front of a fine and well-appointed man-sion. In front of this, the great Sanskritist and translator Sönam Gyatso[331] was seated on a monk's square sitting mat, preaching the Buddhist teachings at length and speaking of many valuable methods for clearing up one's confusion concerning the excellent words of the Buddha.

At about this time, I received many oral transmissions and empowerments from Öngen Rinpoché, such as the complete oral transmissions and empowerments for the cycle of the peaceful and wrathful deities discovered by Karma Lingpa, several of the important transmissions from the Sky Teachings and the works of Karma Chagmé, and The Heart Drop of Yuthok. One night I dreamed of meeting with Lord Karma Chagmé in the form of a cheerful old monk; he gave me many prophecies about my other lifetimes.

During the early and later parts of this year, [35b] Jamyang Khyentsé Wangpo[332] came a couple of times to see me, and studied such texts as the various tables from Chandragomin's work on Sanskrit grammar. He treated me with great deference and respect. This was the first time that I had met with him in person.

On one occasion, I dreamed of a pleasure grove joining heaven and earth, in which there was something like a rock face, with relief carvings of buddhas and bodhisattvas, like actual images reflected in the rock, as numerous as stars. The principal figure was the Lord of Sages with his hand extended; I touched the crown of my head to his hand in faith.

On another night, I had an extremely clear dream of seeing the principal deity Ushnisha Sitatapatra[333] and several of the wrathful goddesses in her retinue; the other deities in her mandala were only briefly visible, but it seemed that most of them were trampling elephants under their feet. The morning after this dream I wrote a prayer of praise and supplication to this deity.

In the ninth month, due to Dabzang Tulku's insistent urging that I undertake the practice of The United Intent Of the Gurus, I studied in detail the traditional performance of the *drupchen* ritual[334] and the fulfillment ritual[335] of The United Intent of the Gurus with Sang-ngak Tendzin, a lama from Garjé. I had to write out some notes commenting on the *sadhana*, and on the tenth day of the month, after an all-day ritual and *torma* offering combined with much prayer, I dreamed that night of being in a lovely residence, where there were two rows of people seated. To the left and right, at the heads of the rows, were Rigdzin Gödem[336] and Namchö Mingyur Dorjé,[337] [36a] both in layman's dress. Next to them were seated two persons in monk's robes, whom I took to be incarnations of Yön-gé Mingyur Dorjé and Rolpai Dorjé. They were all discussing topics from the Buddhist teachings, and this gave me a tremendous sense of confidence. I also dreamed that I raised three white silk banners and performed a *lhasang* ceremony on the roof of a temple filled with gilded tombs.

On the sacred day commemorating the Buddha's descent from the gods' realm,[338] about five of us, me as teacher with a few of my students, began a short retreat on The United Intent of the Gurus, during which we were also practicing the *sadhana* called *Liberation Through Seeing.* One night, I dreamed that I met with the learned and accomplished Karma Chagmé, looking old and in monk's robes; he cleared up a number of key points for me concerning the practice of The United Intent of the Gurus. After that, there were many times when positive signs manifested in the elements on occasions when I was about to perform the *Sun and Moon* practice or a solitary practice of *Liberation through Seeing.*

During the winter, I undertook a retreat on the protective deity Bernakchen in embrace with his consort. At the beginning, I experienced great upset, but later on there were a few signs of success which tallied with the traditional texts. At year's end I attended the *gutor* ceremonies. During one offering of a "tantric inner *torma,*" I had a vision that I was suddenly in the Middle Hall of Samyé Monastery,[339] where the three figures of the abbot Shantirakshita,[340] the teacher Padmakara, and the Buddhist king Trisong Detsen[341] were discussing the Buddhist teachings, along with several other translators and scholars. I felt that I was a realized scholar, seated among them, and then the vision faded. During the praises, I had a fleeting impression of actually seeing [36b] the protective deity Sechok Nakpo; and during the melodic chanting of the praises to the feminine protective deity, I drifted off a bit and saw a very gaudily dressed woman smiling and looking at me and the rest there.

IN THE NEW IRON OX YEAR [1841-1842], I continued to maintain a regular practice. One night, without any strong predisposition to account for the experience, I saw myself become the deity Black Krodhi,[342] my body like a small mountain, with a human skin in my right hand and a skull cup held in my left. Spreading the skin over the entire three realms, I overwhelmed the universe with my splendor. Around this time, there were many other quite marvelous signs. On the evening of the ritual commemorating the tenth day of the first month, I dreamed of being in a huge field where an abundant crop was growing, with irrigation canals carrying water in all directions. Looking up, I saw white clouds gathering in a square pattern in the southwestern sky, and in the center of these I clearly beheld Guru Rinpoché[343] seated, in his aspect as

Padmasambhava. On the fifteenth, the day of the full moon, after having given a transmission of the bodhisattva vow to about seventeen aspirants, I dreamed that night that we all raised a large pole with prayer flags and a victory banner on its tip. This was clearly a sign that in the future there would be many occasions on which I would transmit both traditions of the bodhisattva vow.

In the spring, I went in response to a summons from the Jadra clan,[344] who were patrons of mine, [37a] and performed several ceremonies. There were signs of some disturbance due to environmental disharmony and the activity of *gyalpo* demons.[345] When I performed a ritual to promote prosperity, there were good signs. In particular, when I was closing the "door of prosperity," a large measure of barley spontaneously appeared inside the chest in which we had placed the box symbolic of prosperity. After that, the family's wealth also grew and grew.

In the fourth month, following the instructions of Öngen Rinpoché, a group of about four of us were performing a ceremony for a "circle" to harmonize the environment, the teachings, and the sangha. One night during this, I dreamed I was in an inconceivably huge meeting hall (which I felt was in Lhasa), which was filled inside with images of buddhas and bodhisattvas; in front of these, countless sangha members were performing the activity ritual[346] from *The Discourse on Individual Liberation*,[347] and I dreamed that I and many others were preparing to distribute offerings. There were also excellent dream indications on the night that I received from Öngen the empowerment for Simhamukha according to the tradition of Taksham.[348] He also related that he had dreamed of giving me a copper amulet belonging to him, which was filled with tightly rolled paper on which was written the magnetizing mantra of this deity. But I did not perform this practice intensively after that.

Due to my specific request, in the sixth month we went to the meditation center, where he graciously bestowed on a group of us (seven or so) the complete empowerments and instructions for The United Intent of the Gurus. [37b] On this occasion, I dreamed of Vajradhara Pema Nyinjé seated on a high throne, wearing a new formal outer shawl; he was enthroning me, and I was wearing a slightly shabby shawl with designs worked in gold stitching. Dabzang Tulku said that after receiving such empowerments and oral transmissions as these, that we absolutely must perform a *mendrup* ritual.[349] While he did not have much by way of materials at that time, he prepared the basic substances. A few of us got together whatever we had, and the director of the monastery's pharmacy sent ritual implements to be used in the preparation of medicines. Having received permission from Kyabjé Rinpoché, we made hasty preparations and during the ninth month Öngen Rinpoché presided over the ceremonies as the vajra master, with the group of master and students being about twenty-five, some fine lamas foremost among us. The night we established the outer boundary of the retreat and decorated the shrine room for the performance of the *mendrup* ritual from The United Intent of the Gurus, I dreamed of several disturbing signs, and that Öngen used a sword to split my head in a cross pattern, so that much blood and lymph spilled out. One night during the main practice, I dreamed of finding two *malas*[350] with jeweled ornaments, and due to this occurrence I recalled that this was a dream. Thinking to go and meet Padmavajra,[351] I was traveling by flying when a pleasant voice from the sky proclaimed, "You needn't go. Padmavajra, wearing his scholar's cap and holding a skull cup, is already present here." [38a] Upon this, I awoke.

On another occasion, I dreamed very clearly of meeting the Ninth Lord Karmapa, Wangchuk Dorjé.[352] As I bowed respectfully to him, he spoke many vajra verses about Mahamudra, and my mind became immeasurably joyful. Another time, I dreamed I was in a place where many medicinal shrubs were growing, where an elderly and radiant figure (whom I realized was Samten, a doctor who was related to Situ Rinpoché) was explaining many marvelous things to me about medicine.

On the evening of the ceremony to receive the spiritual attainments of the practice, I dreamed of reliable indications that I was receiving blessings: of three naked young virgin women standing in front of me with their fingers covering their pudenda; of the *tertön* Chöjé Lingpa, smiling and radiant with blessing as he explained many points of medicine rituals to me; and of being served sumptuous food and drink, and so on. Furthermore, whether due to some slight previous karmic connection or whatever, whenever in the earlier or later times in my life I have practiced The United Intent of the Gurus, this *terma* unequalled by any other whatsoever, it seems that there has always been some definite sign of its blessing for me.

At a certain point later on, the evening after I had performed a formal authorization for Phadampa Sang-gyé's[353] lineage of Manjushri for a few of my students, I dreamed of the venerable Karma Chagmé as an elderly monk, who said to me, [38b] "It would be best to use Avalokiteshvara as a deity in which to place your hopes. Then when you die, you take on the suffering of all sentient beings with your compassion, and there is the power to keep your attention from reverting to this world. If you practice the meditation of Manjushri, there is no guarantee of such power. However, there are three rulers under the earth." Immediately upon him saying this, it seemed as though I saw these three rulers to be Phadampa Sang-gyé, Jambhala, and Vasudhara,[354] the three of them orange in color and with complete raiment and ornaments. Upon meeting them, I felt a faith in them grow in me.

On the nineteenth day of the tenth month, as I was beginning a basic retreat on Vajrakila, I dreamed I was on a pleasant hillside, all covered with blue flowers. At a certain point, they all changed into small, white bell-shaped flowers, and Lord Pema Nyinjé was sitting in the midst of them. I was picking flowers, and having gathered many of them, I offered them to him. Another time I dreamed that Gyalwang Karmapa Thekchok Dorjé bestowed on me a dark round stone the size of my thumb, saying that it was a kind of wish-granting gem which he had recovered from a river as a *terma*. And one morning at dawn, as a cheerful sun was rising, I took hold of a dream and made circumambulation around the residence where Lord Pema Nyinjé stayed. On the path I met a *dakini* with the body of a human woman, who approached me with a coquettish air; [39a] as I had a clear impression of us as masculine and feminine deities in union, I experienced the four joys in a stable manner.

On the eighth day of the eleventh month, I dreamed that I was on the roof of a fine house, and looking out to the northeast I could see a mountain with its peak shrouded in a mass of smoky clouds. In the center of these clouds I saw the protective deity Raksha Natha wreathed in a garland of skulls; below him were the two figures of Kshetrapala and Indra, both dark blue, single masculine figures; and below them was Dorjé Draktsen, naked, with wrathful ornaments, and holding a heart and a noose. Finally, I dreamed that these figures were obscured as though by mist, and faded from sight.[355]

AS I WAS APPROACHING the end of my Vajrakila retreat, I had several premonitions of death. Around the twenty-fifth day of the twelfth month, the old chieftain was seized by an illness. He passed away on the twenty-fifth day of the first month of the Water Tiger Year [1842-1843], and up until that point I did all I could for him with whatever power was at my disposal, reading the introductions to the intermediate state, and applying the amulets which liberate through contact[356] as he was dying. Although there were some remains, his passing away took place in a most excellent manner, and everything he left behind was used for a good purpose.[357]

This old chieftain had been pure in maintaining his vows as a fully ordained monk, which he had received from the omniscient Drukchen Rinpoché.[358] He had devotion to, and trust in, lord Pema Nyinjé and other lamas, and never interrupted or lessened his daily recitations and liturgies; as well, he had finished several intensive recitation retreats. He was very active in constructing religious statues and buildings, and in gathering accumulations of merit and awareness,[359] devoting everything he owned to the Buddhist teachings. [39b] He was never associated with any of the major harmful actions, such as the taking of life. And because he met his death so nobly, I feel that he cannot but have gone to a favorable state of rebirth. He was kinder to me than even my father and mother.

When one hundred days were finished, I ended my Vajrakila retreat. In the fourth week after Öngen's death, moreover, as I was performing commemorative rituals from The United Intent of the Gurus, specifically the fulfillment ritual and the purification ritual for cleansing obscurations, there were signs that the deceased was in a state of happiness.

One night I dreamed of a woman with a single eye in her forehead which reflected various images like a mirror. After we had exchanged many symbolic words, she changed into a fine-looking woman. In the center of a fine mansion with four doorways, we engaged in sexual union, and forms began emanating from us, moving toward the doorways. There would have been four forms, but after the two forms for pacifying and enriching activity had been emanated, the illusory dream vision faded away.[360] From the first day of the third month, I was stricken with a condition resembling asthma, which was difficult to diagnose; daily I felt that now I was sure to die. By the fourth month I had improved somewhat, and I performed the *torma* ritual for the goddess Parnashavari from the Sky Teachings, and a short recitation for the outer practice of the longevity *sadhana* entitled The Gathering of Secrets; there were many excellent signs. One night I dreamed of a scroll which I knew to be the speech amulet of some spiritual master; inside was a message that [40a] "were you to be freed from the obstacles of three major crises in your life by praying for the compassion of Orgyen Rinpoché, I say that you would definitely live more than seventy years." I recalled that I prayed every evening with devotion, using the prayer called Clearing Obstacles from the Path, and that occasionally it seemed as though Orgyen, with an assembly of deities to clear obstacles from my path, was actually present, and as though the sky were filled with *vidyadhara*s and *dakini*s. I was then told in my dream, "If you are capable of praying, no other means is needed; you will be totally immersed in that compassion."

Once I dreamed of finding a nine-pointed vajra and a ritual dagger about a cubit in length; thrusting them into my belt, I went on to a certain house, where I found the great bodhisattva Shantirakshita and Khaché Panchen[361] both seated, each on a white silk cushion. They ordered me to come over and choose between them; choosing the great abbot, I lifted him onto my shoulders and went outside to show him to a large crowd of people. I was told, "This is what is meant by 'carrying the enlightenment of the buddhas on your shoulders'."

I received the conferral of life force for Black Hayagriva of Ratna Lingpa's tradition from Lama Sang-ngak. Moving to a residence in the upper part of the monastery, I was performing a recitation retreat for Black Hayagriva when I had a sign in my dreams—of defeating demons while having a stable experience of visualizing myself as the deity.

At dawn on the fifteenth day of the fifth month, I dreamed that the Teacher Shakyamuni [40b] was staying in a certain region, and that I was sitting among the many *arhats*, such as Nada and Kashyapa,[362] who were surrounding him. The Teacher was preparing to bestow some spiritual teaching, and as the excellent pair[363] drew close to him, I knelt and folded my hands in a very devoted state of mind and recited once *The Discourse on the Recollection of the Three Jewels*.[364]

Upon their invitation, I went to visit the Alo Dilgo family.[365] During my performance there of the ritual of the peaceful and wrathful deities, I dreamed nightly of signs that there was a child coming to them. One night, I dreamed of crossing a large river of limpid water, to a white cliff where I "opened the doorway" of the place; whereupon the protective deity Zhingkyong and his feminine consort appeared, with two black people in the form of lions circumambulating them clockwise. They dissolved into the cliff face. From the west of that place there appeared Mahadeva[366] and his consort, each in the form of a red person carrying a hooked elephant prod; I imposed an injunction[367] on them. On another night, I dreamed that I was journeying to India, when I stopped on the road at a place called Palri, where in the company of several companions I performed the feast offering of Vajravarahi. Two individuals were present who were known to me and who were fluent in Sanskrit. I asked them whether the roads were passable to Bodh Gaya and Vulture Peak. They replied that there was an epidemic at Vulture Peak, and that the road was closed to Bodh Gaya by edict of the ruler of that region, but they said, "Here is the way to Pemakö and other places," speaking at length and pointing the way with their fingers. [41a]

At dawn on the fourth day of the sixth month, I dreamed of being in a shrine room where there were five thrones. On the central throne was the Tenth Gyalwang Karmapa, Chöying Dorjé,[368] wearing a black antelope skin[369] but otherwise clad as usual. To his right was the Gyaltsap incarnation, Drakpa Chokyang,[370] youthful with a fair complexion and bloodshot eyes, wearing an orange ceremonial hat. To his right was Zhamar Chökyi Wangchuk,[371] looking very massive and wearing on his head the ceremonial hat called "Bringing Liberation On Sight." To the left of Gyalwang Karmapa was seated Vajradhara Pema Nyinjé, looking no different than he normally did as far as his body type and so forth; his hat changed in color, from red to black and back. I had the impression that below him was seated one of the Pawo incarnations, but the form was not clear. As I met with them, they were all cheerful, impressive, and awe-inspiring.

About this time, my refuge lord said that he was slightly unwell, and graciously arranged a ceremony to "ransom the spirit,"[372] with my lord himself presiding. Beginning on the eighth day, he was stricken anew with a serious case of influenza, but ultimately it did not harm him.

In an audience with Situ Rinpoché I sought his permission for a leave of absence in order to do some practice in retreat at the upper meditation center. At first he was reluctant, but eventually I obtained his promise that I could stay in retreat for three years.

I got rid of all my possessions, large and small, and commissioned religious objects to be made: as the symbol of body, [41b] a very fine set of eleven scroll paintings depicting the deities of The United Intent of the Gurus, together with the protective deities of those teachings; as the symbol of speech, a copy of *The Discourse on the Perfection of Wisdom in Eight Thousand Stanzas*,[373] written in gold ink; and as the symbol of mind, one hundred thousand small *tsa-tsa*s.

At the hermitage, it would seem that at the time of Lord Chökyi Jungné there had been both a meditation center and retreat huts. However, since the Öntrul incarnation Wang-gi Dorjé[374] had later established the lower meditation center, the upper center had been allowed to fall into disrepair as though abandoned, and there was nothing but dilapidated buildings.[375] One day in late autumn, I went to investigate the site and perform a *lhasang* ceremony there. On that occasion, there was no clear path leading to the older site, but as I was climbing up behind the new center, a vulture flew up into the air and I followed after it. As it flew facing eastward from an opening in the rocks, I looked back and beheld the site of the retreat. Going there, I performed a propitiatory *lhasang* ceremony, and positive indications and auspicious circumstances occurred. After that, I was joined by several visiting monks who shared my ideas, and on the foundations of the former lama's residence we began building a small house just to indicate that the site was being used again. One night I dreamed that I was finely dressed in cassock and shawl, giving the empowerment for the cycle of the peaceful and wrathful deities called the Natural Freedom of Enlightened Intent to an enormous crowd, and that it got too late in the day for the *torma* empowerment and the ceremony of conferring the auspicious signs and symbols, so that I had to leave off there and confer those stages the next day. I wondered whether that was in reference to a function that I would come to have later on.[376]

One night, I dreamed of a very pleasant shrine room, in which [42a] the Fourteenth Gyalwang Karmapa was seated. To his right were hung several scroll paintings which seemed to depict his previous incarnations. Whether it came from the paintings or Lord Karmapa himself, I was unable to distinguish, but I very clearly heard the words, "Mind has been definitively described by holy persons"; there would seem to have been some significance to this event.

Following this, aided by several writers I was preparing the biographies of the members of the monastic residence for publication, when the region from Horkhok to Rudam and Lingtsang[377] was hit with a violent earthquake. This caused a great deal of destruction, but there was no damage in the area around the meditation center. Around this time I composed some verses which seem to be something of an autobiographical statement, and so I have included these lines of verse here as an interlude.

> Guru Padmakara, renowned one of the human world,
> venerable chosen deity Tara,
> *dakini*s and *dharmapalas*[378] without exception,
> united as one in the venerable Pema Nyinjé:
> dwell in the center of my heart until my enlightenment!
> Bestow the attainment of simultaneous realization and liberation!
> Grant your blessings that I may lead beings equal to space!
>
> Through positive acts and their equally positive results
> I have attained a human birth and met the Buddhist teachings.

However, I must further my aspirations:

for I was born in a border land, the country of Bön.

Though I have studied much in all the fields of learning,

I lack the intellect to reach the height of wisdom.

[42b]   While I wish to teach and to debate, my acumen is slight.

I have received the three vows in their entirety,

yet faults and failings, large and small, are like falling rain.

My confessions and confirmations of my vows are not authentic.

Although I talk a lot of practice and of meditation,

I have not reached the end of indications of success;

my feelings of confidence are a barren woman's son.[379]

Reinforced and nurtured from beginningless time,

perverse thoughts spring up like gardens in the summertime.

Practice languishes in a lack of effort,

while the ten nonvirtuous actions[380] happen automatically.

Positive qualities are scarcer than a rabbit's horns.

Such is the story of a mortal such as I,

whose behavior is not that of a holy one

but a sham who makes what is not spiritual seem as though it were.

Even though this is the case, by the power of the Three Roots

from an early age my mind has inclined to virtue.

Casting aside the way of Bön, I have entered the door of the
     Buddhist teachings.

Nowadays, dissatisfied with my practice in view and action,

I aspire to follow after those of yore.

I have read the many commentaries in an unbiased way,

and examined the biographies of many learned and accomplished ones.

I cannot abide even seeing books

by those sectarians who chase after fame,

for speaking judgmentally is the way of fools.

Knowing this, I have savored the flavor of things in the cave of
     enlightened intent

of the new and old schools without prejudice.

I have practiced pure view for all the Victorious One's teachings.

Rejecting the Buddhist teachings[381] is a heavy burden which I have
     no wish to carry.

[43a]   I know that a life of simplicity and study alone is dearer
            than public ceremonies,[382] empowerments and formal rituals, and all
                the cultural trappings
            of religion mixed with the eight worldly pursuits.
            I have more faith in the inner meaning of the sutras and tantras alone
            than in all there is to be learned in the fields of knowledge.
            I have more interest in the Buddha's words than commentary,
            for I know that while there are many profound instructions,
            there is nothing which is not complete in the Buddha's words.
            I aspire to definitive truth more than provisional truth,
            and to the pinnacle of the Madhyamaka[383] even more than that.
            I have more faith in correct view than in action,
            and I know that the welfare of others is dearer than my own.
            I trust renunciation more than studying books,
            for it is better to tame the mind even a bit
            than to be very learned in scripture and logic.
            I have more faith in the methods of tantra than of sutra,
            for the unsurpassable view and action of tantra
            makes my hairs stand on end when I even see or hear of them.
            Rather than a lofty position at odds with the Buddhist teachings,
            I would sooner be humble, dying like a dog;
            I always think, "Oh, to die engaged in contemplation
            in empty caves and solitary dales!"

            While I have not had the good fortune to practice
            the profound view and action of sutra and tantra,
            I have no doubts or hesitation about these;
            and though I have not received transmission
            of the various traditions of Buddhism, profound and vast,
            yet I have no cynical thoughts that I have no need of them.
            I am not able immediately to accomplish
            the vast import of the tantras, scriptures and specific instructions,
            but I am not discouraged or thinking of quitting in despair.
            While I have not understood these meanings all at once,
[43b]   I do not think of giving up, for I have the intelligence capable of
                gradual realization.
            Having seen the crux of the Victorious One's skillful methods,

I do not have the nerve to advance my own opinions recklessly,
saying. "This is truth, the rest is stupidity."
Since I have not hidden my mind from myself,
I know that I am not some exalted person,
yet while I must be considered an ordinary mortal,
I still take pride in being in accord with the Buddhist teachings to
    some extent.

In this retreat, in accord with the teachings, casting off useless
    activity,
I will apply myself with vigor: I will not die with regret!
Without encouragement from others, this attitude that will not be
    denied
has been with me from a very early age.

When engaged in nothing but distraction and what is not spiritual,
day and night my lifetime is ground away
as span and force of life grow smaller,
and all my friends, companions, attendants, students, monks and laity,
appall me at the way we drag each other down,
finding blame with one another—
have I any understanding or realization of the Buddhist teachings?
Do I act in the slightest in accord with teachings, guilelessly?
Though I have not the least depth of experience or realization,
I eat and wear only what is misappropriated from those living or
    dead.
Even now, I sell the sacred teachings, gathering possessions
through empowerments, oral transmissions, and instructions.
Furthermore, those acts of Mara[384] of which the Victorious One
    spoke in many ways
come effortlessly to hand;
like a deer that has run into a snare,
[44a] my mind is pained with fear, anxiety and regret.

As I wonder what to do and what is best,
like a widow grieving for her husband dead and gone,
will former karma and present circumstances cause

some virulent disease, impossible to treat,
and shall I die tonight? or tomorrow early?
Helplessness and impermanence
have become my teachers, encouraging me to take heed.

As a bird which is ready to take flight
is swiftly stirred by the wind,
is not this preparation to soon go into solitude
an excellent presage for gaining the accomplishment of my chosen
    deity?

While such were the innermost depths of my feelings, later on I fell entirely under the influence of others, and distractions have become a greater and greater part of my life, so that it dismays me to see how numerous these are. Now I am reduced to aspiring that such aspirations may come about in some future human existence.

While I had received the empowerment for The Union of All Rare and Precious Jewels many times in the past, I thought to receive this from a different lineage of transmission, and so requested the empowerment from Situ Rinpoché. He also bestowed on the hermitage the name of Kunzang Dechen Ösel Ling.[385]

When I returned to my hermitage, I had nothing other than a set of shabby clothes, a small lump of tea,[386] and five small measures of barley. Nevertheless, with another fellow retreatant I began my retreat on the fifteenth day of the sacred ninth month of the Buddha's descent from the gods' realm.

One after the other, I carried out the preliminary practices for that most profound *sadhana*, The Union of All Rare and Precious Jewels, [44b] according to the instruction manual of the great master of awareness.[387] One night, during the period that I was performing one hundred thousand refuge prayers in conjunction with prostrations, I dreamed that I was close to slipping over the edge of a very steep icy abyss, when on the ledge above me appeared Rigdzin Tsewang Norbu,[388] cheerful and smiling and radiant; he pulled me up by the hand and we went to a very pleasant meadow. Another night, I dreamed of the extreme terrors of the Avichi hell of endless torment. Feeling heartfelt love for the other beings there, I began a meditation of *tonglen*,[389] and during this I realized that this was a dream; immediately, I found myself in a beautiful mansion. Another time, I dreamed that Öngen was performing a ritual of purification based on the six perfections.[390] At the end of a sentence he recited, "I, the one who has passed away, offer this bathing." I respectfully suggested that he should have said, "I shall bathe this fortunate one" (meaning myself), whereupon he seemed embarrassed and went away; I hastened after him, and he then bathed me thoroughly in a copper tub. Since Lord Öngen himself had departed for the pure realms[391] not long before that, the words of the purification ritual seemed to be a reminder of that.

One night, I dreamed of a bridge over a large river; on the far side were many people moving down the slope, who I was told were destined for lower rebirths. I said, "I must save them," and saying *mani* and *siddhi* mantras[392] over many pebbles, I cast these from the peak of a hill on the near bank. Many of the people [45a] came across to me and I led them to higher ground up the valley, to a hill which we climbed where there were two caves, one above the other, in which Orgyen and his consort were said to be residing. In the mouth of the lower cave, I could see the face of Yeshé Tsogyal; bowing respectfully, I requested empowerment and she bestowed a special blessing upon me.

During the winter solstice, I undertook a week-long retreat and the annual ritual of Vajrakila to avert negativity. One night, I dreamed of a magnificent temple, in the center of which I saw the great and glorious Vajrakumara,[393] slightly vague as though cloaked in mist. On either side were the ten wrathful deities of Vajrakila's retinue, shining like the rays of the sun on crystal; these were about two or three stories high. At that point, the venerable Taranatha appeared, looking slightly emaciated; placing a *kila* dagger on my head, he recited, "Om vajra kila kilaya sarva vighnan bam hum phat samaya veshayastvam,"[394] and said, "If you, too, add this ending to the mantra, the blessing will come more quickly."

During a seven-day personal retreat on the Venerable Goddess,[395] while I was reciting the supplementary mantras,[396] I dreamed of seeing a woman-sized golden statue of White Tara, said to be the one erected by King Songtsen Gampo[397] at Longthang Drölma.[398] I was filled with deep faith and bowed to her; the statue became the Venerable Goddess in actuality, blazing radiantly and [45b] seated on a slightly unlevel throne in a darkened room.

As I had had many signs of impending death previously, so there were many such premonitions about this time. I dreamed over and over of many women and of taking part in feast gatherings; since for the most part these were obviously signs of my possible demise,[399] I performed a ritual for cheating death.

SINCE ÖNGEN HAD PASSED into peace on the twenty-ninth day of the twelfth month, during the first month of the Water Hare Year [1843-1844] I spent one week performing the fulfillment ritual from The United Intent of the Gurus in his memory. During this time, I lacked any but the most rudimentary possessions to use as offerings and so forth, but my refuge lord provided me with support for a week, so I was able to practice. Over and over during my practices of the development of bodhichitta, Vajrasattva, the offering of mandala and so forth, I had dreams that accorded with those mentioned in the texts. During the *guruyoga* practice and that of the Seven-Line Prayer, I felt some slight refinement in my experience of the nature of mind.

Around this time, I received about five large measures[400] of butter from Situ Rinpoché himself; he said that this was to thank me for having spent almost two summers serving him by extensively editing the master woodblocks for *The Integration of Means and Wisdom* and the Dorjé Drollö texts. Beginning also about this time, the Jadra clan provided my basic necessities for a few years, so that I was at least not impoverished. Although my spiritual master's staff at Palpung would have given me my salary and my share of the donations made to the general assembly of monks, [46a] I did not ask for a thing, and so the obscurations due to misappropriation were less from this time on. In my home valley, an earthquake had destroyed our house and property without leaving a trace, and my old mother showed up. She stayed with me, reciting the six-syllable mantra.[401]

One night—I think it was during my *guruyoga* practice—I dreamed that the Karma Chagmé incarnation, Tendzin Thrinlé, bestowed a complete empowerment and oral transmission for the Eight Commands in a very brief time, following which the main meditation center became divided into nine areas (like a checkerboard with three squares to a side), in which I saw the assemblies of the principal and secondary deities of the Eight Commands as though they were actually present; in particular, the assembly of deities of the *padma* family of speech, together with the guardians, were extremely clear.

In the height of summer that year, Lama Karma Norbu came. I received the following transmissions which he bestowed: the empowerment for the five deity mandala of Chakrasamvara from the Shangpa Kagyü School;[402] the respective formal blessings[403] for the Six Yogas of Niguma, based on his own text; the transmissions for the section concerning the protective deity from *Dispelling All Obstacles*;[404] the extensive, middle-length, and abridged instructions on the Six Yogas, together with supplementary material; and detailed instructions on *The Amulet of Mahamudra, The Stages on the Paths of the Three Kinds of Spiritual Individuals,* and *The Seven Points of Mind Training,* all based on these works by Jonang Jetsün Rinpoché.[405] As well, he related some of his own experiences at random. When I later met with him at my spiritual master's residence at Palpung, he was very delighted to see me, [46b] and spoke at length of how his experiences and realizations had developed. He also said, "Don't make errors in your practice, and we will meet together in the pure realm of Khechara." He was aware that I would not be able to meet him again, since he died afterward.

In the eighth month, the venerable and holy lama Karma Ösel Gyurmé[406] was to bestow the empowerments and oral transmissions from the works by Jonang Jetsün Rinpoché, and so I went to upper Ling province. There were about ten of us gathered, including Dabzang Tulku Rinpoché, and Karma Ösel Gyurmé spent some three months bestowing the empowerments of most of the classes of tantra found in the collected works of Taranatha (the Kalachakra[407] foremost among these), as well as the oral transmissions for five or six volumes of Taranatha's writings. During this time, I experienced in my dreams some significant indications and a great sense that I was receiving blessings.

Following this, I returned to my hermitage, and during the winter solstice undertook a personal retreat focusing on Vajrakila. One night, I dreamed of a temple in the Indian style, with a courtyard surrounded by a low brick wall. Off to one side, I saw an image of the great glorious Vajrakumara, in a style resembling the Nepalese, which I understood to be painted by Khaché Panchen in blood that flowed from his own nose. To either side of the figure, the canvas was filled with depictions of the essential mantra of the deity. This image became more and more radiant, until finally I couldn't bear to look at it. At dawn on the morning after I had completed a ritual to avert negativity, I had an experience in meditation [47a] of looking up at the sky from the mouth of a spacious cave on a cliff side; I beheld very clearly the masculine and feminine aspects of Vajrakumara, formed as though from clouds, and in front of them the guardian of the Vajrakila cycle, Reti, riding on a mule. I then awoke. The following day there arrived a letter from my venerable lord Pema, in which he wrote several teasing yet complimentary verses, such as,

> In the forest hermitage of Kunzang Dechen Ling
> dwells the omniscient lord of *siddha*s. You who have mastered the
>   three solitudes,
> may you be completely victorious in your battle with the four *maras*![408]

and with these words I felt I had received a great blessing from him.

After this, while I was beginning the outer *sadhana* of The Union of All Rare and Precious Jewels, I dreamed one night of meeting the omniscient Dolpo Sang-gyé. I bowed to him, filled with faith, and he bestowed his blessing on me. I also experienced many signs of purifying harmful actions.

FROM THE BEGINNING of the Wood Dragon Year [1844-1845] through the sixth month, I practiced the inner *sadhana* diligently. Throughout this practice I had frequent signs in my dreams, some of which I will relate here. I dreamed of the sun and the moon rising together at dawn, and of putting on a "lotus hat" and fine robes. Going out on the rooftop, I met Vajradhara Pema Nyinjé seated in the middle of a group of people. Having prostrated to him, I sat down to his left, and he gave me his own mala of *raksha* beads. He also gave me several symbolic predictions, and encouraged me with words like, "Very good! Excellent!"

One night, [47b] I dreamed of the venerable Taranatha, quite heavyset and with a ruddy complexion, short in stature but very radiant and charismatic. I thought to myself, "Here is someone who has spiritual attainment. I should request an empowerment to transfer his timeless awareness to me." When I requested this, he placed both hands on my head and gave me a blessing. He then stated that he was still residing in Tsang Province, and that I might visit him later on. He then departed.

Another time I dreamed that Jampa Bumpa[409] of Kathok Monastery[410] arrived, looking heavyset. I asked him to consecrate a statue of the Sage in sambhogakaya aspect and some protection amulets in my possession.

On another night, I dreamed of looking to the east from the rooftop of my dwelling, and in the middle of a gap in the mountains I saw the Seventh Lord Karmapa, Chödrak Gyatso,[411] with his hands in the ritual gesture of "touching the earth." To his right was Chen-nga Chökyi Drakpa,[412] with his hands in the ritual gesture of meditative equipoise,[413] and to his left was Tenpai Nyinjé,[414] with his hands in the ritual gesture of giving spiritual teachings. They were dressed in their usual robes and hats, but their bodies were the size of small mountains.

Once, I dreamed of seeing a gathering of many great scholars of the Indian Buddhist tradition, among whom I was told were Vasumitra[415] and Chandragomin. On another occasion, it was Phadampa Sang-gyé, seated inside a small hut, wearing an Indian shawl of wool; I bowed respectfully, and presented many mandala offerings to him. And another time I dreamed that an old *torma* representing Taranatha had been replaced. [48a] There was a very loud clap of thunder, and I looked out at the sky to behold Ra Lotsawa Dorjé Drak[416] very clearly visible, sitting there.

In yet another dream, I saw the *mahasiddha* Karma Pakshi sitting in a temple, and requested his blessing. Occasionally, I would dream of a steep-sided ravine, in which I would see Mahakala and Mahakali—specifically, Lord Bernakchen and his Lady—as two figures with the heads of ravens; or there would be three of them, black people wearing black cloaks and riding black horses. At first these would be statues, and then they would actually come to life, moving about and showing different expressions.

Once I dreamed that I flew, and traveled to the slopes of a very large mountain; there were many statues, as though spontaneously formed in the rock, and in the middle of these was a realistic statue of Jatsön Nyingpo, to which I offered a seven-branch prayer.[417]

One morning at dawn, I had a clear vision of being seated on my bed and looking up at the mountain behind my retreat house; the one peak became three, and on the central one was the guru Saroruhavajra, embracing a white consort. On the right-hand peak were the masculine and feminine figures of Hayagriva and Vajravarahi in union, and on the left-hand peak was a form like that of the yellow Jambhala. On the front slopes was a divine gem with eight facets. I saw all this very clearly for a short time, and then awoke.

In one dream, I was in a temple. On the central throne was Gyalwang Karmapa Yeshé Dorjé;[418] he was of short stature, with a round face and blood-shot eyes, and was wearing the black vajra crown. [48b] To his left was Gyaltsap Drakpa Chokyang, wearing the orange crown that liberates on sight. To Karmapa's right was Situ Mitruk Chökyi Gocha,[419] seated on a chair in the manner of Maitreya. Around him were many volumes printed on yellow paper; from among these he gave me an Indian manuscript of a tantra.

On another occasion, I dreamed of being in what seemed to be a cultivated valley. On the slopes of the right-hand side was the *mahasiddha* Sang-gyé Nyenpa;[420] he had cut open the torso of a human corpse and pulled out the heart, and was holding it up in his hand. On the left-hand slopes was Gyaltsap Drakpa Döntrup,[421] seated in meditation posture. In the center of the valley was Gyalwang Karmapa Chöying Dorjé,[422] gazing up into the sky and pointing in every direction with a threatening gesture. He seemed to be in the midst of a gathering of emissaries, and was radiant with blessings.

Around this time, I had a dream of a very strong wish to receive the transmission of a definitive lineage of instruction for the four major instruction manuals of The United Intent of the Gurus. In my dream, Lord Pema Nyinjé was overjoyed, and gave me encouragement, assuring me of the existence of such a transmission of teachings. Seated on thrones were the deities Vajradakini and the three-faced, six-armed form of Simhamukha; they effortlessly bestowed on me a blessing of supreme timeless awareness, the unity of bliss and emptiness. I further dreamed, on one occasion, of mounting a ladder into the sky, and of stating that this was a sign that I had attained one of the levels of bodhisattva realization. During a feast offering on the tenth day of the seventh month, [49a] I felt as though I vaguely saw the face of Guru Rinpoché.

In particular, when I had about half completed the inner *sadhana*, some words of Tsel Rinpoché affected me, and this pointed out to me the fundamental nature of mind as an utterly ordinary state[423] beyond conceptual rationalization, simply resting as it is, uncontrived, without the need for the rational mind to fabricate or contrive, to arrest or establish anything at all. I felt a deep certainty of this which was not mere intellectual understanding. Seeing that all my previous efforts at meditation and resting in a non-conceptual state had not gone beyond this conceptual fabrication, I gained some partial conviction regarding the view of space-like simplicity, free of elaboration. It had been the case that my practice of the stage of development was not clear when I was guarding the essence of mind, and the essence of mind was lost when the development stage practice was clear; but now I was convinced that the appearance of the deity was mind, that mind was empty, and that appearance and emptiness were simultaneously present. When I was mindful of the clarity of the appearance, I experienced it from the point of view of its true nature, without the need to seek elsewhere. Nowadays, however, I am no longer able to transform the mindfulness of concepts into a mindfulness of their true nature, and it depresses me to see that times of ever-increasing distractions have caused me to fall under the sway of agitation and confusion.

When I had completed the inner *sadhana*, together with the supplementary practices, I went to see Situ Rinpoché for the purpose of taking part in a ceremony to promote the Buddhist teachings in general, involving the construction of an "effigy of the blade"[424] and the performance of the practice associated with it in the Vajrakila Temple. The preparations were completed in the first half of the eighth month; during the latter half, [49b] about fifteen participants conducted a week-long retreat, led by Dabzang Tulku and others who had already completed those stages prior to this. With the successful completion of the effigy ritual and the week's practice, I went back up to my retreat. Picking up where I had left off, I practiced in succession the secret *sadhana* of the Wrathful Guru, the most secret *sadhana* of the *dakini* Simhamukha, and the longevity *sadhana* from The Union of All Rare and Precious Jewels. Finally, I performed a four-day fire ritual for the four kinds of activity,[425] together with the ritual of Vajrakila to avert negativity and other ceremonies to prepare for the new year.

WHILE PERFORMING THE fulfillment ritual of The United Intent of the Gurus during the first days of the Wood Serpent Year [1845-1846], I experienced incredibly positive signs in dreams, such as finding many shining relics of the Victorious One.

During the second month Dabzang Tulku was requesting the empowerment and oral transmissions for the Eight Commands practice called The Gathering of *Sugatas*[426] from Garwang Tulku of Zurmang Monastery. Since he ordered me to attend as well, I went and received the complete empowerments and oral transmissions. The steward of Palpung, Tashi Chöphel, and someone named Rigdzin from the monastic residence provided a large lump of silver, and using these as basic capital, Dabzang Tulku undertook to supervise arrangements for combined *drupchen* and *mendrup* rituals. I myself, having received the empowerments and oral transmissions, went back up and spent over a month in personal retreat focusing on the practices of the peaceful and wrathful deities from The Gathering of Sugatas.

During the third month we performed the *drupchen* and *mendrup* rituals within sixteen days at the main meditation center, with Dabzang Rinpoché presiding as vajra master over some thirty-odd participants. [50a] With that accomplished, I settled back in my own retreat house and began practicing the outer *sadhana* of the nine deity mandala of Jinasagara. To commemorate the eighth day of the fourth month, I performed the two-day fasting ritual of Avalokiteshvara. During the first night, I dreamed rather vaguely of seeing three forms, of various sizes, of Khasarpana Avalokiteshvara;[427] on the night of the main ritual, I dreamed of seeing a statue of Khasarpana made of gold and copper, which filled the entire sky.

During the fifth month, in accordance with the wishes of Öntrul I went to my spiritual master's residence at Palpung to receive a detailed instruction on the explanatory tantra of medicine, as well as several miscellaneous teachings on important subjects.

In connection with this, I had a meditation experience one day while I was attending the tenth-day ceremony in the sixth month. I very clearly saw a form of Orgyen Rinpoché, at first two-dimensional, like a painting, then actually present. His cloak and coat and other garments were green, and in his right hand he brandished a *kila* dagger and a vajra, while the other details (such as the skullcap in his left hand) were as usual. Although I feel that these kinds of Nyingma ceremonies and rituals can transmit an enormous amount of blessing, nevertheless I have felt that the contamination of impairing my *samaya* connection with this lineage grows stronger with time, even though I later took part in many Nyingma *drupchen* rituals.

Following this, I returned to my hermitage and picked up where I had left off in my practice of the outer *sadhana* of Jinasagara. On the night of the new moon of the seventh month, I dreamed of an inconceivably vast palace, in which were arranged rows of many tall objects, like plates for mandala offerings. [50b] Around the perimeter of these were swirling lakes of blood (which I was told were the lakes of lower realms of rebirth), the banks of which were guarded by the gatekeepers of the hells, who had the heads of tigers and other beasts. To the rear of the palace was seated a buddha (I couldn't tell whether it was Amitabha or Maitreya) surrounded by numerous attendants. There were many people outside the gate, who had to cross those rows of mandala plates to reach the buddha's presence, but they were not able to pass. A lama explained to them that if they would proceed by prostrating while calling upon Bhaisajyaguru, they would arrive in the presence of that buddha. But of these people, some did not know how to recite Bhaisajyaguru's name, while others said that they knew how but had no deep devotion toward this buddha. Most of them could not advance from row to row, but were dragged from their path by these animal-headed figures and thrown into the lakes. Although I knew that I had a great freedom to do what I liked, and could have gotten there by flying, I thought of Bhaisajyaguru's greatness, and passed over eight rows of these stone plates by prostrating, with each prostration including a recitation of the names of the deities of Bhaisajyaguru's mandala known as the Eight Brothers. The buddha then placed his right hand on my head and said, "In the future, in an eon known as Star-like, you will attain buddhahood as [51a] a *tathagata* called Perfected Universal Monarch." I thereupon woke from sleep.

A few nights later, I had a dream of a fertile valley, the sward dotted with flowers; rising from the top of a hill was the entire spectrum of the levels and paths of the Buddhist teachings, laid out in an ascending order which you could see. I dreamed that someone explained it all to me. He spoke at length, of how the foremost among the gods were better off than ordinary worldly people, and how ordained people were superior to gods, while spiritually advanced beings (from "stream-enterers" up to *arhats*)[428] were superior to the ordained. Superior to them all, he said, was Maudgalyayana, and superior to him was Shariputra.[429] He explained the many ways in which each was superior to the other, and how this arose from their coarser or more subtle ways of understanding the meanings of the Four Noble Truths.

Another night, in my dreams I felt that I was about to die, and turning to face the southwest, I flew in that direction, thinking to go to Zangdok Palri.[430] When it seemed that I had gone about halfway on my journey, I saw both Orgyen and his consort, together with a third figure, Vimalamitra,[431] all on the slopes of a verdant col on a very high mountain. Descending to earth, I circumambulated them and made prostrations. Bowing my head, I requested some indication of their intent regarding me, that there might yet be some things for me to accomplish which would make it unnecessary to go to the continent of Chamara. Although they spoke many words of advice, I could not keep them in mind. [51b] At a certain point, I came back to my room. I received a summons stating that I had to come with all haste, whereupon I flew back in return, until I saw my spiritual master's monastic seat in a vivid brilliance. With that thought, I awoke from sleep.

On one occasion, I dreamed that Terdak Lingpa was seated in the center of the courtyard of a beautifully laid-out palace. His face and clothing were just as they are usually depicted in images of him, and he was stout of body and giving off a radiance. With intense faith, I received the four empowerments from his body.[432] When I requested several empowerments and oral transmissions that he might have given, he replied, "You should come to Mindroling; I am still staying there, and will give you whatever empowerments and oral transmissions you need, performing them all in detail." I awoke while thinking that I belonged to the bloodline descended from him.

In yet another dream, I saw my lord guru, Karma Ösel Gyurmé, wearing the three monastic robes, seated inside a particular building at the head of an assembly of people. Below him sat many other people in rows. With great devotion, I received the four empowerments from him through a process of meditation. One large individual told the story of the ordained rulers who invited the glorious Atisha to Tibet,[433] phrasing the marvelous details in an elegant manner, and presented many offering to the spiritual master, who then actually became the glorious Atisha. [52a]

On the fifteenth day of one month, there appeared to me in a dream one who was in essence a *dakini* of enlightened awareness, but in form was a flesh-eating *dakini* with the body of a human woman; she gave me an unshakeable experience of great bliss.

During the ninth month Dabzang Tulku came to assist me in performing the ceremonies of the nine tantras of The United Intent of the Gurus, and we practiced these for many days. One night, I dreamed of the moon, with a dim radiance, crossing the sky toward the south; knowing this to be a dream, I transformed myself into a *garuda*, and flew toward the east. I heard a voice call out from the sky, saying, "Go to the pure realm of Abhirati,[434] where there is water to drink that dispels sickness." And so I flew on my way. Immediately after crossing a high pass, I saw a pleasant land that I took for Abhirati, with dazzling palaces nestled within it. I landed below these, where there was a pond; taking this to be the medicinal waters referred to previously, I gulped down a mouthful. Going inside one of the palaces, I saw a seated blue buddha with sambhogakaya ornaments. Taking this to be Akshobhya, I bowed respectfully, requesting. "I pray that you grant a means of purifying the obscurations of karma, so that I and all sentient beings do not go to inferior states of rebirth!" Breaking into a smile, he spoke the long mantra[435] of Bhaishajyaguru and, following that, many Sanskrit mantras which resembled long mantras of longevity, with words like *Om punye punye* and so forth.[436] [52b] I awoke while thinking that I would go to meet some spiritually advanced person.

From the vajra master Tendzin, I received the empowerments for *The Secret Gathering of Compassion* and other practices, and then returned to my own abode to practice as before. When I received orders that I absolutely must go to Gyalrong to aid the teachings and monasteries, I wished to be of benefit, and so undertook a month-long personal retreat focusing on Kurukulle according to Karma Chagmé's tradition, during which several excellent signs occurred. While keeping up this practice and praying to Dakpo Rinpoché[437] one-pointedly, I dreamed that I found some of the flesh of both Gampopa[438] and Longchenpa, a little of which I ate, saving the rest.

AT THE START OF THE NEW Fire Horse Year [1846-1847], I began the inner *sadhana* of Jinasagara. After this, there was an epidemic of measles,[439] a case of which I contracted. When I had recovered slightly, and was ready to begin the secret *sadhana*, I was stricken with dysentery and came close to dying. Once I had recovered from that, I practiced the secret and combined *sadhana*s, and the offering ceremonies and feasts as extensively as my wealth and provisions would permit. Because I had to perform some small ceremonies on behalf of other people, I further developed a wasting sickness. This practice of Jinasagara, being the quintessential life force of the *dakini*s, is traditionally said to be very hazardous, and so there are many stories of others, too, who have encountered dangers with this practice. For me, though, I just have never experienced a personal retreat more upsetting than this one.

At this time, [53a] I dreamed of a lovely and elegant temple, in the center of which was the thousand-armed, thousand-eyed form of Avalokiteshvara, his body as white as a conch shell. In front of him was the feminine consort named "She of the Six Syllables, Tamer of Beings"; to his right and left were the white forms of "Jewel-holder" and "Holder of Secrets," shining with rays of light. At first these were in the forms of statues, but they then became real, and I bowed to them with great physical, verbal and mental respect.

Another time, I dreamed of flying in the sky in a clockwise direction, speaking much of the great qualities of the pure realms of the buddhas. Finally, I went to Sukhavati, where I briefly saw three figures, the principal form of Amitabha and his two attendants,[440] before I awoke.

On another occasion, I dreamed that the Dzogchen master Sönam Zangpo, truly Dromtön[441] come back to life, had come to Kyodrak. When he said that his practice was Dzogchen and his deity Mahakarunika, and that he explained these both to others as well, I was overjoyed. Immediately after that, I saw a heavyset old lama with a dark complexion, who was turning a prayer wheel with delight.

In the third month, with several of my students I undertook a three-week practice for the longevity *sadhana* of *The Vajra of Meteoric Iron*, as well as the ceremonies for making the pills called "Spontaneous Liberation from Lower States of Rebirth" according to the methods of Jatsön Nyingpo, the longevity chakra[442] of *The Vajra of Meteoric Iron*, and the amulets of *The Heart Essence of Definitive Meaning.*

As part of Palpung Monastery's general calendar of ceremonies, and [53b] especially to aid in the construction of a building to house some new statues of deities, I went to my spiritual master's residence in accordance with Situ

Rinpoché's orders, and a group of seven of us, master and students, performed a ceremony to dispel all harm from the earth spirits.

When I was about to set out for Gyalrong, since I had nothing whatsoever of my own, my spiritual master's residence provided the supplies for my camp, and loaned me the offerings and other necessities that I would require. My refuge lord bestowed a gift of several articles of clothing on me, and the Jadra clan sent several more. Situ Rinpoché bestowed on me the empowerment and conferral of command[443] for the protective deity Bernakchen, and granted me a lengthy interview. We formed our traveling party on the twenty-seventh day of the fifth Tibetan month. As I was leaving the encampment, Nego Kyabtra Tulku arrived from Dongpang Cave. From him I received a letter and an extremely fine painting of the venerable White Tara, painted in the old Kadampa style, both sent by Karma Ngédön, a student who had a *samaya* connection with me. This was definitely a positive indication of auspicious coincidence.

On the way, I visited Öntrul Rinpoché in Zhechen Monastery to offer prostrations and receive his blessing. Crossing the Dzachu River, we reached Parkha, where there were flash floods of a color like vermilion ink, the like of which the local inhabitants said they had never seen before. I was uncertain as to what this was a sign of.

At Datal, we were met by the ruler of Gyiling, who had come from Gulok to escort us. Accompanying his party, we passed through Nyikhok [54a] and arrived among the tent villages of Gulok.[444] Going to see those who invited me, the ruler of Gyiling principal among them, I fulfilled each one's requests. From this point onward, I began to have many bad dreams due to contamination and misappropriation.

From there we continued to a place called Doi Rulak. At dawn one morning while staying there, in a state between a dream and a meditation experience I dreamed of a bearded young man, carrying the tools of a smith, who said, "I have come to escort you. You should follow after me, while I go on ahead." With this, I dreamed that he went away. The next day we came to the beginning of the region of upper Do and saw the spirit mountain of an oath-bound guardian known as Thangyak the Smith.[445] We were met by an escort from Namgyal Monastery in upper Do, including a procession of monks in formal yellow robes. I gave all the empowerments and oral transmissions for the six volumes of works by Jatsön Nyingpo to Chöjé Lama Tenphel Dödön, and to the other lamas and monks, and fulfilled the requests of each of the patrons. One night I dreamed of a chest in that very place, within which I saw a golden-colored form of the protective deity Bernakchen, smiling and radiant, but with the left face slightly soiled and twisted to the right.

Next we passed through Dzirkha and came to Dzamthang.[446] The households of various spiritual masters and the monks of several monastic colleges put on a splendid display of hospitality for us, with formal processions to escort us. I performed the empowerment of Lord Atisha's lineage of Sarvavid Vairochana at the monasteries of Chöjé and at Tsangchung, [54b] and that of Guhyasamaja Manjuvajra[447] for the lamas, monks and meditation center residents of Tsangchen Monastery.

Having fulfilled the wishes of numerous patrons, I arrived at the borders of the Gyalrong states. The ruler of Dzong-gak had made excellent arrangements for our escort and other provisions on the road, and so we came to the monastery of Namgyal Ling. In the capital,[448] I answered the wishes of my hosts by performing rituals focusing on the peaceful and wrathful deities, *drupchö* rituals and empowerments to promote longevity, ceremonies to release people from the effects of negative forces, and so forth.

During our travels, we also received excellent hospitality from those in the capital of Choktsé. Accompanied by two parties of escorts from the ruler of Sokmo[449]—who met us at a greater and lesser distance, respectively[450]—we came to the palace of Karshö, which we made our base for the duration of our stay. I was very impressed when I looked over some of the one hundred or so Bönpo texts stored there, editions commissioned by the ruler of Throkyap. I saw clear signs of guardian deities surrounding them.

From there we journeyed to Throchu. The day we crossed Potsolo Pass, there was heavy snowfall and windstorms, which caused great difficulty to all the lamas and monks in the party. The populace of Otodro honored us with an escort and with their hospitality. Accompanied by escorts and a very elaborate formal procession from Shubha Monastery in Throchu, we continued on to the monastery, where I stayed in the apartment of Chöjé Tendzin Döndrup, in the spiritual master's residence. I questioned the lamas and monks concerning their situations, and sent the steward to the capital of Sokmo with a complete list of their requests. Although quite a lot of barley was collected as offerings when I performed public empowerments to large crowds, on behalf of the monastery's inhabitants [55a] some aides were sent out to raise more support. Some of the monks went to circumambulate Mount Langchen Gyingri and the mountain in Amdo called Dungri.

As for me, there were many disturbing signs, both external and internal, which caused me to undertake a personal retreat and the annual Vajrakila rituals to avert negativity for the coming year and, immediately upon finishing these, to perform a month of personal retreat focusing on the Venerable Goddess. Due to these practices, the negative signs in my dreams changed somewhat, and there were many positive signs. In particular, one night I dreamed of circumambulating a stupa and then setting off toward another building. The path being shrouded in darkness, an old woman was acting as my guide. She said, "At this point, between the old and the new years, there is danger from within and without and in between, from the ghosts of the dead, so take care! Then you will arrive safely." She showed me a staircase which I ascended, and when I reached the top I looked in the distance to behold a stupa of gold about six feet in height. On another occasion, I dreamed of a dark room, inside which, lit up by the rays of the sun, I saw a statue of the Venerable Goddess, golden in color and about a story in height, with a huge fruit held in her right hand. On the night of finishing my retreat, I dreamed of seeing an enormous stupa fashioned of copper and gold. Hoping to make a contribution to promote the Buddhist teachings, I undertook a week-long personal retreat focusing on Kurukulle, during which I had many very disturbing signs.

WITH THE BEGINNING of the Fire Sheep Year [1847-1848], I began an intensive *sadhana* practice for a form of Avalokiteshvara known as "The One Spontaneously Liberating Lower Realms." [55b] I completed one hundred thousand recitations of the long mantra. During the breaks between these meditation sessions, I strenuously practiced methods for gathering the accumulations of merit and awareness, such as prostrations and mandala offerings, and even by night my habitual tendencies made themselves felt for the most part as experiences of compassion and emptiness. I developed more understanding and realization of the excellent speech of the Buddha. In my dreams, there were many signs of the effects of harmful actions and obscurations being purified. I experienced a great descent of blessings. It was also at this time that I composed some verses of praise to the eight great bodhisattvas,[451] a work entitled *The Eight Great Clouds*; this was the first of my compositions signed in my own name.

During this period, I dreamed twice of going to hell realms, only to escape easily with the aid of a companion. On the slopes of a steep mountain, I clearly "saw" my home in a previous lifetime and recalled the circumstances of that lifetime. I dreamed of meeting Gyalwang Karmapa Jangchub Dorjé[452] and

Rigdzin Tsewang Norbu. I dreamed once of Avalokiteshvara, and the Lord of Sages seated under the bodhi tree. Surrounding him on all sides were many gardens, and I saw a radiant person who looked like an Indian mendicant yogi strolling about in these. I was told that this was the noble Maitreya. Feeling an immeasurable faith in all of these, I bowed to them with respect. Pointing at a certain tree, I humbly asked whether that was the bodhi tree under which the victorious Maitreya would attain buddhahood in the future. He replied, "No, not this one. But this bamboo growing here now will at that time [56a] turn into a wish-granting tree, and I will rely upon that to attain victory." On another occasion, the noble and excellent Avalokiteshvara himself manifested in the form of an elderly couple, who were on the point of bestowing the secret empowerment upon me when they said, "Avalokiteshvara is the master of domesticated beasts." They were then transformed into an eight-year old boy who predicted many things to me. He said, "Previously, when you encountered threats to your longevity, you were freed from these through your practice of The Union of All Rare and Precious Jewels. Even now, you should take care to perform these recitations and other practices."

While I was engaged in this recitation practice, I experienced many signs of environmental disharmony[453] in close succession, so I performed the recitation and visualization for averting these forces. When I dreamed of enemies threatening me, some experts in divination with knotted cords also stated that there was the threat of enemies to someone of equal status to me.[454] In the shrine room dedicated to the protective deities, I performed an offering ritual and a ritual to defend myself against enemies. When I was casting out the *torma*, there were excellent signs, such as a large flame shooting out to the west with a roaring sound.

To satisfy the requests of several patrons and to consecrate the meeting hall, I gave a formal authorization to the general assembly of lamas and monks. I gathered up the offerings and services provided to me and, after performing a *lhasang* ceremony, organized my traveling party for the return to our own region in the fourth month.

The night we stayed in a small monastery called Tsakho, I dreamed of a cheerful group gathered at the meditation center of Palpung; as I made prostrations to them, [56b] I saw in the rear of the temple a one-story high image of the masculine and feminine aspects of Chakrasamvara in union, sky-blue in color. To their left was a golden image of White Tara, and in front of that a radiant form of Dorjé Bernakchen. These three images were not drawn or sculpted, but were like rainbows, blazing with rays of light. When we were staying in Dokha, I experienced signs that I could overcome an oppressive force that was afflicting me. One night, as we were camping on Gyatup Plateau, I dreamed of the Four-Armed Mahakala at the head of a line formed by the five deities in his retinue, and dreamed that they had been sent by Kyabjé Rinpoché. And when we stayed at Shing-go, I dreamed of meeting both Akashagarbha[455] and Nivaranavishkambhin, just as they are traditionally described in literature. As I bowed to them with faith, they spoke of me as though talking to someone else, saying, "This child has incurred a fundamental downfall in his *samaya* connection for a very trifling reason." However, they said, the two of them and Kshitigarbha[456] had redeemed me. I myself felt this to be the case, and was overjoyed. I showed my satisfaction to them and thought, "I must meet Kshitigarbha." I went to a temple off to one side, and there came a cheerful-looking monk. He said that he had come to perform a *ganachakra* feast at the Palpung meditation center. I requested that he not deny me his compassion in this life, future lives, and the intermediate state between life and death. [57a] He thereupon took a beer jug in both hands and granted his blessing by placing this on the crown of my head. He placed a nourishing drink in my hand, and I drank it.

At that time in the summer season, it seemed as though it would be easy to cross Potsolo, so we camped there for a day. That night I dreamed of going to a certain building, where two middle-aged monks in Mongolian dress were staying. There I visualized myself in the form of Black Hayagriva of Ratna Lingpa's tradition. I touched the sword in my right hand to their heads, and they bowed respectfully to me.

I told them, "The two of you previously received lay ordination in the presence of both the great Orgyen and Karma Pakshi, so it is very important to maintain your vows accordingly."

They replied, "Sir, having received these vows, we will keep them."

"What are your emanations like?," I asked.

They mentioned many kinds, saying, "White men on white horses, yellow men on yellow horses, red men on red horses, black men on black horses, and so on." I awoke with the thought that these were paternal deities of the Khangsar clan.

We continued to the capital of Sokmo. In response to the grievance issued by the monastery there, a formal decision had been handed down, together with documents that justified the decision. But it seemed that the Buddhist master of Shubha[457] was somewhat zealous in pursuing his own interests and had not relinquished the property that had been levied. His opponent was a family relation of Daro Takkyap, the most powerful advisor in the region, and so the master had not been able to achieve his goal to defeat his opponent and win his case.[458] [57b]

In response to requests, I performed a consecration of the temple and an empowerment for the king and queen. Gathering up the offerings, we left for Namgyal Monastery in Dzong-gak. During a lengthy stopover while I was doing much recitation, I dreamed one night of someone called Dro Lhagyal[459] pointing toward a certain mountain and saying that the Kuntrul incarnation[460] had caused some rather frightening developments in an area close to the capital of Bhu. In addition to a feast and propitiation ceremony of The United Intent of the Gurus (to commemorate the twenty-fifth day of the lunar month), I practiced the *sadhana* and made the amulet that is the representation of enlightened speech according to this practice. I dreamed of seeing Guru Rinpoché, seated in the middle of a squarish white cloud in the sky, and of him changing into the Lord of Sages. I also dreamed of a small whitewashed building, with many prayer wheels installed around it, which I was told was the meditation center of the "illuminating jewel of the mind."

We then struck camp and continued. When we reached a place called Shumidhur near the capital of Bhu, I received a disturbing letter from Kuntrul. Kuntrul and I had never even met, and so had no connection whatsoever, either good or bad, but he had gone against the edicts of Kyabjé Rinpoché, who had been very angry with him and expelled him from the region of Palpung. Kuntrul had gone to the commune of Sertar, where he had sought support from the family of the chieftain. [58a] Gradually they had built up a relationship of priest and patron. At this point, since I was an official representative of Palpung Monastery, Kuntrul wished to settle an old score. By inciting the chieftain's partisan faction to raise an army, and by bribing several of the townspeople, he made plans to have me killed and the rest of my party seized. Because this made our route so hazardous, we had to waste a long time waiting in this place. When I was performing an offering ritual focusing on the protective deities, the odor of the *gugul* incense pervaded everywhere, inside and out, and sparks actually flew from my body time and time again. We practiced the *sadhana* of the protective *ging* deities, and obvious signs of success were clearly visible to all. And while praying over a period of time while meditating on the protection circle of the venerable Tara, I dreamed of numerous gold and copper statues of White Tara, each complete with throne, seat and backrest, all seeming very real and solid with their right hands in the ritual gesture of generosity. I bowed my head to them. All these indications eased my mind.

In that region there were many small monasteries following the extensive lineage of the Jonang tradition. Many of the lamas and monks convened, and I bestowed the complete empowerments of the glorious Kalachakra, instruction on the preliminary practices for its Six Branches of Union,[461] the empowerment of Vajrabhairava,[462] and other transmissions.

Perhaps it was due to the several quite wrathful local spirits, but once for an entire day [58b] it hailed throughout the area, with many bolts of lightning and incessant, overwhelming thunder and sheet lightning. We did whatever protective visualizations we knew, and no harm whatever befell our camp.

Two individuals—one of the evil men who had sworn to kill me and one of the major figures in the chieftain's faction—died unexpectedly, without Kuntrul being unable to protect them. There were also some extremely bad signs. Planning to loot the entire Palpung party, the chieftain's strategists had the majority of his forces lying in ambush. We sent messengers ahead to Dzamthang to gather information, and met several informed envoys, including one of the master's teachers. The majority of our party went into hiding, while a group of five or six of us, myself and some of my students, went ahead, using artful means to reach the master's residence at Dzamthang Monastery. There we found a delegation of several people, led by Kuntrul himself; but since they could do nothing, they went away. With the aid of an escort from the staff of the monastic residence[463] our party arrived safely.

I requested detailed instructions on the Six Yogas of *The Kalachakra Tantra*, together with practical instruction, from a lama named Ngawang Chöphel, who had mastered the study and practice of the Vajra Yoga cycle of the *mahasiddha* Tsangpa Tsang. From other lamas, I also requested such instructions as the word-by-word commentaries on methods for carrying out personal retreats focusing on the oral tradition of Vajrabhairava. [59a]

In that area was located a very powerful temple dedicated to the protective deities, erected by Chöjé Paljor Zangpo. I spent some three days there, performing a propitiatory ritual to the protective deities. One night, I dreamed of seeing first a statue, then the actual presence, of Vajra Panjara Natha,[464] about one story in height; and of seeing the four-armed goddess Rangjung Gyalmo,[465] riding a red mule with a human corpse strapped on like a roll behind the saddle, about three stories high and shining with red rays of light. I understood these as signs that the blessings of the protective deities had not diminished.

In the company of a very large group made up of accompanying escorts from these local groups and guides who had come from upper and lower Do to escort us back, we arrived at Yuthok Namgyal Monastery. While staying there, I gave explanations to some of the lamas and monks on *The Profound Inner Meaning* and the two smaller related treatises. I also gave instructions on the preliminary practices of the Mahamudra tradition.

Since Tashi Gyatso of Gyiling was known for his psychic abilities, I asked him which ceremony I should perform, since many teachers and their attendants from Drinyen Dongshar were to escort me. I received a letter from him, saying that he had been told it would be excellent if I were to lead a ritual at Yuthok Namgyal Monastery to invoke the protective deities to defeat enemies. So together with four others who had completed the requisite recitation practices, I undertook a week-long supplementary recitation. I attended the *gutor* ceremonies which were celebrated at the monastery to end the year. We finished this with a ceremony to expel a *torma*,[466] a fire ritual, and thanksgiving prayers. [59b]

IN THE FIRST MONTH of the new Earth Monkey Year [1848-1849], I finished the remainder of the instructions begun previously. At this time, perhaps as a sign arising from my practicing *The Four Session Guruyoga* and the ritual of "the gift of the body"[467] on a daily basis, I dreamed one night of Gyalwang Mikyö Dorjé[468] and the Drukpa Kagyü master Pema Karpo seated in the courtyard of a temple. I bowed with great devotion to Gyalwang Karmapa and requested him, "Please grant your blessings to my body, speech and mind!" He recited *The Four Session Guruyoga*, beginning, "Namo guru," and when he recited "When the precious spiritual master approaches," there appeared two individuals who seemed to be his attendants, bearing staffs topped by a statue of the Sage and a large stupa. I felt quite inspired as they circumambulated many times, clockwise and counterclockwise. Then Drukpa dissolved into Gyalwang Karmapa. When the section dealing with the *dakinis* of timeless awareness was finished, they all went into the temple, and Karmapa turned into Lord Pema Nyinjé Wangpo, who placed his two hands on my head. He completed the recitation from the line, "Mikyö Dorjé fills the whole of space" to the end, in a divinely mellifluous voice. Further, the sky was filled with emanations of the holy one from India, Phadampa Sang-gyé, and Machik Lapdrön. From Phadampa's forms nectar was flowing like a stream; when I drank from this, my mind was delighted at its sweet flavor. [60a]

I received an urgent message from Kuntrul that he needed to present a grievance, so I went, accompanied by a party from the chieftains of Dokhok and Serkhok,[469] and we met with him in a small valley leading off from the main Do Valley. After several days of discussion, the older members of the group came to an agreement among themselves, at which we restored good relations with some trifling gifts which pleased Kuntrul, such as a horse and some gemstones.[470] The gathering then broke up, and together with our escorts from upper Do we went to the area of Gyiling in Gulok, where I spent several days satisfying the requests of the individuals concerned. The escorts from this area guided us from upper Nyi as far as Tsaptsa.[471]

I then met with Jampai Dorjé, the Öntrul incarnation of Zhechen Monastery, and made him a series of offerings. From him I requested several oral transmissions, such as The Gathering of Secrets and Vajrakila cycles from Guru Chöwang's tradition.[472]

Proceeding in stages, we reached Palpung Monastery during the second month. I had an audience with my refuge lord Vajradhara, who expressed great delight that I had conducted this affair effectively. I offered all the articles and possessions I had received to the administrators of the spiritual master's residence.

In the past, when lamas had been sent in succession to Gyalrong, many monks in their parties had died and all kinds of rumors had abounded. This time, though, none of the lamas or monks in my party had lost their lives, although we sustained a great loss of horses and mules due to mange and other causes. It was also around this time that the monastery of Ba Chödé[473] had attacked Pung-ri Monastery. The Chagdud incarnation had been slain.[474] The majority of lamas and monks were helpless to prevent such events. [60b] The fact that things had turned out as they did for our monastery, that our expedition of teachers and students to Gyalrong had escaped from the clutches of our enemies, brought accolades and congratulations from many.

A lama named Tetsa had given me some ounces of gold, and whatever there was I offered to Kyabjé Rinpoché and requested from him the sublime empowerment of the Kalachakra and the complete instructions for the Six Branches of Union.

At the hermitage, I again met my old mother, who was living quite comfortably there. I took a brief rest and undertook a personal retreat focusing on the Venerable Goddess.

Previously, from an young age I had leisure to write and put great stock even in whatever dreams I had, good or bad; so up until the time I was in upper Do, I kept copious diaries, also recording some accounts of such signs in my recitation and *sadhana* practice as seemed useful. From this point on, though, I kept no records whatsoever of my dreams and so forth; and while there were a few indications of receiving blessings (though I had in no way any ability to develop signs of accomplishment in the various kinds of recitations and *sadhana*s), none of these are clear in my memory, and I find myself deprived of anything of this nature to relate. And besides, the greater my distractions became, the more my positive tendencies were eclipsed and my confused tendencies encouraged. Because it was necessary for me to be involved in all kinds of contamination due to articles offered to me in faith, especially the contamination associated with deceased individuals, from this time on the clear and visionary experiences of my earlier life became obscured; the positive signs in my dreams stopped, [61a] and I dreamed of numerous bad omens. Even the vigor of my experiences and realization in meditation has suffered accordingly, and I find that I am quite dismayed at having had to engage so recklessly in such negative and contaminating activities.

During my trip to Gyalrong, when I reached Tsaptsa I had arranged for the supplies with which to have the volumes of The United Intent of the Gurus written out. Two scribes began this task on the twenty-fifth day of the fourth month.

From this point on, I gradually gathered a few motivated students around me, and taught them Sanskrit grammar, poetics, orthography, astrology, medicine and so forth, according to their individual interests; but it was rare that any of them completed a thorough study of the main and auxiliary texts. Even of those who did finish, it is hard to say whether more than one or two really made any significant contribution as a result.

During this period, the incarnate master Jamyang Khyentsé was residing at Dzongsar. In a letter to me, he related that his elder brother, Gyurmé Döndrup, had shown great promise as one who would promote the Buddhist teachings, but had died in central Tibet. While Jamyang Khyentsé's grief had been inconsolable, he said, "Now that you have successfully returned safe and sound, I am as happy as if I had forgotten my previous grief." He said that it was now imperative that he receive from me a complete transmission of all the empowerments for the classes of tantra of the Jonang tradition. Accordingly, I agreed to this and he came to Palpung Monastery. I myself [61b] moved to Khangsar College in the monastery.[475]

For a fairly large group of lamas and incarnates and monks, Lord Khyentsé himself foremost among them, I used the writings of Jonang Jetsün Rinpoché to give all the empowerments I had previously received for these classes of tantra, principally the glorious Kalachakra; I also gave the oral transmissions for the *sadhana*s and mandala rituals, instructions on the Six Branches of Union, transmission of the seven mandalas of the Ngok tradition[476] according to the set of manuals written by Karma Chagmé, and the blessing ceremonies and instructions for the Six Yogas of Niguma according to the Jonang tradition. Lord Khyentsé himself had been to central Tibet. He said that even though, at that time, the continuous transmission of blessings for these tantra classes of the Ngok tradition remained unimpaired, that nevertheless this set of Karma Chagmé's manuals was inadequate for performing the *sadhana* and other major rituals connected with these practices. He said, "You must definitely produce an adequate set of manuals that includes texts for each of these rituals."

I returned to my hermitage and performed several times the ritual for offering one hundred feasts according to The United Intent of the Gurus. I undertook a personal retreat for about three months for the practice of *The Illuminating Gem of Enlightened Mind*. In the main meditation center, together with Dabzang Tulku I received a complete transmission of the empowerments for The United Intent of the Gurus from Lama Sang-ngak.

At this point, my resources were depleted, and several of my students remarked, "At this rate, it will be impossible to support even you and your mother, let alone the writing out of all thirteen volumes of The United Intent of the Gurus. Better go to the east of here on rounds to collect alms." [62a] I therefore borrowed horses and pack animals from the Jadra clan and went to gather offerings of grain in the eleventh month. Because the influence of the clan of the chieftain of Meshö[477] was widespread at this time, I was well-received wherever I went. I was given gifts from both Dzongsar Monastery and the Dzongsar administrator for the empowerments and formal authorizations that I gave there. I also visited the monasteries of Terlhung and Thramto briefly, and was richly provided with offerings of grain and other goods. I completed my circuit in the twelfth month, returning to immediately perform the ritual of Vajrakila to avert negativity.

IN THE NEW EARTH BIRD YEAR [1849-1850], I began a personal retreat focusing on *The Illuminating Gem of Enlightened Mind* practice, after first doing a week-long retreat to supplement my previous retreat on this practice. When the *sadhana* retreat was finished, I performed the extensive ritual of fulfillment for seven days, and the fire ritual for the four kinds of activity for four days, and so on, doing things in this developmental and extensive way.

Because this year was my thirty-seventh, and therefore the most crucial year of my life,[478] I continued by spending a month each practicing the longevity ritual called The Gathering of Secrets, the outer *sadhana* entitled *Consummate Profundity*, and the practice of White Tara.

Around this time (and I am uncertain as to whether it was earlier or later on in this period), I dreamed one night of a fine fertile meadow, where there was a throne shaped like a boulder of white stone, marked with many self-arisen letters in both Indian and Tibetan scripts. On this throne was seated Guru Padmasambhava. I bowed to him respectfully, and offered a prayer that the obstacles to my longevity be dispelled. He bestowed a blessing on me, and said that this blessing would extend for forty-four years from that date, [62b] without harm coming to me. "At that point," he said, "you will actually meet with me." I later saw a reference to this in the *sadhana* of enlightened mind entitled *Dispelling All Obstacles*, which was discovered by Chokgyur Lingpa.[479]

In midsummer I gathered together a number of scribes and had the texts of The United Intent of the Gurus written out. I also taught Sanskrit grammar to a lama who had come from Thramto. With the coming of autumn, Kyabjé Rinpoché had finished making a new statue, and I went to take part in the ceremony of filling the hollow interior of the precious object with appropriate scrolls containing long mantras. It took several days to prepare for the ceremony, after which the installation of the mantra scrolls[480] was carried out splendidly, with Dabzang Tulku and Zhechen Tulku[481] in attendance. Immediately afterward, Situ Rinpoché himself came, and the whole group of about fifteen of us, master and students, performed a two-day consecration rite based on the mandala of Chakrasamvara. Situ Rinpoché then moved to upper Ling, to the residence of Dabzang Tulku where, in response to our prayers, he bestowed the formal blessing for *The One Hundred Siddhas* from Atisha's tradition, and oral transmissions for many important works of the Karmapas and Zhamar Rinpochés. We, for our part, made mandala offerings of whatever wealth we possessed, and offered ceremonies for the long life of Situ Rinpoché. He then went to the main meditation center. A residence for Situ Rinpoché was required there, and since it was absolutely essential that I go out to help raise funds by collecting offerings of grain, I organized a traveling party to cover the region as far as Meting Dzingkhok and set out to collect alms of grain. I returned from my rounds in the twelfth month, and in accordance with my standing custom I immediately performed a ritual of Vajrakila to avert negativity and undertook a personal retreat focusing on the Venerable Goddess. [63a]

IN THE FIRST MONTH of the new Iron Dog Year [1850-1851], I performed the extensive fulfillment ritual of The United Intent of the Gurus and, in keeping with the requests of several important patrons, I spent about three weeks in a personal retreat (undertaken for both my own and others' benefit) focusing on the longevity *sadhana* called The Gathering of Secrets. On the first day of the second month I went to the spiritual master's residence at Palpung. Öntrul was receiving one hundred empowerments[482] of the longevity practice *The Integration of Means and Wisdom* from Tendzin Tulku of Zurmang Monastery, and I joined him in requesting this transmission. I then received, one after the other, the major and minor empowerments and instructions for the oral lineage of Chakrasamvara; the oral transmissions for the five main volumes and other instruction manuals dealing with Lord Bernakchen, Lady Rangjung Gyalmo, and other protective deities (as well as memorization of the appropriate liturgies); and the complete empowerments and oral transmissions for *The Lake Cliff* from Rolpai Dorjé's *termas*. In return, I offered Zurmang Tendzin Tulku the oral transmissions for the Five Works of Maitreya and other works.

From the third to the fifth month I taught on a number of different subjects—Chandragomin's *Discourse on Grammar, The Profound Inner Meaning*, the two smaller treatises, and the three levels of vows—to many students, principally Kyabché Sötrul. Following this, I returned to my own residence. The woodblocks for the thirteen volumes of The United Intent of the Gurus were finished, and I completed the editing and had boards, wrappings, labels and ties made of the finest quality materials. Gyatrul[483] had come from Palyul, and we began study of Chandragomin's grammar. I also taught a series of subjects, including medicine and astrology, to Pema Lekdrup when he arrived. [63b]

During the earlier and later parts of this year, I wrote a number of small works on unrelated topics, such as my notes for the empowerment ceremony of The United Intent of the Gurus. In particular, in accordance with a directive from Situ Rinpoché, I composed a prayer of praise to Guru Rinpoché entitled *The Eight Omnipresent Omens.*

The throne holder of Nyidzong arrived to receive instruction on the "Single Intent" teachings of the Drigung Kagyü. During the winter solstice, I undertook a personal retreat focusing on Vajrakila and performed a ritual to avert negativity, and following that, one after the other, the *guru sadhana* of *The Heart Drop of the Black Hum* and personal retreats focusing on the dark blue and white forms of the Swift-Acting Jnana Natha.[484] One morning at dawn, during my practice on the white form of the protective deity, there was a definite sign of the deity's presence: I actually saw Lama Karma Norbu sitting in the sky in front of me, with a fair complexion and shining with rays of light.

In the twelfth month Gyatrul had completed his study of the three volumes of Chandragomin's Sanskrit grammar. I began teaching him the basic works on Tibetan grammar. [64a]

DURING THE FIRST MONTH of the new Iron Pig Year [1851-1852], I undertook a personal retreat focusing on Akashagarbha, and performed the confession ceremony and the confession of dreams. On one occasion previous to this, when I had been performing a confession ceremony, I had dreamed of a vague figure saying to me, "Recite the sutras of Manjushri, Avalokiteshvara, and Akashagarbha and your harmful actions and failures in maintaining your vows will be absolutely purified." On this occasion, I also dreamed of seeing an indefinable deep blueness, like the sky, and thinking to myself, "This is Akashagarbha."

The young prince of Dergé[485] sent a directive requiring me to perform a number of practices, which I carried out in due order. As well, it was often necessary throughout that year to respond to the insistent summonses of many important patrons, particularly the Jadra clan, and I performed several ceremonies (especially ones for ensuring their good fortune) and many ceremonies for deceased persons, such as the ceremony of the peaceful and wrathful deities.

By the summer, Gyatrul had finished his studies, and I offered him a name in recognition of his status as a trained grammarian. He then received his full monastic ordination from Situ Rinpoché and returned to his home monastery. During this period, I mostly spent my time in formal meditation sessions, on either Jinasagara or my usual daily practices.

Lama Karma Ngédön arrived from Lithang in the fifth month. He said that I must prepare a detailed astrological chart for the recent birth of the newest prince of Dergé,[486] and so I drew up the calculations, using *The Soft Rain of White Lapis* and the later translations of the Chinese systems of astrology as my sources. Following this, I received orders that I was required to come to Dergé for the ceremonies surrounding the birth, so I went to Lhundrup Teng.[487] I completed ceremonies to offset calamities due to the earth spirits, and performed some major empowerments, as well as a ceremony to ensure good fortune for the younger brother of the king. I then returned home.

During the autumn, I received some transmissions from Lama Sang-ngak: the empowerments and oral transmissions for *The Gem Trilogy of Supreme Compassion* of Sang-gyé Lingpa;[488] the white, black, and red forms of Manjushri; and the oral transmissions for two volumes of uncollected texts dealing with the Eight Commands. Going to upper Ling, I gave the oral transmissions for the Seven Treasuries of Longchenpa to Dabzang Tulku and his students. [64b] Dabzang Tulku bestowed the cycle of empowerments from the Mindroling tradition entitled the Noble Wish-Granting Vase. Together with Dabzang Tulku, I requested the complete empowerments and oral transmissions for the Four Higher Collections of the Heart Drop Teachings from Gönpo Tulku. I also received the empowerments for Vajrasattva according to the tradition of Taksham, and the oral transmission for the Nyingma volume of *The Collected Instructions on the Six-Armed Mahakala*. Gönpo Tulku said that he required instructions for the Six Yogas of Niguma and the Six Branches of Union from *The Kalachakra Tantra*, and so I taught him these. At the meditation center, I requested the empowerments and oral transmissions for Vajrakila according to the tradition of Chöjé Lingpa, and for the complete system of empowerments included in the Sky Teachings.

Having undertaken in extensive detail my annual personal retreat focusing on Vajrakila and a ritual to avert negativity, as well as a personal retreat focusing on the noble Tara, I then undertook a personal retreat focusing on the cycle of the peaceful and wrathful deities called the Natural Freedom of Enlightened Intent, according to the manuals of Karma Chagmé, which present forty-two variations of the mandala.

DURING THE SECOND MONTH of the new Water Rat Year [1852-1853], I ended my retreat, having completed the recitations for the peaceful and wrathful deities. Jamyang Khyentsé Rinpoché having returned from central Tibet, I sent a messenger to offer a scarf of welcome and a scroll painting of one hundred *siddhas*. He sent back a very special statue of Vajrakumara made of yellow bronze, a *terma* discovered by Kunkyong Lingpa; this, he said, was an auspicious sign for dispelling obstacles to our activities for the sacred Buddhist teachings.

In response to a special envoy sent by the Sokmo clan of Meshö,[489] I went to them and for the benefit of those who had died both previously and recently, [65a] I had to spend two weeks performing the ritual of the peaceful and wrathful deities. To Khyentsé Rinpoché, who had come especially, and to about twenty other lamas and incarnations, including Donyön Tulku, I gave the entire collection of empowerments and oral transmissions of The Precious Source of Sadhanas from the Jonang tradition. Khyentsé Rinpoché very graciously bestowed gifts on me, such as a precious "regent" statue,[490] which was a *terma* discovered by Dorjé Lingpa,[491] and a complete set of block prints of the works of Jonang Jetsün Rinpoché. For my part, I requested the empowerment and oral transmissions for the teachings of Guru Chöwang entitled *Dredging the Pit of Cyclic Existence*, and instructions on the *Dzabir* of Khyentsé.

Due to the insistent requests from the young prince of Dergé[492] that I absolutely had to attend the ceremonies for building a new meditation center, I went to Dergé Gönchen, where I performed ceremonies to dispel harm and promote longevity and good fortune. Focusing on the articles housed there, I also practiced the *sadhanas* for liberation through contact and sight from The United Intent of the Gurus. Following this, I continued on my circuit.

Dabzang Tulku had built a new monastic residence in upper Ling, and said that I must perform a major empowerment, which I therefore did. I requested from him the longevity empowerment for Taksham's tradition of Amitabha, and other empowerments.

The king of Dergé and his brother had come to witness the sacred dances for the celebration of the tenth day of the lunar month. In their presence, I performed three days of empowerments, including the one hundred empowerments of the peaceful and wrathful deities. For the older brother, I performed the combined empowerment for Sarvavid Vairochana and the nine deity mandala of Amitayus, and for the younger brother, several formal authorizations. They then departed.

At the main meditation center of Palpung, I met with Situ Rinpoché. [65b] I spent several days giving the formal blessings and instructions for the Six Yogas of Niguma to the retreatants. For several lamas of Throkyap in Gyalrong,

and for a Lama Sakho and others, I followed Situ Rinpoché's instructions and
went to the spiritual master's residence, where I spent several days performing
the formal blessing focusing on the hundred *siddha*s.

During the seventh month Khyentsé Rinpoché came to upper Ling at the
request of Dabzang Tulku, myself, and other teachers and students. Beginning
with the "three white cycles" of the Tshar tradition, and concluding with the
transmission of the goddess Tseringma, he bestowed the complete
empowerments, oral transmissions, and instructions for the collection The
Compendium of All Sadhanas that he himself had recently compiled. He also
bestowed all the following transmissions on us out of his inconceivable grace:

- the empowerments, oral transmissions, and instructions for the Innermost Heart Drop of the Guru
- the empowerments, oral transmissions, and instructions for the entire
  collection of *terma* teachings of the Mindroling tradition
- the empowerments, oral transmissions, and instructions for the *Kila Razor* practice of Vajrakila, The Guru: The Gathering of Secrets, and the
  Black Krodhi *terma* cycle of Nyang
- the empowerments and oral transmissions for *Orgyen With a Retinue of
  Gauri Goddesses* and *The Great Vase of Nectar*
- the oral transmissions for many minor cycles of older *terma*s
- the general empowerment for the Lords of the Three Families[493]
- the empowerments and oral transmissions for the collections *The Manifest Enlightenment of Vairochana* and *The Vajradhatu*
- the explanatory instruction on the overall path
- the empowerments and instructions for the Sixteen Spheres of the
  Kadampa lineage, the oral transmissions for the two volumes of Kadampa
  teachings, and the formal authorization and instruction for the Four Deities of the Kadampa School[494]
- the twenty-five mainstream instructions transmitted by Niguma, the ritual
  transmission of blessings for the white and blue-black forms of the Six-
  Armed Mahakala, [66a] the ritual transmission of blessings and instructions of Sukhasiddhi and *The Combination of Four Deities*, as well as
  oral transmissions for whatever teachings of the Shangpa lineage exist as
  continuous transmissions
- instructions on the texts on Mahamudra and the Six Yogas of Naropa by
  Dakpo Tashi Namgyal[495]

- the empowerments, oral transmissions, and instructions for the Zhijé lineage,[496] according to the manuals of Lochen Dharma Shri[497]
- the empowerments, oral transmissions, and instructions for the Severance cycles of Thangtong Gyalpo[498] and of the Mindroling tradition
- the instruction on the longevity *sadhana* of Druppai Gyalmo[499]
- the empowerment for Kurukulle according to the Tshar tradition, and the instruction on the central channel connected with this, as well as the instructions on the transference of consciousness and the "inconceivable" stage of completion
- the instruction on *The Seven Points of Mind Training* by Gyalsé Thogmé Zangpo[500] and
- the blessing transmission for the collected mantras of Guhyasamaja, Chakrasamvara, and Vajrabhairava.

During these times, I saw a number of good signs in my dreams. I dreamed of being given many relics by Tendzin Tulku, which he said were those of Jetari,[501] and of finding many relics of Tselé Natsok Rangdrol.[502] I dreamed of entering the gate of a palace that I was told was the palace of Zangdok Palri; led inside by a steward, I beheld Guru Rinpoché, with rows of *tantrikas* on either side of him, and requested his blessing. In one dream, I became the four-armed form of Vajravarahi, and bestowed empowerments on several other people with my *kartari* knife.[503]

Khyentsé Rinpoché ended the series of teachings with the transmission of the Northern Treasure tradition of *The Profound Path of Symbol and Meaning*. After we had offered a mandala of whatever we possessed, he returned to Dzongsar Monastery. I went to see those who had summoned me to visit, the Sokmo and Nera clans[504] and others, [66b] and met their expectations by performing a ceremony focusing on the peaceful and wrathful deities, as well as rituals to ensure good fortune.

During the tenth month we journeyed to Dzongsar Monastery, where we stayed in the monastic quarters of the Nera faction. In response to Khyentsé Rinpoché's requests, I offered him several unrelated empowerments and oral transmissions for the Heart Drop of the Dakini and other cycles of the old and new schools of tantra. He in turn bestowed the empowerments, transmissions and instructions of the Dzogchen approach—teachings from the Category of Mind and *The Vajra Bridge* from the Category of Expanse—as well as the empowerment for the peaceful and wrathful deities from *The Web of Magical*

Illusion, the explanatory instructions on *The Heart Essence of Secrets*,[505] and the oral transmissions for the commentaries of Rongzom and Yungtön,[506] together with his, Khyentsé Rinpoché's, instructions and explanations of other tantras. Following this, he also invested me with the authority to transmit these teachings. As part of his kindness, I also received the complete empowerments for the following: the nine deities of Samyak[507] according to the So tradition; the tantra called *The Equal Union of Buddhas*; the five deities of the Arapachana form of Manjushri, The Heart Drop of Naturally Lucid Basic Space; and the authorization for the protective goddess Dhumavati[508] according to the Ngok tradition.

Nowadays, as far as even the most famous lamas and scholars are concerned, other than those who hold their own specific traditions and several mainstream lineages of teaching, there are few who could equal Khyentsé Rinpoché's extremely fine regard and pure view for all the teachings of the Sage without bias, and accounts of their spiritual careers are meager. In particular, in these latter times there are many who, while they themselves do not act forthrightly and do not have a pure spiritual outlook, still speak of the relative superiority and inferiority of different Buddhist traditions, or the relative purity or impurity of different lineages, saying things such as, "Well, at least such-and-such a tradition has empowerments." [67a] To say nothing of other traditions, they are full of meaningless suspicions and resistance concerning even their own traditions, like the proverbial skittish old yak that causes himself to shy.

I, too, although I have been someone who has longed from his heart for the Buddhist teachings, have not turned out to have the mental strength to make up my own mind, and so have not accomplished my wishes successfully. From this point on, however, gradually the lotus of my faith in all the teachings of the Sage (without sectarian distinctions) and in the holders of those teachings unfolded in an unbiased manner. My spiritual career, too, has improved, and I have not committed the grievous fault of rejecting the teachings.[509] All this is due to the grace of this precious lord guru.

I then returned to my home monastery. In the eleventh month, I moved from my spiritual master's residence to the Vajrakila Temple, where Dabzang Tulku and I, accompanied by some of our students, prepared and performed a ritual of ransom focusing on Vajrakila. In the twelfth month we were summoned by the young prince of Dergé to come and direct ceremonies that would remove obstacles to the consecration of the new meditation center. So we went

to Dergé Gönchen and performed the Vajrakila ritual for about a week; as
well, we performed the ritual of "Liberation on Sight" from The United Intent
of the Gurus for the statues to be installed in the meditation center. But when
the consecration ritual was performed by Dziphu Khenpo, the signs, both outward and inward, were extremely disturbing. We returned to Situ Rinpoché's
monastic residence, where Öntrul Rinpoché taught me the methods required
for the "vase consecration" ritual[510] from Supreme Compassion: The Gathering of Secrets. [67b]

THEN, DURING THE NEW YEAR celebrations for the Water Ox Year [1853-
1854], we performed the vase consecration ritual very thoroughly with a large
group of participants, with Dabzang Tulku acting as the vajra ruler and myself
in the role of regent.

It was during this time that I fulfilled a request from a few of my patrons by
going to the hermitage and giving the instruction on longevity practice from
the tradition of Druppai Gyalmo. I began with the preliminary practices and
continued through the instructions on the stage of development and mantra
repetition.

I received two letters from Khyentsé Rinpoché in central Tibet instructing
me to codify the rituals connected with the mandalas of the Ngok tradition. He
had already spoken insistently about this the year before to Dabzang Tulku
and Zhechen Tulku. They both urged me again and again, saying that there
was no way to avoid finishing this task. It had occurred to me that, since I
didn't know what strengths and weaknesses there might be in my successive
rebirths and what the limits of my aspirations might be, this undertaking might
be beyond me, only serving to block my progress toward liberation and harming these teachings. So, previously I had been unable to begin the work and
had abandoned the project. But now that there was such a definite need for
these rituals to be codified, I first needed to develop a sense of resolve. Karma
Chagmé Rinpoché once said,

> I have completed the phase of approach for more than a hundred
>   deities
> and have never once used a harmful mantra or practiced to gain
>   power over anyone.
> So if this is the cycle of activities I complete, it is something worthy
>   of completion. [68a]

At important junctures in life, it is said that someone such as this citation describes should determine the circumstances of one's rebirth and the length of one's life.[511] So I asked Dabzang Tulku (since he met these criteria) if he would first undertake to determine my rebirth. Although his principal deity practice was that of Jinasagara, on this occasion he spent three weeks in retreat, carrying out the phase of approach for Supreme Compassion: The Gathering of Secrets. Once he had thus prepared the substances to be used in determining my circumstances and was embarking on the phase of enactment, Dabzang Tulku dreamed one evening of reading the text of a certain lama's biography in which there was discussion of the life examples of many lamas of the old and new schools of Tibetan Buddhism, as well as those of the Bön tradition, along with accounts of how they benefited beings. Following this he read the lines

> He will definitely prove to be the most sublime adornment
> of these fourteen masters.

Someone had written, as a footnote to this, "This is significant." In the early morning hours, Dabzang Tulku further dreamed of a square field, with four figures of Orgyen Rinpoché holding ploughs, one in each of the four cardinal directions. In the intercardinal directions were four women holding sacks of grain. There was a large crowd gathered.

Dabzang Tulku asked one of the women, "What is happening here?"

She replied, "This is the occasion when Rigdzin Terdak Lingpa was founding Mindroling Monastery. He spent a week practicing meditation on Orgyen Rinpoché and so consecrated the site."

In Dabzang Tulku's mind there arose the thought, "Kongtrul is indisputably an emanation of Minling Terchen."[512] [68b]

Later on, Dabzang Tulku dreamed that I was standing on the roof of a fortress many stories high on the summit of a lofty hill. I was gazing up at the sky again and again and writing on a large scroll what appeared to be some formal request.

In his dream he asked me, "Why are you staring at the sky?"

I replied, "I write down everything I compose after asking the gods about it."

Dabzang Tulku told me afterward that this pleased him enormously and aroused in him a boundless sense of faith and joy, for he thought to himself, "Both the words and the meaning will be excellent and the blessing will be truly great."

When I examined the circumstances of my rebirth for myself, I dreamed that I arrived at a monastic institution that I was told was Mindroling. When I entered a temple, I glimpsed many *tsa-tsa*s set out in lines; I was told that those to my left were the successive incarnations of Terchen, while those to my right were the incarnations of Lochen Dharma Shri. I was not sure who each and every figure represented, but an idea occurred to me: "Suppose this means that there is an additional person to be added to these others, who are the fourteen successive rebirths of Terchen?" Even in my dream, however, I did not reach the conclusion that I was that person. It is sufficient if we take this to be due to some karmic carryover due to a positive connection I forged with this great *tertön* in the past.

I also wrote to Khyentsé Rinpoché asking him to examine my circumstances. As soon as he read my letter, he saw a word in Sanskrit, *udaya*, appearing clearly before his eyes. [69a] This word *udaya* can be translated as "arising" or "flourishing." Khyentsé Rinpoché told me that this was a sign that I would explain the teachings clearly and that my writings would be widely read.

Previously, when Khyentsé Rinpoché had visited Zhung Peshing, the principal seat of the Ngok clan, he received a prophecy that I should codify the rituals of the Ngok mandalas. He related this to Chimé Tulku. As well, one of the lamas of Zhalu Choktrul in Tsang Province was a hidden yogi, an indisputable emanation of Marpa. He had once said something meaningful and prophetic to Zhalu Choktrul: "It would promote the Buddhist teachings if someone in your lineage of students were to write manuals for these tantric teachings of Marpa and spread them." Zhalu Choktrul then went to Khyentsé Rinpoché and said, "I have not yet found someone among my students who is capable of writing these manuals. Would you please look into it?" This led to me receiving these insistent requests over a period of time.

So it was at this point that I asked Khyentsé Rinpoché for this examination. In the first place, he dreamed that he went through a temple to his chambers, where he saw a text wrapped in red cloth on the shrine. Someone told him, "This is the account of Yönten Gyatso's successive rebirths." He thereupon recalled that he should examine this. Thinking, "I must read it very carefully," he unwrapped the text and looked at it. He found a section toward the back of the text with the heading "The Biography of the Spiritual Mentor Lumé Tsulthrim Sherab."[513] [69b]

Someone said, "That's not Yönten Gyatso, that's Lumé," to which he replied, "They are one and the same."

He continued reading and found the accounts of the successive rebirths and life examples very detailed. Among the introductory verses was the following passage:

> Renouncing samsara, he relied on solitude as one would nectar.
> He rejected errors of interpolation and omission in mantra repetition as one would avoid poison.
> With diligence that was like the flow of a river,
> he was graced with visions of his chosen deities and gained sublime spiritual attainment.
> He was freed of the residual karma that brought him diseases caused by *naga* demons.

Following this were accounts of Vajrapani,[514] Ananda,[515] Bairotsana, followed by those of Lumé and his immediate rebirth, Lhajé Zurpoché.[516] After some thirteen such accounts, he came to the section dealing with the lama who was the present rebirth.

In summarizing the extremely detailed account of Lumé's life, Khyentsé Rinpoché recalled mention of Lumé's chosen deity being White Vajrapani and the protective god he relied upon being the white *tsen* spirit[517] named Tsangpa Dungtöchen. He read of Bairotsana's extraordinary experiences due to the intervention of *naga* demons, when Bairotsana brought smallpox on Margyenma.[518] And he told me that he recalled the foregoing verses very clearly.

A second sign came to Khyentsé Rinpoché in his dreams. He dreamed that he was riding a horse, accompanied by four monks on foot. They were traveling to Zabbulung Valley.[519] At Neda, they were invited to the house of a lay tantric master, [70a] who requested empowerments and blessings and served Khyentsé Rinpoché with honor. The dream continued, and to all who asked where they were headed they always replied, "We're going to see Zabbulung, the valley of hidden teachings."

Some rain fell on their journey, and the monks said, "What should we do about the bad weather today?"

Khyentsé Rinpoché replied, "Everything will be fine," and continued on his way.

By afternoon they had reached about halfway up the valley, when they saw a river a small way off, with smoke in the air that indicated a prosperous nomadic encampment. Everyone, old and young, came running through the river to take Khyentsé Rinpoché's blessing. He asked the people how much further there was to go and they explained that he had only completed half the journey.

"Where is the best place to spend the night?" he asked them. They replied that there was no convenient shelter higher up the valley, not even an overhang.

The monks said, "Well, in that case we should stay at your home tonight. Can you put us up?"

"Since you will have to leave early in the morning, we can provide you with lodgings," the nomads replied.

This having been arranged, Khyentsé Rinpoché's party crossed the river to the encampment, where they were shown to a field next to the felt tents, the ground of which was completely covered with white cushions. They were served an evening meal of soup.

They were told that the lama who was the leader of the group was to arrive the next morning at sunrise. Because the lama was very scrupulous about hygiene, [70b] Khyentsé Rinpoché and his students were requested not to make any mess with their *torma* offerings or whatever. Rinpoché spent the evening in meditation.

He then dreamed that after arising the next morning and taking his breakfast, he set off and reached the upper end of the valley, with someone who seemed like his father showing him the way. He reached the place in Zabbulung known as "The Palace where the *Sugatas* Gather." There, in the shadow of a boulder, sat a yogi with a small topknot, dressed in monastic robes. His body was of medium height and build, and he wore a few ornaments. He was sitting like someone taking shelter from the rain. Standing up, the yogi introduced himself:

"I am the *tertön* of Threngpo, Sherab Özer.[520] It is a very auspicious circumstance that you have come. Let us go and discover a *terma*."

Overjoyed, Khyentsé Rinpoché went to the boulder, which the yogi split open to reveal a scroll. Khyentsé Rinpoché said, "Thereupon, the yogi was transformed into you, Guru Guna Samudra,[521] just as you appear now. You said to me, 'You are the custodian of this yellow scroll, so I will give you the oral transmission now.' You then read through it once very well. It seemed to me to contain a section from The Sphere of Freedom dealing with increasing one's intelligence and wisdom and gaining the power of total recall." (It seems that my lord himself had very clear memories of having been Jamyang Khyentsé Wangchuk.[522])

At the end of the fourth month I met with Kyabjé Rinpoché for what was to be one of the last times.[523] He filled his bowl, a fine piece made of jade, [71a] with food and handed it to me. Up to this point, every time I had met with Situ Rinpoché, I had visualized receiving the four levels of empowerment from the mandala of his body. Once, when I was staying in my spiritual master's residence, in the wake of receiving empowerments in this fashion I had a continuous experience of the unity of bliss and emptiness. I think this means that I received Situ Rinpoché's blessing in some small measure.

At about this time, Situ Rinpoché began to feel slightly indisposed. Although he did not show signs of any specific illness, he dictated his will to both Öntrul and Dabzang Tulku. On the evening of the seventh day of the fifth month there were earthquakes and other signs, and he turned his mind toward benefiting others.[524] The two lamas summoned me the next morning, saying that I needed to come and serve as a scribe, so I went to my spiritual master's residence. There, on the basis of his own detailed instructions, preparations were made for the ceremonies to commemorate Situ Rinpoché's passing. I was responsible for writing out most of the important documents. Arrangements were made to sponsor all available offerings, to be made in the presence of his precious tomb in Lhasar Temple at the meditation center of Palpung Monastery, as well as the ritual of *The Heart Essence of Vajrasattva*, to be performed by the residents of the center. On the third cusp day,[525] Lama Sangngak and I, assisted by a number of other masters and students, performed the fulfillment ritual from The United Intent of the Gurus in front of the gilded tomb[526] in Lhasar Temple.

During this time, I had a delightful dream of being on a vast plain [71b] and encountering this lord guru Maitreya.[527] His form was radiant and he was seated on a small throne. The entire environment seemed to change. I bowed to him with great devotion, whereupon he said to me, "The purest dwelling is by a lake. You should request the oral transmission of a mantra from the Lord of Victorious Ones.[528] This is important."

Then, in my dream I found myself in a pleasant spot by a lake surrounded by a ring of snow peaks wreathed in white clouds. Hosts of many gods and goddesses were manifesting everywhere, singing sweet songs of praise. I took this to be a sign of my lord's rebirth being conceived in the womb. I wonder now if this was an indication of the incarnation being born near Namtso Thanglha.

We discussed which offering ceremonies to begin with. Öngen had previously said, "Since the refuge lord himself was widely known to be an emanation of Lord Marpa, in the future the two rituals of Hevajra and Guhyasamaja, being Marpa's principal practices, cannot be omitted." To me he added, "You should codify the *sadhana*s and mandala rituals and detail all the practical methods associated with these."

I replied, "Palpung is one of the main centers of the Kagyü School. Thus, a copy of the edition printed there of the tantras transmitted by Marpa would be very useful." This was agreeable to both Dabzang Tulku and Öntrul, [72a] so I went up to Palpung, thinking only of ways to honor the memory of Situ Rinpoché.[529]

I began the project by arranging the *sadhana* and mandala ritual for the tantra of Hevajra. Among the books in my spiritual master's residence were texts by such authors as Thrükhang Lotsawa[530] and Rinchen Zangpo of the Ngok clan, but the oral transmissions were no longer available.[531] Among the later works was a manual of medium length by the Fourth Zhamar Chen-nga Chökyi Drakpa, which was incontestably part of the Ngok tradition; and in the collected works of Jonang Jetsün Rinpoché I found several texts, like pure gold, dealing with the tantras transmitted by Marpa. I took these two latter sources as my basis.

While I was compiling the texts, Thralep Yeshé Nyima[532] arrived when the requisite period[533] after Situ Rinpoché's passing had elapsed. He brought with him the tantric works of Chen-nga Chökyi Drakpa, which he had received from Öntrul Karma Rinchen (himself a student of Kunkhyap). He had received all the empowerments and oral transmissions for these texts, and so I requested all of these from him. So my lineage of empowerments was totally pure and the line of oral transmission, too, needed no further support from other sources.[534]

At this point Dabzang Rinpoché had gone to Karma Gön Monastery. During the first days of the eighth month we placed the salt used to preserve Situ Rinpoché's remains, as well as the top of his cranium that miraculously survived the cremation, inside the gilded tomb in Lhasar Temple. We spent two days consecrating the tomb, performing the rituals of the "two Vimalas"[535] and that of Jinasagara.

It was at this point that I saw signs in my dreams of the influence of *naga* demons. [72b] Due to some circumstance of moral contamination, I experienced the first onset of my eye disease, and by the next morning no one could open my eyelids. My speech was affected and my senses were dulled. At the same time, a number of others experienced speech difficulties. For seven days at the hermitage, I performed the practice for improving eyesight that is contained in the *terma* of Nyang,[536] and experienced positive signs, such as dreams of the sun and moon rising. However, due to some circumstance of moral contamination or another, my eyesight would occasionally weaken to the point that my eyes burned and I could not stand light. I would have to bandage my eyes with black cloth for several days. This condition has continued to flare up from time to time.

At this point Kyater[537] began a retreat for about a month, performing spiritual practices for my longevity. He reported positive signs in his dreams. On the evening that he finished his retreat and brought me the substances of longevity, I had good dreams that the moon rose, I donned new clothing, found a casket of *terma*s, and so on. I had previously pursued the matter quite persistently with Dabzang Tulku. "While Kyabjé Rinpoché was still alive," I said, "I had no chance to come to any decision. But for me to leave it now would definitely be inappropriate. Please help me by looking into the matter."[538] Dabzang Tulku looked into the situation,[539] but came to no certain conclusion. He said, "For the time being, at any rate, other than you calling him Kyasu Lama,[540] it would be potentially very risky for you to give him the title of a *tertön* or establish a spiritual connection with him by receiving empowerments or instructions. Better not to do it at all." [73a] So on this occasion I did not request longevity empowerments or other transmissions. Kyater then set out in the direction of Terlhung on a fund-raising trip,[541] but had no provisions of his own for the moment. I offered him two sets of clothing, silk greeting scarves, even paper and ink—all that he would need for the trip. It was at that point that some very fine auspicious circumstances were first set in motion for me to practice at Riwo Wangzhu and compose the manual describing the region.[542]

Beginning in the ninth month, I spent some time in personal retreat, meditating on several of my chosen deities, and as well performed the ritual of Vajrakila to avert negativity. Toward year's end, I was joined by a few students in performing the extensive *torma* ritual for the Six-Armed Mahakala. I dreamed of several of the excellent signs mentioned in *The Collected Instructions* for this deity.

DURING THE SECOND MONTH of the new Wood Tiger Year [1854-1855], I concluded my retreat and performed the extensive ritual of fulfillment from *The United Intent of the Gurus*. I went to my late spiritual master's residence, where I instructed those who were to lead the vase consecration ritual.

During the third month Öntrul and I presided as we actually began the ritual. Just as we were approaching its completion, a monk quite suddenly took ill with smallpox, but we did not let that deter us, and finished the ritual in a thorough and excellent manner. Since no other person developed even a single pustule for that whole year, it was evident that this single case was provoked by the power of the *drupchen* ritual.[543] As soon as we finished the ritual, Öntrul and others [73b] went immediately to Paljor Plateau. I came back to the meditation center. Through the kindness of the venerable lama Karma Ösel Gyurmé, I received the empowerments and oral transmissions from the collected works of Jonang Jetsün Rinpoché that I had not previously received. These included the great ordination from the Kalachakra cycle and the empowerments for Hevajra according to the tradition of Shantigupta,[544] the twenty-five deity mandala of Buddhakapala,[545] the Anuttarayoga tradition of *Manjushri Endowed with Secrets*, all the forms of Chakrasamvara, and all the forms of Yamantaka. I presented to Karma Ösel Gyurmé a mandala offering of thanks, offering him as much as my circumstances allowed. On the fourth day of the fourth month I went to preside over a large group in the performance of the ritual of White Tara, the text of which I had newly codified; the ritual lasted for four days. Öntrul returned before long.

I experienced occasional severe bouts of my eye disease and throat troubles. On one occasion, I dreamed that the venerable Taranatha had prepared for a major empowerment that he was intending to confer on me. I had the clear impression of being Tsewang Norbu and serving Taranatha. It seems that Tsewang Norbu attested to the fact that he was the rebirth of Taranatha's regent, Yeshé Gyatso, and the venerable Taranatha himself had said that he, Taranatha, and Yeshé Gyatso were both aspects of the same mindstream. So I felt that my dream had some small significance.

At the beginning of the fifth month [74a] I taught the liturgies and practical techniques associated with the Hevajra practice. I performed the empowerments of Hevajra, Guhyasamaja, and Mahamaya[546] for the monastic community, although I experienced some major signs of disturbance. I attended the Hevajra ritual in memory of Situ Rinpoché in the capacity of vajra master. I also attended one day at each of the other rituals of Guhyasamaja and Mahamaya that were going on in adjoining halls. There were some eight practitioners continually performing the extensive fulfillment ritual from The United Intent of the Gurus at the tomb in Lhasar Temple; when I brought another four people with me, that made for thirteen, master and students, who spent seven days performing the ritual. We also gathered for the rituals of such practices as the cycles of peaceful and wrathful deities transmitted by Jatsön Nyingpo. At the meditation center (since Dabzang Tulku had gone to Karma Gön Monastery), it fell to me to instruct the retreatants for the next eight practices in their schedule. On my way up, then, I gave some teachings and then went to the hermitage.

There, I codified the texts for some thirteen tantras; in addition to those that were already well-known, I included some of the other tantras transmitted by Marpa. These included the *sadhanas*, mandala rituals, and other necessary texts, as well as instructions on the stages of completion, formal authorizations, and cycles concerning the guardian deities. I gave this collection the title *The Tantric Treasury of the Kagyü School*. With this, I completed the work that I had begun the year before.

On a number of occasions (I can't pinpoint when), I dreamed of excellent signs that I was receiving blessings. I received some amazing prophecies concerning the tantras of Marpa. I saw prophecies by Naropa[547] written on the walls of many temples. In the center of a delightful temple, in which all the tantras were housed, [74b] I saw the deity Vajra Chaturpitha Yoga, blue like the sky; it was as though I actually met the deity. And I opened a cloth scroll, said to be a blessed object copied by Rechungpa and Karma Pakshi from Chakrasamvara on Sinpori Mountain; inside I clearly saw the syllables *Om ah hum hrih* in Sanskrit, whereupon I felt faith and received the four levels of empowerment. However, I didn't note these experiences down at the time, so now I can't recall much of what happened.

The evening that I began working on the instruction manual for the longevity practice transmitted by Druppai Gyalmo[548] I dreamed of the stupas in which the eight portions of the Buddha's relics were housed.[549] I felt that this was a very good sign. During this period, there were many who came to me for various empowerments and oral transmissions or to study something, and I would satisfy their individual requests.

From the seventh through the eighth month I was in personal retreat. In response to requests from many people, I wrote my instruction manual on the system of "mental training," or *lojong.*[550] On the evening I began, I dreamed of a *terma* discovered by Duddul Dorjé,[551] said to be the heart of Vairochana, from which many *sharira* relics were growing. I dreamed that I ate some of these relics and gave more to others.

I ended my retreat in the ninth month and went to Dzongsar Monastery to meet with my precious and omniscient spiritual master. He conferred on me the empowerment and ritual ablution for the white form of Vajravidarana[552] according to the tradition of Bari Lotsawa,[553] which took him an entire day. This alleviated my eye troubles somewhat. He also bestowed the empowerments for the Sakya tradition of Vajrakila—the higher activity, lower activity, and the "wrathful liberating empowerment"—and [75a] the instructions for the practice that combines the deities Samyak and Vajrakila. The evening after the preparatory ritual, I dreamed that I met Vajardhara Pema Nyinjé. He conferred on me the oral transmission for the four volumes of his collected works in a very short time, after which he spent a long time ordaining me and entrusting me with these teachings.

Khyentsé Rinpoché also conferred teachings on such cycles as Guhyasamaja, the five stages according to Ghantapada, Mahamaya, Chaturpitha, Samputa,[554] and the unelaborate form of Red Yamantaka, as well as the empowerments for the two Vimalas. He bestowed the oral transmissions for all the texts relating to these cycles, and the oral transmission and practical instruction for *The United Families of Three Kayas* and some minor *termas*. On one occasion during this time, I dreamed of meeting Lord Mikyö Dorjé, who was dressed in the robes of a fully ordained monk. I prayed to him with faith over and over, whereupon he said, "It would be excellent for you to commission a statue of the predecessor."

"Do you mean Chödrak Gyatso?," I asked.[555]

"No," he replied, "I mean the previous Situ, Chökyi Jungné.[556] The form of the spiritual master has great blessing." He went to a temple and I followed him, praying to him all the while. He was holding in his hands something he referred to as "a cow that yields all that could be desired." He spoke many words in a symbolic language I couldn't understand, conferring his blessing on me again and again.

The master of Ngor named Ngawang Lekdrup[557] arrived, and from Khyentsé Rinpoché and this student of his together I requested the empowerment and oral transmission for Vajrapani according to the tradition of Pema Ledrel Tsal, the blessing of Samayavajra,[558] and other transmissions. [75b] For my part, I offered many empowerments and oral transmissions to my all-seeing precious master, and the empowerments of The Guru: The Gathering of Secrets and Buddhakapala to both of them. Once these transmissions had been completed, I responded to requests from several of my patrons, primarily from the Sokmo and Puma clans, and then made a short fund-raising trip to Meshö and Terlhung.

It was about this time that I dreamed one night of the afternoon sun setting behind a mountain pass. There I saw the accomplished master Thangtong Gyalpo, his heavyset form youthful and radiant. There was another *siddha* there, too. Just as the sun set, I was conversing with them when the thought occurred to me, "If I prostrate and pray to them until sunrise, I will surely receive their blessings." With great devotion I offered a few prostrations and prayers, whereupon Thangtong Gyalpo began uttering many prophetic statements. I don't recall most of these, but at one point he said,

> In the past, when the master Padma
> was conferring The United Intent of the Gurus
> at the power spot of the Chimphu uplands in Samyé,
> you were Ngen-lam Gyalwa Chok-yang.[559]
> Your secret name was Palgyi Nyingpo Lodrö Drimé Tsal.
> I was your apprentice, Lhabu Dönyö-Dé.

He seemed to be saying that at that time I was the translator Gyalwa Chok-yang and he was my disciple. [76a] He then told me how we had been connected in all lifetimes since that time, and how in all those lifetimes I had borne the names Pal [Glory] and Lodrö [Intelligence]. This dream seemed to me to indicate my auspicious connection with my all-seeing precious master, since he was indivisible from Thangtong Gyalpo.

In *The Oral Transmission of Ethical Codes* it states,

> Rely on holy people
> like a vine winding itself around a *sala* tree
> and you will be embraced by the glory of their nobility.

And so it was that around this time I felt any sectarian bias or other fixation I held waning, while my study intensified and my understanding flourished. In *The Discourse Requested by Madröpa, King of the Nagas* we find the following passage:

> O kings of *nagas*, thus there are two acts that, for a bodhisattva, are the activity of Mara. What are these two, you ask? They are to lack devotion for spiritual masters and to indulge in arrogance, boasting about oneself. These both are the activity of Mara and a bodhisattva should avoid them completely.

In accordance with this citation, I had previously felt devotion for my spiritual masters and understood that I myself had no positive qualities, so I didn't have a great deal of arrogance. But once I saw the way that this lord acted, it seemed that from that point on I felt even more devotion for this spiritual master and had no pride.

Immediately on returning to the hermitage, [76b] following my lord's instructions I performed a ritual for the sixty deity mandala of Vajrabhairava and my annual ritual for Vajrakila to avert negativity. One night I dreamed that I was oppressed by many *gyalpo* demons. Meditating myself to be Black Hayagriva, I used my sword to annihilate them all without any trace remaining. I bound three women, who I took to be *senmo* demonesses, to oaths and they offered to me the syllables of their life force—*Ni Na Ra Ra Hum Ra*. I gave them the names Dorjé Palmo Tsal, Dorjé Wangdrup Tsal, and Dorjé Yeshé Tsal.

IN THE NEW WOOD HARE YEAR [1855-1856], I undertook a personal retreat on the practice of Hevajra according to the tradition of Marpa; some very auspicious omens occurred on the first day. In three months I had completed the phase of approach, along with the supplementary fire ritual.

In the fourth month I went to Palpung Monastery, attending the vase consecration ritual and group offering rituals. I also presided as vajra master over the Hevajra ritual to commemorate Situ Rinpoché. I received most of the cycles of Ratna Lingpa's teachings from Lama Sang-ngak, and when Dabzang Tulku Rinpoché arrived I requested all the empowerments for *The Complete Gathering of Masters of Awareness*. In response to his request, I offered to him the empowerments and oral transmissions that I had recently codified for mandalas of Marpa's tradition. Kyater also performed an empowerment of Vajrakila at Dabzang Tulku's request.

The previous year, when I had been in retreat, [77a] Dabzang Tulku Rinpoché had arrived unexpectedly one day, insisting, "Today it is crucial that you confer the empowerment for the Mindroling tradition of The Gathering of All Sugatas." I pointed out to him I was unprepared and lacked the *tsakli* cards needed during the ritual.

He replied, "It will be all right to use some other symbols for the empowerment of the deities." We came up with a special mirror from The United Intent of the Gurus and a vajra and bell. That same day I performed the basic empowerment for The Gathering of All Sugatas. Dabzang Tulku said that he had great need of this transmission in the future. It seems that the mirror we used was a *terma* discovered as a sacred object that had belonged to one of the former princes of Tibet.[560]

On this occasion I also performed a number of formal authorizations and other transmissions. From Lama Karsö, I myself received many oral transmissions, including those for the practices of the "Molten Metal" form of Yamantaka of the Drigung Kagyü School, Vajrapani from the Jathang tradition, and the "Haughty Mara" form of Yamantaka.

I returned to the hermitage and immediately put the finishing touches on the manuals for *The Tantric Treasury of the Kagyü School*. In response to some insistent requests from a few lamas and monks of Dzamthang Monastery, I also composed manuals for the practice of Vajrakila called *The Display that Conquers the Maras*. The Nera clan needed the ritual for the *sadhana* of wrathful deities from the Eight Commands to be performed and asked me to participate, but I didn't have time and sent Kyater as my representative.

Kyater wished to meet Dzongsar Tulku Rinpoché[561] and asked me to help him by sending a letter of introduction. Kyater was a person of such fine character and other qualities that no matter how I considered him, he was quite unlike other people, [77b] so I felt that he might be a *tertön*. He had a *terma* called *Lotus Ushnisha*, but he had no letters of authentication,[562] nor had he composed any works of his own. So I wrote a letter asking Dzongsar Tulku Rinpoché to examine the situation. Once the ceremonies for the Nera clan had been completed, Kyater met Dzongsar Tulku, who immediately conferred on him the empowerment for the *Kila Razor* practice of Vajrakila. He spoke to Kyater in great detail and advised him that he must receive from me the empowerment for *The Web of Magic* and an explanation of the tantra. When Kyater returned he told me of this need, and so for him and few others I performed the empowerment of the peaceful and wrathful deities of *The Web of Magic* and a complete explanation of the tantra. We performed the ritual of the tantra and a feast of thanksgiving. From Kyater, I in turn requested the ritual ablution and empowerment for the five deities of ablution according to the Drukpa Kagyü School.

I invited Lama Pema Sang-ngak Tendzin Rinpoché to the hermitage and from him I received all the basic and secondary empowerments for *The Discourse of United Intent*[563] according to the manuals of Nyalpa Delekpa;[564] the eighteen "meanings of A" from the Category of Mind; all the empowerments for Dredging the Pit of Cyclic Existence, the *terma*s of Pema Lingpa,[565] *The*

United Intent that Descends Everywhere, Vajrapani, the Wrathful Guru, the longevity *sadhana* entitled *The Vajra Mala*, and the *terma* cycles of Zhikpo Lingpa;[566] and a number of other empowerments and oral transmissions. [78a] I offered whatever I could to him as a mandala offering of thanks.

During this period my eye disease was flaring up, so I had to rest much of the time. I recited quite a number of liturgies, including the fulfillment rituals from both The United Intent of the Gurus and a cycle focusing on the peaceful and wrathful deities, and performed one hundred offerings to the protective deity Dhumavati as a means of giving thanks for the completion of *The Tantric Treasury of the Kagyü School* and of entrusting her with these teachings. The omens were very positive. On this occasion I dreamed of a huge flood of white water and of the *daka*s and *dakini*s of the twenty-four gathering places engaged in amazing kinds of secret conduct. I undertook a personal retreat focusing on the *Kila Razor* practice of Vajrakila transmitted by Guru Chöwang. I also performed my annual ritual to avert negativity. The *tertön* Chokgyur Lingpa went to Dzongsar, where he and Tulku Rinpoché[567] codified the *sadhana* of enlightened mind called *Dispelling All Obstacles*, after which he returned. During this time a seal of secrecy was placed on the texts. When he told me the situation, I asked him, "Would it be possible for you to confer just the blessing on me?"

He replied, "There was already a need in the past for you to encounter these teachings, but you didn't say anything to me. Since you are my spiritual master, I didn't feel I should offer them to you, so I left it at that. But now there is a pressing need." To establish auspicious circumstances at the outset, I requested of him the longevity empowerment from The Union of All Rare and Precious Jewels. He then conferred on me all the empowerments and oral transmissions for his own *terma* of enlightened intent, the *guru sadhana* of Vimalamitra [78b] and the "empowerment into the four spheres," and empowerments of form, speech, and mind from his *sadhana* of enlightened mind *Dispelling all Obstacles*. These latter empowerments he conferred from memory, using a "regent" statue of Guru Rinpoché. During this time he gave a lengthy account of how he received these *terma*s.

Speaking of the records[568] of his *terma* teachings he said, "There is mention of you being one of the successive rebirths of the great translator Bairotsana. Due to the karmic obscuration that Bairotsana incurred in bringing smallpox on Margyenma, that *naga*'s influence is felt wherever that rebirth occurs, causing such afflictions as smallpox. Your eye disease is due to nothing but this; your eyes are affected by smallpox. From now on you should use the auxiliary practice of Vajradanda[569] from *Dispelling All Obstacles*, meditating on the deity and repeating the mantra; this will definitely cure you." He talked of many such matters. He then returned to his home region.

During this time I had a few excellent signs in my dreams. I dreamed of my refuge lord Vajradhara himself, in a very delighted mood, conferring on me the ablution of Vajravidarana. I had an extremely pleasant dream of being in a large field of fine crops and yellow flowers in the summertime, with many cuckoos singing. In my dreams, the *tertön* Chokgyur Lingpa said to me, "You are the custodian of the third empowerment" and I found a skull cup filled with many pieces of turquoise and coral. But while I had such excellent dreams, I also dreamed of eating mud mixed with manure and vomiting it back up. [79a] This even caused me some nausea by day, and after that it seemed that I experienced greater and greater negative effects due to my unconscious mis-appropriation of property. But once I had received the blessing of Chokgyur Lingpa's *sadhana* of enlightened mind, my eye illness never flared up again. Afterward, the precious lord gave me a text of Vajravidarana, and from then on I did the practice daily, even undertaking a personal retreat at one point. My eyesight cleared up for good, which gave me real confidence in what the *tertön* said to me and in his *terma*s, so different from many things that people in later times have just dug out of the ground or pulled out of rocks!

During the spring equinox, I spent a week in retreat focusing on White Tara according to the tradition of Duddul Dorjé. Previously, it had occurred to me that it would be of benefit in the transmission of all the many important minor *terma* cycles I had received over the years if I were to collect the texts to-gether, and again I summoned up the inspiration behind that project. I now felt that it would be best to include these minor instructions—which after all were cases of less important techniques for purposes that were both beneficial and harmful—in a compilation of the empowerments I had received for the rare *terma*s of the major and more well-known *tertön*s, editing these into a concise format. I asked my all-seeing precious master about this idea. His response was to write four volumes of texts summarizing some minor *terma*s.

He said, "It would be ideal if you were to use these as your basis and write your work, [79b] collecting all the cycles of *guruyoga*, Dzogchen teachings, and Avalokiteshvara practice[570] from the major *tertön*s."

I replied, "That being the case, please compose a table of contents showing which *terma*s should be included and what order should be adopted."

At that point, in order to ensure the completion of the project and obtain permission to undertake it,[571] I did a personal retreat on the practice known as *The Spontaneous Fulfillment of All Wishes: The Treasure Trove of Qualities*, reciting the mantra and prayers. The signs were excellent. Following this I carried out the outer, inner, and secret practices for the longevity *sadhana* called *The Vajra of Meteoric Iron*, as well as the ritual to consecrate blessing pills. One night I dreamed of finding four relics. I was told that three were those of Vimalamitra, Yeshé Tsogyal, and Shelkarza,[572] while the fourth was said to be one worn by Orgyen Rinpoché around his neck and buried by him in a miraculous manner. I had a number of such excellent signs in dreams.

I FINISHED THIS RETREAT on the eighth day of the new Fire Dragon Year [1856-1857], following which I undertook a week of practice on the Vadisimha form of Manjushri, and a week on the consecration of blessing pills. I also had excellent signs in my dreams during this period: I dreamed I was sitting on a throne wearing my formal monastic robe, reading a book written in silver ink, a text of which both the words and meaning were excellent, and I dreamed of seeing the sun and moon rise. When I finished this retreat I went to the meditation center, where I performed the empowerment of Hevajra for the retreatants, as well as the series of transmissions called The Peaceful Garland and The Wrathful Garland, the collection of transmissions for protective deities called The Lightning Garland, and the oral transmissions for all the collected works of my refuge lord. [80a]

From Lama Dampa I requested the empowerments of The Heart Drop of Yuthok and Vajrapani according to the tradition of Jathang, as well as the formal authorization for the practice of Red Jambhala from Karma Chagmé's tradition. In answer to our invitation, Samten Tendzin, the realized master of Ji, arrived. He conferred the empowerment and oral transmission of Guru Chöwang's Eight Commands cycle entitled The Perfection of Secrets, the complete empowerments of the Taksham cycle (including The United Intent of the Chosen Deities and The Guru: The Wish-Fulfilling Gem), the empowerment and oral transmission for the *dakini* Simhamukha according to the tradition of Mati, and other instructions. When these were completed, we made a mandala offering of gratitude to the lama, who then returned to his home.

I performed a ritual for prosperity and protection at Jelo in Meshö, following which I went to Dzongsar and met with my all-seeing precious master, from whom I received the empowerments of Vajrapani Who Vanquishes Death and the Sakya tradition of the Simhanada form of Manjushri. In turn, I offered several oral transmissions to him. That night I dreamed that the *tertön* Chokgyur Lingpa discovered a vase that I was told would spontaneously fulfill all wishes. I asked him to bless me with it. Inside were many blessing pills to be distributed. The day following this dream, I came across the texts for the *sadhana* of enlightened mind *Dispelling All Obstacles*. I returned to my home and started three scribes transcribing the *terma*s I had already collected.

On the twenty-first day of this month I went to see my lord master, who related that the night before (that of the twentieth)[573] he had had a lucid vision of a woman dressed in blue telling him that they should go, whereupon he followed her. [80b] On the path they came to a deep ravine, and the woman flew into the air. He, too, could fly and had experiences that paralleled those found in the accounts such as those of Guru Chöwang's pure visions. During these experiences he briefly saw the countries of India, Tibet, and Nepal. Finally he came upon a mountain with its summit shrouded in mist. As he came closer, the mountain took on more and more clearly the shape of a stupa. As they came very near, he could see both the front and back of the mountain; the front appeared very clearly like a stupa in form, with gateways on the four sides of the "lion throne" base.[574] But in whatever direction they went, the gate was closed and they could not gain entrance.

He asked the woman about the origins of the mountain and she told him, "This is the city of Shantapuri."

He said, "Where does Sherab Özer, the great *tertön* of Threngpo, live around here? I must go and meet him."

She replied, "Here he is called the *daka* named Thöpai Dumbu Tsal. Just now he is living in Tibet. Here gods, goddesses, *daka*s, *dakini*s, and others constantly gather to honor his remains with offerings."

My spiritual master listened at one of the doors and was fascinated to hear sweet music, like the sounds of some exotic instrument. Along with this incredible melody, he could hear amazing passages of verse from the tantras being chanted. The woman said, "This is music from the offering ritual." [81a]

"When Thöpai Dumbu Tsal went to Tibet, what became of him?" he asked.

She said, "While there he remains silent, not speaking, but seemingly immersed in a state of meditative absorption. When he returns from Tibet, he will speak and teach the Buddhist teachings again. That's the difference."

Behind that mountain was a second, darker in color and further off, which she told my spiritual master was Zangdok Palri. They flew there and landed on the summit, where he saw an exceedingly magnificent palace with three stories, which he took to be the immeasurable mansion of Lotus Light. He entered the hall on the ground story, to find the Guru as the king of Sahora surrounded by his eight manifestations, while in the hall on the second story was Avalokiteshvara in the form of Jinasagara, surrounded by the eight great bodhisattvas; in both these halls he beheld statues. When he went up to the hall on the uppermost story, however, he saw something formed of blue light, whereupon, he told me, he awoke from this pure vision.

During the fourth month I went to Palpung Monastery to serve as the vajra master presiding over the vase consecration ritual, which went very well. At Dzongsar, in accord with a summons that Ngari Lama[575] had spoken on his deathbed, I performed an offering ritual for Jinasagara. I requested from my precious lord guru the transmission of the most wrathful form of Hayagriva, the conferral of the exorcism technique based on the five long mantras, and the empowerments and oral transmissions for of Guru Chöwang's The Guru: The Gathering of Secrets. I in turn offered to him the empowerments and oral transmissions for Ratna Lingpa's tradition of Vajrakila, and his longevity *sadhana*s called The Vajra Garland [81b] and The Gathering of Secrets. At the monastery, I presided over the *sadhana* ritual of Hevajra as an offering to my guru, and also attended one day each at the rituals of Guhyasamaja and Mahamaya. Lama Pewang was staying at Dzongsar Monastery, and from him I received the empowerments and oral transmissions for Red Jambhala and Black Krodhi as discovered by Chöjé Lingpa, as well as The Secret Dakini Treasury.

I heard the wonderful news that the incarnation of my refuge lord had been reborn at Namtso, recognized by Gyalwang Karmapa, and invited to Tsurphu. I also received, from Sang-ngak, the empowerments for the white and black forms of Krodhi according to the Sky Teachings. My all-seeing precious master also received these transmissions, following which I returned to my hermitage to carry out the retreat requirement entailed in these empowerments. Ritrul Dargyé Gyatso arrived and I requested several empowerments from him.

I went to Lhasar Temple at Palpung, and the evening I arrived there were some miraculous signs, such as the door opening and closing by itself. I spent several days preparing for a ceremony that would combine a *drupchen* ritual, an empowerment, and a *mendrup* ritual. On the twenty-fifth day of the fifth month my lord guru arrived and, once I had begun by conferring the preliminary phase on my students, attended the ceremonies and participated in the *drupchen* and *mendrup* rituals. With the completion of the phase of accepting the spiritual attainments, we had spent some sixteen days in practice, including several major and minor empowerments. Khyentsé Rinpoché also received from me the empowerments for the Eight Commands practice The Perfection of Secrets, the cycle of peaceful and wrathful deities discovered by Karma Lingpa, [82a] and all the *termas* of Zhikpo Lingpa. I offered him the empowerment for The Conjunction of Sun and Moon transmitted by Sang-gyé Lingpa, and in return he conferred on me, seven times over, the longevity empowerment of Thangtong Gyalpo (the *terma* of enlightened intent discovered by Chöjé Lingpa), whereupon he brought the transmissions to a halt.

About this time, some of my masters and students performed a longevity *sadhana* on my behalf, praying for my long life and kindly making offerings to me. On that occasion, my lord himself composed an explanation of the five aspects of excellence[576] that was exceedingly fine in both wording and meaning. In the text of his talk he referred to the excellent environment as "the third glorious Devikoti,"[577] symbolizing the eye of timeless awareness at the uppermost point of the central channel. Since that name had not been applied to the Palpung area in the past, I took note of his comments. Later, when I asked him the reason for using this term, he said that he had heard it during a clear vision in which the *dakinis* sang a secret song to him. Shortly thereafter, he left.

From Sang-ngak I received the empowerments associated with the seventeen Dzogchen tantras, along with the conferral of life force for the wrathful goddess Ekajati;[578] the formal authorization for the ten holy sites from the tradition of Sang-gyé Lingpa; and a number of oral transmissions, including that of the practice of the deity Aparajita[579] to resolve conflict. From a teacher named Guru Natha, I received several teachings, including the instructions on the completion stage for The Union of All Rare and Precious Jewels. I then returned to my hermitage, where I performed the pacifying *lhasang* offering and other annual rituals and composed several new works. At this point it did not seem fitting to apply the term "treasury" to my new writings on *termas*, [82b] so I began referring to the ten or so volumes as my "garland of *termas*," editing them and sponsoring the publication.

On the twenty-seventh day of the seventh month my all-seeing precious master came down to Palpung Monastery to read the oral transmissions for the thirteen volumes of The United Intent of the Gurus and the main texts for a cycle focusing on the peaceful and wrathful deities. Then, for some twenty or more incarnate masters—some who came from other places (including Shar

Lama from Dergé Gönchen, Pema of Dzogchen Monastery, and others) and some who lived at Palpung Monastery (such as Öngen Tulku)—I gave transmissions based on the manuals prepared by Jonang Jetsün Rinpoché. These included the great ordination ceremony of Kalachakra, all the cycles of Chakrasamvara and Yamantaka, and the instruction manual on the six lineages of transmission by Shantigupta (as translated in more recent times by Taranatha himself). I also gave all the empowerments, oral transmissions, and instructions for my newly codified version of the Eight Commands cycle The Perfection of Secrets.

Lord Khyentsé himself conferred on me the bodhisattva vow according to both the Madhyamaka tradition (according to the manuals used in the tradition of Mindroling Monastery) and the Chittamatra[580] tradition (as arranged by my master himself). With this as an introduction, he then transmitted The One Hundred Instructions of Kunga Drolchok[581] to me very thoroughly, giving a concise overview using a structural analysis; explaining these teachings in detail, using those instruction manuals for which he had received oral transmission; summarizing these hundred instructions using their actual wording; and finally conferring an empowerment using the texts. [83a]

He explained both *The Kalachakra Tantra* and the major commentary on it, entitled *Stainless Light*, according to the methods employed by Butön Rinpoché,[582] and transmitted to me all the manuals used in the Zhalu tradition. At the conclusion, he bestowed on me the text of Taktsang Lotsawa's[583] *General Overview*. We celebrated with a *ganachakra* feast. With all this, Khyentsé Rinpoché ensured auspicious circumstances to entrust me with these teachings.

He gave an oral transmission, with commentary, for *Reciting the Names of Manjushri*. He also conferred the following transmissions: the major empowerment for Amoghapasha;[584] the empowerment of the fifteen deity mandala of the wrathful Black Vajravidarana according to the Drukpa Kagyü tradition; the empowerment of Samyak according to the Khön tradition;[585] the blessing ritual of Hevajra from the Taklung tradition;[586] the empowerment of Chakrasamvara and consort; the formal authorization of the Four-Armed Mahakala; the "speech empowerment" of Chöying; the empowerments of the nine deity mandala of Ushnishavijaya,[587] the thirteen deity mandala of Akshobhya, and the eleven-headed form of Avalokiteshvara according to Nagarjuna's tradition;[588] the conferral ritual of Ushnisha Sitatapatra; the empowerment of Ghrihamatrika;[589] the common blessing ritual of Kamaraja;[590]

the seven-day and three-day courses of the yogic practice of inner heat and the "fire empowerment"; the empowerment of Vajrabhairava; instructions in *The Dakini's Oral Lineage* and other practices; the empowerments and teaching transmissions[591] of The Six Instructions of Maitripa;[592] the instructions of the oral lineage of Kalachakra according to the tradition of Bodong;[593] the blessing rituals of Sahaja and Shavaripa;[594] the teachings entitled *The Inseparability of Profundity and Lucidity*; the sutra tradition ceremony focusing on the Sage; the seven-day course of instruction for the transference of consciousness; the longevity empowerment entitled *Lengthening the Arrow*;[595] the empowerment and oral teaching transmission of Samyak from the *terma*s of Chöjé Lingpa; [83b] and the longevity empowerment from The Sphere of Freedom. After I had received this last empowerment, I experienced some positive omens—on the road home I was given a set of one hundred statues of Guru Rinpoché and had dreams of banks of flowers in full bloom.

On the first evening that Khyentsé Rinpoché was bestowing the three-day instruction on the Lamdré cycle[596] (using the text entitled *Illuminating All the Hidden Meanings*), I dreamed that I arrived in a place that I took to be Ewam in Ngor. I entered an assembly hall, where I saw many golden thrones arranged on either side; it seemed that there was a lama sitting on each of these, but I didn't identify them precisely. There was a vacant throne higher up in the ranks to my right, and I felt that this was my seat. I was told that Ngorchen Dorjé Chang[597] was seated in an alcove at the front of the temple and I went to meet him. I saw him atop his throne, his upper body that of the deity Hevajra, with eight faces and sixteen arms, while his lower body was that of a lama sitting cross-legged. In my dream, I bowed to him with faith.

In answer to a sudden invitation by Gyalsé Mingyur of Tsenri, Khyentsé Rinpoché went there, where I was able to receive from him all the empowerments and oral transmissions for the Heart Drop of the Dakini and The Union of Spiritual Commands: The Peaceful and Wrathful Deities (both discovered by Dechen Lingpa[598]); the oral transmission of Guhyajnana;[599] the oral transmissions for all the *terma*s of Zhikpo Lingpa; and the empowerments and oral transmissions of the collected minor practices of the Longsal tradition.

From Lama Pema Sang-ngak Tendzin I received transmissions of the source texts for Rongzom's tradition of Vajrakila, the commentary on Vajrakila entitled *The Black Vase*, and the collected works of Thrang-go. [84a] Lama Karma Ngédön of Lithang transmitted to me The One Hundred Instructions of Throphu Lotsawa and the mandala ritual of Vajrabhairava according to the Mal tradition[600] (authored by Sönam Seng-gé[601]). Thus, I requested from them the oral transmissions that I hadn't had time to request of my lord guru. In conclusion, I offered them the empowerment of the longevity *sadhana* of Akashagarbha discovered by Yön-gé Mingyur Dorjé and received in turn the instructions for the longevity practice of White Chakrasamvara. With this, the proceedings came to an end and my lord guru departed.

I returned to my home at the hermitage and performed the one hundred offerings to the protective deities and other annual rites. The steward of Situ Rinpoché's monastic residence asked me to help him do fund-raising over the winter. We set out from Palpung with a traveling camp. Passing through Alo Tsetsa and other places, we came to Ngul-khar, where we encamped. That evening I dreamed of meeting Ngari Panchen Pema Wang-gyal and Rigdzin Duddul Dorjé[602] and receiving their blessings. I cannot remember clearly when this was. Later on I dreamed that at the head of the valley was Lambaka, a minor power spot associated with Tsadra, which made me wonder if this was a sign of my receiving blessings.

The evening that we reached Tö-ngo Shö-lhak in Rakchap, I dreamed that Longsal Nyingpo[603] showed me several statues of the deities of the Eight Commands, saying that these statues were those he used for his meditation. He also discovered several relics, but it was necessary to hide them again. The next day, I wondered whether this meant that on my journey I would come across a site of *termas* concealed in a hill. [84b] I asked people if there was such a hill on our route, but was told that there was not. Continuing our journey, we arrived at Dzongshö, where we encamped. That evening I dreamed that Lord Pema Nyinjé showed me a mountain shaped like Yeshé Tsogyal riding on a peacock, in which were a great number of statues of deities. There were several symbolic letters on the cliff face, which confirmed that this was a power spot.

We completed our fund-raising circuit in upper Dzing and turned back, reaching Shoksum. From there, on the tenth day of the eleventh month I set off with a small group of students for Dzongshö. There we performed one hundred repetitions of the feast offering for The Union of All Rare and Precious Jewels, a fire ritual, and the ritual of the gift of the body. That evening I dreamed of a huge temple with a surrounding wall, guarded by protective deities, in which I met Rigdzin Jatsön Nyingpo. He gave me substances that brought liberation on being tasted—a few white pills and a substance that resembled white resin. He said, "Enemies are coming from the east, so you must turn them back." He then mounted a black horse and rode off toward the east.

The next day I went to the highest point of the area and performed a brief ritual of Simhamukha to avert negativity. I also visited most of the caves, in which I found deposits of pitch, red lead, and many powerful and naturally occurring pills that had formed from a spiritual medicine prepared by Guru Rinpoché when he performed a ritual to consecrate a ritual effigy. I saw a grove of white rhododendron bushes, and there were rainbow-colored clouds in the sky. [85a] Later on, when I entered the inner sanctum of the area, I saw a ray of light like an intensely white rainbow shine down from the sun, while a flurry of snow swirled like flower petals. To my left and right were swirling circles of five-colored rainbow light, which lasted the whole morning.

We toured the communities of Meting and then returned to the monastery, where Öntrul told me that he had been invited to central Tibet by Chirlo Choktrul. "You simply must go there in my stead," he said. To dispel any potential problems, I attended the daily rituals in each of the shrine rooms dedicated to the protective deities, after which I returned to the hermitage, where I carried out a personal retreat focusing on the practice called *The Union of the Families of the Three Immortal Kayas*.

On the third day of the twelfth month Chokgyur Lingpa discovered his *terma* called *The Three Categories of the Great Perfection* in the cave of Pema Shelphuk in Dzam-nang. I was informed quite suddenly of these circumstances by both the *tertön* and Tulku Rinpoché, so I immediately set about making preparations for ritual feasts, *torma* offerings, and other necessary rituals. About this time, there was a fierce wind for several days; this is clearly described in my lord guru's biography as the machinations of the local spirits.

I also performed the annual year-end Vajrakila ritual to avert negativity. On the twenty-third day of the month the *tertön* arrived, so we hung banners, blew conch shells, and performed a *lhasang* ceremony to honor him. Snow fell like flower blossoms [85b] and he pronounced all the circumstances to be very auspicious. I served him as scribe, copying such texts as the empowerment ritual for White Amitayus from the original yellow scrolls, and again the auspicious signs were very positive. I dreamed of living into my eighties and of discovering many special cycles associated with the deity Yamantaka. Chokgyur Lingpa conferred on me the empowerments, oral transmissions, and instructions for his own *terma* of Padma Vimaloshnisha,[604] as well as that of *Dredging the Pit of Cyclic Existence* and (as my own personal lot) the form of

Yamantaka called the Lord of Death, from The Seven Profound Cycles, which he had discovered the previous year.

I said, "Prior to this, there was no point in asking, but now it seems that it is timely to ask you to write an account of this place where I live."

The *tertön* replied, "This is one of some twenty-five major holy sites in eastern Tibet, so an account is already concealed as a *terma*. Thus, I don't need to create one." He bestowed on me one of his own *terma*s, discovered in Yephuk Cave—a black stone from Sitavati Grove in India, on which the exalted Nagarjuna had carved an image, called "Blazing Fire," of a protective deity. "But I need a statue in return," he said, so I presented him with an old and very special "regent" statue of Guru Rinpoché that was in my possession.

I told Chokgyur Lingpa, "I have been working on a collection of your more important *terma*s, but now I must ask that you look it over and see what might or might not be appropriate for inclusion." He told me that he had discovered several *terma* caches and the records of teachings they contained, [86a] and that at such times he encountered Guru Rinpoché directly and held conversations with him. "I can recall all of that without forgetting anything," he stated. While on his way back to Jadra, he stopped in Padrak to perform a ritual feast and ceremony of fulfillment. He also discovered the detailed account of the Sengdrak Cliff.

ON THE FIRST DAY of the new Fire Serpent Year [1857-1858], Chokgyur Lingpa received the concise account of the twenty-five major holy sites of eastern Tibet and came to see me. I made offerings honoring him as the one responsible for these *terma*s. While I was examining them, I found many lines of verse that Guru Rinpoché had spoken in response to Chokgyur Lingpa's questions, but I didn't make a list of them at the time. I felt as though he had given me permission to prepare the collection of his *terma*s however I saw fit, due to my commitment to their fundamental purpose because of my karmic connections and aspirations. On the third day of the month I performed a ritual of longevity based on the practice called The Innermost Heart of Immortality as an offering to the *tertön*, and made offerings to him as well. In return, he performed a *lhasang* ceremony and gave a long and very impressive series of instructions.

Chokgyur Lingpa recounted that when he was on his way to formally recognize the status of Tsadra Rinchen Drak as a holy site, he had recurring visions of the Guardian Goddess of Mantra, which caused him to lose consciousness. Finally he applied a symbol to his forehead, using one of Orgyen's seals, and this cleared his mind and he could identify the major practice caves in the area, all of which were naturally occurring. The next day, as he entered the "inner sanctum" of the area, there was a violent wind and a number of other signs of disturbance.[605] He came to Situ Rinpoché's monastic residence, where the concise account of the twenty-five holy places was codified. [86b] The *tertön* then bestowed the principal empowerment for his *sadhana* of enlightened mind *Dispelling All Obstacles*, using a sand mandala prepared in the Lhasar shrine. My precious lord guru also came, and they codified the practice of Hayagriva.[606] Chokgyur Lingpa then bestowed that empowerment and many others, including that of White Amitayus. Then the two masters set off for Dergé Gönchen.

Chokgyur Lingpa told me that both Öntrul and I were needed when he discovered *terma*s at Sengdrak Cliff. So we set off for Namdrak on the fourteenth, accompanied by a group of monks. On the fifteenth, at the Pema Shelphuk Cave in Utsé, the monks assisted us in performing a hundred feast offerings to Vajravarahi and a thousand to Vajrasattva, as well as *lhasang* ceremonies and rituals to the protective deities. My two precious spiritual masters arrived on the sixteenth and we performed a feast offering in the Sungphuk Cave (associated with Guru Rinpoché's enlightened speech) at Utsé. As rainbows shimmered in the sky and many vultures gathered, the *tertön* said that he could see a gathering of *vidyadhara*s and *dakini*s. He discovered a statue of Orgyen called "Chingtsalpa" from a white cliff face. His meditative experience intensified and he went in search of the main site of spiritual power in the area, finding it at Sengphu in the upper part of the valley. We moved our encampment there.

Over three days we performed a hundred thousand feast offerings using the *sadhana* of enlightened mind from the Northern Treasures cycles. On the morning of the twenty-first, Chokgyur Lingpa discovered a *terma* and I made offerings to acknowledge him as the one responsible, using the practice of Vajrasattva. He opened the *terma* the following day and my omniscient spiritual master [87a] gave an explanatory talk. The substances from the *terma* were distributed to us, each according to his lot. Chokgyur Lingpa also discovered an amulet filled with spiritual medicine from Khandroi Drora[607] and another hidden cache of medicinal substances from Sengphu. On the banks of the Tséchu River, he bestowed on us the empowerment for Guru Dewa Chenpo and then departed and we, masters and students, also returned to our home.

We reached the monastic residence of Situ Rinpoché, where we arranged for the party of monks who would accompany me to central Tibet.[608] I gave the empowerment and oral transmissions of Kalachakra and other cycles to several interested parties and also taught in the meditation center, according to my usual custom. From Khardo, I received a letter from the *tertön* Tsewang Drakpa,[609] along with some of the teachings and *samaya* substances he had discovered. My dreams were filled with very disturbing signs. I became absorbed in completing my arrangements of several rituals and in packing and preparing for my journey to central Tibet. I undertook a personal retreat on a newly discovered *terma* focusing on the peaceful and wrathful forms of Ayushpati.[610] In the fourth month I went to Palpung Monastery and took part in the vase consecration ritual and gave empowerments to a large crowd of people, while at the meditation center I conferred the bodhisattva vow and gave other transmissions.

On the eleventh day of the fifth month, our party traveling to central Tibet visited such mountains as Kardzin and Uchétem to secure the sites by making offerings.[611] In the monastic residence, I performed a consecration of Öntrul's statues of Tara, using the practice of Chakrasamvara for two days, followed by three days of a ritual to Tara. Then I set out for Dzongsar to meet my precious omniscient spiritual master. Khyentsé Rinpoché conferred on me some of his own *terma*s, including all the empowerments, oral transmissions, and instructions for the Heart Drop of Chetsün (which was one of his "recollections"[612]), [87b] The Heart Drop of Simhamukha, and the Heart Drop of Bairotsana. In addition, he conferred all the empowerments and oral transmissions for the deity Samyak from The Seven Profound Cycles. He told me of the holy places and statues in the central Tibetan provinces of Ü and Tsang,[613] and gave very detailed and extensive advice, such as the relative importance of the major and minor holy sites, from the point of view of doing spiritual practice there and visiting specific sites. He also sent me off with presents and I returned home.

We packed our camp and left Palpung on the twenty-second day of the sixth month. Proceeding in stages, we reached the steppes of Dogyü. There, Tertön Rinpoché was in retreat at Karma, so I dispatched someone to him with a message. He sent word that I should come to Karma, but the route would have been very circuitous and I needed to stay as the head of the encampment, so the chance to visit him didn't present itself. On our journey, at such places as Tergar, I satisfied the requests of the lamas and *tulku*s along the way; they would greet us and send us off with formal escorts. When we reached Gyama

Tsaldo, we were joined by Tertön Rinpoché himself. He said to me, "I broke my retreat, because if certain circumstances aren't set in place, your endeavors will surely come to naught." He had made the journey with only five stops to encamp. For the time we camped together, he was most kind, bestowing all the empowerments for his *sadhanas* of enlightened mind, as well as for the peaceful and wrathful deities of *The Web of Magic*, the three cycles focusing on Ayushpati, *The Single Kila of Enlightened Mind*, [88a] Padmadakini,[614] Guhya Natha,[615] and other transmissions. He also trained me extensively in the appropriate rituals to promote the Buddhist teachings in general, and those of the Kagyü School in particular. Chokgyur Lingpa then left in the direction of Zurmang.

At Dormarkho, our party was joined by a representative of the Dergé government and many fellow travelers who were on their way to central Tibet. I performed all the *lhasang* ceremonies and gave whatever advice I could. We took the middle route to the north and offered prayers of aspiration at Kumbum Temple in Shak Karma; the signs of the blessings we received were excellent. In accordance with the accepted customs, I dispatched messengers to the central government and to Tsurphu and met escorts from these places at Sangzhung.

We arrived at Ogmin Tsurphu on the second day of the tenth month, having encountered no hazards on our journey. They accorded us elaborate honors, meeting us on horseback with food, drink, and gifts, accompanied by ceremonial music. On the seventh day, which was extremely auspicious, I went to the main temple, where I first beheld the golden visages of "father and son."[616] Later on, when I had a private conversation with Karmapa in his quarters, I offered him an account of my activities as a *tertön* and he was most impressed. On the eleventh day I witnessed Karmapa perform the ceremony of wearing his crown, which brings liberation on sight, and I made offerings to him. Then Karmapa came to our encampment to enthrone the young Situ incarnation and make offerings to him. [88b] The incarnation himself then departed for the Dechen Phodrang Palace. On the fourteenth, in response to Gyalwa Rinpoché's request, I offered to him the empowerments and oral transmissions for the *sadhanas* of enlightened mind from the Tersar[617] cycles, and we performed a feast offering on the fifteenth. I requested of Karmapa a copy of secret prophecies that he had written down in his own hand.

The majority of those in our encampment stayed there, but I went with a group of five or so students to Mindroling Monastery to receive empowerments and oral transmissions. On the road we had the fortunate opportunity to see, for the first time, the statues of Jowo Shakyamuni and Jowo Mikyö Dorjé in the miraculous temples in Lhasa.[618] We also visited the Potala Palace[619] and the statues of the temple of Chagpori,[620] and went to Tsal Gungthang to make offerings, visit holy sites and offer hundreds of lamps. When we got to Yangdzong in the region of Drak, I did a five-day retreat on the Tersar form of Yamantaka and performed several feast offerings and fulfillment rituals. I performed one hundred feast offerings at the cave of Kharchen-phuk Cave, and feast offerings at the lake sacred to Yeshé Tsogyal and the nearby stupa of Khardo.

In this way we eventually arrived at the glorious center of Samyé. We visited all the temples to see the images and offer prostrations, and took part in a ritual to avert negativity that was being performed in the temple of Duddul Ngakpa Ling, in conjunction with the winter equinox. I then went to see the site of Yamalung, where I established a connection with the place by doing a three-day retreat focusing on White Amitayus from the Tersar tradition. The lamas and monks of Mindroling [89a] performed a longevity ritual for me based on *The Innermost Heart of Immortality*.

On the tenth day of the eleventh month, we performed a hundred feast offerings from *Dispelling All Obstacles* at Khangyu Zhalchen and then returned to Mindroling. When we got there, I saw a doorway open on the right side of the central temple. I entered and saw the famous Ngadrama[621] statue of Guru Rinpoché; the face seemed to me to be very white, shining intensely with light. I saw this statue a couple of times more, and the face always seemed white to me. Once I had sponsored the regilding of the face, however, it then appeared golden in color to me.

I spent three days establishing a connection with the solitudes of the Chimphu uplands,[622] spending the time in retreat on the cycle of Hayagriva from The Seven Profound Cycles. We offered one hundred feast offerings in Drakmar Ke'u-tsang Cave, using The United Intent of the Gurus and the cycle of the Eight Commands called The Gathering of Sugatas. In the lower Flower Cave, we established a connection with the place by performing a group ritual and offering ceremony using the Heart Drop of Chetsün. Crossing the river,[623] we reached Tsethang. After a brief visit to the temple of Thradruk,[624] we viewed the clay statue of the Great Scholar and other images near the marketplace of Drada.

We then continued on to Orgyen Mindroling, where the administrators housed us in a small palace next to the monastic residence and showed us great kindness. In the presence of Thrichen Rinpoché, the precious throne-holder of Mindroling,[625] I received the transmissions for all the instructions from the Nyingma *Kama* collection that I had not received before, as well as the empowerments for the forms of Ayushpati [89b] called "Iron-Like" and "Iron Scorpion," the empowerment for *The Innermost Heart of Immortality*, the conferral of Duthrö Mamo,[626] the life force empowerments for two protective deities (the Four-Armed Mahakala and the Guardian Goddess of Mantra), and other transmissions.

From Thrichen Rinpoché's venerable sister[627] I received many oral transmissions, including those for the volumes of the Nyingma *Kama* collection; The Innermost Heart Drop of Guru Chöwang; and The Heart Drop of Vajrasattva. I also received from her transmissions of the *sadhana* of *The Ancestral Line of the Masters of Awareness* and other transmissions from the Northern Treasures cycles; the *sadhana* of enlightened mind called *Tamer of Beings*; *Karmic Connection*; the "three remedial deities"; The Profound Seal of Varahi; the source texts for the practice of Ayushpati; Guru Chöwang's practice of Nagaraksha; and the practice of the Four-Armed Mahakala from the *terma*s of Nyang.

I also received empowerments from the vajra holder Gyurmé Döndrup,[628] such as the empowerment for the *sadhana* of enlightened mind from the Northern Treasures cycles, as well as the conferral of the practice of Jomjé Tsalchen, and the empowerment into Pema Lingpa's practice of the Eight Commands. He granted me instructions on Guru Chöwang's Planting the Black Spike of Mantra in the Heart; The Mother and Child Instructions on Thoroughly Averting Negativity; the stupa design known as "Supremely Powerful"; and The Seven Instructions on Tara. Gyurmé Döndrup also bestowed many oral transmissions on me, including The Complete Gathering of the Eight Commands of Panchen, the Mamo Gangshar cycle discovered by Rashak Chenpo, and the ritual (from the *terma*s of Nyang) called *The Victorious Ransom of the Protective Deities*.

From the monk Tenphel I received oral transmissions for Manjushri, The Great Perfection; the three antidotal deities; the Cow's Udder[629] collections of Loktripala[630] and Duthrö Mamo from Guru Chöwang's tradition; and the Eight Commands cycle The Gate to the Fortress.

In return, I offered to Thrichen Rinpoché and his sister [90a] the empowerments for the seventeen Dzogchen tantras, the Eight Commands cycle The

Perfection of Secrets, and The Lucid Expanse of Ratna Lingpa; the empowerment and oral transmissions for Tsering Dorjé's General Quintessence teachings;[631] all the empowerments and oral transmissions of the Tersar tradition of the deity Samyak (given that I am the specific custodian for these teachings); and White Amitayus.

My companions couldn't stay any longer, so we left on the twenty-third day of the twelfth month, visiting Jampaling and Drapa Ngönshé's[632] temple in Dranang, crossing rivers and mountain ranges until we reached Tsurphu again on the twenty-ninth. There we took part in the year-end *gutor* ceremonies focusing on the protective deities and witnessed the sacred dances.

DURING THE CELEBRATIONS for the new Earth Horse Year [1858-1859], I had an audience with my refuge lord, Gyalwang Karmapa Rinpoché, who granted me a place in the ranks of those performing the rituals. There were many to perform, including a wrathful ritual focusing on Ayushpati[633] from the Tersar cycles. Once they were finished, I planned to do a short pilgrimage in central Tibet; so I went to Lhasa, where I saw the spectacles connected with the annual prayer festival. I had an audience with the regent, Hotoktu Rinpoché,[634] at the Potala Palace, making prostrations and some token offerings to him. Since the sublime incarnation of Situ Rinpoché had taken rebirth in a family indentured to Tashilhunpo Monastery,[635] through the government minister Shedra[636] I requested official permission to travel to Tashilhunpo and take the incarnation along with his parents back to eastern Tibet. This was granted without any problem. [90b]

Nyungné Lama Rinpoché sponsored me to practice in the anteroom outside the sleeping chamber used by Guru Rinpoché, and I prepared elaborate offerings and performed a thousand feast offerings using the practice *Dispelling All Obstacles*. I also performed empowerments and gave instructions to satisfy the requests of Nyungné Rinpoché, some of the cabinet ministers and their families, and several *geshés*.[637] I performed the "one thousand offerings"[638] to each of the two statues of Shakyamuni. In all the chapels I visited in the Potala, I offered ceremonial scarves, sponsored the gilding of the statues, made offerings, and ensured that all the necessary gestures were carried out thoroughly.

In the second month I traveled through Dechen toward Samyé. On Gökar Pass we met with Drukchen Rinpoché,[639] who was on his way to Tsurphu. He expressed great delight at encountering me. On this journey we arrived without any difficulty, for the representatives of the central government had made all the preparations. The majority of our encampment went to Samyé, but I went with a small group to Yamalung and practiced the *sadhana* of White Amitayus from the Tersar cycles. There were people in Yamalung who had gone there to perform the customary rituals sponsored by the central government, and I gave empowerments and oral transmissions to them.

Then we visited Drakmar Drinzang briefly and continued on to Samyé. There we performed a thousand feast offerings based on a *sadhana* of enlightened mind from the Tersar cycles. I offered ceremonial scarves and made offering in the chapels. I sponsored gilding of the statues in the central temple [91a] and offered a thousand lamps. In the Aryapalo shrine I made a connection by performing feast offerings and prayed intently for the welfare of both central and eastern Tibet. On the summit of the Hepori Hill I performed a ritual to bind gods and demons to their oaths of allegiance.

I went to the Chimphu uplands and made feast offerings on a large scale, stopped on the road at the Tashi Ö-Bar stupa, and then continued on to Densa Thil and Zangri Kharmar, where I visited the holy sites and did as much spiritual practice as I was able. At Thradruk Temple in Yarlung, I offered ceremonial scarves, sponsored the gilding of images, and offered a thousand lamps; I also performed a hundred feast offerings in the presence of the "regent" statue of Orgyen. In the temple on Gangpo Hill near Tsethang, I made feast offerings and performed a ritual to bind gods and demons to their oaths of allegiance. I visited Yumbu Lhakhar[640] and the three places called Bumpa[641] in succession, forging a connection with these places and making offerings. On the slopes of the Shampo massif, I performed a ritual of ransom based on the practice of Ngön-Dzok Gyalpo from the Tersar cycles, and while en route we visited the tomb of King Songtsen Gampo.

At Sheldrak, a group of more than thirty of us, master and students, spent seven days in a *drupchen* ritual, alternating the practices of the peaceful and wrathful deities from the Tersar cycle called the Magical Display of Peaceful and Wrathful Deities. From beginning to end, the signs were excellent. It was also on this occasion that I found someone with the lineage for the "seal of entrustment" of The Gathering of All the Dakinis' Secrets.[642]

Crossing Chaya Pass, we descended past the lake of Drigu and arrived at Mawochok in the southern province of Lhodrak. [91b] Here we made offerings and prayers in front of the statues representing the master and his spiritual son,[643] as well as visiting holy sites in the area. En route we performed ritual feasts based on Guru Chöwang's cycle of the Eight Commands at Benpa Chagdor, Guru Lhakhang, and other places. We also saw the famous statue of Vairochana at Khoting.

We spent five days at Chagpurchen in Kharchu, practicing the Tersar *sadhana* of the deity Samyak. We then continued our journey, performing feast offerings in Lhamokhar and Palgyi Phukring, arriving at last at the miraculous palace in Sekhar. We visited the holy sites there, performing extensive feast offerings and making many prayers in front of the statue of Marpa and in Nyanya Lungten-phuk Cave. We visited the sacred lake of Pemaling and the holy sites of the Lhalung Valley and Guru Lhakhang. Passing through the area of Yamdrok, we reached Chagzam Chuwori, where we established a connection with the place by practicing and performing feast offerings. We also performed a ritual to bind gods and demons to their oaths of allegiance. We went to Sinpori specifically to perform a feast offering and make prayers in front of the statue of Chakrasamvara. Continuing on our way, we made a side trip to Zhung Threshing, where we made offerings and prayers at the shrines housing the relics of Marpa and Ngok. Crossing Jela Pass, we stopped to visit stupas on our route and so arrived in Lhasa. There I reported to the authorities that I had performed the rituals requested of me.

In the fourth month we returned to Tsurphu, arriving on the tenth day and witnessing the sacred dances. [92a] At Pema Khyungdzong,[644] I undertook a personal retreat on the deity Vajradanda, as well as one on the Tersar cycle of White Amitayus (to promote Karmapa's long life). On the eight day of the fifth month I ended my retreat in response to a summons from Gyalwang Karmapa. I went to where he and his retinue were encamped for the summer and had an audience with him. I offered the extensive empowerment for White Amitayus to Karmapa. On the tenth day, he also received from me the empowerment for the *sadhana* of enlightened mind called *Dispelling All Obstacles*. Drukchen Rinpoché was there as well, but he said that he would not request Tersar empowerments, since our refuge lord[645] had suffered from poor eyesight since journeying to eastern Tibet. However, on the night of the ninth, Drukpa Rinpoché had several significant signs come to him in his dreams, which cut through his doubt. So on the tenth, about twenty lamas and *tulkus*— including Karmapa, Drukpa Rinpoché, Situ Rinpoché, and Pawo Rinpoché— received the empowerment for one of Chokgyur Lingpa's *sadhana*s of enlightened mind. Following this, I transmitted the cycle of Ayushpati from The Seven Profound Cycles to three masters—Gyalwang Karmapa, Drukpa Rinpoché, and

Chöwang Tulku;[646] to Drukpa Rinpoché because he was the custodian of the Yamantaka Ayushpati teachings, and to Karmapa because he had intended to receive these instructions all along. I offered them the entire transmission of the empowerment, the oral transmission, an explanation of the tantra, practical instructions for practice, and the oral instructions I had received. At the palace of Dechen Podrang, we received all the empowerments and oral transmissions for the cycle of Dechen Lingpa's teachings from Pawo Rinpoché. We returned to Gyalwang Karmapa's seat in Tsurphu, [92b] where I offered the entire range of empowerments and oral transmissions for several cycles—the Magical Display of Peaceful and Wrathful Deities, Dredging the Pit of Cyclic Existence (including the auxiliary practices associated with the protective deities), and the Vajrakila practice called *The Sphere of Enlightened Mind*—to Karmapa and Öntrul. Then, I arranged very meticulously for all the ceremonies planned for by Chokgyur Lingpa, to serve both general and more specific purposes.

The sublime Situ incarnation was invited to visit Nenang Monastery [647] and I accompanied him, visiting the holy sites and stupas. There I also offered to Pawo Rinpoché the empowerments and oral transmissions for the Tersar cycle of Vajrakila. In between these transmissions, I requested from him many rare empowerments and oral transmissions from both the Nyingma and Sarma Schools, teachings that Rigdzin Tulku had received from the previous Pawo.[648] Returning to the area of Tsurphu, I made a thorough attempt to visit the special holy sites, including the statue of Lhachen called "The Ornament of the World" and the cave of Dusum Khyenpa. I made what offerings and prayers I could at these places. On various occasions during my stay at Tsurphu, I was able to fulfill the requests of Gyaltsap Rinpoché[649] by giving him the transmissions of such cycles as Chokgyur Lingpa's *sadhana* of enlightened mind and White Amitayus.

We began our preparations for the return journey to eastern Tibet, consulting astrologers, performing *lhasang* ceremonies, and so on. A small group of us went to Lhasa to offer our final respects to the governor before our departure. At this point in time, the abbot of Radreng was the regent, so he showed us great favor, even sending us off with a ceremonial "treasure scarf" for the *tertön*. [93a] He spoke of the need for this to be returned to him after it had been taken around the whole of greater Tibet. We also visited the two statues of Shakyamuni to offer prostrations and fervent prayers for the success of our venture.

On our return journey, we visited the temple of Neten in Yerpa, the former seat of the Kadampa School in the Phenyul Valley, Taklung, Radreng, and other centers. At Sang-zhung, Choktrul Rinpoché[650] and the rest of us met the welcoming party from Palpung. In the region of Nakchukha, we were joined by a large encampment from Tsurphu, and there were many people who came to request empowerments and to witness the vajra crown ceremony. At several points, our path was blocked by rivers in full spate, and there were so many such halts in our progress that our trip took a long time. Passing through Bershak, Sumdo, and other areas, we reached Gina in the ninth month.

The encampment from Tsurphu had been able to travel with us, so we had requested that they accompany our party. They were sent on to Palpung ahead of us to wait for Gyalwang Rinpoché,[651] who had to visit Karma Gön Monastery that year. In conjunction with that, he received important invitations from all the major and minor lamas and *tulku*s of the monasteries throughout the region, but since every monastery on his route invited him to stay, we were held up for quite some time. But I was able to witness each of the vajra crown ceremonies he performed, and for my part transmitted empowerments and formal authorizations in response to the requests of the respective lamas and monastic communities. At Tashi Umathang, we were joined by Öntrul [93b] and the escort from the Dergé government. The *tertön* Chögyal Dorjé also came, and I requested the transmissions of several cycles of his teachings.[652] As a special means to ensure auspicious conditions in the most general sense, for three days we performed a group ritual of the longevity practice *The Integration of Means and Wisdom*; I also offered a longevity empowerment to Choktrul Rinpoché.

Passing through the region of Zurmang Monastery and other areas, we continued as quickly as possible, crossing the Drichu River in small boats. When we reached Tsagyé Plateau, we were met by an envoy from Dergé, who had been dispatched to welcome Karmapa with a ceremonial scarf. I was dressed like a poor minor official, and was quite upset by this, for I thought, "What a state for me to be in when Karmapa first receives our offerings!" I took this to be a premonition of his personal power starting to come to an end.

From Alo Shega, we continued on to the monastic seat. The morning we set out, Choktrul Rinpoché was experiencing great mood swings, from happiness to sadness, and he was deeply troubled by the difficulties the cold winds caused us. In this and other ways, the rest of our journey was rather inauspicious. We stayed on Gyépa Plateau, accompanied by the mounted escorts sent by the monasteries of the region.

On the morning of the tenth day of the tenth month, we reached the monastery and were received by a large escort of monks in their formal robes, playing ritual music. We presented a mandala offering to Gyalwang Karmapa in the main hall and he blessed each person individually. A feast was served to the participants in this great gathering and Öntrul himself presented each person with a ceremonial scarf. [94a]

I went to the hermitage, where I met my mother, who was in good health. After a few days rest, I performed one hundred ceremonies to the protective deities and other rituals. Over the winter solstice, following my usual custom, I undertook a personal retreat on Vajrakila, followed by a ritual focusing on that deity to avert negativity and a retreat on the Venerable Goddess. It was about this time that Chokgyur Lingpa, having been invited to Dergé, had discovered several *termas* en route. On Thra-o Plain, he had fallen very ill with what resembled blood poisoning, so my master Tulku Rinpoché had gone to perform rituals to dispel the contamination. Once Chokgyur Lingpa had recovered, he continued on to the capital. At Dokhoma he took part in a *drupchen* ritual, using the cycle of the Eight Commands, and performed a ritual focusing on wrathful deities to avert negativity. He sent word to me insisting that I come to participate in the ritual, so I went. I met both masters, as well as Chokgyur Lingpa's mother and son and other family members. I attended the ritual. Tulku Rinpoché gave an incredible lecture. When the *torma* was cast, there were disturbing signs (such as how the winds blew), so the *tertön* went on to practice another ritual to avert negativity for two or three days. I myself performed another kind of ritual to avert negativity, using the practice of The Union of All Rare and Precious Jewels and a ritual based on the sixty deity mandala of Vajrabhairava according to the tradition of Atisha. I also performed all the empowerments for the Nyingma *Kama* collection for my incarnate master, the *tertön*, and the queen and prince of Dergé.[653]

CHOKGYUR LINGPA HAD DISCOVERED an account indicating that a new monastery needed to be founded on Mandala Plateau in Nanktro, as a way of promoting the teachings and benefiting society at large, [94b] so in the new Earth Sheep Year [1859-1860], following this account, the masters and students all went to choose a site. During this time there was a certain kind of snowfall known as "white, red and black," following which there were some negative omens. On Mandala Plateau, we established some auspicious conditions as we gathered to perform a feast offering and my precious and omniscient lord explained tantras of the older and new schools. We completed a ritual to establish a rapport with the local spirits, the concealment of a treasure vase,[654] and certain other rituals, and then returned home. At this point, Chokgyur Lingpa offered many gifts to the prince and his mother, principally a "regent" image of Guru Rinpoché that he had discovered, explaining the importance of the project, and they had agreed to help him. But the monks of Dergé Gönchen were very sectarian in their doctrinal outlook and the royal chamberlain, Tashi Gyatso, feared that harm would come to the Sakya institutions of the area, so out of spite he held the project up.

It was at this stage that Tulku Rinpoché said, "If we can build a temple large enough to need four pillars and an image of Maitreya, this much will be enough to ensure that the troubled times under Nyaké[655] do not affect us." My lord guru then conferred the empowerment of the Heart Drop of the Exalted Goddess of Immortality. I also received several empowerments from the *tertön* himself, including that of the form of Avalokiteshvara known as "Dredging the Pit of Cyclic Existence." I served as scribe when Chokgyur Lingpa codified the activity ritual of the principal *sadhana* of enlightened mind, and Tulku Rinpoché was the scribe for the practice called *The Spontaneous Accomplishment of Goals*, the practice of Vaishravana,[656] and various other secondary texts (such as the *drupchen* manuals for the two *sadhana*s of enlightened mind, the prophetic account, and so forth). [95a]

At the capital, Khyentsé Rinpoché conferred the empowerments for *The Discourse of United Intent*, and led two weeks of practice that combined *drupchen* and *mendrup* rituals. I was able to receive all these empowerments and was entrusted with these teachings as well. The *tertön* installed a statue of Vaishravana in the palace and I performed a ritual of ransom for the young prince; immediately afterward, I returned to Palpung.

There Dabzang Tulku arrived from Karma Gön Monastery and in response to his request, I performed all the empowerments and oral transmissions for the six volumes of Jatsön Nyingpo's teachings, in conjunction with doing the practices involved. Several people came to me requesting instructions on poetics, Mahamudra, and other topics, and I satisfied their needs on an individual basis.

The great *tertön* came to my hermitage and I asked for his help in bestowing still more of his *terma*s and conferring on me the blessings of his direct lineage. He performed an enormous feast offering and prayer ritual. That night I dreamed of Guru Rinpoché in the form of the *tertön* Dorjé Lingpa, conferring on me the blessings of the *terma*s of the one hundred major *tertön*s. I myself could remember having been a student of Dorjé Lingpa in a previous life and, in that incarnation, having received and practiced all his *terma*s. I could also recall being Dungtso Repa[657] during the time of the *dakini* Kunga Bumpa.[658] I thus received the direct lineages for the *terma*s of these two masters.[659] [95b] From Chokgyur Lingpa I then requested an oral transmission for The Spacious Expanse of the View of Dorjé Lingpa (which represented only a portion of his *terma*s, since no others were available), as well as all the empowerments and oral transmissions for The Gathering of All the Dakinis' Secrets and the instructions and blessings for all the texts of *terma*s that I could find. We codified the *drupchen* manual for the primary *sadhana* of enlightened mind discovered by Chokgyur Lingpa and the teachings concerning the Swift-Acting Jnana Natha, which were my personal lot. Chokgyur Lingpa issued a directive to Situ Rinpoché's monastic residence, together with a prophetic account, concerning the need to erect a temple to the great and glorious deity[660] on this important spot, for the sake of the teachings in general and our specific tradition.

He said, "In order to open up the holy site of Tsadra Rinchen Drak, we must first install statues of the guardian deities here to the east, in this mandala of timeless awareness." He performed an investiture for me, conferring on me many empowerments and blessings, especially the instructions for the entire cycle of his own Tersar revelations. He also selected and consecrated the site for the new temple. The vajra master Ngédön performed a ritual of Chakrasamvara to prepare the site, and I myself performed one focusing on Kalachakra for the same purpose. On that day, people viewing from afar saw the two of us surrounded by a ring of brilliant rainbow-colored light. In the fourth month construction of the temple began under the supervision of Öntrul from Situ Rinpoché's monastic residence.

I went to Palpung Monastery [96a] and took part in the yearly vase consecration ritual; the ritual this year, with the *tertön*[661] presiding, was the *sadhana* of Hayagriva from his Tersar cycles. There were sacred dances and he performed a ritual to avert negativity. When these were finished, I returned to my hermitage, where I performed the fulfillment ritual of The United Intent of the Gurus and undertook a personal retreat based on the Heart Drop of the Exalted

Goddess of Immortality. The circumstances at both the outset of the retreat and the conclusion were most auspicious.

Then the great *tertön* arrived. He prepared drawings of the amulets for masculine and feminine protective deities, and constructed shrines for the guardian deities and the *naga*s. He also performed an extensive feast offering and fulfillment ritual at the peak of Uchétem, as well as a *lhasang* ceremony to promote harmony with the local spirits. He pointed out all the naturally occurring sacred formations, moving in a clockwise direction around the site.

On the tenth day of the sixth month Chokgyur Lingpa went to the secret cave of Bairotsana (to the right of Tsadra Rinchen Drak) and discovered the three Secret Sphere cycles, the yellow scrolls containing the account of Tsadra as a holy site, and substances to be used in the construction and filling of the statue of the great and glorious deity.[662] He then returned to the hermitage, where the scrolls were codified. He described the layout of the holy site, including the outer and inner paths of circumambulation, and gave me detailed accounts and practical training in all that was necessary to open the site up and establish the pilgrimage route.[663]

In preparation for Gyalwang Rinpoché's upcoming visit, we observed all the traditional forms, such as sending a formal escort to greet him, and inaugurated a ritual to commemorate the tenth day of the month. I myself saw to the necessary supplies [96b] and then went on a pilgrimage around the sacred site; the signs were extremely positive. I satisfied the great *tertön*'s requests for empowerments and oral transmissions, and he left in a mood of great delight. I performed the entire cycle of empowerments and ritual blessings of the Shangpa School for Donyön Tulku and others. From Dabzang Tulku I received The Heart Drop of Maitripa discovered by Taksham, as well as other transmissions. After I had paid him my respects, he went to Karma Gön Monastery. I undertook another personal retreat on the practice of the Heart Drop of the Exalted Goddess of Immortality, and had clear indications that I would live until the age of eighty, or possibly ninety.

The lay tantric master Thrindu Behu and his students came specifically to meet with me and receive the transmission of the six volumes of Jatsön Nyingpo's *terma*s, so I gave them all the empowerments and oral transmissions. They promised to build a meditation center and maintain an ongoing practice of these instructions. I satisfied the requests of several of my patrons and then went to Meting to collect offerings of grain on behalf of those in the temple and meditation center. I also met with my all-seeing precious master, who bestowed the empowerment of the nine deity mandala of Amitayus. Returning home, I met with Gyalwang Rinpoché, and in response to his request I offered him the oral transmissions and practical instructions for the Eight Commands.

I took up residence at the hermitage of Bongsar and the indications were very favorable. There I instituted a system of continual practice in the shrine dedicated to the protective deities. I did a personal retreat on *The Sphere of Enlightened Mind*, a practice of Vajrakila from the Tersar cycles, and in addition performed the annual year-end *gutor* ceremonies to avert negativity. [97a]

IN THE NEW IRON MONKEY YEAR [1860-1861], I went to Palpung Monastery. On the fifth day of the month commemorating the Buddha's spiritual miracles, Choktrul Rinpoché presided from the throne, while the teaching lamas and scholars expounded the mainstream traditions of the sutras and tantras. I myself gave an extensive explanation of the mandala offering. I presented "ten thousand offerings"[664] from Tsurgar, Palpung, Dergé, and other centers. The following day, after the group meal, I spoke to the gathering, explaining the tantra entitled *The Heart Essence of Secrets* by giving just an overview.

Gyalwang Karmapa conferred the oral transmissions for the collected writings of Düsum Khyenpa and Khachö Wangpo.[665] I gave the oral transmissions for *The Gathered Commands*, the commentary on Buddhist ethics by Mikyö Dorjé, and other works. In response to the insistent requests of Ngédön, the vajra master of the meditation center, and others, I performed the empowerments and oral transmissions for the Jonang collection *The Precious Source of Sadhanas*; *The Peaceful Garland* and *The Wrathful Garland* (including transmissions for the protective deities); and the *sadhanas* of enlightened mind for the Tersar cycles. My dreams were filled with troubling signs, so I returned to my hermitage and practiced the longevity *sadhana The Gathering of Secrets* diligently.

In the third month, as requested by Gyalwang Karmapa, I offered him the empowerments and oral transmissions for my newly completed collection, *The Tantric Treasury of the Kagyü School*. In addition to Karmapa, I performed these for all present. During the fourth month we began the vase consecration ritual, with Karmapa himself presiding as vajra master. [97b] On the day of the empowerment, he gave general teachings and advice, and especially spoke in detail to Öntrul of the last Situ's unfulfilled wishes, such as the crucial need to institute a monastic summer retreat.[666]

In the fifth month Gyalwang Karmapa went to the hermitage, where he presided over a *drupchen* ritual based on The United Intent of the Gurus, a very elaborate ceremony that included a ritual to consecrate sacred medicine. Lord Khyentsé Rinpoché also came, and Karmapa took great delight in receiving from him the transmission of the Heart Drop of the Exalted Goddess of Immortality.

We received an urgent request from the chieftain Nyaké, so Gyalwang Karmapa, Kuzhap Choktrul,[667] and others, including myself, traveled with our students to Drangdil, where we encamped. Karmapa fulfilled all the Nyarong chieftain's requests—performing a ritual cremation for one of his sons who had died, conferring formal authorizations, performing the vajra crown ceremony, and so forth.[668] On our return journey, we detoured to Ting-lhung, where we met my all-seeing master, who was staying in Dagam Wangphuk Cave. Gathering together, we performed an extensive feast offering. Gyalwang Karmapa received transmissions from Khyentsé Rinpoché, including the "ultimate empowerment" for Mahakarunika Chittavishramana,[669] and the cycles of the Heart Drop of the Lotus-Born and the Heart Drop of Chetsün. On this occasion, the auspicious conditions were excellent—just as they are described in the texts—and afterward Gyalwang Karmapa continued on to the monastic seat of Palpung.

I went on to my hermitage, and on the seventeenth day of the sixth month four artisans, a master and his apprentices, [98a] began work on the statues for the Vajrakila Temple. We made elaborate preparations for filling these images with mantras and so forth. A group of four fully ordained monks performed an auspicious ritual to renew their vows and a ceremony to prepare the site. We installed the central axes and secondary supports for the three statues of *herukas*[670] and placed special objects in each of their five places.[671] We also filled the statues with four kinds of relics and more than one hundred thousand of their individual essence mantras.

Gyalwang Karmapa arrived on the ninth day of the eighth month and I offered him my best wishes for his health. I requested a blessing from him and he responded by bestowing the transmissions for the Heart Drop of the Lotus-Born and the *sadhana* of enlightened mind called *The Wish-Fulfilling Gem*, one after the other. On the twenty-ninth day of the eighth month we performed the activity rituals for the protective deities; in this and other traditional ways we began erecting a statue of the Swift-Acting Jnana Natha. In the heart center of the statue we installed a naturally formed statue of that protective deity, and in addition filled the statue with all the objects specifically associated with this deity and (as is customary) the four kinds of relics. The installation of these imbued the statue with blessings. The statues of the principal deities of The United Intent of the Gurus, Kalachakra, Vajrakumara, and the protective deities (in the shrine dedicated to them) were painted and the eyes were opened.[672] Everything was completed by the seventh day of the tenth month, whereupon I gave the artisans ceremonial scarves, gave a party, and sent them off with offerings to pay for their work. [98b] Kuzhap Rinpoché and Öntrul both led a group of some fifteen lamas who had completed the requisite retreats in consecrating the statues over two days, using the ritual of Chakrasamvara. I made them offerings and gave a celebratory party, too.

While it would be good if a meditation center were built at this temple, it is difficult to know what turn events will take, so I sent to my lord guru at Dzongsar Monastery, asking him to determine whether it was worth making the effort to build such a center. Khyentsé Rinpoché had a vision in which he was on a high cliff as the sun was rising and a rain of crystals of all sizes was falling. After that he went into the dwelling of a powerful local spirit, whom he took to be Dri Nyendong. There he opened a door and saw representations of enlightened form, speech, and mind,[673] as well as many treasure troves of various articles. He was told, "Take whatever you want." Inside there was a very fine crystal with eight facets, about a cubit in height, which contained the vivid forms of the host of peaceful deities of the Vajradhatu mandala, formed of rainbow light. Khyentsé Rinpoché saw himself carrying this on his shoulder, feeling great delight. He felt an inkling that he should show this crystal to others, whereupon he lost it and seemed to pass out. Then he found another, although it was smaller than the former and he could carry it in his hands. The night before, Khyentsé Rinpoché had dreamed of the great scholar Vimalamitra appearing in front of him in an amazing globe of light, directly introducing him to the nature of mind in a very extensive way, beginning with a method for transferring consciousness at the time of death. This introduction caused Khyentsé Rinpoché to understand much that he hadn't previously.

When he related to me these excellent signs he had seen, [99a] I made up my mind to establish the meditation center. I went to Situ Rinpoché's monastic residence to request funds that would ensure that the retreat program could begin that year; I took four large lumps of gold and silver to back up my request and offered them to Öntrul. He selected seven people—one to be the retreat master, five to be retreatants, and one to be the lama responsible for the rituals of the protective deities. I assigned them lodgings and used astrology to determine a date for beginning the retreat. Once they had all gathered, to dispel any obstacles at the outset they performed the four-mandala ritual of Tara, one hundred rituals to the protective deities of both the Nyingma and Sarma traditions, and personal retreats on the Secret Sphere cycle of Vajrakila practice. When the ritual to avert negativity had been completed, they began their three-year retreat program. I chose the regular rituals to be performed and the liturgies for the rituals of the protective deities. I also made it my duty to provide the retreatants over time with whatever they needed by way of empowerments, oral transmissions, and instructions. It is on this site that, over the years, some eight temples of various sizes have been constructed, filled with representations of enlightened form, speech, and mind, and provided with offerings, rooms for lodging, kitchens, and so forth; all of this is set forth in detail in my book describing the center.[674] I drew up an equally detailed schedule for the retreatants to follow, from the initial rituals to dispel obstacles through the entire three-year program—the practices focusing on the stages of approach and accomplishment, the regular practices done every month, the daily schedule of four meditation sessions, and so forth.

I was summoned to Dergé to conduct certain rituals, so I went and performed the Vajrakila ritual to avert recurrent cycles of negative energy[675] and (in the temple of Vaishravana) rituals focusing on the protective deities and *lhasang* ceremonies to promote harmony with the local spirits. [99b] Having fulfilled the wishes of the young king and his mother by performing empowerments, ceremonies to free them of the effects of negative energy, and other rituals, I returned home.

On the twenty-fifth day of the eleventh month I began a *torma* ritual of accomplishment focusing on Jnana Natha, a ritual that included people reciting the mantra continuously in shifts.

THIS RITUAL CONCLUDED on the third day of the new Iron Bird Year [1861-1862]. I continued for some time in a personal retreat on the practices of White Tara and the Heart Drop of the Exalted Goddess of Immortality, among others. The all-seeing Khyentsé Rinpoché came to visit me in the third month. On the eighth day, when Jupiter was aligned with the constellation of Gyal, he began a series of consecration rituals from the Mindroling tradition, starting with that of Vajrasattva and continuing with the rituals of The United Intent of the Gurus and the So tradition of the deity Samyak, followed by individual rituals from the Sakya tradition that focused on Kalachakra, Hevajra, Chakrasamvara, and Khechari.[676] During all these consecration rituals, from beginning to end, there were the most excellent signs of positive, auspicious energy. Khyentsé Rinpoché also conferred the empowerments for the four traditions of Hevajra and the "essential" Hevajra cycle,[677] as well as the ceremony for arousing motivation according to the Vajrayana tradition, a number of blessing rituals, and the instructions for the "group explanation" transmission of the Lamdré cycle.[678] He taught the latter very extensively, incorporating all the auxiliary instructions. We performed the tantra rituals, feast offerings, and an offering ceremony to honor the spiritual masters of the Lamdré lineage. He also bestowed the oral transmissions for *The Stages of Approach and Accomplishment for the Three Vajras*, the *Cow's Udder* collection for the eastern Tibetan tradition of the protective deities, and many other texts. I presented him with a mandala offering of thanksgiving and he departed. [100a]

During this period, Khyentsé Rinpoché had a pure vision in which he approached an enormous stupa with four major doors and a fifth in the vase.[679] There were very fine statues and furnishings inside, as well as many texts. He inquired of someone what these texts were and the man pointed out to him that these were the "five great Treasuries," explaining at great length about their importance. Rinpoché told me, "This proves that your destiny concerns these Five Treasuries. You should call the collection of *terma*s you have gathered *The Treasury of Precious Hidden Teachings*." He also related that Gyalpo Pehar[680] had said to him, "Guru Pema entrusted me with watching over the temples of Tibet, even one as small as a pile of grain. But none of you perform the slightest offerings or prayers to me. I am capable of dealing with very great threats; I place great stock in the oath I swore to Orgyen Pema. These days there are recurring ill omens, which indicate that something wicked is afoot." Khyentsé Rinpoché told me that Gyalpo Pehar was irritated due to having high expectations, and that from now on it would be necessary to have a short offering ritual to him performed daily in our shrine devoted to the protective deities.[681]

I then went to Palpung Monastery, where I participated in the annual vase consecration ritual and gave some empowerments to the local populace. All went very well. I helped prepare for, and participated in, a ritual focusing on the Puri form of Ayushpati, which we performed for the sake of Öntrul's long life. I also gave many empowerments and oral transmissions in response to the individual requests of a number of lamas and *tulku*s, and instructed the residents of the meditation center. [100b] In addition to continuing what I had started before, I instituted a tradition of the empowerments and instructions of the Zhijé School.

My lord guru had told me that it was important that there be a stupa to the north of this meditation center, so we selected the site using the rituals of the two Vimalas, planted the central axis, consecrated the *tsa-tsa*s,[682] and thus completed the construction of a "stupa of complete victory."[683] We also gilded the roof, and made preparations around its base to perform a ritual to infuse the site with the blessings of a major holy site. We filled the attic with long mantras, consecrated the temple, and performed a ceremony to install the victory banners.

I spent the rest of my time fulfilling the requests of several of my patrons and doing a few personal retreats until, in the eleventh month, I undertook a retreat on The United Intent of the Gurus. At year's end, I took part in the *torma* ritual of accomplishment focusing on my protective deity.[684]

ON THE FOURTEENTH DAY of the new Water Dog Year [1862-1863], we had the first demonstration by the retreat graduates of their ability to dry cotton sheets through the power of their meditation; I was very gratified to see the warmth they could generate and other real signs of blessings.[685] At the start of the second month they finished the seven-day *sadhana* practice of the oral lineage and so concluded their retreat.

Prior to this, Lama Karma Ngédön had urged me to write a treatise on the three levels of ordination, saying that if I did so he would write a commentary. But my feeling was that there were already any number of treatises on this subject, and that if I were to write a treatise it should be more comprehensive in scope, something that would be of use to people who had not studied much. So in the periods between my meditation sessions [101a] I had been composing the source verses to my treatise *The Encompassing of the Knowable*,[686] a treatise dealing with the three higher trainings.[687] Later, I offered this to my lord guru for his inspection, and on that occasion he gave me great encouragement, saying, "This is definitely due to the blessings of your spiritual masters and the power that comes from having the *dakini*s open up your subtle channels. We will call this *The Treasury of the Knowable*,[688] the first of the five great Treasuries you will produce. Now you must write your own commentary to it."

At this point, word came from Dzongsar that my omniscient and precious spiritual master was ill, so I spent several days performing a ritual to "turn back the escort," a longevity *sadhana*, and a major ritual to invoke the *tenma* sisters.[689] Then I went to Dzongsar, where I sponsored a ceremony for my spiritual master's long life, I offered to him some empowerments and oral transmissions that he had not received before, and in return he conferred on me the oral transmissions for Lalitavajra's commentary on *The Heart Essence of Secrets* and other works.

It was around this time that for several years the uprising led by Nyaké, the enemy of the teachings, flared up again. At a certain point, the queen of Dergé was preparing to flee the capital.[690] Tulku Rinpoché was invited to perform rituals on her behalf, but although he set out he was not able to reach her. There was no choice but for me to go, so I went to Dergé Gönchen. My journey was marked by extremely inauspicious omens. I spent many days in the temple dedicated to Vaishravana, performing a ritual of fulfillment and restoration. Then the queen's two sons were forced to go to Horkhok, so to remove obstacles on their journey I transmitted to them the empowerment of the *sadhana* of enlightened mind *Dispelling All Obstacles*. [101b] I then spent a few more days performing rituals of fulfillment and restoration.

Previously, when I had carried out some ceremonies on the occasion of the young prince's birth,[691] I had dreamed of a very large field lying fallow, with a few tiny flowers growing in one corner. And on another occasion I dreamed of being summoned to Dergé Gönchen, only to find that I didn't recognize anyone I met there. I was told that a woman and many soldiers were residing inside. In my dream, the palace had been largely consumed in a fire, with only the ruins of the Ranang Gate and the window frames left by the flames. I felt deeply saddened at this dream, and it would seem that it was a foreshadowing of things to come.

It was also around this time that I dreamed that the regional representatives of the central government commissioned four victory banners to be installed on the roof of a temple, and that an official confirmation of this, bearing the red governmental seal, had been received. These proved to be signs of the imminent arrival of the armed forces from the Tibetan government.

After I had spent about a month there, the chamberlain told me, "We no longer have the wherewithal to support your stay. There's just enough left to offer you, the lama, and your three monk attendants something for your efforts." So we returned to Palpung, where I attended the annual vase consecration ritual during the fourth month.

In accord with the intentions of the *tertön* Chokgyur Lingpa, a stupa was to be built at the base of Situ's tomb, so we laid the foundation for this after performing the rituals of the two Vimalas to consecrate the site and a *lhasang* offering to propitiate the local spirits. [102a] At Lhasar Temple, we completed the ceremony of the two Vimalas involved in the casting of *tsa-tsas*. Once the ritual installation of the central axis was over, we performed a consecration rite and did extensive work to finish the stupa, which included a depiction of the deity Mahakarunika Chittavishramana that could bring liberation on sight.

I went to my hermitage, where I carried out a number of rituals, including fire rituals associated with the four kinds of enlightened activity,[692] the ritual of the "nine classes of great powerful ones," and a ritual to appease wrath. It was around this time that I decided to give the title *The Treasury of Precious Hidden Teachings* to the collection of *terma*s I had previously gathered, and began the task of arranging the activity rituals, empowerment manuals, instructions, and necessary auxiliary practices associated with these *terma*s. It was also during this year that I was instructed by Öntrul to institute the monastic summer retreat, so I composed practical instruction manuals for the retreat itself and the specific rules governing it. I trained the chant master Rinchen and others in the detailed methods for these observances. Thus the tradition of the summer retreat was instituted at Lhasar Temple.

At the end of the sixth month, on behalf of Situ Rinpoché's monastic residence I spent a week performing a ritual focusing on wrathful deities to avert negativity. In the past, Rigdzin Tsewang Norbu had averted evil forces that threatened to destroy the monasteries of Palpung and Sadri. He had spoken prophetically about the demonic forces that would continue to afflict these areas, as a holdover from the deaths of many powerful people in the region, and of the importance of suppressing these forces by building a Vajrakila Temple and instituting that practice. [102b] Following his directive, Lord Chökyi Jungné had built a Vajrakila Temple and ensured that a lama would always be residing there, performing the rituals of Vajrakila. He also participated once in a *drupchen* ritual focusing on Vajrakila. Later on, in the *terma* records discovered by Chokgyur Lingpa, as well as in that master's pure visions, there were signs that there would be great threats to the Kagyü teachings. So Chokgyur Lingpa spoke insistently to Öntrul of the absolute necessity of holding such a *drupchen* ritual annually. Öntrul had promised to begin the practice this year. In accordance with traditions of the past, the plan was to begin the practice toward the end of the eighth month, so I trained the chant master, shrine keeper, and others thoroughly in the liturgies and practical details of both the "higher" and "lower" activities of the Vajrakila ritual.[693] We began the practice on the fifteenth day. I undertook the responsibility of being the vajra master. Including those who took shifts reciting the mantra continuously, there were some forty of us, masters and students, who performed the stage of approach, focusing on this deity of timeless awareness,[694] followed by that of intimate approach, focusing on the oath-bound guardians and the wrathful mantras. The ritual of "the effigy of the blade" was prepared by a separate group of five individuals, a *khenpo*[695] and his students. On the twenty-ninth day, we planted the *kila* dagger and cast out the *torma* in order to avert negativity. On the day of the new moon, we performed the ritual to accept the spiritual attainments of the practice, the concise "empowerment into the ultimate meaning," and a hundred feast offerings. Finally, on the first day of the next month we completed an elaborate *drupchen* ritual without any problems, and I returned to my hermitage.

Lama Sang-ngak came and I received from him the Guru cycle of Mati, instructions on the Innermost Quintessence teachings, [103a] The Ocean of Pith Instructions, and many other empowerments and oral transmissions. I also undertook personal retreats on the practices focusing on the noble Tara, such as the Heart Drop of the Exalted Goddess of Immortality. In the ninth month I began a personal retreat focusing on my lord guru's practice of Mahakarunika Chittavishramana. During this time I had very positive signs in my dreams, such as finding myself in a vast and pleasant garden of flower beds; in particular, I dreamed of being given the upper portion of Ngadak Nyang Rinpoché's embalmed body and eating a bit of it myself while giving the rest to others. During the waxing phase of the moon in the twelfth month I completed my retreat, having finished an extensive practice of the stages of approach, accomplishment, and enactment. With the retreatants, I then began a series of rituals honoring the protective deities of both the old and new schools, while we changed the *torma*s installed in the shrine room dedicated to these deities. I trained people in the liturgies and rituals for a new practice we were instituting in the lower shrine room—a *dö* ritual[696] of fulfillment focusing on the protective deity Bernakchen. I also attended a day of this ritual. At my hermitage, I practiced the year-end *torma* ritual of accomplishment for my protective deity.

WITH THE COMING OF the new Iron Pig Year [1863-1864], I recited quite a number of liturgies, including an offering ceremony to ensure the spread of the teachings. At Situ Rinpoché's monastic residence, for the benefit of Kuzhap Rinpoché I performed the empowerments of The Union of All Rare and Precious Jewels (which had been the personal practice of the late Situ), Chöjé Lingpa's tradition of Vajrakila, and other transmissions, as well as the ablution ritual of Vajravidarana. I then returned to my residence.

It was around this time that the armies of the Nyarong chieftain occupied Dergé Gönchen [103b] and seized control of the entire administrative region. Rumors abounded of a large force dispatched by the central Tibetan government, under the leadership of the government minister Zhapé Phulungwa[697] and others, that would cause heaven and earth to shake. Word came from Kartok that the chieftain of Ga had passed away and so couldn't come; so, in view of the great difficulties, I went there briefly and performed a ceremony.

There was a holy woman from Drachen named Tsulthrim Palmo who had great faith and was a very accomplished at writing and chanting liturgies. From an early age she had visions of Amitabha with two bodhisattvas, one on either side. While completing the preliminary practices for The Union of All Rare and Precious Jewels and carrying out other practices, she would effortlessly have visions of many of her personal deities. This faithful woman, who kept her *samaya* connection well, had followed Chokgyur Lingpa's advice and served as his guide when he opened up holy sites and as his companion at feast offerings. At this point in time she had fallen ill due to some contamination related to her *samaya* connection, and although I tried my best through giving her empowerments and performing other rituals, she passed away. At weekly intervals[698] I accomplished whatever virtue I could on her behalf, and during my annual observance of an extensive fulfillment ritual from The United Intent of the Gurus, I added a ceremony called *Firelight* to purify her of obscurations, and performed other extensive rituals, including one known as *Dredging the Pit of Cyclic Existence* from the cycle of the peaceful and wrathful deities.

At the end of the first week, I dreamed that I had successfully introduced her to the nature of the intermediate state after death, while after the fourth week I dreamed of showing her the way to the realm of Lotus Light [104a] and of us clearly seeing the entire realm arrayed before us. Later on, my esteemed and all-knowing spiritual master related that he had had a vision in which he clearly heard a *dakini* saying that initially this holy woman Tsulthrim Palmo had taken rebirth as a lowly woman in a charnel ground due to some slight infraction of her *samaya* connection, but that afterward she had reached a pure realm. The *dakini* told Khyentsé Rinpoché that this was due to my positive efforts on Tsulthrim Palmo's behalf, and to the fact that the three levels of obscuration were less dominant in the deceased's mindstream, while the three kinds of maturation were more so.[699] As virtuous acts in memory of Tsulthrim Palmo and a daughter of the Jadra clan, who had also passed away, we prepared for each a hundred thousand *tsa-tsa*s of Akshobhya and erected tiered stupas,[700] for which I performed the rituals of the two Vimalas and the consecration ceremony. Then I left.

The great *tertön* had discovered some *terma*s from Sengdrak Cliff, including a sacred instruction comprising six scrolls and a biography of Guru Padmakara entitled *A Garland of Gems*. But due to several circumstances, he had not codified these. Nevertheless, upon my insistent requests he did codify *The Heart Essence of Enlightened Mind*, a section of instructions dealing with Vajrasattva. He conferred the empowerment and oral transmissions for this on me, saying that he himself had received them after praying to Orgyen Rinpoché. The evening after we had performed the feast offering, fulfillment ritual, and supplication prayers from this cycle, I dreamed that someone who I took to be Lord Pema Nyinjé was inside a temple. As I bowed respectfully to him, he cast from his hands many objects that all turned out to be crystals. [104b] I performed circumambulations on a path encircling the outside of the temple and then gathered up many of the crystals and put them in the folds of my robes.

It was around this time that the queen of Dergé and her son were taken hostage by the Nyarong chieftain, and my mind could find no peace whatsoever. I sent word to Dzongsar Tulku Rinpoché to request that he conduct any ceremonies that would be of use. He would reply every month or so, his letter relating any important divinations or dreams, while he spent his entire time diligently performing these ceremonies. During the second month the armies of Nyarong reached Meting, where they caused enormous destruction. Even some of my major patrons were affected, so I performed a ritual based on the cycle of peaceful and wrathful deities; those with faith and pure *samaya* connection felt some small signs of this benefiting them.

In the third month we began a *drupchen* ritual focusing on Vajrasattva. In previous years I had prayed to my precious lord guru that he kindly consent to write an instruction manual for the Innermost Heart Drop of the Guru, for any number of reasons—for one thing, it would be useful to all the lamas and monks attending this ritual. But he replied that he had absolutely no intention of writing such a manual. Instead he told me, "You are definitely worthy of writing it. The instruction manual for this Mindroling tradition of Vajrasattva is certainly useful as a basis, for it is easy to understand and broad in its application. It covers material that is not dealt with very much in Longchenpa's own writings on the Innermost Heart Drop of the Guru, so you should base you work on the Mindroling manual." He spoke insistently about the value of such an undertaking. [105a] As I lacked the confidence to write such a book, I begged him to divine what the outcome would be if I did agree to do so. On the fourteenth day I offered a large feast, and after praying that night my lord guru dreamed in the early morning that he was sitting in a meadow filled with flowers, on top of a high white cliff overlooking a deep ravine. The sun rose in the east and he felt a sense of delight, whereupon he awoke. Immediately he heard a voice saying, "The heart drop teachings of the supreme secret will blaze ever greater, like a lamp fueled with sesame oil." He took this voice to be that of the *dakini* Shridhara. With this encouragement to write the text, I began composing an instruction manual for the "mother and child" cycles of the Heart Drop teachings.[701] That same evening my dreams were filled with positive signs—images of the sun rising, of many vultures gathering, and so on—and I completed the work.

In the fourth month I attended the annual vase consecration ritual. The learned lama Tashi Özer had arranged for my support during a writing project, so until the end of the seventh month I was engaged in writing the commentary to my *Treasury of the Knowable*. Since Öntrul was forced to go to the Nyarong district,[702] there was no one to lead the summer retreat this year, so I arranged for provisions so that some thirteen fully ordained monks could observe the retreat in the meditation center.

In the eighth month [105b] Kuzhap Rinpoché sponsored the Vajrakila *drupchen* ritual. When I was coming down from my hermitage, my legs became swollen and painful. From the day that the actual ritual began, both lamas and patrons were greatly afflicted by a viral infection. Although I didn't really have the strength to get up, I aroused my resolve and attended the group practice. The illness cleared up on the twenty-ninth, and on the first day of the next month I went back up to my hermitage, where the eruptions on my skin cleared up without a trace. This was a sign of something major affecting the patrons.[703] For a time, then, I made preparations for, and performed, a wrathful ritual focusing on Vajrakila, all the while undertaking appropriate personal retreats and giving empowerments and instructions at the upper and lower meditation centers. With this, the contagion cleared up.

Toward the end of the year I did a personal retreat on the protective deity Sang-gön Mukpo and attended the group *torma* ritual based on the protective deities.

AFTER THE BEGINNING of the new Earth Bird Year [1864-1865], I performed the fulfillment ritual from The United Intent of the Gurus. I also offered many empowerments and ritual ablutions to Kuzhap Rinpoché in order to alleviate some difficulties he was still experiencing. I spent some time carrying out the preliminary practices and the outer *sadhana* of supplication prayers from the *sadhana* of enlightened mind *Dispelling All Obstacles*. With the onset of warmer weather, I resumed writing my commentary on *The Treasury of the Knowable* and also composed texts for rituals to be included in my *Treasury of Precious Hidden Teachings*. Just as had been the case in the past, from time to time I would be constantly involved in meeting the needs of all kinds of groups, large and small, giving empowerments, oral transmissions, and instructions. [106a]

The first group of retreatants finished their three-year, three-fortnight program.[704] This year there was no one to participate in the annual vase consecration ritual, so we held it during the seventh month and I went as I always had. When it was over, I performed a ceremony for Kuzhap Rinpoché to rid him of the effects of some negative force and was preparing to go back up to my hermitage, when I was stricken by some virulent form of contamination and was incapacitated for about a week. From this point onward, whenever I would perform a ceremony to remove negativity or a ritual ablution, this contamination would flare up intensely.

It was about this time that the delegation from the Nyarong chieftain came to Dergé Gönchen and began taking hostages, rounding up all the lamas and notable laypeople who were under that jurisdiction. Although I was contacted by them briefly, by the grace of the Three Jewels the matter was dropped. Then, during the ninth month, there came a great force commanded by the nobleman and government minister Phulungwa and his brother, as well as many able leaders from the executive, military, and administrative branches of the central government. The force included troops from the central Tibetan army, as well as reinforcements from Dragyap, Gonjo, Richap,[705] and other areas. This force recaptured the area around Dergé Gönchen and fought with any in the surrounding area who did not submit. Our monastery of Palpung was in danger of being attacked, since it harbored some who were very hostile to the government force, but just at that point the Dongkham Thripa, the leader of the Dragyap contingent, suddenly fell ill. The commander summoned all who knew the Dergé region and they told him I would be the best one to call in, [106b] so a messenger was dispatched to bring me. Although I was greatly concerned over the Nyarong chieftain and the war he was waging, the divinations turned out well, so I trusted in that fact and crossed over a desolate pass to come down to the military camp at Ngulsip.

Although I performed empowerments, ritual ablutions, and so forth for the Dongkham Thripa, the problem was deeply rooted. I did a divination to determine whether he should stay or leave, and the result indicated that it was preferable that he leave, which he did. I met the great commander and offered him a ceremonial scarf. He ordered me to spend a few days performing offering rites to the protective deities. Once I had finished these, the armies of the Nyarong chieftain approached and there was great tumult and anxiety—an experience that reminded me what circumstances would be in the intermediate state after death. At that point I was required to give counsel and do divinations to find out when the Nyarong foe would strike and from which direction he would come. Such affairs are hardly covered in the explanations concerning divination procedures, so I just spoke whatever came to mind and by the blessings of the Three Jewels everything I said turned out to be accurate. Even the commander was impressed.

On the actual day of battle, the central Tibetan forces were victorious and congratulations were heaped on me. I made a petition on behalf of everyone connected with Palpung, mentioning every name I knew, and this landed well on the ear of the commander, who gave me his promise that everyone under the jurisdiction of Palpung, both the monastery and the surrounding countryside, would be spared any aggression. Then, while the war with the Nyarong forces was still raging, I returned home. [107a]

The next group of new retreatants had to be installed this year, so I began giving the empowerments, oral transmissions, and instructions they would need. We observed the winter solstice as always, with offering rites to the protective deities and a *sadhana* ritual for the Six-Armed Mahakala. I myself began completing the inner *sadhana* and the rest of the stages of practice in *Dispelling All Obstacles.*

Around this time I had many amazing dreams, but I am unable to recall them all. One night, though, I dreamed of an incredible white cloud, shimmering with rainbow light and filled with many Tibetan letters in the "headed" script[706] that held a great deal of significance for me; these letters finally resolved into three *Hum* syllables. Once I dreamed of seeing the brilliant forms of Padmakara and his consort in the clear sky. In another dream I found a sheath containing two scrolls filled with large symbolic script, which I was told were scrolls belonging to Chokgyur Lingpa; I read one of them and deciphered its meaning. After an evening when especially strong obstacles manifested, I dreamed that Dorjé Bernakchen and the Six-Armed Mahakala actually subdued these manifestations, and in the early morning I met the glorious Düsum Khyenpa, receiving the four levels of empowerment from his form in meditation and hearing him grant me special advice.[707]

I also dreamed of the Fourteenth Karmapa discovering a profound *terma* and graciously conferring on me much advice [107b] that seemed prophetic, and of Lord Pema Nyinjé granting some words of instruction about what to accept or reject, after which he adopted an air of someone who is terribly fatigued. It occurred to me later on that this dream might have presaged the obstacles that affected that sublime incarnate being Thekchok Dorjé's mindstream. It was also around that time that Öntrul had been driven from Hor to the region of Nyarong. One night I dreamed of meeting the omniscient Longchenpa and Minling Terchen, both of them very delighted, and of the latter showing me "regent" statues of the Supremely Compassionate One and Guru Rinpoché. In my dream, the neck area of the statue of Guru Rinpoché was slightly damaged. On another occasion I dreamed of Dabzang Rinpoché, who was extremely joyful and made several symbolic gestures; of myself putting on a very sacred and awesome mask of Yamantaka and performing a wrathful dance; and of Minling Terchen and the omniscient lama Longchenpa coming to me and expressing their delight over and over. Once I dreamed of finding a well-formed skull cup filled with a powerful substance, and of keeping this as a support during *drupchen* rituals. One time, in the early morning on the day of the new moon, I dreamed of our Teacher in the garb of a fully ordained monk, surrounded by a retinue and with Shariputra standing behind his throne. Saying, "Come hither,"[708] he granted me monastic ordination. Immediately afterward I joined the ranks for a ceremony to restore and renew monastic vows. I had many such dreams. [108a]

MY RETREAT ENDED during the third month of the new Wood Ox Year [1865-

1866]. The war with the forces of Nyarong had turned in the government's favor toward the end of the last year. The commander was still resident in the area at this time and sent a messenger to fetch me, so I went. For about a month I performed empowerments, ritual ablutions, and the like to offset the effects of negative forces. Lhasar Temple, the great printing house, and other buildings had been used during the conflict as barracks and prisons, so the resulting moral contamination was grievous. The commander told me that a consecration was needed, so I carried out the purification rites, ablutions, and consecrations, as well as the necessary feast offerings, rituals focusing on the protective deities, and so forth. Returning to my area, I attended the annual vase consecration ritual at the monastery. I then went up to my hermitage, where I was constantly involved in many rituals having to do with the war that was going on.

During the fifth month I accompanied Kuzhap Rinpoché to the peak of Uchétem, where we performed a magnificent ceremony to secure the mountain and suppress aggression. At first there were disturbances—a mighty wind rose up, and hail and lightning fell from all quarters—but eventually everything became very peaceful. Descending to Ngo-nang Lhasar, to avert any negativity we performed a ritual focusing on wrathful deities, based on the Eight Commands. When we cast the *torma* out, there were some major omens that I could see with my own eyes, and when the effigy personifying negativity was prepared, others dreamed of signs that the hordes of our foe would be defeated.

In the sixth month another escort arrived to conduct me to Dergé Gönchen, [108b] where I spent two weeks performing ceremonies for the commander—one week on a ritual to free him of the effects of negative energy and one week on longevity practice. I also performed more than a hundred ritual ablutions and longevity empowerments for him. During that time I also incidentally satisfied the requests of many important personages, after which I returned to my home. This year, about ten fully ordained monks observed the monastic summer retreat at my hermitage.

In the eighth month the force under the command of General Thrimönpa[709] annihilated Nyaké and destroyed his fortress down to the foundations. Even the commander himself came to the Hor region. The queen of Dergé and her son, as well as Öntrul Rinpoché, were released from captivity and permitted to return. I offered them empowerments and audiences in response to their individual requests.

The commander ordered me to perform a ritual of victory and ransom based on the protective deities, so I undertook a personal retreat focusing on the Four-Armed Mahakala.[710] Then, during the ninth month, I arranged for all the preparations for the ritual. Dönpal, a lama of Zhechen Monastery, came and, together with a substantial number of other masters and students, we performed the ritual of victory and ransom, which went very well. Dönpal had previously received from Öntrul Rinpoché many empowerments and oral transmissions that I had not myself yet received, so I requested these. I gave some instructions in the meditation center and, having finished these, journeyed back up to my hermitage, where I began teaching Lhaksam[711] and others the Kalapa system of Sanskrit grammar. I also began a personal retreat based on the Swift-Acting Jnana Natha. [109a] While the retreatants performed the annual liturgies in their program, at the winter solstice I myself performed a small ritual focusing on the Eight Commands to avert negativity. At the end of the year I finished my retreat and took part in the *torma* ritual focusing on my protective deity.

DURING THE FIRST DAYS of the new Fire Tiger Year [1866-1867], having graciously ensured peace throughout the eastern provinces, the supreme commander and his forces returned to central Tibet. I went to see him off and offered my best wishes for his health. I also offered to him a ceremony to free him of the effects of negative energy, and a longevity empowerment. The prince of Dergé was ill, so I performed over a hundred longevity empowerments on his behalf before returning home. Phulungwa, commander of the government forces, commended me on the service I had rendered to the government, with my divinations on behalf of his troops being so accurate and my attention to the ceremonies he required of me over the months being so meticulous. By way of compensating me, he conferred on me the deed to the nomadic pastureland in the region of Pa-Ok Tsetru, both the main tract and some smaller plots. For some time these had been the property of whoever was strong enough to take them, but now lay unclaimed. The Dergé government, too, showed their delight with me, as the queen and prince made offerings to me in return for the continual ceremonies I had done on their behalf during the two or three years that they had been under the power of Nyarong.

When Öntrul returned to Palpung, he told me, "It is thanks to your kindness that Palpung Monastery and its surrounding countryside were spared. [109b] Prior to this, the monastic residence has not provided you with anything, but as a sign of our support, henceforth the buildings and land of Naru and Drama will be deeded to the hermitage as long as it endures." Kuzhap Rinpoché was equally effusive in his praise, even giving me a written testimonial.

On the eighteenth day of the month commemorating the Buddha's spiritual miracles, with the sun in the lunar mansion of Hasta,[712] at Lhasar Temple I began giving the oral transmission for the Kangyur to Kuzhap Rinpoché and a number of other lamas, incarnate masters, as well as many faithful students who gathered for this purpose. I began by reading aloud *The Discourse of the Fortunate Eon*. But during the second month, the concentration this task required of me caused my old issue with contamination to flare up intensely and I was held back for quite a few days. Someone named Chögyep and others performed ceremonies on my behalf. At that point I requested the oral transmissions for the "sealed" practices of Jering and Darmo and other texts.[713] On the twenty-fifth day of the second month, having completed the sections on the discourses and the monastic code, I called a break. Dabzang Rinpoché came to my hermitage, where I requested from him the Zurmang tradition of the Heart Drop of the Dakini and other empowerments. I also gave instruction in both meditation centers, upper and lower, as it came time to do so. Starting on the thirteenth day of the third month, I gave the oral transmissions of the extensive, middle-length, and abridged sutras on the Perfection of Wisdom, as well as for three other sutras. Then I returned to the hermitage and took part in a group ritual focusing on Vajrasattva.

In the fourth month I went to the meditation center, where a large tent had been pitched on the meadow in front of the center. There, starting on the fourteenth day, I gave the oral transmissions for [110a] the *Heaped Jewels* and *Garland of Buddhas* discourses.[714] After we performed a major *torma* offering to the *dakinis*, I began reading the tantra section. I had finished about four volumes when I was stricken with a "male disease" that resembled some kind of lymphatic disorder, which proved very debilitating. After about a week, I could just manage to ride a horse, and returned to my hermitage. Dabzang Tulku came once more and performed for me a ritual to dispel contamination and a longevity empowerment. I also requested from him the oral transmissions for many texts from the Tersar and other cycles. At that point, a doctor was able to diagnose that I was suffering from a "cold" condition of the bile and gave me medicine, so that I gradually got better.

I went to Palpung Monastery in the fifth month, and there I witnessed the sacred dances on the tenth day. I performed empowerments for Dabzang Tulku, a group from Dergé, pilgrims from the Jang region, and others. The great *tertön* Chokgyur Lingpa arrived and gave a succession of empowerments and oral transmissions for his own *terma*s that I had not received before, including the "oral tradition" of Vajrakila and *The General Assembly of Mamos.*[715]

On the twenty-fifth day we began a group ritual from The United Intent of the Gurus to consecrate sacred medicine in the main hall, with the *tertön* presiding. During this ritual he experienced some significant omens in his dreams and urged me insistently to write manuals for *drupchen* and *mendrup* rituals. He told me, "This year, any of the usual rituals you might do won't be of any use. [110b] Instead, you must perform a feast for the heroes and heroines."[716] He also came to my hermitage, where he consecrated the statues. In addition, in the shrine room dedicated to the protective deities, Chokgyur Lingpa performed rituals to make offerings to these deities and invoke their enlightened activities. He then left for Dergé Gönchen.

I gave the oral teaching transmission for my *Treasury of the Knowable* to the Ngor master Ngawang Rinchen and others, going through the text quite methodically. From Ngawang Rinchen I requested the oral transmissions for some arrangements of rituals from the Tersar tradition. He said, "It would be fitting to hold your feast at Lhamdo Burmo." We planned to hold it there, but in the eighth month he suddenly returned to my hermitage and told me, "It won't work at Lhamdo Burmo. It would be best to hold it here, so I need to start the preparations today." It was necessary to convene five heroes and five heroines. When they tried to do so, they almost managed to find everyone, but there was still one heroine unaccounted for. I then told Ngawang Rinchen of a girl who was the daughter of my father's brother. My old mother had always referred to her as a niece of our family and had cared for the girl from the time my niece was between five and seven years of age. "She will do fine," said Ngawang Rinchen, and included her in the ranks. He presided over a feast offering and fulfillment ritual based on a *sadhana* of enlightened mind. That night he had a vision of twenty-five women, spiritual practitioners who had been students of the *dakini* Kunga Bumpa in the past. Among them were five who had been blessed by the *dakini*s of the five buddha families. [111a] One in particular, named Sang-gyé Tso, had received the blessings of Buddhadakini. He saw that at that former time he had been Dungtso Repa and had a relationship with this woman. This girl, my niece, was a rebirth of that woman. He spoke to me at length of the situation, telling me that she should not marry, for if she were given to anyone else, the one who married her would not benefit by it. In fact, he said, this would anger the *dakinis* and lead to harm. He wrote a letter explaining that it would be best for my niece to remain as she was, and he applied his seal to this. He gave her the name Chimé Deter Rigdzin Drölma.

I asked him, "If that is the case, since she is living near this monastery, wouldn't it be better for her to become a nun, so as to ensure that no one forms a relationship with her?" He replied, "It wouldn't do for her to have too many duties. Better that she remain a practitioner in retreat."

There were some twenty-five women prophesied to be Ngawang Rinchen's consorts, of whom five lived in the Dergé region. Due to external circumstances, he had not been able to meet some of them, and some women he had met had turned out not to be the actual consorts, an error that had led to some breach of his *samaya* connection. "This girl, however," he said, "is certainly one of the prophesied ones." He told me that he intended to speak with Öntrul later on and outline the situation, saying that he needed to initiate something.

That evening he performed a feast offering [111b] and had a clear impression that Yeshé Tsogyal was beginning to confer on him the records of The United Intent of the Dakinis. Although on this occasion there were plentiful and extremely positive circumstances, it would seem that Jonang Jetsün Rinpoché was certainly right when he said, "As for ensuring excellent auspicious circumstances, the single effort one makes at the outset may be fine, but since such circumstances are conditioned,[717] how could they be permanent? As long as the positive momentum does not go awry, well and good. If, however, some counterproductive condition causes circumstances that are initially auspicious to go awry later on, that single act at the outset was not enough. This is something important that everyone should understand."

The Ngor master Ngawang Rinchen insisted that he needed me to perform the empowerment of the Innermost Heart Drop of the Dakini, so I did so, after which he departed. I myself went to Situ Rinpoché's monastic residence, where I gave the remainder of the oral transmissions for the tantra section of the Kangyur. In response to individual requests from some of the lamas and incarnate teachers, I also performed the empowerments for the "peaceful garland and wrathful garland," the three empowerments (extensive, middle-length, and abridged) from Karma Lingpa's cycle of the peaceful and wrathful deities, Padmavajra, *The Integration of Means and Wisdom*, and other transmissions. The *tertön* requested instructions from me, so I offered him instruction on the Heart Drop of the Dakini and a brief explanation on the basis of the source verses of my *Treasury of the Knowable*. From him I received quite a number

of instructions, including those for *The Distilled Tincture of Meteoric Iron.*
[112a] I then returned home.

From the fourteenth day of the ninth month to the tenth day of the eleventh,
I undertook a personal retreat focusing on the deity Vajra Sitatapatra, an auxiliary practice from The Profound Longevity Practice of the Three Roots. During
this retreat, one night I dreamed of meeting Phadampa, whose demeanor was
very impressive, and of discussing the extent of my realization with him. I also
has a dream in which I was convinced that Orgyen Rinpoché was still living in
Tibet. I went into a certain temple and found that whom I had taken for Orgyen
was in fact Chokgyur Lingpa. I prostrated to him with great devotion and
received the four levels of empowerment from him in a process of meditation.
My dreams during this retreat were entirely consistent with those I had previously during my retreat on The United Intent of the Gurus. During this time I
also undertook a personal retreat focusing on the form of Yamantaka called
Ayushpati, using a practice from The Seven Profound Cycles.

Meanwhile, the great *tertöns*[718] had together discovered a *terma* from the
cliff of Taktsang Tsodrak in Rongmé Karmo. Chokgyur Lingpa was staying at
that time in Dagam Wangphuk Cave and sent word that I should come immediately. So on the tenth day of the eleventh month I finished my retreat and
went to see him. He was delighted to see me and we codified, among other
teachings, *The Four Doctrines of the Guardians of the Teachings*, the five
Heart Essence cycles, the six basic *sadhana*s, and the fulfillment ritual for the
shvana goddesses. He performed the ritual from *The Four Doctrines of the
Guardians of the Teachings* to cast a *torma* in each of the four cardinal directions. I requested many transmissions from his Tersar tradition. My precious
lord also came [112b] and bestowed the basic empowerment for his Heart
Drop of the Siddhas and other transmissions.

We then journeyed to Khangmar Monastery, where Chokgyur Lingpa inaugurated a *drupchen* ritual based on his *sadhana* of enlightened mind. During
the dances in the feast offering, he caused an amazing display of blessings to
manifest. My lord guru, Khyentsé Rinpoché, bestowed the "ultimate empowerment"[719] for the *sadhana* of enlightened mind called *Wrathful Dynamic Energy*, using the actual yellow scroll to perform the ceremony. He gave an
extensive explanation of *The Stages on the Path: The Heart Essence of Timeless Awareness*[720] and an explanation of *The Stages on the Path of Secret Mantra*. From Chokgyur Lingpa I received the empowerment for the basic *sadhana*,
and he conferred profound and extensive advice for this practice.

Chokgyur Lingpa composed a speech and investiture ceremony when the governor of Dergé was installed, and conducted the ritual known as *The Blazing Jewel of Temporal Rule*.[721] He also codified some teachings that formed part of the auspicious circumstances of this occasion. Then the great *tertön* went to Kathok Monastery in answer to a formal invitation. As for me, I returned home, where I gave empowerments and taught in the upper and lower meditation centers.

AFTER THE CELEBRATIONS for the new Fire Hare Year [1867-1868]—the first year in the fifteenth sexagesimal cycle[722]—I undertook my annual personal retreat on Vajrakila and concluded with a ritual to avert negativity. During the second month I went to Dzongshö, where the great *tertön* Chokgyur Lingpa was staying, having asked his permission to do so the last time we had met. There we codified several yellow scrolls, including the remainder of the teachings concerning the *shvana* goddesses and the secret record of prophecies. My lord guru also came and took part in a *drupchen* ritual based on the newly codified version of the Eight Commands called The Gathering of All Sugatas. [113a] He gave us direct introduction to the aspects of enlightened form, speech, mind, qualities, and activity, each associated with one of the five places on the body. Seating me on a throne made of stones, the two of them invested me with the title of a *tertön* and performed a ceremony for my long life.[723] Each of these masters discovered a profound *terma*, after which we went to the ancestral estate of the Alo Dilgo family to begin a *mendrup* ritual focusing on the Eight Commands. We then journeyed together to Pema Shelri. We performed feast offerings at such places as Ösel Shelphuk Cave (associated with Bairotsana), and the two masters also opened Orgyen Sangphuk Cave. Each of them discovered a cache of *terma*s. The great *tertön* even urged me to try, and I came out of the Orgyen Sangphuk Cave with a casket of *terma*s in my hands and offered it to him. Then the *tertön* went to Dzogchen Monastery in response to an invitation. I returned to my home, where I attended the vase consecration ritual in the fourth month.

Prior to this, every year or two Kuzhap Rinpoché would repeatedly suffer from a loss of speech due to fissures opening up in his tongue. I performed a ritual to free him of the effects of negative energy many times over, and both Dabzang Tulku and the *tertön* performed any number of ritual ablutions and ceremonies to dispel contamination. But Kuzhap Rinpoché's condition only worsened. At this point I performed the specific rituals for his long life, feast offerings, and ceremonies to turn back the escort that I deemed appropriate according to *The Secret Prophecy*. His health gradually improved. To promote the Buddhist teachings, [113b] I performed a major ritual of ransom based on the *mamo*s, and at my hermitage carried out the fulfillment ritual from The United Intent of the Gurus.

When the *tertön* came back from Dzogchen Monastery, he performed a ritual to commemorate the death of Ön Lama and he heard the sad news that Dabzang Tulku had passed away, so there were more commemorative ceremonies. At Palpung Monastery, the *tertön* intended to conduct a *drupchen* ritual, so to clear away potential obstacles to that, he began by presiding over a short feast offering with sacred dances in Palchen Temple at my hermitage. Then he went to the main hall at the monastery and oversaw the *drupchen* ritual and sacred dances, using the basic *sadhana* of enlightened mind as the foundation and incorporating two other such *sadhana*s as auxiliary practices. As part of the very elaborate proceedings, he also performed a ritual in honor of the date commemorating "the abbot, the master, and the king."[724]

At the hermitage, my old mother was stricken with an illness, so Kuzhap Rinpoché, his brother, and the precious *tertön* presided over a group composed of all the important lamas, performing more than thirteen hundred empowerments, including those of the peaceful and wrathful deities and Sarvavid Vairochana.[725] When she passed away, my omniscient lord came from Dzongsar and he and the *tertön*, together with the foremost of the retreat graduates, performed the direct introduction and transference of consciousness for her.[726] I used about half of all that I possessed to sponsor acts of virtue that would bring her excellent help.

When the *tertön* set off again, I escorted him part of the way. As soon as we had camped for the night, [114a] he gave me the text of The United Intent of the Dharmapalas and entrusted me with the teachings, whereupon there suddenly came what seemed to us to be very positive omens—a scattering of hail and the sound of thunder from the east. My lord guru also accompanied us to escort Chokgyur Lingpa as far as Kyapché Gotö. It was at this point that the great *tertön* was leaving for central Tibet. Although he had some important instructions to leave with me, along with his written directive, I was not able to carry out a single one of these. When he later returned and was staying on Alo Paljor Pass, I myself was with one of my patrons; when Chokgyur Lingpa's summons reached me by messenger, I set off to see him. At that time he was having visions of countless major holy sites and had combined some four *terma*s—including the record of The United Intent of the Dakinis—into one. He expressed his delight and said, "Now these must be finished in the presence of the one who discovered them." He also revealed a profound *terma* in Zhitro Shelphuk Cave.

Chokgyur Lingpa then went to the Chayang ancestral estate, where he performed a consecration and a ritual to ensure prosperity. During these ceremonies, the Kathok Situ incarnation[727] came and made offerings to the *tertön*, who was overjoyed at this auspicious connection and spoke about matters that seemed to pertain to the future destiny of this Situ incarnation. Having codified several yellow scrolls, Chokgyur Lingpa then journeyed to Palpung by way of Yuthok.[728]

He told me I should go to identify the holy site of Khamphuk Cave in Dzong-chen, so I followed his advice and went there. From the outset the circumstances were quite positive [114b] and I could clearly identify self-manifesting caves and other places at this holy site. The external signs were also excellent—while I was performing a feast offering in Khamphuk Cave, a great number of vultures gathered and ate the feast, while amazing displays of rainbows shone in the sky. I then returned to my hermitage, to which my lord guru also came. We began a *drupchen* ritual based on the So tradition of the deity Samyak. Khyentsé Rinpoché also gave a large number of empowerments and oral transmissions, including an explanation of *The Ornament of Higher Realization* according to Rongtön's system of exegesis;[729] the oral transmissions for supplementary volumes of the Tengyur; cycles of teachings from the early Kadampa School; and several *terma*s that I had not received before.

When he was bestowing the empowerment for The Spacious Expanse of the View discovered by Dorjé Lingpa, on the night of the main body of the ritual, my lord dreamed that he himself was transformed into a woman named Dorjé Tso, the wife of a householder at Layak in the southern province of Lhodrak, and was living an ordinary worldly life. At a certain point, her husband said to her, "Our family's lama is coming, so we must prepare a seat." She swept the room clean and laid out the seat, whereupon someone she took to be Dorjé Lingpa arrived—a short, corpulent lama with a small topknot and long tresses of hair, wearing a yellow sleeveless vest. She requested his blessing[730] and served him. That evening she went into his room [115a] and they spent the time in various kinds of love play, as he held her hands, kissed her, embraced her, and so forth. Things became a bit vague, as one minute he seemed to be Dorjé Lingpa, and the next minute Jonang Jetsün Rinpoche, the one indistinguishable from the other. Upon arising in the morning, she served him as before. The lama mounted his horse and left, accompanied by several monks on foot.

On his seat the woman found something like a small box, covered with silk and vibrating. She said, "Our family lama has left something behind," and picking it up she ran after him calling out his name. She caught up with him and placed the box in his hands. He told her that this was a box filled with his *terma* substances[731] and said, "The fact that I left it behind is most auspicious, so you must take care of it." Because she was a woman and conscious of the fact that she might, for example, have to move to another region,[732] she told him, "I can't take care of it for you. I'm unable to keep it. I don't know what to do." He consoled her, saying, "It doesn't matter. Just keep it for a while and I'll be back for it." She said, "I don't know where or when I'm going. I really can't take care of it for you, so please give me your blessing."

Opening the box, he took out a large yellow scroll and began reading the title: "Herein is contained the great catalogue of *The Oral Transmissions of Secret Mantra*." [115b] He continued to read the entire text aloud; it seemed to be an index of many of Dorjé Lingpa's *terma*s, both those that were already famous and those that were not. He then returned the scroll to the box. He then placed the box on her head and said, "Take care of this for me, and my next incarnation will come to claim it from you."

She thought, "While I am getting on a bit in years, this lama is still young, so there is no possibility of his next incarnation being born to me."[733] She asked the lama, "When will he be coming, sir?" He replied, "He probably won't be coming until at least five hundred years from now." She took the box and was preparing to go back home when she thought, "This lama is truly Orgyen, so I should ask him where Kongtrul's mother has taken rebirth." She asked him this, and he replied, "She was born in a watery environment." Dorjé Tso was very saddened by this and cried, "What kind of 'watery environment'? And what's to become of me?" The lama said, "Well, things are much better for her now. But you should do the practice of Akshobhya[734] for her."

Khyentsé Rinpoché said that at this point in the dream, his thought was that the phrase "watery environment" referred to some amazing situation of her enjoying a mansion made of gems, fine ornaments, and so forth. And while he was thinking this, he awoke.

He told me that this memory of Dorjé Tso was always clear in his mind.

And since there is no way for us accurately to fathom the emanations of those who dwell on high levels of realization, it is plain to me that she was one of my master's embodiments. Around this time I myself dreamed of finding a white conch shell [116a] and a mala adorned with four golden counters. Since it would seem that Dorjé Lingpa died toward the middle of the seventh sexagesimal cycle,[735] almost five hundred years have passed since then.

During the time Khyentsé Rinpoché was staying with me, he had many visions. In particular, one night Yeshé Tsogyal spoke to him at great length, giving him clear prophecies and advice of both a general and very specific nature. She described how the *tertön*s to date had come and spoke of the need to finish the record of The United Intent of the Dakinis. Following this vision he described only this much to me, but spoke no more of the experience. And although I asked him a few times to clarify something about how the record was to be dealt with, he didn't devote any energy to it. Since it was not a good time for Khyentsé Rinpoché to go to or stay at the *tertön*'s encampment, I feel that he took this as a sign that the auspicious circumstances to finalize the record were blocked and that the cache of *terma*s would not be discovered. He did, however, codify the practice combining the deities Samyak and Vajrakila, which was the first part of his oral lineage,[736] and performed the ritual to avert negativity.

In the eleventh month Khyentsé Rinpoché left for his monastery to preside over a *drupchen* ritual based on Vajrakila. He gave extensive transmissions, including an explanation of the fragmentary basic tantra[737] and the empowerment, oral transmission, and explanation for his oral lineage of Vajrakila. Then, in the twelfth month he came to my hermitage, where he gave an explanation of the basic tantra of Chakrasamvara and many oral transmissions I had not received before, including some texts from the long historical tradition of the Nyingma School [116b] and works from the collected writings of the great *tertön*s. When I performed a ceremony for his long life and a feast offering in his honor, he had a very significant vision. Once I had made offerings and a formal mandala offering, Khyentsé Rinpoché left for Situ Rinpoché's monastic residence. I participated in the annual *torma* ritual for accomplishment based on my protective deity.

AT THE NEW EARTH DRAGON YEAR [1868-1869], I went to the monastic residence to receive the collection called *The One Hundred Transmissions of Narthang*, which was being conferred. I then returned home, where I undertook several personal retreats. At the end of the first month I attended the annual vase consecration ritual.

Since I had planned to give the empowerments and oral transmissions for *The Treasury of Precious Hidden Teachings* this year, the Lingtrul incarnation of Dzogchen Monastery and other lamas and *tulku*s began arriving during the second month. From Lingtrul I received the oral transmissions for texts in the Tengyur that I had not received before. On the twenty-fifth day of this month I went to the meditation center, where I began giving the oral transmissions for the Indian sources of the Mahamudra tradition to a gathering headed by Kuzhap Rinpoché. From Lingtrul I received many empowerments and oral transmissions from the Northern Treasures cycles—including the extensive empowerment for the *sadhana* of The Ancestral Line of the Masters of Awareness and Unobstructed Enlightened Intent—as well as *The Guru: The Ocean of Gems* of Pema Lingpa, and other traditions.

The year before, when Tulku Rinpoché visited me he told me that next year I should give the empowerments and oral transmissions of *The Treasury of Precious Hidden Teachings* for the first time. He promised that he would be the main sponsor to request them and gave me detailed advice on who else should receive them, as well as on the *drupchen* ritual and offerings that should accompany these transmissions. [117a] This being the case, I hoped he would come soon, so I waited for his arrival, giving and receiving other important empowerments and oral transmissions until after the start of the fourth month. But although he had intended to set out from Dzongsar, he was afflicted by some illness that affected his hands and feet in turn. I received a letter from him explaining how unwell he was and so I began reading some oral transmissions from *The Treasury of Precious Hidden Teachings* on the tenth day of the month.

After I had finished these, it was clear that he was unable to come, so we performed a Vajrasattva *drupchen* ritual for seven days. I then began giving the transmissions with the empowerment of The Gathering of Sugatas, Nyang's *terma* of the Eight Commands, and then continued with the collection known as The Precious Vase Yielding All Desirables and all the so-called mother and child transmissions of *The Treasury of Precious Hidden Teachings*—all kinds of empowerments, blessings, authorizations, and conferrals of life force,[738] as well as instruction manuals and four volumes of "sealed" practices. I finished all of these on the fifteenth day of the seventh month. I accepted extensive offerings from Situ Rinpoché's monastic residence, as well as what individuals gave me in gratitude for the transmissions. Then the gathering dispersed.

At the hermitage, I performed a commemorative ceremony for my old mother and the fulfillment ritual from The United Intent of the Gurus. I then went to Chayang for a short rest. Pelek, the steward, came and I gave him instruction in Mahamudra. I received large lumps of silver as offerings for enough provisions to support the hermitage. Then, after satisfying the requests of several of my patrons, I returned home in the ninth month. [117b]

Öntrul had given new instructions that this next year I was to oversee the vase consecration ritual, the monastic summer retreat, and the Vajrakila *drupchen* ritual. At the same time, I assigned eight lumps of silver to provide offerings and provisions for the meditation center at the hermitage. The former retreatants finished their program, and when I had time I began the process of giving empowerments, oral transmissions, and instructions to the new group who would participate in the third retreat. I spent one session daily as a kind of personal retreat using the practice of Vajrakila from Khyentsé Rinpoché's oral lineage, combining this with a Vajrakila ritual to avert negativity that I performed on the winter solstice. Things were very stressful for me, for I was having many health problems due to internal disturbances, while there were many demands from Öntrul and others for empowerments, oral transmissions, and instructions. Still, I performed my usual rituals—the annual *torma* ceremonies, the offerings to the protective deities, and the *torma* ritual of accomplishment based on my protective deity.

IN THE FIRST MONTH of the new Fire Serpent Year [1869-1870], since most of the signs I was experiencing in my dreams were disturbing, I spent some time in personal retreat, using a combination of the outer *sadhana* and the *terma*s from the longevity practice The Gathering of Secrets, as well as *Consummate Profundity*.

I invited Öntrul to come in the second month and a group of fifteen of us, master and students, requested from him one hundred repetitions of the rituals and empowerment for the longevity practice *The Integration of Means and Wisdom*. During this time I had several excellent signs in my dreams. Once I was free of my retreat commitments, I continued writing my arrangements of rituals for *The Treasury of Precious Hidden Teachings*.

In the fourth month I went to attend the vase consecration ritual. Although Kuzhap Rinpoché presided as the vajra master, this time I experienced a lot of disturbance. In the meditation center [118a] I transmitted the two systems of the bodhisattva vow to Kuzhap Rinpoché and the retreatants. At the hermitage, I performed the fulfillment ritual from The United Intent of the Gurus.

I had planned to write a commentary on *The Hevajra Tantra*, and to request permission for this I performed the *guru sadhana* of Marpa in conjunction with more than a hundred repetitions of rituals to purify myself of obscurations. I also practiced means to gather merit and deepen awareness, prayed, and performed feast offerings and fulfillment rituals. I began writing methodically, beginning with the chapter on the vajra family in the first section. In the tradition of explanation deriving from Marpa and Ngok, there has been no one definitive method of exegesis as there is, for example, in the Sakya tradition. Nowadays, the two commentaries most widely used are Ngok's *Like a Jeweled Ornament* and the venerable Rangjung Dorjé's commentary. But the former is entirely an explanation of the "hidden import" of the text, while the latter emphasizes the meanings of the words themselves, but the description of the deity is somewhat imbedded, which makes it difficult to use when one is explaining it (or listening to the explanation) in connection with the basic tantra. Chen-nga Chökyi Drakpa[739] bases his treatment on so many Indian commentaries that his explanation is not easy to understand. Such ancient explanations as the commentaries of Ram and Tsak are extremely unclear. The commentary by Thrinlépa[740] is somewhat clearer, and the excellent commentary by Dakpo Tashi Namgyal is so fine that I kept it aside as an overview. Taking the meaning of the words as my primary concern, I sought to clarify them further in light of the hidden meaning and, distinct from that, the ultimate meaning. [118b]

Going to supervise the monastic summer retreat, I taught *The Highest Continuum*,[741] *The Profound Inner Meaning*, and *The Hevajra Tantra in Two Chapters*, completing both a thorough explanation and a ritual in honor of the tantra. Returning up to my home, I began writing my commentary to *The Highest Continuum*.[742] Toward the end of the eighth month I went to preside as master over the Vajrakila *drupchen* ritual. Then, during the ninth month I finished my commentary on *The Highest Continuum* and just then received a most positive affirmation—from Dzongsar my precious lord sent me a seal and some fine representations of the eight auspicious substances.[743] In response to an insistent request from Sertal Lhatsé Tulku and his students, I went to Situ Rinpoché's monastic residence and gave all the empowerments and oral transmissions for the peaceful and wrathful deities of *The Web of Magic*, for *The Discourse of United Intent*, and for the Category of Mind.[744]

In answer to a summons from the regional government, I went to Dergé Gönchen, where I performed a ritual focusing on wrathful deities to avert negativity, a ceremony to promote prosperity, and some empowerments that people wished to receive. Khangsar Khenpo[745] also requested several empowerments from me, and once these were finished I went on a tour to raise funds for some statues that were being constructed. My travels took me through Alo, Ngé, Dzomtok, and Tsetsa, as far as Pewar, and I responded to requests from many patrons along the route.

ON THE FIRST DAY of the new Iron Horse Year [1870-1871], I performed a ritual at the holy site of Arap to acknowledge it as a major holy site and infuse it with blessings. At the monasteries of both Pewar and Palpung, [119a] I gave such empowerments and instructions as were required of me and, having finished these, I returned to my hermitage.

At the end of the first month I performed ceremonies for the health of the new Situ incarnation at the monastic residence, as well as a ritual focusing on wrathful deities at Lhasar Temple. During the second month I spent a week at the hermitage performing ceremonies for the health of Öntrul—a longevity *sadhana* and a ritual of ransom—and performed a longevity empowerment for him daily.

In Dergé, many divinations had resulted in prophecies indicating the interference of a malevolent spirit called Arté and word had been sent about four times that my presence was required. But due to the fact that many powerful masters had tried to best Arté and not succeeded, and the fact that someone as insignificant as I did not have such power in the slightest, I had repeatedly asked to be relieved of this obligation. This had not been granted, however, and the last time the summons came, I saw a positive sign of emerging victorious in my battle with this obstacle, so I agreed to go.

While I was making preparations, Rigdzin Drölma fell ill with what seemed like influenza, after which she suddenly lost consciousness and fell into a faint. I performed whatever medical rites I could; she recovered, but from then on suffered constantly from poor health due in part to her susceptibility to premonitions. When I was someone with few needs and staying in strict retreat, I made do with whomever attended me, often just getting by, but there was no really trustworthy monk who stayed with me. Later in life, when my building projects and other activities became more numerous, the people who helped me were very humble, such as my old mother and others, who looked after my affairs. [119b] Other than this, I have never followed the custom of great lamas and their monastic residences, so there has been no one I called my steward or secretary. If any monk is my better, I consider him in charge, so to speak, but I give short shrift to those who are my inferiors—thieves, liars, and so forth. As for my equals, however, it is a sign of the times we live in that I do not find anyone reliable, someone incapable of hypocrisy and worthy of a long-term association. I have made no efforts to seek out monk attendants, and since my old mother passed on, my niece[746] has served me in her place.

I reached Dergé Gönchen on the nineteenth, but the day before that at Thanggyal Temple[747] there was a disturbing omen—the large lamp that burned constantly on the shrine overflowed when it was filled. Beginning on the twentieth, I gathered with several students at Sipgön Monastery to perform a practice of intense mental focus for a week. On the twenty-ninth we also performed rituals to suppress negativity and dispatch the spirit. We concluded by conducting a fire ritual to invoke wrathful energy the following day, and a pacifying *lhasang* offering during the waxing phase of the moon. Around this time, Khangsar Khenpo told me that he had had a telling dream of countless beings, whom he took to be *gyalpo* demons, fleeing the monastery to go elsewhere. While the whole process had gone successfully, in such situations there can be peace for a time, after which things flare up anew and the negativity must again be suppressed. If one is not able to heal the situation for good, there will not be any lasting benefit.

During that time, people were also conducting ceremonies in the main hall. [120a] As well, I received orders that I was to perform a major ritual of ransom from *The General Assembly of Mamos* of the Tersar tradition. Accordingly, I made preparations and then performed the ceremony in the most extensive manner, both the basic ritual and its auxiliary practices. Nowadays, of all the general rituals in use, this is perhaps the finest. Once I had satisfied requests for empowerments and rituals to promote prosperity, I returned home, where I began writing my commentary on *The Profound Inner Meaning* and teaching Chandragomin's system of Sanskrit grammar to Lhaksam.

In the fifth month I went to Changri in response to a summons to attend a vase consecration ritual there. I attended a similar ceremony at Palpung Monastery in the sixth month, but my old condition due to contamination flared up and for several days I was not able to take part in the group ritual. Around this time we heard the tragic news that the great *tertön* had departed for the pure realms[748] at Netengang. When we had finished the ceremony, I transmitted the empowerment and oral transmissions for Vimaloshnisha to the group. I requested the oral transmissions for the collected works of Dolpopa from Lama Karma Saljé. (For several years before and after this, I requested from various lamas many empowerments and oral transmissions that were rare and that I had not received previously.)

I completed my commentaries on *The Profound Inner Meaning, The Treatise Distinguishing Ordinary Consciousness from Timeless Awareness*, and *The Treatise on Buddha Nature*. Rangjung Dorjé's own commentary to his *Profound Inner Meaning* is primarily a treatment of certain difficult points[749] and is so deep as to be hard to understand. The overview by the Fifth Zhamar [120b] does not contain a complete commentary on the entire source text. And while there are many other commentaries to this work, either the lineage of transmission has been lost or they do not seem to me to be of appropriate length. For the basis of my commentary, I selected the concise but clear text entitled *Illuminating Garlands of Light*, by the first Thrinlépa. I also included material from other sources, including a very special explanation by the great translator Sönam Gyatso, in the form of notes based on the lectures of the great Tsurphu Jamyang, and the lecture notes written down by Tsewang Kunkhyap when Lord Chökyi Jungné was explaining this text.

During the monastic summer retreat I taught on the three levels of ordination and the entire texts of *The Profound Inner Meaning, The Hevajra Tantra in Two Chapters*, and *The Highest Continuum*, as well as performing a ritual in honor of the tantras. Gradually, I also wrote an overview of *The Hevajra Tantra in Two Chapters*. During this period I had very positive signs in my dreams; for example, I dreamed of Vajradhara Pema Nyinjé being very pleased with me and encouraging me, placing a crystal mala around my neck.

In the ninth month a daughter of Dokhar, the central government minister, was due to arrive in the kingdom to be married to the prince, and my presence was required to perform ceremonies to offset any potential problems. I went in answer to the summons and satisfied everyone's expectations. Then, in the tenth month, Kuzhap Choktrul was preparing to set out for the central province of Tibet, so I performed a longevity empowerment and other means to remove obstacles. I also escorted him part of the way, accompanying him to the banks of the Drichu River. [121a]

After that I went to the Chayang estate. The line of oral transmission had been lost for the nine volumes of the Second Zhechen Rabjam's collected works. Dorjé Rabten of Dzogchen Monastery had heard that I had previously received this transmission from Öntrul Rinpoché, so he came bearing the texts and I gave the entire oral transmission. During this process my mind was quite disturbed on several counts—I saw signs that Kuzhap Rinpoché had encountered major obstacles (primarily those inflicted by *gyalpo* demons) and I had dreams in which someone who resembled my old mother spoke very angrily, uttering many prophetic statements that this year was not a good time to journey to central Tibet. Returning home, I followed a directive I had received from Kuzhap Rinpoché to perform a powerful ritual of ransom based on Dorjé Drollö and some additional rituals of offering to the protective deities.

Once these were finished, I responded to my lord guru's summons and went to Dilgo to carry out spiritual practices for the sake of his sister and satisfy the requests of several patrons. After that I went briefly to the area of Meting and then on to Dzongsar, where I had an audience in the presence of my all-seeing precious master. He required many empowerments and oral transmissions from me, which I offered to him. He bestowed many on me in return. In particular, in accord with a prophecy that came to him, Khyentsé Rinpoché conferred on me the empowerment and oral transmissions for The Profound Drop of Tara, as well as the empowerment and oral transmissions for The Profound Drop Uniting the Families of the Three Roots, a practice that had recently come to him in a pure vision. [121b] He gave me a scroll painting of the Guardian Goddess of Mantra, which was imbued with the presence of the deity, and at the same time performed the conferral of life force for this protective deity. During this ritual I felt a sense of awe, as though the goddess herself had actually come, with my breath short and my body unable to move. I asked Khyentsé Rinpoché to use his psychic abilities to determine the destiny of the teachings of Palpung, and the signs he saw in his dreams were somewhat disturbing—for example, he saw a mountain being consumed by bloodthirsty demons.

ON THE FIRST DAY of the first month of the new Iron Sheep Year [1871-1872], I dreamed that Pema Ösel Do-ngak Lingpa[750] bestowed an empowerment on me, which he told me was the basic empowerment for *The Complete Union of the Intent of the Peaceful and Wrathful Forms of Samantabhadra.* He bestowed this as a series of the four levels of empowerment, and in between he conferred a number of smaller empowerments and instructions, so that I had the impression that I had received fifteen complete cycles of teachings. The morning after this dream, Khyentsé Rinpoché gave me some texts to examine, which were from the teachings connected with his "*terma* of enlightened intent,"[751] The Complete Union of the Intent of the Three Roots, and honored me with the knowledge that I was to be their custodian. He also bestowed on me the blessing ritual for the guru principle, which is the first of The Seven Profound Cycles discovered by Chokgyur Lingpa, and the blessing ritual for the *heruka* form of Vajrasattva according to Marpa's tradition.

I discussed an idea of mine with Khyentsé Rinpoché. I had already received teachings from the traditions of the Eight Lineages of Accomplishment. So that these transmissions would not go to waste, I had thought to gather all the most important empowerments, instructions, and spiritual advice in a single collection. [122a] When I suggested this plan to Khyentsé Rinpoché, he told me that he himself had written about twenty small volumes of instruction on these subjects, but that he had a big problem in that the empowerments were not complete. "Your idea is excellent," he said, "and you should put this collection together and call it *The Treasury of Spiritual Advice*." He drew up a list of some ten volumes of oral transmissions and spiritual advice, such as the "red" and "black" volumes of the Lamdré tradition, and composed histories of the lineages of my *Treasury of Precious Hidden Teachings* and *Treasury of Spiritual Advice*. Khyentsé Rinpoché told me that I should write an instruction manual for the *Eight Cycles of the Path*.

The night of the nineteenth, after I had agreed to write this book, my lord guru had a significant dream. He found himself in a region of India renowned for its medicinal plants, in a pleasant and dense grove of sandal and aloe wood trees. Seated on a small throne of aloe wood was Khenchen Dorjé Chang, Jampa Kunga Tendzin,[752] wearing a formal monastic robe and beaming with a cheerful and radiant smile. Khyentsé Rinpoché bowed to him in devotion and the master said, "It is excellent that Kongtrul Rinpoché and you are writing about Lamdré."

Khyentsé Rinpoché replied, "But sir, my master and I haven't written anything about Lamdré. Beginning this year, we have simply made a small collection of the empowerments, oral transmissions, and instructions."

As though he hadn't heard, [122b] Jampa Kunga Tendzin repeated, "It is excellent that you are writing about Lamdré. In the past, the glorious Lama Dampa Sönam Gyaltsen[753] planned to write an instruction manual on all nine cycles of this path. But aside from his four major works on the basic instructions, he never wrote a manual dealing with the last eight cycles. If that were to be completed now, is would serve to fulfill the intent of Lama Dampa. Here is a volume from the oral lineage of Lamdré. You should offer it to Kongtrul Rinpoché." Thereupon, Jampa Kunga Tendzin took a text of medium size, wrapped in red cloth, from under his arm and placed it in Khyentsé Rinpoché's hands. Khyentsé felt quite amazed, for up until then he had never heard of something called the "oral lineage of Lamdré." He wondered, "Why must this be given to Kongtrul?" Jampa Kunga Tendzin smiled and said, "Kongtrul is my family." "And who is 'your family'?," Khyentsé asked him. "He is Müchen Sang-gyé Rinchen,"[754] came the reply.

At that, Khyentsé Rinpoché reflected, "Sang-gyé Rinchen was the lama from whom Jamgön Kunga Drolchok has received the Chakrasamvara cycle and other teachings when he was eleven or twelve years of age. The rebirth of Drolchok was Taranatha, and his rebirth in turn is Kongtrul. [123a] This might mean that Drolchok and Sang-gyé Rinchen were, so to speak, of identical mind, but I'm not sure he meant that Kongtrul was actually Sang-gyé Rinchen's rebirth." Immediately Jampa Kunga Tendzin said, "That's it exactly! Müchen Sang-gyé Rinchen and Kunga Drolchok were such that their mindstreams were identical."

Then Khyentsé Rinpoché conferred on me a number of gifts, including five very special statues (one of them a statue of Tara that was reputed to speak, which had been used by the exalted Nagarjuna in his meditation practice and which Khyentsé Rinpoché had brought back with him from Zabbulung Valley in the Shang region), some twelve volumes of advice and instruction, and a pair of objects representing the principle of enlightened mind. I returned to my hermitage, bearing these all with me, and continued with my usual schedule of personal practice, lectures, and so forth.

Khen Lama Tashi Özer was usually in residence to oversee the hermitage, so in order to encourage others in their virtuous endeavors, I went to attend a *drupchen* ritual that was being planned at the holy site of Tashi Nenang in Yuthok. The morning that our journey brought us up behind the holy site, we saw a five-colored rainbow coming from the east and a two-colored one coming from the west, meeting in the middle. These lasted from sunrise to midday. First of all, at the highest point on the land I performed a *lhasang* ceremony of atonement and a ritual to bind gods and demons to their oaths of allegiance. In the very center of the site, we conducted a *drupchen* ritual based on the *sadhana* of enlightened mind *Dispelling All Obstacles*, which finished on the eighth day of the second month. With care and attention, we then performed the ritual to infuse the place with the blessings of a major site. [123b]

On Paljor Plateau, for a group led by Lama Tashi Özer, I performed the empowerments for the entire range of mandalas in the Karma Kagyü School, as well as the basic and secondary empowerments for the *sadhana*s of enlightened mind from the Tersar tradition. I then returned to my home. The year before, Rigdzin Drölma had conceived, and when I now asked my lord guru to name the child he said, "Last year a woman came to me saying that the son of Rigdzin Drölma would be a rebirth of Rongpa Galo.[755] Since she said his name would be Namgyal Dorjé, it would be excellent to name the boy that." He gave me a letter with his seal, conferring the auspicious name of Jamyang Namgyal Dorjé on the boy. He said, "In the future he should become learned in the Kalachakra system."

In the second month I conducted a Vajrasattva *drupchen* ritual, which also incorporated a ritual to consecrate medicinal pills. Phunrapa, the governor of Nyarong,[756] had come to have an audience with my lord guru, who said my presence was required, so I went in response to his summons. While there, I received from my precious lord the empowerment from Butön's tradition of Kalachakra, as well as all the empowerments, oral transmissions, and instructions for The Heart Drop of Longchenpa,[757] all of which he was bestowing on the governor at the time. The governor insisted that I should conduct a ritual to ensure his longevity, so I spent a week performing many longevity empowerments. I requested an empowerment from the "tantra tradition" of Vajrakila[758] from my lord guru. [124a] He had a significant dream in which he was explaining the story of how Tzagyépa Dorjé Seng-gé extended his spiritual master's lifespan through the practice of Vajrakila, and while he was preparing for the empowerment[759] he had a pure vision in which he received the direct lineage[760] from Nanam Dorjé Dudjom,[761] after which he bestowed the empowerment in a very extensive manner.

I returned home to my monastery, where in the fourth month I participated in the annual vase consecration ritual and performed empowerments for the public at large. An emissary from Phunrapa arrived, summoning me to Dzongsar Monastery, where I presided over a ceremony that Phunrapa sponsored for my precious and omniscient spiritual master's long life. Phunrapa was planning a large project to smelt mercury and he requested Khyentsé Rinpoché to direct it. Rinpoché replied that henceforth he had no intention of leaving his quarters, and explained to Phunrapa that I was the only other person who knew the process. This led Phunrapa to require that I come to the region of Nyarong.[762] At this point in time, the owner of the arable land of Khanglep in Meshö Hakda had been penalized by Phunrapa, who placed all the revenues from this land at the disposal of my hermitage, to sponsor a group ritual focusing on the deity Kalachakra, which Phunrapa insisted be performed annually to suppress the effects of the barbarian uprising of Gönpo Namgyal. I consulted with my master and prepared a meticulous list of items needed for this project, which I gave to the governor. As well, rain was scarce at that time and I had many liturgies to recite, including some to bring rain.

This year, Tsadra was a holy site to be visited by all,[763] [124b] so I made a précis of the account that Khyentsé Rinpoché wrote, which dealt with the benefits of circumambulating the place and other topics. When I had returned to my home, during the sixth month Öntrul and several others joined me in mapping out the circumambulation route.[764] We did everything according to Khyentsé Rinpoché's explanations, taking the necessary provisions and performing the lhasang ceremonies, offerings of a golden libation,[765] feast offerings, aspiration prayers, and so forth. When we were performing a lhasang ceremony and an offering of a golden libation in front of the tree marking the northern entrance to the site, from the east there came a rainbow that covered half the sky, like a blue-green field on which many other colors were overlaid, reaching from the east toward the south and lasting the entire morning.

In the record of holy sites that Chokgyur Lingpa had previously discovered as one of his termas, there was no mention of this site, but later on my lord guru discovered another terma, in which there was a listing of the marks Guru Rinpoché's left with his body at Pal De'u. Based on this, we searched for these marks and found them.[766] We also found several other signs—naturally occurring phenomena that had not been there before, notably Tashi Palphuk Cave and a white A letter about one story high.

During the sixth month, every afternoon a whitish rainbow with an opaque appearance would spread from west to east, covering half the sky. Many people gathered to join the procession that constantly circumambulated the holy site along the designated path. Everyone got along without quarreling or fighting, and those who had to carry or lead animals that went blind or lame did not experience the slightest fatigue, despite the four ravines and eight gullies to be crossed. [125a] We may take these facts to be signs of success.

At this point in time, at the hermitage there were many pilgrims coming to view the Tara statue, so the days were spent entirely in dealing with the press of people. I was told that when I went to Reti Lake to do ceremonies to bring rain, all the people doing circumambulations could see above the lake a cloud with a like a "source of phenomena"[767]—which stayed there for a long time. As well, it rained.

On the tenth day of the sixth month, I identified the holy site of Pal De'u and also laid out the path for circumambulating the site. Two of Öntrul's attendants sponsored a *mendrup* ritual based on The United Intent of the Gurus, which was performed at Palchen Temple in the hermitage. On the second day, a cymbal that had no visible flaw in it shattered; later on it seemed that this was a foreshadowing of the master and his attendants suffering an interruption of their material support.

During the seventh month in conjunction with rituals I was performing for the general populace of Lharu, I carried out a powerful ceremony of suppression, a *lhasang* offering, a ritual of ransom, and other rites, following which I performed an extensive consecration ceremony from the *sadhana* of enlightened mind *Dispelling All Obstacles* to infuse this major holy site with blessings. With the intention of bringing happiness to the region, I also performed a ritual of ransom involving three offerings—"medicine," *rakta*, and *torma*[768]— from *The General Assembly of Mamos.*

Prior to this, my precious lord guru had codified a record of some three holy sites that were associated with Tsadra. [125b] At this point, in response to a request someone made, I journeyed to Pemadrawa, which is sacred to Lingtsa Tenkyob.[769] On this occasion there were rainbows and other positive signs and omens. I performed a pacifying *lhasang* offering, a ritual to bind gods and demons to their oaths of allegiance, and a consecration ritual to infuse this important site with blessings. I laid out the path for circumambulation and, having thus identified this holy spot, I departed.

In the hall of the summer retreat, I gave instructions to the participants in the retreat, including the three levels of ordination, *The Highest Continuum*, *The Profound Inner Meaning*, and *The Hevajra Tantra*, which I introduced by giving the empowerment. I gave a series of explanations on the concise summaries from my *Treasury of the Knowable*. Once these were finished, I went to my hermitage, where I undertook a personal retreat on the cycle of Vajrakila called The Crucial Point, including the supplementary recitations.

In the eighth month I went to the Vajrakila Temple to participate in the annual ritual of accomplishment focusing on Vajrakila. Once that was completed, I performed a ritual for Situ Rinpoché at his monastic residence—a ritual that focuses on a wrathful form of Guru Rinpoché know as Mekhyil and is designed to avert negativity, and in conjunction with that a major ritual of ransom focusing on the nine *gyalpo* demons and *senmo* demonesses. There were some significant signs of disturbance. By giving empowerments, oral transmissions, and instructions, I satisfied the requests of many lamas and monks who came from various places, some of them important figures, some quite ordinary people. At the hermitage, I continued my personal retreat while editing the drafts of some of the commentaries I had already written.

On the day of the new moon in the eleventh month, old lama Sang-ngak passed away, but although I was summoned rather insistently I chose not to break my retreat and so did not go to where he had died. While I was engaged in a personal retreat focusing on the deity Samyak according to Guru Chöwang's tradition, [126a] I had some amazing dreams. I dreamed of finding a double handful of fresh myrobalan fruit,[770] the kind called "Completely Victorious." At dawn on the day that I accepted the spiritual accomplishments of the practice, I dreamed of someone explaining to me the significance of a great many symbols found in the methods for accepting such accomplishments. But this person told me, "Although you have accomplished the practice of this chosen deity, there are not more accomplishments to accept than those of The United Intent of the Gurus." Immediately, I beheld an enormous statue of Padmavajra with green light shining from it and being reabsorbed back into it.

I also undertook personal retreats for other cycles, such as Chokgyur Lingpa's practice of Zangjangma and the oral lineage of Samyak. One night I dreamed that nine *mahasiddha*s of the holy land of India had gathered in the temple; the identities of most of them were vague, but I clearly remember Vajraghantapa,[771] who was with his consort, and Kukuripa,[772] who was unaccompanied. All of them enjoyed the company of the same consort, as they joined in the gathering for a feast. Such a display of timeless awareness, involving these amazing symbols and their underlying meaning, awakened understanding in me that I had never had before. I carried out the annual recitations I was accustomed to do, as well as participating in the year-end *torma* ritual of accomplishment. During this ritual, the nectar in the skull cup on the shrine increased in volume and came to a boil, until it was on the point of spilling over.[773]

KUZHAP RINPOCHÉ HAD RETURNED from central Tibet. On the tenth day of the new Water Monkey Year [1872-1873], he arrived and presented us with gifts. As a gesture to give thanks for his successful travels, he performed more than a hundred feast offerings based on The Union of All Rare and Precious Jewels. [126b] He departed after we had given a formal tea to celebrate his visit. Around this time I experienced several signs of negative energy affecting me. I had several dreams in response to these signs, such as one of the deity Ayushpati crushing this negativity with his mallet, and of me taming this energy by meditating myself as the wrathful deity Vajrakila and reciting the mantra.

I ended my retreat on the twenty-third of the month. Beginning on the twenty-fourth, about thirty of us, master and students, participated in a *drupchen* ritual focusing on the deity Samyak according to the So tradition of the *kama* lineage of the Nyingma School, following the newly prepared manual for this ceremony. During this time I experienced some positive signs in my dreams—of drinking fresh rainwater from the ledges of an amazing, self-manifesting stupa and of conferring an empowerment on many people while sitting on the upper ledge that symbolizes the immeasurable attitudes;[774] of seeing vast, lush beds of yellow flowers in the summertime; of finding many crystals protruding out of the earth; of seeing many fields filled with abundant harvests; and of having marvelous experiences of perceiving symbols and meanings connected with my future lifetimes.

The retreatants completed their program. The governor of Nyarong sent his steward to invite me to visit, so I made preparations to depart. I left the hermitage on the twelfth day of the second month. At Dzongsar I met with my precious lord guru, who conferred on me the symbols of the five principles of unending adornment[775] and a ceremony to promote my longevity. He told me of the need for me to expand my works on the refining of mercury and the preparation of medicinal tinctures, making these clearer and more extensive, [127a] and urged me to begin writing several works as auxiliary treatises to my *Treasury of the Knowable*, including a commentary on *Poetics: The Source of Riches*. At this time, I dreamed of journeying to Ngor Monastery where I beheld, in a special chapel of Khangsar Khenpo, eight stupas made of gold and an image of Khechari that seemed like the actual deity. One night I dreamed of meeting Gyalwang Karmapa Chöying Dorjé, who looked old, with his hair in a topknot, and was surrounded by his family members. I bowed at his feet and mentally recited the lines that begin with the words, "In all lifetimes, may I . . . ," and so forth.[776] Speaking aloud, I said, "In this and all future lives, may Gyalwang Karmapa hold me in his compassion!" Karmapa granted my request and gave me advice, saying, "I have something to give you. Hold on to it and don't lose it!"

Leaving Dzongsar, I paused on my journey at Pawang Bongmo in the region of Takhok to perform offerings of *lhasang* and a *ganachakra* feast. Arriving at the fortress of Rigyal, I spent several days making preparations for the process of refining mercury. On the first day of the third month I began by offering a golden libation and performing the feast offering from The Heart Drop of Yuthok and the offerings to the guardian deities. There were excellent signs as we commenced the work—rainbows appeared and rain began to fall. [127b] Step by step, I requested practical instruction and we were very successful in refining the mercury and preparing medicinal tinctures. Mindful of the usefulness of these procedures, I wrote a practical manual on the preparation of medicines and a book of instructions concerning the use of crystals. During this time I had several amazing dreams, the import of which was difficult for me to fathom, and one night I dreamed that the great *tertön* Chokgyur Lingpa gave me a cycle of teachings focusing on the *dakini* principle. Looking at one of the yellow scrolls in particular, he explained several of the symbols to me. He also conferred on me a scroll containing four strings of wrathful mantras to deal with all manner of epidemics, saying, "These will protect you on your journeys." I also had visions of several places where *terma*s were concealed in the area and saw a record of these.

Once we had finished the process of refining the mercury, we performed a ritual of consecration based on the sambhogakaya form of Bhaishajyaguru. At the insistent request of the governor, I performed some transmissions that he felt were necessary for several thousand lamas and monks; these transmissions included the two traditions of the bodhisattva vow, the empowerment for the Eight Commands called The Gathering of Sugatas, the major empowerment of Kalachakra called "the child's entrance," and the blessing ceremony for the practice of the feminine principle from The Heart Drop of Longchenpa.

Having honored all the requests made of me, I started on my return journey, traveling to Öpung Monastery in Pheltsa. After performing a number of empowerments and oral transmissions for the lamas and monks there, I continued by stages until I reached Meshö. [128a] I paid my respects to my precious master at Dzongsar Monastery and then continued to my home.

In the fifth month I carried out the appropriate rituals that are performed annually during this month, including an offering ceremony on the tenth day and a pacifying *lhasang* offering. The house of Sokmo in Meshö was intending to sponsor a ritual to promote the Buddhist teachings; I was ordered by the Dergé government to oversee preparations for a major ritual of ransom from the Tersar tradition, focusing on the *mamos*, so I went to Meshö. The day that this ritual was performed, there were powerful and disturbing signs. Once this ritual was completed, my precious lord guru instructed me that I needed to perform rituals in some of the holy places to the east, rituals to bind gods and demons to their oaths of allegiance and to infuse these sites with blessings. When I performed such rituals, first at Pema Shelphuk Cave, there were signs of disturbance, just as there had been in the past. On my return trip, the lamas and monks of Dzongsar Monastery and Pema Dorjé, a *khenpo* of Dzogchen Monastery, asked me to give some transmissions. In response to their request, I performed the major ceremony to confer the bodhisattva vow, as well as the oral transmissions for the meditations of the "Sons of the Buddha" and the ritual focusing on these eight great bodhisattvas.

In the past, my lord guru had codified a text describing a holy site associated with a Bönpo shrine called "the Yulgé Pula stupa." Now, however, he said that I needed to be sent specifically to open up this area. I discussed the circumstances with Khyentsé Rinpoché in great detail. Then, traveling by way of the Bönpo monastery in Changlung Valley, I continued on, accompanied by Changtrul, the incarnate master of Changlung. We reached the stupa at a point where three roads met. [128b] Beginning with a *lhasang* offering to establish harmony, as well as an impressive ceremony to suppress negativity, we then carried out a short practice based on the three principles of longevity, prosperity, and spirituality. Changtrul and other Bönpo practitioners in the assembly established their individual retreat centers. I identified the features of the area in detail, including the primary holy site, the hills to the right and left, the cave that bore self-manifesting marks of spiritual accomplishment, and so forth. I also laid out the outer and inner routes for circumambulation. In addition, I carried out whatever was needed at other sites—Dzing Thrawoné and the crystal cliff of Sheldrak in Yulung Valley. At Phadam Shelri and Dagam Wangphuk Cave I performed a hundred feast offerings. Having accomplished these and other tasks, I returned home by way of Dzongsar.

Once back home, I performed empowerments for Thromgé Tulku[777] and Adzom Tulku[778]—all the empowerments for *The Discourse of United Intent*, the peaceful and wrathful deities of *The Web of Magic*, and the Category of Mind. In response to requests from Öntrul, Getrul[779] of Kathok Monastery, the son of the *tertön* Chokgyur Lingpa,[780] and Lama Pema Norbu,[781] I made preparations at my hermitage for the empowerments and oral transmissions of *The Treasury of Precious Hidden Teachings* to be given a second time. All the oral transmissions were read by the vajra master Lama Ratna. We began on the tenth day of the seventh month and had completely finished the empowerments and transmissions by the fifteenth day of the ninth month. No sooner had we begun than a letter arrived from the Tenth Lord Situ, along with a scroll painting of Vajrapani. When the transmissions were finished, I received offerings [129a] and a ceremony for my long life was performed; the auspicious circumstances—including the offerings of gold, turquoise, a crystal bowl, and a vajra that I was given—were excellent.

Then Öntrul told me that he himself would not be able to transmit these teachings, and that any advanced practice of them would be difficult for him; he did, however, promise to look into arranging for an edition of the texts to be published.

The chieftain of Ling had told me on several occasions that he fully intended to come and receive these empowerments and oral transmissions, but he did not attend this time. From Dzongsar, my lord guru sent word that this chieftain was a very spiritual ruler who lived only for the Buddhist teachings, and that therefore I should go to him. So I made preparations to leave my hermitage. First of all, I intended to greet the *tertön* Tsewang Drakpa, who was coming to Rongyap, but I was unable to arrive in time, instead reaching my home region on the third day of the tenth month, at which point the *tertön* had arrived in time to greet me! We stayed in the local monastery, where I had the opportunity to examine the thirteen volumes of his newly discovered *termas*. In front of the holy site in the region, in a white tent we performed a *lhasang* ceremony and a ritual to bind gods and demons to their oaths of allegiance. The sacred mountain in that place was so high that at that time of year it was covered in snow and we were unable to reach it. I satisfied the requests of the residents of the monastery and the surrounding region; I also performed the complete empowerments and oral transmissions of the *sadhana* of enlightened mind *Dispelling All Obstacles,* for the *tertön*, his consort, and their two children. Prior to this, my lord guru [129b] had told me that it would be excellent for me to receive a longevity empowerment from the *tertön*, so I requested one of him.

I then departed for Dzong-go in the region of Ling, where I began giving the empowerments and oral transmissions of *The Treasury of Precious Hid-*

den Teachings to many lamas and incarnations, such as Zhechen Rabjam and Jedrung, as well as the Ling chieftain and the rest of the large gathering. I also performed the following series of empowerments: the Noble Wish-Granting Vase collection from the Mindroling tradition; the peaceful and wrathful deities of *The Heart Essence of Secrets*; *The Discourse of United Intent*; the eighteen "techniques of A" from the Category of Mind; the Innermost Heart Drop of the Guru; the Innermost Heart Drop of the Dakini; nine volumes of the Nyingma *Kama* collection, the three major practices of the Eight Commands; *The Vajra Bridge* from the Category of Expanse; and the Mindroling tradition of *The Profound Meaning of Ati*. This series also included the complete oral transmissions and instructions for the Four Higher Collections of the Heart Drop Teachings and the rest of the foregoing collections.

In response to an insistent invitation from the governor of Denchö, I journeyed to the Chödé Palace, passing on the way through Namling. At the palace I made preparations to consecrate about three hundred treasure vases and perform the three-stage ceremony[782] to infuse the place with the blessings of a major holy site; these tasks I accomplished over five days, at the same time carrying out a personal practice of a *sadhana* of enlightened mind. I then went to Drenthang, where I performed a ritual to bind gods and demons to their oaths of allegiance and a consecration ceremony to bless this as a major holy site. I also performed whatever empowerments were necessary, for smaller groups and in large public settings.

THEN, AT THE NEW WATER BIRD YEAR (the year in which I turned sixty-one [1873-1874]),[783] I returned to Chödé. I was met by the lamas and monks of several monasteries, including Zhang-gu and Tse-drum, and gave Mahamudra instructions by way of establishing a connection with them. [130a] I performed a consecration ceremony at the palace and satisfied requests for a longevity empowerment and other functions, after which I continued on my way. At Seng-gé Namdzong I performed a *lhasang* ceremony and rituals to cleanse the mountain, bind the gods and demons to their oaths, and bless this as a major holy site. The weather was very mild and warm, as though it were summertime. I also performed a ceremony to bless the temple of Tara as a major holy site.

At the monastic residence of Namling I performed a ritual to promote prosperity, as well as rituals to cleanse and consecrate the main temple and the shrine to the protective deities. Having satisfied the needs of the patrons, I journeyed on to Dzong-go, where I gave transmissions from the Kagyü School—the empowerments and oral transmissions of Varahi, Chakrasamvara, and Jinasagara, and instructions on Mahamudra and the Six Yogas—to Jangtrul of Ringu Monastery and his students, the chieftain of Ling, and others. Once I had completed the necessary preparations and practices, on the roof of the palace I performed a ritual to bind the local gods and demons to an oath of allegiance and a ceremony to bless the area as a major holy site. When all this was finished, I departed from Dzong-go.

On my way home, as I neared Dergé, I receive a letter summoning me to the great monastery there. On the fifth day of the second month I reached the new palace that had been built, where I attended a ceremony of monastics and lay patrons at Chemchen to celebrate the enthronement of Khangtön. I completed preparations for the rituals of Vajrakila, *Kingkang*, and the earth spirits, and met a few requests for empowerments, after which I went to the Chayang estate, [130b] where I recited some liturgies.

When I returned to my hermitage I was met by many visitors from upper Ga, including Rongta Tulku, Dzithang Chöjé, and Palchim Anyé. I fulfilled their individual requests in order. In the fourth month I received orders from Dergé to go to Changra, so I set out, attending a vase consecration ritual. I also performed a ritual focusing on the wrathful deities from the Eight Commands and a *gyaldö*[784] ritual. Returning home, I carried out my annual recitations and performed an extensive consecration of the hall for the summer retreat. For the rest of this year, I performed my usual duties, installing the third group of retreatants at the hermitage and giving empowerments, oral transmissions, and instructions at the lower meditation center. I also continued working on my writings, composing new texts as needed.

Dzongsar Tulku Rinpoché sent word that it would be good for Kuzhap Rinpoché to spend some time in retreat, but even though letters were sent to Dergé the permission was not forthcoming. It fell to Öntrul and myself to press the matter. Hoping it would be of some benefit in the long run, we explained the reasoning behind this plan to the government in as helpful a way as we could and, with every expectation that we would receive official permission, I offered the empowerment and oral transmission for Dorjé Drollö to Kuzhap Rinpoché and he began his retreat.

As always, I gave empowerments and instructions to the participants in the monastic summer retreat. [131a] In the shrine of the protective deities at the hermitage, we installed new *tormas* to represent the deities of both the old and new schools, as well as preparing the "life force" chakras and "spirit stones"[785] and filling the representations with mantras. I also attended the group ritual in the Vajrakila Temple.

In the ninth month I served as vajra master during a combined *drupchen* and *mendrup* ritual focusing on The United Intent of the Gurus, sponsored by Öntrul in the summer retreat hall. On this occasion I had several excellent dreams that I was receiving the blessings of the practice. In particular, I dreamed of a *mahasiddha* (though I wasn't sure who), who was in essence Orgyen Rinpoché and from whom I requested empowerment. He conferred the vase and secret empowerments directly on me, and then everything vanished from sight and I was directly introduced to the blissful sensations that elicited the potential in me to receive the third empowerment, that of wisdom and timeless awareness. Then the dream faded, and I had a meditative experience prior to awakening in which I clearly heard the following words spoken:

> Samantabhadra's enlightened intent is originally pure.
> Like a globe of crystal, it is flawless.
> With the conferral of the empowerment into the dynamic energy of
>   awareness,
> may you be inseparable from the primordial protector!

Thereupon I awoke. On the afternoon that the medicines were being sifted and blended, I had a violent headache and was unable to attend the group ritual. I dreamed of a charnel ground and following that the signs I experienced were rather disturbed.

For a large group that included Dragyap, Sertal Lhatsé Tulku, and others, I had to give many empowerments, oral transmissions, and instructions on a continual basis, [131b] including the Four Higher Collections of the Heart Drop Teachings, the Category of Expanse, *The Highest Continuum*, and an explanation of my own *Treasury of the Knowable*. From the eleventh month onward, I undertook personal retreats focusing on *The Oral Lineage of Vajrakila* and *The Heart Drop of the Profound Meaning of Ati*, as well as carrying out my annual practices. While I was practicing *The Heart Drop of the Profound Meaning of Ati*, I dreamed one night of Zurchung Sherab Drakpa,[786] his body enormous and resplendent, acting as though offering someone a full measure of barley and then saying, "I have nothing more than this." I thought to myself, "He is truly a *heruka*," and felt faith grow in me. On another occasion I dreamed of an ancient temple in which I saw a huge statue of Tara, which I was told had been the image used by King Songtsen Gampo for his meditations and which seemed to be draped with the bowed forms of arrogant demons. The next morning I thought, "This is an indication that my karmic obscurations, such as those due to misappropriating property, have gotten much worse." This feeling left me saddened. Prior to this, Kuzhap Rinpoché—who had found that retreat life did not suit him—had repeatedly requested permission to be excused from his duties and was becoming increasingly frustrated. The day he reached Palpung Monastery on his way from Dergé to Dzongsar, he made a real point of some of his grievances. A number of badly motivated monks cast much blame on Öntrul and me. I sent Kuzhap Rinpoché a letter detailing these abuses and received in reply a copy of a scathing tract he had issued. This was a sign that a major disruption of *samaya* was about to occur.[787] My precious lord guru sent word from Dzongsar that such a great threat to the teachings [132a] could cause enormous damage, and that it was best if we just let everything be. Although the Dergé government undertook no action, Kuzhap Rinpoché was unable to forget his grudge and let things be, but continued to engage in heated remarks until Tsering Döndrup, the head steward of Dergé, had to settle the matter. Most of the grievances turned out to be baseless and empty accusations, and some of the evil monks who had been instigators were imprisoned, while Öntrul was sent to stay at Drenthang and I was confined to my own residence. For his part, Kuzhap Rinpoché gave me his pardon and told me that he had never turned against me and had borne no ill will toward me at any point during the proceedings. Toward the end of the year, I performed the offering ceremonies and intensive rituals focusing on the protective deities.

IN THE NEW WOOD DOG YEAR [1874-1875], during the month commemorating the Buddha's spiritual miracles, I carried out my usual recitations. I also composed my commentary to *The Stages on the Path: The Heart Essence of Timeless Awareness* in its entirety.[788] During the third month, Getrul of Kathok Monastery, wanting to receive all the instructions for *The Treasury of Precious Hidden Teachings* that he had not been able to receive previously, sent an escort to invite me. So I went to Kathok Monastery, where I satisfied the requests of many lamas and incarnate masters, as well as viewing the statues of the deities there. [132b] I had long had the desire to see the images in this monastery, including the famed "hundred thousand images," so I made some small efforts at prostrations and circumambulations.

Following this, I had hopes of staying in this place for a while, but at Palpung Monastery Öntrul had suddenly passed away due to some contamination connected with *samaya*.[789] In view of the urgency of the situation (because there was no one to oversee the commemorative ceremonies), two old monks sent messengers repeatedly to urge me that it was imperative that I come, so I quickly returned to Palpung. Two emissaries from the Dergé government oversaw the practical details of the ceremonies, while I shared what I knew about Öntrul's wishes concerning the distribution of his possessions. His personal effects were thus distributed among the lamas and members of the monastic community. The ceremonies were sponsored throughout by several lamas, and once they were completed I also sponsored a week-long fulfillment ritual based on The United Intent of the Gurus. When Öntrul was still alive, he had gathered enough to sponsor the publication of *The Treasury of Precious Hidden Teachings*, as well providing tea for thirteen hundred people.[790] This had all been left with his steward Pelek. On this occasion, once his commemorative ceremonies had been completed, the expenses included tea for about fifteen hundred, and I left the funds for publishing *The Treasury of Precious Hidden Teachings* once again with Pelek. In Öntrul's private chambers in Palpung Monastery, Kuzhap Rinpoché and I joined a large group of monks to perform a ceremony.

For the most part, the general monastic population of Palpung had absolutely no conflict with me on the level of the teachings or our *samaya* connection. [133a] But it would appear that there were a few people who, perhaps due to previous karma, felt some kind of disharmony with me. At about this time I received a letter from my precious lord guru. In it he said, "Up to now, you have explained and spread the teachings in that monastery through empowerments, oral transmissions, and instructions. You have taught people the practical techniques of the *drupchö* and *drupchen* rituals of both the old and new schools, and presided as vajra master over these rituals. You have even taught the secular arts and sciences. As well, you have spent such a long time at the retreat center. After all this, such accusations against you are most heinous. The lama responsible for this should be killed: that's all there is to it. As the great Lord Atisha once said, 'One should go a hundred leagues from a place where strife has occurred.' What's done is done, but it will definitely threaten your longevity and harm you in other ways, so you shouldn't set foot inside that monastery again!" But my own thought was that the minds of these people might have been disturbed by demons of broken *samaya*,[791] and I felt only compassion for them, not the slightest malice. But as soon as I had repaid Öntrul's kindness to me, I felt my mind turn away from all these lamas and monks, and for fourteen years I did not go near the monastery, which meant that my teaching activities at the meditation center effectively came to a halt as well. Although I could have gone to any monastery I chose, whether of the old or new schools, [133b] I thought of my *samaya* connection with Lord Pema Nyinjé and his brother and for the time being decided to stay where I was at the hermitage.

In the sixth month I visited Dzongsar, where I performed a week-long ritual of the longevity practice The Gathering of Secrets for my lord guru's long life. I also performed a ceremony as an offering to the Bönpo *tertön* Tsewang Drakpa and the others present—a large nonsectarian gathering of lamas and incarnate masters of all schools, as well as their patrons and others among the faithful. This *tertön* spoke of quite a number of rituals that should be performed and of the need for a hundred thousand feast offerings, based on the Heart Drop of the Exalted Goddess of Immortality, to be carried out in major holy places. I and my attendants committed ourselves, each man to do ten thousand of these feast offerings, and we went to our respective places and performed these rites, after which we returned to Dzongsar; we had performed ten thousand feast offerings in each of the meditation caves at Tsadra, Palphuk Cave in Tashi Nyida, Zhitro Shelphuk Cave, Pal De'u, and other holy places.

In the eighth month a messenger came from the queen of Dergé in Meshö, requiring my presence at combined *drupchen* and *mendrup* rituals based on the Eight Commands. Accordingly, I went to Tashi Phodrang.[792] The royal family of Dergé also attended. As we began the *drupchen* ritual, the weather turned summer-like and there were other excellent signs. Following my lord guru's instructions, every day I explained some of The Stages on the Path: The Heart Essence of Timeless Awareness. Finally, I brought the proceedings to a conclusion by giving the major empowerment in private to the aristocrats and others (according to a list that had been drawn up) and the more public empowerment [134a] to the group at large.[793] I petitioned the Dergé government for the additional funds needed to publish The Treasury of Precious Hidden Teachings and received a promise that my project would be taken under consideration. The queen spoke of the need for me to fill the statues she had commissioned with mantras, and of the fact that she wanted to support me. On this occasion I spent a week performing the rituals to prepare the chakras of the *yaksha* spirits[794] and the consecration of treasure vases using the practice of the white form of the Six-Armed Mahakala. I dreamed of a shower of white flowers falling and when I had finished the rituals and was reciting the concluding prayers of benediction, there was thunder and a terrific downpour and other excellent signs.

I went to Dzongsar Monastery to meet with my lord guru. Having received several important empowerments and oral transmissions from him, I continued on to my home. Having carried out a number of recitations, I went to Dergé Gönchen on the twenty-second day of the ninth month. The next day I prepared for the rituals to consecrate the treasure vases and chakras, and for the unveiling of the hanging that brings liberation on sight.[795] Khen Tashi Özer and other lamas performed these rites, step by step. The regent of the house of Thartsé[796] and I prepared the long mantras, purified and consecrated the substances to be placed inside the statues, and performed other preliminaries. Then it came time to fill the great statue of Shakyamuni and that of Orgyen Rinpoché, as well as the stupas and the gilded roof ornaments. We performed the appropriate rituals in each case, leaving no detail overlooked. [134b] Then Thartsé Rinpoché performed a three-day ritual of consecrating, while I performed the two-day ritual based on Chakrasamvara. In this way we finished all that was necessary to the project. I then went to Chayang.

Tashi Samphel, the chamberlain of Atri, was sponsoring a *drupchen* ritual at a place called Rameshvara, known in the local dialect as Rawé. The morning I set out on the road there, I saw a very vivid rainbow and other excellent signs. We began the *drupchen*, using the *sadhana* of enlightened mind *Dispelling All Obstacles*. In my dreams I had positive signs, such as seeing the *daka*s and *dakini*s of the twenty-four gathering places dancing, but there were also signs of me consciously undermining some positive circumstance. Once the ritual was over, I performed both the private and public empowerments. During the *drupchen*, we had made preparations for the ritual to bless the site as a major holy place, so at the highest point of the land we spent two days during enduring heavy winds as we performed such ceremonies as the rituals to bind gods and demons to their oaths and to bless the site as a major holy place, as well as a hundred feast offerings. The weather was so bad that some of the patrons later took this to be a bad sign.

I then returned to my hermitage. [135a] On the day of the winter solstice, I performed a ritual of Vajrakila to avert negativity, an offering ceremony to the protective deities (during which the representational *torma*s on the shrine were replaced with new ones), and a ritual of accomplishment focusing on my protective deity. I also undertook a fairly long personal retreat based on the deity Vijaya, one of the auxiliary practices from the Heart Drop of the Exalted Goddess of Immortality.

THE STEWARD PELEK ASSUMED responsibility for publishing my three-volume commentary to *The Treasury of the Knowable* during the next year, that of the Wood Pig [1875-1876], and he also intended to begin the work of publishing *The Treasury of Precious Hidden Teachings*. So around the time of the new year, I had no time for attending any other liturgies than the *drupchö* rituals in the meditation center, for I was busy composing rituals for inclusion in *The Treasury of Precious Hidden Teachings*.

During the second month I asked Rigdzin to sponsor a ritual, and for about sixteen days I, together with Khenpo Könchok Özer of Dzogchen Monastery and others, took part in combined *drupchen* and *mendrup* rituals based on The United Intent of the Gurus. During this time, in my dreams there were excellent signs of *dakini*s gathering and so forth, and I also dreamed of meeting Orgyen Rinpoché in his aspect as the king of Sahora, bearing a fine arrow of long life. On the morning of the twentieth day the *khenpo*, Lama Pema Norbu, and others went to the hall for the summer retreatants.

When Öntrul died the previous year, it had not been possible to cremate his remains. Now we performed four separate ceremonies at the same time and offered his body to the flames. On that day there were rainbows and other very positive signs. In fact, since his passing the year before, [135b] everyone had seen many rainbows over the months that followed.

Getrul and Dotrul from Kathok Monastery came to receive the empowerments and oral transmissions that had been newly added to *The Treasury of Precious Hidden Teachings*. I gave empowerments and oral transmissions to the son of Chokgyur Lingpa and others who had been entrusted with his *terma*s. The young son of the Dilgo clan, Jamyang Gelek, had taken monastic ordination and wanted to pursue an intensive spiritual practice, so I gave him the empowerments, oral transmissions, and instructions for The Union of All Rare and Precious Jewels. In these and other ways I was continually engaged in fulfilling the needs of many individuals.

The *tertön* Tsewang Drakpa came to Dzongsar Monastery. This *tertön* was a person whose activities were quite amazing. In accord with an injunction by

Chöjé Rinpoché, a *dakini* in the form of a vulture had offered a cache of *terma*s to him at Pema Shelri; all the *tertön*'s companions had witnessed this event. The list of empowerments and instructions I had received[797] was in sorry shape, so to make it more presentable we had it rewritten, including a decorative title page. I took great pains with the writing, going over the main part of the list in detail with Lhaksam, and we finished about half. From Lama Gönpo Dorjé of Pheltsa, I received all the instructions from the Taksham cycle of *terma*s that I had not yet received, primarily those concerning the three main *sadhana*s of enlightened intent. I received both empowerments and oral transmissions in their entirety.

On the holy day commemorating the Buddha's descent from the gods' realm, I went to Lhamdo Burmo, where I performed a *lhasang* ceremony and a feast offering. The signs and circumstances were excellent. [136a] Having taken care of the necessary liturgies to be performed at the hermitage, I went to Dzongsar, where my precious lord guru was extremely delighted to see me. There were still several texts from his *terma* of enlightened intent, The Three Roots: The Heart Drop of Utter Lucidity, which had not been codified, so I served as the scribe when he did this. He then bestowed the basic empowerment, the longevity empowerment, and the empowerments for enlightened form, speech, mind, qualities, and activities. Due to the many visions Khyentsé Rinpoché had, these teachings were later expanded. Rinpoché also gave the empowerments and oral transmissions for his rediscovered *terma*, The Gathering of All the Dakinis' Secrets, in the order they had come to him.[798] During this time, Khyentsé Rinpoché fell violently ill over and over due to the strain of his schedule. I offered him the oral transmissions for the volumes concerning the six-faced form of Yamantaka and the Mamo Gangshar cycle, as well as the empowerment and oral transmission for Sang-gyé Lingpa's Vajrakila cycle, Quintessence of Enlightened Mind. Khyentsé Rinpoché told me that the night after this Vajrakila empowerment, he dreamed of being in a black felt tent. His mother was there, stoking a rather fitful fire with dung. Rinpoché himself was lying down with his head pillowed on a yellow leather bag. His old mother wailed, "You are so feeble! To think that we, mother and son, should have come to this!" Outside, the tent was surrounded by a crowd of many rough men brandishing knives. They called out so loudly that Rinpoché was frightened speechless. In the back of the tent was a high throne, on which I was seated, [136b] reciting the essential mantra of Vajrakila—"Om vajra kili kilaya" and so forth[799]—in a loud voice. The men outside said, "Listen, that's the sound of a demon! Flee! Flee!" And they dispersed, so that in his dream Khyentsé Rinpoché felt a joyful sense of relief. He told me that this meant that while he had felt that he was meeting a great obstacle, the Vajrakila empowerment had averted it.

A group of about twenty lamas, incarnate masters, and scholars, including my lord guru, as well as Khangsar Khenpo Rinpoché and others, received the transmission of my *Treasury of the Knowable*. This took about ten days, as I combined the source text with my commentary in an oral transmission that involved explanations. Once this was completed, we recited prayers of aspiration and benediction, and Khyentsé Rinpoché was effusive in his praise of what he called "a treatise for the ages." He advised the recipients that they must teach and promulgate this text in their respective monasteries, whereupon they each promised to do so—Khen Rinpoché at Ngor and so on—although I have no idea whether they remembered to or not. The night after we performed a fire ritual of magnetizing energy from The Gathering of All the Dakinis' Secrets, my lord guru had a very special vision, while I myself had some amazing dreams.

I urged Khyentsé Rinpoché to take care to ensure that the direct line of transmission for the empowerment of the Mamo Gangshar cycle remained intact. He thereupon passed on this direct line of transmission just as he himself had received it from Orgyen Lingpa[800] in a pure vision. [137a] He instructed me to arrange the activity ritual and empowerment manual, impressing the importance of this on me. During that time, Tamdrin Wangmo, the holy woman of Shik-kya, arrived and Khyentsé Rinpoché conferred on her the empowerment and instruction on the transference of consciousness from The Union of All Rare and Precious Jewels. He also told me that he himself needed a formal authorization for the practice of White Tara, which I offered to him. That very afternoon, however, he fell seriously ill. This put a halt to all of the unfinished projects I was carrying out with my spiritual master, as important as they were.

While I was staying at the encampment, I gave brief explanations of the tables found in Chandragomin's Sanskrit grammar and other topics to the excellent scholar Mipham Gyatso[801] and others. During this time I had many lucid and significant dreams—of numerous gatherings of women and of various symbols being explained to me—but I have not written these down, fearing that it would prove too wordy.

About the time Phunrapa, the governor of Nyarong, received an order from the Dalai Lama[802] in central Tibet saying that either my lord guru or I had to come to Lhasa to carry out the preparation of "precious pills," which involved the refining of mercury.[803] Phunrapa insisted that I be the one to go, which upset me very much and even made me physically unwell. I respectfully insisted that I be excused from this duty, but felt that the governor was not going to relent. Just then word came from central Tibet that the Dalai Lama had passed away,[804] at which point all discussion of this project naturally came to a halt.

About the twentieth day of the twelfth month, Khyentsé Rinpoché's health improved somewhat and I requested an audience to receive his blessing. [137b] He told me that he had had three significant dreams, one of which involved the "spirit lake" of Remati far to the northwest, and the "spirit mountain" near it,[805] which provided protection to the region on both the outer and inner levels. Someone he knew from before gave Khyentsé Rinpoché a letter written in red ink, in which he read that if barbarians were to make offerings and throw a spirit catcher into the lake, this would harm the Buddhist teachings in general, and the two of us in particular. The man also told Rinpoché that he needed a guide, for he had been lost for a long time, so my spiritual master showed him his path. In that letter was a couplet that read, "The harm caused by the *dö* ritual will be dispelled by performing feast offerings. The harm caused by the *torma* offerings will be dispelled by woven cloth." This meant that a ritual of ransom involving the scattering of cloth would be necessary, so Khyentsé Rinpoché said to me, "As soon as you reach your home, it is crucial that you perform a wrathful ritual of ransom based on Vajrakila." His rediscovered *terma, The Vajra Nectar,* had been codified and Rinpoché gave me copies of the texts and charged me with the responsibility of maintaining these teachings. Spending some time to satisfy the needs of some patrons along the way, I returned to my hermitage, where I performed the accomplishment ritual of my protective deity, as was my custom.

DURING THE CELEBRATIONS of the new Fire Rat Year [1876-1877], I gave the transmission of the Innermost Heart Drop of the Guru to the retreatants. Once I had finished that, I had further duties to attend to. I gave the empowerments, oral transmissions, and instructions for the Category of Mind and *The Vajra Bridge* from the Category of Expanse to several of the retreat graduates and the two Lhatrul incarnations.[806] I performed a major empowerment of the masculine and feminine protective deities for the Sang-gyé Nyenpa *tulku;*[807] I also satisfied the needs of many others, including some of his relatives. [138a] During the waning phase of the moon, with some thirteen others who has completed the intensive retreat of Vajrakila, I performed the wrathful ritual of ransom. There was a powerful sense of disturbance.

At the beginning of the second month we began a *drupchen* ritual focusing on Vajrasattva, and on the twenty-third I began giving the empowerments and oral transmissions for The Precious Source of Sadhanas to Kuzhap Rinpoché, Öngen, Chöjé Tulku of Dzamthang, and others. This transmission was finished on the twenty-third of the third month, after which I performed the blessing for the Eighty-Four *Mahasiddhas*[808] and the entire succession of empowerments from the Sky Teachings. In the fourth month I went to Tashi Nenang, where Garjé Drodok[809] was sponsoring combined *drupchen* and *mendrup* rituals focusing on the Eight Commands. The outer and inner aspects of the *drupchen,* including the empowerment, went very well, and we performed several hundred feast offerings. On the road from Tashi Nenang I visited Chayang and also satisfied the needs of several of my patrons. In the fifth month I went to Meling Dordrak in answer to the insistent invitation of the *tulku* of the monastery, who was planning to institute a new schedule of observing the tenth day of the lunar calendar.[810] I performed rituals to banish hindrances and consecrate the ritual dance costumes and other objects. I finished the main *drupchö* ceremony and a concluding fire ritual, as well as the private and public empowerments, after which I returned to the hermitage.

I offered Kuzhap Rinpoché a ceremony for his long life and gave him some presents, whereupon we went to our summer encampment, where we began a *drupchen* ritual based on the So tradition of Samyak. [138b] I was continually giving empowerments and oral transmissions to meet the needs of many of the individuals gathered there. During the waning phase of the moon in the sixth month, in response to an order from Dergé I went to Dzongsar Monastery, where I performed rituals to promote the Buddhist teachings and benefit the government, including elaborate rituals of ransom focusing on the *mamo*s and *tenma* sisters. Although the plan was that all the supplies necessary for the rituals would be provided by the Dergé authorities, there was nothing forthcoming, so I borrowed all that I needed from Tulku Rinpoché. My dreams and other signs at this point were very disturbing. Then I received for the first time the news that I was being summoned to Dergé to direct preparation for the building of a "stupa of great power" there. I requested the oral transmission for Nyang's *Thorough Instruction on the Guru* and other texts from my precious lord. I also met Namdor from whom I received a formal authorization for the practice of Manjushri, as well as my formal investiture as a lama.[811]

On this occasion, my lord guru had a pure vision, in which he found himself on an eight-stepped mountain, shaped like a stupa, which he took to be Mount Kailash.[812] There was a cave in which he saw signs of *terma*s concealed, and he entered it, wearing his formal monastic robe and carrying a monk's alms bowl and staff. While Khyentsé Rinpoché was taking part in a feast offering inside the cave with several women, the sun rose in the east; as it shone there, were rainbows and showers of blossoms, whereupon Orgyen Rinpoché came and sat on a ledge in front of Khyentsé Rinpoché, adopting the posture of Maitreya. [139a] He was carrying something orange that resembled an urn. He held this to the three places on Khyentsé Rinpoché's body,[813] saying, "This is the empowerment that combines four mainstream transmissions of tantras, explanatory commentaries, and pith instructions. Once Orgyen Rinpoché had uttered the mantras "Kaya abhishincha om," and so forth,[814] Khyentsé Rinpoché was on the point of asking that the urn be placed in his hands, when he saw something that he ate. It was sweet to the taste and he felt the melting liquid filling his body. Then Orgyen Rinpoché told him, "Recite the Seven-Line Prayer a hundred thousand times and Orgyen Pema will enter your being."[815]

Following this, the vision faded, but Khyentsé Rinpoché said, "This is timely; it is very important to complete the hundred thousand repetitions of the Seven-Line Prayer." I replied, "Of course you, my lord, constantly feel the presence of Orgyen Pema within you. But although I can't entertain any such hope, I will see that these repetitions of the prayer are completed, for that will serve as a cause for me to be guided by Orgyen Pema in the future." And I immediately sent offerings to individual retreatants in various places, especially at my own hermitage, sponsoring them to do the repetitions and thus ensuring that the prayers were done.

Khyentsé Rinpoché instructed me that we needed to arrange for the empowerments and oral transmissions of *The Treasury of Precious Hidden Teachings* to be given that year at Dzongsar Monastery. So I returned home and began gathering together the things I would need—the texts, the small diagrams and ritual implements used in the empowerments, and so on—after which I went back to Dzongsar. When I was close to reaching it, half the sky filled with rainbows, the like of which I had never seen before—with many layers of five-colored bands and large and small spheres of light, [139b] all shifting and changing. At Dzongsar, I met with all those who had come for the empowerments, including the Gyatrul incarnation from Palyul Monastery, the Moktsa incarnation[816] from Kathok Monastery, the Rabjam and Gyaltsap incarnations from Zhechen Monastery, the Jédrung of Ling, the two Lhatrul incarnations, and Khenpo Akön from Dzogchen Monastery.

On the twenty-fifth day of the seventh month, at Lhasar Temple we began a *drupchen* ritual based on the Eight Commands practice The Gathering of Sugatas. Once we had completed the preliminary phase of the ritual, I bestowed the successive empowerments that confer personal benefit and the ability to benefit others. During the eighth month, for the previously mentioned lamas and incarnations, as well as for the scholar Rabjampa Kunzang Sönam and others, I gave the empowerments and oral transmissions that my lord guru didn't need to receive. I also gave the oral transmissions for a number of volumes, including those of The Guru: The Gathering of Secrets. At a certain point during this period, Pawo Rinpoché[817] came to Palpung Monastery, so I went to meet him. At my hermitage, I requested him to perform a consecration ritual and a longevity empowerment; I made offerings and sponsored a formal dinner for him, as well as taking him on a brief tour of the images and temples. I then returned to Dzongsar Monastery, where I picked up where I had left off with the empowerments and oral transmissions I had been giving. Pawo Rinpoché also came to Dzongsar, where I satisfied his requests; we began with the empowerment for Hevajra according to the tradition of Marpa, following which I gave the oral transmissions for my overview and commentary on The Hevajra Tantra, as well that on The Profound Inner Meaning. [140a] He also listened to many other oral transmissions I gave, including the entire Garland of Lightning cycle of rituals associated with the protective deities.

This year the group who had been in retreat were to finish their program, so that a fourth group could start its retreat. So in the eleventh month, having finished the empowerments for The Treasury of Precious Hidden Teachings, I returned to the hermitage to give the empowerments, oral transmissions, and instructions that the new group of retreatants needed to begin. I also drew up a manual of guidelines and advice for them.[818] This took half the month, after which I returned to Dzongsar and continued giving the oral transmissions that had been left unfinished. By the sixth day of the twelfth month I had completed these, including four volumes of teachings bearing the seal of secrecy and the oral transmissions of other useful texts. Beginning on the seventh day, we gathered in Khyentsé Rinpoché's chambers and I began giving the oral transmissions for a number of texts that my precious lord guru wished to receive.

DURING THE CELEBRATIONS for the new Fire Ox Year [1877-1878], while I was giving the oral transmission for the volumes concerning Ayushpati called *The Iron-Like Scorpion,* Chagla Khentrul arrived from central Tibet. He wanted to join our group of master and students to receive the empowerments and oral transmissions for Unobstructed Enlightened Intent (from the Northern Treasures cycles) in their entirety. As well, I gave Khentrul the empowerments, oral transmissions, and instructions for the Innermost Heart Drop of the Guru, as well as those for several other cycles of the Northern Treasures that he had not received before. Following this, Khentrul sponsored a ceremony and made offerings to us, master and students, and then departed.

On the third day of the second month [140b], I finished the rest of the oral transmissions and began the rest of the empowerments, which I completed on the thirteenth day of the third month. For Kuzhap Khampa, who came especially to receive these transmissions from me, as well as for Thartsé Pönlop[819] and his students, Dzogchen Tulku,[820] and others, I performed the entire five-day major empowerment[821] for the glorious Kalachakra, followed by the instructions for the Vajra Yoga system of the Six Branches of Union.

Then I spent another seven days in my lord guru's chambers, giving all the empowerments and oral transmission for the collection entitled the Noble Wish-Granting Vase. I also gave the instructions associated with *The Treasury of Precious Hidden Teachings* in their proper order. As a rite of thanksgiving, we performed more than one hundred offering ceremonies to the guardian deities.[822] My precious lord guru directed a ritual based on the nine deity mandala of Amitayus and a ceremony to promote my long life; as well, he gave me a large quantity of gifts. I also received offerings from the other lamas and *tulku*s for the transmissions I had given.

During this time I had a dream in which Gyatrul from Palyul Monastery gave me what seemed like a golden balance, treating me with great respect. I gave the balance back, placing it around his neck, and entrusted both him and Moktsa Tulku to uphold these teachings, reciting prayers of benediction at length. In accordance with my dream, Gyatrul has gone on to bestow the transmission of *The Treasury of Precious Hidden Teachings* three times. While for Moktsa Tulku, although he was an exceptional and holy master who upheld the teachings, his life was cut short by an obstacle. [141a]

Chokgyur Lingpa and others had received many prophecies of the need to erect a "stupa of great power" at Tsezuldo. In more recent times, malevolent spirits had gathered in increasing numbers there, until the road was impassable due to the great disturbances people encountered there. Over time, the Dergé government had repeatedly sent orders that I was to oversee the building of the stupa. At this point, however, an escort arrived to take me to Tsezuldo, and once I had received detailed instructions from my lord guru on the entire procedure from start to finish, I set out.

Going first to my hermitage, I collected the texts and other things I would need, after which I proceeded to Tsezuldo in Alo, where Tashi Gelek, the representative of the Dergé government, was seeing to the preparations. We were joined by others, powerful practitioners who had completed personal retreats on the practices we would use—masters such as the *tertön* Tsewang Drakpa and the lamas and *tulkus* of Dorjé Drak Monastery.[823] Master and students, together we performed a ritual based on Vajrakila, beginning with the taming of the site, the exorcism, and the ritual dances. We made a *lhasang* offering to establish harmony and an offering of a golden libation, and performed a ritual to bind gods and demons to their oaths of allegiance. We sought out the power center of the site, where we laid out the diagram of the serpent Mahoraga,[824] buried the treasure vase, and so forth. We then prepared the chakra diagram and other necessary articles. As for the spirit stones for the demons who are harbingers of foes, death, ruin, discord, and broken *samaya*, these needed to be sought in the four cardinal directions and in the center of the area. All the psychic impressions I had of where to find these proved to be accurate, which gave me confidence in our endeavor.

On the third day of the fifth month Khen Lama Tashi Özer and others [141b] performed an auspicious ceremony to restore and reaffirm their monastic vows,[825] after which we laid the foundation for the stupa. We ensured that all the auspicious circumstances described in the traditional texts were put in place. Everyone spoke of the positive signs we saw, such as the rainbows that appeared at daybreak.

On the ninth day we broke up into separate groups, who performed the rituals of casting the *torma* and suppression in an excellent manner. At Pomdrak, the *tertön* had discovered a cache of substances that were to be sealed inside the stupa, the most important of which was some of the salt that had been used to preserve the remains of the Buddhist king Songtsen Gampo.[826] So on the tenth day, we performed a feast of the heroes and heroines and opened the *terma* cache. On the eleventh day we began building the lower portion of the stupa, and on the nineteenth we performed the investiture ceremony to join the lower and upper structures. We then carried out the stages of accomplishment and enactment, and on the day of the new moon we invited the deities to reside permanently within the great stupa as their abode. We brought the project to its conclusion with a feast offering, a fulfillment ritual, a fire ritual, and other ceremonies. As the remaining outer layers of the stupa were being constructed, in response to an urgent request we went to the far shore of the Drichu River.

Kuzhap Rinpoché had had to go the year before suddenly to central Tibet, where he still was. This year the signs concerning the fate of the Buddhist teachings were very disturbing, so I went to Drölma Drakar on Ngay Pass.[827] There I performed a hundred feast offerings and, on the top of the hill, a ritual to avert negativity. The whole thing went very well; there were rainbows and other positive signs. After I had satisfied the wishes of my patrons, [142a] I returned to the stupa at Tsezuldo. I performed the ritual to consecrate the entire site, as well as erecting a shrine to the *genyen* spirits,[828] carrying these duties out in great detail. Then, in the sixth month, I set out for home.

At Palpung Monastery, I was told that a ceremony to quell foes was needed in the temple of the protective deities, the specific aim being that this would promote the Buddhist teachings, so I attended this ceremony as instructed. I also took care of many duties, such as giving both private and public empowerments and instructions to the retreatants at the hermitage and to other groups.

In the seventh month, in answer to a previous summons I went to Dzongsar to carry out a practice based on the Seven-Line Prayer at its major holy sites. At the monastery I joined with my lord guru in performing a ritual purification for the rebirth of the *tertön* Chokgyur Lingpa,[829] as well as a ritual to confer blessings on the child, a formal investiture, and prayers of benediction. During this time my impressions and other signs were excellent. I was also told that outside the building there were rainbows and showers of blossom-shaped drops of rain.

As a means to ensure that I could discover *terma*s for The United Intent of the Three Roots, my lord guru told me, "This is how you should accumulate recitations of the Seven-Line Prayer." Armed with these instructions, I went to Pema Shelphuk Cave, where I spent eight days and seven nights meditating and reciting prayers. During this time, one morning I had a clear impression that symbols of the form, speech, and mind of the deity Jambhala had formed naturally on a cliff face in the valley below. Within the *Jam* syllable was the inscription of a name, and in particular I could clearly see the green *Jam* syllable.[830] In the wake of this vision I had the impression that it would be excellent if the people living in the upper valley were to perform rituals to promote prosperity. Once I had performed a hundred feast offerings, as well as rituals of offerings to the protective deities and fulfillment, I crossed the pass [142b] and spent a week reciting liturgies and practicing at the cliff of Taktsang Tsodrak in Rongmé Karmo. I had dreams that included both disturbing and excellent signs. The morning that I finished my retreat, the *rakta* offering on the shrine overflowed and spilled onto the floor.

The queen mother in Dergé had previously sent an emissary summoning me, for she was planning to hold combined *drupchen* and *mendrup* rituals focusing on the Eight Commands. At this point, I set out in answer to her summons. While en route, I performed a ritual to purify obscurations for a patron of mine who had died. I stayed the night at the patron's home, and early the next morning his daughter came to see me and gave me a bolt of green silk and a statue of Tara. I fell back asleep briefly and dreamed, as I had in the past, of being menaced by *gyalpo* demons and using the meditative absorption of Vajrakila to quell these threats. As well, two *dakinis*, one larger and one smaller, wearing tiaras set with corals, gave me many prophecies encoded in symbolic language.

I continued on to the palace of Tashi Phodrang, where I met with the royal family and the lamas and monks of the monastery, who had also assembled. We began the rituals on the seventh day of the eighth month and spent a week each on the *drupchen* and *mendrup* rituals. During this time I had many clear and positive dreams. I dreamed of meeting Minling Terchen, who in my dream was practicing in a cave on the cliff face of the Chimphu uplands in the region of Samyé; it was a pleasant day, with warm weather and rainbows. The two *dakinis* reappeared, telling me that there was a very important *terma* of wealth objects concealed to the east. I met a very impressive lay tantric master whom I took to be a *tertön*; [143a] I asked for his help in discovering this *terma*, and he promised to do so, which made me feel joyful.

Upon awakening I could recall the details about the *terma* quite clearly, and I also had clear impressions of my precious lord guru giving me several prophecies and explaining to me the meaning of symbols found in many yellow scrolls, as well as many mental images of the region where the *terma* was concealed and the hidden teaching itself. During the ceremony to accept the spiritual attainments of the *drupchen*, the queen mother presented me with a lotus crown and the lay participants sponsored a ritual for my long life. I concluded this by performing a major empowerment in private for the aristocrats, Dzogchen Rinpoché,[831] Lingtrul, the *tertön*'s incarnation,[832] Dongkam Tulku,[833] and others, as well as empowerments that were more public, including one for the whole gathering. We performed a group ritual for the "one hundred holy sites" associated with the peaceful and wrathful deities, as well as an extensive "one thousand offerings" ceremony on the day of the new moon. With all of this, once we had offered the relics of the seven previous buddhas,[834] everyone saw the whole of Meshö Valley filled from top to bottom with rainbows.

I then set out for Dagam Wangphuk Cave, where I began a personal retreat on the fourth day of the ninth month. That first evening, I dreamed that Orgyen Rinpoché himself, taking the form of my lord guru Khyentsé, showed me a volume of yellow pages on which many columns of symbolic letters were written. He opened the book and explained the symbolism of the whole work to me, beginning with an instruction on how to chant the Seven-Line Prayer. Although I had many other significant dreams, I did not record them. During this time there were many shimmering white rainbow clouds; [143b] in particular, on one occasion about half the sky was covered for a long time by wispy rainbow clouds, like *kusha* grass, that came from the west toward the east.

I also had some meditative experiences. For example, at one point, I found myself entering a large stupa, only to be told that due to harm inflicted by an injurious earth spirit there was a flaw on the southwest corner of the lowest step; if the view and philosophy of the Jonang tradition were restored to its former glory, I felt, the stupa would have no such flaw.[835] In a similar vein, someone who appeared to be a scholar read to me from many writings that discussed the need for the respective systems of other philosophical schools to be preserved just as the founders had envisioned.

On the twenty-fifth day I performed a hundred feast offerings and the rituals for the protective deities. Once these were finished, I set out for Pema Shelri, were I began another personal retreat. One morning I had a meditative experience, a vision in which I saw a white *dakini* wearing silks and bone ornaments, holding a vajra and bell. She then changed and I clearly saw her holding a longevity vase in her right hand and a lotus surmounted by a gem in her left, wearing a tiger skin skirt. On another occasion, I dreamed of seeing a life-sized statue of the venerable Milarepa, his skin and garment white, his long locks of hair covering his back, his hands crossed behind his back, and holding a hand drum and thighbone trumpet. I bowed with respect to this image, which changed into the actual presence of Milarepa, who brought his hands in front and crossed them [144a] to give me his blessing.

By this point I had completed more than one hundred and five thousand, three hundred repetitions of the Seven-Line Prayer. I performed feast offerings, fulfillment rituals, and offerings to the protective deities in all the caves of this holy place. On my journey back, I stopped one night at Gyang Nepotsa. There I dreamed of many signs that there were *termas* in Dzongshö.

On the seventh day of the tenth month I went to the "great palace"[836] of Deshek Düpa in Dzongshö, where I performed feast offerings at each of the five holy sites. On the tenth day, at the great meeting hall—the holy site associated with the principle of enlightened mind—we made preparations for a "one hundred offerings" ceremony and other rituals, after which we celebrated with more than a hundred *ganachakra* feasts.

Both Tulku Rinpoché and Chokgyur Lingpa had spoken of the need for a temple on a particular power spot in this area, but due to the passing of Öntrul and other events this temple had never been built. I began discussing a project of mine, to see whether a simple tiered stupa could be erected. From this point on, the representative of Palpung became quite inspired by this idea and said that he would see to having the foundation of the temple laid. The local official from Rakchap also said that he would contribute. With such excellent circumstances coming together, plans were made for a meditation center to be built the next year and funds were assigned for that purpose. On my way back I satisfied the needs of some of my patrons and performed a ritual to promote the Buddhist teachings at Dzebum Phodrang.

During this whole period I had dreams of which the portent was difficult for me to determine. [144b] I dreamed of many signs connected with holy places and *termas*, and of many gatherings of women.[837] I dreamed of a building that seemed to be a temple on a holy mountain, in which I met someone who combined Dakpo Rinpoché and Jatsön Nyingpo in him inseparably; I prayed to him with devotion and he gave me the text *The Jewel Garland of the Sublime Path*. In one dream, I met Pema Nyinjé Wangpo and Gyalwang Karmapa Thekchok Dorjé; they expressed great delight at seeing me and told me, "We want to receive a number of transmissions from you, including your *termas*." I dreamed of gods and demons associated with both the Buddhist and Bönpo traditions vowing many times over to cure diseases that afflict herd animals. I also dreamed, among things, of Tulku Rinpoché conferring a tall scholar's cap on the "regent" statue in my possession and piling heaps of gems six inches high around it, a sight which filled me with delight. Early one morning, I had a clear impression of seeing in the sky an enormous sphere of light ringed with rainbows, in the center of which was the glorious Vajrasattva surrounded by many deities of the one hundred peaceful and wrathful families; thereupon the vision faded.

On the first day of the twelfth month I reached Dzongsar Monastery, where I met with my precious, omniscient spiritual master; who spoke to me about various things with obvious delight. I asked him again about my cycle of instructions concerning the Seven-Line Prayer and he gave me five auspicious articles and paper to write on, insisting that I must write something down. [145a] That evening I dreamed of donning a new formal monastic robe of orange cloth and finding many bamboo pens. A *dakini* with her hair hanging freely, who resembled Jetsün Namgyal of Tsurphu,[838] gave me a record of *terma*s written in symbolic script on cloth and tied up with a small iron *kila* dagger. She told me, "We two must discover these." Early the next morning my lord guru himself had a dream in which, he later told me, he gave me statues of the buddhas of the five families, four of them complete and one with its lower body missing. In the dream he said to me, "You must repair this one," and I replied with some trepidation, "That will be difficult." This seemed at the time to be a prediction of future events.

On this occasion, my spiritual master showed me some articles that the guardian deities of the *terma*s had actually offered to him and gave me blessing with them; these included a vajra made of a metal called *dhaiksham*, which was Guru Rinpoché's personal implement and the physical support[839] for the cycle, and the "regent" statues of Tsogyal from Zabbulung Valley. Since these articles had come to him so effortlessly, he wondered aloud whether there were actual cycles of teachings associated with them to be found. But nothing came of this later on, and it would seem that Khyentsé Rinpoché returned the vajra, along with many scrolls and *terma* substances, to the guardian deities to hold in trust, for after he passed away none of these articles was to be found.

Once, when a wild and mentally unbalanced monk came to him for a blessing, [145b] this caused Khyentsé Rinpoché's health to be very disturbed. In response to this, I composed several works, including a method for chanting the Seven-Line Prayer. I also finished teaching the major commentary on Chandragomin's system of Sanskrit grammar to Mipham Gyatso and others.

One night I dreamed of meeting Zhamar Palchen Chökyi Döndrup,[840] who seemed very youthful, and of finding myself inside a very finely appointed temple, in which I saw Amitayus, surrounded by more than a thousand buddhas, all of them the color of gold and radiant. I also had dreams in which I found many relics, scrolls, and the skull of Sang-gyé Nyenpa[841] in surprising ways.

Having given empowerments and instructions to satisfy the needs of many people who had gathered there, I then returned to my hermitage, where I performed offering rituals to the protective deities, during which the *torma* representations on the shrine were changed, and the *torma* ritual of accomplishment focusing on my protective deity. I also welcomed many visitors.

DURING THE CELEBRATIONS for the new Earth Tiger Year [1878-1879], I was very busy carrying out my usual recitations, giving empowerments and instructions to the retreatants, and editing my *Treasury of Precious Hidden Teachings*. In the second month, with Rigdzin serving as sponsor, we began combined *drupchen* and *mendrup* rituals focusing on The United Intent of the Gurus. At the same time as the *drupchen*, there were other large groups performing separate ceremonies—a fulfillment ritual, a Vajrakila practice, and a longevity practice. During this time there were signs that I was receiving blessings. In particular, one night I dreamed that my all-seeing precious master [146a] placed in my hands a vajra about a foot long and a white conch shell about nine inches long, saying that these came from Lhamdo Burmo. He also held a vajra and bell in his hands and showed them to me. In my dream, we codified an average-length *sadhana* of Gesar and immediately a group of several of us, master and students, arranged some quite remarkable *torma*s and offerings and performed the ritual based on that *sadhana*. During the *mendrup* ritual, I dreamed of a wandering monk who appeared out of nowhere and poured what looked like *solgangpa* medicine[842] out of a hollow horn and gave it to me, saying, "This is the very best of medicines for disorders of the lower abdomen; it can cure all kinds of diseases."

In the third month I traveled both to satisfy the requests of my patrons and visit Dzongsar Monastery, but there I found that my lord guru was unwell. I spent my time giving teachings such as The One Hundred Instructions of the Jonang School to the many lamas and *tulku*s who wanted to receive them, checking texts that had been edited, and so forth. I also wrote a *sadhana* associated with the Seven-Line Prayer. During this time, one night I dreamed that Lochen Dharma Shri sent me a letter and an accompanying scroll from

Mindroling Monastery, which I read. That morning, I dreamed I was visited by a large blue woman who said she was Kalaratri,[843] whose left leg was pointing skyward. She thrust herself between my thighs. Next to her was a naked red woman wearing jeweled ornaments who looked on, smiling. There was also a group of about four other women, [146b] one of whom was Rigdzin Drölma, who gave me a *kila* dagger about eighteen inches long, made of the finest copper. Delighted with this, I held it and read a letter that my lord guru had sent me. As I deciphered the contents of this letter in my dream, I saw that it contained a remarkable catalog of *terma* caches.[844]

I returned home in the fifth month, where I performed my customary duties, including the major empowerment for Kalachakra. Orders came from Dergé that summoned me to Changra. There I performed ceremonies to promote the teachings and benefit the secular government, including a ritual to banish demons and the consecration of many treasure vases. There were signs that *nyen* demons were gathering to create mischief, so I went to the places affected to deal with the problem. On my way back I consecrated the stupa at Tsezuldo and erected a cairn to Thanglha.[845] In all the places I visited I performed feast offerings and satisfied the needs of my patrons, after which I returned to the hermitage.

The rebirth of Dabzang Rinpoché came to see me, accompanied by other lamas, *tulku*s, and leaders from the community of Gegyal, and for them I gave the empowerments and oral transmissions for the majority of the mandalas of the Kagyü tradition. The *tertön* Tsewang Drakpa, who lived in my home region, had sent me letters over a period of time, insisting that I must visit the area this year.

For this and other reasons, I went first to Dzongsar Monastery, where I met with my lord guru. He spoke to me of many things that I was to commit to memory. [147a] In particular, Khyentsé Rinpoché told me of some of his extraordinary visionary experiences, including a pure vision in which he received profound empowerments from one who was the inseparable unity of Indrabodhi and Saraha.[846]

Khyentsé Rinpoché had studied with more than two hundred masters in both eastern and central Tibet, four of whom he considered his primary masters. He told me, "I would have liked to discuss my realization with the other three if they were still alive, but they have all passed away. Now you are the only one left, so now I have something I must discuss with you." He then briefly described the ways in which his experiences had developed in practicing both the structured and unstructured aspects of the stage of completion. I found that I myself had had no comparable experiences or realizations in the slightest. But if I were to assess his realization on the basis of all that I have understood from studying many instruction manuals from both the old and new schools, I would say that he had gained mastery over the three aspects of the subtle channels, subtle energies, and *bindus*, and that his practice of breath control had purified most of his subtle energy within his central channel. From the perspective of the Mahamudra approach, he had realized the "one taste" of everything;[847] while from that of the Dzogchen approach, he had realized the full expression of enlightened intent, experiencing all sensory appearances without bias, as expressions of the nature of mind. When I understood this, I felt a certainty that Khyentsé Rinpoché was none other than the great Orgyen and Vimalamitra themselves. I in turn had some minor points of my practice to discuss with him, and his response was that I had gained the stage of "awareness reaching full expression" according to the *trekchö* system.[848] In intervals between our sessions, I taught a brief overview of Chandragomin's system of Sanskrit grammar to the master of the house of Thartsé and his students, [147b] gave the empowerments and oral transmissions for the cycle Unobstructed Enlightened Intent to Palyul Tulku and Gyalrong Tertön, and gave many transmissions that were requested by large numbers of lamas and *tulku*s.

In the ninth month Khyentsé Rinpoché presided over a short *drupchen* ritual based on the rediscovered *terma* cycle of Drimé Kunga[849] that focuses on Jinasagara, during which Rinpoché gave the entire range of empowerments, oral transmissions, and instructions for this cycle. I prayed to Khyentsé Rinpoché for the permission that would allow me to pass on this profound empowerment in turn. During the empowerment he focused his attention on me most intently, which led me to an experience of what true unchanging bliss must be like. Khyentsé Rinpoché then was delighted and conferred his permission on me, whereupon I felt that my connection with the Vajrayana had truly become something meaningful.

It was at this point that Khyentsé Rinpoché said to me, "Up until now you have been of great service to me. From now until you are seventy-three years old, there will certainly be no obstacles whatsoever to your longevity, but after that things will depend on the merit of the teachings and of beings."[850] After he had spent a day performing the feast offerings for Tsokyé Dorjé[851] and Dorjé Drollö from my cycle focusing on the Seven-Line Prayer, Rinpoché said that he had beheld the entire universe to be the mandala of Tsokyé Dorjé and in other ways felt enormous blessing from the practice.

When it became necessary for me to go to Rongyap,[852] I asked Khyentsé Rinpoché if it was a good idea. He devoted some thought to this and said that it was an excellent plan. On the night that I decided to go, my lord was actually visited by Lhatsün Tsangpa,[853] who gave him a scroll of paper. After Khyentsé Rinpoché read this, Lhatsün Tsangpa said, "You all are planning several projects. [148a] It would be inappropriate for you not to perform a hundred feast offerings according to The Trilogy of the Two Doctrines of the Guru." There were other equally surprising pieces of advice, and Rinpoché told me that we should follow them. The following day we performed the hundred feast offerings according to The Trilogy of the Two Doctrines of the Guru, a rediscovered terma teaching originally discovered by Gya Lotsawa;[854] as well, Rinpoché graciously bestowed the pith empowerment for this cycle. For those whom he had appointed his successors, he also most deliberately conferred the prayers of supplication and aspiration and the formal blessing for Vajrakila from this *terma* cycle.

I then continued on to my home region, where I was met by an escort of several masters and students, who had been held up gathering provisions. We arrived at the Bönpo monastery in Rongyap, where we performed group rituals for two *sadhana*s of enlightened mind from the Tersar tradition. We also performed the mandala offering ritual of Tara several times and, on the tenth day, the feast and fulfillment ritual from The United Intent of the Three Roots. That night I dreamed of a *dakini* with luxuriant hair, perhaps in her twenties, who came to me and gave me some very attractive things, such as a banner of brocade, as well as an exquisite scholar's cap, some texts, and about seven vajra and bells. At the time I felt that I understood the meaning of one or two of these symbols. Someone said to me in my dream, "Hold on to these and they will prove useful for a few years." I felt joyful and happy at this.

At that point in time the *tertön* Tsewang Drakpa had gone to Lhokhok to give spiritual guidance and had not yet returned, so a group of us, master and students, began a *sadhana* practice based on my cycle based on the Seven-Line Prayer. [148b] We had just started the practice of the spiritual master as dharmakaya when a number of auspicious events occurred—a letter from Kuzhap Rinpoché arrived from Puwo, as well as one from Pungri Tulku that came with a crystal from Tsari[855] and the "secret menses" of Varahi.[856]

During the practice I saw many excellent signs in my dreams. As well, I was given a piece of the *mahasiddha* Karma Pakshi's mummified flesh, on which a white syllable had spontaneously appeared, still attached to the flesh; this gift delighted me and I thought that I should prepare it to be used as a "mother culture" and so share it with others.[857] I also had clear impressions of the omens connected with that holy site. I went to a large white boulder, which people called "the white tent," in front of the site, where we performed a *ganachakra* feast. There were excellent signs, such as rainbow clouds and a flock of many white and brown vultures landing near us.

I summoned a chant master from Ling and gave empowerments and oral transmissions for the Bön community. Then the *tertön* Tsewang Drakpa returned and I took part in a *drupchen* ritual based on the *sadhana* of enlightened mind called *The Wish-Fulfilling Gem*, including a ritual to consecrate sacred pills and a public empowerment at which the pills were distributed to the populace. Together, the *tertön* and I performed a *lhasang* ceremony, an offering of a golden libation, and a ritual to bind the gods and demons to their oaths of allegiance. I identified Pema Lhatsé as one of the eight "emanated" holy sites[858] at which beings were guided through enlightened activity—specifically, the holy site connected with the guiding of beings through the principle of the *padma* family—and I circumambulated the site, pointing out the route with my finger. Just as before, there were rainbow clouds, flocks of vultures, and so forth, and for two days the weather became as warm and pleasant as in summertime. [149a] As well during this time, every day at twilight there appeared a rainbow of bluish-green light that moved from the west like a blanket unfurling, to touch the peak of this holy site. One night around this time, I dreamed of an aristocratic man who was requesting a longevity empowerment from me; as his offering, he placed before me a garland of various jewels and some fine pieces of turquoise and coral, which he said weighed as much as three large lumps of silver. This was obviously an omen concerning my longevity.

I left many gifts for the Bönpo monastery, including a piece of property to provide income; representations of enlightened form, speech, and mind; shrine articles; musical instruments; sacred dance costumes; even sitting mats. To benefit the monks themselves and improve their living quarters, I appointed Khardo Chönam to oversee matters by keeping accounts, giving training, directing projects, and so forth.

A son of the Entok clan in Den had died, and I received an insistent summons saying that it was imperative that I come. So I went there and performed a ritual to purify obscurations affecting the deceased's consciousness. I also satisfied requests from patrons at places along my route, such as Nyen and Sakar. I then continued on to Drugu Dilkhar in Marong, where I met up again with the *tertön*. We performed a *lhasang* ceremony, an offering of a golden libation, and many feast offerings. There is a marvelous account of this place, that it was blessed when Guru Rinpoché used his miraculous powers to throw a piece of stone here from Zangdok Palri.

On the evening of the tenth day of the eleventh month I dreamed of what seemed at first to be a very ordinary building. But when I opened the door, [149b] I found myself in a remarkable, delightful, and elegantly-appointed temple. In the center of this was Tsokyé Dorjé. Above his head was Dechen Gyalmo,[859] dancing in space, appearing just as she is described in the practice focusing on the feminine principle found in The Heart Drop of Longchenpa. To Guru Tsokyé Dorjé's right were Padmakara and Padmasambhava, and to their right Pema Gyalpo and Loden Choksé. To the Guru's left were Dorjé Drollö and Seng-gé Dradrok, and most especially Shakya Seng-gé and Nyima Özer, the latter pair's forms being intensely radiant.[860] Nyima Özer was gazing at Bairotsana, who was seated in front of him, and his left hand was placed on Bairotsana's head as he conferred many oral transmissions on him. In my dream, I observed them for a short time.

Once I had finished my duties in that area, I returned to Rongyap, where I performed feast offerings, fulfillment rituals, offerings to the protective deities, and so forth, after which I went to a place in Pema Lhatsé called Karyak. In the record of the twenty-five holy places in eastern Tibet there is the following passage:

> Karlung is a cliff face shaped like a lotus cap;
> at the peak of the cap is Orgyen's meditation cave.

Just as this passage indicates, I found a white escarpment with three high points. It was difficult for anyone to ascend to the central one, so there had never been anyone seeing or hearing of a meditation cave there, but I went looking for it nonetheless, holding on to the vegetation and using rope ladders. Midway, set back in from a kind of ledge in the cliff face, I found a large and spacious cave and, at the back, a life-sized naturally occurring image of Padmasambhava. To the right of this cave was the "cave of the spiritual mentor," [150a] while to the left was the "cave of immortality and longevity." I discovered footprints in the rock and other visible signs of the presence of Guru Rinpoché and other accomplished masters of both the Bönpo and Buddhist traditions. Having received some small signs of spiritual attainments—some statues and holy substances—I began my descent, but a violent wind arose and made the return journey difficult.

I went to Ling because of a summons that required my presence there. I participated in a *drupchen* ritual based on Ratna Lingpa's cycle of Vajrakila and satisfied other requests made of me, after which I crossed over into Nyen and traveled through Khardo Rongkha. I performed feast offerings and other rituals at Sheldrak Ö-dzong, a major holy site at the head of the valley. That night I dreamed that I beheld the four-armed form of Avalokiteshvara, the "Guide of Beings," and joined in a feast gathering of *daka*s and *dakini*s in the palace of Chakrasamvara. I continued on to the Duddul Tseiphuk Cave and arrived the next day at Khardo Monastery, with the sky filled with rainbows. There I satisfied requests from both the monastic community and the local populace.

ON THE DAY OF THE NEW Earth Hare Year [1879-1880], in answer to the directive of the *tertön* Tsewang Drakpa, I went to Dzödong Temple and performed a consecration ritual, a ceremony to establish this as a holy site, and a ceremony for the longevity of Kuzhap Rinpoché, which led to several prophetic signs. I then went to Tashi Tsekdzong in Tsang-rong. That day there were amazing signs—rainbows shining with light, vultures and crows gathering, and so forth. [150b] At Chimé Phuk Cave, which is associated with Vimalamitra, I performed a feast offering focusing on Vajrakila and, in accordance with the usual custom, a *lhasang* ceremony and an offering of a golden libation. Once these tasks were completed, I returned homeward.

An order came from Dergé requiring my presence there, and en route I stopped at Lhadrang Monastery in upper Ön, where I satisfied the requests of the lamas and monks. Continuing on to Dergé Gönchen, I prepared all the primary and secondary articles for the rituals to fill the statues of the gurus and wealth deities with long mantras and to perform the respective *sadhana*s. Many masters and students, including the royal family of Dergé, participated in a very well-performed ritual of *sadhana* practice, focusing on the gurus and wealth deities and including shifts to recite the mantras continuously. Once I had satisfied all the requests made of me, I continued my homeward journey, passing through Chayang.

I arrived back at the hermitage during the second month. Although I had an injury that bothered me somewhat, I performed a number of ceremonies. I was completely occupied with fulfilling requests for empowerments and oral transmissions and with editing the rituals from *The Treasury of Precious Hidden Teachings.* Öngen and others were insisting that I must attend the vase consecration ritual this year, so I went. In addition, I reconsecrated the new images in Lhasar Temple and practiced on behalf of Tsulthrim Gyatso, the old attendant of Khyentsé Rinpoché from Dzongsar Monastery.

In the fifth month the *tulku* of Dorjé Drak sent word that I must attend a *mendrup* ritual focusing on the Eight Commands, so I went there. Once the ceremonies were completed, I returned home. [151a] I filled many large and small statues, including the previously constructed statue of Vajrasattva Heruka, with long mantras and consecrated them. Rigdzin Drölma was setting out on a pilgrimage to central Tibet, so I performed empowerments, *lhasang* ceremonies, and other rituals to facilitate her journey, after which she set out. I was kept busy with my obligations, such as the oral transmission for the concise medical work *Ewam* that Lama Pema Norbu requested. I also went to Dzongsar Monastery, where I spent a long time giving empowerments, oral transmissions, and instructions to satisfy the needs of many people who had gathered there. Because my lord guru's health was precarious, I only asked for a brief audience.

That year a new meditation center was being constructed in upper Dzong, so I went there, satisfying the needs of my patrons along the way. A day or two before I was to arrive, I dreamed one night of being swept away in a flood, only to have Tara pull me out by the hand and deliver me to safety. I also dreamed of being met by an escort of monks in formal regalia more splendid than the feathers of a peacock. In one dream, I found several caches of *terma*s in accord with a prophecy from Tulku Rinpoché and opened the seals on these to find two volumes of texts, the first part of one closely resembling texts from The Heart Drop of Longchenpa, and the other volume containing several important chapters of history and prophecies.

When I arrived in upper Dzong, the work on constructing the new meditation center had already been going on for about a year. I performed the *ganachakra* feast from The United Intent of the Three Roots a few times, [151b] and for a few days a group of three of us, master and students, performed an intensive *sadhana* ritual focusing on the rediscovered *terma* of Drimé Kunga focusing on Jinasagara. On the day we concluded, I performed a public empowerment in conjunction with the concluding ceremony to consolidate the spiritual attainments of the practice. During this empowerment there were some very auspicious signs. I received a letter from Dabzang Tulku,[861] accompanied by the gift of a fine turquoise, and Lhodrak Sungtrul sent me a shawl of orange wool from central Tibet. As well, the weather during this period was exceptionally mild and there were rainbow-tinged clouds and other excellent omens.

For some time there had been prophetic accounts that told of the necessity of building a stupa at Sé Khardo in order to avert invading forces at the Tibetan borders. In accord with this fact, I received word from the Dergé authorities that I must go there. As well, the *tertön* Tsewang Drakpa arrived and we traveled together to the palace of Dergé, where we drew up plans for the stupa. In conjunction with a Vajrakila practice, I performed the suppression ritual.[862] At Sé Khardo I performed a *lhasang* ceremony to establish harmony and an offering of a golden libation, and performed a ritual to bind the gods and demons to their oaths of allegiance. We sought out the power site[863] of the area, and while we were performing the suppression ritual, a hawk suddenly fell from the sky and died there, which everyone talked about as an excellent sign.

The stupa was built stage by stage and we then filled it with long mantras and performed the consecration ritual. After satisfying the needs of my patrons in that region and on the road back, I returned to Dzongsar Monastery. When I met with my precious lord guru, [152a] he told me of a dream in which he had seen right in front of him a very special "regent" statue that resembled Padmasambhava. It was an amazing image, complete with a throne, a thousand-petaled lotus seat, a backrest, and was housed in a small chapel.

He asked a woman what this was and she replied, "This is Bairotsana's representative."[864] To this he retorted, "But it's not Bairotsana, it's Padmasambhava!" She said, "The two of them are identical, there is no distinction between them." Immediately Khyentsé Rinpoché heard what sounded like the word "pig," whereupon the chapel housing the statue exploded into fragments. The statue itself tilted to one side, so that Rinpoché was deeply concerned that it might be broken. He awoke at that point in a very upset state of mind.

Rinpoché then related that he had fallen asleep and dreamed again, this time of meeting Zhechen Öntrul. He asked Öntrul what the former dream had indicated and Öntrul replied, "That was a sign that Kongtrul will face a real crisis next year."

"What kind of crisis?," Khyentsé Rinpoché asked.

"The crisis spiritual masters face when their time has come," was the reply. Öntrul continued, "I myself passed away at the age of sixty-eight, and Kongtrul will be sixty-eight next year."

"What can be done to help?" asked Khyentsé Rinpoché.

Öntrul told him, "If Kongtrul goes into a strict retreat for a year, during which time he doesn't meet anyone and focuses on the stages of approach and accomplishment—especially the practice of *The Lotus Distillation*—really practicing deeply, there will be no problem."

Not only did Khyentsé Rinpoché have these dreams, [152b] but he told me of other negative omens. He said, "When Kuzhap Choktrul was first setting out from central Tibet to return to his monastic seat, seven of the finest lamas in his entourage passed away, including Lama Gönwang. While they were en route, many more lamas died, a Lama Sang-ngak among them. Word has come that Kuzhap Rinpoché won't return until next year. All this means that you definitely should not stay at the Palpung hermitage, so it is important that you do your retreat in places around here. Since the *tertön* is still with us, we will have him do a divination to determine which places would be suitable."

I myself returned to my residence. While I was performing the year-end *torma* ritual focusing on my protective deity, the front part of the large *torma* crumbled.

DURING THE CELEBRATION for the new Iron Dragon Year [1880-1881], as in the past I took part in two *drupchen* rituals, one after the other, focusing on Vajrasattva and the *kama* tradition of Samyak. I then gave the retreatants whatever advice I could and they completed their program. The *tertön* Tsewang Drakpa arrived and told me that he had performed a divination according to the wishes of Kuzhap Rinpoché's household. It indicated that Pema Shelphuk Cave, Karmo Taktsang, and Dagam Wangphuk Cave were completely inappropriate sites for my retreat. Upper Dzong proved favorable, and when the *tertön* stayed for a day at Nya-lhung, the signs were also favorable. He said that he had also relayed this news to Dzongsar Monastery.

It was time for me to perform feast offerings and rituals to avert negativity on the major mountain peaks and at the four major holy sites of the region, [153a] and the *tertön* accompanied me to the nearby places and we performed the rituals together. The *tertön* told me that since the caves of Thukjé Könphuk and Dagam Wangphuk were holy places associated with longevity, I should plan to do a year of retreat in each at some point, and accordingly I did so.

For those who were to conduct the ritual of Chakrasamvara according to Vajrapani's[865] *Commentary on the Beginning Section*, I performed an extensive empowerment for this cycle—both the preparatory phase and the actual empowerment—as well as giving other transmissions. By this point, the woodblocks for printing about forty volumes of *The Treasury of Precious Hidden Teachings* were ready, so I worked with a very altruistic editor and prepared the texts for publication. When the arrangements for this were more or less in place, I set out for my hermitage, encountering buffeting winds and other signs that the local spirits were displeased.

At Dzongsar I met my precious lord guru, and on the tenth day we performed a feast ritual for The General Assembly of the Three Roots, which he had finished codifying. Khyentsé Rinpoché bestowed the empowerment, oral transmissions, and instructions for this practice in great detail; he told me that he felt disturbances at the outset, but that eventually there came a sense of peace. He also conferred the transmissions for his rediscovered *terma* teaching The Five Remedial Deities, as well as the Blazing Vajra tradition of Vajrapani and the prayer of Ngari Drupchen based on the six-syllable mantra.

On the morning that I was leaving, Rinpoché's health was much improved and he said that further teachings had been codified. Prior to this, he had codified the outer *sadhana* for the longevity practice of The Heart Drop of Mitra, but now the inner and secret sadhanas had been finished [153b] and with delight he conferred on me the empowerments for these further elements of the practice.

I had dreamed that someone read to me a text that I was told had been authored by Lochen Dharma Shri of Mindroling Monastery; I had a clear impression of a table of contents for the work. I came to Khyentsé Rinpoché with this experience and all my more recent insights, going back some time. He gave me a great deal of advice, including the observation that if I found even a single stone at Dzongshö, it would be unwise to lose it. I then set off, arriving at the hermitage on the fourteenth.

On the fifteenth, I performed an extensive version of a *lhasang* ceremony and an offering of a golden libation. I then established the outer boundary[866] for my personal retreat, which I began on the seventeenth. I carried out the practices focusing on the guru, chosen deity, and *dakini* in their proper order, reciting many mantras for each. During the breaks between my meditation sessions, I spent all the time I could composing rituals for inclusion in *The Treasury of Precious Hidden Teachings*. I had a number of confused dreams that indicated disturbances cropping up.

Then one night I dreamed of a temple that I felt I myself had erected. On the right side of the hall I saw Red Hayagriva with three faces and six arms,[867] with the retinue figures all complete on the deity's seat. The form was about one story high and shone with a brilliance that made it difficult to look at. Another time I dreamed of a temple with splendid appointments, in which many *siddha*s were seated in rows. To my left was Shantigarbha,[868] very clearly visible, holding a *kartari* knife, and enjoying the company of a *dakini* with whom he was engaged in amorous play.

My retreat dwelling, which had been built previously, involved some risks, since it was rather close to the edge of the cliff; [154a] among other problems, water flooded down the cliff face onto it. There was no temple as such, just a sort of nomad's dwelling. The whole situation was so unsuitable that it became essential to have new buildings constructed. By way of my mother, I sent word to the king of Dergé, explaining my predicament. Both the Dergé government and that of Shok sent laborers. Once I had completed my retreat on the guru practice, I performed the ritual of Hevajra to prepare the ground, whereupon we laid the foundation and the plan of the buildings.

Jamyang Gelek,[869] who had finished his retreat at Palpung, came by way of Dzongsar; he assumed the bulk of the responsibilities, and from that time to this it is he who has been primarily responsible for all the activities carried out at this center, especially the construction of the statues and so forth. Concerning this person, when my lord guru and I were staying together in Paljor and Jamyang Gelek came to see him, Khyentsé Rinpoché told me, "There is a connection between the two of you as spiritual master and student, for you are a rebirth of Döndrup Gyalpo, a lay tantric priest of the Nyang clan, while he was once Tsélé Rinpoché.[870] The fact that you took The Union of All Rare and Precious Jewels as one of your main meditation practices is a karmic holdover of that lifetime when you were together. How very fine!" At any rate, there is certainly a connection between us based on our shared aspirations. During the periods between the demolition and clearing of old buildings and the construction of new ones, I moved for a time to the caves of Wangchen-phuk (a holy site associated with the principle of enlightened speech) and Tsitta Sangphuk (a site associated with that of mind) [154b] and continued my retreat. By the eighth month my new retreat dwelling was finished, and three artisans began building the niches for the statues of the deities and preparing the pigments for painting these. The central image constructed was that of Orgyen Zahorma, with many statues of gurus and deities as his retinue; over time we finished filling these images with long mantras and consecrating them.

In the ninth month Rigdzin and his attendants arrived at the outset of a pilgrimage they were undertaking, and I met with them for a brief time. During this period I had several dreams in which I saw omens of demonic activity and other disturbing signs, but for the most part there were many omens of definite benefit for my longevity, such as dreams about stupas and *tsa-tsa*s. I also dreamed of a few things that struck me as amazing but were difficult to interpret.

On one occasion I dreamed of arriving at the central temple in Samyé Monastery. As I was reciting a seven-branch prayer and offering many confession prayers in the presence of the main statue, off to my right I saw the actual form of Red Chakrasamvara according to the tradition of Luhipa, as well as Gya Zhangtrom,[871] looking still in their prime. The *tertön* Chokgyur Lingpa seemed to come down from the sky and land on the grass. He said, "I am very attached to my sister, for the bliss that she confers through the process of melting is very intense." So saying, he gazed upward, and off in the southwestern sky [155a] I beheld a mass of white light shaped like a stemmed lotus. I had a dream of the omniscient Chökyi Jungné bestowing on me the formal authorization for the practice of White Manjushri. In one dream I met Karma Chagmé, who told me many accounts of beings being liberated; I touched my head to his heart center, praying to him with deep devotion and formulating many aspirations.[872] I dreamed of seeing a human-sized standing form of the Four-Armed Avalokiteshvara, and of finding a large crystal and polishing the lower portion, only to find that the stone changed into a radiant white statue of the omniscient Dolpopa. In one dream, I met my lord guru, standing in warm sunlight and holding in both his hands a statue of a white figure that I took to be Maitreya, a standing figure with the hands in the gesture of perfect generosity and clad in white silk robes. My spiritual master told me, "This is a *terma* that was discovered at the meditation retreat center of Palpung," and placed the statue on my head as he chanted many verses, conferring a blessing on me and arousing in me a boundless sense of delight. I dreamed of a woman of fine appearance who fell ill and whose body took on a deathly pallor; she then revived and her color returned, whereupon she uttered several cryptic prophecies. Chokgyur Lingpa came to me in a dream, wearing bulky bone ornaments, to show me by gestures that he was entrusting me to codify several new *terma*s of his, and that it would be excellent for these to appear. [155b]

I also dreamed of a lama handing me a skull cup of a golden color, with the design of an eight-spoked wheel inside. He told me, "This is from the skull of a fine lama. It would be wonderful if you used it as your drinking vessel." Not long after this, something very auspicious happened in connection with this dream, for Dzogchen Rinpoché gave me the cup made from Bairotsana's skull, which was a *terma* discovered by Taksham.[873]

During the winter solstice I performed three days each of certain rituals to avert negativity—the *torma* ritual from Ratna Lingpa's cycle of Vajrakila, the *torma* ritual from The Gathering of All the Dakinis' Secrets, and the averting ritual of Ratna Thöthreng[874] from the Tersar tradition. When these rituals were completed, I undertook an extensive personal retreat focusing on the *sadhana* called *The Heart Essence of Enlightened Activity* from The United Intent of the Three Roots. I received many presents from Dzongsar Rinpoché,[875] including a long, sleeveless monk's vest and offering utensils.

This year, with the completion of the statues housed in the meditation center, in the light of the rising sun there appeared white rainbow-like rays, so bright as to be hard to look at, going off to the right and left, and three times there fell thick showers of blossom-like flakes of snow. Nothing like this had ever seen before.

The incarnation of Karma Chagmé came, and I gave several transmissions to satisfy his requests. During this whole year I had no greater need to meet people and receive guests than what I have described, so my spiritual practice flourished and I was able to finish many of the sections of *The Treasury of Precious Hidden Teachings* in the breaks between my meditation sessions.

DURING THE CELEBRATIONS for the new Iron Serpent Year [1881-1882], I was visited by Dzogchen Rinpoché, [156a] who came to receive the transmissions for my instructions concerning the Seven-Line Prayer, so I gave the entire cycle of empowerments and oral transmissions. Following that, for about three nights running I experienced a great many confused thoughts, but I still wrote the part of this cycle concerned with the feminine principle. I spent some time in strict personal retreat, focusing on my usual practices.

In the fourth month I felt a sense of disturbance, with signs indicating the influence of *gyalpo* demons. This marked the resurgence of the negative force of contamination that had afflicted me previously. I suddenly developed an illness, and on the following day a letter arrived from Kuzhap Rinpoché, in which he told me that I must accept the confessions of those who had previously quarreled with me. These troublemakers had never entertained the slightest intention of expressing regret or confessing their wrongdoing, and even though some three or four years had passed, none of them had said a single word to me. Although Kuzhap Rinpoché tried to act on their behalf, nothing came of it—at least nothing that you would find discussed in the teachings—but I am certain that I felt not the slightest trace of malice toward them. I replied to Kuzhap Rinpoché, saying that even if they had some *samaya* connection with me, the number of years that had already passed meant that all the degrees of contradiction, impairment, transgression, and violation had already occurred,[876] and that I could certainly see no way for this to be purified and our *samaya* connection restored by mere *pro forma* gestures. Kuzhap Rinpoché intended to come and see me during the fifth month. The sense of this negative energy of contamination became extremely palpable and I had to forego several of my meditation sessions. As soon as he had arrived, my boils burst and I felt slightly better. [156b] I requested an audience with him and fulfilled his request to perform a few empowerments.

During the earlier of the two sixth months,[877] I completed the requisite number of mantras for my retreat, as laid out in the source texts for the practices. I performed a hundred feast offerings, a *lhasang* ceremony, and other rituals, after which I concluded my retreat. During this time I had many random dreams, but no time to write all of them down. But I did dream on two occasions of seeing the spirit of a monk who had been knifed to death[878] robbing the spirit of someone in our retreat center, and of oppressing that monk's spirit by meditating on *The Wrathful Display of Vajrakila* and causing it to flee. I also was startled awake on these occasions.

One night I dreamed I was reciting a prayer that begins, "The sun in the southwest . . . ," and so forth. As I did so, I felt deep longing as I contemplated Orgyen Rinpoché's enormous kindness to human beings in his lifetime in this realm and to bloodthirsty demons in later times.[879] Immediately I beheld Guru Rinpoché himself as a large and heavyset lama, his form a dark red. Earlier in life I had acquired two fine crystals, one larger than the other, and the thought now occurred to me that this had been an omen that I would prosper. Finally, I felt great devotion to Guru Rinpoché and he stretched out both hands and placed them on my head. I received the four levels of empowerment.

In another dream I found myself in a fine temple. The principal images were murals of Avalokiteshvara Khasarpana and White Tara, but there were many other images painted in gold; at first these all seemed to be drawings, but finally, to my delight, I saw them become the actual forms of the deities, majestic and shining with light. There was a huge pile of *tsa-tsas* in the right hand doorway. [157a] Someone told me that these needed to be consecrated, for they were to serve as the focus for people of the region to do prostrations and circumambulations. I performed a consecration ritual.

I had clear impressions of having been both Yön-gé Mingyur Dorjé and Khyungdrak Dorjé[880] in previous lifetimes. I dreamed of meeting someone with a body of golden hue; I felt with great devotion that this was the buddha Ratnagarbha, and was bathed in the radiance from his visage. In one of my dreams, I found myself in a temple, sitting on a small throne and dressed in fine robes, gazing upward at the blessed and radiant presences of such masculine deities as Chakrasamvara according to the tradition of Luhipa, Hevajra, and Mahamaya, and such feminine deities as the Four-Armed Goddess.[881] Behind me was a large gathering of people chanting the long mantra of Amitayus in a low murmur, and I joined in the chanting. I dreamed that the guardian deity Red Kshetrapala revealed himself to me in his dismounted form, and that I beheld the forms of Yamaraja and Brahmanarupa.[882] In conjunction with the practice of The United Intent of the Three Roots, I performed an extensive consecration of the statues in the meditation center, using the ritual called *The Source that Yields Virtue and Excellence* from the Mindroling tradition.

During the latter sixth month, with a large number of my students I participated in a lengthy *drupchen* ritual based on The United Intent of the Three Roots. I also performed offering rituals and thanksgiving ceremonies to the protective deities of the old and new schools. I gave many empowerments and oral transmissions connected with the cycles of the Seven-Line Prayer to the son of Serpa Tertön and a number of others who gathered from all directions for this purpose. [157b] I made feast offerings at holy sites and in caves, after which I went to Dzongsar Monastery. There I met with my precious lord guru, to whom I offered all the empowerments and oral transmissions for the Taksham cycle of The Guru: The Wish-Fulfilling Gem; the practice transmitted by Mati[883] called *The Wish-Fulfilling Gem that Embraces Everything*, and Dechen Lingpa's Heart Drop of the Dakini. A great many people had gathered at Dzongsar, including Dzigar Choktrul, and I satisfied their individual requests for various empowerments, oral transmissions, and instructions. I also gave the oral transmission for my *Treasury of the Knowable* as well as for *The Profound Inner Meaning*, the two short treatises, and other texts.

I then returned to my hermitage, where I gave the appropriate empowerments, oral transmissions, and instructions needed by the five new candidates who were beginning their retreat program. I then performed the annual Vajrakila ritual to avert negativity, as well as the installation of new *torma*s on the shrine and the offerings to the protective deities. I prepared new lists of the texts housed in the several temples, ensuring easier searches, and other useful features, after which I went directly to Dzongsar Monastery. There I did a detailed edit of the latest volumes of my *Treasury of Spiritual Advice* that had been published.

DURING THE CELEBRATIONS for the new Male Water Horse Year [1882-1883], I spent my time in spiritual practice and the recitation of prayers. The master of Thartsé and his students came expressly to see me, and on the fourteenth day of the month commemorating the Buddha's spiritual miracles I performed the preparatory ritual of the nine deity mandala of Jinasagara, followed by the main empowerment on the fifteenth. [158a] This began a series of empowerments and oral transmissions that included the five deity mandala of Chakrasamvara, the Vajradhatu mandala of the Yogatantra class, the mandala of The Deities of the Five Classes of Tantra[884] from the Shangpa tradition, all the Chakrasamvara cycles (such as Vajrapani's *Commentary on the Beginning Section*, from the Jonang tradition), all the cycles of Yamantaka, and my large and newly edited collection, *The Tantric Treasury of the Kagyü School.* These transmissions were completed on the twenty-first day of the third month.

At the outset of this series, I dreamed of being in a finely-appointed temple, in which I found myself in the actual presence of the two teachers of sutra and tantra[885] (whose forms were rather indistinct) and Sachen,[886] whose face was white with a reddish tinge. I prayed to them with devotion. Then the Fourteenth Gyalwang Karmapa entered and I escorted him to his place, a seat strewn with pink flowers. I was given many relics, including one of Karmapa's teeth, which resembled a white conch shell. In another dream my lord guru was holding a yellow scroll of many sheets, about a foot long, which he said was a *terma* discovered by Duddul. He showed me the decorative *lancha* script and I asked him to bless me with the text. He also explained to me the structure of the basic instruction manuals, the "mother" and "child" texts. After we had made preparations for the ritual of Lekden[887] according to the Tersar tradition, that evening I dreamed of the clouds in the sky parting to reveal the actual form of Lekden, to whom I cried out with longing three times. [158b]

At this point, Kuzhap Rinpoché, Dzogchen Rinpoché, the Gemang incarnation,[888] Lingtrul, Kuchen of Palyul Monastery,[889] Gyarong Yatrul, Tertön Mingyur Tulku, Adzom Drukpa, and many other lamas and *tulku*s came specifically to receive the empowerments and oral transmissions for *The Treasury of Precious Hidden Teachings*. As a preliminary means to dispel obstacles we read the Kangyur collection aloud,[890] performed feast offerings and fulfillment rituals, and offered confession. Then, to begin the transmissions, within the context of a *drupchen* ritual focusing on The United Intent of the Gurus, I gave the major and minor empowerments of this cycle. Kuzhap Rinpoché then had to leave. For the other lamas and *tulku*s who had gathered, beginning on the nineteenth day of the fourth month, for the fourth time I gave the empowerments and oral transmissions for *The Treasury of Precious Hidden Teachings*. These were completed by the first day of the eighth month, whereupon the majority of the lamas and *tulku*s returned to their home regions.

On the tenth day of that month I performed a *ganachakra* feast at Khandroi Drora. That morning at dawn, I had a kind of visionary meditative experience in my dreams. In the sky in front of me, I clearly saw the form of Orgyen Nangsi Zilnön.[891] Under his seat were two lines of verse, which I read and committed to memory; the import of these lines was that, for the sake of promoting the Buddhist teachings and benefiting all beings in general, and for my, the yogin's, benefit in particular, I should complete thirteen *drupchen* rituals in an unblemished environment and with spiritual companions whose *samaya* connection with me and each other was not impaired.

The masters of Ngor and his students, Dzogchen Rinpoché, the *tertön*'s rebirth, and others—some thirty people in all—promised me that they would study, teach, promulgate, and practice the instructions found in my *Treasury of Spiritual Advice*, [159a] so at the outset I performed for them a major *torma* empowerment focusing on the *dakini*s.[892] On the fifteenth day of the eighth month I began giving the empowerments, oral transmissions, and instructions from *The Treasury of Spiritual Advice*. These were finished by the fourteenth day of the tenth month. On the fifteenth day, in conclusion we very methodically performed a *ganachakra* feast and, at Khandroi Drora, an offering ceremony for the "one hundred families of yoginis." I also gave the empowerments and oral transmissions for the Khön tradition of Samyak, and for the white and black forms of Vajravidarana. Dezhung Tulku[893] came, and in response to his specific requests I gave an overview and explanation of *The Hevajra Tantra* according to the Ngok tradition. The lamas and *tulku*s then returned to their home regions.

During the winter solstice, while I was performing the annual ritual of Vajrakila to avert negativity, for two nights running I heard the laughter-like cry of owls on Rapsel Plain. Being an older person with some experience, I knew this to indicate a grave possibility for something calamitous to occur, but when Gelek made some remark about "being superstitious about bird calls," I became self-conscious and let it go.

During the sun's northward progress,[894] I finished a personal retreat on the Venerable Goddess, including supplementary mantra repetitions, after which I went to Dzongsar Monastery. There I requested an audience with my precious lord and paid my respects. On the twenty-fifth day, he bestowed on me the empowerment and oral transmissions for the cycle The Guru: The Wheel of Supreme Bliss, a rediscovered *terma* from Gyatön Pema Wangchuk. I made an offering to the monastery to sponsor a ritual for the reading of the Kangyur to avert negative omens. [159b] I also explained the situation to my lord guru, and on the twenty-ninth day he conferred the empowerment for the practice of Hayagriva called Liberating All Arrogant Ones,[895] rediscovered by Drugu Yangwang Tsal. In conjunction with that, Khyentsé Rinpoché oversaw an all-day group ceremony and a ritual to avert negativity that lasted halfway through the night. The next day I felt extremely disturbed at first, but gradually calmed down until I felt quite at ease; my spiritual master remarked that he felt no serious problem would come of these omens. Then, in his enormous kindness to me, my spiritual master bestowed an extensive series of empowerments, oral transmissions, and instructions, including the practice of Tara transmitted by Yakchar Ngönmo, called *Freedom from All Fear*; the Hayagriva cycle of Lord Molmi Khyil, the Lotus cycle of peaceful and wrathful deities transmitted by Nyima Seng-gé; the cycle of Black Jambhala transmitted by Balpo A-Hum; the seven cycles of instructions of the Zhijé School from Lhatsün Ngönmo; the Kurukulle form of Padmadakini from Rongzom Chökyi Zangpo; *The Treasure of the Enlightened Mind of Samantabhadra* from Mangpo Jangchub Lingpa; *Vajra Nectar* from Ramo Shelmen; *Supreme Compassion: The Lamp That Illuminates Meaning*, a practice of Avalokiteshvara from Drodul Letro Lingpa;[896] and *The Heart Essence of Light*, the *guru sadhana* of Drimé Kunga. I also received transmissions for several *terma* cycles that I had not received before.

Many times over the years, I had felt that a very important purpose was being served by the Tersar traditions of teachings, given that they are profound instructions that were intended for our times, to guide anyone in whatever way necessary. Even more important were more ancient *terma* cycles from the past, whose names one doesn't even meet with nowadays, but I did not have the good fortune to be able to locate other noble or famous individuals still living, [160a] who could transmit these to me. During this period of time, however, I had the opportunity to be with my precious lord, who is authenticated in vajra prophecies and in my own direct experience to have been a true master of the seven modes of transmission.[897] In cases where only fragments existed of hidden teachings discovered by authentic *tertön*s in the past, he was able to codify these instructions. This opportunity was in some part a fulfillment of my repeated prayers. As Orgyen Rinpoché said,

> You don't hold gold in esteem,
> and gold doesn't fall into the hands of the poor.
> You don't hold the teachings in esteem,
> and the teachings don't fall into the hands of the unfortunate.[898]

I feel that my fortune has been incredibly good to have effortlessly found what is so hard to find—all the teachings my heart could desire. In cases where there were still texts available for more ancient *terma*s, but the line of empowerment and oral transmission had been broken, I had only to pray to Khyentsé Rinpoché and Guru Rinpoché himself would appear to him in the form of the respective *tertön*, conferring the lineage of direct transmission on my spiritual master. As for his newly codified *terma*s, the *dakini*s and *terma* guardians would offer him the actual yellow scrolls, and the codified texts would include the stages of development and completion, as well as activity rituals, concise but complete in meaning, profound and condensed—his *Molten Gold* practice, for example. Khyentsé Rinpoché seemed to be delighted with each and every text, every section, of teachings that could be considered *terma*. [160b]

DURING THE CELEBRATIONS for the new Water Sheep Year [1883-1884], my lord guru had a vision of the great *tertön* Sang-gyé Lingpa. This master told him, "It is excellent that you and Bayo Chözang—who was both my spiritual master and my student—have managed to promulgate many ancient *terma*s anew. However, if you can accomplish this with some twenty-five more ancient *terma*s, this will fulfill Guru Rinpoché's enlightened intent. For both of you, too, this will ensure that your lives and destinies will be completely fulfilled. As a way to dispel hindrances to this undertaking, it is crucial that you pursue spiritual practice and perform feast offerings at major holy sites." Shortly after Khyentsé Rinpoché related this vision to me, I wrote the details down and offered this account to him, but he said nothing. I wondered whether he was displeased that I had done so.

Khyentsé Rinpoché also bestowed on me the oral transmissions for the commentary on the "Single Intent" interpretation of the Drigung Kagyü School, the treatise on the three levels of ordination from the Taklung School, and other works. At one point he fell ill and it was up to me to satisfy the requests of the many people gathered there, including giving the empowerment for The Complete Gathering of the Eight Commands. I also finished my new editions of several cycles of teachings. During this period, one morning at dawn I dreamed of donning a crown of the five families and upper and lower vestments[899] and then entering a large temple. There was a gathering made up entirely of lay tantric priests, [161a] who were performing an activity ritual, all of them chanting and playing music. At the far end of the temple were the actual presences of the Guru in the form of the Three Roots, the masculine and feminine protective deities in union, and other deities. Off to one side were many practitioners chanting the six-syllable mantra *Om mani padme hum* in a pleasing murmur. I went outside to a nearby cliff face, a pilgrimage site where I found several crystals. There was also a small crystal stupa with its vase slightly damaged; as soon as I picked it up, it grew into a radiant crystal stupa about a foot and a half tall. The bottom broke off, and I put the spire in the folds of my robe, giving the lower portion to my attendant to carry. In my dream, we then went up and over a mountain pass.

Around this time, a mild form of smallpox began spreading throughout the region around the monastery and everyone fell ill. On the eleventh day of the second month Khyentsé Rinpoché's health improved slightly; he recounted the histories of his rediscovered *terma*s in great detail and I wrote down an account of these. On the thirteenth I went into his presence and he told me, "Regardless of what prophecies of future events may come, it is completely inappropriate to write these down or otherwise record them. It is best not to hold on to such things, but just to let them go. Now that you have written things down, once something is written down it must be held onto, so we should prepare some accounts dealing with spiritual practice." [161b] So we compiled several detailed accounts—of thirteen undisturbed holy sites that could easily be reached by pilgrims; of *terma*s with unbroken lineages, which focused on gurus, chosen deities, and *dakini*s; and of methods to practice longevity *sadhana*s, both old and new. Khyentsé Rinpoché also offered ingots of silver to sponsor me in my practice of *drupchen* rituals.

I went up to Dzongshö, where I spent several days in a personal retreat using a practice that focused on the feminine principle. About the twentieth of the month I contracted smallpox but did not fall seriously ill, and after about ten days I recovered. However, I immediately developed a blood and subtle energy condition that nearly killed me. I recovered from this after seven or eight days, only to be further stricken by a particularly virulent form of lymphatic disorder. Several doctors made a great fuss about this, saying that there was some fundamental problem with my lymphatic system. I also heard people talking about applying spiritual remedies.

By the fifth month I was feeling somewhat better, so when Khenpo Rinchen Dargyé[900] arrived I was able to perform several empowerments and oral transmissions from the Tersar cycles of Chokgyur Lingpa and other teachings. As well, Gyatrul of Palyul Monastery came specifically to receive the empowerments, oral transmissions, and instructions that had not been included in *The Treasury of Precious Hidden Teachings* previously, so I gave these to him. The prince of Ling came, accompanied by his lay and monastic retinue, and I satisfied their individual requests. Given that I was still ill, I went to the hot springs of Dzumtsa and Tingtsa to take the healing waters. This eased my symptoms—the burning and itching, the pustules, and the swellings.

I felt much better than before, so for the first of the *drupchen* rituals I was to undertake I went to Dagam Wangphuk Cave, where I nominally took part in a ritual based on the Heart Drop of the Exalted Goddess of Immortality. [162a] On this occasion, however, we had only the barest essentials in the way of offering utensils and so forth, and couldn't make any further preparations. As well, there were only eleven of us, master and students, so even the shifts of people doing ongoing mantra repetition didn't happen as they should have.[901] As we neared completion, in the middle of the night a monk who was mentally unstable went to the top of the cliff above and hurled rocks down on us, forcing everyone to flee inside the cave. So there were great disturbances, and my lymphatic disorder flared up again, until I felt as though I were sitting in a fire.

Beginning at this point, every time I performed a feast offering I had no idea whether the spiritual character of my companions was unimpaired or not, as I myself had no psychic insight about this. But to ensure that at least the letter of the prophecies was observed rather than being ignored, I insisted that a young, morally pure girl attend the *ganachakra* feasts. When the *drupchen* rituals were completed, there were many who gathered to receive an empowerment, so I would perform a public empowerment each time. I would then return to take the waters at the hot springs, and so healed gradually.

For the second *drupchen* ritual, I went to Pema Shelri, where we began the practice of the *sadhana* of The Ancestral Line of the Masters of Awareness from the Northern Treasures cycles. This time there were more participants than previously, including Lama Paljin, a retreat master from Yilhung Yakzé, and his students. As well, Lama Pema Norbu and Lama Tsering[902] arrived from the hermitage. We made the necessary preparations and carried out the practice, incorporating daily offering ceremonies and other rituals to make the format more extensive as we progressed. When we completed the *drupchen*, there were rainbows and other excellent signs.

The third *drupchen* ritual was performed at Dzum Tsangkar and was based on the cycle The Guru: The Wheel of Supreme Bliss discovered by of Gyatön Lama. [162b] On this occasion there were more than twenty participants, for Lama Yönten, a Severance master from Palpung, came with his students. I stayed for a day or so in an empty meditation center on this spot, but due to the negative influence of a demon inhabiting the place, my health was disturbed and I did not have a pleasant time of it.

We undertook the fourth *drupchen* ritual, based on *The Heart Essence of Light*, the *guru sadhana* of Drimé Kunga, at the holy site of Thrawo in Dzing. My health was improving gradually. By this time I had completed the three *guru sadhana* practices.

The fifth *drupchen* ritual was at the "palace" of Deshek Düpa in Dzongshö, where we began our practice of The Supreme Gathering of Commands discovered by Orgyen Lingpa. During this *drupchen*, at dawn on the tenth day of the month I had a dream. From what I took to be the direction of Lhasa, Drenpa Namkha[903] and his sister, Yeshé Tsogyal, approached, carrying a sealed letter that came from the north, which they gave to me. Inside I found an image of the eleven-headed form of Mahakarunika with a consort. They also gave me a scroll containing prophecies and advice, as well as about five fine crystals. During this time, Moktsa Tulku of Kathok Monastery came to give me gifts, and I performed an ablution ritual and one hundred repetitions of a longevity empowerment for him. I also satisfied the requests of several of my more important patrons, after which I journeyed through Rakchap on my way to Pewar. When I was close to reaching Arap Nenang, from the west there appeared a rainbow that covered half the sky, of many colors but with a predominant shade of dark bluish-green. There were many spheres of light, large and small, [163a] surrounded by rings of rainbow light. This all lasted a long time. Those who had some knowledge of the region said that they had never seen the like of this before, and took it to be something quite marvelous.

In front of the holy site of Godawari, I stayed in a new meditation center that Garjé Drodok had built inside a cave. Since he undertook to support us, a group of eight of us, master and students, did a group retreat for the deity Vajra Amrita.[904] We then prepared the substances for the ablution ritual of Amritakundali[905] and the incense of Humkara,[906] after which we began the intensive practice of *madana*.[907] At the outset the entire area, inside the cave and out, was permeated by the healing odor of medicines. The thought occurred to me that the way things turned out was indicative of my receiving blessings. Around this time I dreamed of a lay tantric practitioner whom I took to be Ramo Shelmen, who was dressed in blue robes and gave me many medicinal substances.

We then began the sixth *drupchen* ritual, based on the cycle of Vajra Amrita. We performed the *sadhana* of liberation, the outer *sadhana*, and the rituals to consecrate medicinal substances and pills, as well as the fire rituals connected with the four kinds of activity and the fifth—the sublime accomplishment of enlightenment. We finished with a feast of the heroes and heroines and other ceremonies to conclude the *drupchen*, We also performed the enactment of the six modes of freedom.

I then went to the holy site of Rameshvari in Atri, where Tashi Samdrup (a member of the Solpön clan) had built a new meditation center. There to begin with, a group of fifteen of us, master and students, undertook a group retreat based on the practice of the flawless Jinasagara. Then, under the sponsorship of the Solpön clan, we began the seventh *drupchen* ritual, based on the practice of Jinasagara. [163b] During this time, morning and evening a red light would tinge the mountains, and at midday the clouds and surrounding environment would take on a reddish hue. At night, several people could hear the sound of the six-syllable mantra being chanted, without being able to determine which direction it was coming from—up, down, inside the meditation center, or outside. The signs in my dreams were very positive—five women appeared and made symbolic gestures to me, I found crystals, and so on—and, in particular, I dreamed of meeting the glorious Düsum Khyenpa and of touching my head to his heart center, such that our minds merged.

Having completed the practices of three of my chosen deities on this site, I set out and on the way stopped at Evam Monastery, where I performed a consecration ritual and some empowerments. There I also came close to encountering someone with whom I had an issue of broken *samaya* connection, which caused me to suffer from extremely high blood pressure when I continued my journey. I spent several days at the estate of Chayang. As soon as my health improved I set out for Tashi Nenang, where I stayed in the new meditation center. The merchant of the Hotsé clan of Alo undertook to support us, so I began with a personal retreat based on the practice of Black Krodhi, a *terma* discovered by Nyang Rinpoché. For the eighth *drupchen* ritual, we used this practice of Krodhi and completed it with feast offerings and so forth. I also fulfilled the requests of many people, both the highborn and commoners.

When I was close to departing on my return journey, I has some troubling dreams of something disastrous happening to Kuzhap Rinpoché and of death threatening those in the meditation center at Palpung. On the twenty-fifth day of the eleventh month I crossed the pass and reached my hermitage, where I attended the rituals to install new *torma*s on the shrine and make offerings to the protective deities. [164a] At the start of the twelfth month I began a personal retreat focusing on the practice of Hayagriva called *Liberating All Arrogant Ones*, which I finished on the morning of the new moon.

AT THE OUTSET OF THE NEW Wood Monkey Year [1884-1885], I undertook a personal retreat on the practice of The Gathering of All the Dakinis' Secrets. The previous group of retreatants had finished their three-year program and left retreat. This year, there were several people who planned to start the program, but only after a delay, on the twelfth day of the later of the two second months.[908] Rigdzin Drölma had arranged for combined *drupchen* and *mendrup* rituals based on The United Intent of the Gurus, and I attended in the capacity of vajra master. These were completed during the waxing phase of the moon in the third month.

I then performed the empowerment of Ratna Lingpa's tradition of Vajrakila for the two *tulku*s of Tsedrum, as well as the transmissions requested by Tsawa Rinchen Namgyal and the empowerments and oral transmissions for the mandalas of the Kagyü tradition for a group that included Zhechen Tulku and

Lama Tashi Chöphel. In my breaks I maintained a rigorous schedule of editing ritual texts.

During the fourth month, in front of the cliff face of Pawo Wangchen Drak, under the sponsorship of Kuzhap Rinpoché a group of about forty-five of us, master and students, began the ninth *drupchen* ritual, based on the cycle of Mamo Ngöndzok Gyalpo from The Seven Profound Cycles. We arranged for a group of people to perform a separate ritual, a major ritual of ransom. There were evident signs of disturbance, such as lightning and hailstorms during the middle of the night.

During the waning phase of the moon, I went to a place in front of Pemakö in Lhamdo Burmo. There I found that the necessary preparations had been made under the auspices of the Dergé government. A group of fifty-five of us, master and students, [164b] began the tenth *drupchen* ritual, based on The Gathering of All the Dakinis' Secrets, alternating this with the five fulfillment rituals. We had a number of pleasant experiences—a rainbow appeared around the highest point of the site during the feast offering on the twenty-fifth day, and banks of summer flowers, quite unlike the usual kind, blossomed in profusion. By this time I had completed three practices focusing on the *dakini* principle.[909]

Finishing this *drupchen* ritual during the waxing phase of the moon in the fifth month, I made my way in stages back to my hermitage, where I performed the entire series of empowerments from the Sky Teachings for many retreatants, old and new. As well, I transmitted the empowerments, oral transmissions, and instructions for all the extant practices of the Shangpa School to Tsaptsa Tulku, who had come specifically to receive them.

In the sixth month I completed a personal retreat on a seven-day longevity practice in Dorjé Aphuk Cave in Meshö Rongmé, after which I went to the cliff face of Dorjé Drakmar in Munang. There I found that the queen mother of Dergé had made all the necessary arrangements. Since this was the site of the *terma* of Drugu Yangwang Tsal, a group of thirty-five of us, master and students, began the eleventh *drupchen* ritual, focusing on the practice of Hayagriva called *Liberating All Arrogant Ones*. Khyentsé Rinpoché had prepared a concise version of the practice, including the feast offering.

Once we had completed this *drupchen*, I went to Karmo Taktsang in Rongmé, where a comparable group of us began the twelfth ritual, based on the Mindroling tradition of Vajrasattva. We carried it out in a thorough and extensive manner, with feast offerings and so forth. Then, crossing Sidu Pass, I reached Pema Shelphuk Cave.

There we began the thirteenth *drupchen* ritual, [165a] based on the general *sadhana* of the five-family mandala of Amitayus—the cycle of instructions focusing on the principle of longevity from The Seven Profound Cycles, which all concern deities of the Three Roots. On the first day, Khen Lama Tashi Özer returned from central Tibet. He presented me with statues of the three deities of longevity[910] and other gifts, and so the omens were extremely positive. We performed extensive feast offerings, and in conjunction with the ceremony of accepting the spiritual attainments of the practice when we were concluding the *drupchen*, we performed a fire ritual that emphasized enriching activity. Khen Lama and others performed a ritual to turn back the escort and one to promote my longevity.

After these were concluded, I went to Dzongsar Monastery, where I met with my precious and omniscient guru. He conferred on me the empowerments and oral transmissions for Nyang Rinpoché's practice *Supreme Compassion: The Guide of Beings*; the complete empowerments for *The Sun of the Lucid Expanse*, a mother tantra cycle from Dorjé Lingpa; the oral teaching transmissions for a whole range of tantras; the Hum Cycle; and the empowerments, oral transmissions, and instructions for the Heart Drop cycles. Khyentsé Rinpoché told me that while he was conferring the teaching cycles from Dorjé Lingpa, he had the experience of seeing Dorjé Lingpa actually present in the sky in front of him, and of their minds merging as one. Among the four "Gatherings" discovered by this *tertön*, Khyentsé Rinpoché had received some text in symbolic script concerning The Gathering of the Dakinis' Commands and intended to codify this teaching further, but later distractions interrupted this plan. He also bestowed on me the complete range of empowerments for *The Sealed Visions* of the Fifth Dalai Lama; instructions on the process of distilling and retaining the subtle essences of the body; and the oral transmissions for his arrangements of the basic ritual and that of the Mindroling tradition of Vajrasattva.

Around this time the regent of Riwoché[911] arrived, [165b] and in response to his requests I gave the transmissions for three cycles—the Eight Commands, The United Intent of the Gurus, and Vajrakila—as well as the oral transmission of meditation instructions for the ritual of the Buddha and the eight great bodhisattvas; the pith empowerment from The United Intent of the Three Roots; and an empowerment to promote his longevity. After satisfying his requests, I continued on to Dongshö.

There, I transmitted several of the tantric cycles from *The Tantric Treasury of the Kagyü School* to the incarnation of Lodrö Nyima of Thrangu[912] and his students; and the empowerment, oral transmission, and instruction for Tarayogini to Kunzang Sönam and several people from Dzamthang Monastery. Norbu Tendzin and Tertön Sögyal[913] of Nyarong arrived, and for them I gave the empowerments and oral transmissions for the Ushnishavijaya cycle of Zhikpo Lingpa, my *sadhana* based on the Seven-Line Prayer, and the *Hum Sadhana* of Dorjé Drollö. From the Nangchen area came the masters Drupwang Tsoknyi,[914] Kyodrak, Dungtrul, and Saljé, as well as their students, and I satisfied their individual requests as well. From Drupwang Tsoknyi, in turn, I received complete instructions on the Oral Lineage cycle for the path of skillful means and on the "five stages" found in *The Innermost Gathering*, Ratna Lingpa's so-called *sadhana* of enlightened mind. From Dungtrul I received the empowerment for Chakrasamvara from the Barom Kagyü tradition.[915] I performed feast offerings and other rituals in the various practice caves in the area and then, in accord with my precious lord's previous orders, I went to Dzongsar Monastery at the end of the tenth month.

There, on the twenty-fifth day of the month, I began giving the oral transmissions for The Collected Tantras of the Nyingma Tradition to a large and noble gathering, my lord guru foremost among them. On the twenty-fifth day of the eleventh month Khyentsé Rinpoché conferred the empowerment, oral transmissions, and instructions for White Varahi, a rediscovered *terma* from Garwang Letro Lingpa. Once I had finished the oral transmissions for the Nyingma tantras, [166a] I gave other oral transmissions, using edition published by the Dergé printing house[916] of such works as the nine-volume collection of the Eight Commands cycle The Gathering of the Sugatas (one of Nyang Rinpoché's *termas*), and the Seven Treasures and the Trilogy of Being at Ease by Longchenpa.

DURING THE CELEBRATIONS for the new Female Wood Bird Year [1885-1886], on the first "victorious day"[917] I completed the foregoing oral transmissions and began reading through the collected works of Jonang Jetsün Taranatha; by the eighth day of the second month I had completely finished offering the oral transmissions for all eighteen volumes. I also satisfied individual requests, such as the empowerments and oral transmissions for Dechen Lingpa's cycle, The Heart Drop of the Dakini, which I performed for the *tertön*'s son, Tsewang Drakpa, and others.

I returned to my hermitage, reaching it on the fifth day of the third month.

But I was completely exhausted and suffering from highly elevated blood pressure. Still, I performed the major Kalachakra empowerment at the request of the *tertön*'s son, of Jamyang Drakpa of Khargo, and of the Kalachakra practitioners at Palpung Monastery.

The previous year, Rigdzin Drölma had fallen ill, and although I carried out all the medical procedures and rituals possible, she had shown no improvement. I spent two days performing one hundred and eight repetitions of an empowerment that focused on the peaceful and wrathful deities and was designed to aid someone dying, but she did not live. About ten retreat graduates, including Lama Ngöndrup, the vajra master of the meditation center, performed the transference of consciousness, while many practitioners who had completed the requisite personal retreats carried out rituals from both the old and new schools, to purify her mindstream of obscurations. Once these began, I too attended occasionally. I also requested aid from the masters who were best at guiding the deceased's consciousness—especially the "fathers and sons" of the Karma Kagyü and Drukpa Kagyü Schools[918] and my lord guru. I had offerings made on her behalf at the major religious centers of central Tibet, [166b] and made donations to the monastic communities. Her remains were cremated in the middle of four fire rituals being performed around the pyre. In such ways, I took pains to ensure that her memorial rites were very thorough and positive. During this time, the responsibility for sponsoring these rites was carried out by the deceased woman's elder brother, Tsering Döndrup. He was very generous in sponsoring offerings to the Three Jewels, commissioning statues, and so forth. Regardless of the task, great or small, he proved very reliable and capable, never putting anything off, but dealing with it right away. In particular, whatever I asked him to see to, no matter how difficult—whether the writing out of texts, the carving of woodblocks, the renovations to a temple, or what have you—he did whatever he could in every case, and thus was of inestimable benefit.

The Tönpa Jetsünma arrived specifically to receive the empowerment, oral transmissions, and instructions for *The Wish-Fulfilling Gem* from the Innermost Heart Drop of the Guru, so I transmitted these to her in detail. During this time, I dreamed that the Jetsünma gave me a handful of crystals and turquoise stones, and her maid gave me a handful of turquoise stones as well.

I undertook a personal retreat focusing on the deity Vijaya, and once that was completed I performed the ritual of one thousand offerings to Vijaya. At both the outset and the conclusion of this retreat, extremely positive signs occurred quite naturally. Then Tsering Döndrup sponsored the final commemorative rites, including the preparation of a hundred thousand *tsa-tsa*s, the erection of a multi-storied stupa, the rituals of the two Vimalas, and the ceremony to install the central axis, down to the concluding prayers of aspiration and other acts of virtue.[919]

Pressing invitations had come to me from Kathok Monastery, where both Donyen and Moktsa Tulku had passed away, [167a] but I had no time to go there; I did, however, make offerings and sponsor commemorative acts, as well as perform ceremonies and prayers from a distance.

In the sixth month I went to Dzongshö to meet Dzogchen Rinpoché, who came specifically to receive transmissions from me. I gave the entire range of empowerments, oral transmissions, and instructions for the cycle of the six-faced form of Yamantaka from the Nyingma *Kama* collection; the Dzogchen cycle called The Spacious Expanse of the View, from Dorjé Lingpa; and The Heart Drop of the Cycle of Hum. I also transmitted to him all the empowerments, oral transmissions, and instructions that I had recently added to the collection, which especially included rediscovered *terma*s. For Tertön Sögyal, Lhaksam, and others, I performed the empowerment for the peaceful and wrathful deities of *The Heart Essence of Secrets*, and I gave the explanatory instructions for *The Profound Inner Meaning* to Dezhung Tulku and others. To several lamas and monks of Dzamthang, I gave the empowerment for Tarayogini. In these and other ways I satisfied the needs of individuals.

I also participated, with a group of about forty others, for more than two weeks in an elaborate ceremony that combined *drupchen* and *mendrup* rituals based on The United Intent of the Three Roots. We were visited by the venerable Pawo Rinpoché,[920] Yangtrul of Palyul Monastery, and others, and I did my best to satisfy their specific requests. On this site in Dzongshö we built a "stupa of enlightenment"[921] as a representation of enlightened mind, in addition to founding a college for the study of logic. I used the gold I had collected en route, and also finished some other fine projects to commission statues.

In the eleventh month I returned to Dzongsar Monastery, where I met with my precious lord guru. We had some extraordinary conversations, as he related to me how recently he had undergone a vision of meeting Indrabhuti— the "middle one," also known as King Jah[922]—and Saraha, [167b] inseparable from one another, and of receiving the cycle of techniques relating to the path of skillful means[923] that are known as the "forty groups of four." He also had a dream of the Situ incarnation journeying to a place that seemed to be on the border between India and Tibet, which he said indicated where the rebirth would take place.

While Khyentsé Rinpoché was bestowing the entire range of empowerments and oral transmissions for Dorjé Lingpa's Gathering of the Guru's Commands, he had a vision one morning at dawn. In this vision, he was approached by the princess of Ling, Jamyang Tsulthrim Wangmo, who had a new jacket made of brocade, over which she wore a maroon shawl of the finest silk. She was carrying a vase that held a bouquet of amazing flowers, the like of which Khyentsé Rinpoché had never seen before. She said, "These are indisputably flowers that the exalted and sublime Nagarjuna planted on the Mountain of Glory to the south,[924] but they have become a bit withered in the interim. If you sprinkle them with some of the vase water from the ritual for the Gathering of the Commands, it will restore them." She offered him the flowers and he sprinkled on them vase water from the Gathering of the Guru's Commands that he had on the table in front of him, whereupon the flowers immediately bloomed much more fully than before. They had many rings of petals and were of various colors, so lovely that he couldn't stop looking at them. The princess of Ling said, "Aryadeva is definitely eight years old by now." She then departed. In Khyentsé Rinpoché's opinion, this clearly proved that I was Aryadeva.[925] He said, "We must insert the name of Aryadeva [168a] in the prayer to your previous incarnations that Karmapa wrote. You have very clear signs of habit patterns connected with *The Four Hundred Verses*."[926]

During this time, I also occupied myself with fulfilling the requests of many who came to receive empowerments, oral transmissions, and instructions, as well as continuing to arrange rituals for inclusion in my *Treasury of Precious Hidden Teachings*. On the sixth day of the twelfth month word came from Palpung that Kuzhap Choktrul Rinpoché[927] had passed away. An envoy came, bearing a letter from Öngen Tulku that stated that I must come immediately, since I was familiar with the commemorative rites to be performed. So I set out. We spent about three days performing a ritual to the guru in front of the remains. There had existed an account detailing the resources that were to be used for such commemorative rites, dating from the time of the two previous incarnations, but with the passage of time there was little in the way of assets, either belonging to the administration of Situ Rinpoché's monastic residence or his personal estate. I drew up a list of such possessions as had not already been let go, to be dedicated as offerings for the rites. His remains were cremated in the traditional manner. With the other responsible parties, headed by Öngen, I made a very careful accounting of what remained in Situ Rinpoché's upper and lower chambers—spiritual articles, clothing, personal possessions, and so on. We established seed money for the gilding of Situ Rinpoché's tomb, but the responsibility for finishing this had to lie with Garjé Drodok, and so word was sent to him. Until the end of the third week I took part in the recitations in some small way, but then I went briefly to the hermitage. [168b]

During this time I dreamed that I met Ngadak Nyang Rinpoché, looking very cheerful and delighted. I offered him a present and requested his blessing. He said a few words to me in a mood of great delight, telling me for instance that the blessings of many group rituals, including rituals to consecrate vases, had formed on the surrounding mountains as a kind of lustrous deposit.

DURING THE CELEBRATIONS for the new Fire Dog Year [1886-1887], I went to the monastic residence. Three projects were under way. The incarnation of Öntrul had been reborn as the son of Pawo Rinpoché, and funds were needed to secure his release.[928] Since the incarnation and his students were residing in Nangchen, an escort was needed to invite him to Palpung; and a party was being organized to go on a fund-raising trip to sponsor the gilding of the previous Situ's tomb. I gave very thorough counsel to these groups, after which I journeyed to Dzongsar Monastery.

There I offered the empowerments, oral transmissions, and instructions for the five mandalas of the oral lineage of the Karma Kagyü tradition to my precious guru, the master of Ngor and his students, the incarnation of Rolpai Dorjé from Zurmang Monastery, and others. I also performed the basic rituals, such as the "holding of speech." To Dzögön Tulku and his students, I transmitted the empowerment for the nine deity mandala of Jinasagara according to the Karma Kagyü tradition, as well as the empowerments, oral transmissions, and practical methods for The Peaceful Garland and The Wrathful Garland. The Tsenri Netrul incarnation requested the empowerment into the cycle of peaceful and wrathful deities called The Gathering of the Guru's Commands, discovered by Dechen Lingpa. To Lhaksam Tenpai Gyaltsen, I gave an explanation and overview of *The Hevajra Tantra*, and explanatory teachings on *The Profound Inner Meaning*, the two smaller treatises, and *The Highest Continuum*. From the lord among scholars, Lama Mipham Gyatso, [169a] I requested oral teaching transmissions for his own compositions—his major commentary,[929] as well as his commentary on *The Ornament of the Middle Way*; his commentary on the chapter concerning wisdom from *Engaging in the Conduct of a Bodhisattva*; his overview of *Dispelling Darkness in the Ten Directions*, which is Longchenpa's commentary to the tantra *The Heart Essence of Secrets*; and his commentary on *The Recollection of the Three Jewels*. Then, during the third month, I returned to my hermitage.

There, a group of some fifty-five participants, master and students, performed elaborate rituals, beginning with the vase consecration from the cycle of the flawless Jinasagara, and continuing with the longevity practice, the fulfillment ritual, and a Vajrakila practice. These rituals were finished within the space of ten days. I gave the oral transmissions for the Indian sources of the Mahamudra tradition to Öngen and the Tenga incarnation of Zurmang Monastery, and also satisfied Tenga Tulku's requests for empowerments and oral transmissions.

After finishing these duties, I went to Palpung Monastery during the fourth month to attend the annual vase consecration ritual. I spent several days at Situ Rinpoché's monastic residence, performing rituals to promote prosperity, and then performed the ritual of one thousand offerings to Ushnishavijaya at the hermitage.

In the fifth month Pawo Rinpoché and his son[930] arrived and we formally enthroned the Öntrul incarnation in an elaborate ceremony. They then planned to depart together for Pawo Rinpoché's seat in central Tibet, promising to return once Öntrul had attained his majority. We offered all honors to them and they set off. In response to orders from Dergé, I set off for Chagri, where I performed an extensive ritual of vase consecration, as well as giving such empowerments and oral transmissions as were required of me, including the "oral lineage" cycle of Vajrakila. I also satisfied requests for such ceremonies as a consecration of the palace. [169b] I offered twenty-five repetitions of the longevity empowerment from Druppai Gyalmo to Dziphu Khen Rinpoché, from whom I requested the formal authorization for the practice of White Tara as transmitted by Bari Lotsawa.

I then left for Paljor Plateau. In accord with the request of Khen Lama Tashi Özer, I took part with about eighty others in a *drupchen* ritual focusing on the healing principle of Vajra Amrita, participating throughout the entire program of preparation, main practice, and conclusion. Returning eventually to my hermitage, I gave the entire cycle of empowerments, oral transmissions, and instructions for my *guru sadhana* based on the Seven-Line Prayer to Lama

Chöying of Gegyal, Tendzin Namgyal (the brother of Dabzang Tulku), and others.

I put aside a few of my obligations, such as the plan for me to attend the feast offering at Burmo, and in the eighth month went to Dzongshö. This year, the gathering of great lamas from the upland and lowland regions did not attract many participants. The residents of Dzamthang, the Chokling incarnation,[931] and a few others had only minor requests for me to teach, so my time there was quite relaxed. I was able to complete many of the arrangements of rituals to be included in my collections—*The Tantric Treasury of the Kagyü School*, *The Treasury of Precious Hidden Teachings*, and *The Treasury of Spiritual Advice*.

I went to Dzongsar Monastery in the eleventh month. I gave the empowerments, oral transmissions, and instructions for The Union of All Rare and Precious Jewels to the Dodrup incarnation, and explanatory teachings on *The Stages on the Path: The Heart Essence of Timeless Awareness* to the Khamtrul incarnation,[932] as well as fulfilling many other requests for teachings. Then, conferring over a period of time with my precious lord guru, I wrote my *Biographies of the One Hundred Revealers of Hidden Teachings.*[933] For the more well-known figures, there seemed no need to include more details than a brief and basic account, [170a] and so I wrote out a simple listing, fearing that otherwise the text would become too wordy. Still, I felt confident that my work was superior to the five or six prior collections of such biographies of *tertöns* that I had read.

Through the kindness of my guru, I received empowerments and oral transmissions, including those for *Protection from All Lower Rebirths*, The cycle of Mahakarunika from Dorjé Lingpa; *Sublime Light of Timeless Awareness*, the longevity *sadhana* from Ngari Panchen; and many minor but authentic *termas* for which I had not previously received transmissions.

In the twelfth month I returned to Palpung Monastery. The Fifteenth Gyalwang Karmapa[934] was to arrive soon, and so I helped make whatever preparations were necessary for the welcoming escort and so forth. On the tenth day, I accompanied the escort to the nearby meadow of Druzhi Gyepa, where I had the good fortune of first beholding the visage of Gyalwang Rinpoché. My experience of this occasion was very pleasant indeed. The skies were clear, the earth still unfrozen, and the weather as warm as summertime. Karmapa reached Palpung Monastery by the eleventh of the month. On the twelfth, in the smaller chambers of Situ Rinpoché, we made our first spiritual connection, for I performed a purifying ritual[935] and a formal authorization for the practice of White Tara as my offerings to Karmapa.

I then returned to my hermitage, where I entered a personal retreat focusing on the "oral lineage" tradition of Vajrakila in conjunction with a longevity practice. My precious lord divined that I would need to offer empowerments and oral transmissions to Gyalwang Rinpoché, and so I performed rituals to offset any potential obstacles. About six lamas from Dzamthang, who had all completed the requisite retreats, came [170b] and after we had made the necessary preparations we spent seven days performing the ritual of the sixty deity mandala of Vajrabhairava, from Bari Lotsawa's ritual of Simhamukha to avert negativity, and seventy thousand repetitions for the feast offering and fulfillment ritual from the rediscovered *terma*, The Combined Practice of the Three Roots. Thirty thousand repetitions were also done by people in Dzongshö, making a total of one hundred thousand repetitions that were completed.

ON THE THIRD "VICTORIOUS DAY"[936] of the new Fire Pig Year [1887-1888], Gyalwang Karmapa, Jé-ön Chöwang Tulku,[937] and their students came especially to see me. They presented me with abundant gifts and prayers for my long life. The monastery also sponsored the offering of representations of enlightened form, speech, and mind and a day-long ritual focusing on White Tara. On the tenth day, Gyalwang Karmapa and his retinue installed themselves at my hermitage, and took part in the tenth-day feast offering based on the Secret Sphere cycle. I offered the empowerment to them. On the eleventh day, I performed the preparatory phase of the empowerment for the nine deity mandala of Jinasagara, and began the teachings with a single session on the preliminary practices of the Mahamudra tradition and *The Jewel Ornament of Liberation*.[938] Over time, combining empowerments with teaching sessions, I gave the empowerments, oral transmissions, and instructions for the entire range of mandalas of the Karma Kagyü tradition, as well as *The Tantric Treasury of the Kagyü School*. I offered the major empowerment for the masculine and feminine protective deities in union to Gyalwang Karmapa in private, in the shrine room dedicated to those deities, and performed the *torma* empowerment for these principal protective deities, and the formal authorizations for their five retinue figures, for the lamas and monks of Karmapa's encampment. The instructions on the main body of Mahamudra practice and the Six Yogas, as well as the oral transmissions for the mandalas and auxiliary texts, [171a] were finished by the waxing moon of the third month. While I was giving the transmissions for *The Tantric Treasury of the Kagyü School*, first the venerable Khamtrul, then Dzögön Jedrung Tulku, Dabzang Tulku, and other lamas and *tulku*s from the southern regions arrived, until the hermitage had no room for anyone else to stay and we were forced to call a halt to the teachings.

I accompanied Gyalwang Karmapa and his retinue back to Palpung Monastery. On the seventh of that month we made preparations for the ritual of one thousand offerings in front of the great gilded tomb. We performed a ritual focusing on the eight great bodhisattvas, and I offered the formal ceremony for conferring the bodhisattva vow, according to the Madhaymaka tradition, to about one hundred masters and students, Gyalwang Rinpoché foremost among them. Then, on the eighth day, in front of the great gilded tomb we performed the ritual of one thousand offerings and I offered the ceremony for the bodhisattva vow according to the most elaborate format of the Mahayana approach. On the ninth day, Karmapa took up residence in the temple for the monastic summer retreat.

I began giving the transmissions for *The Treasury of Spiritual Advice*. Starting with the teachings on *Parting from the Four Attachments* from The One Hundred Instructions of Kunga Drolchok, I spent about four days finishing these instructions and transmitting the Kadampa teachings connected with the sources found in my *Treasury of Spiritual Advice*. I then performed the ritual from the Kalachakra cycle for the acceptance of students, as well as the preparatory phase of the empowerment. On the auspicious date of the fifteenth day of the third month, from the main stages of the empowerment I performed that of the "entrance of the child" and the "general sublime empowerment," followed by the "special sublime empowerment" on the sixteenth. On the seventeenth, I offered the empowerments of the vajra master—those of both the "ruler" and the "great ruler"—to Gyalwang Karmapa in private.[939] [171b]

I asked the general administrator Garjé Drodok to sponsor a *drupchen* ritual focusing on the Eight Commands, and we spent several days preparing for this. Karmapa went to Lhasar Temple in Palpung Monastery. We began the *drupchen*, establishing the outer boundary on the twenty-fourth of the month. By the fifth day of the fourth month we had completed the main practice of the *drupchen* ritual, based on the Gathering of Sugatas, and a *mendrup* ritual. I performed the empowerment for *The Major Record of Discourses* for some of the lamas and *tulku*s (Gyalwang Karmapa foremost among them) and the empowerment for the ongoing daily practice for about a hundred people. These were completed with elaborate ceremonies on the seventh day of the month, and for a time I went to my hermitage to rest.

On the fifteenth, in the temple for the monastic summer retreat I continued with the transmissions of the Kadampa teachings, beginning with the technique of the Sixteen Spheres and finishing the remaining transmissions. Then, step by step, I transmitted the ripening empowerments and ritual blessings, the liberating instructions of spiritual advice, and the supportive oral transmissions for the teachings that are fundamental and essential to the Eight Lineages of Accomplishment, including the following: the Lamdré cycle; the Dakpo Kagyü; the Shangpa Kagyü; Dampa's systems of Zhijé and Chö; the Vajra Yoga tradition; the Stages of Approach and Accomplishment from Orgyenpa;[940] the cycle of Mahakarunika Chittavishramana; the collection The One Hundred Instructions; other more minor instructions, especially those of the traditions of Throphu and Bodong; and, once those were completed, the three Categories (of Mind, Expanse, and Direct Transmission) of the Early Translation School, the minor instructions found in the collected works of Longchenpa, and other teachings.[941] These were finished by the tenth day of the sixth month. [172a] Once I had finished offering these teachings, I brought everything to a positive conclusion with a teaching on the longevity practice associated with White Tara.[942]

I then returned to my home area, where I visited Burmo and other holy sites briefly to perform feast offerings, after which I went to Dzongshö. Gyalwang Rinpoché was staying here, for his great encampment had been struck and he was journeying to the region of Lithang in response to an invitation to visit there. He performed a consecration ritual for the temple in Dzongshö and visited the holy sites in and around the area. I rendered what service I could and he then left. I satisfied any number of requests for teachings from the many who had gathered there already or who did so over the next while—including Somo Tulku of Gyalrong, Khargo Tulku, Bakha Tulku and his brother from Lhodrak, the chieftain Taiji of Markham, the men and women of the family of the chieftain of Lithang, and the lamas and monks of Gonjo. I also wrote as much as I could, arranging rituals for inclusion in my Treasuries. After installing long mantras in the statues of the protective deities and consecrating them, I went to Dzongsar Monastery, reaching it during the waning phase of the moon in the tenth month.

My lord guru was ailing slightly, so I offered to perform a ritual ablution.

He was enormously kind to me, and I was able to receive from him a number of transmissions, including the following:

- *The Innermost Heart of Immortality*
- all the lineages he held for instructions based on *The Trilogy of Natural Freedom* and other works by Longchenpa
- his direct lineage for the empowerment, oral transmissions, and instructions based on The Sole Sufficiency of Great Perfection cycle from Rinchen Lingpa
- the empowerments and oral transmissions for the five cycles of *sadhana*s found in The Heart Drop of the Accomplished Masters
- detailed instructions on The Four Cycles of Garlands that Forge the Path
- the empowerments and oral transmissions [172b] for *Eight Commands of the Accomplished Master*, as well as the instructions and an explanation of the tantras and commentaries
- the fivefold stage of completion from the Eight Commands cycle called the Gathering of Sugatas
- the five stages of The Perfection of Secrets
- the four major instructions from the cycle called Natural Arising
- instructions on the Universal Gathering of Sugatas from Longsal
- all the empowerments, oral transmissions, and instructions for Dorjé Lingpa's Gathering of the Chosen Deity's Commands: The Complete Perfection of Secrets and
- the empowerments, oral transmissions, and instructions for the Heart Drop of the Three Families from Chokgyur Lingpa

Khyentsé Rinpoché also conferred a profound honor on me by performing feast offerings to dispel any potential obstacles to my giving the empowerments and oral transmissions for my *Treasury of Precious Hidden Teachings*. He sponsored specific ceremonies on my behalf, such as the rituals of *The Heart Sutra* and of Tara, personally distributing gifts of silver to about one hundred and sixty lamas and monks.

I returned to my hermitage on the seventeenth day of the twelfth month. I attended the group *torma* rituals focusing on the protective deities.

DURING THE PERIOD OF THE NEW Earth Rat Year [1888-1889], the old group of retreatants was due to finish its program, so I gave them necessary em-power-ments and oral transmissions, such as those for The Peaceful Garland and The Wrathful Garland. I also transmitted the ordination of the bodhisattva vow according to the Madhyamaka tradition to the retreatants at both medita-tion centers, upper and lower. I also undertook a personal retreat focusing on Padmachandali, an expression of the feminine principle of longevity. Since the practice of Vajrasattva had been used the year before, this year we began a *drupchen* focusing on the deity Samyak.

Gyalwang Karmapa also attended. Given that he had insistently urged me the previous year to pass on to him the empowerments and oral transmissions for *The Treasury of Precious Hidden Teachings*, he intended to receive them at this point. It was necessary to begin these with a *drupchen* ritual combined with a major empowerment focusing on the Eight Commands. [173a] Since Karmapa had already received the empowerment for the Gathering of Sugatas, we now used Guru Chöwang's Perfection of Secrets as our basis. For this purpose, I went from the hermitage down to the meditation center. Gyalwang Rinpoché installed himself in the temple for the summer retreat. On the day of the new moon,[943] I performed the rites of boundary closure and the prepa-ratory phase of the empowerment. On the first day of the month we started the *drupchen* ritual, beginning with the investiture and the adorning of the mandala. We spent seven days on the main practice, after which we per-formed the stage of accepting the spiritual attainments of the practice, and I offered the entire major empowerment and that for the ongoing daily prac-tice as well.

Once we had finished taking down the boundary cairns and so on, we be-gan the transmission of the great *Treasury of Precious Hidden Teachings*, start-ing with the empowerment and instructions for the glorious Vajrasattva, the sovereign lord of the one hundred buddha families.[944] I gradually completed all the empowerments and related instructions. We then completed the follow-ing transmissions from both the Atiyoga and Mahayoga classes:

- the cycles connected with the peaceful and wrathful deities
- the practices focusing on the Three Roots in general
- the outer and inner *sadhanas* of the Guru
- the three levels of such practice (that is, of dharmakaya, sambhogakaya, and nirmanakaya)
- the wrathful forms of the Guru

- the cycles concerning the chosen deities of the *sadhana*s of The Eight Commands in general
- the specific cycles of the peaceful and wrathful forms of Manjushri, the deity of enlightened form and
- the specific cycles of the peaceful expressions of the *padma* principle of enlightened speech, including those of Amitabha, Amitayus, and—from the cycles concerning Mahakarunika—Ratna Lingpa's Supreme Compassion: The Gathering of Secrets, including the empowerment focusing on the one thousand buddhas.

We then called a temporary halt to the transmissions.

At this point, on the tenth day of the third month there was a conjunction between the constellation of the Victor and the planet Jupiter, and so Gyalwang Rinpoché accompanied me to the main meeting hall of the monastery, the meditation center, and the hermitage, performing rites of consecration in each. [173b] On the fifteenth day, merely by way of establishing some auspicious interdependence between us, I offered Karmapa an explanation of the source verses for the first four chapters of my *Treasury of the Knowable*, and of the sutras, tantras, and secular fields of knowledge in general.

On the sixth day of the fourth month there was another conjunction between the constellation of the Victor and Jupiter, so a large gathering was called, at which we prepared the pills of Manjushri and Sarasvati.[945] Gyalwang Rinpoché went to the monastery to preside over the annual vase consecration ritual.

Some of the Dergé nobility had planned this year to go on pilgrimage to the holy sites of central Tibet, so I went specifically to Dergé Gönchen to see them off. I performed one hundred and eight repetitions of a longevity empowerment. Having paid my respects, I satisfied the needs of several of my patrons on the route back. I gave empowerments and other transmissions to some who were also traveling to central Tibet, and then returned home.

The temple complex of Lhasar was very comfortable and spacious, so we moved there on the third day of the fifth month and picked up where we had left off before.[946] Beginning with *The Condensed Intent of Profound Meaning* of Pégyal, found in the section on Mahakarunika in my *Treasury of Precious Hidden Teachings*, I transmitted the following teachings:

- the rest of the section on Mahakarunika
- the wrathful aspect of Hayagriva, both red and black forms

- the section on the principle of enlightened mind, including Samyak, the peaceful and wrathful deities, and Vajrapani
- the section on the principle of enlightened qualities, including Vajra Amrita
- the section on the principle of enlightened activity, including Vajrakila
- the section of The Imprecations of the Mamos
- the section of The Wrathful Mantra Curse
- the general and specific practices for taming the classes of arrogant ones
- the sections dealing with *dakini*s such as Varahi, Krodhi, Tara, and other feminine deities
- and the sections dealing with the masculine and feminine protective deities.

In addition to these transmissions concerning the Three Roots and the protective deities, [174a] I passed on several cycles of Bönpo teachings discovered by authentic *tertön*s of the Nyingma School, which I had felt it necessary to include in my collection, as well as techniques to enact enlightened activities in general and the specific ones of pacification, enrichment, magnetizing power, and wrathful intervention. I also transmitted teachings associated with the Anuyoga class, including the new *terma* cycle entitled The Vajra Array, and, from the Atiyoga class, the cycles that unite the enlightened intent underlying the three transmissions of Vimalamitra, Padmakara, and Bairotsana, as well as the General Quintessence, the Innermost Quintessence, and general collections of spiritual advice.

I concluded the transmissions with the empowerment for the longevity practice The Gathering of Secrets, bringing the whole series to a close on the thirteenth day of the seventh month. At the thanksgiving ritual, Karmapa performed feast offerings on a grand scale, including one hundred feast offerings based on the cycles of The United Intent of the Gurus and The Spontaneous Accomplishment of Goals. He performed a ceremony to promote my longevity and bestowed many gifts on me. During this time, the oral transmissions were all read aloud by Khen Lama Tashi Özer.[947] Then I spent a day or two reading out the texts for which he had not yet received transmission. When everything had been carried out without omission or interpolation, I returned to my hermitage. Karmapa's main encampment had moved to the region of upper Ga. From Bakha Tulku, I received several empowerments and oral trans-missions from the teaching cycles of Pema Lingpa.

On the fifteenth day of the eighth month I went to Dzongsar Monastery and offered a ceremony to promote my lord guru's longevity; the indications were extremely auspicious, and I was inspired by the delight he showed. I continued on to Dzongshö, where I satisfied the individual requests of a number of spiritually motivated lamas and *tulku*s. [174b] But the majority of my time there was spent writing as much as I could, finishing what I had not yet completed by way of manuals for personal retreats, instruction manuals, and arrangements of empowerments.

I returned to Dzongsar Monastery on the fourteenth day of the tenth month. There I met Gyatrul, who had come back from Gulok. For a small group that included my lord guru and Gyatrul, I gave some transmissions from the Kagyü tradition—The Peaceful Garland, The Wrathful Garland, the cycle of protective deities called The Garland of Lightning, the formal authorizations for the masculine and feminine protective deities and their five retinue deities, and the complete major empowerment for The United Intent of the Chosen Deities of Taksham, according to the background teaching found in *The Major Universal Commitments*.

Khyentsé Rinpoché had already received the empowerments and oral transmissions of the Sky Teachings from Gyatrul. Then, for myself and a few others, on the tenth day of the eleventh month Khyentsé Rinpoché began giving us the transmissions in turn, starting with the cycles concerning Amitayus. On the twenty-fourth day, he concluded the series on a positive note by conferring the empowerment for the *terma* of enlightened intent focusing on White Amitayus. We thus received the entire range of empowerments, oral transmissions, and instructions from the Sky Teachings—both teachings that are explicitly recorded in the accounts of this cycle and those that are not, as well as the *terma*s of enlightened intent—and in addition the oral transmissions for the biographies of Namchö Mingyur Dorjé and Karma Chagmé Rinpoché and the latter's arrangements for the empowerment rituals of the Sky Teachings. Khyentsé Rinpoché concluded with the entire series of empowerments and oral transmissions from the whole cycle of Duddul Dorjé's *terma*s. These finished during the waning phase of the moon in the twelfth month.

Both Khyentsé Rinpoché and Gyatrul urged me to give the empowerments, oral transmissions, and instructions from my cycle based on the Seven-Line Prayer, as well as the teachings on the feminine principle.

ON THE FIRST DAY OF THE NEW Female Earth Ox Year [1889-1890], [175a] I completed my transmissions on a positive note with the empowerment for the "combined practice"[948] and the longevity empowerment from The Union of All Rare and Precious Jewels. I then offered them the following transmissions: the ritual blessings for the Eighty-Four *Mahasiddha*s according to the Jonang tradition; the empowerments and oral transmissions for the *guru sadhana*s of Marpa, Milarepa, and Dakpo Lharjé;[949] and concise instructions on "blending and transference,"[950] the Six Yogas, and Mahamudra. I also gave the formal authorization for the practice of White Tara to Thartsé Khen Rinpoché, and that of the secret *sadhana* of Hayagriva for all those who had gathered. Khyentsé Rinpoché performed a ceremony to promote my longevity and bestowed many gifts on me.

I then went to Palpung Monastery, where I met with Gyalwang Rinpoché. He devoted a great deal of energy to determining the circumstances of Kuzhap Rinpoché's rebirth.[951] I began giving the series of empowerments, oral transmissions, and instructions for the sixth group of new retreatants. I also satisfied request for teachings from the constant stream of people coming from all directions; in one case, for example, I gave the oral transmissions for some eighteen auxiliary texts to several motivated individuals. I continued writing out arrangements of rituals for inclusion in *The Treasury of Precious Hidden Teachings*. I gave instructions on *The Highest Continuum* and *The Profound Inner Meaning* to Lama Tashi Chöphel.

In the third month I went to Lhasar Temple to begin the process of installing long mantras in Kuzhap Rinpoché's tomb[952] and in the statue of Maitreya being erected in honor of the new incarnation. I made elaborate preparations, preparing the chakras of the *yaksha* spirits, filling the treasure vases, performing the ritual to consecrate the long mantras, and so forth. [175b] Having offered the long mantras to the tomb and statue in the proper order, I performed the rituals of visualizing the deities, imbuing them with blessings, and installing the central axes using the rituals of the two Vimalas. The final installation and rite of consecration were finished by the third day of the fourth month, after which I went to my hermitage.

The general administrator and principal lamas of Palpung had gone to Lithang to search for the new Situ incarnation and escort him back. I became caught up in all kinds of projects—giving the empowerment for the Heart Drop of Chetsün and other cycles to many motivated people, making preparations for *drupchen* rituals, and so forth.

Gyalwang Karmapa had gone to Dzongsar Monastery and received from Khyentsé Rinpoché the empowerments and oral transmissions for The Compendium of All Sadhanas and other collections, as well as all kinds of oral teachings. Once these were completed, Karmapa left Dzongsar and was invited back to Lhasar Temple. Once his party had been properly installed in their quarters with great care, the master Karmapa, with more than one hundred and eight of his students, participated in a *drupchen* ritual focusing on The United Intent of the Gurus, which also involved a *mendrup* ritual, secondary fulfillment rituals, longevity practices, and a Vajrakila ritual. These began on the twenty-third day[953] and were concluded in a very thorough manner on the fifth day of the waxing moon in the fifth month. I made offerings to Gyalwang Rinpoché—very special representations of enlightened form, speech, and mind (in particular, a naturally occurring statue of Tara); nine measures of silver pieces; one hundred and eight bricks of fine quality tea; and more than three hundred horses and other pack animals. As exemplified by Chöwang Tulku's offerings of a full measure of silver pieces, [176a] the nobility and government officials all made greater or lesser offerings, according to their means. I urged the monastic community, administrators, and others to offer whatever they had, which amounted to more than a hundred bricks of fine quality tea. I offered to Gyalwang Rinpoché the empowerments and oral transmissions for The Deities of the Five Classes of Tantra (from the Shangpa tradition) and for Tarayogini, as well as the ritual to confer the "life force dagger" of Shvana[954] (from the Tersar tradition). From him in turn I requested the empowerment for the *guru sadhana* he had authored, and the oral transmissions for *Sargachupa*, the account of his previous lifetimes, and for the ritual to promote prosperity that focuses on the protective deities.

The rebirth of Kuzhap Rinpoché[955] had been escorted back from Lithang, and Gyalwang Karmapa performed the formal tonsure ceremony,[956] the naming ceremony, and the enthronement without any hindrances, completing these in a very thorough manner. I offered a ritual ablution to the Drukpa and Situ incarnations, and performed a longevity empowerment for them both and for the nobility of Tsurphu. When Karmapa's great encampment was struck and they left for Lhokhok, I joined the escort and saw Karmapa off with wishes for his good health, after which I went to Burmo and other places to perform feast offerings. I continued with the empowerments, oral transmissions, and instructions for the retreatants at my hermitage, picking up where I had left off.

I began writing detailed accounts of the contents of *The Treasury of Precious Hidden Teachings* and the lineages through which these teachings had been transmitted. In the seventh month I went to Dzongshö, where I spent a month finishing the accounts of the contents and the lineages, as well as the arrangements of rituals. During this time, I dreamed one night that Minling Terchen came and consecrated the statues there. [176b] He advised me intently that it was crucial that the teaching lineages of the Mindroling tradition continue, and that The Heart Drop of the Dakini was an important cycle. On another occasion, I dreamed that Lochen Dharma Shri spoke to me, relating many special words and meanings that I had never heard of before.

Gyatrul of Palyul Monastery arrived, and I gave all the empowerments and oral transmissions from *The Treasury of Precious Hidden Teachings* that he had not received in the past. To the noble lady of the Khyung-nak clan and others who had gathered, I gave the empowerments, oral transmissions, and instructions for *The Treasury of Spiritual Advice*. This took more than two months, after which those who had received these empowerments and teachings returned to their home regions.

In the tenth month I undertook a personal retreat focusing on Vajrakila in the cave of Dzong-chen. I performed the ritual of the effigy of the blade during the waning phase of the moon.[957] During this tenth month Tsaptsa Tulku came and I transmitted to him the thirteen great commands focusing on the Six-Armed Mahakala. I also needed to give the complete instructions on Mahamudra to him and the retreatants at Dzongshö, after which Tsaptsa Tulku left to return home. I went to Dzongsar Monastery to meet with and pay my respects to my lord guru. I spent several days receiving oral transmissions from him. He gave me a number of gifts, including a painting of the thirteen principal and secondary deities of the Heart Drop of the Exalted Goddess of Immortality, to be installed at the hermitage, as well as his hand bell and monk's shawl.

During the waxing phase of the moon in the twelfth month, I arrived back at my hermitage. Beginning on the thirteenth day, I undertook personal retreats that focused in succession on the nine "unchanging deities" that were the primary practice of Maitripa. At the end of the year, [177a] during the ritual of accomplishment a flaw appeared in the great *torma*.

DURING THE CELEBRATIONS for the new Iron Tiger Year[958] [1890-1891], another performance of the *torma* ritual of accomplishment, *The Great Torma Ritual That Dispels Obstacles*, was undertaken, and I was told that everything went very well. The king and ministers of Dergé had returned from Lhasa the previous year, and Tsering Döndrup had been sent as their representative. I ended my personal retreats toward the end of the second month. A group of about forty of us, masters and students, performed an elaborate *drupchen* ritual based on the "higher activity" for the cycle of Vajrakila called The Unsurpassable Innermost Secret. This finished during the waxing phase of the moon in the third month, and afterward I gave the major empowerment to several very important personages—most especially Kuzhap Choktrul—and the concise empowerment to the others. I satisfied many requests for teachings from people who came from all directions; for example, I gave the empowerment, oral transmissions, and instructions for the Heart Drop of Chetsün to the Lhokham incarnation and his son, as well as to many realized yogis from Gechak. Beginning on the fifteenth day of the third month, I performed the three-day major empowerment into the Kalachakra cycle to Kuzhap Choktrul and the retreatants. Lho Jedrung Tulku came from Nangchen and I satisfied his requests for many empowerments and oral transmissions, especially for the Ironlike cycle of Ayushpati.

During the fourth month we began a *drupchen* ritual focusing on Vajrasattva. Then, in response to insistent urging by the *tulku* of Dorjé Drak, I went to that monastery. I participated in combined *drupchen* and *mendrup* rituals focusing on the Natural Arising cycle of the Eight Commands. This finished during the waxing phase of the moon in the fifth month, and for the participants in the ritual, principally the lamas and *tulku*s, [177b] I performed the major empowerment for the Natural Arising cycle, as well as a public empowerment for the crowds who gathered.

Having made feast offerings at Pal De'u, Burmo, and other places, I returned to the hermitage, where I performed a consecration for the newly installed images and offerings in the temple and carefully edited the volumes of *The Treasury of Precious Hidden Teachings* that had already been printed. On the tenth day of the sixth month sacred dances were being held at Palpung Monastery, and in response to the administrators' insistence that I attend, I did so. The monastic and lay officials of Dergé were also in attendance, and I performed a longevity empowerment for them and held audiences with them.

I went to Dzongsar Monastery during the waning phase of the moon. I met with my lord guru just after he had finished a personal retreat focusing on the Ratön tradition of Vajrakila. He was very gracious, bestowing on me some of the substances of spiritual accomplishment and a ceremony to summon the forces of longevity. The *tulku* of Dzakha,[959] Kunzang Namgyal, had arrived and Khyentsé Rinpoché was receiving some empowerments and oral transmissions from him. To begin with, Dzarkha Tulku conferred the oral transmissions for the collected works of Tselé. He then gave a complete series of empowerments and oral transmissions, beginning with The Vajra Heart Essence of the Three Kayas, a *terma* discovered by Longsal, and including Longsal's Vajra Heart Essence; the oral lineages of Vimalamitra and King Songtsen Gampo; The Intense Blazing of Timeless Awareness; the Eight Commands cycle of The Innermost Gathering; the cycle of The Innermost Secret Guru; and the rediscovered Magic cycle of Dampa Deshek. He also gave the instructions for The Vajra Heart Essence and The Intense Blazing of Timeless Awareness, as well as the oral transmissions for the collected works, biography, and visionary accounts,[960] [178a] and the three volumes of his own arrangements of the empowerments of Duddul and Longsal. I received all of these transmissions. From my lord guru I received the empowerments for the peaceful deities of the Eight Commands cycle of the Gathering of Sugatas, for the longevity practice, and for both the peaceful and wrathful aspects; some twelve teachings on such topics as the source verses and commentary to *The Stages on the Path of Secret Mantra*; instructions of Duddul Dorjé on the Dzogchen approach and the *bardo* states; and the oral transmissions for the volume of Zhechen Öntrul's collected writings and the complete "mother and child" collections of Desi's *Supplement*.[961]

I myself fulfilled many requests for teachings from a number of lamas, *tulku*s, and monks, including such teachings as the cycle of Khyungpo. I also completed many arrangements of rituals, including the cycle of the Eighty-Four *Mahasiddha*s.

Then, during the waning phase of the moon in the eighth month, I went to Dzongshö. Over time, I wrote out the instruction manuals to be included in *The Treasury of Precious Hidden Teachings*. I made feast offerings at the holy sites and in the caves in the surrounding region. I gave instructions to Dorshul Khandro and the retreatants, and satisfied the requests of many aspirants for empowerments and teachings. Toward the end of the tenth month, I also performed a ritual of Vajrakila to avert negativity.

In the eleventh month I went back to Dzongsar Monastery, where I met with my lord guru, paying my respects and having conversations with him. There were by now so many people making requests for audiences with Khyentsé Rinpoché that, by this point, his attempts to bring forth *terma*s had to be put aside. As far as empowerments and oral transmissions were concerned, he could only confer these on very infrequent occasions, for he had absolutely no time. For several days I was kept busy greeting visitors and answering letters for him. Then I left him and arrived at the hermitage, [178b] where I participated in the annual ceremonies to replace the *torma*s on the shrine and perform offering rituals focusing on the protective deities. In the twelfth month I completed a personal retreat on the Siddha cycle of the Eight Commands.

DURING THE PERIOD OF THE NEW Iron Hare Year [1891-1892], I undertook a personal retreat focusing on Jatsön Nyingpo's cycle of the Eight Commands. On the twentieth day, I performed the ritual for averting negativity from the Wrathful Display cycle. Then, during the second month I installed long mantras in some of the gilded statues, most importantly that of White Tara. When I was performing the consecration ritual, I was given a painting of the three deities of longevity, and there were other excellent and auspicious circumstances. During this time, one night I dreamed that I had crossed an enormous ocean of very white milk, and while I was returning back over it I was struck for a time by how radiant it was, bathed in my dream by the light of the sun. I also dreamed that I was given two prophetic letters, a primary one and a derivative one, which I was told came from Dergé.

I began to focus my attention on rendering service to my precious lord guru. About twenty of us, master and students, spent several days performing a *drupchö* ritual focusing on White Tara. We also performed the ceremony of one thousand offerings to the three deities of longevity. During the third month a group of about thirty people, master and students, participated in a *drupchen* ritual based on the Heart Drop of the Exalted Goddess of Immortality, including very extensive feats and offerings. I experienced excellent signs in my dreams, and conferred the extensive empowerment on Kuzhap Choktrul and others. I sent Jamyang Namgyal Dorjé[962] and some of his students to Dzongsar to perform rites to promote the longevity of my omniscient guru. [179a] I selected the finest representations of enlightened form, speech, and mind, as well as the best clothing and other goods, and sent these along with three measures of silver coins; so I was able to feel satisfied with the material offerings I made to him.[963]

Machen Tulku of Taklung came to see me, and I spent about one-and-a-half months performing empowerments for him. These included the entire range of empowerments, oral transmissions, and instructions for *The Tantric Treasury of the Kagyü School*; the five-day major empowerment into the Kalachakra cycle; the major empowerments for the *sadhana* of enlightened mind and Vajrakila cycles from Ratna Lingpa; and the primary and secondary empowerments for The Heart Drop of Yuthok. We had made a truly heartfelt connection, and he then departed.

I made a special trip to Dzongsar Monastery, where I pleaded urgently with my precious lord to reinstate the lines of transmission for the initial and intermediate empowerments from the Zhijé School, which had become interrupted. His response was most gracious.[964] I also received from him the instructions for the six transmissions from Rongtön concerning the Perfection of Wisdom tradition. Word came to me from the Dergé government that it was essential for me to attend a vase consecration ritual, so I traveled with great difficulty to Chagri, where we began the ritual. I performed a ritual to ensure release from negative forces for Khen Rinpoché, the king and prince of Dergé, and members of the aristocracy. I performed several empowerments in response to their wishes, and, as requested, on the roof of the palace I performed a ritual to bind gods and demons to their oaths of allegiance and a consecration ritual to infuse this important site with blessings. In response to insistent requests from the lamas and monks of Dergé Gönchen, I performed a Vajrakila ritual to avert negativity and a fire ritual. [179b] At the monastery, I spent several days performing rituals of cleansing and blessing, after which I visited Burmo and other sacred sites on my trip back, performing feast offerings, and then arrived at my hermitage.

I was suffering from a case of diarrhea, and so spent several days resting. Then, in the seventh month I went to Dzongshö. Dzarkha Choktrul had come there, too, and a group of about fifty of us, masters and students, began on the seventh day to perform combined *drupchen* and *mendrup* rituals focusing on the Eight Commands cycle of the Gathering of Sugatas. In response to the requests of the sublime Dzarkha Tulku, Lama Paljin, Sa Khandro, and others, I performed a number of empowerments, both elaborate and concise, including *The Major Record of Discourses*. Once I had made offerings to the lamas and monks and brought my stay to a conclusion, I went to Dzamthang specifically to meet with five retreatants, to whom I gave the "sublime empowerment" for the Kalachakra cycle and the empowerment for Tarayogini. I also gave teachings as requested by other motivated individuals.

Lamas and *tulkus* who were motivated to receive empowerments and oral transmissions from me kept arriving. Beginning on the first day of the eighth month, I gave a series of transmissions to the sublime Dzarkha incarnation, Jedrung of Ling, the Situ incarnation of Kathok Monastery, Gyalsé Tulku, the younger Barphuk Tulku, and many others who had gathered there. These transmissions included the entire range of major and minor empowerments for The United Intent of the Gurus and the oral transmissions for the thirteen volumes of teachings in that cycle, [180a] and finished on the first day of the tenth month. The lamas and *tulku*s returned to their home regions. From Dzarkha Tulku I received instruction in the six *bardo* states according to the cycle of peaceful and wrathful deities from Karma Lingpa, as well as the oral transmissions for the collected works of Longsal and the volumes of the Supreme Gathering of Commands. I gave the thorough instruction for the Mahakarunika cycle of Karma Chagmé to Lama Orgyen Lhundrup of Sertal and others, and also satisfied requests for teachings from many others who gathered from all directions. For Tsepak,[965] I gave explanations and instructions for *The Highest Continuum*, *The Profound Inner Meaning*, the two smaller treatises, and *The Stages on the Path: The Heart Essence of Timeless Awareness*. I performed feast offerings, fulfillment rituals, ceremonies for the dead, and was generally able to satisfy all the requests made of me.

I then went briefly to Dzongsar Monastery, where I met with my precious lord guru. As his health was somewhat worse, I offered to perform the cleansing ritual *Dispelling All Contamination of Broken Samaya*.[966] I also spent several days satisfying the requests of people who gathered from all directions. Khyentsé Rinpoché bestowed on me nine very special representations of enlightened form, speech, and mind, to be installed in the stupas that would entomb his remains, and gave me advice on what training I should offer to the *tulku*s of Palpung.

I returned to my hermitage at the beginning of the eleventh month. On the day of the winter solstice, I performed a ritual of Vajrakila from The Seven Profound Cycles to avert negativity. I began a personal retreat focusing on the practice of the "Molten Metal" form of Yamantaka; this finished on the day of the new moon. Öntrul was returning to Palpung Monastery this year from central Tibet, [180b] and so I went to meet him and offer a meal. I performed the longevity empowerment from The Union of All Rare and Precious Jewels, the *torma* empowerment for Mahakala and consort, and the oral transmissions for the liturgies used during the year-end *gutor* ceremonies focusing on the protective deities. Beginning on the third day of the twelfth month, I undertook successive personal retreats focusing on the Secret Sphere cycle—the *guru sadhana*, the practice of the masculine aspect, and the practice of the feminine aspect.

ON THE FIRST DAY OF THE NEW Water Dragon Year [1892-1893], a group of fifteen of us, master and students, spent three days performing a *drupchö* ritual based on the Heart Drop of the Exalted Goddess of Immortality. We also performed a group ritual for seven days, using the longevity practice *The Integration of Means and Wisdom*; I gave the empowerment to Kuzhap Choktrul and others. I performed the ordination ceremonies for transmitting the bodhisattva vow from both mainstream traditions[967] for Kuzhap, Öntrul, the Jedrung of Riwoché, Phakchok, and a group of about ten prospective retreat graduates (for the groups in both the upper and lower meditation centers were due to finish their programs this year). I then spent about two weeks in a personal retreat focusing on recitation of the six-syllable mantra of Hayagriva from The United Intent of the Chosen Deities.

In response to the wishes of the two *tulku*s from Riwoché, on the twenty-fifth day of the month I began giving a series of transmissions to the two of them, Kuzhap Rinpoché, Öntrul, and others. I began with the empowerment for the five deity mandala of Chakrasamvara according to the Shangpa tradition, and continued with the complete instructions for this tradition's "ten fundamental transmissions," its "later mainstream transmissions," its transmissions associated with the blue-black Mahakala, its five components (root, trunk, branch, flower, and fruit), its *sadhana* practice called *The Combination of Four Deities*, and its practice of the inseparability of the guru and the protective deity. I also gave the transmission for the Ayushpati cycle from Zhangtrom and that of the Vajrakila cycle from Ratna Lingpa; the major empowerment for the Secret Longevity cycle; [181a] the Kamtsang tradition of Mahamudra and the Six Yogas; and the empowerment and oral transmissions for the *guru sadhana* of the Secret Sphere cycle. Once these were finished, the recipients returned home.

From Dzongsar came word that my precious guru's health, while slightly worse than before, was not obviously disturbed or gravely threatened. He said, "Although you are practicing a great deal, using rituals to promote my longevity, there is no problem for the moment. I'll be better by the twentieth of the second month." I took this to be true. But nothing I could do proved to be of use, and I received a letter to the effect that Khyentsé Rinpoché had passed quite naturally into the state of peace on the morning of the twenty-first. As soon as I received word, I went there with all haste and performed the cleansing of his remains and so forth. On the morning of the twenty-fourth, in the presence of his sacred remains, I prayed for him to arise once more from the

spacelike state of utter lucidity, and made offerings and prayers of supplication and aspiration until my mind felt satisfied. I prepared the remains, wash-
ing them, placing syllables on the power points, and attaching amulets according
to the individual traditions of the old and new schools.

I spent five days in the presence of Khyentsé Rinpoché's remains, practicing a ritual of Vajrasattva in conjunction with a ritual to the guru. On the
twenty-seventh day, Thartsé Khen Rinpoché performed a ritual to the guru.
On this occasion I offered empowerments to Khen Rinpoché and received
them from him, and made prayers of supplication and aspiration to invoke his
innate compassion, all without error and in accord with tradition. [181b] After
the ritual to the guru on the twenty-ninth day, we requested that the deities
depart. On the day of the new moon, Khen Rinpoché, Pönlop,[968] the chant
master of the monastery, and I led four rituals surrounding the remains, which
we offered to the flames of the pyre. For three days afterward, we made offerings in front of the structure housing the ashes, and observed all other appropriate honors. Then, up to the third weekly cusp point we performed, in
succession, the fulfillment ritual from The United Intent of the Gurus, a *drupchö*
ritual focusing on Jinasagara, and *The Two Teachings of the Guru*. The head
steward, Khyentsé Rinpoché's brother Kalzang Dorjé, was very generous in
providing funding for the commemorative rites, including ten very important
articles to be installed in the stupa I was constructing. I myself offered two
measures of silver pieces as a contribution toward the commemorative ceremonies. I also gave five ounces of silver to Khyentsé Rinpoché's attendants
and gave then what practical advice I could. I conferred the empowerments for
The Equal Union of All Buddhas, and the three empowerments (extensive,
middle-length, and abridged) for the Heart Drop of the Exalted Goddess of
Immortality, to both Thartsé Khen Rinpoché and his regent, Pönlop Zhapdrung.

I then left Dzongsar Monastery and returned to my hermitage. Once there,
however, I still performed appropriate rituals on the cusp days when they occurred, as well as rituals to the guru and prayers of supplication and aspiration.
At the end of the requisite number of days,[969] some thirteen of us, master and
students, performed a *drupchö* ritual based on the Padmavajra cycle—the
mandala of the Eighty-Four *Mahasiddhas*—as extensively as possible, and
make offerings and offered prayers of dedication on a large scale. [182a] For
the long mantras to be installed in Khyentsé Rinpoché's stupa, I commissioned
about ten people to spend about one-and-a-half months printing these from
woodblocks and rolling them.

I gave the entire series of empowerments, oral transmissions, and instructions for my *guru sadhana*, based on the Seven-Line Prayer, to the Kuchen incarnation of Palyul Monastery, who came to receive these. For Khenpo Rinchen Dargyé of Karma Gön Monastery, I performed many empowerments and gave many oral transmissions and supplementary instructions from the Tersar cycles of Chokgyur Lingpa.

During the earlier of the two fourth months, I went to Lhasar Temple in Palpung Monastery for the specific purpose of installing the long mantras in the stupa that had previously been constructed there. Khen Lama Tashi Özer, Lama Lodrö Zangpo[970] (who had been an attendant to my lord), and many other lamas and *tulkus* had gathered. Jamyang Gelek accepted the responsibility of sponsoring the project. We performed the necessary preparations—preparing the chakras of the *yaksha* spirits, the treasure vases, and other kinds of chakras; consecrating the long mantras; preparing the central axis; and so forth. We spent many days on the rituals of cleansing and consecration. It proved easiest to locate the stupa to the right of Vajradhara Pema Nyinjé's tomb in Lhasar Temple, so we began by performing the rite of claiming the earth, followed by the stages for installing the long mantras, carrying out the process of visualization and dissolution very extensively.

On the day of the new moon, after taking temporary ordination to ensure auspicious circumstances,[971] we performed the ritual of the two Vimalas to insert the central axis into the stupa. We then spent several days actually installing the long mantras. [182b] Once this was complete, about seventeen of us, masters and students (principally Öngen and Öntrul), performed a two-day ritual of consecration based on the nine deity mandala of Jinasagara, finishing this on the eighth day of the month. We also prepared the "articles that bring liberation on sight" according to the cycles of The United Intent of the Gurus and The Intense Blazing of Timeless Awareness. This stupa had formerly been, in my opinion, destined to be the most important of the representations of enlightened mind that I would construct, but now that it had come to serve as a memorial to my precious lord guru as well as being his tomb, it became the primary repository for the *tsa-tsas* containing his ashes and other such objects.[972]

I went to the hermitage, where I spent several days satisfying requests for teachings from people who had gathered from all directions. In accord with a letter she had sent me previously, the queen of Dergé came to Palpung Monastery to participate in a *drupchen* ritual, so I set out once again for Lhasar Temple.

We began on the twentieth day of the later fourth month. More than eighty people, masters and students, were participating in either the main ritual or one of the four ceremonies being conducted off to the side. We combined a *drupchen* ritual based on the Eight Commands cycle the Gathering of Sugatas with a *mendrup* ritual focusing on Vajra Amrita, and concluded during the waxing phase of the fifth month.

I went to my hermitage, where there were many new arrivals, including the Zhechen Gyaltsap, Lodrö Tulku, and others, whose individual requests I satisfied. Dzasak, the governor of Nyarong, came with many gilded statues, so I performed the rites of installing the long mantras and consecrating these statues. [183a] I spent many days giving the empowerments and oral transmissions for some important cycles—including The Peaceful Garland and The Wrathful Garland and the arrangements of the empowerment rituals for the Sky Teachings—to Kuzhap Choktrul, Öntrul, the retreat graduates, and others. Word came that the Gyatrul incarnation of Palyul Monastery,[973] the *tertön* Tsewang Drakpa of Dalung Valley, and the queen mother of Dergé (while in Changra), had all passed away between the twentieth and the twenty-ninth days of the fifth month. Although I received very insistent invitations to assist at each of these funerals, I was feeling the burden of my advancing years and my illnesses were flaring up, so I couldn't honor a single invitation, but had to send my apologies in all cases. I had received funds from my participation in the commemorative rites for Khyentsé Rinpoché and other spiritual practices, so I used these to make extensive offerings and to sponsor each of many groups to perform appropriate rituals; to these efforts I added any and all prayers of dedication and aspiration that I knew.

At the beginning of the sixth month I went to Dzongshö. There I met Lama Norbu Tendzin, who had come specifically to request from me the empowerment for the Supreme Wheel cycle of Vajrapani and other transmissions. I performed all the appropriate transmissions to satisfy him. I began giving the oral transmissions for The Collected Tantras of the Nyingma Tradition to a few who had gathered for that purpose, including Dzarkha Choktrul, Zhechen Gyaltsap, Jamyang Tulku of Kathok Monastery, and the two princesses of Lingtsang. Palyul Monastery once more sent extensive funds and gifts to be used toward Khyentsé Rinpoché's commemorative rites, so I sponsored large groups to perform rituals, and made offerings and prayers of dedication as extensively as possible. Dzasak, the governor of Nyarong, was journeying to central Tibet, and on his way he stopped to see me. [183b] I spent several days

244 The Autobiography of Jamgön Kongtrul

conferring the empowerments, oral transmissions, and instructions for the three categories of *guru sadhana*, the Dzogchen teachings, and Mahakarunika, as well as the empowerment for *The Prayer in Seven Chapters* from the Total Union cycle and other teachings. In the eighth month I finished the oral transmissions for the tantras, and we held a celebration, involving a feast offering, at Khandroi Drora on the first day of the ninth month. Dezhung Tulku arrived, and I satisfied his wishes with the empowerments, oral transmissions, and instructions for the five deity mandala of the red form of Yamari,[974] as well as the instructions on *Mahamudra: The Ocean of Definitive Meaning*.[975] I transmitted the entire range of empowerments for the *sadhana* of enlightened mind discovered by Taksham, entitled *Refined Gold*, to Ripa Tulku, Doshulwa, and others. I also gave many teachings requested of me by Tsenri Lama and others.

On my way home I stopped at Dzongsar Monastery, where I performed feast offerings and made prayers of supplication in my lord guru's chambers. In response to a request from the master of Ngor and his students, I gave him, Mipham Gyatso, Norbu Tendzin, and others the explanation and oral transmission for the glorious *Kalachakra Tantra* and its commentary, as well as the complete manuals written by Butön Rinpoché and his "heart son" Rinchen Namgyal.[976] In Dzongsar there were projects with which I had planned to help, such as the consecration of the newly built meeting hall and the temple of Tsé Lhakhang.

I then went to my hermitage. This year, it was time for the ninth group of new retreatants to begin their program. Initially, I began giving them what they would need—the successive empowerments, oral transmissions, and instructions, as well as the schedule of practices and my advice and guidelines. [184a]

Dzogchen Tulku's party was returning from Lhasa, and he decided to come and see me. I requested a longevity empowerment from him and showed him all honors. I undertook a personal retreat focusing on the oral lineage tradition of the combined practice of Samyak and Vajrakila. I also performed the annual ritual of Vajrakila to avert negativity.

Jamyang Namgyal Dorjé had been stricken with a virulent and contagious illness resembling tuberculosis. Within a few days his lymph had become poisoned, so I performed various empowerments. While rites were being done for him, shortly after midday on the twenty-eighth of the tenth month, he passed away suddenly. I did whatever I knew how to in such cases—supplication prayers, pointing out the nature of mind to him, placing on his body amulets that brought liberation through touch, and so forth. There were signs that the pointing out had taken effect, for his body remained upright and its luster did not fade. After three days, with the vajra master Lama Döndrup performing the transmission of the transference of consciousness, there was the sound of "Eek!" and Jamyang Namgyal Dorjé's luster faded, he slumped over, and blood flowed from his nostrils, all of which were signs that he had gained freedom.

Together with some retreat graduates who had all completed the stages of approach and accomplishment, I performed the rituals and offering ceremonies on the weekly cusp days very thoroughly and extensively. I invited Dzogchen Rinpoché, the Pönlop of Ngor,[977] the two Öntruls of Palpung Monastery, and other masters. I dedicated offerings to great spiritual masters without any sectarian bias, but mainly to Situ, Pawo, and others of the Karma and Drukpa Kagyü Schools. I sponsored rituals of one thousand offerings at the three major religious centers in the Lhasa area,[978] [184b] supportive practices at individual monasteries, and in such ways ensured that fundamental positive forces were established on a large scale. When we cremated his remains with four rituals taking place surrounding the pyre, the indications were excellent— the sky was completely clear, the next morning there was a whitish rainbow stretching from east to west, and during that day there were remarkable cloud formations and rainbows.

When the forty-nine-day period was finished, I had a dream in which Jamyang Namgyal Dorjé seemed to be even more lustrous and well-clad than he had been in life. He was called to the north by a messenger and said he had to go, and in my mind's eye I clearly saw the house from which the messenger had come. Following that, I had a visionary experience in which someone whose form was unclear gave me a text, which turned out to contain many very special teachings on the outer, inner, and secret levels of *sadhana* practice for the goddess Khechari. When I examined the text, I saw a passage stating that the goddess Khechari had given Jamyang Namgyal Dorjé a nectar pill, and that as soon as his consciousness had been transferred, he had gained freedom in the immediacy of basic space. When I awoke from this vision, I felt very glad.

This man had come to me when he was just a little boy first learning to speak, and had recited the Seven-Line Prayer clearly. Later on, he proved to be very intelligent and endowed with positive karmic tendencies. He had finished the four hundred thousand repetitions of the preliminary practices for the Mahamudra approach, and even trained somewhat in the main practice. As well, he had completed personal retreats focusing on the Vajrakila cycle from Ratna Lingpa and the Mahakarunika cycle of Supreme Compassion: The Gathering of Secrets in an excellent manner. He had planned to do more practice over time, and I had entertained hopes that he would become a lama [185a] and be of benefit to himself and others. But this monastery has been plagued by an evil force from the past, and due to the times we live in nowadays, all those who show promise of doing good for themselves or others fall prey to obstacles. This man, for instance, did not live beyond his twenty-third year.

During this time, the king and prince of Dergé arrived and I performed a ritual to ensure release from negative forces, longevity empowerments, and so forth on their behalf. I satisfied the wishes of many who came from all directions, including five lamas from Dzamthang, to whom I gave the sublime empowerment for the Kalachakra cycle, as well as oral transmissions for the Six Branches of Union. In accord with a divination by Dzarkha Tulku, I made arrangements for, and performed, a ritual of the Eight Commands cycle of The Wrathful Display. With the retreatants, as usual I participated in the ceremonies to replace the *torma*s on the shrine, as well as the offerings to the protective deities and the Mahakala rituals.

DURING THE WAXING PHASE of the moon in the new Water Serpent Year [1893-1894], I carried out my usual spiritual practices and recitations, and a group of twenty-one of us, master and students, spent three days in Thongdröl Lhakhang Temple performing a *drupchö* ritual based on the Heart Drop of the Exalted Goddess of Immortality. I transmitted the empowerment and oral transmissions for the *guru sadhana* of Milarepa and other teachings to the Barom Kagyü master Gönchung Tulku of Kyodrak and his students.[979] The year before I had received a directive from Dragyap to perform a ritual, so during the waning phase of the moon a group of about forty of us, master and students, began a *drupchen* ritual based on The United Intent of the Gurus. We concluded on a grand scale with a celebration, including a hundred feast offerings, on the sixth day of the second month. Then, in Drölma Lhakhang Temple, I spent three days performing a *drupchö* ritual focusing on Tara, [185b] followed by three days of one focusing on the three deities of longevity. Throughout these months, during my breaks I wrote as much as I could, completing the texts needed for inclusion in my *Treasury of Spiritual Advice*.

From the monasteries of both Zhechen and Dzogchen came very insistent requests that I go there, and an envoy was sent to take care of my duties in my absence, but I was feeling the weight of old age, and the omens were also a bit disturbing, so I sent back gifts and offered my deepest apologies. On the twenty-first of the month a large group of us performed a ritual based on Padmavajra as a commemoration to my precious lord guru.

In the third month, Kuzhap Choktrul,[980] Öntrul, Trungpa Tulku of Zurmang Monastery,[981] the incarnation of Chokgyur Lingpa, and many others gathered, and I performed the empowerments for the entire range of mandalas of the Kagyü tradition, as well as the empowerments for The Guru: The Gathering of Secrets and other cycles. For the *tertön*'s incarnation in particular, I gave all the empowerments, oral transmissions, and instructions from Chokgyur Lingpa's *terma*s that he had not received previously. The retreatants were performing a *drupchen* ritual focusing on Vajrasattva, and I attended for about three days and also conferred the extensive empowerment at the conclusion of the ritual. In the fourth month I gave the oral transmissions for some seven volumes of my own miscellaneous writings to the *tulku*s, Lama Tashi Özer, Lama Tashi Chöphel, and others.

A letter, together with a present, had come from my lord guru's brother, Kalzang Dorjé, in Dzongsar, and in response to his request I spent several months around this time [186a] using my breaks to write the biography of my precious and omniscient guru.[982] On this note, interspersing the text with verse would merely be the caprice of a poet, so it didn't seem to matter whether this biography contained them or not. As for the main point—Khyentsé Rinpoché's life example—he seemed to me to be such an embodiment of the infinite and amazing that someone such as I couldn't possibly recount his life with complete accuracy. But it seemed very important that the text be as detailed as possible, even though it was only from the viewpoint of what I had seen for myself. Khyentsé Rinpoché had left no personal account of what he did from year to year, and there was no one among his attendants who had retained clear knowledge of the events, so I based my account on Khyentsé Rinpoché's own verse summary of his life. In addition, I set down what I had heard, without exaggerating or diminishing anything. The signs while I was writing this biography were extremely positive—those who had received empowerments and oral transmissions from Khyentsé Rinpoché sent their support and sponsored a ceremony to promote my longevity, during which Ön Lama of Dragang came and presented me with a sitting mat of the finest quality, bearing the design of crossed vajras.[983]

To the vajra master of the meditation center and other masters and students, I gave the empowerments for the initial and intermediate transmissions from the Zhijé School. To the monks and laymen, I gave the empowerment for Chakrasamvara, according to the tradition of Ghantapada;[984] the instructions for the Five Stages;[985] and the empowerments, oral transmissions, and instructions for the rediscovered *terma* of *The Guru Chakrasamvara*. [186b] And to Tsedrum, Khargo Tulku, and others, I gave the instructions for the Six Yogas of Naropa. Having finished such duties for the time being, I traveled to Dzongshö in a leisurely fashion.

At the beginning of the fifth month, Lhatrul of Palyul Monastery and Dzonggak Tulku arrived. They were on their way to a new monastery founded in Gulok, and stopped on their route specifically to meet me. They presented me with substantial offerings and I gave them the empowerment, oral transmissions, and instructions for the *guru sadhana* of the Secret Sphere cycle. I also gave the oral transmission for *The Profound Path in Seven Sections*. Dzonggak Tulku was quite ill, and so he stayed for a while so that I could examine him and make a diagnosis. He had tried everything—medicine, rituals, techniques to remove obstacles, empowerments—but the underlying problem to his illness was a disorder of the phlegmatic humor, which grew worse until he passed away into a state of peace. He left abundant contributions toward his commemorative rites, and I practiced as much as I could on his behalf, performing rituals until the requisite period of time had elapsed.

I gave the empowerments, oral transmissions, and instructions for the cycles of Rolpai Dorjé's *terma*s, which he discovered in both lakes and rock faces, to Trungpa Tulku of Zurmang Monastery, who came specifically to receive these from me. The formal authorizations associated with the guardian deities of these teachings were implicitly included in the transmissions.[986] The lines of transmission for the rituals to confer the life force of these guardians had become broken in the Zurmang monastic complex, because the strictures governing the transmission of them between the high lamas and *tulku*s had been too strictly enforced. Although the lineages remained nominally intact among a few of the retreat graduates, two distinct ways of practicing them had emerged, and Trungpa Tulku had never received these transmissions from me.

On the third victorious day[987] during the waning phase of the moon, a group of more than thirty of us, master and students, [187a] began a *drupchen* ritual based on Ratna Lingpa's longevity practice *The Gathering of Secrets*. We ensured that the outer and inner *sadhanas*—all three stages of approach, accomplishment, and enactment—were completed within twenty-one days, so that we finished on the thirteenth day of the seventh month. We also held a group prayer session as an extension of the *drupchen* ritual, specifically for the purpose of increasing our own and others' fundamental positive qualities.

This year, Demönpa, the governor of Nyarong, came to Meshö to conduct an investigation into the social unrest toward the king and ministers of Dergé. Over time he sent many gifts, and over and over again I had to arrange group rituals focusing on Tara and the protective deities, in response to the general and more specific requests he made. During the seventh month I also gave the whole range of empowerments, oral transmissions, and instructions for The Innermost Heart Drop of the Guru to seven retreatants from Gonjo, the two princesses of Ling, and others. For the sake of these retreatants, I also performed the ordination ritual for the bodhisattva vow according to the Madhyamaka tradition, and gave a few of them complete instructions for the Mahamudra approach.

Around this time, over a few months I wrote for many days, composing a manual for personal retreat focusing on the nine deity mandala of Kalachakra, an arrangement of the empowerment ritual for the feminine aspect found in the Secret Sphere cycle, a manual of instruction for the stage of completion in this practice, and other texts. On the tenth day of the ninth month, I went to the new meditation center that had been built, where the retreatants offered me a ceremony to promote my longevity. Due entirely to the kindness of my precious lord guru, my lifespan has been extended so as to reach the length indicated in the later prophecy he uttered concerning this. [187b] As well, I myself have had dreams over time that seem to tally with this.

It was during this period, though, that my dreams became slightly disturbed. In any case, my life's main work—my Five Treasuries—had been completed, along with the table of contents and the manuals concerning the lineages of these teachings. Other than a few minor texts, nothing remained unfinished. The woodblocks for these collections were also close to completion, and so there was nothing left over to weigh on my mind.

These days, my allotted span of life was coming to a close. I knew that once one's time is up, even if the Buddha were to come along, he could do nothing to avert it. Still, due to a few trifling concerns (not the least of which were the insistent entreaties by those who place some kind of hope in me), I requested the *tertön* of Dzarkha, Lerab Lingpa,[988] to divine what lay ahead. The *tertön* in turn asked Dzarkha Tulku to investigate this matter as well, and the two of them came to a similar conclusion. They stated categorically that many repetitions of a ritual were indicated, and that if these were performed, I would face no great hindrance or harm in the following year, other than the inevitable process of aging. I completed three hundred thousand repetitions of the fire offering ritual focusing on the *dakinis* (for this was the ritual that was indicated). During the waning phase of the moon in the ninth month, two lamas from Kathok Monastery, both named Nüden, and the monastic community prepared and performed a ritual based on the Eight Commands, to "clear the ground," so to speak. Three practitioners had to be appointed to practice a longevity *sadhana* on my behalf, and when the *sadhana* of *The Intense Blazing of Timeless Awareness* had been completed, they performed a major ceremony employing an effigy to ransom my life force from demonic influences, [188a] as well as ten thousand repetitions of *The Immaculate Tantra of Confession* and one hundred thousand feast offerings. From the two sections of the hermitage, Gelek and Tsering Döndrup made sure that these rituals had been performed. The thought was always in my mind that these rituals—the fire offerings, *The Immaculate Tantra of Confession*, and so forth—were something that needed to be done whether I died or not, but as my body continued to deteriorate, this served as an example that inspired me to use positive forces to counteract negative circumstances.

Dezhung Tulku arrived and I gave him whatever teachings he needed, including an oral transmission, with explanations, of *The Highest Continuum*, and instructions in the seven points of mental training.[989] The governor and his retinue arrived at the beginning of the tenth month, and I satisfied their requests by giving them whatever empowerments and oral transmissions they wished. I performed *ganachakra* feasts and made extensive prayers of benediction in the various meditation caves in the area. I performed a thousand repetitions of the feast offerings from the cycles of The Union of All Rare and Precious Jewels and The Gathering of All the Dakinis' Secrets. In addition, I finished whatever else came up due to the requests of individuals. I then returned homeward, and on the way stopped at Dzongsar Monastery to perform the feast offering based on The Combined Practice of the Three Roots in my precious guru's private chambers. I then continued on to my hermitage.

I gave empowerments and oral transmissions in response to individual requests from the senior and junior chaplains to the prince of Dergé, the monks of Drak-nak Monastery in Gonjo, and others. I then undertook a personal retreat focusing on the Vajrakila cycle of Chöjé Lingpa, and performed the annual ritual of Vajrakila to avert negativity. I had commissioned a fine gilded statue of White Tara, [188b] and installed the long mantras inside and consecrated it, and in conjunction with this undertook a personal retreat.

In the twelfth month I undertook retreats focusing on three "oral lineages"— Hayagriva, the *mamo* goddesses, and Vajra Amrita. At the end of the year, I participated briefly in the *torma* ritual of Mahakala.

ON THE FIRST DAY OF THE NEW Wood Horse Year [1894-1895], I turned eighty-two years of age. Beginning on the second day, I was stricken with a virulent illness, some kind of contagious infection. In particular, my chronic coughing fits, which had been ongoing, upset my health, and I was completely unable to sleep. Tsering Döndrup became concerned and asked the lamas of Kathok Monastery and Dzarkha to determine what was going on. A great deal of uproar ensued, with people running here and there performing supportive rituals. For my own part, intending to purify myself of obscurations, during that first month (the month commemorating the Buddha's spiritual miracles), I sponsored the monastic community of Palpung to recite the six-syllable mantra *Om mani padme hum* one hundred million times. To each of the more than three hundred participants, I gave a gift of silk and three ounces of silver. The Dergé nobility and the lamas and monks of Palpung, including Situ Rinpoché and his brother, sponsored individual rituals to promote my longevity. The retreatants performed a *drupchö* ritual focusing on Tara many times over. Due to such efforts, one would have expected anyone's illnesses to clear up, but given the weight of my advancing years, it was difficult to hope that my health would undergo any improvement.

CONCLUDING REMARKS

For some time, Khen Lama Tashi Özer [189a] and Lama Orgyen Lhundrup of Sertal had both urged me on many occasions of the need for me to write my autobiography. As well, the great scholar, Lama Tashi Chöphel, made a similar request and provided me with paper and writing materials.[990] Given all of this, it is inevitable that I have written at least this much, if only to keep myself awake at times when I was comfortable enough and had no hope of giving or receiving any more empowerments, oral transmissions, or teachings.

In general, I gained a special working basis with this precious human existence. Its special features have included the seven qualities of a higher state of rebirth and the four great influences with which it is endowed.[991] The meaningful result of this was that I entered the doorway of the Buddha's teachings; and not only that, for I have encountered the Vajrayana, the approach of the secret mantras, which is something that almost never occurred in the past, almost never occurs in the present, and almost never will occur in the future. Like someone who has journeyed to the fabled Isle of Gold, I have had the free will to achieve whatever I wanted.

Such circumstances seem practically impossible ever to find within the bounds of samsara, but even though I have enjoyed them, due to the powerful influences of my karma and past aspirations, as well as the fact that my personal freedom has been sacrificed for others, I have not truly been able to apply myself to the essentials of spiritual practice in the way that I intended. Instead, I have been distracted by an uninterrupted process of projects—activities that I never intended to pursue. Nevertheless, from an early age I have, as a matter of course, rejected things of this world. I have not been given any title as some great incarnation.[992] I have not been burdened with the effects of unintentional misappropriation incurred by anyone overseeing a monastery. [189b] I have had no need for any such activities, but rather have, up to the present, strived solely at positive and spiritual activities.

This is the very essence of what someone's biography should contain, and up until my thirties I had not been affected by any misappropriation of support offered by the faithful or offerings made on behalf of deceased individuals. Since that time, however, the negative effects of such unintentional misappropriation has become a heavier and heavier burden to me. My clear inner vision and positive qualities have become more obscured, while the effects of my harmful actions, moral failings, and negative habits have become more prevalent. As one of the sutras states, "It is a more grievous fault for someone to violate their ethical discipline and become involved in misappropriation than for an evil person to kill a thousand people every day." There is no one—not me, not anyone else—who doesn't affirm the three levels of ethical discipline. But on the level of the vows for individual liberation,[993] as long as a monk doesn't openly consort with women, he is deemed to be keeping his vows purely; monastic administrators and lamas don't attach any importance to the other fundamental downfalls of a monastic.[994] As for the bodhisattva vow, the fundamental flaws—of mentally abandoning another being or engaging in the four negative attitudes[995]—seem to have become the actual practices in which people engage! So why even mention the *samaya*s associated with the four levels of empowerment in the highest level of tantra, *samaya*s that have vanished like a rainbow fading, when people engage in most of the primary and secondary downfalls of the *samaya* of the mantra approach without even thinking about the consequences.

The causes of all these situations is said to be the four ways in which moral failings occur—that is, due to ignorance, lack of respect, heedlessness, and a plethora of afflictive emotions. [190a] First, as for ignorance, if most of those who are given the titles of a lama or *tulku* nowadays haven't the slightest clue about the three levels of ordination—about what constitutes the guidelines to be observed or the various degrees of infractions, transgressions, or violations that can be incurred—how can we expect the rank-and-file monks to know? Second, although someone might not have a deeply-held lack of respect for the training, without knowledge there can be no real respect; and those who, worse still, deliberately flout their ordination are committing an egregious mistake. Third, it is necessary to cultivate heedfulness, mindfulness, and alertness, for if one is unable to do so, one's physical, verbal, and mental behavior falls under the sway of heedlessness. Fourth, people born in these times of spiritual degeneration are subject to afflictive emotions that are growing steadily more powerful, so people for the most part are under the sway of one or another of the three emotional poisons.[996] Due to such flaws, I myself am constantly plagued by the nagging dread that there is no destiny for me but some lower state of rebirth. The foregoing amounts to my concluding remarks.

ACTIVITIES

The superb accomplishments of holy people are well-known as the "nine modes of the holy" and the "three spheres of activity." Although there is no question of my having any of these in the true sense, I do have certain accomplishments that serve merely as partial approximations. Let me discuss these under the headings of the three spheres of activity—that of erudition, which includes study and contemplation; that of renunciation, which concerns meditative stability; and that of projects, which concerns other undertakings.

STUDY AND CONTEMPLATIONS

Transmissions Received

Concerning the first sphere of my activities, I have accepted the three levels of discipline, which is the precious foundation for all one's positive qualities, [190b] and to the best of my ability have adhered to the training for each level. I studied a number of more exoteric subjects to the point where I no longer needed to rely on anyone other than myself. These subjects included the three Sanskrit grammars of the Kalapa, Chandra, and Sarasvata systems (the source texts and auxiliary treatises); a concise overview of the field of epistemology;[997] the arts of painting, sculpture, and the layout of immeasurable mansions;[998] medicine (the Four Tantras and practical experience); the Chinese system of astrology; and metrics, poetics, and etymology and nomenclature, including the source verse of *The Treasury of Immortality* and its commentary.[999]

As for the more esoteric teachings, I have received detailed explanations of the following texts of the general Buddhist tradition: *The Ornament of Higher Realization, The Entrance into the Middle Way, The Treasury of Higher Teachings*, and *The Highest Continuum*.

I have also received detailed explanations of the following extraordinary texts of specific traditions:

- *The Kalachakra Tantra* and its major commentary (explanations from the Zhalu tradition and oral transmissions of the instruction manuals by Butön and his students)
- the root *Chakrasamvara Tantra* and its commentary (an explanation of Lord Tsongkhapa's *Illuminating All the Concealed Meanings*)
- *The Hevajra Tantra in Two Chapters* (explanations in both the Sakya and Ngok traditions, and oral transmissions of the instruction manuals of the two schools)
- explanations of the fragmentary root tantra of Vajrakila and *Reciting the Names of Manjushri* and
- the venerable Rangjung Dorjé's works—that is, *The Profound Inner Meaning, The Treatise Distinguishing Ordinary Consciousness from Timeless Awareness*, and *The Treatise on Buddha Nature*.

From among the teachings of the Nyingma School, I have received an extensive explanation of the root tantra entitled *The Heart Essence of Secrets* according to the commentary by Lochen Dharma Shri of Mindroling, as well as receiving oral transmissions of *The Imprint* and other ancient commentaries. [191a] I also have studied in detail, according to the traditional methods, explanatory instructions on *The Garland of Views* and *The Stages of the Path of Secret Mantra*. In most of the above cases I committed the source verses to memory, and in all cases I read and reflected deeply on the commentaries.

I have received the oral transmissions for the precious Kangyur—the collection of the Victorious One's words translated into Tibetan, which are the primary sources of the sacred teachings of Buddhist tradition—on two occasions, as well as the oral transmissions for the twenty-five volumes of The Collected Tantras of the Nyingma Tradition and for the texts from the Tengyur collection for which lineages of oral transmission still exist today (this amounts to more than twenty volumes).

I have received all the empowerments and oral transmissions for the following cycles:

From the Kriya Tantra class (the basic level of the Vajrayana), I have received transmission for:

- The Protectors of the Three Families; The Array of the Threefold Samaya
- the forty-seven deity mandala of Bhaishajyaguru; cycles associated with the *tathagata* family (including the cycles of the two Vimalas, Ushnisha Sitatapatra, the two traditions of Akshobhya, and the five protective goddesses)
- cycles associated with the *padma* family (including Amoghapasha, the thousand-armed, thousand-eyed form of Avalokiteshvara, and the nine deity mandala of the "Deathless Drumbeat" form of Amitayus)
- and the white and dark blue forms of Vajrapani.

From the Charya Tantra class, I have received transmissions for the cycle of The Manifest Enlightenment of Vairochana and the five deity mandala of the Arapachana form of Manjushri.

From the Yoga Tantra class, I have received transmissions for:

- the Vajradhatu mandala
- the Manjushri cycles of Dharmadhatu: Lord of Speech and Secrecy
- the mandalas of The Tantra of Refinement and Shakyamuni with the Ninefold Ushnisha

- the basic transmissions of the two traditions of Sarvavid Vairochana and
- the auxiliary transmissions of twelve mandalas.

As for the Anuttarayoga Tantra class, I have received transmissions for cycles from the mother tantras in detail:

- for the glorious Kalachakra, the usual and special empowerments from the three traditions of Ra, Dro, and Tsami as transmitted by the Jonang, Zhalu, and Kamtsang Kagyü Schools, and the Great Precept cycle [191b]
- for Hevajra, the empowerments for the four Sakya traditions with all their subdivisions, the nine deity mandala and Nairatma from the tradition of Ngok, and the "abridged family" mandala based on *The Vajra Pavilion*
- the empowerment based on *The Sealed Vajra Locket,* as well as transmissions connected with the root *Chakrasamvara Tantra*—that is, Vajrapani's *Commentary on the Beginning Section,* the tradition of Luhipa, the body mandala and five deity mandala from the tradition of Ghantapada, the tradition of Krishnacharin, the Bhramahara system, the thirteen deity mandala from the tradition of Maitripa
- the feminine cycles, including the thirty-seven deity mandala of Varahi, Naropa's tradition of Khechari, the Chal tradition of the goddess with the two faces (symbolizing the two levels of truth), Arthasiddhi, and Shantigupta's tradition of Varahi
- concerning the explanatory tantra of Chakrasamvara: the cycles of The Source of Commitment; The Qualities of Refinement; The Six Universal Monarchs; Manjuvajra Chakrasamvara and Wrathful Chakrasamvara with One Hundred Thousand Arms (both based on the newer translation of the texts); the "Donkey-Headed" form of Chakrasamvara; the seventeen deity mandala of Varahi; the Vajradaka cycle; the three combined lineages of *The Ocean of Dakas*; the "Great Visage" form of Varahi and *The Source of Varahi* (both based on the newer translation); and the wrathful form of Vajrasattva
- other mother tantra transmissions, such the cycle of Chakrasamvara Avalokiteshvara Padmajala, the five deity mandala of Kurukulle, Tarayogini, and others that will be discussed later.

As for the father tantras, I have received the empowerments for a number of cycles, as well as the oral transmissions for their respective manuals of instruction, and I have studied these instructions in detail:

- for Guhyasamaja, the tradition of Nagarjuna, Guhyasamaja Manjuvajra, and Atisha's tradition of Guhyasamaja Avalokiteshvara
- for Yamari, the five- and thirteen deity mandalas of Red Yamari, the Zhang tradition of Black Yamari, and the cycle of the six-faced Yamari
- for Vajrabhairava, the mandala of Vajrabhairava surrounded by a retinue of eight reanimated corpses, [192a] the thirteen deity mandala, the tradition of Kyo, the forty-nine deity mandala, the deity surrounded by eight wrathful goddesses, and the nine deity mandala in the tradition of Mal
- the Mahachakra form of Vajrapani and
- the Anuttarayoga tradition of *Reciting the Names of Manjushri.*

THE EIGHT LINEAGES OF ACCOMPLISHMENT

Nyingma

The first of the eight great mainstream lineages of spiritual accomplishment famed in the land of Tibet is that of the Early Translation School—that is, the Nyingma—which includes three traditions: *kama,* or long historical transmissions; *terma,* or hidden teachings; and *daknang,* or pure visionary transmissions.

From the *kama* tradition, I have received the empowerments, oral transmissions, and instructions for all the lineages still currently available, including the following:

- the three cycles of *The Discourse of United Intent, The Web of Magic,* and the Category of Mind
- the Equal Union cycle
- the three traditions of Black and Red Yamari
- the two traditions of Samyak
- the three traditions of Vajrakila
- the two traditions of Dredging the Pit of Cyclic Existence
- the cycle of the Eight Commands called The Gate to the Fortress
- the white and black wrathful forms of Vajravidarana and
- the works of the omniscient Longchenpa, including his great Seven Treasuries, his Trilogy of Being at Ease, his miscellaneous works and, most especially, the Four Higher Collections of the Heart Drop Teachings.

From the *terma* tradition, I have received the empowerments, oral transmissions, and instructions for all the lineages of the great *tertöns* that are still available, from those of Sang-gyé Lama,[1000] Sherab Dorjé Bum, and Chökyi Drakpa[1001] to the "three sublime nirmanakayas" (Ngadak Nyangral Nyima Özer, Guru Chöwang, and Rigdzin Gödem), the famous masters with the title "Lingpa" (especially the five great Lingpas[1002]), Pema Ledrel Tsal, the three named Drimé, Jatsön Nyingpo, Duddul Dorjé, Longsal Nyingpo, [192b] Taksham Nüden Dorjé, Yön-gé Mingyur Dorjé, and Rolpai Dorjé, down to those of Pema Ösel Do-ngak Lingpa and Chokgyur Dechen Lingpa. I have received the transmissions for their collected works (especially those of the *tertön* Sherab Özer in one volume and those of Minling Terchen in fourteen volumes), biographies, spiritual advice, and songs, as well as for all the minor *terma*s for which transmissions still exist.

From the tradition of pure visions and oral lineages, I have received the empowerments and oral transmissions for lineages from many major and minor *tertön*s, especially Lhatsün Namkha Jigmé, Nyida Longsal,[1003] Namchö Mingyur Dorjé, the great Fifth Dalai Lama, Jigmé Lingpa, and Thukkyi Dorjé.[1004] I have also received the oral transmissions for the Sky Teachings and the collected works of Jigmé Lingpa and other masters, including those of Tselé Natsok Rangdrol in six volumes, those of the two Zhechen Rabjam incarnations in nine volumes, those of Zhechen Gyaltsap in two volumes, and those of Öntrul Rinpoché in one volume.

Kadampa

From the cycles of the second lineage, the precious Kadampa, I have received the following:
- the empowerments, formal authorizations, and instructions for the Sixteen Spheres and the Four Deities
- the detailed instructions on the precious Kadampa volumes [193a] known as The Father's Teachings and The Sons' Teachings
- the source text *The Stages on the Path to Enlightenment* and its middle-length commentary by Sharawa[1005]
- *The Blissful Path of Refined Gold*
- *The Oral Transmission of Manjushri*
- instructions on Putowa's[1006] *Scriptural Teachings*, together with the extensive commentary and essays

- Chégom's[1007] *Pith Instructions*, including *The Heaped Jewels* and miscellaneous writings
- Dolpawa's[1008] *Blue Udder* collection
- the miscellaneous writings of Naktso Lotsawa,[1009] Dromtön, Kharakpa,[1010] and others
- the *Mountain Teachings* of Gyergompa[1011]
- *The Seven Points of Mind Training* and the major oral lineage of detailed instructions on this
- *The Compendium of All Excellent Explanations*
- Langri Thangpa's[1012] *Eight Verses* and Khampa Lungpa's[1013] *Eight Practice Sessions*
- instructions on miscellaneous writings from the new Kadampa tradition[1014] (including *The One Hundred Collected Instructions on Mental Training*, the collected writings of Gyalsé Thogmé Zangpo, and the precious Lord Tsongkhapa's *Three Principal Aspects of the Path*) and
- the oral transmission for *The Great Spiritual History of the Kadampa School.*

Sakya

The third of these lineages is that of the Sakyapa, whose spiritual advice is based on the Lamdré system. From among these teachings, I have received the following:
- the transmission of the bodhisattva vow according to the tantric approach
- the four traditions of empowerment for Hevajra, followed by the primary and secondary instructions from the "group explanation" transmission of the Lamdré cycle and the formal blessings as appropriate
- the oral transmissions for the *Yellow Volume, Red Volume*, and *Blue Volume* of the Lamdré system [193b]
- explanations of *The Hevajra Tantra in Two Chapters*, including the seven indispensable source texts
- the formal blessing of Naropa's tradition of Khechari, as well as instructions and oral transmissions for the associated volumes and
- on numerous occasions, the empowerments for the Anuttarayoga classes of tantra and formal blessings and authorizations for the series of instructions known as the Thirteen Golden Teachings.

Marpa Kagyü

The fourth lineage is that of the Kagyü, the oral lineage from Lord Marpa. From among the cycles of these teachings, I have received the following oral transmissions:

- the two volumes of Indian sources on Mahamudra
- the Indian sources on the Six Yogas, including *The Standard of Authentic Instruction* and the *Vajra Verses of the Oral Lineage*, and the longer and shorter original sources
- the combined collections of Marpa's and Milarepa's songs
- the single volume of Dakpo Rinpoché's collected writings
- the empowerments, oral transmissions, and instructions for the root cycles of the oral lineage (the extensive version from the tradition of Rechungpa, the middle-length from that of the Kamtsang Kagyü, and the shorter from that of Ngamdzong)
- the cycles of instructions of the "disembodied *dakinis*" and
- the four scrolls of the oral lineage.

From the individual traditions of the Kagyü—that of the seat of Dakpo, Tsalpa, Phakmo Druppa, Throphu, Drukpa (or Lingré, with its three branches of upper, lower, and middle), Yang-gönpa, Barawa, Taklung and Drigung[1015]— I have received the instructions on Mahamudra and the Six Yogas; explanations of the "Single Intent" and other interpretations; and the major text of instructions on Mahamudra by Martsang Yeshé Gyatso.

In particular, [194a] from the Kamtsang Kagyü tradition, I have received the empowerments for the five practices of the glorious Düsum Khyenpa and the nine and five deity mandalas of Jinasagara; and authorizations for The Peaceful Garland and The Wrathful Garland of deities, and those for the collection of protective deities called The Lightning Garland. I have also received the oral transmissions for the following:

- the single volume of Düsum Khyenpa's collected works
- the miscellaneous writings of the venerable Rangjung Dorjé, Khachö Wangpo, Wangchuk Dorjé, and others
- the commentary on ethics and the volume of short essays by the Eighth Karmapa, Lord Mikyö Dorjé
- the collected works of the all-seeing Chökyi Jungné and Lord Pema Nyinjé Wangpo
- a number of writings from the Zurmang Kagyü School and

- the twenty-odd volumes of the collected works of Karma Chagmé of Nedo, from his *Mountain Teachings*, background instructions, and detailed instructions on Mahakarunika, to his works on rituals of ransom.

Shangpa Kagyü

From among the teachings of the fifth lineage, the Shangpa Kagyü, I have received the following:
- the major empowerment for The Deities of the Five Classes of Tantra (which the learned and accomplished Khyungpo Naljor received from Vajrasana[1016])
- the ten transmissions concerning the Six Yogas
- the later source transmissions
- the thirteen major transmissions for the protective deity
- instructions on the Five Golden Teachings from the tradition of Niguma
- the practical methods for the Six Yogas of Sukhasiddhi
- the *sadhana* called *The Combination of Four Deities* transmitted from Rahula[1017] and
- oral transmissions for the Indian and Tibetan source texts and instruction manuals, comprising some five volumes.

Zhijé (Pacification of Suffering) and Chö (Severance)

As for the cycles of the sixth lineage, that of Zhijé and Chö, I have received the following transmissions: [194b]
- the entire range of empowerments and formal blessings for the initial, intermediate, and later transmissions, as well as their respective instructions
- the oral transmissions for the single volume of Phadampa Sang-gyé's miscellaneous works and Lochen Dharma Shri's instruction manuals
- the empowerments and instructions for the first transmission of the Chö teachings (from Rangjung Dorjé), the intermediate transmission (from Jamyang Gönpo[1018]), and the later transmission (the tradition of Gyalthang)
- the oral transmissions for the single volume of Chö sources (authored by the brahmin Aryadeva and Machik Lapdrön) and

- the three volumes of Chö sources from the Zurmang and Gyalthang traditions.

Dorjei Naljor (Vajra Yoga)

From among the teachings of the seventh lineage, that of Vajra Yoga, I have received the following:
- the empowerments for both the Jonang and Zhalu traditions of Kalachakra
- instructions on the Six Branches of Union
- the oral transmissions for some of the Indian sources and the manuals concerning the stages of development and completion, the *sadhana*, and the mandala rituals.

Dorjé Sumgyi Nyendrup (Stages of Approach and Accomplishment for the Three Vajras)

Concerning the eighth lineage, that of The Stages of Approach and Accomplishment, I have received the oral transmissions for the instructions and other volumes concerning the Stages of Approach and Accomplishment for the Three Vajras, including the sources containing advice from the great *siddha* Orgyenpa and their commentaries.

I have also received transmissions for several collections, including the following:
- The Vajra Garland of Maitriyogi
- The One Hundred Instructions of Narthang
- the formal blessing for the Eighty-Four *Mahasiddhas*, as well as instructions on the Six Yogas and the oral transmissions of the instruction manuals
- The Precious Source of Sadhanas collection from the Jonang School
- the thirteen volumes of The Compendium of All Sadhanas assembled by my precious lord guru
- the empowerments, oral transmissions, and instructions for The Six Instructions of Maitripa
- a number of minor instructions from the Throphu, Bodong, and other traditions [195a] and
- (on two occasions) The One Hundred Instructions of Kunga Drolchok.

WRITINGS AND THE FIVE TREASURIES

Given that I have studied the teachings of the Victorious One extensively and without sectarian bias, the mark of all this study is to be found in my writings. Foremost among these are my great Treasuries, but I did not initially plan these and the thought that I should assign the name "the Five Treasuries" never entered my mind. However, once I had finished many works due to the insistent requests of my spiritual masters and mentors, my all-seeing guru, Jamyang Khyentsé Wangpo, prophesied on the basis of his pure vision that I would produce these five Treasuries, and bestowed on me what amounted to tables of contents for each collection of teachings.

The Treasury of the Knowable

The first of the Five Treasuries is *The Encompassing of the Knowable*.[1019] This begins with an introductory section—the part that is "positive at the outset."[1020] It discusses the title of the work, as well as the formal verses of homage and my statement of intent as the author.[1021]

The main body of the work—the part that is "positive in the interim"—comprises ten major sections. These discuss the following topics:

- the universe as the field in which beings are guided spiritually
- the Buddha as the teacher who guided them
- the cycles of the Buddhist teachings that are the means of guidance
- the ways in which these teachings spread in India and Tibet
- the three levels of ethical discipline that serve as the foundation of spiritual practice
- a detailed analysis of the study undertaken at the outset of the spiritual path
- a detailed analysis of contemplation as the intermediate phase
- a detailed analysis of meditation as the final outcome
- the paths and levels that are traversed through these last three processes and
- the eventual way in which the fruition is gained.

Each of these ten sections has four subsections. [195b] Through these discussions, one can also come indirectly to understand the Hinayana, the Mahayana, and the special enlightened intent underlying the Early Translation School's approach of the vajra pinnacle of utter lucidity.[1022] To summarize these sections, the fifth deals with the higher training of ethical discipline, the sixth and seventh with that of wisdom, and the eighth with that of meditative stability; thus they constitute the core of the work, while the rest of the sections deal with secondary topics that are the causes or results of these higher trainings.

The conclusion—the part that is "positive in the outcome"—brings the work to its completion by discussing the nature and value of the treatise and the way it was composed; as well, this part contains prayers of aspiration and benediction.

The source verses, the summary and overview, and the line-by-line commentary comprise three volumes.

The Tantric Treasury of the Kagyü School

The second of the Treasuries, *The Tantric Treasury of the Kagyü School*,[1023] takes as its basis the "seven mandalas of Ngok," the primary tradition of the lineage that has come down from the master Marpa. Some transmissions received from other sources have also been included in the collection.

The sections concerned with the mother tantras[1024] are as follows:

• the section on Hevajra, including the nine deity mandala. While this follows a format which resembles that found in the tradition of Saroruhavajra, it would seem that Nagarjuna is considered the source of this transmission. This section also includes instructions on "blending and transference" according to the individual traditions of Naropa and Maitripa; the fifteen deity mandala of Nairatma; and the Hevajra mandala known as the "gathered family," according to the explanatory tantra *The Vajra Pavilion*

• the section on Chakrasamvara and Vajravarahi according to the Kamtsang Kagyü School, including the five deity mandalas for both deities; instructions on the Six Yogas; the mandala of the "six universal monarchs"; and the twenty-nine visualizations for self-consecration deriving from *The Sealed Locket*

• the section on Mahamaya, including the five deity mandala and instructions on the three yogas of form, mantra, and phenomena

• the section on Vajra Chatuhpitha,[1025] [196a] including the sixty-two deity mandala of the Yoga of Space cycle and the cycle of the feminine principle of the thirteen deity mandala of Jnaneshvari, as well as the instructions on the practice of Vajra Chatuhpitha

- the section on Buddhakapala, including the twenty-five deity mandala, as well as the teachings according to the tradition of Shantigupta.

The sections concerned with the father tantras are as follows:
- the section on Guhyasamaja, including the tradition of Nagarjuna as well as the instructions on the Five Stages
- the section on *Reciting the Names of Manjushri*
- the section on the five deity mandala of Red Yamantaka and the Mal tradition of Vajrabhairava surrounded by a retinue of eight reanimated corpses (these two are not lineages that come from Marpa, but there exist transmissions of the empowerments and oral transmissions, as well as manuals written by the Eighth Karmapa and Fourth Zhamarpa, and so these two cycles have been included so as to complete the three families of the father tantras)
- the section on Vajrapani, which contains the five deity mandala of Chanda from the tradition of Rechungpa

In all of these cases, new versions of the *sadhana*s, mandala rituals, auxiliary liturgies, fire rituals, and so forth were prepared for the collection.

The transmissions from other sources include the empowerments and authorizations for the Wish-Fulfilling Wheel form of White Tara, the tradition of Vajrasattva transmitted from King Jah, Vijaya, Green Tara, Vajrapani, and the three guardian deities of these teachings—Tantra Natha, the goddess Dhumavati, and the goddess Tseringma. The collection includes the most important old texts associated with these cycles, as well as any necessary new works that were prepared for inclusion.

To serve as background teachings for the collection, I composed a commentary on the Mahayana treatise entitled *The Highest Continuum*; an overview and word-by-word commentary on the glorious root tantra *The Hevajra Tantra in Two Chapters*; [196b] commentaries on the works of Lord Rangjung Dorjé—*The Profound Inner Meaning, The Treatise Distinguishing Ordinary Consciousness from Timeless Awareness*, and *The Treatise on Buddha Nature*. In all of these works I sought primarily to facilitate understanding.

This collection also includes teachings from the *kama* tradition of the Nyingma School:
- one volume dealing with the Khön tradition of Vajrakila, including the activity ritual and the rite of "higher activity," both written by the venerable Taranatha (In response to an insistent request from the lamas and

monks of Dzamthang Monastery that these two texts had to be supplemented, I added my own compositions, primarily the wrathful empowerment of liberation and the *torma* ritual for averting negativity)
- a section on the Khön tradition of Samyak, which includes three parts—
  the *sadhana*, the mandala ritual, and the daily practice
- a section on the So tradition of Samyak, which includes the manuals for
  the *drupchen* ritual and personal retreat
- a section on the six-faced form of Yamantaka, which includes the *sadhana*,
  mandala ritual, and empowerment manual and
- a section on the wrathful white and black forms of Vajravidarana, which
  includes the activity rituals and empowerment manuals.

The Treasury of Precious Hidden Teachings

The content of the third of the Treasuries, *The Treasury of Precious Hidden
Teachings*,[1026] can be summarized by the following verses:

> As for earth *termas*,[1027] Sang-gyé Lama was the first to discover one,
> followed by Gyaben Dorjé Ö, Guru Hung Barwa,
> Gya Lotsawa Dorjé Zangpo, Lhatsün Jangchub Ö,
> Zhangtsün Darma Rinchen, Rongzom Chökyi Zangpo,
> Drapa Ngönshé, Sherab Dorjé Bum, Drigungpa Chökyi Drakpa,
> Nanam Tupgyal, Zhangtrom Dorjé Ö-Bar,
> Khyungpo Palgyi Gewa, Gya Phurbu Ngön,
> LharjéNupchung, Lhatsün Ngönmo,
> Rashak Chöbar, Uru Shakya Ö,
> [197a] Druptop Ngödrup, Nyangral Nyima Özer,
> Ramo Shelmen, Drugu Yang-wang Ter,
> Chupo Tokden Gendün Gyaltsen, Tulku Bakhal Mukpo Dong,
> Kunpang Dawai Özer, Ngadak Molmi Khyil,
> Sumpa Jangchub Tsulthrim, Kyangpo Drakpa Wangchuk, Driben
>   Sherab Lama,[1028]
> Taklung Sang-gyé Önpo Könchok Sé, Nyalpa Nyima Sherab,
> Yak-Khyar Ngönmo, Burbu Ja'u Gön,
> Balpo A-Hum, Ajo Palpowa,
> Changmen Döndrup Dargyé, Rongmen Nyimai Ö,
> Dampa Marpo, Kalden Jipa,

Khampa Mezor, Khala Mebarwa,
Khampa Thramo, Drangti Gyalné Kharpuwa,
Dugu Rinchen Seng-gé, Tsang-Ring Sherab,
Lama Drum, Yöndak Kharnakpa,
Guru Chökyi Wangchuk, the four yogic masters of *terma*s,
Jomo Menmo, the great Dungtso Repa,
Gyatön Pema Wangchuk, Khampa Nyima Drakpa,
Guru Jotsé, Khandro Kunga Bum,
Tseten Gyaltsen, Vajramati,
Khyakdorpa, the three lay tantric masters named Wangchen,
Kyebu Zangling Wangchuk, Yeben Yabön,
Pema Ledrel, Gyalsé Lekpa,
Drimé Özer, Meben Rinchen Lingpa,
Bönpo Lhabum, Yang-bön Ritrö Paseng,
Dragom Chökyi Dorjé, Yarjé Orgyen Lingpa,
Nyida[1029] Sang-gyé, Sherab Mebar,
Drampa Kunzang, Gyalsé Dorjé Lingpa,
[197b] Zangpo Drakpa, Orgyen Sang-gyé Lingpa,
Drimé Lhunpo, the venerable Drimé Kunga,
Langpowa Palgyi Gyaltsen, Rigdzin Gökyi Demtruchen,
Thangtong Gyalpo, Druptop Karma Lingpa,
Palden Jamyang Lama, Samten Dechen Lingpa,
Drodrul Ratna Lingpa, Pema Lingpa,
Chokden Dorjé, Drodul Letro Lingpa,
Pema Kunkyong Lingpa, Orgyen Do-ngak Lingpa Chokden Gönpo,
Orgyen Tennyi Lingpa Pema Tsewang Gyalpo, Ngari Panchen Pema
Wang-gyal Dorjé,
Tsering Dorjé, Gyama Mingyur Letro Lingpa Kunga Palzang,
Rinchen Phuntsok, Mati Ratna,
Garwang Orgyen Zhikpo Lingpa, Ngari Rigdzin Lekden Dorjé,
Threngpo Drodul Lingpa Sherab Özer, Nesarpa Khyentsé Wangchuk
    Do-ngak Lingpa,
Tashi Topgyal, Epo-chok Garwang Letro Lingpa,
Pema Rigdzin, Langpo Chagdepa Tashi Tseten,
Rigdzin Jatsön Nyingpo, Duddul Nüdenpa,
Jangchub Sempa Dawa Gyaltsen, Orgyen Terdak Lingpa Pema
    Garwang Gyurmé Dorjé,

Rigdzin Chenpo Longsal Nyingpo, Taksham Dorjé Samten Lingpa,
Mingyur Dorjé Drakpo Nüden Tsal,
Kuchok Ngak-gi Dorjé, Latö Takmo Guru Önsé Khyungthok,
Chöjé Lingpa, Kundrol Yungdrung Lingpa,
Ratön Topden Dorjé Pema Tsewang Tsal, Khampa Rinpoché
    Ngawang Kunga Tendzin,
Rigdzin Thukchok Dorjé Hum-nak Drodrul, Kunzang Dechen
    Gyalpo Mönlam Dorjé,
Rigdzin Chenpo Rolpai Dorjé, Rongtön Pema Dechen Lingpa,
Kathok Rigdzin Tsewang Norbu, Tsasum Terdak Lingpa Garwang
    Namchak Dorjé,
Drimé Lingpa, Ta'u-Rong Rokjé Lingpa Drodul Tsal,
[198a]   Garwang Chimé Dorjé, Dorjé Thogmé Tendzin Da-ö Dorjé,
Rangdrol Tingdzin Gyalpo Dawai Özer, Chögyal Dorjé,
and Pema Ösel Do-ngak Lingpa,
down to Chokgyur Dechen Zhikpo Lingpa.

The cycles of *terma*s of enlightened intent, direct oral lineages,
and pure visions include those of
Jangchub Sempa Dawa Gyaltsen, Öntön Kyergangpa Chökyi Seng-gé,
Kathokpa Dampa Deshek, Yuthok Yönten Gönpo,
Geshé Tsöndru Drakpa, the venerable and omniscient Rangjung
    Dorjé,
Palden Dorjé of Phenyul, Drupwang Dawapa,
Rechen Paljor Zangpo, Bodong Tokden Sang-gyé Gönpo,
Druptop Tsulthrim Zangpo, the omniscient Pema Karpo,
Ur-nyön Chödrak, Lhatsün Namkha Jigmé Tsal,
the Fifth Dalai Lama, Nyida Longsal,
Mingyur Dorjé, Duddul Rolpa Tsal,
Khedrup Karma Chagmé, Kunzang Chö Dorjé,
the one named Ngawang, Dorjé Drakpo Tsal,
the omniscient Jigmé Lingpa, Palri Tulku Pema Chöjor Gyatso,
Ngapö Gegen Pema Gyeypa, Situ Pema Nyinjé Wangpo,
Chagmé Karma Tendzin Thrinlé, and Pawo Tsuklak Chökyi Gyalpo.

In this way, the collection takes as its basis the essential empowerments
and usual instructions for the most widespread cycles of earth *terma*s, *terma*s

of enlightened intent, pure visions, and direct oral lineages.[1030] To these I added my new compositions as necessary—*sadhana*s, activity manuals, empowerment manuals, manuals for personal retreat, instruction manuals, and so forth. As well, the smaller cycles of instructions, the rarer transmissions, and the sources [198b] and old manuals of minor *terma*s are all collected; wherever clarification was needed, I composed supplements. Thus, the collection runs to more than sixty medium-sized volumes of texts. Such texts as *The Stages on the Path: The Heart Essence of Timeless Awareness* and other Tersar texts needed to be included in this collection, as well.

The Treasury of Spiritual Advice

For the fourth of the Treasuries, *The Treasury of Spiritual Advice*,[1031] because of my deep faith in the Eight Lineages of Accomplishment that developed in Tibet, I spent a great deal of effort in seeking out the ripening empowerments and liberating instructions transmitted by the extensive lineages of all of these systems. Although no one could have the time to put all of these teachings into practice, they were collected so that the advice my spiritual masters had imparted would not go to waste. I also thought that while the famous traditions were widespread enough, it might be possible to ensure that some very rare transmissions, which were on the point of disappearing, might at least be preserved as lineages of words.[1032] In addition, it is my feeling that to hear these essential teachings of the sutras and tantras even once gives purpose to our lives as human beings. With this altruistic motivation, I collected the quintessential elements of these eight systems of practice, as well as their most profound ripening empowerments and liberating instructions.

Nyingmapa

The first system, that of the Early Translation School, or Nyingma, consists of the "three yogas." The first of these three sections is that of the Mahayoga approach. This section includes *The Concise Path* by Buddhaguhya; the precious master Padmakara's *Pith Instructions: The Garland of Views*, together with a commentary, and his *Sphere of the Mamos' Activity*; and the concise instructions on *The Heart Essence of Secrets* by the omniscient Longchenpa. [199a]

The Anuyoga section includes teachings on the four stages of yoga connected with *The Clarification of Bliss*, and extracts from the intuitive techniques of meditation from the *Discourse of United Intent*.

Of the three categories—outer, inner, and secret—of the Atiyoga section, the outer Category of Mind surveys the fundamental tantra and explanatory commentaries, and includes the empowerment for *The Eighteen Meanings of A* and the instructions from the tradition of Kham, Nyang, and Aro. The inner Category of Expanse surveys the fundamental tantra and explanatory commentaries, and includes meditation methods, the blessing ritual of the guru, and instructions. The secret Category of Direct Transmission surveys the fundamental tantra and explanatory commentaries, and includes the empowerment and instruction for the Innermost Heart Drop of the Guru; the secret cycles of the omniscient master of the Buddhist teachings, Longchenpa, including his instructions for the cycle of Being at Ease in Mind Itself and The Trilogy of Natural Freedom, his instructions on the tantra *Dredging the Pit of Cyclic Existence*; and the rituals to honor the gurus of the Heart Drop lineage and to make offerings to the seven classes of guardian deities of these teachings.

Kadampa

The section dealing with the second system, the Kadampa, consists of three parts—the source texts, the spiritual advice, and the pith instructions. The section on the source texts includes the primary source—*The Lamp for the Path to Enlightenment* and its autocommentary—as well as commentaries on the stages on the spiritual path and other instructions.

The section on the spiritual advice includes the primary source—*The Seven Points of Mind Training*—as well as the instruction manual on this theme called *The One Hundred Collected Instructions on Mental Training* and other texts.

The section on the pith instructions includes the source text—*The Bodhisattva's Garland of Gems*—as well as the empowerment and instructions for the Sixteen Spheres and the auxiliary authorizations and instructions concerning the Four Deities.

From the "new Kadampa" tradition, so named by Jé Rinpoché,[1033] I have included his treatise *The Three Principal Aspects of the Path*, as well as the text *Mahamudra: The Main Path of the Victorious Ones*, and the definitive instructions.

To supplement these teachings, I have included the rituals to confer the bodhisattva vow from both traditions of that ordination. As well, there are some associated texts—[199b] instructions on the Madhyamaka view, a ritual to honor the gurus of the Kadampa School, and transmissions connected with Kartari-dhara Mahakala[1034] (the guardian deity of these teachings) and Lord Atisha's tradition of White Jambhala.

Sakyapa

In the section dealing with the third system, that of the spiritual advice concerning Lamdré ("The Path and Its Fruition"), are found the primary source— *The Vajra Verses*—and its commentaries, as well as the source text on *The Inseparability of Samsara and Nirvana*, with the instruction manuals and explanatory essays concerning this text.

The section also includes the empowerment for the "pith instruction" tradition of Hevajra; texts from the extensive, more direct, and extremely direct lineages of the Lamdré teachings; the instructions on threefold purity according to the tantra *The Vajra Pavilion*; the "eight later cycles concerning the spiritual path"; and the "spiritual connections of the six avenues." The auxiliary instructions include those concerned with *Parting from the Four Kinds of Attachment*; a ritual to honor the gurus of the Lamdré School; and the authorization for the eight deity mandala of Vajra Panjara Natha, the guardian deity of these teachings.

Kagyüpa

In the section concerning the fourth system, that of the Kagyü School of the powerful master Marpa, the common teachings include the fundamental source of the Mahamudra approach—the glorious *Tantra of the Uncorrupted State*— as well as commentaries authored by Saraha, Shavaripa, Tilopa, Naropa, Maitripa, Marpa, Milarepa, and Gampopa.

The uncommon teachings include the authentic texts that are the primary source for the Six Yogas, as well as the vajra verses of the intimate oral lineage, the smaller and larger original texts, and the three cycles of Tilopa's, Naropa's, and Marpa's clarifications of the intimate oral lineage. This section also includes the empowerment for the masculine and feminine aspects of the glorious Chakrasamvara mandala according to the tradition of the intimate oral lineage. The fundamental advice and instructions included are the three treatments of the intimate oral lineage (the extensive, middle-length, and abridged), the nine doctrines of the "disembodied *dakinis*" by Rechungpa, [200a] and the "four rolled scrolls" of Tsurtön's[1035] intimate oral lineage.

This section contains instructions—primarily those concerning Mahamudra and the Six Yogas—from the individual subschools of the Dakpo Kagyü tradition, the four major ones being the primary one associated with the monastic seat of Dakpo, the Tsalpa of Guru Zhang,[1036] the Karma Kamtsang (with its branches of Zurmang and Nedo), and the Pakmo Drupa. Of the eight minor branches of the Pakmo Drupa Kagyü, the section contains teachings from the Drigung, Taklung, Throphu, and Lingré Kagyü (also known as the glorious Drukpa School, with its three subdivisions of upper, lower, and middle). There are also works by Yang-gönpa and Barawa.

In addition, the section includes a ritual to honor the gurus of the Kagyü School in general, and transmissions concerning the protective deities of these teachings—the Four-Armed Mahakala and the goddess Dhumavati.

Shangpa Kagyü

In the section concerning the fifth system, that of the Shangpa Kagyü School, the primary sources are the vajra verses, and their commentaries, concerning the Six Yogas (the root), Mahamudra (the trunk), the three methods of "carrying on the path" (the branches), and the "deathless state" (the fruition), as well as the fundamental texts concerning the forms of the goddess Khechari (the flowers). The two collections of ritual blessings are the two cycles of teachings that establish the guidelines for receiving blessings—the six transmissions of the pivotal blessings, and the later basic transmissions. The section also contains the entire teachings from the direct lineage of Thangtong Gyalpo; the instructions written by the venerable Taranatha for the extensive lineage; and the practice cycles for Sukhasiddhi and *The Combination of Four Deities*. There is a ritual to honor the gurus of the Shangpa tradition, the authorizations for the *dakinis* of the five classes [200b] and the Swift-Acting Jnana Natha. The section also includes the thirteen major transmissions associated with the protective deity, the practice of *Penetrating the Heart*, and the transmission for Kshetrapala.

Damchö Duk-ngal Zhijé (Sacred Teachings for the Pacification of Suffering)

The section dealing with the sixth system, that of Zhijé School, includes the tantra fragments that are the primary sources, as well as miscellaneous writings of Phadampa Sang-gyé and all the empowerments and ritual blessings for the three transmissions of these teachings—early, middle, and later—as well as for the protective deities. There are the instruction manuals for these themes written by Lochen Dharma Shri, and Nyedo Sönam Pal's[1037] instructions on the Zhijé teachings.

The auxiliary branch of the Zhijé system is that of The Sacred Teachings on the Object of Severance.[1038] This section includes the primary sources for this approach, written by Aryadeva and Machik Lapdrön—including *The Teaching Essays, The Further Essays, The Heart Essays,* and *The Pinnacle Jewel of Wisdom*—and the profound Heart Drop teachings. As for the ripening empowerments, three traditions are included, those of the Zurmang, Jamyang Gönpo, and Gyalthangpa. The spiritual advice includes the instruction manuals for the three transmissions—early, middle, and later. There is an activity ritual focusing on the feast offering, and one to honor the gurus of the Zhijé School.

Dorjei Naljor (Vajra Yoga)

The section dealing with the seventh system, that of the profound path of Vajra Yoga, includes the primary source—the quintessential *Kalachakra Tantra*—as well as instructions from the intimate oral lineage of Kalachakrapada and some small source texts by Shavaripa. There is the *sadhana* and offering ritual for the nine deity mandala, the extraordinary sublime empowerment and its instruction manuals and auxiliary texts, all authored by Jonang Jetsün Rinpoché. The section includes *The Profound Path: The Sphere of Nectar,* [201a] the middle-length treatment of the Six Branches of Union from the tradition of Anupamarakshita; and the concise version entitled *Touching the Tip of the Tongue to the Palate.* There is a ritual to honor the gurus of the tradition of the Six Branches of Union, as well as the authorizations for the form of Kalachakra with consort and the protective deity Vajravega.[1039]

Dorjé Sumgyi Nyendrup (Stages of Approach and Accomplishment for the Three Vajras)

The section dealing with the eighth system, that of The Stages of Approach and Accomplishment for the Three Vajras, includes the primary source (which was bestowed on the *mahasiddha* Orgyenpa by Vajravarahi and the *dakinis* of the four families). There is also the explanatory commentary to this, as well as the instruction manuals and the methods for meditating to bring the stages of approach and accomplishment to consummation in a single sitting.

Miscellaneous Instructions

The ninth section of this collection contains a number of unrelated teachings— spiritual advice that derives from various traditions. These include the bless- ing ritual and instructions concerning the Eighty-Four Mahasiddhas; the individual empowerments and instructions for The Six Instructions of Maitripa; the cycles of Mahakarunika Chittavishramana and The Threefold Quintessen- tial Meaning as transmitted in the Zhalu tradition; the five definitive instruc- tions on Avalokiteshvara; Thangtong Gyalpo's practice associated with the six-syllable mantra; the Mahamudra instructions and *The Sutra Ritual of the Sage* from the Bodong tradition; the instruction on *chandali*[1040] and the trans- ference of consciousness transmitted by Rechen Paljor Zangpo; the "mother transference" of Rongtön; the instructions on the "seven lines of specific trans- mission" according to the new translations of the Jonang tradition; and various kinds of alchemical procedures.

The collection concludes in a positive manner with the authorizations for the three deities of longevity, the intimate oral lineage of the seven-day longevity *sadhana*, the instructions for the longevity practice of White Tara according to the tradition of Bari Lotsawa, and a ritual to honor the three deities of longevity.

The Extraordinary Treasury

For the fifth of the Treasuries, *The Extraordinary Treasury*,[1041] my lord guru, Jamyang Khyentsé Rinpoché, [201b] provided a token table of contents. And while a large number of yellow scrolls and sacred *samaya* substances fell into my hands, these were for the most part lost due to circumstances of place and time. In some of these cases, it would seem that due to the collective lack of merit in the world, the result was what the proverb refers to as "whistling in the wind," so there is no advantage to my even mentioning them here. In the seven volumes of this collection are contained my own miscellaneous writ- ings that pertain in some way or another to the Five Treasuries as a whole; my all-seeing precious master, Jamyang Khyentsé, catalogued these in a table of contents that has fifteen headings—the number that is the date of the full moon in the lunar month.[1042]

TEACHING ACTIVITIES

If we consider my activities in explaining the teachings, I have taught many times—to people of high station and low—such subjects as the basic texts of Tibetan grammar; the three Sanskrit grammars of the Kalapa, Chandra, and Sarasvata systems; works on metrics and poetics; the Four Tantras and medical treatises; and the Indian and Chinese systems of astrology.[1043] But of all my students, none proved greater at being able to teach others in turn than Lama Karma Ngédön of Pangphuk and the tutor Lhaksam Tenpai Gyaltsen.

I have taught such texts as *The Profound Inner Meaning, The Hevajra Tantra in Two Chapters*, and *The Highest Continuum* on many occasions and, having received an explanation of the tantra *The Heart Essence of Secrets* from the great *tertön* Chokgyur Lingpa, passed this teaching on to monks in colleges, *khenpo*s, and others. I have conferred the oral transmissions for the precious Kangyur once; for The Collected Tantras of the Nyingma Tradition [202a] twice; for selected portions of the Tengyur several times; for my *Treasury of the Knowable* four times; for my *Tantric Treasury of the Kagyü School* seven times; for my *Treasury of Precious Hidden Teachings* five times; for my *Treasury of Spiritual Advice* three times; for the Noble Wish-Granting Vase of the Mindroling tradition eight times; and for The Precious Source of Sadhanas of the Jonang School three times.

As well, there has hardly been any transmission I received that I have not passed on at least once, especially in the Kagyü and Nyingma Schools. In the latter part of my life, people gathered in such great numbers to receive empowerments, oral transmissions, and instructions from me that I was required to move from group to group, going to each one many times over. My only hope in doing this has been that it might help the teachings continue and be of some small benefit to the minds of his listeners. I have never criticized those who were hard up and could not provide any kind of formal offering, but provided whatever they wished for. And that is not all, for whenever my health has permitted I have done whatever was in my power to perform even such small favors as divinations, astrological readings, and exorcisms, without ever complaining or feeling discouraged. When wealthy people gave me a lot of things, I would accept these, but only with the thought that it was due to the greatness of the Buddhist teachings, never engaging in any false modesty and claiming, "Oh, I'm not someone who *ever* accepts things." Whatever I have received in the way of material offerings, be it large or small, [202b] other than providing food and support for me and my retinue of monks, has not been wasted in inappropriate ways, but has been used entirely to finance the construction of the three kinds of representations or to sponsor *drupchen*s and other rituals.

MEDITATION

Concerning the second sphere of my activities, that of renunciation—which is to say, my practice of meditation—from the time that I enrolled at Palpung Monastery at the age of about twenty, I undertook a few personal retreats and kept up a daily practice. From the time that I turned thirty and took up residence at my hermitage, where I still live currently, and up to the present time, I have undertaken a schedule of personal retreats on a continual basis. It has always been my intention to rely on the three kinds of solitude[1044] and focus uniquely on a one-pointed practice of the stage of completion, in both its structured and unstructured aspects. However, what with the empowerments, oral transmissions, and instructions that I have requested from or given to others, and in particular the duties involved in producing my Five Treasuries, I have fallen under the sway of ever-increasing distractions—which I nonetheless presume to be spiritual endeavors—and so things truly have not turned out as I planned.

During my stay at the meditation center at Palpung Monastery, I carried out the practices in accord with the general tradition, beginning with four hundred thousand accumulations of the preliminary practices for the Mahamudra approach, and continuing on through the personal retreats on the stages of approach and accomplishment. Here at Tsadra Rinchen Drak, initially I practiced The Union of All Rare and Precious Jewels. I trained in all seven stages of the preliminary practices—the taking of refuge (in conjunction with prostrations), the arousal of bodhichitta (in conjunction with the technique of sending and receiving), and so forth—until I experienced the requisite signs. I then carried out the outer, inner, secret, and most secret *sadhana*s, the longevity *sadhana*,

[203a] and the enactment of the four kinds of activity, practicing each stage until I had repeated the requisite number of mantras.

Since that time, at various times over the years I have completed personal retreats focusing on the stages of approach and accomplishment for a number of cycles. These retreats have included the following practices from the Sarma Schools:

- the Kagyü traditions of the nine and five deity mandalas of Jinasagara (which I have also kept up as the core of my daily practice)
- the glorious Kalachakra
- for Chakrasamvara, the tradition of Luhipa and the Kamtsang Kagyü tradition of the five deity mandala
- for Hevajra, the tradition of Marpa and Ngok, and that of Saroruhavajra
- the five deity mandala of Mahamaya
- Guhyasamaja Akshobhyavajra
- Black Yamari
- the nine deity mandala of Vajrabhairava
- the Mahachakra form of Vajrapani
- the Shangpa tradition of the body mandala of The Deities of the Five Classes of Tantra
- Druppai Gyalmo's tradition of Amitayus
- Mati's tradition of White Manjushri
- Atisha's tradition of White Tara (I have completed the stages of approach and accomplishment for this deity many times over)
- the white and blue-black forms of the Six-Armed Mahakala; and the Kagyü tradition of Mahakala and Mahakali in union.

I have also done retreats on the following practices from the Nyingma School:

- Guru Chöwang's cycle of The Guru: The Gathering of Secrets
- the Northern Treasure cycle of The Sadhana of the Ancestral Line of the Masters of Awareness
- Gyatön's cycle The Guru: The Wheel of Supreme Bliss
- Sang-gyé Lingpa's tradition of The United Intent of the Gurus
- the *guru sadhana* of Drimé Kunden, *The Wish-Fulfilling Gem*
- the *terma* of enlightened intent called The Heart Drop of the Lake-Born One
- the two *sadhanas* of enlightened mind from the Tersar tradition—*Dispelling All Obstacles* and *The Wish-Fulfilling Gem*

- Chöjé Lingpa's tradition of The Combined Practice of the Three Roots
- *The Secret Path*, a *guru sadhana* focusing on Dakpo[1045]
- the practices of The Heart Drop of the Black Hum [203b]
- the chosen deities of the Eight Commands—that is, The Gathering of Sugatas; The Perfection of Secrets; Natural Arising; and The Supreme Gathering of Commands (in these cases, I have made at least some connection through undertaking retreats)
- the Eight Commands cycles of Jatsön Nyingpo, the Heart Essence of Spiritual Attainment
- the Natural Freedom of Enlightened Intent cycle of the peaceful and wrathful deities
- the *terma* of enlightened intent focusing on the goddess Vijaya
- the cycles called United Intent—that is, Manjushri Vadisimha; Manjushri Ayushpati; Black Kingkara; Yamantaka; and Amitabha
- the longevity *sadhana* called The Gathering of Secrets
- *The Vajra of Meteoric Iron*
- *The Innermost Heart of Immortality*
- the cycles of Mahakarunika—that is, King Songtsen Gampo's tradition; The Guide of Beings, from the *terma*s of Nyang; Dredging the Pit of Cyclic Existence; my lord guru's cycle of Chittavishramana; and the flawless Jinasagara
- the cycles of Hayagriva—that is, Liberating All Arrogant Ones; the *Six-Syllable* practice from The United Intent of the Chosen Deities; and the practices of Black Hayagriva from both Nyang and Ratna Lingpa
- the Mindroling tradition of Vajrasattva
- Guru Chöwang's cycle of the nine deity mandala of Samyak
- the Tersar cycle of Vimalamitra
- Vajra Amrita
- Guru Chöwang's Razor cycle of Vajrakila
- Ratna Lingpa's cycle of The Unsurpassable Innermost Secret
- Chöjé Lingpa's cycle of The Sphere of Enlightened Mind
- my lord guru's oral lineages—The Mind Drop of Yamantaka, The Heart Drop of Hayagriva, The Profound Drop of Samyak, The Sublime Drop of Amrita, The Crucial Drop of Vajrakila, and The Crucial Drop of the Mamos
- the Seven Profound Cycles of Chokgyur Lingpa—the Magic cycle of peaceful and wrathful deities, [204a] and the cycles for Yamantaka, Hayagriva, Samyak, Vajrakila, and the *mamo*s

- the *dakini* cycle of Black Krodhi from the *termas* of Nyang
- The Gathering of All the Dakinis' Secrets
- the Tamer of Maras cycle of White Tara
- the Heart Drop of the Exalted Goddess of Immortality
- the cycle of Vajradakini Sitatapatra and
- the cycle of Padmadakini Kurukulle.

From among these practices, I have also participated many times in *drupchen* rituals focusing on the cycles of the Eight Commands, Vajrakila, Tara, and others.

I have also made at least some connection with my own *terma*, The United Intent of the Three Roots; the stages of approach and accomplishment for both the masculine and feminine aspects from the Secret Sphere cycle; the Six Yogas of Naropa and Niguma; the Vajra Yoga system; and the Heart Drop cycles of the Dzogchen approach. As well, since the practices of Mahamudra and *lojong* mental training are so easy to apply, they have been the focus of my practice on a daily basis.

PROJECTS

Concerning the third of my activities, this comprises my other undertakings.[1046]

Kunzang Dechen Ösel Ling

Buildings

Here at my hermitage, it had been my thought that it would be good to have a temple and perhaps four residences for retreatants. At that time, Chokgyur Lingpa prophesied that temples on this site were, in fact, necessary, and so accordingly we first laid the foundations for my residence. After that, I dedicated all the funds that came my way toward the construction of the temples and meditation center, and over time these were built. There are eight temples: the primary structure of the Palchen Lhakhang and the secondary buildings, which are the temples of the Lama Lhakhang, the Sung-rap Khang, the Thongdröl Lhakhang, [204b] the Drölma Lhakhang, the Neten Khang, the Thukdam Khang, and the Gönkhang.

Statues

The principal statues in the Palchen Lhakhang ["Temple of the Great and Glorious Deities"] are those of three *herukas*—Vajrasattva, Samyak, and Chakrasamvara—each one story high. There are also statues of Kalachakra in union with consort, the deities of The United Intent of the Gurus, and Vajrakumara.

The statues in the Lama Lhakhang ["Temple of the Guru"] include those of the founders of the Eight Lineages of Accomplishment.[1047] In the Gönkhang ["Temple of the Protective Deities"], the principal statue is that of the Swift-Acting Jnana Natha, and there are clay statues depicting the most important protective deities of the old and new schools of Buddhism.

In addition, in the Palchen Lhakhang there are statues made entirely of gold and copper. The larger-sized statues are two statues of the Lord of Sages, Orgyen as the king of Sahora, Amitayus, and Green Tara. The intermediate-sized ones, one hundred and seven in number, include the thirty-five deities from *The Ritual to Confess Faults*, the Eight Brothers of Bhaishajyaguru; the twenty-one forms of Tara, and the eight manifestations of the Guru. The one hundred and fifty-five smaller-sized statues include one hundred and three images of Amitayus.

In the Sung-rap Khang ["Temple of the Scriptures"], the largest statues are those of the Lord of Sages, the master Krishnacharya, and the Guru (with two flanking figures). There are statues of middling size, including ones of the buddhas of the three times,[1048] the thirty-five buddhas from *The Ritual to Confess Faults*, and ten others of various deities.

In the Thongdröl Lhakhang ["Temple That Brings Liberation On Sight"], the primary representation is a statue of Tara that has been known to speak on occasion. The other large statues are those of Vajrasattva Heruka, and the two principal goddesses of the Heart Drop of the Exalted Goddess of Immortality.[1049] [205a] There are statues of their fourteen retinue figures and two sets of statues—one of middling size, the other smaller—depicting the forms of Tara that protect one from fear. There are statues of the seven buddhas of the past carved in white sandalwood, and of the eight great bodhisattvas carved in red sandalwood: these all have thrones and backrests, and are housed in individual shrines.

In the Drölma Lhakhang ["Temple of Tara"] is a statue of White Chinta-manichakra Tara[1050] that is one story high. The larger statues include Guru

Nangsi Zilnön, Guru Dewachenpo,[1051] Vajrasattva, the eleven-headed form of Avalokiteshvara, and Vimalamitra. There are twenty-five statues of intermediate size, including twenty-two of the Buddhist elders and their retinue.

In the Neten Khang ["Temple of Elders"] there are two middle-sized statues of the Lord of Sages, and statues of the Lord surrounded by the Buddhist elders, all carved in white sandalwood and housed in a fine shrine. There are also statues of the elders and their retinue in gold and copper, as well as nineteen other assorted statues.

The principal representations housed in the Thukdam Khang ["Temple of Meditation"] are three "regent" images—*terma* discoveries—that are furnished with thrones and housed in individual shrines. There is a large statue of the four-armed Avalokiteshvara known as the Guide of Beings, cast in Kashmiri bell metal. There are statues of gurus from all schools, without sectarian bias, and chosen deities—twenty-seven of large size, made of gold and copper, and eighty-six of intermediate size and eighty of smaller size made of bell metal and other metals. In the outer courtyard are twenty-five middle-sized statues, including those of the twenty-one forms of Tara (with White Tara being the principal one).

There are eleven statues made of bell metal and gold in the Gönkhang, making a total of some five hundred and seventy-five statues in all the temples. [205b]

Paintings

As for the scroll paintings, there are twenty-five rooms with paintings dealing with themes from the classes of tantra. There are also two sets of paintings in the "gold style"[1052]—one set, in seven rooms, depicts the one thousand buddhas, with the seven previous buddhas as the central figures; the other set, in nine rooms, depicts the one thousand forms of Orgyen, with Orgyen Rinpoché and his eight manifestations being the central figures. There are two sets of paintings focusing on The United Intent of the Gurus—one depicting fifteen deities, the other eleven. Five paintings are concerned with themes from *The Discourse on the Grand Display*. There are three paintings that deal with the "golden garland"[1053] of Kagyü masters (with Marpa, Milarepa, and Dakpo Lharjé as the central figures), and three rooms with paintings of the sixteen elders. In the Palchen Lhakhang is a painting of a man-sized figure of Amitayus, and paintings one story high depicting the Lord of Sages; the thousand-armed, thousand-eyed form of Avalokiteshvara; and the gurus of the Kagyü lineage, with Situ Chökyi Jungné as the central figure. In Neten Khang Temple, five rooms contain paintings of the sixteen elders. In the main hall are three paintings depicting the one hundred and eight *tertön*s. There are a number of scroll paintings of varying sizes (large, intermediate, and small) in the different temples—a total of three hundred and ninety-five in all.

There are *tsakli* cards with ceremonial parasols[1054] that depict the deities of Karma Lingpa's cycle of the peaceful and wrathful deities; the Padmavajra cycle; the longevity practice *The Integration of Means and Wisdom*; and the Tersar Magic cycle of White Amitayus. There are some forty-eight large paintings of mandalas from both the Nyingma and Sarma Schools, as well as a great many painted mandalas and *tsakli* cards, principally connected with my *Tantric Treasury of the Kagyü School, Treasury of Precious Hidden Teachings*, and *Treasury of Spiritual Advice*. These were all collected with great effort.

Texts

As for the scriptures housed here, the precious words of the Buddha in their Tibetan translation—the Kangyur—and auxiliary texts comprise some one hundred and seven volumes. There are also the following main collections:

- The Collected Tantras of the Nyingma Tradition, in twenty-six volumes
- the Buddha's discourses that address the definitive meaning of the teachings, in nine volumes
- twelve volumes containing *The Discourse in One Hundred Thousand Stanzas*
- the Tengyur—the authoritative Indian commentaries in their Tibetan translation—in two hundred and ten volumes [206a]
- the Four Higher Collections of the Heart Drop Teachings and
- the Seven Treasuries of Longchenpa and his Trilogy of Being at Ease.

In all, the hermitage houses more that fourteen hundred volumes of scripture printed with woodblocks.

There are also about six hundred and ninety-three volumes of handwritten manuscripts, including the following:

- the manuals for the Eight Lineages of Accomplishment

- the teachings of the Shangpa tradition, in eight volumes
- the Eight Commands cycles—that is, The Gathering of Sugatas in nine volumes, The Perfection of Secrets in four volumes, and Natural Arising in two volumes
- the Ironlike cycle of Ayushpati, in two volumes
- The United Intent of the Gurus, in thirteen volumes
- many collections of source texts, primarily those of Jatsön Nyingpo, the Mindroling tradition, and Chöjé Lingpa
- my *Treasury of the Knowable*, in three volumes
- my *Tantric Treasury of the Kagyü School*, including my three commentaries on *The Profound Inner Meaning*, *The Hevajra Tantra in Two Chapters*, and *The Highest Continuum*, in six volumes
- my *Treasury of Precious Hidden Teachings*, along with the "sealed" teachings, in more than sixty volumes
- my *Treasury of Spiritual Advice*, in ten volumes and
- my own collected writings, in seven volumes.

Representations of Enlightened Mind

The great gilded tomb[1055] is in Lhasar Temple at Palpung Monastery. At the hermitage, in the Palchen Lhakhang there are some sixty-four representations of enlightened mind, including a stupa of the "glorious inviolable" style, a "stupa of timeless awareness" (a style found in the Kalachakra cycle), two sets of eight stupas housing relics, and several stupas in the Kadampa style. The details concerning the special substances installed inside these stupas are clearly set forth in the accounts that I have written. [206b] According to a *terma* that is an inventory to Tsadra Rinchen Drak:

> When this inventory appears on the surface of the earth,
> the enlightened form, speech, and mind of the *heruka*s
> will be transferred here from the pinnacle pure realm.

In addition, while there was already an image of a *heruka* in Zur Ukjalung Valley, the time during which it could bring benefit to beings in the region was drawing to a close, so the great *tertön* Chokgyur Lingpa prophesied that instead this site of Tsadra Rinchen Drak would serve as a fount for the teachings; so it is my opinion that this place has a very special significance.

SAppointments

I have gathered all the necessary appointments and articles for these buildings, as well. In the temples are canopies, flat banners, and cylindrical banners; offering utensils (especially water bowls and butter lamps); articles for both *drubchö* rituals (according to the Sarma traditions) and *drupchen* rituals (according to the Nyingma tradition); musical instruments (drums, flat and hollowed cymbals, conch shells, long horns, *gyaling* trumpets, and thighbone trumpets); and rows of benches and mats for seating people. In the steward's office and kitchen are all of the necessary articles, such as copper pots and cauldrons, kitchen utensils such as ladles, containers for food and condiments, and so on. Everything has been assembled with care and effort.

Retreat Program

Here, those who enter the retreat program begin by training their minds through the common preliminary practices, in conjunction with study of *The Jewel Ornament of Liberation* and other literature dealing with the developmental stages on the spiritual path. They then carry out a process of accumulations and refinement involving the uncommon preliminaries, followed by the guru yogas. Once these are completed, their practice focuses on the stages of approach and accomplishment for the five deity mandala of Chakrasamvara and the cycle of The Deities of the Five Classes of Tantra, both from the Shangpa tradition. They then spend about a year and a half practicing all the Shangpa teachings, [207a] both the principal and secondary ones. During the remaining half of the second year, they focusing on the stages of approach and accomplishment for the nine deity mandala of Kalachakra and develop some familiarity with the vajra yoga system of the Six Branches of Union. During the final year, the retreatants' practice focuses on Vajrasattva and Samyak, as well as completing all the practices involved in the Innermost Heart Drop of the Guru.

On an annual basis, three tantras are read aloud—*The Kalachakra Tantra*, *The Hevajra Tantra in Two Chapters*, and *The Chakrasamvara Tantra*. The retreatants perform the following rituals:

- during the first month, a ritual honoring the anniversaries[1056] of Marpa, Milarepa, and Dakpo Lharjé, which involves wearing cotton robes[1057] and chanting *The Ocean of Songs*[1058]
- in the second month, a feast offering and fulfillment ritual from The

Heart Drop of the Masters of Awareness to honor the anniversary of Minling Terchen, and a three-day *drupchö* ritual based on the Shangpa tradition of The Deities of the Five Classes of Tantra to honor the anniversary of the venerable Taranatha

- in the third month, a seven-day *drupchö* ritual focusing on the Kalachakra practice, including a ritual honoring the one hundred families of yoginis
- in the fifth month, the fulfillment ritual from The United Intent of the Gurus
- in the ninth month, the ritual focusing on the gurus of the Shangpa lineage, in honor of the anniversary of Khyungpo Naljor
- in the twelfth month, the ritual focusing on the lineage of the Heart Drop teachings, in honor of the anniversary of the omniscient Longchenpa
- as for the rituals focusing on the protective deities, in the eleventh month there are incidental rituals involved in changing the permanent *torma*s on the shrine, while at the end of the year there is the *torma* ritual of accomplishment focusing on the Swift-Acting Jnana Natha.

On the holy days of the fourth month the retreatants are to practice on a large scale, gathering the accumulations and performing the ceremony to restore and renew their vows.

On the seventh day of every month there is a *drupchö* ritual focusing on Vajrasattva, performed in honor of Lord Pema Nyinjé. On the eighth day, the retreatants practice the longevity *sadhana* The Gathering of Secrets and perform a *drupchö* ritual focusing on White Tara. [207b] On the tenth day there is the ritual of The United Intent of the Gurus, and a feast offering based on some appropriate *guru sadhana* and the practice of Vimalamitra. The offering ritual honoring Kalachakra is performed on the fifteenth day, and on the twenty-fifth day a *drupchö* ritual focusing on Chakrasamvara and the rituals for the white and red forms of Khechari, which are performed in alternate months. Various offering rituals focusing on the protective deities are done on the twenty-ninth day. On the day of the new moon, the ritual of Samyak according to the So tradition is performed; as well, *The Tantra of the Essence of Secrets* is recited during the six months when the days are long enough, while *Reciting the Names of Manjushri* is recited during the six months when the days are short. In fact, all the tantras have related rituals for reciting them aloud, and these are performed as appropriate.[1059]

On a daily basis, every morning there is a group ritual in the Palchen Lhakhang, in conjunction with which there is a ceremony to restore and renew

one's vows on the three levels of ordination. In the evenings, there are fulfillment rituals and offering rituals focusing on the protective deities of both the
Sarma and Nyingma Schools. I have laid out a step-by-step schedule for the
daily schedule of four practice sessions. Every month, on the days of the full
and new moon, those who have received novice vows or full monastic ordination take part in their respective ceremonies to restore and renew their vows. I
have detailed the practice schedule for the retreatant in charge of the shrine to
the protective deities in another text.[1060] To ensure that the teachings (primarily
those of the three turnings of the wheel[1061]) endure for a long time, on the
eighth day of every month the residents of the Neten Khang perform the ritual
from Sang-gyé Lingpa that focuses on the elders.

All the foregoing constitutes a rough overview.

Dzongshö Retreat Center

In Dzongshö, furthermore, in the Guru Lhakhang ["Temple of the Gurus"],
the principal statues are those of Orgyen as the king of Sahora, Amitabha,
Amitayus, Jinasagara, [208a] Vajrasattva, Samyak, White Tara, the Sixteen
Elders, and the gurus of the Eight Lineages of Accomplishment. In the Thukné
Lhakhang ["Temple of the Abode of Enlightened Mind"], there is a statue of
the Lord of Sages one story high, as well as clay statues depicting the eight
great bodhisattvas, Padmasambhava, Green Tara, and protective deities of the
Sarma and Nyingma Schools (the Swift-Acting Jnana Natha foremost among
them). As far as their contents and so forth, the statues have been prepared in
an authentic manner.

In my own residence, there are large and small statues made of copper and
gold—principally a statue almost two feet high of the Master[1062] as the king of
Sahora—and more than twenty scroll paintings. There are also more than five
hundred volumes of block print texts, including especially the Kangyur, the
Tengyur, and The Collected Tantras of the Nyingma Tradition, as well as texts
from the *kama* and *terma* traditions, the collected works of other masters, commentaries, liturgical arrangements, and other texts. This place and the temple
are fully furnished with offering utensils, lamps that are kept burning continuously, musical instruments, benches and mats for seating groups, and so forth.
There are supplies to support seven retreatants.

Every year, the monastic communities of the region gather to perform the
ritual of reading the Kangyur aloud. During the month commemorating the

Buddha's spiritual miracles, they perform the ritual focusing on the eight great bodhisattvas; during the fourth month, the fasting ritual; and in the ninth month, the ritual based on *The Discourse on Liberation*. I have also instituted a tradition of feast offerings being performed on the tenth days of the waxing and waning phases of the moon, and offering rituals on the twenty-ninth day of every month. [208b]

In the chapel of Tashi Chökhang, there are permanent installations of statues made of copper and gold (especially those of the Lord of Sages and Guru Rinpoché), scroll paintings, and so forth. There are fine mural paintings at the Bön monastery in Rongyap.

I have requested that the Dergé administration take responsibility for the funding of various projects: for the erection of statues of the two teachers of sutra and tantra,[1063] and statues of the guardian deities; for the providing of flat and cylindrical banners, musical instruments, benches and sitting mats; for the providing and repair of costumes for ritual dances; for funds to sponsor the annual summer retreats and offering rituals; for the support of the retreatants in charge of the shrines to the protective deities. Thus, I have ensured that these projects will continue to receive support as long as they require it.

CONCLUDING VERSES

I am at a loss to claim that this is the authentic life example of a holy
person;
I regard it as only slightly better than the common behavior of lowly
folk.
This narrative describing my life is rather haphazard,[1064]
but while it may give a wise person pause, might it not please a fool?
May the Jewels grant their blessings that this account that I have
written
will never be a cause of anything harmful to myself or others,
but rather that the force of goodness will grow
so that all connected with this will find meaning therein and embrace
a vast scope of activity!
Sarvatha kalyanam maogala bhavantu![1065]

ENDNOTES

1. These are knowledge as a profound insight into the true nature of reality and detailed knowledge of things in all their multiplicity; together, these two kinds of knowledge constitute the omniscience of buddhahood.

2. Tib. *Dorjé Chang*. The "primordial buddha" epitomizing dharmakaya in the Sarma Schools of Tibetan Buddhism. One's personal master in Vajrayana practice is identified with Vajradhara; Kongtrul, for example, refers to Situ Rinpoché as "Vajradhara," "my refuge lord Vajradhara," or "Vajradhara Pema," and the tenets and principles of the Vajrayana are termed the "commands of Vajradhara."

3. The secret name of Guru Rinpoché, or Padmakara, conferred on him during his time wandering in the charnel grounds of ancient India.

4. This is a prayer to Situ Pema Wangchok Gyalpo, Kongtrul's root guru. Situ was considered an emanation of Padmakara, or Guru Rinpoché (the Indian master who was primarily responsible for establishing Buddhism in Tibet in the eighth century), who is here referred to by his "secret name" of Dorjé Thöthreng Tzal; this name was conferred on Padmakara by *dakini*s when he was pursuing his Vajrayana practice in the charnel grounds of ancient India.

5. The principles of enlightened form, speech, and mind, termed "secret" because they are hidden from the perceptions of the ordinary mind.

6. The Sanskrit term *Mahakala* is a generic reference to a class of masculine protective deities; the feminine form is *Mahakali*.

7. The Sanskrit term *nirvana* entails several levels of meaning. There is a "lower level" nirvana, attained when one's mindstream is liberated from rebirth within the cycle of samsara. Here, however, Kongtrul is referring to a nirvana that is described as "nonstatic," or "not confined to any specific limit"—that is, the transcendence of the extremes of ongoing confusion in the cycle of ordinary existence on the one hand, or the peace of mere personal salvation from suffering on the other. This latter sense of nirvana is based on the principle of enlightenment for all beings without exception.

8. Faith in Buddhist traditions is a multifaceted experience. Traditional texts enumerate three aspects of faith—awe, emulation, and conviction. To this a fourth aspect, that of incontrovertible faith, is often added. See, for example, *The Jewel Ornament of Liberation*, pp. 19-21 (H. V. Guenther, trans.) and pp. 64-66 (Khenpo Konchog Gyaltsen Rinpoche, trans.).

9. These are the Jataka stories, compiled by the Indian Buddhist master Aryasura. They have appeared in several English translations—*The Gatakamala, or Garland of Birth-Stories by Aryasûra*; *Stories of the Buddha, being Selections from the Jataka*; and *Once the Buddha Was a Monkey: Arya Sura's Jatakamala*.

10. Taranatha (1575-1634) was a great scholar and writer of the Jonang School, whose

controversial position on "qualified emptiness" (*zhentong*) contributed to its suppression by the central Tibetan government in the seventeenth century. Kongtrul discusses Taranatha in his account of his former lives.

11. An epithet of the Buddha Shakyamuni.

12. An epithet of the Buddha Shakyamuni.

13. The reference here is uncertain; possibly Kongtrul is quoting the Sixth Zhamar of the Kagyü School, Chökyi Wangchuk (1584-1630), or one of the Garwang incarnations of Zurmang Monastery (RT). Alternatively, this may be a reference to a guru of Karma Chagmé, or the Ninth Karmapa Wangchuk Dorjé (1556-1603) (ADD).

14. A central concept in all Buddhist systems is the structure of the spiritual path—the process by which one develops from an ordinary state to that of perfect enlightenment. The most common schema is the Mahayana description of five paths (which are serial processes) and ten levels of realization (which, taken together constitute the third and fourth of the five paths, the fifth constituting the level of buddhahood and the path of "no more learning"). The path of application is the second of the five paths; the path of seeing is the third, entailing a stable, yet still incomplete, realization of the true nature of reality. For a detailed discussion by an esteemed Kagyü master of the qualities that are experienced on these paths and levels, see Chapters 18 and 19 of *The Jewel Ornament of Liberation* by Gampopa.

15. This probably refers not to the bodhisattva of compassion, but to the Indian Buddhist author of the same name.

16. An expression denoting buddhas and bodhisattvas.

17. According to the *Tibetan-English Dictionary of Buddhist Terminology* (p. 39), these are: living in a harmonious environment, relying on holy mentors, developing one's aspirations through prayer, and gathering merit.

18. For the Tibetan people, "Tibet" refers to the central provinces of Ü and Tsang, while the eastern provinces are known as "Kham." They refer to the entire region (including the western provinces of Ngari) as "greater Tibet." People from the eastern provinces are quite clear on the point that they are Kham-pa, not Bö-pa—"(central) Tibetan"—just as Canadians are touchy about being called "Americans" (in the sense of being citizens of the United States).

19. According to the *Bod rgya tshig mdzod chen mo* (p. 808), the four rivers are the Drichu (Yangtze), Machu (Huang-ho, or Yellow River), Ngulchu (Salween), and Dachu (Mekong). The six ridges defined by these river valleys are Zalmogang, Tsawagang, Markhamgang, Poborgang, Mardzagang, and Minyak Rabgang. See *The Nyingma School of Tibetan Buddhism: Its Fundamentals and History*, vol. 2, Map 10.

20. The Drichu River, which has its headwaters in eastern Tibet, becomes the Yangtze in China.

21. According to *Rimay Philosophy of Kongtrul* (p. 1), Sharda refers to the Dzachu (Yalung) River, which lies to the north of the Drichu; this places Kongtrul's birthplace at the eastern end of the Zalmogang Ridge, which is bisected by the Drichu.

22. This is a reference to the Vajrayana schema of the five buddha families of the mandala; the *padma*, or lotus, family is associated with the transmutation of ordinary patterns of desire and attachment into a discerning quality of timeless awareness. The lotus family figures prominently in the Tibetan systems of Buddhism; Tibet is held to be the particular sphere of influence for Avalokiteshvara, the bodhisattva of compassion and a prominent archetype of the lotus family, as was Padmasambhava, who more than any other master was responsible for bringing the Buddhist teachings to the Tibetan people. The twenty-five greater regions are classified according to these five principles in five groups of five; they are listed in *The Nyingma School of Tibetan Buddhism: Its Fundamentals and History*, vol. 2, pp. 181-182; it would seem that the sixth entry in this list, Pema Shel-ri, corresponds to the region that Kongtrul is calling Pema Lhatsé.

23. Literally, "Back of the Ravine."

24. The Bön tradition is the spiritual system prevalent in Tibet before the introduction of Buddhism, which began in the eighth century. With its own large corpus of teachings and a monastic system that parallels that of the Buddhists, the Bön tradition is still alive today, even in refugee communities outside of Tibet, although historically the number of adherents has been significantly smaller than that of Buddhism since the latter's acceptance as the state religion of the Tibetan rulers.

25. Tso ("lake") is a common ending to women's names, especially among the nomadic tribes of Tibet.

26. The *garuda* is a bird deriving from Indian mythology. It hatches fully-formed from the egg, and so is a metaphor for someone with a high degree of spiritual realization.

27. Tib. *Kuntuzangpo*. The personification of the primordial state of buddhahood.

28. Puwo is a region in southeastern Tibet, near the border where the Brahmaputra River enters the northwestern Indian province of Arunachal Pradesh.

29. Gyalrong, or Tsawa Gyalmorong, is a large region far to the east of Puwo, southeast of Kongtrul's birthplace and close to the old border with China.

30. Literally, "Pass From Which the Garuda [Brood] Scattered."

31. This is a general term ("Enjoyment of Space") for the pure realm of enlightened being associated with *dakinis*—feminine deities such as Vajrayogini.

32. Milarepa (1052-1135) was the famous yogi and saint whose songs have inspired Tibetans ever since they were compiled by Tsangnyön Heruka Rüpai Gyenchen (1452-1507); they have been translated into English in several versions. See *The Life of Milarepa*, *The Hundred Thousand Songs of Milarepa*, *Drinking the Mountain Stream*, and *Miraculous Journey*.

33. Khyungpo Naljor (978/990-1127) was a Tibetan master who made seven journeys to India, studied with over one hundred and fifty gurus (including the two *dakinis* Niguma and Sukhasiddhi), and founded the Shangpa Kagyü lineage of Tibetan Buddhism, which Kongtrul did so much to revivify in the nineteenth century with his inclusion of the core teachings of this lineage in his collection, *The Treasury of Spiritual Advice*. An account of Khyungpo Naljor's life is found in *Like An Illusion: Lives of the Shangpa Kagyu Masters*, pp. 44-92.

34. A reference to the Khyungpo clan; the Tibetan word *khyung* is the equivalent of the Sanskrit *garuda*, a term for a mythological bird like an eagle or roc, the mount of the Vedic god Indra.

35. This term refers to teachings that are concealed as "hidden treasures" and revealed, often centuries later, by a qualified master known as a *tertön*. For a detailed discussion of this tradition of teachings, see *Hidden Teachings of Tibet*.

36. A Bönpo master who lived from 1360 to 1385.

37. Ling, or Lingtsang, is an area near Kongtrul's birth region, to the northwest of Dergé.

38. While it is possible that Kongtrul was conceived due to a secret liaison between his mother and Khyungpo Lama Yungdrung Tendzin, it is more likely that the childless couple approached the lama and asked him to provide them with issue by fathering a child with Kongtrul's mother. This would also ensure the continuation of Khyungpo Lama's family line—an important consideration in Tibetan religious culture.

39. The calendar adopted by Tibetans in 1027, which combines elements from the astrology of India (primarily that found in *The Kalachakra Tantra*) and China, is based on a sixty-year cycle of twelve animals in combination with five elements. See *Tibetan Astrology*, pp. 18-31. The New Year falls in February or March, depending on the lunar cycle, and so the Tibetan year overlaps two years of the Western calendar.

40. Manjushri is a bodhisattva who embodies the wisdom of all buddhas, and one of a number of "deities of wisdom" on which Vajrayana Buddhist practitioners meditate in order to awaken such wisdom in themselves.

41. The idiom signifies the ideal process of making offerings, attributed to the mythical bodhisattva Samantabhadra (as distinct from the use of the same name to refer to the primordial state of buddhahood), whose enormous powers of meditative stability allow him to fill the reaches of space with mentally created offerings.

42. Laypeople in Tibet traditionally wore lighter-colored clothing, while monastics word darker maroon robes.

43. The term refers specifically to castles built in a style that originated with the pre-Buddhist tradition of Bön; such edifices were associated with places sacred to local spirits (RT).

44. *Torma*s are offerings formed of dough and butter, often quite elaborate and highly

colored. Because fine foods, fruits, flowers, and other objects suitable for offering on a shrine were scarce in Tibet, the custom developed of making *torma*s as substitutes. Depending on the context, a *torma* may symbolize the presence of a deity, an offering to that deity, or a focus for certain rituals performed in conjunction with meditation on that deity.

45. The *lhasang* is a form of offering ceremony much used in Tibetan culture that predates the advent of Buddhism but was incorporated into the new religion's repertoire. It involves liturgies and prayers recited in conjunction with the burning of offerings in a fire, especially fresh juniper branches that have been moistened, so as to produce clouds of thick, white smoke. The *lhasang* is a way of honoring deities and other embodiments of spiritual principles, as well as one of establishing harmony with local worldly spirits and forces, to ensure their support for one's virtuous undertakings; in the latter case, it is described as a kind of benevolent bribe.

46. The Bönpo monastery of Menri is located roughly halfway between Zhigatsé and Lhasa, in a side valley north of the Tsangpo River, in the south central province of Tsang. Menri was founded in 1405 by Nyamé Sherab Gyaltsen, and became the foremost training center for the Bönpo faith in the entire Tibetan region.

47. The Tibetan term *yungdrung* is the equivalent for the Sanskrit *svastika*, an ancient symbol of auspiciousness and immutability in many Asian cultures; it is found in both Bön and Buddhist contexts in Tibet. It is interesting to note that Kongtrul was given the reverse name of that of his biological father, perhaps as an oblique recognition of his true parentage.

48. This refers to any way in which the recipient of an offering may incur some moral flaw in accepting it. This contamination (Tib. *kor-drib*) may be due to some fault on the part of the person making the offering (perhaps in how they acquired the article being offered), or due to the recipient taking it under false pretenses or otherwise misappropriating it. When one accepts offerings and does not then put them to the use intended by the donors, one incurs a negative karmic consequence, even if the error is not intentional. Great masters can suffer to some extent from this problem, given that their position in Tibetan society required them to accept large numbers of offerings constantly, without always being aware of the source of the goods offered or the donor's intentions. There are various ways in which it is held that one can be adversely affected by such contamination, involving such factors as food, clothing, and companions; this contamination impairs one's spiritual experiences and progress.

49. The term *tokden* ("realized one") usually refers to someone involved in advanced yogic practice. This lama was obviously one of the first to exert a spiritual influence on the young Kongtrul; in Volume 11 of Kongtrul's writings we find an account of the memorial tomb of this lama.

50. Presumably a Bönpo center in Kongtrul's home region (RT).

51. This is a reference to advanced yogic practices—the structured phase of the stage of completion in Vajrayana practice—that involve physical postures, breathing exercises, and visualizations in order to harness and control subtle energy in the mind and body for the purpose of effecting states of realization.

52. One of the common Tibetan epithets of Guru Rinpoché, or Padmakara, the Indian master who is credited with establishing Buddhism in Tibet in the eighth century.

53. The Seven-Line Prayer is the most well-known invocation to Padmakara; the Vajra Guru mantra (*Om ah hum vajra guru padma siddhi hum*) is the basic mantra associated with him.

54. Situ Pema Nyinjé, also known as Pema Nyinjé Wangpo (1774-1853), was the ninth Tai Situ incarnation of the Karma Kagyü School. During the first half of Kongtrul's life, he was one of the most famous and influential lamas in eastern Tibet.

55. Dzogchen Pema Rigdzin (1625-1697) was the first Dzogchen Rinpoché incarnation and founded Dzogchen Monastery in 1684 or 1685. This became one of the six most important monasteries of the Nyingma School in the greater Tibetan region. These six were: Dorjé Drak and Mindroling in the higher elevations of central Tibet, Zhechen and Dzogchen in the middle elevations of eastern Tibet, and Kathok and Palyul in the lowlands of southeastern Tibet.

56. Möngyal Pema Gyalpo was a Bönpo master who was alive during Kongtrul's early years; his monastery, Menri Möngyal, was on the border between Dzachukha and Lingtsang, close to Ringu Monastery (RT).

57. Moma Kunshé Thikpo ("Diviner with Accurate Knowledge of Everything") was the principal caster of divinations during the time of Gesar of Ling, the semi-legendary king of eastern Tibet. The style of language used by the diviner in Kongtrul's dream is reminiscent of the Gesar epics (RT).

58. This is a Bönpo method of divination that involves holding a cord and casting it with a flick of the wrist so that it forms knots, the patterns of which are then read (RT).

59. This cryptic and metaphoric language is typical of diviners; the basic import here is of a very positive result.

60. The monastery of Zhechen Tennyi Dargyeling, one of the major Nyingma monasteries in eastern Tibet, was founded in 1735 by the second Rabjam incarnation, Gyurmé Kunzang Namgyal. The successive Rabjam incarnations have been associated with Zhechen Monastery; the present incarnation, Jigmé Chökyi Seng-gé (b. 1966), is the seventh of the line and the grandson of the late Dilgo Khyentsé Rinpoché, Rabsal Dawa, who was himself a rebirth of Jamyang Khyentsé Wangpo. Rabjam Rinpoché lives in Kathmandu, Nepal, where he directs the center of Zhechen Tennyi Dargyeling founded in exile by his illustrious grandfather in the

early 1980s. The Karma Kagyü monastery of Palpung Thupten Chökhorling was founded in 1727 by the eighth Tai Situ incarnation, Situ Panchen Chökyi Jungné. It became the major Kagyü monastery in eastern Tibet and the seat of the Tai Situ incarnations.

61. In eastern Tibet, there are several common ways of forming affectionate nicknames. Someone's personal name is shortened and a prefix or suffix is added. Here, the name Ata is likely derived from the name Tashi. See *Among Tibetan Texts: History and Literature of the Himalayan Plateau*, pp. 276-277, n. 38.

62. Tsari, or Tsaritra, is one of the most important holy places in Tibet. It is a small region between the southern province of Dakpo and the Indian border. Blessed by Padmakara and Vimalamitra, it became an important site of pilgrimage for the Kagyü schools after the Drukpa Kagyü master Tsangpa Gyaré Yeshé Dorjé visited there. The Kagyüpas hold Tsari to one of the sacred sites described in the tantras of Chakrasamvara, one of the most important deities whose meditation is practiced in the Kagyü systems. See *Tibet Handbook*, pp. 224-227.

63. Because of his central importance to the Tibetans' world view, Guru Rinpoché, or Padmakara, is often referred to simply as "the Guru." I have capitalized the word in such cases to distinguish this usage.

64. One of the principal *mahakalis*, or wrathful feminine protective deities.

65. This is a practice designed to give one facility with aiding one's own consciousness or that of another in leaving the body at death. The skin eruptions on the crown of the head that Kongtrul mentions are one of the signs that the practitioner has gained a degree of proficiency in the practice.

66. This physical sign is taken to indicate that one has gained a sufficient degree of proficiency in the technique to be able to transfer one's own consciousness at the time of one's death.

67. Dergé was the administrative and cultural center of that area of eastern Tibet; by Kongtrul's time, its government enjoyed a semi-autonomous status with respect to the central authority of the Dalai Lama's cabinet, and exercised a loose form of control over the surrounding regions that included the collection of taxes.

68. The reference is obscure, but probably refers to a Bönpo ritual (RT).

69. One of the five sambhogakaya buddhas of the basic Vajrayana mandala principle.

70. These are a group of eight well-known manifestations of "the Guru"—that is, Guru Rinpoché, or Padmakara—in which he is held to have appeared on particular occasions for specific purposes.

71. Bernakchen is a principal protector of the Kagyü School and the special protector of the successive Karmapa incarnations. Perhaps Kongtrul sees his early fascination with this deity as a premonitory sign of his future connection with the Kagyü.

72. Namgyal Ling was a Kagyü monastery in Denkhok (RT).

73. *The Discourse on Pulse Diagnosis and Urinalysis* constitutes the second chapter of

the "later tantra of activity," one of the four source tantras of the Buddhist medical tradition in Tibet.

74. Orgyen and Orgyen Rinpoché are popular Tibetan epithets for Guru Rinpoché.

75. This is a reference to an event in Padmakara's life story. The ruler of the kingdom of Sahora in ancient India (roughly equivalent to the present state of West Bengal and the country of Bangladesh), enraged at what he saw as Padmakara's seduction of his daughter, tried to immolate them both in a huge fire, but Padmakara transformed the fire into a lake. The king repented and offered his kingdom to Padmakara, who transformed it into a center of spiritual teachings. The entire episode is recounted in *The Life and Liberation of Padmasambhava*, vol. 1, pp. 234-274.

76. Born in 1786, Tsewang Dorjé Rigdzin was the forty-third generation of the kings of Dergé. He wrote the history of his royal house; see *A Genealogy of the Kings of Dergé: sDe-dge'i rgyal-rabs*. Known in his later life as Dergé Yabchen, he renounced his throne to become a monk and scholar in 1826, eventually authoring a commentary on *The Hevajra Tantra*.

77. The families of these administrators owned estates near Dergé, probably on the banks of the Drichu River, which becomes the Yangtze in China (RT).

78. These are rituals focusing on the protective deities, held every year just before the New Year's celebrations, to offset negative influences that could affect events in the forthcoming year.

79. Given the fact that Tibet has suffered repeatedly at the hands of invaders of Mongol extraction, this metaphor is a common one.

80. Despite its lofty-sounding name, this would have been a regional administrative center that also served as a prison.

81. Chamdo, located at the confluence of the Ngomchu and Dzachu Rivers, which join to form the Dachu, or Mekong, River, is the site of the oldest and most important Gelukpa monastery in eastern Tibet, Kalden Jampaling, founded around 1440 by Jangsem Sherab Zangpo, a student of the great Tsongkhapa Lobzang Drakpa (1357-1419), founder of the Gelukpa School.

82. The Menri school of painting, established in the early fifteenth century by Menla Döndrup Gyalpo of southern Tibet, was one of the earliest indigenous schools developed in Tibet, combining the Indian and Nepalese styles that had been the dominant influences up to that point with the new influx of Chinese influences. See *Among Tibetan Texts: History and Literature of the Himalayan Plateau*, pp. 251-258.

83. Although it was not a standard practice, it would seem that on occasion the Dergé government established an encampment in the hills of the region (RT).

84. Rudam is a mountainous region to the northeast of Dergé, in which Dzogchen Monastery is located.

85. Henceforth in his autobiography, Kongtrul refers to the Chödé chieftain, Tsephel of the Khangsar clan, as "the old chieftain."

86. Rather than signifying the incarnation of a specific master, this title refers to one of a line of incarnations of someone originally related to the principal incarnation of a monastery—perhaps a younger brother, cousin, or nephew; the successive incarnations would retain the title, even though there was no family connection in that generation. The Zhechen Öntrul mentioned here was Jamgön Lama Gyurmé Thutop Namgyal (b. 1787).

87. Denkhok was the region north of the town of Dergé, under the jurisdiction of the kings of Dergé and bordering the kingdom of Ling.

88. The title Jamgön (Manjushri, the Protector), which also came to be applied to Kongtrul later in his life, is affixed to the names of highly revered lamas in recognition of their erudition and wisdom.

89. Kongtrul often refers to this master as Zhechen Öntrul, or Jamgön Lama. Zhechen Öntrul Gyurmé Thutop Namgyal (b. 1787) was the master of many great figures, including the Nyingma masters Dza Paltrul Rinpoché Orgyen Chökyi Wangpo (1808-1887) and the second Kathok Situ incarnation, Chökyi Lodrö (1820-1879?).

90. This is a system of divination using white and black pebbles to determine how the interaction of five elements—wood, fire, earth, metal, and water—will affect someone's physical health, life force, personal power, and prospects for success (RT).

91. Skt. *Kavyadarsha*. An Indian Sanskrit work on poetics by the seventh-century author Dandin, which was translated into Tibetan in the thirteenth century and became the principal source for the study of poetics.

92. A work of lists and groupings of technical terms.

93. This is the study of word derivations, the use of technical vocabulary, and categories of topics. It is one of the five minor fields of learning in the Buddhist tradition; the others are poetry, metrics, drama, and astrology. The five major fields are art, medicine, Sanskrit, epistemology, and the Buddhist teachings themselves.

94. The Nyingma master Gyurmé Tendzin Pelgyé was a student of Thrinlé Chödrön, a Dzogchen master who was the daughter of the Mindroling throne holder Thrinlé Namgyal (1765-1812). Thrinlé Chödrön was also noteworthy in that she was one of Jamyang Khyentsé Wangpo's Dzogchen masters.

95. *The Mirror of Poetics* is divided into three major sections: "The first gives definitions and classifications of various literary forms, and describes the ornate eastern Gaudi and the simpler southern Vaidarbhi style of classical Sanskrit writing, together with intermediate variations. It also specifies the gunas or virtues of poetic expression. The second section explains and illustrates the thirty-five alaokaras or figures of speech which embellish literary language. The third further discusses the yamaka, another embellishment which consists of alliterative repetition of syl-

lables, and goes on to deal with chitrabandha or unusual literary techniques, and also discourses on the doshas or blemishes of expression." (*Dandin: Tales of the Ten Princes*, p. xiv).

96. The two basic works on Tibetan grammar—*The Thirty Consonants* and *The Application of Affixes*—are held to have been authored by Thönmi Sambhota, a minister under the Tibetan king Songtsen Gampo, who journeyed to India in the seventh century and designed the script for the written Tibetan language, basing it on an existing Indian script.

97. An abbreviated form of empowerment ritual that follows a simple format in which the master authorizes the student to meditate on a given deity by transmitting blessings based on the principles of the deity's enlightened form, speech, and mind.

98. Skt. *Manjushri-nama-samgiti*. This is the first text in the tantra section of the Kangyur, the collection of Tibetan translations of teachings considered to be the words of the Buddha, and is commonly used by practitioners as a liturgy to awaken powers of understanding.

99. A number of systems dealing with Sanskrit grammar were introduced into Tibet, with Tibetan translations of their source texts being prepared; the most common systems were those known as the Chandra, Kalapa, and Sarasvata systems. The Chandra system is named after Chandragomin, a seventh-century Indian Buddhist lay master who authored *The Discourse on Grammar* (Skt. *Chandra-vyakarana-sutra*), a Tibetan translation of which exists in the Tengyur collection.

100. Hayagriva (Tib. *Tamdrin*) is the wrathful aspect of Avalokiteshvara, the bodhisattva of compassion.

101. The term "peaceful and wrathful deities" (Tib. *Zhithro*) refers to a mandala of forty-two peaceful and fifty-eight wrathful deities that are associated with the experiences one's mind undergoes in the intermediate state after death, or *bardo*. Each of the deities corresponds to a specific aspect of an individual's mind-body complex. It was a very common practice in the eastern provinces of Tibet for lamas to perform such rituals when people died or were very ill. The ritual referred to here is specifically designed to lead someone's consciousness away from negative states and toward more positive ones. Often rituals are performed many times over, in an abbreviated format, in order to reinforce the effect.

102. Dzong-go was the main monastery in Ling Province; the head, referred to as the Ling Jedrung, was always a son of the king of Ling (RT).

103. The monastery of Ogmin Orgyen Mindroling was founded in 1670 by Rigdzin Terdak Lingpa, near the head of the Drachi, a side valley that branches off the main valley of the Tsangpo River on the south bank, almost opposite the site of Samyé. It became the largest and most important Nyingma institution in central Tibet and produced a distinctive style in ritual arts and music that remains a

standard of excellence to this day. Rigdzin Terdak Lingpa was the first "Minling Thrichen" (Great Throne Holder of Mindroling); the current Thrichen, the twelfth in the line, lives at the Mindroling branch founded in Dehra Dun, India.

104. The Union of All Rare and Precious Jewels (Tib. *Könchok Chidü*) is a *terma* cycle that focuses on different aspects of Guru Rinpoché—outer, inner, secret, and most secret. Discovered by the *tertön* Jatsön Nyingpo (1585-1656), it became one of the most popular and widely practiced *terma* cycles, used by practitioners of all schools of Tibetan Buddhism.

105. Skt. *rasayana*; Tib. *chülen*. These are based on the principle that all matter contains a nutritive essence from which an advanced practitioner can gain sustenance, through the power of meditation and certain rituals. Masters of this technique are credited with nourishing themselves by eating rocks, flowers, and so forth.

106. The Northern Treasures are a group of practices and teachings based on *termas* discovered by Rigdzin Gödem in the fourteenth century.

107. A holy site in the hills above Palpung, blessed by Guru Rinpoché during his time in Tibet.

108. Pilgrimage was a major element in Tibetan religious life. See *Sacred Ground* for an informative essay and a translation of one of Kongtrul's own works on the subject.

109. Longchenpa Drimé Özer (1308-1364), also known as Longchen Rabjampa, was arguably the greatest scholar the Nyingma School of Tibetan Buddhism ever produced. Although much of his prodigious literary output has been lost, his Seven Treasuries remain standards for study to this day. Rather than being a connected series, they are individual treatises that stand on their own, each one exploring a particular theme that relates to the Dzogchen, or Great Perfection, system of the Nyingmapa. A project to translate these Treasuries into English is underway under the auspices of the late Chagdud Tulku Rinpoché and the Tibetan Heritage Institute. Two of the works have already appeared—*The Precious Treasury of the Way of Abiding* with its autocommentary, *The Exposition of the Quintessential Meaning of the Three Categories*, and *The Precious Treasury of the Basic Space of Phenomena* (with its autocommentary, *A Treasure Trove of Scriptural Transmission*).

110. The Sanskrit term *sadhana* (Tib. *druptap*, "means of accomplishment") here refers to a liturgy associated with a deity practice, often quite concise and used for personal practice.

111. Tib. *Guru Drakpo*. A wrathful manifestation of Guru Rinpoché.

112. This refers to the single form of a male deity, without a feminine consort.

113. A *kila* dagger is a symbol of the deity Vajrakila, used on a shrine as a focus for meditation and depicted being held in the deity's hand; its three-sided blade

represents the resolution of the three negative emotional patterns of attachment, aversion, and ignorance into their true nature.

114. "Doors to *termas*" are avenues, usually physical, through which concealed teachings may be revealed.

115. This field of study focuses on the formation of words and various forms of metered verse used in liturgies and poetry.

116. The *Kalapa*, or *Kalapasutra* (also known as the *Katantra*), is a Sanskrit work by an Indian author known variously as Ishavaravarman, Sharvavarman, or Sarvavarman; *The Discourse of Sarasvata* is known in Sanskrit as the *Sarasvata-vyakarana-sutra*. These constitute two of the simpler and more well-known systems; Kongtrul's main emphasis, however, was on the more scholarly and challenging presentation found in *The Discourse on Grammar* by the Indian Buddhist master Chandragomin. For illuminating accounts of the development of this field of studies in Tibet, see *A Survey on Sanskrit Grammar in Tibetan Language* and Chapter 14, "Buddhist Literary and Practical Arts According to Bo dong paṇ chen Phyogs las rnam rgyal," in E. Gene Smith's *Among Tibetan Texts: History and Literature of the Himalayan Plateau.* pp. 190-199.

117. An epithet for Padmakara, or Guru Rinpoché.

118. This is a very well-known *terma*, a prayer invoking the blessings of Padmakara.

119. In the deity practices of Vajrayana Buddhism, the principal deity is often "crowned" by the form of another deity, resting on top of the principal deity's head. This smaller form, termed the "master of the (buddha) family" (Tib. *rigdak*), indicates the particular family of the mandala schema that is associated with the principal deity.

120. Another well-known *terma* of prayers to Padmakara, discovered by Drapa Ngönshé in the 11th century.

121. A monastic complex might include one or more such residences, whose function was to ensure continuity of its administration and the transmission of teachings. Such residences were often (though not exclusively) associated with incarnation lines, with the next incarnation inheriting the residence from his predecessor. A single residence might also be associated with a number of tulkus or lamas (RT).

122. When Thönmi Sambhota, minister to the Tibetan king Songtsen Gampo in the seventh century, journeyed to India to research the development of a written Tibetan language, the *lancha* script of northern India is said to have served as the model for the "headed" (*u-chen*) script of Tibet and the *vartu* for the "headless" (*u-mé*) script.

123. A great master such as Öntrul Gyurmé Thutop Namgyal would only occupy his residence sporadically, spending much of his time in retreat somewhere in the region of the main monastery (RT).

124. The ordination is usually intended to be kept for the remainder of one's life; the

fact that Zhechen Öntrul suggested this arrangement has a prophetic touch to it, as though he was aware of the compromising situation Kongtrul would face the next year at Palpung.

125. This idiom refers to the ordination ceremony conferring the complete vows of a *bhikshu*, a fully ordained Buddhist monk. In the Tibetan tradition, the vows are usually conferred to a group of three individuals.

126. An epithet for the Nyingma, the oldest school of the Tibetan Buddhist tradition. It is called the Early Translation School because its teachings are based on translations of texts done during the period between the reigns of the Tibetan kings Trisong Detsen (reigned 756-797) and Ralpachen (reigned 814-836), before King Langdarma began his persecution of Buddhism after his elder brother Ralpachen's assassination. The life of the great translator Rinchen Zangpo (958-1055) is usually taken as the beginning of the Later Translation Schools; these form the basis for the Sarma, or "new," schools of Tibetan Buddhism, which include virtually all the schools other than the Nyingma. The Early Translation School is noted for its interpretive and lyric style (Tib. *dön-gyur*, "translation of the meaning"), the Later Translation Schools for a more literal, technically accurate, style (Tib. *tsig-gyur*, "translation of the words"). The Nyingma School, and its Dzogchen teachings in particular, constituted Kongtrul's first exposure to the Buddhist tradition and continued to exert enormous influence on him throughout his life.

127. The three bases of the Buddhist monastic tradition are a common theme for writers within this tradition. They are the summer retreat (a three-month period devoted to intensive study and practice), the monthly ceremony to renew vows, and the ceremony to determine specific infractions of the vows.

128. The Gyaltsap incarnations of Tsurphu are an important line within the Kagyü School. Since the time of the Sixth Karmapa, Thongwa Dönden (1416-1453), their function has been to act as regents (Tib. *gyaltsap*) in the periods between the passing of one Karmapa and the enthronemnt of the next. The first Gyaltsap, Goshri Paljor Döndrup, lived from about 1427 to 1489. The Gyaltsap incarnation at the time Kongtrul is discussing would have been the ninth, Drakpa Yeshé, who was born in 1821 (and thus would have been about thirteen or fourteen at the time) and died in 1876.

129. The "translated word of the Buddha"; the canon (usually in one hundred and eight volumes) of the Tibetan translations of ethical codes, sutras, tantras, and other sources, almost exclusively from Indian originals, of texts that are considered the authoritative teachings of the Buddha (although this term is not confined solely to the Buddha Shakyamuni).

130. Skt. *Arya-bhadrakalpika-nama-mahayana-sutra*. This text is the first in the sutra section of the Kangyur. It is always the first text read when the oral transmission

for the Kangyur is conferred. The sutra discusses the one thousand buddhas who, it is held, will appear during this age. An English translation has been published as *The Fortunate Aeon.*

131. The "translated treatises"; the canon (in more than two hundred volumes) of the Tibetan versions of authoritative commentaries (mostly Indian in origin) on the source texts of the Kangyur.

132. Tib. *Nyingma Gyübum.* The tantras of the Early Translation School, or Nyingma, were first collected by Zurchen Shakya Jungné (1002-1062). When the codification of the Kangyur and Tengyur began under the direction of such Sarma masters as Butön Rinchendrup (1290-1364), there was a consistent policy of excluding the Nyingma tantras from the collection, usually on the basis of the argument that Indian originals for these texts could not be validated. It was only when the Eighth Situ Rinpoché, Situ Panchen Chökyi Jungné (1700-1774), edited the Dergé woodblocks of the Kangyur that several of the more important Nyingma tantras were included. The *Nyingma Gyübum* went through a number of handwritten editions until the first woodblocks were carved in the late eighteenth century, under the auspices of Tsewang Lhamo, a queen of Dergé who was a student of the great Jigmé Lingpa. The collection contains the source tantras for the Mahayoga, Anuyoga, and Atiyoga systems of the Nyingma.

133. The famed Jonang master, Dolpo (or Dolpopa) Sherab Gyaltsen (1292-1361) was also known as Dolpo Sang-gyé ("The Buddha of Dolpo," after his home region). He did much to systematize the philosophical school of "qualified emptiness" (Tib. *zhentong*) in such works as his *Ocean of Certain Meaning.* For a detailed discussion of his life and philosophy, see *The Buddha from Dolpo: A Study of the Life and Thought of the Tibetan Master Dolpopa Sherab Gyaltsen.*

134. The Third Karmapa (1284-1339). On the basis of his study with Longchenpa's guru Kumaradza and a vision of the early Dzogchen master Vimalamitra, Rangjung Dorjé developed a synthesis of teachings on the nature of mind, infusing the Mahamudra teachings of the Kagyü with those of the Heart Drop (*Nyingthik*) lineage of Dzogchen. For a brief account of Rangjung Dorjé's life, see *The History of the Sixteen Karmapas of Tibet*, pp. 55-58. *The Profound Inner Meaning* (Tib. *Zabmo Nangdön*) is a detailed treatise on the underlying principles of spiritual practice according to the higher classes of tantra.

135. The United Intent of the Gurus (Tib. *Lama Gongdü*) is one of the most important *terma* cycles of the Dzogchen tradition; it was discovered by Sang-gyé Lingpa (1340-1396).

136. This is probably a reference to work known as *The Collected Instructions of the Mani Mantra* (Tib. *Mani Kanbum*), which contains the teachings focusing on Avalokiteshvara and is attributed to the seventh-century Tibetan king Songtsen Gampo. Concealed as a *terma*, it was discovered by Sang-gyé Lingpa.

137. Tib. *Pema Kathang*. Perhaps the most popular biographical account of Padmakara, or Guru Rinpoché, this is a *terma* that was discovered by Orgyen Lingpa (b. 1323).

138. Tib. *Kathang Dé-nga*. These five works, which are *termas* also discovered by Orgyen Lingpa in the fourteenth century, are standard sources of information on early Tibetan history.

139. Jigmé Lingpa (1730-1798) was a Nyingma master whose most important contribution was his *terma* of enlightened intent, the cycle of The Heart Drop of Longchenpa (Tib. *Longchen Nyingthik*). Three of the nine volumes of his collected works constitute the source texts for this cycle.

140. Tib. *Dom-sum Nam-ngé*. The definitive Nyingma work on the interrelationship between the disciplines of the Hinayana, Mahayana, and Vajrayana approaches, authored by Ngari Panchen Pema Wang-gyal (1487-1542).

141. This grouping of practices constitutes the basic mandala of the Mahayoga class of the Nyingma tantras. Five—Yamantaka, Hayagriva, Samyak, Vajra Amrita, and Vajrakila—are classified as "transcendent" practices; one, The Imprecations of the Mamos (*Mamo Bötong*), a "boundary" practice; and two, Praises and Offerings to Worldly Gods (*Jikten Chötö*) and The Wrathful Mantra Curse (*Möpa Drak-ngak*), "mundane" practices.

142. Karma Lingpa was a fourteenth-century *tertön* who discovered, among other *termas*, the most important and widely-practiced cycles focusing on the mandala of the one hundred peaceful and wrathful deities; this cycle contains detailed teachings on the *bardo*, or intermediate, states.

143. Tib. *Döjoi Bumzang*. A collection of empowerments and their related *sadhanas*.

144. Nyang Rinpoché, or Ngadak Nyang-ral Nyima Özer (1136-1204) was one of the greatest of the early *tertöns*.

145. Tib. *Dorjé Sempa*. One of the sambhogakaya buddhas, referred to as the "source of all mandalas" and associated with the principle of purification.

146. Tib. *Öpamé* ("Infinite Light"); one of the sambhogakaya buddhas of the five families of the basic Vajrayana mandala, Amitabha is associated with the Realm of Bliss (Skt. *Sukhavati*; Tib. *Dewachen*) and the practices commonly known as "Pure Land Buddhism," which constituted an important element in all schools of the Tibetan tradition.

147. A very concise empowerment ritual, often used in transmitting the blessing and practice of a wrathful or protective deity.

148. The six-syllable mantra is *Om mani padme hum*, the mantra of Avalokiteshvara, the bodhisattva of compassion.

149. The "mandala offering" is a symbolic exercise of visualizing the entire universe filled in one's imagination with everything worthy of offering and presenting

this to a vajra master as a formal way of requesting that a transmission of some kind be bestowed.

150. Implicit in this statement of the old chieftain is the fact that Palpung Monastery, as the politically more important institution, was exercising its right to conscript the talented young Kongtrul from Zhechen; it was only his recognition as an incarnation "belonging" to Palpung that kept him from being similarly requisitioned from Palpung by the Dergé authorities.

151. That is, Jamgön Rinpoché Gyurmé Thutop Namgyal.

152. Jamgön Rinpoché's choice of this phrase would seem to have been prophetic; the ordination name Kongtrul received later in his life at Palpung was Yönten Gyatso (Ocean of Qualities).

153. The title indicates the elder of one or more Öntrul incarnations in a given monastery. Karma Thekchok Tenphel, the Palpung Öngen, became Kongtrul's mentor.

154. A standard work on astrology (RT). The charts referred to are not personal charts, but tables to determine planetary configurations and the interactions of the elements.

155. This is possibly Jampa Kunga Tendzin (1776-1862), the grand abbot of Ngor Monastery, a master of the Lamdré lineage of the Sakya School and one of Jamyang Khyentsé Wangpo's teachers.

156. In Tibet, respect was shown to invited guests by going out to meet them on their journey and escort them back to one's residence. The farther the distance the escort went out, the more respect was being indicated.

157. This refers to lumps of silver roughly the size of a horse's hoof.

158. In Denkhok (RT).

159. Dergé Gönchen ("the great monastery of Dergé"), also known as Lhundrup Teng, was founded in 1448 by Thangtong Gyalpo, under the auspices of Lodrö Tobden, the thirty-first in the succession of the kings of Dergé.

160. Palyul Namgyal Jangchub Chöling, founded in 1665 by Rigdzin Kunzang Sherab (1636-1698), was one of the two most important Nyingma monasteries in southeastern Tibet, the other being Kathok. For information on the monastery and lineage of Palyul, see *A Garland of Immortal Wish-fulfilling Trees: The Palyul Tradition of Nyingmapa.*

161. This was presumably because the Nyingma administration of Palyul requisitioned Palden Chögyal's services rather than allowing the Kagyü authorities to enlist him. He is implying that the same could happen to Kongtrul if the talented young man were to go to Palyul Monastery.

162. Here the honorific title (Tib. *Kyapgön*) refers to the Ninth Situ Rinpoché, Pema Nyinjé Wangpo, the highest ranking tulku at Palpung.

163. Literally, "the Victorious Ones, Father and Sons." The "Father" refers to the Gyalwa Karmapa, the "Sons" to the secondary incarnations of the Kagyü School, such as the Tai Situ and Zhamar incarnations.

164. This is a title that Kongtrul often uses in referring to his root guru, the Ninth Tai Situ, Pema Nyinjé Wangpo.

165. This refers to a particular style of writing in which each syllable of a poem fits in a square on a grid. The poem then consists of many shorter poems that can be read by following a line of squares in any direction.

166. That is, the old chieftain, who had initiated Kongtrul's move from Zhechen to Palpung almost eight months earlier.

167. That is, Kongtrul's mentor at Zhechen Monastery, Jamgön Gyurmé Thutop Namgyal.

168. Since Öngen already knew of the previous ordination, he may not have insisted on the formal dissolution ceremony, since it was clear that Kongtrul already felt compromised enough (RT).

169. The "Great Scholar" was the twelfth-century Kashmiri master Khaché Panchen Shakyashribhadra, who reintroduced the lineage of the monastic ordination through western, or upper, Tibet after the persecutions of King Langdarma had destroyed the monastic structure in the ninth century.

170. This was the full name of the Ninth Situ Rinpoché. The Tai Situ incarnations are held to be emanations of the bodhisattva Maitreya, who in the future will become the buddha following Shakyamuni.

171. This refers to the structure of the complete ordination ceremony, in which the aspirant takes the vows of a layman, a novice monk, and a fully ordained monk, one after the other. Even if the first two stages of ordination have been taken in the past, they are taken again during this ceremony.

172. It is common for monastic ordination names to be quite lengthy and ornate. The "Karma" prefix indicates ordination in the Karma Kagyü School; the rest of Kongtrul's name could be translated "Ocean of Qualities, All-Pervasive Enlightened Activity, Glorious and Noble One." He signed many of his works with the shortened name Karma Yönten Gyatso.

173. That is, of Situ Rinpoché.

174. A common design in Tibetan scroll paintings, inspired by Chinese themes, depicts six symbols of longevity—a cliff face, a river, a tree, an old man, a crane, and a deer.

175. From this point onward, Kongtrul often refers to the Ninth Situ Rinpoché with some variation of the epithet "my precious lord of refuge" (Tib. *Kyabjé Rinpoché*), instead of a more specific title.

176. It was common for numerous incarnation lineages to be associated with any given large or important monastery. Following the lifetimes of Kongtrul and Jamyang Khyentsé Wangpo, for example, Palpung Monastery housed incarnations of the Tai Situ, Öngen, Kongtrul, and Khyentsé lines, among others, while Zhechen Monastery was home to a number of incarnation lineages, including

the Rabjam, Gyaltsap, Öntrul, Kongtrul, and Khyentsé lines (ADD). The first Palpung Kongtrul incarnation was Khyentsé Özer (1904-1953), who was the son of the Fifteenth Karmapa, Khakhyab Dorjé; the second was Karma Lodrö Chökyi Seng-gé Tenpai Gocha, who was born in 1954 and died tragically in an automobile accident in India in 1992; his rebirth, Chökyi Nyima, was recognized by the Seventeenth Karmapa, Orgyen Trinlé Dorjé, in 1996, and is currently being trained at the late Jamgön Kongtrul's center in Pullahari, Nepal. The first Palpung Khyentsé incarnation was Karma Khyentsé Özer (1896-1945); the second, still living in India, was born the son of a Bhutanese nobleman. The first Zhechen Kongtrul incarnation, Pema Drimé Lekpai Lodrö (1901?-1960), was the teacher of Chögyam Trungpa Rinpoché (1940-1987); the second was born as the eldest son of Trungpa Rinpoché. The first Zhechen Khyentsé was Dilgo Khyentsé Rinpoché, Rabsal Dawa (1910-1991), who founded a new Zhechen Monastery in Kathmandu, Nepal, after leaving Tibet when the Communist takeover occurred; the second Zhechen Khyentsé was born in 1993, the son of Tsikhé Chokling Rinpoché (who is an incarnation of Chokgyur Lingpa).

177. The Seventh Pawo Rinpoché (1718-1781) of Nenang Monastery in central Tibet, who died in 1781. The Pawo incarnations are an important line in the Karma Kagyü School. Given that Situ Pema Nyinjé Wangpo was born in 1774 and would only have been about seven at the time of Pawo Tsuklak Gawa's death, Pawo Rinpoché may have left his advice in the form of a letter.

178. The Fourteenth Karmapa, Thekchok Dorjé (1798-1868). The Karmapas, with their monastic seat at Tsurphu in the Tölung Valley west of Lhasa in central Tibet, have been the supreme heads of the Kagyü School since the days of the First Karmapa, Düsum Khyenpa (1110-1193).

179. The Drukchen Rinpoché was the head of the Drukpa Kagyü subschool. Given that the Drukchen referred to had already advised Situ Pema Nyinjé Wangpo by 1833, it would seem to be a refence to Eighth Drukchen Kunzik Chökyi Nangwa (1768-1822), because the Ninth Drukchen Jigmé Mingyur Wang-gyal (1823-1883) would only have been about ten years old.

180. The eighteenth-century master Belo Tsewang Kunkhyap of Zurmang Monastery was a close student of the Eighth Situ Rinpoché, Situ Panchen Chökyi Jungné.

181. Rigdzin Tamdrin Gönpo was an eighteenth-century holder of the lineage of Ratna Lingpa's *termas*.

182. Due to political circumstances, a more powerful school could prohibit the recognition of an incarnation associated with another school. One famous example is that of the Zhamar Rinpochés of the Kagyü School. The Tenth Zhamar, Mipham Chödrup Gyatso (1742-1792), while on pilgrimage to Nepal, was accused by the Gelukpa-dominated central Tibetan government of complicity in a Nepalese invasion on the southern Tibetan border. The government confiscated the Zhamar's

lands and banned recognition of the incarnation. It was only due to the petition of the late Sixteenth Karmapa, Rangjung Rigpai Dorjé (1924-1981), that the government permitted the lineage of incarnations to be reinstituted.

183. It was this Kuntrul (a minor Kagyü incarnation from Golok) who became something of personal nemesis for Kongtrul years later, in 1847.

184. Kongtrul is an abbreviation of KONGpo Bamteng TRULku, the "incarnation from Bamteng in Kongpo Province" (in the south of Tibet).

185. Tib. *Drupthap Rinchen Jungné*. A collection of empowerments and related sadhanas from the Jonang tradition, compiled by Taranatha (1575-1634).

186. Ratna Lingpa was a major *tertön* who lived from 1403 to 1479.

187. Atisha (982-1054) was an Indian Buddhist master whose personal name was Dipamkara Shrijnana. Born into a royal Bengali family, he studied with a number of Buddhist masters. Undertaking a difficult sea voyage to Sumatra, Atisha remained there for twelve years, studying with a master named Dharmakirti, from whom he received the teachings on cultivating bodhichitta that became the core of the "mental training" (Tib. *lojong*) system of practice first developed by the Kadampa School founded by Atisha's students in Tibet. Returning to India, Atisha taught at the famed monastic college of Vikramashila and other institutions. Atisha was invited to journey to Tibet by the "royal monk" Yeshé Ö (947-1024) (ex-ruler of the western Tibetan province of Ngari) and his grand-nephew Jangchub Ö (984-1078). In addition, Atisha's chosen deities, Tara and Avalokiteshvara, appeared to him in visions, further convincing him of the necessity of his teaching in Tibet. There, he began teaching the fundamentals of Buddhism and became a key figure in inspiring the later spread of the teachings in Tibet. The most important of Atisha's more than twenty works was *The Lamp for the Path to Enlightenment*, in which he set forth the three spiritual models that became standards for explaining the various levels of the Buddhist teachings—the practitioner seeking a better rebirth, the one seeking individual salvation from suffering, and the one seeking universal enlightenment. For an account of Atisha's life, see *Atisha's Lamp for the Path to Enlightenment*, pp. 7-21

188. That is, Öngen and others.

189. The first Karma Kagyü monastery in eastern Tibet, founded in 1147 by the First Karmapa, Düsum Khyenpa, on the banks of the Dzachu River in eastern Tibet, about one hundred and twenty kilometers west of Dergé. It was the residence for the first seven Tai Situ incarnations, until the Eighth Situ, Chökyi Jungné, founded Palpung Monastery in 1717.

190. Karma Chagmé (1613-1678), who often signed his works with a Sanskritized version of his name, Raga Asya, was a Karma Kagyü master who codified the Sky Teachings (Tib. *Namchö*), a cycle of *termas* of enlightened intent discovered by Namchö Mingyur Dorjé (1645-1667). His incarnations were affiliated

with the Nyingma monastery of Palyul in eastern Tibet, because that monastery maintained the lineage of the Sky Teachings. A Chagmé Tulku named Sang-ngak Tendzin was a student of the Fourteenth Karmapa, Thekchok Dorjé (1799-1869); this is likely the incarnation to whom Kongtrul is referring.

191. Dzigar was a Drukpa Kagyü monastery about one hundred kilometers southeast of Dergé. The First Dzigar Choktrul was Sönam Gyatso (1608-1669); in 1834, the incarnation attending the oral transmission was likely the Fifth Dzigar Choktrul, Chökyi Nyima (b. 1799?), or perhaps the sixth incarnation, Ngawang Tenpai Nyima.

192. Saga, the fourth month of the Tibetan lunar calendar, generally corresponds to late May and early June of the Western calendar. It is considered an especially auspicious time for spiritual endeavors, since it includes the days commemorating the birth, enlightenment, and passing of the Buddha Shakyamuni. The fifteenth day of this month is the day of the full moon, also considered auspicious for spiritual undertakings.

193. These latter two cycles are also *termas* discovered by Ratna Lingpa.

194. Tib. *Thukjé Chenpo* ("The Supremely Compassionate One"); an epithet of Avalokiteshvara, the bodhisattva of compassion.

195. Tib. *Dorjé Phurpa*. A wrathful masculine protective deity associated with the principle of enlightened activity, Vajrakila is one of the deities in the Eight Commands cycle.

196. These are two cycles that focus on Yamantaka, the wrathful form of Manjushri.

197. The main monastery of the Jonang tradition, Takten Phuntsoling was originally founded by Kunpangpa Thukjé Tsöndrü (1243-1313) as Jonang Phuntsoling, but later renamed during the lifetime of the great Jonang master Taranatha (1575-1634), only to be absorbed into the Gelukpa School during the time of the Fifth Dalai Lama (1617-1682) and eventually renamed as Ganden Phuntsoling. The woodblocks of the original Jonang works were preserved, but making copies of these texts was forbidden until one of Kongtrul's contemporaries, Zhalu Ribuk Tulku Losel Tenkyong, persuaded the authorities to allow an edition to be printed.

198. The Fourth Drukchen of the Drukpa Kagyü School, Pema Karpo (1527-1592), was a prolific and seminal writer whose works are central to the Drukpa Kagyü School.

199. Tib. *Jonang Thrigya*. A collection of instructions found in cycles of less widespread teachings that are nevertheless considered valuable and important.

200. For certain cycles of teachings, it is traditional for the oral transmission for each text to be given three times, at least one of which is a slower "teaching transmission."

201. Tib. *Namshé Yeshé*.

202. Tib. *Deshek Nyingpoi Tenchö*.

203. Yuthok Yönten Gönpo the Elder (eighth-ninth centuries) was Tibet's foremost scholar of medicine of the time, and served as royal physician to King Mé Aktsom and his son, King Trisong Detsen. He was renowned as Bhaishajyaguru, the Buddha of Healing, in human form.

204. Vajrayana techniques of deity yoga involve several distinct stages—approach (Tib. nyenpa), accomplishment (drubpa), and enactment (léjor). Each of these stages involves specific visualizations and mantras, and has its own function. Approach is the process of familiarizing oneself with the deity and the meditation (likened to first becoming acquainted with a powerful and influential figure), accomplishment is that of consolidating and deepening that familiarity (likened to developing a deeper friendship with the individual), and enactment is that of using the practice of the deity to achieve specific goals (likened to enjoining a favor from the individual). The first two stages are usually done in a strict retreat, with a requisite number of mantras to be recited or a specific period of time to be spent in the practice of the meditation. The third stage is then carried out at the successful conclusion of the retreat, and often involves specific rituals (such as homa, or fire rituals). In common Tibetan parlance, the term nyendrup refers to an intensive retreat emphasizing the first two stages; it is translated throughout the text simply as "personal retreat."

205. This would seem to be a reference to the tantras found in the Kangyur.

206. Tib. Yuthok Nyingthik. A cycle of spiritual and medical teachings based on the original teachings of Yuthok Yönten Gönpo the Younger (1126-1202), a descendant of the original Yuthok Yönten Gönpo and one of the main figures in the development of the Tibetan medical tradition.

207. Tsa-tsas are small figurines cast in clay, depicting small stupas or forms of deities. The interior chambers of temples and stupas are filled with large numbers of these before the building is consecrated.

208. The Sanskrit term stupa (Tib. chörten) refers to a monument of varying styles that incorporates architectural features that correspond to components of the spiritual path and qualities of the awakened state of buddhahood. A stupa is considered a representation of enlightened mind, just as images are representations of form and books those of speech.

209. In Vajrayana systems of practice, advanced practitioners may have consorts, who may or may not be actual sexual partners but whose function is to inspire and nurture the practitioner's realization and activities. The fact that Situ Rinpoché was a fully ordained monk would not necessarily have precluded the idea in Kongtrul's mind of him having such a consort, if only on the symbolic level of the dream.

210. Maitreya, the bodhisattva who will become the next buddha of our eon, is unique in Buddhist art in being depicted sitting on a throne in the Western fashion, rather than cross-legged.

211. Yeshé Tsogyal was a queen of Tibet and the principal consort to Padmakara during his time in that land. She was directly responsible for the concealing of most of the *terma*, or hidden treasure teachings. Her life story has been translated as *Sky Dancer, Mother of Knowledge,* and *Lady of the Lotus-Born.*

212. Abhayakara, or Abhayakaragupta, was an Indian Buddhist master (late eleventh-mid twelfth centuries), who may be one and the same as Abhayadattashri, author of a commentary on the songs of the Eighty-Four *Mahasiddhas*, a famous group of highly accomplished Vajrayana masters of ancient India.

213. Sok-ön Rigpai Raldri, also known as Sok-ön Kazhipa or Ratnabhadra, was a Kagyü master who tutored the Sixth Karmapa, Tongwa Dönden (1416-1453).

214. That is, Palpung Öngen Thekchok Tenphel. Such honorific titles as *Choktrul* ("Sublime Incarnation") and *Rinpoché* ("Precious One") are often added to the "basic" name of a *tulku*. For example, Kongtrul often refers to the Tenth and Eleventh Situs as "Kuzhap Choktrul," a reference to them being further rebirths of his guru the Ninth Situ Pema Nyinjé Wangpo.

215. These five are all important practices in the Karma Kagyü School, known collectively as the Five Personal Practices of Düsum Khyenpa, the First Karmapa (Tib. *Düsum Khyenpai Thukdam Nam-nga*). Vajravarahi (Tib. *Dorjé Phamo*, a feminine deity) and Chakrasamvara (Tib. *Khorlo Demchok*, a masculine deity) are two of the most important deities of the mother tantras in the Anuttarayoga class of the Sarma Schools. Jinasagara (Tib. *Gyalwa Gyatso*) is a form of Avalokiteshvara in union with a feminine consort, and thus also pertaining to the highest, or Anuttarayoga, class of the Sarma tantras. Sarvavid Vairochana (Tib. *Kunrik Nampar Nangdzé*) and Akshobhya (Tib. *Mikyöpa*) are two of the sambhogakaya buddhas of the five families of the basic Vajrayana mandala; their practices, which pertain to the more introductory class of Kriyatantra, are associated with purifying one's consciousness of the effects of negative karmic patterns, and so they are often employed to benefit deceased individuals.

216. Amitayus (Tib. *Tsépamé*, "Infinite Longevity") is an aspect of the sambhogakaya buddha Amitabha, and is associated with the principle of longevity.

217. The Second Karmapa, Karma Pakshi (1204-1283), was noted for his extraordinary spiritual powers; a *guru sadhana* focusing on him was revealed as a *terma* by Yön-Gé Mingyur Dorjé (b. 1628/41).

218. One of the Eight Lineages of Accomplishment (Tib. *drup-gyü shing-ta gyé*) that developed in Tibet, the lineage of Chö ("Severance") was based on the teachings of the Tibetan woman master Machik Lapdrön (1055-1145). See *Machig Labdrön and the Foundations of Chöd* and *Machik's Complete Explanation: Clarifying the Meaning of Chöd.*

219. These are three teaching manuals by the Ninth Karmapa, Wangchuk Dorjé. For English translations of the extensive and intermediate manuals, see *Mahamudra,*

The Ocean of Definitive Meaning and *The Mahamudra Eliminating the Darkness of Ignorance*, respectively. A commentary on the abridged manual by the Kagyü master Khenchen Karma Lodrö (b. 1933), the Ninth Thrangu Rinpoché, has appeared as *Pointing Out the Dharmakaya* in the December 2000 issue of *Shenpen Ösel*.

220. In this case, the practices referred to are the Six Yogas of Naropa, a set of advanced practices transmitted particularly in the Kagyü and Geluk Schools.

221. Tib. *Lhabap Düchen*. One of the four most important holy days in the Tibetan Buddhist calendar, the twenty-second day of the ninth month commemorates the Buddha's return to the human realm, which he left for a period in order to instruct the rebirth of his mother in the realm of the gods.

222. A ritual of the Kriyatantra class (the first of the four classes of the Sarma Schools, or of the six classes recognized by the Nyingma). Usually lasting two days, the ritual involves meditation on a thousand-armed form of Avalokiteshvara and repetition of many prayers and mantras. Fasting, bathing, and other forms of ritual purification are an integral part of the ritual, which was widespread and popular in Tibet, often done in "sets" of eight or more at one time. The Indian Buddhist nun Shri (Tib. *Gelongma Palmo*) is held to have formulated the ritual in ancient times based on her experience of being cured of smallpox by using the practice.

223. These are epithets (Tib. *Tönpa* and *Thuppai Wangpo*) for the Buddha Shakyamuni.

224. Tib. *Sangwai Dakpo* ("Lord of Secrets"). A common epithet of Vajrapani, the bodhisattva embodying the principle of the spiritual power of all buddhas; to Vajrapani was assigned the function of codifying the tantras once they were taught by buddhas, in a process similar to that of a scribe and editor. Milarepa's student Rechungpa Dorjé Drakpa (1083-1161) was considered to be an emanation of Vajrapani.

225. These are the scrolls on which many *terma*s are written.

226. Another name for Yön-gé Mingyur Dorjé (ADD). Mingyur Dorjé (b. 1628/41) was a student of Karma Chagmé (1613-1678) and a *tertön* who discovered, among other teachings, the *guru sadhana* of the Second Karmapa, Karma Pakshi.

227. Dorjé Drollö, one of eight major manifestations of Guru Rinpoché, is an extremely wrathful form held to subdue negative forces and protect the *terma* teachings, aiding in their discovery.

228. A prominent mountain and well-known landmark on the route between Dergé and Palpung (ADD).

229. Hor is a region about one hundred kilometers to the east of Dergé.

230. The preliminary practices (Tib. *ngöndro*) are a set of spiritual exercises designed to prepare the student for more advanced Vajrayana practices. The instruction manual used today in the Karma Kagyü tradition was authored by Kongtrul later

in his life, and has been published in an English translation as *The Torch of Certainty*.

231. These *mahasiddha*s, or highly accomplished masters, are the Indian progenitors of some of the most important lineages of teachings associated with the Chakrasamvara tantras. For more details on the life of Krishnapada, also known as Krishnacharya, see Kongtrul's accounts of his past lives in this volume.

232. The Monkey Month is usually considered the seventh in the general Tibetan calendar, but there is an alternate system relating to the *terma* tradition, in which it is the fifth month; this latter case fits the internal chronology of this year in Kongtrul's life most conveniently. The tenth day and tenth month are particularly sacred to "the Guru," that is, Padmakara.

233. Chamara is the legendary subcontinent to the southwest, to which Padmakara went when he left Tibet in order to subdue bloodthirsty demons who were threatening to overrun the human world. Padmakara is held to still be residing in his pure realm above this subcontinent, containing the demons with his spiritual power.

234. A format for group practice that is less elaborate than that of the *drupchen* ritual, usually without closed retreat boundaries or shifts of practitioners reciting mantras day and night.

235. That is, Situ Rinpoché.

236. Hevajra (Tib. *Kyé Dorjé* or *Gyépa Dorjé*) is a deity of the Anuttarayoga class of tantras; this practice and the study of this tantra are widespread in the Sarma Schools of Tibetan Buddhism.

237. A *mahasiddha* of ancient India.

238. That is, Terdak Lingpa Gyurmé Dorjé (1646-1714), who founded Mindroling Monastery in 1670 and was instrumental in collating the original collection of the Nyingma teachings known as *kama*—that is, teachings handed down generation after generation in an extensive historical lineage, as distinct from the *terma*s, which were concealed in the past and continue to be revealed under appropriate circumstances. A *tertön* is someone who is a rebirth of one of Padmakara's students and able, in that lifetime, to reveal *terma* teachings hidden during Padmakara's time in Tibet. See *Hidden Teachings of Tibet*, pp. 71-93 and 157-163, for a discussion of the nature and role of *tertön*s.

239. A thin, gauze-like material stamped with designs, used as covering for scroll paintings to protect them from smoke and other kinds of damage.

240. The first Dabzang Tulku, Karma Ngédön Tenpa Rabgyé (1808-1864 or 1867), was a student of Situ Pema Nyinjé Wangpo and Kongtrul, and a teacher of Khenchen Karma Tashi Özer.

241. In addition to the Three Jewels—Buddha, Dharma, and Sangha—that constitute "sources of refuge," or key spiritual principles, in the general Buddhist context,

555

555555

55

the Vajrayana traditions speak of the Three Roots—Guru, Chosen Deity, and Dakini—as further principles upon which spiritual practice is based. One's personal gurus and those of the historical lineage are the root of blessings; the chosen deities upon which one meditates in Vajrayana practice are the root of one's spiritual attainment; and the *dakinis* and *dharmapalas* are the root of auspicious interdependence and enlightened activity.

242. Chöjé Lingpa Dzamling Dorjé, also known as Orgyen Rokjé Lingpa, was a *tertön* who lived from 1682 to 1725.

243. Skt. *Sukhavati*; Tib. *Dewachen*. The Realm of Bliss, the pure buddha field associated with the buddha Amitabha and the western direction, is the focus for the "Pure Land" schools of Buddhism. This approach gained enormous popularity in Tibet, though it was never regarded as a separate school, being rather an important element in all of the schools.

244. The text has the common abbreviations for the actual mantras of the deities mentioned—*muni* (from *Om muni muni mahamunaye svaha*), *tare* (from *Om tare tuttare true svaha*), *mani* (from *Om mani padme hum*), and *vakyé* (from *Om vageshvaraye svaha*). Shakyamuni is the name of the historical Buddha. The practices of various forms of the feminine deity Tara (Tib. *Drölma*) are enormously popular in the Tibetan tradition. Avalokiteshvara (Tib. *Chenrezi*) and Manjushri (Tib. *Jampal* or *Jamyang*), two of the eight great bodhisattvas of the Mahayana tradition, are archetypes of compassion and wisdom, respectively.

245. These are all lower-lying, forested regions in the southeast of Tibet, near the border with the Indian province of Arunachal Pradesh.

246. Literally, "in the eight directions," that is, the four cardinal and four intermediate directions.

247. A master of the ancient Indian Buddhist tradition, Shantideva was the author of the standard Mahayana source, *Engaging in the Conduct of a Bodhisattva* (Skt. *Bodhicharyavatara*).

248. Tsurphu Monastery (called *Ogmin*, the Tibetan equivalent for the Sanskrit term *Akanishtha*, after the pinnacle pure realm of the buddha Vairochana) was founded in 1187 by the First Karmapa, Düsum Khyenpa; it was the seat of the Karmapas in central Tibet, located in the Tölung Valley west of Lhasa.

249. Kongtrul refers to his guru, Situ Pema Nyinjé Wangpo, as "my lord Pema (Nyinjé)."

250. Yeshé Nyingpo (1631-1694) was the seventh Zhamar incarnation of the Karma Kagyü School; the present incarnation Chökyi Lodrö, born in 1952, is the thirteenth in the line. With their seat of Yangpachen in central Tibet, the Zhamar Rinpochés have played an important role in the transmission of the Kagyü lineage.

251. That is, that he was receiving blessings from the feminine deities that he relied on in meditation (RT).

252. The Sky Teachings are a collection of *terma*s revealed by the seventeenth-century prodigy Namchö Mingyur Dorjé in his early teens, and codified by Karma Chagmé.

253. This refers to the Tibetan custom of wrapping texts, which are stacks of long, narrow, loose pages, in cloth and attaching flaps of cloth to one end of the bundle to identify the contents.

254. Tib. *Sangwa Düpa*. The *Guhyasamaja Tantra*, regarded as being the first tantra taught by the Buddha Shakyamuni (albeit in a sambhogakaya form as the deity Guhyasamaja), is also the earliest Buddhist tantra that Western scholarship has been able to verify. It is part of the class of father tantras of Anuttarayoga (the highest of the four classes of tantra generally recognized by the Sarma Schools), and summarizes all the key points of the Vajrayana path and the fruition to which it leads. For detailed information on *The Guhyasamaja Tantra*, see *Yoga of the Guhyasamajatantra: The Arcane Lore of Forty Verses*.

255. Tib. *Ngapa Rinpoché*. A common epithet of the Fifth Dalai Lama, Ngawang Lobzang Gyatso (1617-1682), who is also referred to as "the Great Fifth." He is remembered for his ecumenical outlook and tolerance of all schools of Buddhism in Tibet.

256. A Kagyü monastery in eastern Tibet, Nedo Sang-ngak Dechenling was the principal seat of the Nyingma *tertön* Namchö Mingyur Dorjé and the Kagyü master Karma Chagmé, and the center of the Sky Teachings lineage. Because of Karma Chagmé's affiliation with the Kagyü School (he studied with the Tenth Karmapa, Chöying Dorjé), a Nedo Kagyü lineage developed as a branch of the Karma Kagyü.

257. Gyalwang ("Lord of Victorious Ones") and Gyalwa ("The Victorious One," which is also an epithet for a buddha) are honorific titles given to the Karmapa incarnations; Kongtrul uses both titles indiscriminately in his account.

258. The Fourteenth Karmapa, Thekchok Dorjé, who lived from 1798 to 1868, was another of Kongtrul's major Kagyü gurus.

259. The Eighth Tai Situ, Chökyi Jungné, also known as Situ Panchen ("Situ the great scholar"). He was born in the same general region as Kongtrul. His principal teachers were the Twelfth Karmapa, Jangchub Dorjé (1703-1732), and the Eighth Zhamar, Palchen Chökyi Döndrup (1695-1732). He became famed for his erudition, and visited Nepal, India, and China as well as traveling throughout the greater Tibetan region. His writings cover the entire range of religious and secular fields of study in the Tibetan tradition. In 1717 Situ Panchen founded Palpung Monastery, which became the seat of the Tai Situ incarnations.

260. That is, the Thirteenth Karmapa (1733-1797).

261. That is, the Fourteenth Karmapa, Thekchok Dorjé.

262. The Dzogchen, or Great Perfection, approach of the Nyingma School of Ti-

betan Buddhism speaks of four visions that define the path of practice known as *tögal*, or "making the final leap." The stage termed "the direct experience of the true nature of reality" (Tib. *chönyi ngönsum*) is the first of these four visions; that of "the enrichment of meditative experience" (Tib. *nyam gongphel*) is the second.

263. The Kagyü monastery of Zurmang Dütsi Thil (the foremost of the three branches referred to) was located at the far western end of the Zalmogang Ridge in eastern Tibet, the same ridge on which Kongtrul's birthplace of Rongyap was located. Zurmang was founded in 1423 by Drung Masé Tokden Lodrö Rinchen (b. 1386), a student of the Fifth Gyalwang Karmapa, Dezhin Shekpa (1384-1415).

264. The First Karmapa of the Kagyü School (1110-1193).

265. Naturally occurring images are images that spontaneously appear on the surfaces of rocks and so forth, as though "growing out" from within the rock in bas-relief. Such manifestations are found throughout the Tibetan and sub-Himalayan regions, and are held to be the product of great spiritual merit on the part of individuals or whole groups of people in those areas.

266. Skt. *Chandoratnakara*. A work on poetics and metrics by the Indian Buddhist author Sarvaja-ratnakara-shanti.

267. According to Alak Zenkar et al., *Bod rgya tshig mdzod chen mo*, p. 2929, the term used here refers to a format often used to adorn the title pages of Tibetan books, involving three lines of identical text in different scripts—*lancha, vartu,* and Tibetan "headed" script.

268. Ga is a region to the northwest of Dergé, beyond Lingtsang.

269. A ceremony associated with the incarnation lineage of the Karmapas, in which the Karmapa sits before an audience and dons a crown, the sight of which confers an enormous blessing.

270. Zurmang Dütsi Thil was the principal seat of the Zurmang subschool of the Karma Kagyü. The Trungpa incarnations were the main tulku lineage associated with the Zurmang complex. The incarnation referred to here would have been the ninth Trungpa incarnation, Karma Tenphel. An informative account of this school is found in *Born in Tibet*, the autobiography of the eleventh incarnation, Chögyam Trungpa Rinpoché.

271. These are pills unique to the Karmapas, who oversee their preparation and give them to students as blessings.

272. Someone in charge of the stores of medicines kept in a monastery's pharmacy, to be dispensed to anyone in need, whether lay or monastic. Since the time of the First Tai Situ, Chökyi Gyaltsen (1377-1448), who was a great physician, Palpung Monastery had always maintained an extensive inventory of medicines (RT).

273. Tib. *Mengyila*; the Buddha of Healing, or "Medicine Buddha."

274. Possibly this title refers to the incarnation of a relative of a former Karmapa

(RT). This may be a reference to the Jé-ön Chöwang Tulku referred to later in Kongtrul's autobiography, although the "mo" suffix, which is technically feminine, might indicate a woman.

275. That is, Karmapa and Situ Rinpoché.

276. This refers to a ceremony in which a master is offered these symbols as a gesture to help ensure longevity and success.

277. Tib. *rigpa tsépep*. The third of the four visions of the *tögal* path of Dzogchen practice.

278. This is probably a form of the goddess Tara that is associated with practices that enhance one's spiritual and material success.

279. This would seem to be the same Yungdrung Phuntsok who had prophesied Kongtrul's spiritual potential.

280. These are a group of worldly guardian spirits.

281. These are references to different kinds of *dakini*s, of which the Achi sisters are specific manifestations.

282. Ga is a region more than two hundred kilometers to the northwest of Dergé.

283. The first month of the Tibetan lunar calendar.

284. This ordination ceremony is the Mahayana equivalent of the monastic and lay ordinations on the level of the *Pratimoksha*, or Individual Liberation, discipline.

285. *Jangchub Sempa* is the Tibetan equivalent for the Sanskrit term *Bodhisattva*; *Lodrö Thayé* in Tibetan means "Boundless Intellect."

286. Such images are also found among the ashes of the cremated remains of advanced practitioners.

287. The relics that form during the cremation of a spiritually advanced person may be of two kinds. The more common form, called *ringsel* in Tibetan, are tiny, very hard, white bead-like formations; the more rare form (called *sharira* or *chitta sharira* in Sanskrit and *dung* in Tibetan) are larger and of five colors.

288. Each "set" of the ritual covers two days; there is a partial fast the first day, with no solid food taken after midday, and a total fast (including water) the second day.

289. One of eight great bodhisattva archetypes in the Mahayana tradition, Nivaranaviskambhin embodies the principle of spiritual purification.

290. It was Chökyong Zangpo (1441-1527) who produced the first complete bilingual translations of the Sanskrit lexicon *The Treasury of Immortality* (Skt. *Amarakosha*) by the sixth-century Buddhist author Amarasimha and its commentary, the *Amarakosha-tika-kamadhenu* by Subhutichandra.

291. Rigdzin Jatsön Nyingpo (1585-1656) was a *tertön* who discovered the cycle The Union of All Rare and Precious Jewels, which was one of Kongtrul's principal spiritual practices.

292. Padmakara is the most common alternative name for Guru Rinpoché.

293. Tib. *Seng-gé Dongma*; an extremely wrathful *dakini* depicted with the head of a lioness.

294. The "old" (Tib. *Nyingma*) school was founded by Padmakara, the Indian abbot and scholar Shantirakshita, and the Tibetan king Trisong Detsen in the eighth century. The "new" (Tib. *Sarma*) schools are those that developed following the new wave of translations from India, from the eleventh century onward—including the Sakya, Kagyü, and Kadampa (later, Gelukpa) Schools.

295. One of the two major stages of Vajrayana meditation, involving emphasis on the visualization of the forms of deities and the repetition of mantras. The second stage, that of completion, involves a structured phase of advanced yogic exercises and an unstructured phase of formless meditation.

296. Marpa Lotsawa Chökyi Lodrö (1012-1097) was the Tibetan master who made several journeys to India, where he studied with Naropa and other great gurus. He founded the Kagyü School, that was later organized into a monastic framework by Gampopa, who was the student of Marpa's principal student, Milarepa.

297. Nesar Tashi Chöphel became one of Kongtrul's close students, who edited the collection of Kongtrul's writings and authored the account of Kongtrul's final years and the funeral ceremonies that is included in this volume.

298. Dharmakara is the Sanskritized form of Chökyi Jungné, the name of the Eighth Situ; his *Great Commentary on the Chandra System* (Tib. *Tsandrapai Tikchen*) is the standard work on the subject in the Kagyü School.

299. Sazang Mati Panchen Lodrö Gyaltsen (1294-1376), a master of the Sakya and Jonang Schools, wrote a major commentary on the source text of the Kalapa system of Sanskrit grammar.

300. The "Ön" prefix denotes that Chimé Tulku was related (possibly in a previous lifetime) to Tai Situ Rinpoché or some other important lama (RT).

301. The title is an abbreviation and could apply to any of several works with similar titles (RT).

302. These are *The Treatise Distinguishing Ordinary Consciousness from Timeless Awareness*, and *The Treatise on Buddha Nature*; these two texts, and *The Profound Inner Meaning*, were authored by the Third Karmapa, Rangjung Dorjé, and have become standard texts for study in the Kagyü Schools.

303. Nyarong is a region to the east, between Dergé and Hor.

304. That is, Karma Ngédön Tenpa Rabgyé (1808-1864), also known as Mendong Tsampa Rinpoché ("Precious Retreatant of Mendong," a monastic hermitage he founded in 1867). Among his works are well-respected commentaries on some of the more popular prayers used in the Kagyü School, as well as a series of brief biographies of the Karmapas. It was Lama Karma Ngédön who initially requested that Kongtrul write a short verse summary of the three levels of discipline—Hinayana, Mahayana, and Vajrayana—on which he, Ngédön, would compose a

commentary. Kongtrul later wrote the source verses for what would become his *Treasury of the Knowable*, and also wrote the commentary himself when Lama Ngédön was too ill to fulfill his commitment. Ngédön did, however, compose a brief survey of the three levels of ordination.

305. Lithang is an area some two hundred and fifty kilometers to the southeast of Dergé.

306. Prophecies contained in a *terma* cycle indicate not only who the *tertön* will be (that is, who will reveal the *terma*), but who will act as "custodian" (Tib. *chödak*) of the teachings, entrusted with their codification and propagation.

307. The literal Tibetan idiom is "rock never hit bone."

308. "Sok" does not here refer to Mongolia (which is "Sokyul" in Tibetan), but to an area in north central Tibet on the trade route between the eastern provinces and Lhasa (RT). Zamkha could mean "near the bridge," possibly a reference to a place near a river crossing in this area.

309. The name of Guru Rinpoché's palace (Tib. *Pema Ö*) in his pure realm of the Copper-Colored Mountain (Tib. *Zangdok Palri*).

310. The literal idiom refers to the point in a *tertön*'s life at which the record of the *terma*s he or she is to reveal in that lifetime is conferred in a vision of Guru Rinpoché.

311. A important feminine guardian figure, Tseringma was a local spirit in the region of Mount Everest who was bound by an oath to uphold the Buddhist teachings.

312. A crown with five petal-like plaques, on which are depictions of the buddhas of the five families of the mandala; one of the sambhogakaya ornaments, echoing the adornments of the sambhogakaya deities, worn by participants in such Vajrayana ceremonies as fire rituals.

313. Also known as Nagamati, Nagabodhi was a student of the Indian Buddhist master Nagarjuna and received the transmission of that master's Vajrayana lineage. Nagabodhi was a *siddha* renowned for his realization of Mahamudra.

314. The bone ornaments are part of the ritual garb worn during certain Vajrayana rituals.

315. A concise ritual of empowerment, also termed "conferral of life force."

316. Tib. *Shinjé Shé*. The wrathful form of Manjushri, the bodhisattva of wisdom, and one of the deities in the Eight Commands cycle.

317. Karma Norbu was a lama of Ringu Monastery in Lingtsang, who transmitted the Shangpa Kagyü teachings to Kongtrul (RT). Mokchokpa Rinchen Tsöndrü was the principal student of Khyungpo Naljor and his successor as holder of the Shangpa Kagyü lineage; see *Like An Illusion: Lives of the Shangpa Kagyu Masters*, pp. 93-108. The Six Yogas of Niguma, transmitted within the Shangpa Kagyü School, are a parallel system of practices to the Six Yogas of Naropa of

the Karma Kagyü; the practices in the two systems are identical in name and function, although the details of visualization differ. Niguma, from whom the Shangpa practices derive, was an Indian woman master who was one of Khyungpo Naljor's principal gurus.

318. One of the Eighty-Four *Mahasiddhas* of India, the master Luhipa transmitted an important lineage of teachings focusing on *The Chakrasamvara Tantra*.

319. A form of Tara included in the Anuttarayoga class.

320. The official in a monastery responsible for enforcing the regulations governing the lives of the monks, and for administering punishment for infractions.

321. A familiar way of referring to Situ Pema Nyinjé Wangpo.

322. These small cards (Tib. *tsakli*) depict deities, ritual implements, animals, and other symbols (such as the parasol mentioned, one of a group of eight auspicious symbols), and are used during empowerments to focus the student's attention as an aid to the transmission process.

323. A custom of offering one hundred of each of a set of traditional offerings, including lamps, bowls of water, food, incense, and so forth.

324. A Tibetan translator and master of the late eighth and early ninth centuries; see Kongtrul's accounts of his past lives.

325. Kongtrul included these translations of the works of Tilopa, Naropa, and other Indian masters in the Kagyü section of his *Treasury of Spiritual Advice*.

326. Such *termas* (termed *gongter* in Tibetan) were originally concealed by being "sealed" by Guru Rinpoché within the mental continuum of one of his intimate students. At some point in the future, when circumstances were appropriate, the *tertön* (who was the rebirth of the original student) would experience the "unsealing" of the memory and the *terma* could be revealed. While there is a striking similarity to the means of transmission called *dak-nang* (pure visionary experience), the two processes are considered to be distinct.

327. Tib. *Néten Chudruk*. These constitute a group of *arhats* to whom the Buddha Shakyamuni entrusted his teachings, and who spread those teachings in various regions around India and in other realms. See *The Nyingma School of Tibetan Buddhism*, vol. 2, p. 173.

328. Tib. *Yenlakjung*. One of the Sixteen Elders, Angiraja spread and maintained the Buddha's teachings in the region of Mount Kailash.

329. Lhatsün Namkha Jigmé (1597-1650) was a *tertön* who is credited with being primarily responsible for establishing the Vajrayana Buddhist tradition in Sikkim, on the Indo-Tibetan border.

330. A powerful local spirit of Tibet.

331. The translator Thrükhang Lotsawa Sönam Gyatso (1424-1482) was a Kagyü master who also wrote several synopses of major Mahayana scriptures.

332. In 1840, Kongtrul first met Jamyang Khyentsé Wangpo (1820-1892), who was

to become perhaps the single most important guru in his life. Although nominally a master of the Sakya School, Jamyang Khyentsé Wangpo was, like Kongtrul, one of the truly nonsectarian masters, who received and passed on transmissions from all of the viable lineages of his day. He and the Nyingma *tertön* Chokgyur Lingpa (1829-1870) were Kongtrul's principal colleagues in spearheading the *ri-mé*, or nonsectarian, movement in eastern Tibet in the eighteenth century. Later in his account, Kongtrul often refers to Jamyang Khyentsé Wangpo as simply "my lord guru," "my precious lord guru," or "my all-seeing precious master."

333. Tib. *Tsuktor Dukarmo*. A peaceful feminine protective deity.

334. An elaborate format for group retreat, involving closed retreat boundaries, lengthy rituals, and shifts of practitioners maintaining a continuous mantra repetition day and night. This format is given particular emphasis in the Nyingma School, dating from the time that Guru Rinpoché introduced it to his Tibetan students.

335. A ritual to restore and renew one's *samaya* commitments as a Vajrayana practitioner.

336. Rigdzin Gödem was a *tertön* who lived from 1337 to 1409; his *terma*s form the core of the Northern Treasure cycle.

337. Namchö Mingyur Dorjé (1645-1667) was the *tertön* who discovered the Sky Teachings (Tib. *Namchö*) cycle.

338. This is the twenty-second day of the ninth lunar month, commemorating the return of the Buddha to the human realm after leaving to teach the rebirth of his mother in a realm of the gods.

339. The first Buddhist monastic institution in Tibet, built in the eighth century through the combined efforts of Padmakara, Shantirakshita, and the Tibetan king Trisong Detsen.

340. An Indian master invited by King Trisong Detsen to oversee construction of the first Buddhist monastery in Tibet at Samyé. When Shantirakshita could not overcome the obstacles posed by the demons of Tibet, he urged the king to invite Guru Rinpoché, who was then able to establish the Buddhist teachings in the Land of Snows.

341. Trisong Detsen was primarily responsible for bringing the Buddhist teachings to Tibet by inviting the Indian abbot Shantirakshita and the master Padmakara to his country in the eighth century.

342. Tib. *Thröma Nakmo*. Krodhi is a wrathful feminine deity whose practice is associated with that of Severance (Chö).

343. The Indian master who was instrumental in bringing Buddhism to Tibet in the eighth century. For information on Guru Rinpoché and his role in the Tibetan traditions of Buddhism, see *Guru Rinpoché: His Life and Times*.

344. The Jadra family was one of the wealthy clans, which also included the Lukdra and Nedra, from whose ranks the ministers of Dergé were selected (RT).

345. In Tibetan lore, a kind of demon that is male and often appears in the form of a Buddhist monk; *gyalpo* literally means "king" or "ruler."

346. A ritual format that is designed to carry out a specific ceremonial function, or to invoke the energy of a deity in order to accomplish some kind of beneficial activity or purpose.

347. Skt. *Pratimoksha-sutra.* The basic Buddhist source on the monastic code.

348. Taksham Nüden Dorjé was a *tertön* born in 1655.

349. An elaborate group ritual format, often performed in conjunction with a *drupchen* ritual, for the preparation and consecration of pills compounded of medicinal and sacred substances. The resulting "medicine" imparts a spiritual blessing to those who partake of it.

350. A *mala* is a string of beads (technically meant to number one hundred and eight) on which prayers or mantras are counted, similar to the function of a Catholic rosary.

351. Another name of Padmakara, or Guru Rinpoché.

352. The Ninth Karmapa (1556-1603) authored important commentaries on the Mahamudra teachings of the Kagyü School.

353. Phadampa Sang-gyé was a twelfth-century Indian master who visited Tibet and who codified the teachings of the Zhijé School, one of the Eight Lineages of Accomplishment in Tibet.

354. Jambhala (Tib. *Dzambhala*) and Vasudhara (Tib. *Nordzinma*) are masculine and feminine deities of wealth, respectively.

355. All of these figures are either protective deities or guardians (that is, worldly spirits bound by oaths to protect the Buddhist teachings.

356. These are amulets that are prepared and consecrated through rituals, to be then worn by living persons or affixed to corpses to transmit blessings. A section of Kongtrul's *Treasury of Precious Hidden Teachings* is devoted to such techniques.

357. The idiom is an expression in the dialect of Kongtrul's region that refers to the custom of using a deceased person's personal possessions to sponsor rituals and other religious works (ADD).

358. Given Khangsar Tsephel's age, this would most likely have been the Eighth Drukchen, Kunzik Chökyi Nangwa (1768-1822).

359. This is an idiom for spiritual practice as a process of augmenting positive qualities and insights in oneself.

360. The four forms would have corresponded to the four kinds of enlightened activity—pacifying, enriching, magnetizing, and wrathful—but Kongtrul's vision was incomplete.

361. That is, the twelfth-century Kashmiri master Khaché Panchen Shakyashribhadra.

362. Kashyapa, one of the Buddha Shakyamuni's ten closest students on the *shravaka* level, was renowned for the qualities he derived from his spiritual training; he

codified the *Abhidharma* teachings after the Buddha's passing, and served as the first of the Buddha's seven successors.

363. Shariputra and Maudgalyayana, two of the Buddha Shakyamuni's closest students, renowned as exemplars of the *arhat* model of Hinayana practice.

364. A short Mahayana sutra describing the qualities of the Buddha, Dharma, and Sangha.

365. This family was famous in eastern Tibet for the spiritual masters who were among its members. These included the late Dilgo Khyentsé Rinpoché (1910-1991). For information on the Alo Dilgo family, see *Journey to Enlightenment: The Life and World of Khyentse Rinpoché, Spiritual Teacher from Tibet*, pp. 12-13.

366. Tib. *Lhachen*. A deity associated with the acquisition of wealth and power, held to be a form of the Hindu god Shiva adopted by Buddhist practitioners.

367. Tib. *kagö*; a ritual used to suppress the effects of negative forces or influences.

368. Chöying Dorjé lived from 1604 to 1674.

369. This skin, worn over the left shoulder, is an emblem associated with Avalokiteshvara, the bodhisattva of compassion. The Karmapas are considered to be human emanations of Avalokiteshvara. According to Indian Buddhist lore, the black antelope is a creature of great compassion that avoids harming any insect life when it browses.

370. The Fifth Gyaltsap of the Kagyü School (1617/8-1658).

371. The Sixth Zhamar (1584-1630).

372. Such rituals are often performed to offset the effects of illness or life-threatening circumstances.

373. One of the Prajnaparamita Sutras of the Mahayana approach.

374. Situ Ön Wang-gi Dorjé was a younger brother of the Eighth Situ, Chökyi Jungné (1700-1774) and a teacher of the Ninth Situ, Kongtrul's guru Pema Nyinjé Wangpo (1774-1853).

375. This became the site on which Kongtrul founded his personal retreat center, which he refers to as his "hermitage" (Tib. *yangthrö*), as distinct from the meditation center (Tib. *drupdra*) located at a lower elevation and closer to the main monastery of Palpung.

376. That is, he would become overly busy bestowing empowerments.

377. This defines an area of hundreds of square miles to the north and east of Dergé.

378. The Three Roots of Vajrayana Buddhism are referred to in these lines. The gurus (exemplified by "Guru Padmakara" in the first line) are the root of blessing. The chosen deities, Tara among them, are the root of spiritual attainment. *Dakini* is a term for feminine deities that are embodiments or expressions of enlightened being, and *dharmapala*s are protective deities; together they constitute the third of the Three Roots, that of the enlightened activity that removes obstacles on the spiritual path.

379. That is, nonexistent; a common expression.
380. The ten nonvirtuous actions comprise three physical actions (killing, stealing, and sexual misconduct), four verbal actions (lying, abusive language, calumny, and idle gossip), and three mental attitudes (covetousness, ill-will, and wrong views about the nature of reality). They are nonvirtuous in that they create and reinforce negative karmic patterns that cause harm to both those who engage in them and those who are the objects of the actions.
381. That is, holding sectarian attitudes.
382. The expression is often used pejoratively, to indicate rituals performed by those who make a profession of selling their services.
383. The "Middle Way" school of Buddhist philosophy, regarded by all Tibetan schools as the pinnacle view of the sutra approach.
384. Mara is the Buddhist personification of all the evil and negative forces binding one's mind to the cycle of ordinary existence. When the Buddha was about to attain enlightenment under the bodhi tree, Mara sent his armies and beautiful daughters to try unsuccessfully to distract the future Buddha from his quest.
385. Literally, "All-Noble and Supremely Blissful Center of Utter Lucidity."
386. Tea leaves were moistened and pressed into bricks, lumps of which could be broken off as needed.
387. That is, Rigdzin Jatsön Nyingpo, the *tertön* who discovered The Union of All Rare and Precious Jewels.
388. Rigdzin Tsewang Norbu (1698-1755) of Kathok Monastery, an incarnation of Guru Rinpoché's student Nupchen Namkhai Nyingpo, was a teacher of the Eighth Situ, Situ Panchen Chökyi Jungné.
389. A technique that is part of the system of practice known in Tibetan as *lojong* ("mental training"), *tonglen* ("sending and taking") meditation involves reversing one's usual egocentric attitude by mentally "sending" one's happiness and positive karma to others while "taking on" their suffering and negative karma.
390. These are the six transcendent principles of the Mahayana path of Buddhism— generosity, discipline, patience, diligence, meditative stability, and wisdom.
391. That is, passed away.
392. These are popular names for the mantras *Om mani padme hum* and *Om ah hum vajra guru padma siddhi hum*, the mantras of Avalokiteshvara and Guru Rinpoché, respectively.
393. Tib. *Dorjé Zhönnu*; another name for the deity Vajrakila.
394. The basic mantra of Vajrakila is *Om vajra kila kilaya sarva vighnan bam hum phat*; the ending *samaya veshayastvam* signifies one successfully upholding one's *samaya*, or formal commitments in tantric practice.
395. Tib. *Jetsünma*; an epithet of the deity Tara.

396. In reciting a requisite number of mantras to complete the formal requirements of a Vajrayana practice, one usually recites an additional number—the "supplementary mantras"—to compensate for having recited some of the original set of mantras inattentively or incorrectly at times.

397. The Tibetan king Songtsen Gampo was born in 569 and reigned from 581 until his death in 650.

398. The name of a temple dedicated to the goddess Tara, located between Lingtsang and Dergé. The main statue of Tara, which is held to have spoken on occasion, was commissioned by the Chinese princess Kongjo, one of the wives of the sixth-century Tibetan king Songtsen Gampo. The temple is said to have been built under the direction of Smritijnana, an Indian master who came to Tibet in the eleventh century. (ADD).

399. For Tibetans these female "escorts" imply impending death. The death of a spiritual master or advanced practitioner is described as a process of his or her consciousness being led by an escort of *daka*s and *dakini*s from this world to a pure realm of enlightened being. Ceremonies to "turn back the escort" are performed to promote longevity. As Kongtrul notes here, another kind of ceremony that can be performed is one designed to "cheat death" by averting the circumstances that would otherwise prove fatal to the individual.

400. The amount a pack animal can carry on its back.

401. *Om mani padme hum*, the mantra of Avalokiteshvara.

402. The Shanga Kagyü is not a branch of the Marpa Kagyü, although many of its teachings are transmitted within the latter system. The Shangpa Kagyü is an independent school founded in the eleventh century by Khyungpo Naljor ("Lama Shang").

403. These are actually ceremonies similar to empowerments, but more concise in format.

404. The protective deity of the Shangpa Kagyü School is the Six-Armed Mahakala. Kongtrul adopted this form as his personal protective deity.

405. That is, Taranatha.

406. Karma Ösel Gyurmé was a Karma Kagyü master whose teacher, Chabtsa Tulku Karma Ratna, studied with Belo Tsewang Kunkhyab of Zurmang Monastery.

407. One of the Anuttarayoga tantras, *The Kalachakra Tantra*, is generally classed as the highest, or "nondual," tantra. It presents an overview of the ground, path, and fruition of the spiritual process, discussing these points with respect to the universe as macrocosm, the human individual as microcosm, and the meditation on the deity Kalachakra based on this tantra. *The Kalachakra Tantra* is also the source of an elaborate system of astrology that became the basis of the Tibetan calendar after the introduction of the tantra to Tibet in 1026/7. See *The Kalacakra*

Tantra: Rite of Initiation and *The Wheel of Time Sand Mandala: Visual Scripture of Tibetan Buddhism.*

408. The four *maras* (Skt.) are personifications of forces and circumstances that bind one to ordinary states of cyclic existence. They are: the *mara* of one's mind-body aggregates, the *mara* of "the Lord of Death" (that is, one's mortality), the *mara* of one's negative emotions, and the *mara* of "the child of the gods" (that is, the subtle distraction of meditative bliss that blocks the mind from gaining more profound levels of realization).

409. Jampa Bumpa was a master of the Nyingma *kama* teachings who lived from the late twelfth to the early thirteenth centuries. He was a guru of the Second Karmapa, Karma Pakshi (1204-1283). Getsé Mahapandita Gyurmé Tsewang Chokdrup (1761-1829) and the subsequent line of his incarnations (the Getrul *tulkus*) associated with Kathok Monastery are incarnations of Kathok Jampa Bumpa.

410. Located almost one hundred kilometers southeast of Dergé, Kathok Dorjé Den was founded in 1159 by Kathok Dampa Deshek (1122-1192) and became one of the major Nyingma monasteries in eastern Tibet.

411. The Seventh Karmapa lived from 1454 to 1506.

412. Another name for the Fourth Zhamar, Chödrak Yeshé (1453-1524), who was a student of the Seventh Karmapa.

413. The *mudra*, or gesture, of resting the hands palms up in the lap, with the right hand lying in the left.

414. The personal name of the Eighth Situ Chökyi Jungné ("Situ Panchen") (1700-1774). In Kongtrul's dream, the Karmapa was thus flanked by the two next highest incarnations of the Kagyu School—the Zhamar (represented by the fourth incarnation) and the Situ (represented by the eighth).

415. Vasumaitra was a master of the Sarvastivadin School of early Indian Buddhism.

416. The translator Ra Lotsawa Dorjé Drak lived from 1016 to 1198.

417. A common format including the "branches" of homage, offerings, confession, rejoicing in the virtue of others, requesting that the Buddhist teachings be transmitted, entreating enlightened beings not to pass from this world, and dedicating the virtue of one's own spiritual practice to the enlightenment of all beings. This format is considered to lie at the very core of the twofold process of spiritual development—the removal of negative factors in one's makeup and the augmentation of positive ones.

418. The Eleventh Karmapa (1676-1702).

419. The Fourth Situ Rinpoché (1542-1585).

420. Sang-gyé Nyenpa Tashi Paljor (1445-1510) was a student of the Seventh Karmapa, Chödrak Gyatso (1454-1506), and a teacher of the Eighth Karmapa, Mikyö Dorjé (1507-1554); as such, he was a vital link in the mainstream transmission of the Mahamudra teachings of the Kagyü School.

421. The Fourth Gyaltsap (1550-1617).

422. The Tenth Karmapa (1604-1674).

423. The Tibetan term *thamal gyi shépa* is used in the Mahamudra tradition to refer to the nature of mind as a state of utter simplicity, beyond any and all conceptual elaborations, and hence "ordinary."

424. A *torma* made for a ritual to invoke wrathful energy to eliminate obstacles to, for example, the spread of the teachings. It would be hurled in a certain direction at the conclusion of the ritual, as a symbolic weapon driving away negativity.

425. These are activities to pacify negative circumstances; to enrich positive qualities; to gain power over one's perceptions and so influence others and the phenomenal world in a positive way; and to intervene directly to remove negativity.

426. The largest of the Eight Commands cycles, The Gathering of Sugatas (Tib. *Deshek Düpa*) was discovered by Nyangral Nyima Özer (1124-1192).

427. A form of the bodhisattva of compassion ("The One Who Enjoys Space").

428. The teachings of the basic Buddhist approach speak of four levels of attainment by such spiritually advanced beings, or *aryas*—one who has "entered the stream," one who will "return once," one who will "return no more," and an *arhat*. A "stream enterer" is one who has removed the factors that are to be removed on the path of seeing (the third of the five paths of the *shravaka* path), but who has not removed the factors that are to be removed on the path of meditation (the fourth path). A "once-returner" is one who has removed the first six of the nine factors that pertain to the realm of desire and are to be removed on the path of meditation, and so will only be reborn in the realm of desire once more. A "nonreturner" is one who has removed all nine factors that pertain to the realm of desire and are to be removed on the path of meditation, and so will no longer be reborn in the realm of desire. An *arhat* is one who has removed all factors that pertain to the three realms of samsara and are to be removed on the path of meditation, and so has conquered the four *maras*.

429. Maudgalyayana and Shariputra were two of the Buddha Shakyamuni's ten closest students on the *shravaka* level; the former was noted for his spiritual powers, the latter for his wisdom.

430. Zangdok Palri ("Copper-Colored Mountain of Glory") is the Tibetan term for the pure realm of Guru Rinpoché, to which he departed on leaving Tibet. It is associated with the southwest direction.

431. An Indian master of the early Dzogchen lineage, Vimalamitra was contemporary with Guru Rinpoché and also taught in Tibet.

432. This refers to a process of meditating on rays of light shining from various chakras, or centers, on a master's or deity's form—forehead, throat, heart, and navel—and being absorbed into the corresponding places in one's own body.

433. An eleventh-century ruler in Western Tibet named Yeshé Ö began prepara-

tions to invite the Indian Buddhist master Atisha to Tibet, in order to reform what the ruler felt were corruptions of the teachings. He was assassinated before he could accomplish his mission, but his nephew and successor Jangchub Ö did invite the master. Both rulers were ordained Buddhist monks as well as secular rulers.

434. Abhirati (Tib. *Ngön-ga*, "Manifest Joy") is the pure realm associated with the eastern direction and the buddha Akshobhya.

435. The Sanskrit term *dharani* refers to long mantra formulas that primarily emphasize the principles of enlightened form and speech as they apply to a given deity, as distinct from the shorter "heart essence" mantras (Skt. *hridaya*; Tib. *nyingpo*), which emphasize the principle of enlightened mind.

436. *Punye* is a form of the Sanskrit term *punya*, or "merit."

437. Another name for the early Kagyü master Gampopa Sönam Rinchen (1079-1159).

438. The early Kagyü master Gampopa Sönam Rinchen (1079-1159), the main student of Milarepa, was the founder of the Kagyü School as a monastic tradition. For an account of his life, see *The Life of Gampopa, The Incomparable Dharma Lord of Tibet.*

439. Living at high altitudes in a relatively microbe-free environment, Tibetans were especially susceptible to infectious diseases.

440. That is, the bodhisattvas Avalokiteshvara and Vajrapani.

441. Dromtön Gyalwai Jungné (1004/1005-1064) was Atisha's first Tibetan student and the first master of the Kadampa School of Tibetan Buddhism.

442. In this context, chakras are depictions, printed on paper, of concentric circular patterns filled with mantras and seed syllables, representing the mandala of a deity in the form of letters and thus embodying the principle of enlightened speech. There are rituals to consecrate these chakras, which are finally folded and tied up with colored thread, to be placed on shrines or worn by practitioners as a kind of amulet.

443. A concise form of empowerment ritual, often used in the case of minor protective deities or guardian figures.

444. In areas where nomad tribes lived, permanent villages were rare; most people lived in tent communities, which could be moved seasonally to graze the herds they kept.

445. A local spirit of the region.

446. A plateau region about two hundred kilometers northeast of Dergé.

447. Tib. *Sangwa Düpa Jampai Dorjé*. One of the main forms of the deity Guhyasamaja.

448. Although terms such as "king" (or "ruler"), "kingdom," and "royal capital" are used in reference to many regions of eastern Tibet, the terms are slightly hyperbolic honorifics. These regions were not, in fact, independent states, but were to

some degree subservient to the government of Dergé, and even to that of the central Tibetan authorities. (RT).

449. This self-styled "ruler" is not to be confused with the Sokmo clan, from whose ranks the ministers to the kings of Dergé were selected. The clan would never use the title "ruler," but would reserve this for their ruler in Dergé (ADD).

450. To show greater respect, those inviting honored guests would often send out two parties to meet and escort the guests back. One party would travel farther out, the other would wait a shorter distance from the hosting monastery or residence.

451. The eight great bodhisattvas are Mahayana archetypes who embody specific spiritual qualities, such as wisdom, compassion, benevolent power, and so forth. They are: Manjushri, Avalokiteshvara, Vajrapani, Kshitigarbha, Nivaranaviskambhin, Akashagarbha, Maitreya, and Samantabhadra (not the same as the primordial buddha).

452. The Twelfth Karmapa (1703-1732).

453. The term refers to any kind of negative energy or influence that may or may not be consciously directed toward one.

454. That is, another lama (RT).

455. Akashagarbha is another of the eight great bodhisattvas of the Mahayana tradition, who are archetypal embodiments of specific qualities.

456. Tib. *Sayi Nyingpo*. One of the eight great bodhisattva archetypes of the Mahayana tradition.

457. That is, the previously mentioned Chöjé Tendzin Döndrup.

458. It would seem that the Shubha Chöjé was allied with Palpung Monastery, and that Kongtrul had been sent to mediate an agreement, hopefully in the Shubha Chöjé's (and thus Palpung's) favor (RT).

459. Likely a local spirit.

460. As Kongtrul mentions earlier in his account, this Kuntrul incarnation had been hastily installed during a dispute between Palpung and the House of Khamba, an event that led to the problems currently affecting Kongtrul and Palpung.

461. The Six Branches of Union (Tib. *Jorwa Yenlak Drukpa*) are advanced yogic practices associated with the practice of Kalachakra, comparable to the Six Yogas of Naropa.

462. Tib. *Dorjé Jikjé*. A form of Yamantaka, the wrathful aspect of the bodhisattva of wisdom Manjushri; one of the principal deities of the father tantra section of the Anuttarayoga class.

463. That is, the estate of Dzamthang Monastery.

464. Tib. *Dorjé Gurgyi Gönpo*. The principal protector of the Hevajra teachings and, by extension, the Sakya School that transmits these teachings.

465. One of the main *mahakalis*, or feminine protective deities.

466. A ritual used to combat or defeat the efforts of an enemy to harm one (RT).

467. *The Prayer of the Four Sessions* is a *guruyoga* focusing on the Eighth Karmapa, Mikyö Dorjé; it was authored by Mikyö Dorjé himself, and is a standard practice among followers of the Kagyü School. The gift of the body is an auxiliary practice used in the system of Chö, or Severance; through a process of meditation and visualization, the practitioner transforms his or her physical body into offerings that are given to various guests.

468. The Eighth Karmapa, Mikyö Dorjé (1507-1554), was the author of *The Four Session Guruyoga* (Tib. *Thunzhi'i Lamai Naljor*), a standard practice of the Karma Kagyü School.

469. Two districts in the province of Golok (RT).

470. Particularly in eastern Tibet, justice was traditionally administered through such *ad hoc* gatherings. If someone had a grievance against someone else, they would agree on a judge or judges and arrange a meeting to take place on neutral ground. The judges were often lamas or chieftains, and their decision was binding on both parties. Someone thus selected to serve as a judge needed no formal or legal authority beyond the acceptance of the two parties in question, and might only serve in this capacity on a single occasion. Sometimes, though, an individual might gain renown for making fair decisions and be called upon frequently. The previous Zhechen Rabjam incarnation (1910-1959) was often consulted in this capacity (RT).

471. An important Kagyü monastery in Lingtsang, Tsaptsa was in fact larger than Palpung and housed about one thousand monks (RT).

472. Guru Chöwang (or Chökyi Wangchuk) was a *tertön* who lived from 1212 to 1270.

473. A monastery of the Gelukpa School located to the southeast of Dergé (RT).

474. The Chagdud *tulku*s were an ancient line of important Nyingma incarnations based in the Nyarong region of eastern Tibet. According to the late sixteenth incarnation, Chagdud Rinpoché Pema Gargyi Wangchuk (1930-2002), the Chagdud incarnation was arrested by forces sent by the central government in Lhasa, who bound him and threw him alive from a cliff.

475. This college was probably sponsored by the Khangsar clan that rendered service to Palpung Monastery and the Situ Rinpochés for many years.

476. The Ngok tradition is based on the teachings of Ngoktön Chöku Dorjé, one of the four main students of Marpa the Translator.

477. An area near Dzongsar Monastery in the Dergé region (RT).

478. According to Tibetan astrology, a "crucial" year, during which momentous events can take place for better or worse, occurs whenever the animal of one's birth year in the twelve-year cycle recurs. For women, it is the second time this recurs that is most significant; for men, the third time. Because Tibetans include the period of gestation in calculating age, this would be a woman's twenty-fifth year and a man's thirty-seventh by Western reckoning.

479. Chokgyur Lingpa (also known as Orgyen Chokgyur Dechen Lingpa) was a *tertön* who lived from 1829 to 1870 and was one of Kongtrul's most influential allies in establishing the *ri-mé*, or nonsectarian, movement. For a short account of this master, see *The Life and Teaching of Chokgyur Lingpa*. Previously Kongtrul referred to him as Kyater or Kyasu Lama. This change in title may reflect the fact that the *tertön* had gained credibility; the problem of false *tertön*s was an ongoing issue, and often a trial period was used to determine the validity of the *terma*s a given person discovered, before other masters would authenticate the discoverer as a genuine *tertön*.

480. Part of the ritual to consecrate statues and stupas involves filling the inner cavity with these small mantra scrolls. Until the consecration process has been completed, the statue or stupa is not considered to serve as an authentic representation of enlightened being.

481. Probably the Zhechen Rabjam incarnation (RT).

482. This does not refer to one hundred different empowerments, but to a hundred repetitions of a concise version of the empowerment ritual in question, done to reinforce the effect.

483. The Gyatrul incarnation Pema Do-ngak Tendzin Ngésang Chökyi Nangwa (1830-1892) was the second throne holder of the Nyingma monastery of Darthang in Golok Province, and became the seventh throne holder of Palyul Monastery.

484. These are forms of the Six-Armed Mahakala, the protective deity of the Shangpa Kagyü school, also known as the Swift-Acting Jnana Natha (Tib. *Nyurdzé Yeshé kyi Gönpo*).

485. Tsewang Dorjé Rigdzin, the forty-third generation of the kings of Dergé, had three sons—Damtsig Dorjé Tsering Namgyal (b. 1811), Tsewang Phuntsok Tenkyong (b. 1822), and Tsewang Dorjé Dradul (b. 1823). Kongtrul here is referring to either the middle or youngest son, or possibly both.

486. This would have been Chimé Takpai Dorjé, the grandson of Tsewang Dorjé Rigdzin.

487. That is, Dergé Gönchen.

488. Sang-gyé Lingpa was an important *tertön* who lived from 1340 to 1396. His principal discovery was the *terma* cycle entitled The United Intent of the Gurus (Tib. *Lama Gongdü*), with which Kongtrul had a strong connection.

489. The Sokmo family was one of the group known as the Dergé Dungkor, who traditionally supplied government ministers to the kings of Dergé. The Sokmo family is distinct from the king of Sokmo mentioned earlier (RT).

490. These are statues of Guru Rinpoché, made by his own students and blessed by the Guru himself. They were concealed as *terma*s and a number of them have been discovered. The term "regent" refers to the fact that their sacredness is such

that to be in their presence is the equivalent of being in that of Guru Rinpoché himself.

491. A *tertön* who lived from 1346 to 1405; see Kongtrul's accounts of his past lives.

492. Given that Tsewang Dorjé Rigdzin's grandson would only have been a year old, Kongtrul is again referring to either Tsewang Dorjé Rigdzin's second son, Tsewang Phuntsok Tenkyong, or his third, Tsewang Dorjé Dradul.

493. That is, the bodhisattvas Manjushri, Avalokiteshvara, and Vajrapani, associated with the "families," or principles, of enlightened form, speech, and mind, respectively.

494. These four deities are Shakyamuni Buddha, Avalokiteshvara, Tara, and the wrathful deity Achala.

495. The former text has been translated as *Mahamudra: The Quintessence of Mind and Meditation*, the latter in *Teachings of Tibetan Yoga*. Dakpo Panchen Tashi Namgyal lived from 1512 or 1513 to 1587.

496. One of the Eight Lineages of Accomplishment that developed in Tibet, the Dukngal Zhijé (Pacification of Suffering) School was founded in the twelfth century by the Indian master known to Tibetans as Phadampa Sang-gyé. Its teachings are based on the Prajnaparamita Sutras, the Buddha's discourses on the perfection of wisdom through the realization of emptiness.

497. Lochen ("Great Translator") Dharma Shri (1654-1718), who is also known as Minling Lochen, was the younger brother of the *tertön* Terdak Lingpa Gyurmé Dorjé, the founder of Mindroling Monastery.

498. Thangtong Gyalpo Tsöndrü Zangpo was a Nyingma master who lived from 1361 to 1464.

499. A woman *siddha* of the Indian Buddhist tradition.

500. Gyalsé Thogmé Zangpo (1295-1369) was an early Kadampa master whose writings include a much-studied commentary on Shantideva's *Bodhicharyavatara*.

501. An Indian Vajrayana master, Jetari was one of the Eighty-Four *Mahasiddhas*.

502. Tselé Natsok Rangdrol (b. 1608) was a master of the Nyingma School and wrote many important commentaries; he studied with the *tertön* Jatsön Nyingpo (1585-1656).

503. The Sanskrit work *kartari* (Tib. *driguk*) refers to a knife with a crescent-shaped blade like a cleaver and a handle formed of half of a vajra. Many wrathful deities are depicted bearing a *kartari* knife, which symbolizes the cutting through of ordinary, confused states of perception and thought.

504. Two of the Dergé Dungkor group (RT).

505. *The Heart Essence of Secrets*, or *Guhyagarbha*, is the primary source of the teachings of tantra in general, and Mahayoga in particular, for the Nyingma School. It has been the subject of numerous commentaries; the expanded *Nyingma Kama* collection compiled by the late Dudjom Rinpoché contains some sixteen

volumes dealing with this source, including Lalitavajra's commentary, which is one of the earliest surviving treatises.

506. Rongzom Mahapandita Chökyi Zangpo was an eleventh-century Nyingma master whose writings were some of the earliest to systematize the Nyingma teachings. Yungtön Dorjé Palwa lived from 1284 to 1365.

507. Tib. *Yangdak*. One of the deities of the Eight Commands cycle.

508. Tib. *Dusölma*; a form of Shri Devi (a principal *mahakali*, or feminine protective deity) practiced by the Kagyü School, due to her association with the Kagyü founding father Marpa the Translator and his student Milarepa.

509. That is, through being sectarian.

510. This ritual is similar to the Mani Dungdrup (also known as Mani Rimdu) that is commonly performed in Tibet and the Himalayan region. The lay community surrounding a monastery gathers with the monastics to collectively recite a large number of mantras (typically one hundred million), during which time a vase of water and sacred pills are consecrated through the blessings of the ritual. At the conclusion, the vase water and pills are distributed to all the participants (RT). The vase consecration ritual is a major way in which the lay and monastic communities interact on a formal level, and so was and is widely observed as an annual event.

511. To determine whether one has the necessary qualities to carry out the task in question.

512. Minling Terchen (the "great *tertön* of Mindroling Monastery"), also known as Terdak Lingpa Gyurmé Dorjé, was born in 1646 and died in 1714. In 1676 he founded the monastery of Mindroling, which became one of the most important Nyingma monasteries in Tibet. In addition to his *terma*s and other writings, Minling Terchen was the first to codify the thirteen volumes of the *kama* teachings of the Nyingma School.

513. Lumé Tsulthrim Sherab was a master of the *vinaya*, or monastic codes, in late tenth and early eleventh centuries and participated in the restoration of the Buddhist teachings in central Tibet following the devastation wrought by King Langdarma; see Kongtrul's accounts of his past lives.

514. Tib. *Chakna Dorjé*. The bodhisattva of spiritual power, appearing in both peaceful and wrathful forms.

515. The Buddha Shakyamuni's cousin and personal attendant.

516. Zurpoché (or Zurchen) Shakya Jungné (1002-1062) was a Nyingma master of the *kama* teachings.

517. *Tsen* are considered to be warrior-like spirits who guard specific regions in Tibet, especially mountain passes; it was considered prudent for travelers on horseback to dismount when passing through such a spirit's territory, lest the spirit be moved to anger by a seeming show of disrespect and cause the animal to throw the rider.

518. Margyenma, also known as Tsepongza Margyen Metok Drölma, was one of King Trisong Detsen's queens. She conspired to turn the king against the translator Bairotsana, who had refused her advances, and have him exiled. Bairotsana's spiritual power was such that the queen contracted smallpox as a result of her harmful actions, but Bairotsana incurred negative karma as well, due to causing this affliction. As a result, Bairotsana's incarnations (including Kongtrul) are held to have suffered as a result from skin diseases, which are inflicted on human beings through the influence of *naga*s.

519. Zabbulung Valley is an important pilgrimage site in the Shang region of the central Tibetan province of Tsang, west of Lhasa.

520. Sherab Özer (1518-1584) discovered the Sphere of Freedom (Tib. *Droltik*) cycle.

521. Guna Samudra is the Sanskritized form of Kongtrul's name, Yönten Gyatso.

522. Jamyang Khyentsé Wangchuk (1524-1568) was the fourteenth holder of the abbatial throne of Zhalu Monastery, a branch of the Sakya School.

523. The Ninth Situ, Pema Nyinjé Wangpo, died in 1853; the Tenth Situ, Pema Kunzang Chögyal, was born in the following year.

524. That is, passed away.

525. According to Tibetan custom, commemorative ceremonies are held during a period of forty-nine days after someone's death, with a "cusp point" occurring every seven days.

526. This refers to the tomb of the Eighth Tai Situ, Situ Panchen Chökyi Jungné, at Palpung Monastery (ADD).

527. That is, Situ Rinpoché.

528. Tib. *Gyalwang*; that is, the Gyalwang Karmapa. At this time, in 1853, this would have been the Fourteenth Karmapa, Thekchok Dorjé.

529. Kongtrul conceived of his collection called *The Tantric Treasury of the Kagyü School* as a memorial to his guru, Tai Situ Pema Nyinjé Wangpo (RT).

530. That is, the Kagyü master, Thrükhang Lotsawa Sönam Gyatso (1424-1482).

531. In order for a lineage of oral transmission (Tib. *lung*) to continue, each generation a living holder of the transmission must read the text aloud to someone who will carry on the transmission to the next generation. In certain cases, due to any number of circumstances, such continuity could be lost, even though the texts themselves were still in existence.

532. Yeshé Nyima was the sixth Thralep incarnation of the Kagyü School.

533. That of forty-nine days.

534. Of paramount importance in Tibetan Buddhist schools, especially in the matter of Vajrayana teachings, is that of a pure and unbroken lineage of transmission from one generation to the next.

535. These rituals belong to the Kriyatantra class, the first of the lower, or introduc-

tory, levels of tantra. They are performed in conjunction with the construction of stupas. The "two Vimalas" are the buddhas who are the central deities of their respective mandalas—Vimalarasmi (Tib. *Özer Drimé*) and Vimaloshnisha (Tib. *Tsuktor Drimé*).

536. A practice focusing on the deity Avalokiteshvara, found in Kongtrul's *Treasury of Precious Hidden Teachings*, in the section dealing with illnesses.

537. An epithet of Chokgyur Lingpa; an abbreviation of Kyasu Tertön —"*tertön* of the Kyasu clan," the name of Chokgyur Lingpa's clan.

538. That is to say, the authenticity of Chokgyur Lingpa and the *terma*s he revealed (RT).

539. The implication is that he meditated on the matter to determine whether it was a case of an authentic *tertön* or not, and whether Kongtrul should accept Kyater (that is, Chokgyur Lingpa) as one of his teachers.

540. "Lama of the Kyasu clan," another epithet of Chokgyur Lingpa.

541. The Tibetan term here is one that harks back to the custom of Buddhist monks in India going on rounds every day to beg for their food. As more stable monastic communities developed, lay people would often come to the monastery to make offerings or sponsor meals in return for teachings they received, a custom observed in many Buddhist countries to this day. In Tibetan society, it became part of the duties of important lamas or incarnations to make journeys throughout their regions on a regular basis, traveling with an entourage and soliciting offerings of food, money, and so forth from the local populace in the area they visited. In return, the lama would confer empowerments, teachings, and blessings on the populace. Such fund-raising trips provided a major source of income and support for large monasteries. This symbiotic relationship between the monasteries and local lay populations was designed to guard against the "selling" of the teachings becoming endemic, for the teachings and offerings were meant to be freely given on both sides without expectation.

542. Such manuals describe the spiritual qualities of a region and pinpoint the holy sites.

543. Powerful spiritual practice is regarded as often "stirring up" illness and so forth, not due to it being their cause, but rather by it causing the underlying karma to mature more rapidly. Given that this karma would have matured in any case, having it do so under such circumstances ensures that one is purified of it more quickly and under some kind of control.

544. A *mahasiddha* of the ancient Indian Buddhist tradition.

545. Tib. *Sang-gyé Thöpa*. A deity and cycle of the mother tantras of the Anuttarayoga class.

546. Tib. *Gyuthrul Chenmo*. A tantra and deity of the mother, or yogini, tantra section of the Anuttarayoga class of the Sarma Schools.

547. The principal Indian master (who lived from 1016 to 1100) of Marpa the Translator, who in turn was the founder of the Kagyü School in Tibet.

548. Kongtrul included this work in Volume 1 of his *Tantric Treasury of the Kagyü School.*

549. Following the Buddha Shakyamuni's passing into nirvana, his remains were cremated and the ashes and relics were divided among eight tribes attending the funeral ceremony, to be taken back to their home regions and enshrined in stupas.

550. Based on Mahayana techniques for developing love, compassion, and altruism, the *lojong* system was developed by the early Kadampa masters and later spread throughout all schools of Tibetan Buddhism. Kongtrul's commentary, which he included in his *Treasury of Spiritual Advice*, has been published in English translation as *The Great Path of Awakening.*

551. The *tertön* Rigdzin Duddul Dorjé (1615-1672) was one of the founders of the Nyingma monastery of Kathok in eastern Tibet.

552. Tib. *Dorjé Namjom*. A deity associated with purification and the removal of obstacles.

553. Bari Lotsawa Rinchen Drak (1040-1112) was an early Tibetan translator and a master of the founding father of the Sakya School, Sachen Kunga Nyingpo (1092-1158).

554. One of the Chakrasamvara cycle of tantras.

555. By "predecessor," Kongtrul assumed in his dream that the Eighth Karmapa, Mikyö Dorjé, was referring to the Seventh Karmapa, Chödrak Gyatso.

556. The Eighth Tai Situ, "predecessor" to Kongtrul's guru, the Ninth Tai Situ, Pema Nyinjé Wangpo.

557. Ngawang Lekdrup (b. 1811) held the office of Pönlop ("Teaching Master") at the Sakya monastery of Ngor and was a master of the Tsokshé lineage of the Lamdré system of teachings based on *The Hevajra Tantra.*

558. Tib. *Damtsik Dorjé*. The practice of this deity is done to restore one's *samaya* when one has committed infractions.

559. Ngen-lam Gyalwa Chokyang was one of Guru Rinpoché's twenty-five intimate students in the eighth century. He was master of the Hayagriva teachings and one of a group of seven men who were the first to receive monastic ordination in Tibet.

560. Presumably one of King Trisong Detsen's sons.

561. "Precious Incarnation of Dzongsar Monastery"; an epithet of Kongtrul's guru Jamyang Khyentsé Wangpo.

562. It was customary for highly respected and realized lamas to be asked to write letters verifying the authenticity of *tertön*s or their teachings, to allay any suspicions people might have.

563. Tib. *Gongpa Düpai Do*. The primary source of the Anuyoga teachings of the Nyingma School.

564. A fourteenth-century Nyingma master.

565. Pema Lingpa was a major *tertön* who lived from 1450 to 1521.

566. Zhigpo Lingpa Gargyi Wangchuk Tsal was a *tertön* who lived from 1524 to 1583.

567. Kongtrul often refers to Jamyang Khyentsé Wangpo ("Dzongsar Tulku Rinpoché") simply as Tulku Rinpoché ("The Precious Incarnation").

568. Before *tertön*s can fulfill their destiny of discovering *terma*s, they first receive transmissions of accounts called "records," which outline the nature, and often the number, of the *terma*s they are to discover in that particular lifetime.

569. Tib. *Dorjé Bechön*. A wrathful protective deity.

570. One criterion for classifying a *terma* cycle as a major one is that it must contain elements that relate to these three kinds of practice.

571. Partly as a means of self-effacement, Tibetan Buddhist authors observe a process of requesting permission from the Three Roots—that is, the gurus of their lineage, their chosen deities, and the *dakini*s and protective deities—before undertaking any major work of composition.

572. Also known as Dorjé Tso, Shelkarza was one of Guyru Rinpoché's highly accomplished woman students.

573. Tibetan dates are counted from sunrise to sunrise.

574. The "lion throne" is the square base on which a stupa sits; it is decorated with bas-relief sculptures of rampant snow lions.

575. Before the Khyentsé line of incarnations began with Jamyang Khyentsé Wangpo, the two main *tulku*s associated with Dzongsar Monastery were the Ngari and Dong-na incarnations (RT).

576. Just as the Mahayana approach emphasizes the arousal of the altruistic resolve of bodhichitta at the outset of any spiritual teaching or practice, the Vajrayana approach speaks of five aspects of excellence as the correct motivation or attitude. The Vajrayana practitioner maintains awareness of the excellent environment as the pinnacle pure realm of Akanishtha; the excellent occasion as the timeless and ever-present moment; the excellent teacher as the embodiment of the primordial buddha Samantabhadra; the excellent students as deities by their very nature; and the excellent teaching as the natural expression of the true nature of phenomena. In calling this "pure view" (*dak-nang*) to mind, the practitionsser is not pretending, but rather recognizing the innate purity underlying our ordinary, confused perceptions.

577. Here Khyentsé Rinpoché is referring to the area around Palpung as having the same sacredness as two other holy sites bearing the name Devikoti, one in India and the other on the southeastern border of Tibet and Assam. The location of holy sites on the surface of the earth is held to correspond to the structure of the channels and chakras in the subtle body of the practitioner.

578. A wrathful feminine deity, Ekajati is one of the most important protective deities of the Dzogchen tradition.

579. A deity associated with wealth, one of the retinue of a major deity of wealth, Vaishravana.

580. The "Mind Only" school of idealist Buddhist philosophy.

581. Kunga Drolchok (1507-1565/6) was a master of the Jonangpa School; his rebirth was Taranatha.

582. Butön Rinchendrup (1290-1364) was a scholar of the Zhalu branch of the Sakya School; he edited one of the early versions of the Kangyur collection, from which he excluded tantras belonging to the Nyingma School on the grounds that their authenticity was questionable, fueling a controversy that echoes to the present day. The Zhalu tradition of Butön specialized in the Kalachakra system.

583. Taktsang Lotsawa Sherab Rinchen was a Sakya master who was born in 1405.

584. A form of Avalokiteshvara, the bodhisattva of compassion.

585. The ancient Khön clan of Tibet, which has produced masters of the Sakya School from the time of its founding, also has ties with the Nyingma School that date from the eighth century, when Khön Nagendrarakshita received transmissions from Guru Rinpoché.

586. Taklung Monastery, the main center of the Taklung Kagyü School (one of the eight minor branches of the Kagyü), was founded in 1180 about one hundred and twenty kilometers north of Lhasa, on the site of an earlier Kadampa monastery, by Taklung Thangpa Tashi Pal (1142-1210).

587. Tib. *Tsuktor Namgyalma*. A feminine deity associated with the principle of longevity.

588. Nagarjuna was the Indian Buddhist master primarily responsible for formulating the tenets of the Madhyamaka, or Middle Way, school of Buddhist philosophy.

589. A feminine deity ("Mother of the Planets").

590. Tib. *Döpai Gyalpo*. One of the wrathful deities associated with the ten directions.

591. An oral transmission (Tib. *lung*) is usually done very rapidly, with the master reading the words of the text aloud to the students at high speed. No attempt is made to communicate or understand the meaning of the individual words; the blessing lies in simply hearing the sounds. In the case of a teaching transmission (Tib. *tri-lung*), the text is still read rapidly, but at a speed that allows the students to follow the sense of the text. Obviously, a teaching transmission takes longer to confer but is considered a greater blessing.

592. Maitripa was one of the Eighty-Four *Mahasiddhas* of ancient India.

593. The Bodong tradition stems from the teachings and writings of the encyclopedic scholar, Bodong Panchen Choklé Namgyal (1376-1451); see Kongtrul's accounts of his past lives.

594. These are two *mahasiddhas* of ancient India.

595. During rituals to promote longevity, an "arrow of longevity" (Tib. *tséda*) is placed on the shrine as one of the supports for meditation. Its length is carefully measured before and after the ritual, and it is taken as a good sign if the arrow is found to have lengthened.

596. The Lamdré (Path and its Fruition) teachings, which focus on *The Hevajra Tantra*, are among the core teachings of the Sakya School of Tibetan Buddhism.

597. This may be a reference to several historical figures: Ngorchen Kunga Zangpo (1382-1456) was the founder of the Ngor branch of the Sakya School and the first grand abbot of its main monastery; Ngorchen Könchok Lhundrup (1497-1557) was the tenth grand abbot of Ngor and an important writer in the Lamdré lineage; Ngor Khenchen Jampa Kunga Tendzin (1776-1862), also one of the grand abbots of Ngor Monastery, was a teacher of both Khyentsé and Kongtrul.

598. Dechen Lingpa lived from 1663 to 1713; see Kongtrul's accounts of his past lives.

599. Tib. *Sangwa Yeshé*; a feminine deity, or *dakini*.

600. The translator Mal Lotsawa Lodrö Drakpa was a teacher of Sachen Kunga Nyingpo (1092-1158), the founder of the Sakya School.

601. Gorampa Sönam Seng-gé (1429-1489) was one of the most brilliant and controversial writers of the Sakya School.

602. Ngari Panchen Pema Wang-gyal (1487-1542) was a Nyingma master whose most famous work is *The Definitive Explanation of the Three Levels of Ordination*. Rigdzin Duddul Dorjé (1615-1672) was a *tertön*, as was his student, Longsal Nyingpo (1625-1692); their *terma*s became integral elements in the Kathok lineage of teachings.

603. Longsal Nyingpo (1625-1692) was a *tertön* whose *terma*s form an important part of the teachings transmitted in the lineage of Kathok Monastery.

604. A form of the bodhisattva of compassion, Avalokiteshvara.

605. Such obstacles, even including seeming "interference" by Ekajati (the "Guardian Goddess of Mantra"), often attend undertakings of great importance. A common Tibetan saying states that "profound teachings and practice involve profound obstacles."

606. One of Chokgyur Lingpa's *terma*s.

607. Literally, "Dancing Ground of the *Dakini*s."

608. The purpose of this journey was to escort the newly recognized Tenth Situ back to Palpung Monastery from the Karmapa's monastery of Tsurphu, where the young incarnation had been living since his recognition.

609. A *tertön* of the Bön tradition.

610. Tib. *Tsédak* ("Lord of Longevity"). The peaceful aspect of this deity is a form of Manjushri; the wrathful aspect is a form of Yamantaka, the wrathful aspect of Manjushri.

611. The Tibetan idiom, *ri-tö* ("praising the mountains"), refers to the custom of performing *lhasang* rituals and raising prayer flags on mountain tops to ensure one's success in an important undertaking (RT).

612. These are recollections (Tib. *jé-dren*) of events that occurred in a previous lifetime of the one recalling them; such memories can serve as the basis of teaching transmissions.

613. Jamyang Khyentsé Wangpo wrote a guide to these holy sites.

614. A feminine deity of the *padma*, or lotus, family, associated with the mastery of the enlightened activity of power ("mganetizing activity").

615. A protective deity.

616. That is, the Fourteenth Karmapa, Thekchok Dorjé, and the newly recognized Tenth Situ, Pema Kunzang Chögyal.

617. Tersar, or "Newly Revealed Hidden Teachings," is a collective term for *termas* revealed in more recent times; specifically, it here refers to those of Chokgyur Lingpa—the Chokling Tersar cycles.

618. That is, the temples of Jokhang and Ramoché, which house these famous statues of the Buddha.

619. The residence of the Dalai Lamas in Lhasa.

620. A small hill near the Potala Palace, site of a major center for astrological and medical studies.

621. "Looks Like Me." When the statue was installed for consecration, Guru Rinpoché saw it and remarked, "It looks like me." He then performed the consecration and stated, "Now it *is* me."

622. A region in the hills above Samyé Monastery, where there are many caves blessed by Guru Rinpoché and other great masters of the past.

623. The Tsangpo River, which flows from its source in western Tibet through the central and southeastern provinces and becomes the Brahmaputra of northwest India.

624. An important temple in the valley south of Tsethang, Thradruk was founded by King Songtsen Gampo, who ruled from from 627 to 650, and was one of the three principal temples during the reign of King Trisong Detsen.

625. This would have been Gyurmé Yizhin Wang-gyal, the son of the great throne holder Thrinlé Namgyal (1765-1812).

626. A feminine protective deity.

627. The sister of Gyurmé Yizhin Wang-gyal was Jetsün Thrinlé Chödrön, who was also an important teacher of Jamyang Khyentsé Wangpo.

628. Not the deceased elder brother of Jamyang Khyentsé Wangpo, but a lama of Mindroling Monastery.

629. The term "Cow's Udder" (Tib. *Bébum*) refers to a compendium of numerous short instructions, often rare, that have been collected from various sources.

630. A wrathful protective deity.

631. Tib. *Kyiti*. These are teachings of the Dzogchen approach, as indicated by the – *ti* suffix (*Ati, Kyiti, Yangti*, etc.).

632. Drapa Ngönshé (1012-1090) discovered the *terma* cycle of the four medical tantras.

633. The ritual referred to involves a *torma* that is cast outside as a means of averting negativity (ADD).

634. This was the abbot of Radreng Monastery, Ngawang Yeshé Tsulthrim Gyaltsen (1816-1863), who served as the regent from 1844 until his death, during the minorities of the Eleventh Dalai Lama, Khedrup Gyatso (1838-1855/1856), and the Twelfth Dalai Lama, Thrinlé Gyatso (1856-1875).

635. Founded in 1447 by the First Dalai Lama, Gendun Druppa (1391-1474/5), Tashilhunpo was the main Gelukpa monastery in Tsang Province and residence of the Panchen Lama incarnations.

636. Shedra Wangchuk Gyalpo was a powerful minister in the cabinet of the Twelfth Dalai Lama.

637. A *geshé* is one who has passed a series of examinations to determine scholastic excellence; the title, which was first adopted by the early Kadampa masters, derives from the Tibetan *gewai shenyen*, the equivalent of the Sanskrit *kalyanamitra*, or "spiritual mentor."

638. A variation on the "one hundred offerings," involving one thousand of each of a set of traditional offerings.

639. The Ninth Drukchen, Jigmé Mingyur Wang-gyal (1823-1883).

640. An ancient fortress, one of the oldest buildings in Tibet, associated with the reign of King Songtsen Gampo in the seventh century.

641. Takchen Bumpa, Gonthang Bumpa, and Tsechu Bumpa.

642. This seal of entrustment is conferred by holders of a lineage on their successors, empowering these students to pass on the transmission in their turn. In finding such a person, Kongtrul was in a position to receive the transmission himself. The Gathering of All Dakinis' Secrets is a *terma* cycle discovered by the woman *tertön* Jomo Menmo.

643. That is, Nyangral Nyima Özer and Guru Chöwang.

644. A retreat site on a cliff face, associated particularly with the Second and Third Karmapas. See *The Power Places of Central Tibet: The Pilgrim's Guide*, p. 126.

645. That is, the Karmapa.

646. The Chöwang Tulkus were rebirths of the *tertön* Guru Chökyi Wangchuk (1212-1270), who in turn was considered the incarnation of the enlightened speech of the eighth-century Tibetan king Trisong Detsen. According to Kongtrul (see *Enthronement*, p. 109), the first Chöwang Tulku was the nephew of the Twelfth Karmapa, Jangchub Dorjé. The *tulku* Kongtrul refers to here (who was the nephew

of the Fourteenth Karmapa, Thekchok Dorjé) must therefore have been the second, or even the third, in the line of Chöwang incarnations.

647. The seat of the Pawo Rinpoché incarnations of the Karma Kagyü School is Nenang Monastery, founded in 1333 by the First Zhamar Rinpoché, Tokden Drakpa Sengé, near the Karmapas' seat in Tsurphu.

648. That is, the Eighth Pawo, Tsuklak Chökyi Gyalpo (late eighteenth-mid nineteenth centuries).

649. That is, the ninth Gyaltsap incarnation, Drakpa Yeshé (1821-1876).

650. Kongtrul refers to the Tenth Situ, the rebirth of his guru Situ Pema Nyinjé Wangpo, as Choktrul Rinpoché ("The Precious Sublime Incarnation") or Kuzhap Choktrul ("The Venerable Sublime Incarnation"). He later applies the same titles to the Eleventh Situ, following that incarnation's birth in 1886.

651. That is, the Fourteenth Karmapa, Thekchok Dorjé.

652. Chögyal Dorjé (1789-1859) discovered a *terma* cycle focusing on the deity Guru Drakpo (the wrathful form of Guru Rinpoché). He died the following year.

653. The queen, Chöying Zangmo, was the widow of Damtsig Dorjé, the forty-fourth generation of the kings of Dergé. Her young son, Chimé Takpai Dorjé, would have been seven or eight years old at this time.

654. Rituals are employed to consecrate "treasure vases" (Tib. *terbum*)—vases filled with jewels and other valuable substances and sealed—that are then buried at specific sites to consecrate a region, protecting it from obstacles and promoting prosperity.

655. A popular epithet for the warlord Gönpo Namgyal of Nyarong province, who waged war over much of eastern Tibet, even capturing Dergé in 1862. For a well-researched article on Gönpo Namgyal's military campaigns, see Tashi Tsering, "Ñag-ron mgon-po rnam-gyal: A 19th Century Khams-pa Warrior," in *Soundings in Tibetan Civilization*.

656. A wealth deity, Vaishravana is one of the four gods who are kings of the cardinal directions.

657. Dungtso Repa the Elder, Sherab Gyaltsen (late thirteenth-early fourteenth centuries), discovered a *terma* cycle of teachings on the nature of mind that had been concealed by the Kagyü master Gampopa.

658. The fifteenth-century woman master Kunga Bumpa was a student of Dungtso Repa the Elder and a teacher of Dungtso Repa the Younger.

659. That is, Dorjé Lingpa and Dungtso Repa.

660. An epithet of either Vajrakila or Samyak.

661. That is, Chokgyur Lingpa.

662. This epithet could refer to either Samyak or Vajrakila; practices focusing on both deities are found in Chokgyur Lingpa's Three Cycles of the Secret Sphere (the third deity is Vajrasattva).

663. The Tibetan idiom, "opening the doorway and laying the path," refers to the practice of a spiritual master identifying a sacred site and delineating its function and boundaries. The route would be used by pilgrims to circumambulate the site and visit all of its special features in order to accrue merit (RT).

664. A variation on the "one hundred offerings," involving ten thousand of each of a set of traditional offerings.

665. The Second Zhamar Rinpoché (1350-1405).

666. The summer retreat, observed in some form by monasteries in all Buddhist countries, is one of the "three bases of purification" in the Buddhist monastic code (the other two being the monthly ceremony to renew monastic vows and the ritual to determine infractions of the rules of conduct). The summer retreat begins on the sixteenth day of either the sixth or seventh month of the Tibetan calendar and lasts for three months, during which time the monastic community is cloistered in strict retreat and the participants devote themselves to study and spiritual practice.

667. That is, the Tenth Situ, Pema Kunzang Chögyal; Kongtrul refers to him as *Kuzhap Choktrul*— that is, the "Sublime Incarnation of Kuzhap" (Kuzhap having been Kongtrul's name for the previous Situ, his guru Pema Nyinjé Wangpo).

668. It is clear that Gönpo Namgyal was a force to be reckoned with, and exerted considerable influence in eastern Tibet at this time, due in large part to his excesses as a military dictator.

669. Tib. *Thukjé Chenpo Semnyi Ngalso*. A form of the bodhisattva of compassion, Avalokiteshvara.

670. The term *heruka* (which is described as being of Sanskrit origin) is a generic term referring to wrathful masculine deities.

671. The five places, corresponding to the five major chakras, or subtle energy centers in the body, are the crown of the head, throat, heart center, navel, and genitals.

672. The last step in any painting of a guru or deity is the filling in of the pupils and irises of the eyes, which are left blank up to the very last. A formal ceremony often accompanies this "final touch" by the artist.

673. That is, religious objects such as statues and paintings (representations of form); scriptural texts (representations of speech); and stupas, vajras, and bells (representations of mind).

674. Translated into English as *Jamgön Kongtrul's Retreat Manual*.

675. Certain kinds of negative energy are cyclical in nature, for example recurring every generation in a family to bring similar catastrophes each time.

676. Tib. *Khachöma*. A form of the feminine deity Vajrayogini.

677. These are found in Volumes 17-20 of Khyentsé's collection, The Compendium of All Classes of Tantra; see Appendix.

678. The Lamdré teachings of the Sakya School, can be transmitted in one of two ways. The more common format, known as *Tsokshé* ("explanation to the group"), involves less detail and is more suited for large groups of students. The more intimate format, known as *Lopshé* ("explanation to the student"), is a very detailed approach and involves more intensive training of fewer participants by the presiding master.

679. The doors are set into the cubical base of a stupa; they may be simple alcoves containing statues or, if the stupa base is large enough to contain a shrine room, actual doorways into that room. The roundish structure on top of the base is the vase, into which is set an alcove (called a "door") that contains a statue.

680. A powerful spirit of Tibet, Pehar was converted by Guru Rinpoché to protect the Buddhist teachings. Originally associated with Samyé Monastery, the first Buddhist institution in Tibet, in the twelfth century Pehar was relocated to Nechung Monastery in the Lhasa area; since that time, Pehar has inspired the state oracles of Tibet—a succession of mediums who have advised the government of the Dalai Lamas and their regents.

681. Pehar is one of a class of protective deities who have worldly origins; these are formerly malevolent or demonic figures that have been bound, by Guru Rinpoché or other masters, by an oath to protect the Buddhist teachings. Such worldly guardians are considered by Tibetans to have personalities that often require a spirit of negotiation on the part of the practitioner.

682. The construction of a stupa involves a mast-like central pole, or axis, around which the spire is built. Large numbers of *tsa-tsa*s are prepared and consecrated to fill the inner chambers of a stupa.

683. This is one of the eight major styles of stupa construction, all of which commemorate events in the Buddha's life. The stupa of complete victory, also known as the stupa of enlightenment, commemorates Shakyamuni's attainment of buddhahood under the bodhi tree in Bodh Gaya.

684. Kongtrul's personal practice focused on the Swift-Acting Jnana Natha, the Six-Armed Mahakala. This deity is also the main protective deity of the Shangpa Kagyü School that Kongtrul held in such high regard.

685. This test is often used to assess a practitioner's success in the practice known as "the inner heat" (Skt. *chandali*; Tib. *tummo*), one of the Six Yogas.

686. The *Shéja Kunkhyab*, also known as *The Treasury of the Knowable* (*Shéja Dzö*). One of Kongtrul's famed Five Treasuries.

687. Consisting of source verses and a lengthy autocommentary, *The Treasury of the Knowable* is arranged around a central theme of these trainings—ethics, mind (that is, meditation), and wisdom (see Appendix). Within this framework, Kongtrul discusses the entire range of subjects within the Buddhist tradition, including more secular subjects such as medicine and the arts. A section of

Kongtrul's *Treasury of the Knowable* has been translated as *The Teacher-Student Relationship*. A long-term project to translate this work was started by Kalu Rinpoché Rangjung Kunkhyab (1905-1989) as the International Translation Committee. The Committee has already produced two volumes—*Myriad Worlds* and *Buddhist Ethics*.

688. *Shéja Dzö*. The other common title for the *Shéja Kunkhyab*.

689. The twelve *tenma* sisters are powerful spirits indigenous to the Tibetan region; they were among the most important of such spirits tamed by Guru Rinpoché and bound by oaths to serve and protect the Buddhist teachings.

690. The queen, Chöying Zangmo, and her two sons were taken hostage by Gönpo Namgyal.

691. Chimé Takpai Dorjé was born in 1851.

692. These are activities that pacify negative factors, enrich positive factors, exert power as a positive influence, and invoke wrathful energy as a means of direct intervention to avert negativity; these four are collectively referred to as ordinary *siddhi*s, or spiritual attainments, involving skillful manipulation of the phenomenal world, as distinct from the sublime attainment of enlightenment itself.

693. The practices associated with the Vajrakila mandala are of two kinds—the "higher activity" focuses on the attainment of enlightenment, the "lower activity" on the enactment of wrathful activity to overcome obstacles to the spread of the Buddhist teachings and the progress of practitioners.

694. The Vajrayana teachings distinguish between deities that are sambhogakaya manifestations of enlightened mind, which are termed "deities of timeless awareness" (Tib. *yeshé kyi lha*), and "worldly guardians" (Tib. *jikten kyi sungma*), that is, worldly beings that have been bound by great masters to an oath to protect the Buddhist teachings.

695. A *khenpo* is one who has completed an advanced degree of scholastic studies in any of the Buddhist schools of Tibet.

696. *Dö* rituals (which have their origins in Bön, the pre-Buddhist tradition of Tibet) serve either of two purposes—that of honoring deities (that is, embodiments of enlightened being) or worldly gods and local spirits, and (as in this present case) that of appeasing or averting negative spirits or forces.

697. Phulungwa Tsewang Dorjé was a minister in the central government who was charged with the task of defeating the forces of Gönpo Namgyal of Nyarong.

698. These are the "cusp points" that recur during the forty-nine day period after someone's death.

699. The three levels of obscuration are those of a fundamental ignorance concerning the nature of reality, of afflictive emotions, and of karma. The three kinds of maturation are physical, verbal, and mental.

700. Kongtrul wrote a text describing the construction of such tiered stupas, based on

the earlier works of the scholar Butön Rinchendrup; see *Principles of Tibetan Art*, vol. 2, pp. 84-85 and 95.

701. The Four Higher Collections of the Heart Drop Teachings are actually five in number. The two cycles referred to as the "mother" cycles are The Heart Drop of the Dakini, deriving from Padmakara, and The Heart Drop of Vimalamitra, deriving from his contemporary, the Dzogchen master Vimalamitra. Longchenpa composed two cycles (termed the "child" cycles) that are further refinements of these—The Innermost Heart Drop of the Dakini and The Innermost Heart Drop of the Guru. The fifth collection is Longchenpa's Innermost Heart Drop of Profundity, which is a synthetic reworking of the preceding four. Taken together, these five collections are the basis for the experiential approach to the Dzogchen teachings, which is called the "Heart Drop" (*Nyingthik*); Longchenpa's Seven Treasuries are the basis for a more scholarly approach to these teachings.

702. Due to a summons from the Nyarong chieftain Gönpo Namgyal.

703. Jamgön Kongtrul and all his successive incarnations suffered from chronic skin disorders. This is held to be a karmic residue from Kongtrul's previous life as the Tibetan translator Bairotsana. Bairotsana incurred this karma when he was exiled from central Tibet due to the machinations of Trisong Detsen's queen, Tsepongza, after refusing her advances (RT). See *The Life and Liberation of Padmasambhava*, vol. 2, pp. 459-462.

704. For a complete account of the program followed in Kongtrul's retreat center, see *Jamgön Kongtrul's Retreat Manual*.

705. These are areas to the southwest of Dergé; the central Tibetan forces would have been joined by reinforcements as they passed through these areas on their way to do battle with Nyarong Gönpo Namgyal.

706. Tibetan texts are usually written in one of two styles—"headed" (*u-chen*), which is also the style used in woodblocks, and "headless" (*u-mé*), which is more cursive. For letters and more informal documents, a running hand known as *khyuk-yik* is employed.

707. The process of receiving the four levels of empowerment in meditation involves visualizing rays of light shining from various centers on the guru's or deity's form and touching the corresponding points on one's own body.

708. According to accounts in the literature of the *Vinaya* (the Buddhist ethical and monastic codes), during the Buddha's lifetime he would ordain someone simply by saying, "Come hither."

709. Gönpo Namgyal was defeated by the central Tibetan government's forces under General Thrimönpa Chimé Dorjé. The Nyarong chieftain and his family were burned alive when the government forces set fire to Gönpo Namgyal's fortress in 1865.

710. This protective deity is particularly associated with the Karma Kagyü School and its Mahamudra teachings.

711. This is most likely Lhaksam Tenpai Gyaltsen, who became a *khenpo* of Palpung Monastery.

712. This is one of seven particularly auspicious conjunctions described in Tibetan astrological works. See *Tibetan Astrology*, pp. 132-143. *Hasta* ("The Hand") is the Indian term for the eleventh (in some treatments the thirteenth) lunar mansion; it contains five major stars, giving it its name, and may correspond to the constellation Corvus.

713. Because of their secret nature, certain texts are termed "sealed" (Tib. *kagyama*).

714. These are two of the largest and most important Mahayana sutras.

715. *Mamos* are wrathful, *dakini*-like figures that may be feminine deities (expressions of enlightened mind) or worldly goddesses.

716. This is a term for a feast offering attended by equal numbers of men and women.

717. That is, produced through the coming together of certain causes and conditions, and hence subject to dissolution when those causes and conditions no longer pertain.

718. That is, Dechen Chokgyur Lingpa and Jamyang Khyentsé Wangpo.

719. This term denotes a very streamlined empowerment format, which focuses on the ultimate meaning of the transmission without a lot of detail or elaboration. Many *terma* cycles include such abbreviated empowerments, which are also convenient when a master wishes to confer the blessings of the cycle and time does not permit the more extensive and complete transmission.

720. This text, known in Tibetan as *Lamrim Yeshé Nyingpo*, has been translated into English as *The Light of Wisdom*.

721. This is an auxiliary practice from the Northern Treasure cycles.

722. The Tibetan calendar is based on a sixty-year cycle, derived from the combination of a cycle of twelve animals in conjunction with five elements. The Fire Hare Year is considered Year One of any given cycle.

723. The *tertön* title that Kongtrul received on this occasion was Chimé Tennyi Yungdrung Lingpa.

724. That is, the abbot Shantirakshita, the master Padmakara, and the king Trisong Detsen, whose united efforts established Buddhism in Tibet in the eighth century.

725. These are rituals of purification and are often performed when someone is nearing death, or once they have died (in order to aid the spiritual progress of the deceased's consciousness).

726. When people die, lamas may conduct rituals of introducing them to the nature of mind just as in the case of living students, for it is felt that effective contact with the deceased is still possible. Similarly, lamas will perform the technique to transfer the deceased's consciousness to a higher rebirth or a pure realm, even

though the actual moment of death (which is the ideal point for such transference to be effected) has already occurred.

727. One of the students of the Eighth Tai Situ of the Karma Kagyü School, Chökyi Jungné (1700-1774), was a lama of Kathok. Following the Eighth Situ's death, this lama instituted the custom of recognizing a parallel line of Situ incarnations at Kathok; thus, the Palpung Situs were Kagyü masters, while the Kathok Situs were Nyingma (RT). The first Kathok Situ was Chökyi Seng-gé (b. c. 1775). The two incarnations mentioned here would have been the Second Kathok Situ, Orgyen Tenpa Namgyal Kunkhyen Chökyi Lodrö (1820-c. 1879) and the Third Kathok Situ, Chökyi Gyatso (1880-1923/5).

728. A place in Dzamthang about two hundred kilometers to the northeast of Dergé.

729. Rongtön Sheja Kunrik (1367-1449) was a Sakya master associated with the monastery of Nalendra north of Lhasa.

730. The term used here refers to the common practice of a master placing his or her open hand, palm down, on the crown of a student's head to convey a blessing.

731. *Terma*s are sometimes in the form of sacred objects or substances that convey blessings, rather than being texts.

732. For example, following her husband.

733. She is thinking that his prophecy about his next incarnation coming to her is an indication that she will become pregnant with his *tulku*.

734. This is another ritual of purification performed for the benefit of a deceased person, to purify the consciousness of causes that could lead to rebirth in lower realms.

735. The seventh sexagesimal cycle was from 1387 to 1446. Dorjé Lingpa lived from 1346 to 1405.

736. The "oral lineage" was one of some seven modes of transmission that Jamyang Khyentsé Wangpo received in his lifetime.

737. Kongtrul's own last work was his commentary on this fragment of *The Vajrakila Tantra*.

738. These are various kinds of Vajrayana transmission ceremonies, from the most extensive format to the most concise.

739. The Fourth Zhamar Rinpoché (1453-1524).

740. Karma Thrinlépa (1456-1539) was a student of the Seventh Gyalwang Karmapa, Chödrak Gyatso (1454-1506).

741. Skt. *Uttaratantra*. One of the Five Works of Maitreya, *The Highest Continuum* is the fundamental Mahayana source on teachings concerning *tathagatagarbha*—the "buddha nature." There exist several English translations; see *The Uttaratantra of Maitreya*; *The Changeless Nature*; and *Buddha Nature*.

742. This has been published in English translation as *Buddha Nature*.

743. These substances are associated with events in the Buddha's life, which imbue them with significance. They are: a mirror, yogurt, *durva* grass, *bilba* fruit, a conch shell whose spiral form turns clockwise, a medicine called *giwang*, vermilion powder, and white mustard seed. These and other auspicious symbols are often cast in metal or painted on *tsakli* cards, to be placed on shrines as symbolic offerings.

744. These are some of the main sources, respectively, for the Nyingma teachings of Mahayoga, Anuyoga, and Atiyoga.

745. This is presumably a reference to Khenpo Ngawang Sönam Gyaltsen (c. 1835-c. 1895) of the house of Khangsar; he was the fifty-fifth grand abbot of Ngor Monastery. Because Dergé Gönchen was a Sakya monastery, there were many masters from the Sakya monasteries of central Tibet who came to study or teach there.

746. That is, Rigdzin Drölma.

747. Located in the town of Dergé, below the monastery of Dergé Gönchen, and dedicated to Thangtong Gyalpo, the founder of the great monastery.

748. That is, had died.

749. There are a number of different styles of commentary in Buddhist writing. Some commentaries are quite exhaustive and thorough, while others are only treatments of selected topics in the source text which have been found to be problematic.

750. This is Jamyang Khyentsé Wangpo's *tertön* title.

751. These are *terma*s that, rather than being concealed texts or other physical objects, are transmissions that were "locked" within the mindstream of one of Guru Rinpoché's students, to be revealed in some future lifetime, when the seal on the memory is released.

752. Jampa Kunga Tendzin (1776-1862) was one of Ngor Monastery's grand abbots (*Khenchen*) and one of Jamyang Khyentsé Wangpo's important teachers (and so, for Khyentsé, Vajradhara, or Dorjé Chang).

753. Lama Dampa Sönam Gyaltsen (1312-1375) was a Sakya master of the Lamdré system of teachings.

754. For details on the life of Müchen Sang-gyé Rinchen (1450-1524), see Kongtrul's accounts of his past lives.

755. Possibly a reference to either Ga Lotsawa Zhönnu Pal (twelfth century) or Ga Lotsawa Namgyal Dorjé (1203-1282).

756. Pokpön Phunrapa Tsering Palden had assisted the government minister Phulungwa in commanding the forces that defeated Nyarong Gönpo Namgyal. After the rebel chieftain was killed in 1865, Phunrapa was given control of Gönpo Namgyal's domain.

757. Tib. *Longchen Nyingthik*. An important cycle of teachings that Jigmé Lingpa (1730-1798) received in a series of three visions as a *terma* of enlightened intent,

The Heart Drop of Longchenpa is perhaps the most widely practiced cycle of Dzogchen teachings in modern times.

758. A tradition expounded by Jigmé Lingpa in his works.

759. An empowerment ritual involves a preliminary phase of self-empowerment, during which the master who is conferring the empowerment receives the transmission from the mandala of deities through a process of meditation and is then able to transmit the empowerment to others.

760. The term "direct lineage" (*nye-gyü*) implies that the transmission comes directly from the source (a deity or master) to the recipient, without anyone else intervening.

761. One of Guru Rinpoché's twenty-five intimate students in the eighth century, Nanam Dorjé Dudjom was renowned for his yogic powers gained through mastery of the practice and teachings of the wrathful deity Vajrakila.

762. This process, used in the preparation of medicinal compounds, had been lost in central Tibet and Kongtrul was instrumental in training people there to revive the tradition (RT).

763. The idiom refers to the fact that, due to various circumstances, a particular holy site may occasionally become the "place of choice" for anyone undertaking pilgrimage to visit (RT).

764. Around each holy site there would be a particular route for pilgrims to follow when circumambulating the site as a means of gaining merit.

765. A ritual with pre-Buddhist origins in Tibet, in which a goblet filled with wine and a sliver of gold is offered, usually to wrathful deities or worldly guardian spirits.

766. There are many sites at which Guru Rinpoché or other masters left footprints, handprints, and other marks in solid rock.

767. A tetrahedronal shape, a symbol for the true nature of reality that is the context within which all phenomena arise; its three-sided form symbolizes three principles—the ground of being, which is emptiness; the spiritual path, which is based on the fact that phenomena lack ordinary characteristics; and the fruition, which is beyond any speculation.

768. These three offerings are specific to Vajrayana rituals. "Medicine" is consecrated alcohol, symbolizing the transformation of impure substances into their pure analogues. *Rakta* (literally, "blood") is an offering symbolizing the transmutation of ordinary desire and attachment. On the shrine used in such a ritual, the *torma* will occupy a central position, flanked a small skull cup (usually worked in metal) on either side, containing the offerings of "medicine" and *rakta*.

769. A local spirit associated with the region.

770. Myrobalan is highly prized for its medicinal properties.

771. One of the Eighty-Four *Mahasiddhas*, also known as Ghantapada.

772. Kukuripa was another of the Eighty-Four *Mahasiddha*s and a teacher of the founder of the Kagyü School, Marpa Lotsawa Chökyi Lodrö (1002/12-1097).

773. Such events are considered very auspicious signs, indicating the success of the practice.

774. Each feature of a stupa's architecture symbolizes some aspect of the spiritual path, or some quality of the enlightened state of mind.

775. That is, symbols of enlightened form, speech, mind, qualities, and activity. These would usually be (respectively) a statue, a text of scripture, a stupa or bell, a longevity vase, and crossed vajras.

776. The complete prayer is: "In all lifetimes, may I never be separate from the true guru, but enjoy the splendor of the Buddhadharma. Having perfected the qualities of the spiritual paths and levels, may I swiftly attain the state of Vajradhara!"

777. The Thromgé clan of the Thromthar region near Nyarong produced many great spiritual figures for centuries; the most recent was the late Sixteenth Chagdud Tulku, Pema Gargyi Wangchuk (1930-2002). The Thromgé clan had strong ties with Kathok Monastery and its Longsal Nyingpo cycle of *terma*s. The reference to "Thromgé Tulku" is not clear; two of Kongtrul's contemporaries were Thromgé Kundun Tulku Sönam Rinchen (a student of the great Nyingma scholar Gyurmé Tsewang Chokdrub (1761-1829)) and Thromgé Do-ngak Tendzin (who studied with the Second Katok Situ, Chökyi Lodrö (b. 1820)).

778. Adzom Drukpa Drodul Pawo Dorjé (1842-1924) was an important figure in the lineage of the Heart Drop (*Nyingthik*) teachings of the Nyingma School. Among his other teachers were Jamyang Khyentsé Wangpo, Mipham Naymgyal Gyatso, and the Second Kathok Situ, Chökyi Lodrö, and his students included the Third Kathok Situ, Chökyi Gyatso, and Dilgo Khyentsé Rinpoché.

779. The Getsé Tulku ("Getrul") incarnation line is one of the most important associated with the Nyingma monastery of Kathok. When Tsewang Lhamo, the queen of Dergé, commissioned the first woodblock edition of The Collected Tantras of the Nyingma Tradition (prepared between 1794 and 1798, the year of Rigdzin Jigmé Lingpa's death), the famous Getsé Mahapandita, Gyurmé Tsewang Chokdrup (1761-1829), was one of the principal editors. The second Getsé incarnation, Tsewang Rigdzin Gyatso, lived from about 1830 to about 1885; the third Getsé Tulku was Gyurmé Tenpa Namgyal (1886-1952). Kongtrul's students could have included the second and third Getsé Tulkus.

780. Jigmé Tsewang Norbu.

781. Pema Norbu was a graduate of the three-year retreat program at Kongtrul's hermitage of Kunzang Dechen Ösel Ling.

782. A ritual invoking the blessings of the protective deities, the protection of the gods of samsara, and the support of local spirits.

783. In the Tibetan way of calculating age, a person is one year old at birth and adds a year each Losar, or New Year. Thus, a person born shortly before Losar would be considered two years old by Tibetans, but only a few weeks or months old by Westerners.

784. The *gyaldö* ritual is a way of honoring worldly gods and local spirits.

785. The literature dealing with the practices of the protective deities describes certain kinds of stones that are held to contain the "spirit" of a given deity. These stones are installed on shrines as symbolic representations of these deities.

786. Zurchung Sherab Drakpa (1014-1074) was a Nyingma master of the early *kama* lineage.

787. Because the Tenth Situ was the rebirth of Kongtrul's guru the Ninth Situ, Pema Nyinjé Wangpo, it was crucial to Kongtrul that he maintain harmonious relations with the tenth Situ, despite the fact that the personalities involved obviously led to conflict at times.

788. This commentary has, in large part, been translated into English as *The Light of Wisdom*.

789. When the *samaya* connection between master and student is disrupted or impaired, it can have negative effects on both.

790. Because of the large populations in Tibetan monasteries, one of the most common forms of support was for patrons to sponsor tea and food, which would be served during group rituals. This custom originated in India when, even during the Buddha's time, rulers and other wealthy patrons of the Buddhist teachings would sponsor meals, in return for which members of the monastic community would give teachings to the patrons.

791. The breaking of *samaya* is held to have very serious consequences. Those who do so may, in the worst cases, be reborn as demons whose activity is one of fomenting further disharmony by influencing others to break their *samaya* commitments.

792. The residence of the ruling family in Dergé.

793. Empowerments given in more private circumstances were more elaborate and involved often lengthy explanations by the master conferring the transmission. Those performed in public were usually abbreviated and focused on the conferral of blessings; this would be more practical, given that the majority of those receiving a public empowerment would be uneducated, even illiterate.

794. A kind of amulet used in the preparation of treasure vases; *yaksha* spirits are associated with the principle of prosperity.

795. The phrase "liberation on sight" (Tib. *thong-dröl*) is sometimes used to refer to extremely large hangings, called *thangka*s, which depict deities or great masters. These can cover an entire wall of a building (in some cases, an entire hillside) and are only put on display during particular holy festivals.

796. The main monastery of the Ngor branch of the Sakya school was located south of Zhigatsé, in the central province of Tsang. The office of abbot rotated among the representatives of four noble houses—Thartsé, Luding, Phendé, and Khangsar (not the same clan that included the patrons of Palpung Monastery).

797. These "accounts of teachings received" (Tib. *thob-yik*) by masters are very useful as historical sources, to establish lineages and determine dates when other masters lived. Such lists can be enormous; the late Dudjom Rinpoché of the Nyingma School left a three-volume record of the transmissions he received in that lifetime.

798. Certain *terma*s are initially discovered and then concealed again, to be rediscovered when circumstances are more propitious. This particular *terma* was originally revealed by Jomo Menmo (1248-1283), a woman *tertön*, who concealed it again until it was rediscovered by Jamyang Khyentsé Wangpo in the nineteenth century.

799. The essential mantra in full is *Om vajra kili kilaya sarwa vighnan bam hum phat.*

800. Orgyen Lingpa (b. 1323) was a *tertön* who discovered *The Account of Padma* and other chronicles of early Tibetan history.

801. Mipham Gyatso (1846-1912), also known as Jamgön Ju Mipham Namgyal Gyatso, or Jamyang Namgyal Gyatso, was the greatest Nyingma scholar and writer of recent times. Among other masters, he studied with Kongtrul, Jamyang Khyentsé Wangpo, and the great Nyingma master Paltrul Rinpoché, Orgyen Jigmé Chökyi Wangpo (1808-1887). Mipham's writings, in more than twenty volumes, cover a vast range of topics and continue to be standard sources for scholastic study in the Nyingma School.

802. The Twelfth Dalai Lama, Thrinlé Gyatso (1856-1875).

803. These "precious pills" (Tib. *rinchen rilbu*) are a highly esteemed medicine.

804. Thrinlé Gyatso died in 1875 at the young age of twenty.

805. Lakes, mountains, and other features of the natural world can be imbued with the "spirits" of local gods; this concept predates the introduction of Buddhism into Tibet.

806. There is a Lhatrul line of incarnations associated with the Nyingma monastery of Palyul; the first Lhatrul, Pema Garwang Tendzin (1852-1935), was the fourth holder of the abbatial throne of Darthang Monastery, a Nyingma center in Golok Province; his rebirth, the Second Lhatrul, Lhundrup Gyatso, was born in 1939. The second Lhatrul incarnation to whom Kongtrul refers may be the Lhalung Sungtrul incarnation of the *tertön* Pema Lingpa (1450-1521); in 1876, this would have been the eighth incarnation, Tenpai Nyima (1843-1891).

807. During Kongtrul's lifetime, the *tulku* was the Eighth Sang-gyé Nyenpa.

808. These are a group of legendary masters from the Indian Buddhist tradition, who lived during the flowering of the tantric teachings in that country. Information on

the lives of such semi-mythic figures is sketchy. See *Buddha's Lions: The Lives of the Eighty-Four Siddhas* and *Masters of Mahamudra: Songs and Histories of the Eighty-Four Buddhist Siddhas.*

809. The general administrator of Palpung Monastery.

810. The tenth day of each lunar month is considered especially sacred, and it is common for ceremonies to be held to commemorate it.

811. Presumably to provide Kongtrul with the necessary authority to direct this important government project.

812. Mount Kailash, a holy mountain in western Tibet and an important site of pilgrimage, has a distinctive dome-shaped peak, reminiscent of certain styles of stupas.

813. That is, forehead, throat, and heart center.

814. The mantra translates roughly as "I confer the empowerment of enlightened form," and similar mantras would have been uttered concerning the principles of speech and mind. The act of Guru Rinpoché touching the urn to Khyentsé Rinpoché's body while reciting these mantras constitutes a process of empowerment.

815. The Tibetan idiom (*lha bap*) here means that Khyentsé Rinpoché will be imbued with Guru Rinpoché's blessings, as though being "taken over."

816. The Moktsa incarnations are among the most important associated with Kathok Monastery. The First Moktsa, Namkha Chöwang, who was born in the early seventeenth century, was a teacher of the famous Getsé Mahapandita, the first Getsé *tulku* of Kathok Monastery. One of Getsé Mahapandita's students was the Second Moktsa, Chöying Dorjé, who in turn was one of Jamyang Khyentsé Wangpo's gurus; the Third Moktsa was Jigdral Thutop Dorjé. Kongtrul's students could have included the second and third Moktsa *tulkus*. The Fourth Moktsa was Jigdral Chökyi Langpo; the present incarnation, the Fifth Moktsa Rinpoché, Jigdral Choklé Namgyal, is spearheading efforts to restore Kathok Monastery in the wake of its destruction during the Cultural Revolution. With the support of the late Sixteenth Chagdud Tulku, Pema Gargyi Wangchuk (1930-2002), Moktsa Rinpoché has also founded a branch of Kathok at Pharping in the Kathmandu Valley of Nepal.

817. The Ninth Pawo, Tsuklak Nyinjé (d. 1911).

818. This has been translated as *Jamgön Kongtrul's Retreat Manual.*

819. That is, the Thartsé Pönlop of Ngor Monastery, Jamyang Loter Wangpo (1847-1914), who is mentioned later in Kongtrul's autobiography. He was one of Jamyang Khyentsé Wangpo's closest students and helped his master compile both The Compendium of All Sadhanas and The Compendium of All Classes of Tantra.

820. The fifth Dzogchen incarnation, Thupten Chökyi Dorjé (1872-1935), who would have been only five or six years old at this time.

821. In its most elaborate form, the empowerment for the Kalachakra cycle takes five days to confer.

822. Ceremonies honoring the protective deities would be performed upon the successful conclusion of any major undertaking.

823. Originally founded in Tsang Province in about 1610, Thupten Dorjé Drak was relocated in 1632, when the third Rigdzin incarnation of the Northern Treasures tradition, Ngagi Wangpo (1580-1639), was forced to flee from the ruling faction of Tsang princes. He moved the monastery to a side valley north of the Tsangpo (Brahmaputra) River, and Dorjé Drak became one of the two most important Nyingma monasteries of central Tibet, the other being Mindroling.

824. Tib. *Toché*. A ruler of the *naga*s, who is invoked in rituals to consecrate a site on which a temple or other sacred structure is to be built. Because the *naga*s are held to control the elements and influence both natural events (such as rainfall) and human affairs (such as illnesses), every attempt is made to ensure their cooperation when the environment is disrupted

825. The rituals involved in stupa construction and consecration require a high degree of moral purity on the part of the participants.

826. Salt was used to preserve and prepare corpses for cremation or embalming, and needed to be changed frequently as it desiccated the body and absorbed fluids. Such salt would be distributed to the faithful as a blessing.

827. Kongtrul presumably went there to dispel any possible obstacles to Situ Rinpoché's safe return and so promote the stability of the teachings.

828. These are certain local spirits of Tibet whom Guru Rinpoché bound with oaths that they protect the Buddhist teachings. Part of this binding process involved the master conferring ordination on these spirits as lay Buddhist practitioners (Tib. *genyen*).

829. This would seem to be the Neten Chokling incarnation, born in 1873. There was also a line known as the Tsikhé Chokling incarnations. The present third Neten Chokling incarnation maintains a center in northern India; the second Tsikhé incarnation, the second son of the late Urgyen Tulku Rinpoché, lives in Kathmandu, Nepal and is the father of the rebirth of Dilgo Khyentsé Rinpoché.

830. *Jam* is the seed syllable (the symbol of speech) of the wealth deity Jambhala; the appearance of these symbols augured well for Kongtrul in his undertakings.

831. The Fifth Dzogchen Rinpoché, Thupten Chökyi Dorjé (1872-1935), who was only a small child at the time.

832. That is, the rebirth of Chokgyur Lingpa.

833. Ngawang Damchö Gyatso, the Dongkam incarnation of the Gelukpa monastery of Dragyap Tashi Chödzong.

834. That is, the Buddha Shakyamuni and the six buddhas preceding him. Three of these are the first three of this age (Shakyamuni usually being counted as the

"fourth buddha"), and three are the last to appear in the preceding age. Relics from all seven of these buddhas are still held to exist.

835. The Jonang School's controversial position on emptiness was partially responsible for its suppression by the Tibetan government.

836. This refers to a topographical formation rather than to a building.

837. Such dreams are considered signs of the energy associated with *dakinis*.

838. Not identified; possibly a female relative of one of the Karmapas.

839. Such physical supports serve to symbolize the principles embodied in the teachings of a *terma* cycle, and are used as central objects on shrines and foci for meditation.

840. The Eighth Zhamar (1695-1732).

841. That is, the original Sang-gyé Nyenpa, the Kagyü Mahamudra master Tashi Paljor (1445-1510).

842. A medicinal herb that is used to treat skull fractures, joint pain, and fever due to toxins.

843. Tib. *Dütsenma*. One of the figures depicted as being trampled underfoot by such Anuttarayoga deities as Chakrasamvara and Vajrayogini; she embodies the emotional passions that ordinarily bind one's mind to the cycle of rebirth.

844. All these dream images are indications of Kongtrul's role as a *tertön* and the blessings of *dakinis* sustaining him in carrying out this mission.

845. An important local spirit in eastern Tibet, associated with a major mountain range.

846. Indrabodhi (or Indrabhuti) was the name of several kings of ancient India who became masters of the Vajrayana teachings; see Kongtrul's accounts of his past lives. Saraha was one of the Eighty-Four *Mahasiddhas* of India, famed for his songs of realization that continue to inspire practitioners to this day; see *The Royal Song of Saraha* and *Ecstatic Spontaneity: Saraha's Three Cycles of Doha*.

847. "One taste" (Tib. *ro-chik*) is the term for the third of the four yogas, or levels of realization, in the Mahamudra system of teachings.

848. The term "awareness reaching full expression" (Tib. *rigpa tsépep*) is one of the four levels of realization—the "four visions" (Tib. *nangwa zhi*) of the Dzogchen approach. In the *trekchö* system of practice, it is the second of these four visions.

849. The *tertön* Drimé Kunga was born in 1357.

850. The flourishing of the Buddhist tradition adn the collective merit of beings in the worldare held to be factors that contribute to a given spiritual master's longevity.

851. A form of Guru Rinpoché ("The Lake-Born Vajra").

852. This is Kongtrul's birthplace.

853. A local spirit.

854. The *terma* cycle The Trilogy of the Two Doctrines of the Guru (Tib. *Lama Tennyi*

Korsum) was originally discovered by the *tertön* Gya Lotsawa Dorjé Zangpo; the reconcealed *terma* was discovered anew by Jamyang Khyentsé Wangpo.

855. A holy site near the border between southeastern Tibet and the Indian state of Arunchal Pradesh.

856. This is likely a reference to a naturally occurring mineral or medicinal substance of a vermilion color.

857. Sacred substances are used as "starters"—which can be preserved over many years, even centuries—to consecrate larger quantities of herbal preparations that can then be distributed to many people as a way of sharing blessings.

858. That is, sites that by their sacred nature, as physical manifestations of the enlightened activity of buddhas, are akin to nirmanakaya emanations.

859. "The Queen of Supreme Bliss"; the form of Yeshé Tsogyal upon which the practitioner meditates as part of the teachings found in The Heart Drop of Longchenpa.

860. These are the archetypes known as the Eight Manifestations of the Guru (Tib. *Guru Tsengyé*). Padmakara and Padmasambhava are the most common names (both roughly meaning "Lotus Source") and forms associated with Guru Rinpoché. Pema Gyalpo ("Lotus King") is the ideal ruler, while Loden Choksé ("Intelligent Sublime Aspiration") is the model of a perfect student. Dorjé Drollö ("Vajra Paunch") and Seng-gé Dradrok ("Lion's Roar") are wrathful forms to eliminate negativity and remove obstacles to spiritual progress. Shakya Seng-gé ("Lion of the Shakya Clan") represents the monastic ideal, and Nyima Özer ("Rays of the Sun") is the model of a tantric yogi.

861. The second Dabzang *tulku*, who would have been about eleven or twelve at the time.

862. Cycles focusing on wrathful deities include rituals designed to suppress negative forces or influences.

863. This would be the place at which the spiritual energy of the area was most concentrated, and so would be the focus for most of the rituals surrounding this process of consecrating a holy site.

864. See *The Mirage of Nectar* in this volume for details concerning the translator Bairotsana.

865. This is a reference to an Indian Buddhist author named Vajrapani, not to the bodhisattva of spiritual power.

866. When one enters into retreat, there are several levels of boundaries that are established. The outer boundary is the physical area to which the retreatant is retricted; the inner and secret levels of the boundary concern the retreatant's attitude and motivation.

867. This form of Hayagriva is known as the "Secret Sadhana" form adn was transmitted as part of the Shangpa Kagyü School.

868. Shantigarbha was one of the eight Indian *vidyadharas* who transmitted teachings to Guru Rinpoché.

869. Jamyang Gelek was a member of the famous Alo Dilgo clan and had previously received teachings from Kongtrul and completed a three-year retreat program under Kongtrul's direction. He became one of Kongtrul's most trusted attendants.

870. "Tsélé Rinpoché" is presumably the Nyingma master Tsélé Götsangpa Natsok Rangdrol (b. 1608); I have not positively identified "Döndrup Gyalpo," but a Döndrup Chökyi Gyalpo of the Drigung Kagyü School lived from 1668 to 1718, and thus may have met Tsélé Natsok Rangdrol.

871. According to Kongtrul's *Biographies of the Hundred Tertöns*, Zhangtrom was a rebirth of the Tibetan master Nupchen Sang-gyé Yeshé.

872. Tibetans define prayer as falling into two categories—supplication (Tib. *sol-dep*), in which one invokes a source of spiritual refuge and support, and aspiration (Tib. *mön-lam*), in which one directs one's own intention in a positive direction.

873. Tasham Nüden Dorjé was a tertön for in 1665.

874. An aspect of Guru Rinpoché associated with the principle of wealth and prosperity.

875. Another name for Kongtrul's guru Jamyang Khyentsé Wangpo.

876. These are terms for varying degrees in the breaking of one's *samaya*, from the least to the most severe. These are determined in part by the length of time that elapses before the one responsible for the break attempts to repair and restore the connection. In the case of a serious breach, once three years have elapsed it is felt that the breach of *samaya* is irreparable.

877. The Tibetan systems of astrology result regularly in months being "doubled" to give a year of thirteen months, which brings the lunar calendar back in line with the yearly solar cycle; for a number of reasons, there are also "extra" or "missing" days in any given month, for example, two ninth days, or the twelfth day followed by the fourteenth, with the thirteenth day omitted.

878. Tibetans believe that a violent death can result in one's consciousness taking rebirth as a vengeful spirit.

879. Guru Rinpoché left Tibet in order to tame the demons of the island of Chamara to the southwest and prevent their invading our human realm.

880. Not identified; possibly the eleventh-century Sarma translator Getsul Khyundrak.

881. Probably a reference to a form of the feminine protective deity Shridevi.

882. The last three figures mentioned are protective deities.

883. That is, the Sakya and Jonang master Sazang Mati Panchen Lodrö Gyaltsen (1294-1376).

884. The central transmission of the Shangpa Kagyü School founded by Khyungpo Naljor is that of The Deities of the Five Classes of Tantra (Tib. *Gyüdé Lha-nga*),

based on a tantra called *The Ocean of Jewels* (Tib. *Rinchen Gyatso*). Khyungpo Naljor received this transmission from his master Vajrasana in India (*Like An Illusion: Lives of the Shangpa Kagyu Masters*, p. 52), but the text of the tantra itself is no longer extant in either Sanskrit or Tibetan. The mandala of the Deities of the Five Classes of Tantras, in fact, integrates the mandalas of the five major cycles of the Anuttarayoga class, the highest of the four classes of tantra recognized by the Sarma Schools—the five being Guhyasamaja, Mahamaya, Hevajra, Chakrasamvara, and Vajrabhairava.

885. That is, the Buddha Shakyamuni and Padmakara.

886. Sachen Kunga Nyingpo (1092-1158), the founding father of the Sakya School.

887. Lekden is considered the "original" of the protective *mahakala* deities, from which the other forms are derived.

888. Gemang Monasery was a branch of the Nyingma monastery of Dzogchen.

889. The third Kuchen, Orgyen Do-Ngak Chökyi Nyima (1854-1906).

890. It was customary to have a group of monks read volumes of the Kangyur aloud as a protective blessing, particularly at the outset of a major project.

891. "Orgyen Who Overwhelms the Phenomena World with Splendor." A form of Guru Rinpoché in which he sits in a loose crosslegged posture with his right hand brandishing a vajra and his left cradling a skull cup containing a vase in his lap. This is the form depicted in the famous Ngadrama statue that Kongtrul saw at Samyé Monastery during the winter of 1857-1858.

892. The *dakinis* are entrusted with the safeguarding of the Vajrayana teachings, so their blessings would be invoked at the outset of the transmission.

893. This is most probably the second Dezhung Lungrik *tulku*, Nyendrak Lungrik Nyima (c. 1840-1898).

894. The period following the winter solstice.

895. "Arrogant ones" (Tib. *drek-pa*) is a general term for the gods and demons of cyclic existence.

896. A sixteenth century *tertön*.

897. These seven modes are those of *kama*, earth *termas* (*sa-ter*), reconcealed *termas* (*yang-ter*), *termas* of enlightened intent (*gong-ter*), recollections (*jé-dren*), pure visions (*dak-nang*), and oral lineages (*nyen-gyü*). Jamyang Khyentsé Wangpo was remarkable for having received all seven kinds of transmissions in one lifetime.

898. The sense of this citation is that one must value something in order to be worthy of it.

899. These are the ritual garments worn during a *homa*, or fire ritual.

900. A Kagyü scholar who was the author, among other works, of several commentaries on the Six Yogas of Naropa and associated practices. He was also a holder of the *terma* lineage of Chokgyur Lingpa (which he received from the *tertön*'s

two sons, Tsewang Drakpa and Tsewang Norbu) and the abbot of one of Chokgyur Lingpa's three monasteries.

901. During a *drupchen*, participants maintain shifts throughout the day and night, so that at least a few people are continuously reciting the mantra of the deity that is the focus of the ritual.

902. A graduate of Kongtrul's retreat program at Kunzang Dechen Ösel Ling.

903. Drenpa Namkha was a Bönpo master who became a student of Guru Rinpoché and a translator of Buddhist works. The reference to him as Yeshé Tsogyal's sister seems to be symbolic rather than historical.

904. One of the deities of the Eight Commands cycle, Vajra Amrita (Tib. *Dorjé Dütsi* or *Dütsi Yönten*) is associated with the principle of enlightened qualities in general, and the consecration of medicines in particular.

905. One of the ten wrathful deities associated with the ten directions (four cardinal, four intercardinal, zenith, and nadir), Amritakundali (Tib. *Dütsi Khyilwa*) is often invoked at the outset of major rituals to eliminate any negative influence.

906. Humkara (Tib. *Humdzé*) is the name of another of the ten wrathful deities, but also that of one of the eight Indian *mahasiddha*s who taught Padmakara. It is not clear whether the reference here is to incense prepared by a method that focuses on the practice of the deity or one that was developed by the master.

907. A Sanskrit term for alcohol, used as a code word in the tantras to refer to the preparation of consecrated medicines, of which alcohol was a consituent. The ritual use of alcohol (or any other normally suspect substances or activities) in Vajrayana practice was not taken as license; certainly in monastic settings, the function was largely symbolic.

908. The Tibetan lunar calendar requires an extra month to be inserted every thirty-three months, in order to bring it back into line with the solar year. See *Tibetan Astrology*, p. 153.

909. That is, the first *drupchen* ritual, based on The Heart Drop of the Exalted Goddess of Immortality cycle; the eighth, based on the Black Krodhi cycle of Nyang; and the tenth, based on The Gathering of All the Dakinis' Secrets.

910. Amitayus, the white Tara, and the goddess Ushnishavijaya.

911. Located more than two hundred kilometers southwest of Dergé, Riwoché Tsuklakhang was a Taklung Kagyü monastery founded in 1276 by Sang-gyé Ön Drakpa Pal (1251-1296).

912. Thrangu Monastery was an important Kagyü institution in eastern Tibet.

913. Tertön Sögyal (1856-1926), also known as Lerab Lingpa or Nyala Sögyal, was a teacher to the Thirteenth Dalai Lama, Lobzang Thupten Gyatso. Lerab Lingpa's rebirths include Sogyal Rinpoché, author of *The Tibetan Book of Living and Dying* and one of the most active teachers of Tibetan Buddhism in the West, and Khenchen Jigmé Phuntsok Jungné (b. 1936), who directs a thriving community

of scholars and practitioners at his center in the Sertar Valley of Golok in northeastern Tibet.

914. This was the First Drupwang Tsoknyi, who was an emanation of both Milarepa's disciple Rechunga and the *tertön* Ratna Lingpa. The present incarnation, the Third Drupwang Tsoknyi, was born in 1966, a son of the Kagyu-Nyingma master Tulku Urgyen Rinpoché.

915. One of the four major branches of the Kagyü School, the Barom Kagyü was founded by Darma Wangchuk (1127-1199/1200).

916. The printing house near Dergé Gönchen, established in 1729 by King Tenpa Tsering, became famous for its excellent standards of editing and production, as well as for the eclectic range of its publications.

917. In Tibetan astrology, this term refers to one of six days in any given lunar month— three during the waxing phase of the moon (the third, eighth, or thirteenth) and three during the waning phase (the eighteenth, twenty-third, or twenty-eighth). Thus, the first victorious day was the third of the month.

918. That is, the Karmapa, Situ Rinpoché, Zhamar Rinpoché, Gyaltsap Rinpoché, and Drukchen Rinpoché.

919. These practices and rituals were further observances for the benefit of the deceased Rigdzin Drölma's consciousness.

920. The Ninth Pawo incarnation, Tsuklak Nyinjé (d. 1911).

921. One of eight traditional stupa designs commemorating major events in the Buddha's life, the stupa of enlightenment is connected with his attainment of enlightenment under the bodhi tree at Bodh Gaya in India.

922. An ancient Indian king and Vajrayana Buddhist master; see Kongtrul's accounts of his past lives.

923. This is a generic term for techniques relating to advanced yogic practices that harness one's subtle energies and lead to practice with a sexual consort.

924. A place in south India where Nagarjuna lived and meditated; also the site of his death. In *Indian Buddhist Pandits*, Lobsang N. Tsonawa (p. 116, n. 39) equates this with present-day Nagarjunakonda in Andhra Pradesh.

925. Aryadeva was an Indian Buddhist master, the main student of the great philosopher Nagarjuna; see Kongtrul's account of his past lives.

926. Skt. *Chatuh-shataka*. A commentary by the third century Indian Buddhist philosopher Aryadeva on his master Nagarjuna's *Source Verses on Wisdom* (Skt. *Prajnaparamita-mula-madhyamaka-karika*).

927. That is, the Tenth Situ, Pema Kunzang Chögyal.

928. In the somewhat feudal system of Tibetan society, it was often necessary to pay a substantial sum to the government of an area in which an incarnation was reborn, to recompense the local authorities for the loss when the incarnation and his (or, in rare cases, her) family were taken to the incarnation's monastery.

929. Mipham Rinpoché authored a two-volume commentary on *The Kalachakra Tantra.*
930. That is, the new Öntrul incarnation mentioned earlier.
931. There were two lines of *tulkus* recognized following the death of Chokgyur Lingpa in 1870. The Tsikhé incarnation was Könchok Gyurmé Tenpai Gyalsten; the Neten incarnation was Pema Gyurmé Thekchok Tenpai Gyaltsen (1873?-1927). It is not clear which incarnation Kongtrul met at this point.
932. The Khamtrul incarnations are associated with the Drukpa Kagyü School. This would have been the Sixth Khamtrul, Mipham Tenpai Nyima (1849-1907). The present incarnation, the Ninth Khamtrul, was born in India in 1980.
933. Commonly known in Tibetan as *Tertön Gyatsa*, this work is included in the opening volume of Kongtrul's *Treasury of Precious Hidden Teachings.*
934. Khakhyab Dorjé (1871-1922), who at that time would have been about sixteen years of age.
935. A ritual to counter the effects of moral contamination or other negative influences.
936. This would be the thirteenth day of the first month, but considering that the tenth day is referred to later in the same paragraph, this might be in error, the second "victorious day," or the eighth day, being intended.
937. The title Jé-ön Tulku is the higher honorific form of Öntrul, and here refers to the fact that the first Chöwang Tulku had been a nephew of the Twelfth Karmapa, Jangchub Dorjé, and so the line of Chöwang incarnations were still considered "relatives" of the line of Karmapas. This Chöwang Tulku was, in fact, the nephew of the Fourteenth Karmapa, Thekchok Dorjé.
938. The most well-known text on the "graduated path" (*lam-rim*) in the Kagyü School, authored by Gampopa (1079-1159). Several English translations have appeared; see *The Jewel Ornament of Liberation* and *The Jewel Ornament of Liberation: The Wish-Fulfilling Gem of the Noble Teachings.*
939. These are all stages in the most elaborate form of the Kalachakra empowerment.
940. Orgyenpa Rinchen Pal (1229/30-1309) was a student of the Second Karmapa, Karma Pakshi (1204-1283).
941. These are all transmissions included in Kongtrul's collection, *The Treasury of Spiritual Advice*, which he began conferring at the beginning of the third month. The "eight practicing lineages" of Tibet are the Nyingmapa, Sakyapa, Kadampa (including the "new Kadampa," or Gelukpa), Marpa Kagyü, Shangpa Kagyü, the system of Pacification and Severance, the Vajra Yoga system, and the system of Approach and Accomplishment.
942. It is traditional to conclude a major cycle of transmissions with a teaching that focuses on longevity, in order to establish circumstances of auspicious interdependence.
943. The thirtieth, or last, day of a Tibetan lunar month.

944. This is the Mindroling tradition of Vajrasattva, which Kongtrul placed at the beginning of the empowerments in his *Treasury of Precious Hidden Teachings*; this cycle is highly regarded as a model for all Mahayoga practices.

945. Tib. *Yangchenma*. Sarasvati is a feminine deity of wisdom, the consort of Manjushri.

946. That is, in Kongtrul's transmission of his *Treasury of Precious Hidden Teachings* to Karmapa.

947. Because of the constraints on time and energy that are involved in the conferral of large collections of teachings, it would often be the case that one master would prepare for and confer the empowerments, while another master would confer the oral transmissions (often while the primary master was preparing for the next set of empowerments).

948. A *sadhana* combining the forms of several deities in a single format, such as a practice focusing on all Three Roots of Vajrayana practice.

949. "The Physician of Dakpo"; another name for Gampopa, who was a doctor before he became a monk and began his spiritual training under Kadampa masters..

950. Tib. *sé-pho*. This term refers to the process of blending one's pure awareness with basic space and transferring that awareness into the utterly lucid state that is the true nature of reality.

951. That is, the birth of the Eleventh Situ, Pema Wangchok Gyalpo, who lived from 1886 to 1952.

952. That is, the tomb of the previous Situ, the tenth incarnation Pema Kunzang Chögyal (1854-1885).

953. That is, the twenty-third of the fourth month.

954. A class of goddesses in the retinue of Vajrakila.

955. That is, the Eleventh Situ, Pema Wangchuk Gyalpo.

956. The formal acceptance of someone into the Buddhist tradition, usually performed in conjunction with the conferral of the vow of refuge.

957. The waning phase of the moon was more favorable for rituals invoking wrathful energy.

958. Both the woodblock and the printed edition have "Hare" in error. The Iron Hare was the following year, 1890-1891, for which both versions read (correctly) "Hare."

959. An affiliate of Kathok Monastery.

960. These are all teachings associated with the Nyingma masters Longsal Nyingpo (1625-1692) and his teacher Duddul Dorjé (1615-1672).

961. Desi Sang-gyé Gyatso (1653-1705) served as chief secular minister under the Fifth Dalai Lama, and then as regent following the Great Fifth's death. His writings include works on sciences such as astrology and medicine; his *Supplement* is a commentary on the medical tantra *The Tantra of Pith Instructions*.

962. Kongtrul's grandnephew, the son of his niece Rigdzin Drölma.

963. Given that the practices Kongtrul uses at this point are concerned with promoting longevity, it is clear that there were signs that Jamyang Khyentsé Wangpo was approaching the end of his life.

964. I.e., Khyentsé Rinpoché somehow reinstated these lines and passed them to Kongtrul; see below, on 186b, where Kongtrul gives these two transmissions to the vajra master from the meditation center and others.

965. One of the graduates from Kongtrul's retreat center, mentioned by Tashi Chöphel in his account of Kongtrul's students.

966. The purpose of such a ritual would be to offset any negative effects of infractions of *samaya* that Kongtrul or others might have committed with respect to Jamyang Khyentsé Wangpo.

967. The two traditions of the bodhisattva vow derive from the Indian Buddhist tradition. The "lineage of extensive activity" originated with Maitreya, the bodhisattva of loving kindess, and passed through the Indian master Asanga; the "lineage of profound view" originated with Manjushri, the bodhisattva of wisdom, and passed through the Madhayamaka philosopher Nagarjuna.

968. That is, Jamyang Loter Wangpo (1847-1914).

969. This refers to the period of forty-nine days that is traditionally observed as the period for commemorative rites following someone's death.

970. Also known as Jangchub Sempa Lodrö Zangpo.

971. This is a twenty-four-hour ordination consisting of eight vows of abstaining from taking life, stealing, sexual activity, lying, taking intoxicants, wearing adornments, singing and dancing and using high seats, and eating after midday. Although most, if not all, of the participants in this consecration process would have been fully ordained monks, the temporary ordination provided an additional element of ritual purity.

972. The ashes of a person's cremated remains are often mixed with the clay used to cast *tsa-tsa*s, as a way of conferring blessing on the deceased or (in the present case) conferring the deceased master's blessing on the tomb.

973. According to *A Garland of Immortal Wish-fulfilling Trees*, p. 98 (where the year of death is given as 1891 rather than 1892), he passed away on the twenty-second day of the fifth month.

974. Tib. *Shémar*. An aspect of the wrathful deity Yamantaka.

975. This is the most extensive of three commentaries on Mahamudra by the Ninth Karmapa, Wangchuk Dorjé.

976. Rinchen Namgyal (1318-1388) was one of Butön Rinchendrup's main students and the author of an instruction manual based on his master's teachings on *The Kalachakra Tantra*.

977. The Ngor Pönlop was Jamyang Loter Wangpo (1847-1914), a master of the

intimate Lopshé transmission of the Sakya School's Lamdré lineage. Jamyang Loter Wangpo was one of Jamyang Khyentsé Wangpo's main student, and helped his master compile two large collections of Vajrayana teachings, *The Compendium of All Sadhanas (Druptap Kuntü)* and The Compendium of All Classes of Tantra (*Gyüdé Kuntü*). See Appendix.

978. These are the major monasteries of the Gelukpa School, and became powerful forces on the Tibetan political scene: Ganden, founded in 1409 by Tsongkhapa Lobzang Drakpa (1357-1419), who was its first throne holder; Drepung, founded in 1416 by Tsongkhapa's student Tashi Palden (1379-1449); and Sera, founded in 1419 by Jamchen Chöjé Shakya Yeshé (1354-1435), another of Tsongkhapa's students.

979. Kyodrak was a monastery of the Barom Kagyü School in eastern Tibet. Kongtrul himself authored the *guru sadhana* focusing on Milarepa, as well as the empowerment manual; both texts are found in Volume 1 of Kongtrul's collected works, *The Treasury of Extensive Teachings* (also known as *The Extraordinary Treasury*).

980. That is, the young Eleventh Tai Situ, Pema Wangchok Gyalpo, who would have been about seven or eight years old at this time.

981. This would have been the tenth Trungpa incarnation, Chökyi Nyima.

982. Kongtrul's biography of Jamyang Khyentsé Wangpo is included in his collected writings, *The Extraordinary Treasury*.

983. The symbol of crossed vajras denotes stability and longevity.

984. Ghantapada was one of the Eighty-Four *Mahasiddha*s of the Indian tradition of Vajrayana Buddhism.

985. The stage of completion according to *The Guhyasamaja Tantra*.

986. That is, without separate rituals of authorization having to be performed; when one had received the main cycle of empowerments, the more minor transmissions for the protective deities were often considered to be included. In this regard, Paltrul Rinpoché of the Nyingma School once remarked that having received the empowerment for the ruler on the throne, he had no need to for the empowerment for the watchdog by the threshold!

987. That is, the twenty-eighth.

988. That is, Tertön Sögyal (1856-1926).

989. The seven-point format is one of the most popular forms of *lojong*, or mental training, based on a work by the early Kadampa master Chekawa Yeshé Dorjé (1102-1176). Kongtrul's commentary on this form of mental training has been translated as *The Great Path of Awakening*. Another treatment, based on the explanations of the late Dilgo Khyentsé Rinpoché, has been published as *Enlightened Courage*.

990. One common way to encourage someone in Tibet to write something for you

was to offer them the paper, pens, and ink, which were more valuable commodities than in our culture.

991. The seven qualities of a higher state of rebirth are: good family, fine body, long life, freedom from illness, good fortune, wealth, and great wisdom. The four great influences are those of living in a conducive environment, relying on holy people, formulating aspirations, and gathering merit.

992. Presumably he is referring to the fact that the Kongpo Bamteng Tulku, whose title he received, was no major figure in the hierarchy of things, and to the fact that, in his opinion, he was only given the title for essentially political reasons.

993. This refers to the lay and monastic ordinations that pertain to the Hinayana level of the Buddhist teachings. They emphasize harmlessness and nonviolence, as means to purify one of negative karma and reinforce positive tendencies that lead to higher state of rebirth and the liberation of an *arhat*, a state of personal salvation from suffering.

994. The four "defeats" that destroy a monastic ordination are to murder a human being, to steal anything of real value, to engage in sexual activity with a partner, or to lie about one's spiritual attainment.

995. According to Gampopa, these four are "(i) to deceive spiritual teachers and persons worthy or worship; (ii) to make others feel ashamed without cause; (iii) out of spite to say improper things to a Bodhisattva who has adopted an enlightened attitude; and (iv) to behave meanly to sentient beings." (*The Jewel Ornament of Liberation*, H.V. Guenther, trans., p. 145)

996. Although both versions of the text consulted have *dus gsum gang rung gi* ("in any one of the three times"), the context strongly suggests the alternative reading of *dug gsum gang rung gi* ("of one or another of the three emotional poisons")—that is, attachment-desire, aversion, and ignorance.

997. This field of study concerns the process of cognition, of how we can gain accurate knowledge of things through either direct experience or inference.

998. Depictions of such "mansions" constitute the primary element in mandalas, whether painted or drawn in colored sands; the study of their traditional proportions and layout was important for the preparation of such mandalas for use during rituals. Occasionaly, three-dimensional models would be constructed.

999. These are two Sanskrit lexicons by Indian authors—the *Amarakosha* by the sixth-century Buddhist author Amarasimha and its commentary, the *Amarakosha-tika-kamadhenu* by Subhutichandra. *The Treasury of Immortality* was the most popular of the Sanskrit lexicons studied by Tibetans, because its Indian author was a Buddhist and its commentary followed the Chandra system of Sanskrit grammar. The translator Chökyong Zangpo (1441-1527) of the Zhalu branch of the Sakya School produced the first complete bilingual translations of these works.

1000. The first *tertön*, who lived from 1000 to 1080.

1001. Chökyi Drakpa (1595-1659) was the twenty-first abbot of Drigung Thil Monastery and the first Chungtsang incarnation of the Drigung Kagyü School. He was a student of Jatsön Nyingpo (1585-1656) and revealed teachings classified as "pure visions" (*dak-nang*).

1002. These are: Sang-gyé Lingpa (1340-1396), Dorjé Lingpa (1346-1405), Ratna Lingpa (1403-1479), Pema Lingpa (1450-1521), and Karma Lingpa (fourteenth century).

1003. Rigdzin Nyida Longsal was a *tertön* active in the seventeenth century.

1004. The fourth Dzigar incarnation (1740-1798), also known as Dorjé Drakpo Tsal.

1005. Sharawa Yönten Drak (1070-1141) was an early Kadampa master and a teacher of the First Karmapa, Düsum Khyenpa.

1006. Putowa (or Potowa) Rinchen Sal (1027-1105) was one of the "three brothers"—the main students of Dromtön Gyalwai Jungné.

1007. Chégom Sherab Dorjé was an early Kadampa master.

1008. Dolpawa Sherab Gyatso (1059-1131) was student of Putowa Rinchen Sal.

1009. The Kadampa master Naktso Lotsawa Tsulthrim Gyalwa (1011-1064) was a student of Atisha and one of the early translators of the Sarma Schools.

1010. This is most likely a reference to the early Phadru Kagyü master Kharakpa Drakpa Gyaltsen (1186-1271).

1011. Gyergompa Zhönnu Drakpa (1090-1171) was a Kadampa master who studied with Jayulwa Zhönnu Ö (1075-1138); the latter was also one of the masters with whom Gampopa studied before he met Milarepa.

1012. Langri Thangpa Dorjé Seng-gé (1054-1123), a student of Putowa Rinchen Sal, was an important Kadampa master in the lineage of the mental training (*lojong*) teachings.

1013. Khampa Lungpa Shakya Yönten (1023-1115) was a student of Dromtön Gyalwai Jungné (1004/5-1064), who in turn was Atisha's foremost Tibetan student and the founder of the Kadampa School.

1014. That is, the Gelukpa School founded by Tsongkhapa Lobzang Drakpa.

1015. The Kagyü School includes four major and eight minor branches. The four major branches were founded by masters who were either students of Gampopa or of his nephew Dakpo Gomtsul (1116-1169)—the Karma (or Kamtsang) Kagyü by the First Karmapa, Düsum Khyenpa (1110-1193), the Barom Kagyü by Darma Wangchuk (1127-1199/1200), the Tsalpa Kagyü by Zhang Tsöndrü Drakpa (1123-1193), and the Phadru Kagyü by Phamo Druppa Dorjé Gyalpo (1110-1170). The eight lesser branches were founded by eight of Phamo Druppa's students—the Drigung Kagyü by Jikten Sumgön (1143-1217); the Drukpa Kagyü by Lingjé Repa Pema Dorjé (1128-1188) (this branch includes the lineages of Yang-gönpa Gönpo Dorjé (1213-1258) and Barawa Gyaltsen Palzang (1310-

1391)); the Taklung Kagyü by Taklung Thangpa Tashi Pal (1142-1210); the Throphu Kagyü by the brothers Gyaltsa Rinchen Gön (1118-1180) and Kunden Repa (1148-1217), and their nephew Throphu Lotsawa Jampa Pal (twelfth century); the Marpa (or Martsang) Kagyü by Marpa Druptop Sherab Seng-gé, the Yelpa Kagyü by Druptop Yeshé Tsekpa (also known as Sang-gyé Yelpa, b. 1134), the Gyazang Kagyü by Zarawa Kalden Yeshé Seng-gé (d. 1207), and the Shuksep Kagyü by Gyergom Chenpo Zhönnu Drakpa (1090-1171). A number of these branches are no longer extant as distinct schools, having been absorbed into one or another of the other branches. For two informative essays, see E. Gene Smith, "Golden Rosaries of the Bka' brgyud Schools," in *Among Tibetan Texts: History and Literature of the Himalayan Plateau*, pp. 39-51, and Lobsang P. Lhalungpa, "The History of the Kagyupa Order," in *The Life of Gampopa, The Incomparable Dharma Lord of Tibet*, pp. 117-139.

1016. One of Khyungpo Naljor's main Indian gurus.

1017. Rahula was one of the Indian gurus of the Tibetan master Khyungpo Naljor, founder of the Shangpa Kagyü School.

1018. Jamyang Gönpo was a master of the Severance lineage who studied under Gyalwa Döndrup, one of the sons of the Tibetan woman master Machik Lapdrön, who was largely responsible for codifying the Severance teachings in the twelfth century.

1019. Tib. *Shéja Kunkhyab*, also known as *The Treasury of the Knowable (Shéja Dzö)*.

1020. A common theme in Buddhism is that the Buddhist teachings are "positive at the outset, in the interim, and in the final outcome."

1021. There is a tradition, going back to the Indian Buddhist university of Vikramashila, that an authentic Buddhist work should follow a standard format. The elements mentioned here are part of that format.

1022. An epithet for the Atiyoga section of the Dzogchen approach.

1023. Tib. *Kagyü Ngakdzö*.

1024. The tantras of the Anuttarayoga class are classified into three categories—father tantra, mother tantra, and nondual tantra. Father tantras emphasize the lucidity aspect of mind and the transformation of anger and aggression; mother tantras place more emphasis on the aspect of emptiness and the transformation of desire and attachment; nondual tantra gives equal emphasis to both aspects of the nature of mind, and deals with the transformation of ignorance. The category to which a given tantra is assigned may vary from one school to another.

1025. Tib. *Dorjé Denzhi*. A masculine deity of the mother tantra section of the Anuttarayoga class.

1026. Tib. *Rinchen Terdzö*.

1027. Earth treasures (Tib. *sa-ter*) are texts or other physical objects concealed in the earth, rock faces, and so forth. See *Hidden Teachings of Tibet*, pp. 77-79.

1028. These three are grouped together as "the three *tertöns*" (Tib. *Tertön Sumtsok*).

1029. Or Nyila (according to Kongtrul's own *Biographies of the One Hundred Revealers of Hidden Teachings*).

1030. Although the way in which *termas* of enlightened intent are discovered seems remarkably similar to the transmission method known as "pure visions" (Tib. *dak-nang*), the distinguishing factor lies in the fact that, in the former case, the teachings is concealed—that is, "planted" in the mindstream of an individual as a latent memory—and entrusted to that individual, so that some future rebirth of that person will be able to access that particular memory and thus "discover the *terma*."

1031. Tib. *Dam-Ngak Dzö*.

1032. The ideal form of transmission is that of a "lineage of meaning," in which the actual experience of spiritual realization is transmitted from master to student; failing that, a transmission of at least the necessary information ("words") ensures that the lineage remains unbroken from generation to generation.

1033. That is, the Gelukpa School founded by Tsongkhapa Lobzang Drakpa (Jé Rinpoché, "The Precious Lord") (1357-1419).

1034. Tib. *Gönpo Driguk*. "The Mahakala Wielding a *Kartari* Knife."

1035. Tsurtön Wang-gi Dorjé (eleventh to twelfth centuries) was one of Marpa the Translator's four principal students, the others being Milarepa (1052-1135), Ngoktön Chöku Dorjé, and Marpa Dowa Chökyi Wangchuk (1042-1136).

1036. Zhang Tsöndrü Drakpa (1123-1193), who founded the Tsalpa Kagyü, one of the four main branches of the Kagyü School.

1037. Nyedo Sönam Pal (1217-1277) was a master of the later transmission of the Severance teachings.

1038. Tib. *Damchö Dükyi Chöyul*.

1039. Tib. *Dorjé Shuk*.

1040. Tib. *tummo*. The "inner heat"; an advanced Vajrayana practice of the stage of completion, and one of the Six Yogas.

1041. Tib. *Thunmong Mayinpai Dzö*. This constitutes Kongtrul's collected writings that do not fit into any of his other collections, and is also known as *The Treasury of Extensive Teachings* (Tib. *Gyachen Kadzö*).

1042. A current edition of Kongtrul's collected writings (Paro, 1976) fills some twenty volumes.

1043. Both of these served as historical influences on the development of Tibetan astrology.

1044. That is, physical, verbal, and mental isolation from involvement in distracting activities.

1045. That is, Dakpo Lhajé, or Gampopa.

1046. This is a general category for projects such as construction, printing, and so forth, that Kongtrul either commissioned or directed.

1047. These founders are the figures most associated with these eight lineages—Guru Rinpoché (Nyingma), Atisha (Kadampa), Sachen Kunga Nyingpo (Sakya), Marpa Lotsawa (Marpa Kagyü), Khyungpo Naljor (Shangpa Kagyü), Phadampa Sang-gyé and Machik Lapdrön (Zhijé and Chö), Dolpo Sang-gyé Sherab Gyaltsen (Vajra Yoga), and the *mahasiddha* Orgyenpa (Stages of Approach and Accomplishment for the Three Vajras)

1048. Probably Kashyapa (the buddha prior to Shakyamuni) as the buddha of the past, Shakyamuni as the buddha of the present, and the bodhisattva Maitreya as the buddha of the future.

1049. The two goddesses referred to are White Tara (in her form as the Exalted Goddess of Immortality) and Ushnishavijaya, another deity associated with longevity.

1050. Tib. *Drölma Yizhin Khorlo*. A form of the deity Tara associated with longevity.

1051. Guru Dewachenpo is a form of Guru Rinpoché found in the *terma* cycles of Chokgyur Lingpa.

1052. A style in which the figures and background are all done in gold paint, with other colors used only sparingly for highlighting. Such paintings are considered more valuable, partly due to the amount of gold employed.

1053. A poetic term for the succession of masters in an uninterrupted lineage of transmission.

1054. These cards are often affixed to the tops of *torma*s, when they are covered with parasols of colored silk as adornments.

1055. This is the tomb of Kongtrul's guru, Situ Pema Nyinjé Wangpo.

1056. Such rituals commemorate not the birthdays of masters, but the dates on which they passed away ("attained nirvana").

1057. In honor of the yogic element of the Kagyü School, the example for this having been set by Milarepa ("Mila the Cotton-Clad").

1058. This collection, containing the Kagyü masters' songs of realization, has been translated as *The Rain of Wisdom*.

1059. Kongtrul gives far more detail in his manual describing the meditation center and three-year, three-fortnight retreat program; see *Jamgön Kongtrul's Retreat Manual*.

1060. See *Jamgön Kongtrul's Retreat Manual*, pp. 144-150.

1061. A standard way of classifying the Buddha Shakyamuni's teachings is to divide them into three phases—the three "turnings of the wheel of the Buddhadharma." The first phase was based on the Four Noble Truths (the truths of suffering, the origin of suffering, the cessation of suffering, and the path leading to that cessation). The second phase concerned teachings on *shunyata* ("emptiness") as the true nature of reality. The third and final "turning of the wheel" dealt with definitive statements concerning ultimate reality, and most especially contained teachings on *tathagatagarbha*, the "buddha nature." A question that has been much debated over the centuries has been which teachings the Buddha intended to be definitive—that is, taken "as given," without interpretation— and which are provisional, and thus open to interpretation. Much of the controversy in the Tibetan traditions has hinged on the question of which category a given teaching should be assigned to.

1062. An epithet of Guru Rinpoché.

1063. That is, the "Lord of Sages," or Buddha Shakyamuni, as the teacher of the sutra approach and Guru Rinpoché, or Padmakara, as the teacher of the tantric approach.

1064. Literally, "goats and sheep herded together."

1065. As is customary in Tibetan works, Kongtrul gives this closing invocation ("May everything be auspicious always!") in Sanskrit.

THE MARVELOUS
GEM-LIKE VISION

An Account of the Passing and Funeral Observances
of the All-Seeing Lord,
the Venerable Jamgön Ngag-gi
Wangchuk Yönten Gyatso

BY NESAR KARMA TASHI CHÖPHEL

[1b]   Namo guru sarvajna-darsha guna samudraya![1]

Although they have primordially discovered the unchanging vajra
     realm, eternal and sacred by its very nature,
they appear in the perceptions of we who are to be guided,
guiding us by seeming to take birth and to die.
I bow to the sublime spiritually exalted beings who perform
     boundless miracles.

Through the force of a single, unfathomable state of timeless
     awareness,
they have the power to extend an instant over an eon,
and through the ten powers[2] they are so very courageous
that they are not subject to defeat in battle with the Lord of Death.

When the merit of those to be guided—which is like a vessel of
     water—is destroyed,

the guides—like reflections of the sun and moon therein—vanish.
In accord with the place and times, their enlightened activities come
    to an end
and for the time being their sublime forms seem to disappear.

[2a]   Nevertheless, until this world of conditioned existence is emptied,
    the motivation and activity of bodhisattvas
    is ceaseless and always amazing,
    so the enlightened activities of venerable gurus continue to flourish.

For the time being, the sun of the rupakaya,[3] this single amazing
    treasury,
is not shining, but has set into the realm of utter lucidity.
At such a time, with the seeds of this wonderful account
I will plant something that will cause the faith of intelligent people to
    grow.

Truly great and spiritually advanced beings—those who are sublime nirmanakaya incarnations—have already, from beginningless time, rid themselves of the habitual patterning that brings about death and rebirth, for they have experienced in full the genuine state of embodiment that is deathless. Nevertheless, though birthless, in the perceptions of other beings they seem to be born; and though deathless, they seem to die and pass away. This serves to inspire those who cling to things as permanent and to encourage them to practice a spiritual discipline. When great beings turn their intention to other concerns that benefit those who are to be guided, [2b] it is their special function that they can withdraw their physical embodiments and pursue other avenues of enlightened activity.[4] Thus, what characterizes these beings is far beyond the scope of an ordinary being's imagination.

Such being the case, in actual fact our holy lord guru[5] had awakened to manifest enlightenment[6] within the basic space of the great buddha Vairochana's inexhaustible timeless awareness. The splendor of his magical emanations, which guide beings in any way necessary, cannot be measured with any accuracy, but is like the gathering of clouds in the upper reaches of worlds throughout the ten directions.[7] He was the exalted Ananda, the foremost among those who received teachings in the presence of the Victorious One. He was the great nirmanakaya emanation and translator Bairotsana, who met Orgyen, the

king of the Buddhadharma. He was these and many others, for he appeared in
the marvelous forms of countless masterful beings on the tenth level of realization, reaching the furthest limits of the paths and levels of realization. He
was the hero Thöpai Dumbu Tsal in the western land of Shantapuri, and in the
future he will awaken to buddhahood as the glorious Adhimukta, in whom the
marvels of the thousand victorious ones of this eon will be realized.[8] He has,
therefore, vanquished the demonic hordes of the Lord of Death and become a
truly perfect buddha.

And that is not all, for Kongtrul Rinpoché's embodiment in this lifetime as
a great and exalted being was prophesied in numerous texts; among all the
notes resounding from the conch shell of the Buddhadharma, these texts that
concern the definitive meaning of the Buddha's teachings are the repositories
of the nectar-like speech of the Victorious One, the Lion of the Shakyas. [3a]
Furthermore, because Kongtrul Rinpoché is imbued with the strength of the
ten powers, he can see that there is real purpose in continuing his presence,
without degeneration or decrepitude, for a long time—throughout this eon, in
fact. So he is certainly someone whose continued presence could not fail to be
of benefit!

All the ways in which he seemed to stay or go, to age and weaken, in this
world were entirely in the perceptions of other beings whom he was to guide.
It is the case with some gurus that they have great qualities but fail to live out
a full life span, or that they enjoy a long life but have no great impact on
nurturing the teachings or other beings through their activities. While this is so
in other cases, our holy guru and glorious protector (whose name it is difficult
for me to utter), this great all-knowing and all-seeing master, was someone
whose longevity and activities seemed to vie to outdo one another. Such a case
as this has never been seen in recent times in Tibet, the Land of Snows, and
discerning people can understand this for themselves by closely examining
Kongtrul Rinpoché's amazing personal history and activities, so there is little
need for me to speak of these matters. You can learn more from the autobiographical accounts of the lord himself, which deal with his outer, inner, and
secret levels of experience, than from this brief account that I have written.

The detailed accounts of Kongtrul Rinpoché's inner and secret levels of
experience show that he upheld the principles of the early masters of the
Kadampa School.[9] All of his qualities were hidden, like a candle burning inside a vase, [3b] and he did not even allude to them obliquely. Rather, he was
always saying things like, "I am a very ordinary person. My destiny is most

likely some lower state of rebirth. I haven't had the slightest hint of any supernormal states of perception, lucid visions, or signs of accomplishment. I have merely undergone an excellent training due to the kindness of my learned and accomplished gurus, but now even that is gone, for I have forgotten it." Speaking in such ways, he adopted a low profile.

Still, when it was appropriate, he would admit to his realization being that of "supreme freedom from elaboration." He would say, "On occasion I have mere glimpses of what it is like to blend mind and sensory appearances of day and night." In actual fact, though, it is certain that Kongtrul Rinpoché truly experienced the realization of the "one taste" of samsara and nirvana, and what more could there be than that to serve as the account of his inner experience?[10]

As for the secret level, this can be ascertained from the few passing references in his extensive autobiography to his visions, to prophecies he received, to his perception of the minds of beings in the intermediate state after death, and so forth, which he tends to mention as though they were simply dream images. In his later years he never slept at all, although it seemed to everyone who was in his presence that he did; this is an authentic sign of his having "blended day and night."

As a matter of fact, I myself heard Kongtrul Rinpoché say, "Even if I am not an actual emanation of Jonang Jetsün Rinpoché, I am certain that it would be all right to consider me as one of his main students, someone for whom he felt great affinity." The student he meant was Taranatha's regent Yeshé Gyatso, whose mindstream was identical to the venerable Taranatha's. [4a] On another occasion Kongtrul Rinpoché said that, in a clear state of visionary experience (not simply a dream), he saw all the subtle channels in his body, filled to overflowing with the Sanskrit vowels and consonants. This is certainly a case of a lofty state of inner experience, for he actually perceived the entire configuration of channels and syllables that constitute the structure of the vajra body.[11]

In his late twenties, Kongtrul Rinpoché underwent a vision in which he journeyed to Zangdok Palri. He spoke to me at length about what happened—how he received blessings and prophecies from the Guru and his consort, but this event is only mentioned briefly in his extensive autobiography.

Kongtrul Rinpoché had a cat that lived with him, of which he was very fond. When it died, he made an offering on the animal's behalf to his refuge lord, Pema Nyinjé, who that very day performed a ritual focusing on the deity

Padmavajra to guide the dead animal's consciousness. Kongtrul Rinpoché said, "The ritual was successful, and thanks indeed to my guru's compassion I have a very clear impression that my cat has definitely achieved a fine human rebirth." I heard him say this and other such things.

Because in the ultimate sense Kongtrul Rinpoché actually dwelled on a level of advanced spiritual development, there should be no need to consider such trifling spiritual experiences, visions, and omens. But I am discussing them, without exaggerating anything, as some small means of nurturing faith in the minds of us spiritually immature people who are preoccupied with things of this world. We common mortals, who are the most ordinary of all and who are subject solely to our confusion, can only assess him on the basis of certain indications [4b] that he saw the world of all appearances and possibilities to be like the play of a dream or an illusion.

Whoever came to see him—no matter how famous, powerful, or wealthy they were—not only did Kongtrul Rinpoché not indulge in flattery to please them, but he found such meetings tedious. Even though they offered him much wealth—many lumps of silver or whatever—he would show no delight, only saying, "They should be given a good blessing cord."[12] When others would say to him, "This is very important," or "This is a nice offering," or "So-and-so has such firm faith in you," he would agree politely that this was so, that such-and such was indeed nice, indicating his pleasure, but by the next day the matter had passed completely from his mind. He never belittled low-born or humble people, and if he even heard of someone being given a bad name by others, for example, it would upset him greatly.

With people of the upper classes, Kongtrul Rinpoché maintained a very dignified and distant manner, never engaging much in conversation with them. But he loved people who were humble and who acted quite naturally without putting on airs. He would chat quite freely with them, giving them his leftover food with his own hands.[13] He was always giving bits of food to birds, dogs, and other animals after blessing these morsels by reciting mantras over them.

His pure perception extended everywhere without bias, so that he would only ever praise anyone, saying "So-and-so is good." Even if someone suspicious and devious came along, Kongtrul Rinpoché would never utter so much as a word of reproach. He would always remark, "Only a buddha can know the true measure of an individual, so what point is there in trying to determine if what we see is the whole picture?" [5a] While in the depths of his heart he was precisely aware of what was true or false, good or bad, no matter what happened—even something that would distress or upset anyone else—he would only say, "Of course this could happen! What might not happen where ordinary circumstances are concerned?" Showing no sign of anxiety, he would show his love all the more.

Other than following the polite conventions of others, he never indulged in trying to defeat enemies or protect friends, for his heart lay solely with the teachings and he lived quietly, devoting his time to teaching, writing, spiritual practice, and meditation. Other than this, he did not engage in any worldly activities whatsoever.

Kongtrul Rinpoché used to say, "From an early age up to the present, I have only been concerned with the teachings and have had no energy for carrying the burden of worldly affairs. The Buddha's words, the commentaries on these, oral transmissions, pith instructions, sutras and tantras, and secular fields of knowledge—no matter what anyone has done concerning any of these, I have no difficulty understanding, without hesitation, that the key point of such-and-such is this or that. But as for the activities of this world, which deal with defeating enemies or protecting friends—things such as business and profit making, contending with enemies, legal disputes, and so forth—when I hear someone discussing these my reaction is, 'What purpose does this extraordinary person aim to accomplish by saying such a thing?' Other than feeling mild surprise, I don't see any point to these things." Someone as unworthy as I, who had at least had enough merit to hear him say these words, in fact heard him say them many times over. And it is my opinion that when intelligent people consider even this much well, [5b] they will understand whether or not Kongtrul Rinpoché was a ruler among renunciants, a yogin disenchanted with the world, and a spiritual being for whom all was like an illusion.

Rinpoché would say, "I am aware that some have doubts, thinking, 'How can I have renunciation when there is nothing greater than protecting one's friends?' But it was my wish to be a 'child of the mountains,' wearing the mist as my clothing and living alone like the wild animals, without enemies or friends, frequenting only solitary places, such as the valley of Gawalung in Puwo,[14] in a random manner. But Pema Nyinjé, who is Vajradhara, would not give me permission to do so, and so I stayed in this area. From that point on, people began showing up haphazardly in my retinue. This was due to some karma I accrued in the past, so there was nothing to be done about it. Now, of course, I have no choice but to look after them." This statement showed the scope of his conduct as a bodhisattva, and those of us who have been part of his retinue know that we were extremely fortunate. So much for my somewhat parenthetical remarks.

When it came to promoting the Buddhist teachings or benefiting other beings, Kongtrul Rinpoché did not indulge for a moment in discouragement, fatigue, or apathy, [6a] saying only, "What better way is there to spend one's human life?" He was truly someone with what is called "a profoundly inscrutable heart," for it was difficult for anyone to fathom the true depths of his mind on any level, outer or inner. The more you came to know him, the more profound he proved to be. That, plus the innocent, seemingly childlike conduct he showed toward others, constitute his ultimate personal history, but ordinary people can be excused for failing to appreciate this fact.

In brief, Kongtrul Rinpoché perfected all the limitless and precious qualities common to those who uphold the teachings of the victorious ones, for he spent his entire life in hearing, contemplating, and meditating on those teachings, and in explaining, writing about, upholding, and propagating them. In addition, this lordly master sought teachings without any sectarian bias, so that there was virtually nothing which he had not studied, from the ordinary fields of secular knowledge (beginning with his first learning to read and write) to the extraordinary teachings of the Vajrayana—including the "three repositories" of the teachings and the empowerments, oral transmissions, pith instructions, explanations, and even the most minor practical techniques associated with the four classes of tantra.[15] If you examine the extensive record of teachings he received, which fills two entire volumes, it seems as though he spent his entire life solely in hearing teachings. If you take into account his activities in conferring empowerments, oral transmissions, and instructions from both the *kama* and *terma* traditions, it seems as though he spent his life solely engaged in transmitting teachings. There are some who, after gaining some rudimentary understanding from desultory study, desire to write and be published, jotting down a few essays in order to become famous or controversial and calling these efforts their "collected works." [6b] Kongtrul Rinpoché was not like this. His works consist of more than ninety volumes—foremost among these his marvelous Five Treasuries—which have served as a life-support system for the dying transmissions of the teachings, without sectarian bias. If you consider these facts, it seems as though he spent his life doing nothing but writing. If you look at the ways in which he pursued his spiritual practice, undertaking personal retreats for a vast array of methods from the old and new schools of both sutra and tantra, it seems as though he was sealed away in a retreat center for his whole life. My lord guru was definitely someone who exemplified the incredible conduct of a spiritually advanced being. I am not exaggerating or misrepresenting things because he was my guru; it will be clear to anyone with intelligence whether or not I am relating what was actually the case.

Kongtrul Rinpoché continued to engage in such an amazing array of superb activities until he reached the age of eighty-seven. Then, at a certain point he began to turn his attention toward benefiting others to be guided.[16] But during that whole year he gave no definite indication whatsoever of his passing, even in his private conversations with his most intimate students or trusted attendants. To a lowly person such as me, who served and waited on him over a long period of time, he did say the following: "Now all my important tasks are finished, especially my great Treasuries. [7a] My life's work is complete. If I were to die tomorrow, there would be nothing more for me to worry about. My health is poor, so it would be fine with me if I were to cast off this broken-down illusory body, which causes such problems for me and others, but up until now I haven't been able to stop breathing. And speaking generally, what joy is there in dying? In particular, it is certain that I carry a heavy burden due to misappropriating a great deal of property. But I have experienced the grace of the teachings of the Lord of Sages in general. More especially, I have encountered the secret mantra approach of the Vajrayana and have not impaired the most basic *samaya*s and vows to which I have committed myself. And while I have not avoided impairing or breaking my secondary commitments, I have tried not to treat the methods of confessing and of reaffirming my vows too casually. So even if I cannot hope to be reborn in some pure realm, I might at least gain a human rebirth. I pray that I will be reborn where I don't have to eat meat." I myself heard him say such things again and again.

It was obvious that Kongtrul Rinpoché prayed continually and one-pointedly to be reborn in the Realm of Bliss. On special holy days, he would perform various rituals to Amitabha, especially his favorite, the ritual discovered by Taksham. While it was difficult to determine what the core of his personal practice was, it is my feeling that he primarily used the two *sadhana*s of Jinasagara from the Kagyü tradition, for the nine deity and five deity mandalas.[17] On one occasion, General Sönam Topgyé of Horkhang Dzasak sponsored a specific prayer ritual for Kongtrul Rinpoché's long life. Rinpoché joined the ranks of those performing the longevity *sadhana* called *The Gathering of Se-*

crets, and during the entire phase in which the guru's longevity is ensured, from beginning to end, [7b] his mind never wandered and he had a clear vision of the entire array of the Realm of Bliss, as though he were actually there. He said, "There is indeed great blessing in this cycle of Ratna Lingpa's teachings. Perhaps this old man can hope for the Realm of Bliss after all." The lord guru spoke these words to me, a worthless and common person, and it is my feeling that his mind blended with the expanse of Khyungpo Naljor's and that he dwells in Amitabha's pure realm.[18]

When Kongtrul Rinpoché was eighty-five or eighty-six, he showed more signs of gradual aging—his health slowly worsened, his eyesight began to fail, and so on. In particular, during the fifth month of the Fire Bird Year [1897-1898], without him showing any visible signs of illness, Kongtrul Rinpoché underwent a change of heart. That is to say, for many days from morning until night he regaled his attendants and others in his retinue with countless and varied stories of the religious and secular histories of India and China, from early times until the present day. He would especially speak at length of the way in which Belo Tsewang Kunkhyap served Jamgön Chökyi Jungné by carrying out the latter's projects after his passing, of how Lord Pema Nyinjé passed away, of how these masters were commemorated in general and by the erection of this or that tomb in particular, and other such matters. When the foremost of his intimate students, Khenchen Chöjé Tashi Özer, [8a] heard of this from his guru's attendants, he went immediately into Kongtrul Rinpoché's presence and began preparations to offer a ritual ablution designed to purify any flaws in his *samaya* connection with his guru, but instead Kongtrul Rinpoché spent the day relating these same stories to Tashi Özer!

When medicine was offered to him, he would not take it. When asked about his meals, he would speak very lofty words born of his deep inner confidence, saying, "It's true I did eat and drink in the past, but what use would it be to eat or drink anything now?" He remained immersed in a state of meditative absorption, experiencing the unity of bliss and emptiness. It seemed as though all his former states—physical, verbal, and mental—had undergone a change. His Holiness Tai Situ, Khenchen Lama Tashi Özer, the king of Dergé (accompanied by his relatives, ministers, and retinue), the lamas and monks of Palpung Monastery, devoted patrons, and others, whether they were close to Kongtrul Rinpoché or not, gathered and prayed fervently that Kongtrul Rinpoché would live longer. At one point he promised to do so, whereupon he immediately reverted to his former condition and manifested signs of illness.

Not long after that, though, he seemed to recover. It was at that point that I and several other lowly people went to the meditation center of Kyodrak in upper Amdo to help restore the teachings there in accord with the wishes of Tai Situ. When I returned, toward the end of the sixth month in that year, I went to offer prostrations to my lord guru, who seemed quite recovered. [8b] During the conversation we had, Kongtrul Rinpoché stated, "Yesterday my mind and perceptions shifted, as though something previously blocked was freed. I felt as I never have before. Pure devotion, disenchantment with the world, renunciation, love, compassion, realization of emptiness—all of these became obvious to me, just as they are described in the teachings, and I thought, 'It would be so fine if I could die while in this frame of mind.' But these proved to be ephemeral experiences, which gradually faded away. Now my mindstream has once more become intractable like the earth in winter." It was on the basis of such comments that at that point I thought to myself, "My guru is surely preparing to depart for a pure realm, but in response to our prayers for his longevity he has granted us his blessing to extend his life, and he is confirming that he will remain for a short time as a protector of the teachings and of beings."

From that point onward, Kongtrul Rinpoché's health went up and down, but steadily worsened. Nevertheless, from time to time he accomplished whatever activities he could, conferring empowerments and oral transmissions, giving teachings, writing treatises, and so forth. We began combined *drupchen* and *mendrup* rituals based on the So tradition of the great and glorious deity Samyak. At the outset, Kongtrul Rinpoché conferred the ripening empowerment on the participants. He also attended the ceremonies for a few days as the presiding master and bestowed extensive teachings on many of the sublime masters attending the ritual, including all the empowerments and oral transmissions for The Three Roots: The Heart Drop of Utter Lucidity—a *terma* of enlightened intent discovered by Lord Do-ngak Lingpa[19]—and the major empowerment for the higher phase of activity from the Sakya tradition of Vajrakila.[20] [9a]

During the winter of that year, he fell ill a number of times, but always recovered. From the precious and venerable Lama Tashi Özer, Kongtrul Rinpoché received a number of transmissions. These included the empowerment for Chakrasamvara and consort from the oral tradition of Rechungpa and the oral transmissions for the works of Orgyen Namdrol Wangpo and the ancient manuscripts of Tsangnyön,[21] the collected oral teachings of the Kadampa

School as compiled by the Sokpo Thoyön Lama Döndrup Gyaltsen,[22] and the three works by Dakpo Tashi Namgyal known as the "Three Rays of Light"—*Rays of Sunlight* (his commentary on *The Hevajra Tantra in Two Chapters*), *Rays of Moonlight* (his detailed commentary on Mahamudra),[23] and *Rays of Gemlight* (his general overview of the tantric approach).

On the ninth and tenth days of the twelfth month, in response to a request from Horkhang Jedrung Lama, Kongtrul Rinpoché bestowed both the preliminary and main phases of the great empowerment for the *sadhana* of enlightened mind called *Dispelling Obstacles on the Path*, a new *terma* discovered by Chokgyur Lingpa.[24] At the close of the year, his health took a real turn for the worse, to the point that we feared for his life, but he still undertook a week-long personal retreat on White Tara according to Lord Atisha's tradition.

ON THE MORNING OF the first day of the new Earth Pig Year [1899-1900], he performed an offering ritual to White Tara. I was present as one of the participants, and on that occasion Kongtrul Rinpoché's health improved. He showed no sign of illness and with a delighted expression exclaimed, "This White Tara is a special deity of longevity, [9b] and thanks to her blessings I can guarantee that I will not die for another year or so." For several days he continued to express his delight, taking part in the New Year celebrations and conversations.

In the second month I served as his secretary, taking dictation and reading passages from texts to him. He composed several works, including his special and most excellent explanations of the Vajrakila cycle in his moderately long commentary on the fragmentary source tantra translated by Sakya Pandita.[25] In his free time he continued his other spiritual activities on a daily basis, conferring minor empowerments and oral transmissions. He instructed me to complete the final portion of the precious record of teachings he received, and after pinning down those I couldn't recall, I am still clearing up a few difficult points.

That year, in the fourth month, Jamyang Loter Wangpo, the precious Pönlop of the Thartsé house of Ngor Monastery, came to see Kongtrul Rinpoché, who received from him transmissions that he had not received before. These included teachings from the Yogatantra class—the explanatory tantra entitled *The Vajra Pinnacle*, the secondary tantra entitled *Complete Victory over the Three Realms*, and the auxiliary teaching entitled *The Gathering of the Family*

of the Sublime and Glorious One. As well, he received the transmissions of
the Vajra Garland collection of Abhayakaragupta, Chakrasamvara according
to the oral lineage of Ngamdzong, and the Secret Conduct cycle of Thangtong
Gyalpo. Receiving these empowerments, as well as many oral transmissions,
occupied Kongtrul Rinpoché until the eighth month. During this time there
were not many others present and he told me, this lowly person, to participate
in all the empowerments and oral transmissions, no matter how more or less
important. "You also should request these," he said, "and this will be useful to
the continuity of these teachings in the future." Kongtrul Rinpoché had great
hopes for me in this regard, [10a] but unless he was thinking of some other
lifetime, it is plain for all, high and low, to see that not a sesame seed's worth
of benefit has come of this, for me or for others, and in the face of that I
wonder if there has been, in fact, some harm done. In any case, he said, "At
this point I myself have no hope of transmitting or propagating these teachings. They are simply the last teachings this old man has received on the point
of his death. Someone like you has done well to receive these transmissions.
The lower classes of tantras, and especially the source and explanatory tantras
of the Yogatantra class, are rare, for they are not found in this region. No one
carries out the formal practices. There is no better performance of the rituals
for the higher and lower classes of tantra than that found with Pönlop
Rinpoché,[26] so in addition you should take at least some note of the preparations for the empowerments, the way they are conferred, and other practical
techniques. I trust that we who are receiving these empowerments now won't
ignore their value. They carry a very powerful store of blessings. These
empowerments have been very useful to me." With great delight, he would
say such things again and again. Kongtrul Rinpoché bestowed the transmission of his new commentary on the fragmentary Vajrakila tantra on Pönlop
Rinpoché, Lodrö Seng-gé,[27] and the rest of us over three days, interspersing
the oral transmission with his explanations.

During that summer, he stayed in his cottage in the hermitage garden, passing the time quite pleasantly in holding conversation, writing, bestowing
empowerments and instructions, [10b] and in other ways answering people's
individual needs. In the sixth month the venerable Situ Rinpoché (who was
preparing to move to his monastic encampment for the summer retreat[28]) came
with his retinue to see Kongtrul Rinpoché, who gave him much advice on both
general and specific points, speaking quite freely. Situ Rinpoché asked him to
come to his monastic seat in the tenth month, to which Kongtrul Rinpoché

replied, "This old man will still be holding on to life and will seek an audience with you."

Kongtrul Rinpoché made extensive offerings to Pönlop Rinpoché for the empowerments, as well as offering him prayers for his long life. He instructed me to write the letter that accompanied these. By and large, he did not make such requests, for he took no pleasure in compositions with many verses and clever stylistic flourishes. Now, however, he said to me, "This time the letter accompanying the offerings should be very fine, so write it with many pleasing verses at the beginning and end. This will be the fruition of the useful fact that you have no difficulty composing verses. Don't worry about formal meter, for none of you will be up to it. The most important subject you should write about is the kindness that I, an old man, have been shown while receiving these present transmissions, which are the teachings I have received on the point of my death."

Then, on the first day of the ninth month he stayed in his chambers and when night fell he felt unwell and couldn't sleep. Next, he fell ill with the lymphatic and skin disorders that had troubled him before. [11a] He experienced a variety of other symptoms as well—bile-like blood coughed up in his spittle, high blood pressure, edema in his legs, and so forth—which gradually worsened. During this time, Kongtrul Rinpoché would say, "If this old man had been able to die last year, when he was having such unusual experiences, it might have served some purpose. Will this present illness prove to be fatal?" When his attendants asked what ceremonies were required, he replied, "You need do nothing beyond a small ritual to avert misfortune. But it is important to sponsor the greater community of Palpung Monastery to recite a hundred million mantras of the Vajradanda Vajrapani." Although Khen Lama Mangala[29] then came and all of us, master and students, performed the appropriate rituals—a major *torma* ritual to avert the Lord of Death, a rite to turn back the escort of *dakinis*, a ritual ablution, and so forth—Kongtrul Rinpoché did not recover but only continued to worsen. Pönlop Rinpoché and Khen Lama presided over the retreatants as they quickly performed a *ganachakra* feast and fire ritual focusing on the *dakinis*, as well as thousand-fold offerings to the three deities of longevity, but nothing changed from before.

One day, he told his attendant, the holy Tsering Döndrup, that it would be a good idea to gather together the most important of his sacred objects. The attendant asked him, "Is this a sign that you are going to pass away, Rinpoché?" He answered, "Not so, [11b] but it will ensure that there is no problem when it actually comes to that. Haven't you seen what it's like when people in your family died?"

It was about that time, when the holy Khen Lama was performing a *dakini* ritual to dispel contamination and a ceremony for Kongtrul Rinpoché's long life, that Pönlop Rinpoché came and offered Kongtrul Rinpoché a silk scarf, requesting that he live longer. Khenchen Lama shed tears as he begged Kongtrul Rinpoché, saying at length how necessary this was—in general for the teachings and all beings, more specifically for this region, especially for the venerable Situ, and in particular for his inner retinue. Khen Lama asked that out of his great love for us he not abandon us, but live longer.

Kongtrul Rinpoché replied, "All right. In response to the request of you, a fine student who upholds the teachings, I will certainly aspire to extend my life a bit." After that he did not speak much at all, but remained in profound meditation, praying while telling the beads of his mala. Following this, on the evening of the twenty-seventh day of the eleventh month of the Earth Pig Year,[30] Khen Lama came into his presence and asked, "Sir, how is your health now? Has it improved?" Kongtrul Rinpoché responded by saying, "At present I have no pain or illness at all. I am quite well." He sat up straight, telling the beads of his mala. I am told that when people came to see him that evening, he would hold up his mala and say, "Come here."[31] [12a]

At about midnight, he entered into the state of equipoise, like the space inside a shattered vase dissolving into the basic space of supreme dharmakaya that permeates all of space, the inexhaustible state of utter lucidity.

Some reflections of my own:

> Alas! Today the sun of the Buddhadharma,
> unequalled by a million suns and moons, has set.
> Is it possible that this victory banner of the teachings—
> unrivalled by the ordinary banners of monarchs—can have fallen?
> A gem, made lovely by the thousand-fold radiance
> of the marvelous legacy of the charioteers of old,
> fell into the hands of those of us with merit.
> Our mentor, who let fall a rain of all our spiritual wants and needs,
> how can we bear the fact that you are gone, dissolved into basic space?
> The teachings are like a lake from which the swans have fled,[32]
> and beings are like the blind deprived of their guide.

Such is my realization, I who will henceforth be denied this spiritual
   protector.
Virtuous mentor, motivated by compassion,
now I have little chance of finding someone such as you.
We who were to be guided, placing our hopes in you,
are lost in a forsaken land. How little compassion you have![33]
Your smiling face, suffused with the compassion in your heart,
and your helpful speech, with advice flowing forth—
now these are but memories that I recall,
for I have no chance to see or hear you and this saddens me.
Now, like the distance between heaven and earth

[12b] is that between you and us unfortunate ones who relied solely on
   your compassion.
How will these eyes of mine
ever behold your sublime embodiment of inexhaustible timeless
   awareness?

COMMEMORATIVE RITES

Immediately upon Kongtrul Rinpoché's passing, his intimate student Khenchen
Chöjé[34] performed the methods for stabilizing our master's meditation according to the pith instructions found in the precious classes of tantra. Kongtrul
Rinpoché's body, which was sitting upright, was clad in his monastic robes
and his head was crowned with his meditation hat. Other than this, he was left
undisturbed for three days, to allow him to rest in the utterly lucid basic space
of dharmakaya. At midnight on the third day, once his enlightened intent had
dissolved into the basic space of reality, there occurred signs—just as they are
explained in the tantras—of his arising from this state of utter lucidity: the
earth and the hills around quaked slowly three times with a low rumble.
   At that point, the two gurus,[35] both vajra holders, prepared a bath and washed
Kongtrul Rinpoché's precious bodily remains thoroughly with water scented
with saffron. They wrote the syllables of the body chakras and the blessings
for the sense organs on dark blue paper, writing in a special decorative script
with gold ink, according to the respective traditions of the higher and lower
classes of tantras, and placed these precisely at the appropriate places on
Kongtrul Rinpoché's body, along with amulets that bring liberation upon con-

tact and numerous tantric scriptures. They wrapped the body completely in fine white cloth from Benares, interspersing the layers of cloth with powdered medicinal herbs. His head was crowned with a topknot and a crown of the five buddhas, [13a] his body was clad in upper and lower vestments, and a vajra and bell were placed in his hands. All these preparations, of clothing him in the garb of the sambhogakaya, were carried out by the holy Khen Lama, assisted by fully ordained monks, and performed in accord with the traditional texts. Kongtrul Rinpoché's body was then placed on a high and beautiful throne, the table in front of it filled with fine and extensive arrays of offerings.

For the next week, the ritual of making offerings to the guru was performed, including the acceptance of the four empowerments. The ritual was performed in a very satisfying way by Pönlop Vajradhara and Khenchen Lama Rinpoché, as well as by me and other participants. During this time, there were signs that those who guard the forces of good[36] were mourning. The weather turned worse. All the hills and valleys lost their luster and looked dull. All the glaciers, cliff faces, peaks and hills guarded by the local spirits changed; everyone could see in them faces covered with tears, and it seemed very clearly as though these rock formations were all bowing their heads. The birds created quite a din with their increased chattering.

It was at this point that Tai Situ Rinpoché arrived with his retinue. Saddened at heart, he presented offerings and made sincere prayers. As well, there was an uninterrupted stream of people, high and low, [13b] who came to view the remains and to present offerings. The time passed with them praying and making whatever offerings they could, according to their means, in order to gather merit. They were allowed to view the remains, like a wish-fulfilling gem, and were given water that had been used to bathe the body; in such ways, there was no impediment to the guru's activity bringing purpose to all connected with him.

Then, on a day that was favorable astrologically, the precious remains were consigned to the fire. There were four separate rituals performed in conjunction with the cremation ceremony. Pönlop Rinpoché presided over the ritual of Hevajra according to the Sakya tradition; Khenchen Lama Tashi Özer, that of Vajrasattva from the tradition of Mindroling Monastery; the vajra master Lama Döndrup,[37] that of Akshobhya from the tradition of Lord Atisha; and Gyalsé Dechen Tulku from Dzögön Monastery, that of Sarvavid Vairochana.[38] These rituals included fire-offering ceremonies, in which fine woods such as red and white sandalwood and fragrant juniper boughs were offered to the flames.

Even after the cremation was complete, Kongtrul Rinpoché's heart was not touched by the fire, but remained as a support for the merit of those to be guided.[39] On that day there was a great snowfall, turning the hills and valleys white. Then the structure containing the funeral pyre was sealed overnight. The following day the fire was doused with milk and saffron water and the bones were collected and placed in an urn. This, too, was clad in the sambhogakaya garb and kept in state for a further day.

It was at this point that Kongtrul Rinpoché's attendant, the steward Tsering Döndrup, [14a] began making offerings on Kongtrul Rinpoché's behalf, dispensing these without a trace of avarice, as though opening up the enormous doorway to the treasury of space.[40] He made offerings of tea and silver to all the major institutions and their branch monasteries, such as Palpung, Kathok, Palyul, Dzongsar, Dergé Gönchen, Chakra, Paljor Pewar, Dorjé Drak, Dzingön Khak, and Dzongshö. These uncountable offerings were to sponsor personal spiritual practice and group rituals. As well, there were periodic ceremonies commemorating Kongtrul Rinpoché's passing, including the following rituals: Chakrasamvara; Vajravarahi; *Supreme Compassion: The Gathering of Secrets*; *Dredging the Pit of Cyclic Existence*; Karma Lingpa's cycle of the peaceful and wrathful deities; the Mindroling tradition of Vajrasattva; Naro Khechari; Sarvavid Vairochana; and the *gurupuja* ritual honoring the masters of the Eight Lineages of Accomplishment. In the presence of the tomb of Situ Chökyi Jungné, Lama Pönlop Dzatrul of Dzamthang led an offering ritual of Kalachakra. In short, there were very impressive and extensive offering ceremonies and other beneficial rituals associated with the tantras of both the old and new schools. Two hundred rows of oil lamps were offered without fail on a daily basis. Each of the lamas present was honored with pure and fine offerings, impressive and all of excellent quality—first and foremost the symbols of enlightened form, speech, and mind,[41] [14b] as well as such offerings as tea, silver, silk, animal skins, and horses.

On the tenth day of the second week after Kongtrul Rinpoché's death, we first heard the pleasing sound of rolling thunder coming from the southwest. In front of Kongtrul Rinpoché's bed in his chambers, on the tenth day Khenchen Lama,[42] myself, and our students performed the *ganachakra* feast based on *The United Intent of the Three Roots*. Just as we were concluding the ritual and reciting the verses to stabilize the presence of the deities,[43] something quite unplanned occurred. In the main temple, the Yangtrul incarnation of Palyul Monastery had been presiding over a ceremony in honor of Kongtrul

Rinpoché—a ritual focusing on the cycle of peaceful and wrathful deities from Karma Lingpa. Once they finished the ritual, they took the urn containing Kongtrul Rinpoché's bones and ashes and escorted it with all honors to his chambers. They arrived just as we were finishing, and there were other such auspicious circumstances as well.

In addition, offerings were made to great lamas and extraordinary spiritual mentors, and they themselves enlisted support, so that they could perform commemorative rites as appropriate and in a very thorough manner. We were provided with clear records of how these donations were used. As well, offerings were made throughout the central Tibetan provinces of Ü and Tsang—especially to the two statues of the precious Lord Shakyamuni,[44] as well as to the three major religious centers in the Lhasa area and other monastic seats and meditation centers—to sponsor rituals of one thousand or one hundred offerings, the regilding of statues,[45] and tea and food for the monastic communities. Tea offerings were sponsored for the communities of monasteries of all schools, without sectarian bias, and especially at Tsurphu in Tölung. In order to request that he perform commemorative rites, a splendid array of offerings was made to the Gyalwang Karmapa—the three representations,[46] bolts of silk and cotton, gold and silver, hides, and pack animals. [15a] Such articles were also offered to the sacred presence of our lord of refuge, the Dalai Lama.[47] In brief, commemorative rites were held by most of the lamas and at most of the monasteries throughout the three regions of Kham, Ü, and Tsang, with spiritual practice being performed on a vast scale that was as laudatory as it was unparalleled.

KONGTRUL'S TOMB

As for Kongtrul Rinpoché's great tomb, it is a "stupa of enlightenment" one tall story high, authentic in its proportions and complete in its construction. The smaller tomb, installed in his chambers, is a "stupa of the descent from the gods' realm."[48] Both of these are covered in equal parts of gold and copper, with a great deal of silver overlay (ornamental spirals and so forth) and inset stones—turquoise, coral, agate, crystal, and others—making them a feast for the eyes. They were sponsored by the prince of Dergé, the excellent Buddhist layman Jigmé Tsewang Duddul,[49] who with great faith, devotion, and enthusiasm provided funding for the metalworkers to be brought in and supported.

Through his admirable endeavors, these stupas were completed in a very short time—within that year, in fact. Using the ritual of the two Vimalas, we installed the central axes, and then prepared the bones and ashes—refining, cleansing, and pulverizing them—after which they were cast into *tsa-tsas*. We ensured that other essential tasks, such as installing the long mantras, were carried out in accord with authentic principles and techniques. The "treasure chests"[50] were filled with objects that are, for the most part, very holy. These included the "regent" image known as Tashi Palbar [Radiant Auspicious Splendor], a *terma* discovered by my lord himself[51] as the representation of enlightened form in his United Intent of the Three Roots; [15b] a great many scrolls of *termas*, including the entire scroll for that same cycle; and relics from the seven previous buddhas. These objects were reverently installed in the chests.

Within the alcove in the spherical body of the large stupa, we installed an image that would provide a source of liberation upon sight. This statue, radiant with blessings, depicts our Teacher[52] and was carved by the exalted Nagarjuna with his own hands in white alabaster from Vulture Peak in the holy country of India. Carried by Indian traders, it came to Tibet and made it a central country, like the Vajra Seat.[53] In more recent times, the statue came into my lord's possession.

In these ways, pure and unerring methods were used to ensure that these tombs are authentic and entirely worthy of people's trust as objects of homage and worship. The installation of the long mantras was carried out in the traditional manner, and with great emphasis on purity, by a large group of participants, both novices and fully ordained monks, presided over by two masters—the great scholar and master of the teachings, Khenchen Chöjé Mangala Rasmi,[54] and the lama Jangchub Sempa Lodrö Zangpo.[55]

During the waxing phase of the moon, the holy time of the fourth month,[56] the tombs were consecrated. As vajra masters who had completed the requisite retreats, Tai Situ, Thartsé Pandita of Ngor Monastery,[57] and Khenchen Chöjé each presided over a large gathering of participants. They performed the rituals of Hevajra, Chakrasamvara, and Vajrasattva, which constituted the actual consecration rituals, lasting two days in each case. As expressions of timeless awareness, the deities were invited to reside within the tombs, so that they became superb repositories worthy of honor by the worlds of humans and gods. [16a]

One can now view the major tomb in the Lhasar Gyüdé Lhakhang[58] at Palpung Monastery. It is to the left of the precious tomb of Vajradhara Pema

Nyinjé. The other tomb is in the outer vestibule of the Thukdam Khang in Kongtrul Rinpoché's chambers at the hermitage. It was arranged that offerings would be made regularly in front of these tombs, and that lamps would be kept burning continuously. Once all this had been spontaneously accomplished without hindrance, gifts of tea, silver, silk, cotton, horses, pack animals, and so forth were made to the artisans involved—the statue makers, calligraphers, woodworkers, smiths, and metalworkers, as well as their assistants. They had been provided with fine food and drink, and were delighted with the commissions. Thus, everything was carried out in an entirely positive way, with no taint of anything negative.

I have written a lengthy inventory for Kongtrul Rinpoché's precious tomb under another title.[59] But although there exist detailed records of the extensive expenses and materials used, it would be a disservice if I felt self-righteous about these. As well, I harbor no illusions that nothing important remained to be done following these meager efforts. You can judge for yourself from the resuslts of these noble undertakings.

Lama Rinpoché Tashi Özer provided ornamental facades of the finest gold, inset with corals. The monasteries of Palpung, Kathok, Palyul, and others gave some fine donations of copper and other materials. By way of showing her gratitude, the young woman Ayudharma,[60] who had been an attendant of my lord guru, [16b] demonstrated her noble and altruistic motivation by sponsoring the offering of a garland of one hundred lamps every day during nine days of the commemorative rites to her guru, as well as sponsoring one hundred thousand repetitions of *The Aspiration to Noble Conduct.* She also offered several crystals and pieces of turquoise to be used as insets on his great tomb, and a garland of small agates to form the ornamentation around the doorway to the vase of the smaller tomb. Even such seemingly small contributions as these were offerings made out of faith in our guru, who was Vajradhara himself, and so were not wasted, for his positive influence ensured that people could have trust in, and see the authenticity of, devoting their efforts to such a project.

OTHER COMMEMORATIVE PROJECTS

Similarly, a statue of Kongtrul Rinpoché was installed in his chamber, along with a statue of Maitreya complete with a throne, both made of gold and copper. As well, it had long been the intention of my lord guru to have a painting done of the wrathful goddess Krodhi in a charnel ground—the specific configuration of the charnel ground spoken of in the source texts—and a fine example of this was completed. In one corner of the courtyard of Palpung Monastery, a tiered stupa called "The Great Repository of Tablets" was built, topped by a large, fine banner of victory made of gold and copper and filled with all the proper contents.

In accord with the directives from the lay and monastic administrations of Dergé, arrangements were made for Kongtrul Rinpoché's Five Treasuries and other works to be preserved at the great printing house of Dergé—woodblocks, wrappings, storage shelves, registers, and indices—so that these would continue to provide benefit for posterity. In the case of any new texts that my lord had intended to include, the work was finished immediately after the foregoing activities were completed. [17a]

The following year, on the anniversary of Kongtrul Rinpoché's passing, a ritual to honor his memory was held in the Palchen Temple at the hermitage. The protector Maitreya—Tai Situ—and Lord Khenchen Lama both presided over a group of more than fifty participants, performing a *drupchen* ritual based on a *sadhana* of enlightened mind focusing on Vajrasattva, a *terma* cycle from the Mindroling tradition. This included a ceremony to prepare and consecrate sacred pills and was completed within a week. I joined a group of ten in Kongtrul Rinpoché's chambers to perform the *gurupuja* ritual and prayers honoring the eight approaches of spiritual accomplishment. At the retreat center, a stupa was constructed to house some of Kongtrul Rinpoché's remains. The ritual focusing on the two Vimala mandalas and the installation of the central axis were performed, and earth and stone from the tomb were used in casting *tsa-tsa*s. Supplementary texts to Kongtrul Rinpoché's collected works—such as the record of the teachings he received—were ready to be written out or carved on woodblocks. We strove to complete these. In brief, we thoughty of ways to fulfill Kongtrul Rinpoché's intentions, and have tried and are still trying to carry out such positive undertakings.

In another context, at the great monastic seat of Dzongshö (the sacred place in which the five principles of enlightened qualities are united), Jamyang Gelek, who had been one of Kongtrul Rinpoché's principal attendants and students, led a group of forty people in reciting liturgies during the forty-nine-day period following Kongtrul Rinpoché's passing. [17b] During the following summer, they finished casting hundreds of thousands of *tsa-tsa*s. Even now, he is in the process of overseeing the construction of a prayer wheel containing one hundred million Vajrasattva mantras, in honor of Kongtrul Rinpoché's memory. Jamyang Gelek continues to strive with constant devotion at flawless ways to fulfill his guru's intentions. He has surpassed his guru in the service he has rendered in constructing buildings and the images they house at this second major seat, which is a great power spot on the earth. The evidence of his success can be seen in the wake of such efforts, and it would be only fitting, by way of describing the qualities of this individual, if some account were to be prepared that discussed the location and buildings of this monastic seat.

KONGTRUL'S STUDENTS

As for my lord guru's holy tutors and gurus, you can learn about them from his lengthy autobiography and the introduction to the record of the teachings he received. Kongtrul Rinpoché also told me that it was necessary for a rough list of his principal students to be included with his autobiography. In answer to his wishes, let me relate this here.

In general, those who were kindest to Kongtrul Rinpoché and functioned as both teacher and student to him included the Gyalwang Karmapa Thekchok Dorjé, Drukchen Rinpoché, Pawo Tsuklak Chögyal, Jamyang Khyentsé, Chokgyur Lingpa, the older Öngen Thekchok Tenphel, Lobzang Rinpoché, and the Mindroling throne holder Gyurmé Yizhin Wang-gyal and his sister. His root guru, however, was for him the sovereign lord of the vast array of buddha families and mandalas, through whose grace Kongtrul Rinpoché received the three levels of ordination, who introduced Kongtrul Rinpoché directly to the essence of his mind as dharmakaya, [18a] and who was inseparable from Vajradhara. This root guru was his lord of refuge, Tai Situ Pema Nyinjé Wangpo. Likewise, there is mention (in Kongtrul Rinpoché's great autobiography) of the most important gurus who served as his spiritual mentors even as they received kindness from him—primarily the Gyalwa Karmapa Thekchok Dorjé and the great scholar of Zhechen Monastery, Gyurmé Tendzin Phelgyé[61]—as well as in the prayers he wrote to them, which form part of his miscellaneous collected works. One can learn about these masters in these sources.

In his later life, the primary lama, or spiritual mentor, who relied on Kongtrul Rinpoché was the one famed as Jamyang Khyentsé Wangpo Kunga Tenpai Gyaltsen Pal Zangpo. He was the foremost among all the vajra disciples who imbibed the nectar of Kongtrul Rinpoché's vast and profound teachings—the prominent pinnacle of the banner of victory, so to speak. This omniscient and fearless spiritual master, Khyentsé Rinpoché, was the crown jewel amidst a vast array of learned and accomplished masters, had no sectarian bias, and was unparalleled on this earth, for he was indisputably the master of the entire range of the Sage's teachings. My own lord guru was shown enormous kindness by Khyentsé Rinpoché, for he received from Khyentsé Rinpoché empowerments, oral transmissions, instructions, explanations—even practical demonstrations[62]—for teachings of sutra and tantra, *kama* and *terma*, Nyingma and Sarma. [18b]

Khyentsé Rinpoché was thus the foundation for Kongtrul Rinpoché's truly vast assimilation of the teachings, so vast that no one could compare to him. Kongtrul Rinpoché himself told me on many occasions, "It goes without saying that, from early on in my life, I had not been lacking in an unbiased respect for the teachings, but nothing had actually opened my eyes to the state of pure vision, in which I could hold all of these teachings in my mind without any contradiction. Since I met Khyentsé Rinpoché, however, I have felt a natural sense of freedom, in that I am confident that I can hold any and all of the Sage's teachings in perfect balance, without seeing any inconsistency between them. Meeting him was also, for me, the dawning of my real familiarity with the Buddhadharma."

In an extraordinary way, Khyentsé Rinpoché was the catalyst who, in a timely manner, awakened in Kongtrul Rinpoché the amazing and profound mystery of his aspirations to discover profound *terma*s.[63] Directly and indirectly, it was Khyentsé Rinpoché who provided support for Kongtrul Rinpoché to discover these *terma*s, by establishing the profound circumstances that would ensure this. It was Khyentsé Rinpoché who spoke prophetically of the great Treasuries in a personal directive to Kongtrul Rinpoché, guiding him initially along that path of action like the rising sun showing the way. Khyentsé Rinpoché's role was like that of one *garuda* born before another.[64] In such ways, his influence on Kongtrul Rinpoché was boundless. My own guru, Jamgön Lama, in turn bestowed on Khyentsé Rinpoché the immeasurable nectar of spiritual teachings—a vast ocean of advice from the Sarma and Nyingma teachings, especially the *terma* tradition—and engaged in extraordinary activities to remove obstacles to Khyentsé Rinpoché's physical well-being.[65]

This situation exemplifies the following fact: In brief, from the time they were incarnate as the Buddhist king Trisong Detsen and the translator

Bairotsana, the "single eye of the world"—as patron and priest—on up to the present, through a succession of rebirths that were pure embodiments, [19a] these two masters have been inseparable, aiding one another. The circumstances of their extraordinary motivation and aspiration remind one of the metaphor of the harmony between the sun and the lotus,[66] with each serving as the other's foremost teacher and student. On the one hand, Khyentsé—who was Vajradhara, and the protector Manjushri—spoke highly of Kongtrul Rinpoché, showering him with utterly devoted praise like so many bouquets of lilies, composing a prayer that begins with the words, "Prophesied by the Victorious One, Jamgön Lama, who is Vajradhara, is a great mainstay of spirituality in our world . . . ," in which Khyentsé Rinpoché extols Kongtrul Rinpoché's great qualities in elegant phrases that resound in all directions and times. Khyentsé Rinpoché also at one point signs himself "the least of his[67] vajra disciples." To put it briefly, the inspiring renown of "the two gurus who are the protector Manjushri"—that is, they are not thought of as two separate figures—still is heard up to our present day in every corner of the central and greater Tibetan regions, as well known as the wind itself to all, from the most learned scholars to the simplest cowherds. The situation that accounts for this fact is something that one can learn about by hearing of the activities of these two lords and thoroughly examining their life histories.

In present times there are two masters to whom Kongtrul Rinpoché entrusted his entire transmissions of teachings and who serve as his true regents. They are the "two victorious ones, father and son"—that is, the fifteenth Gyalwang Karmapa incarnation, Kunzang Khakhyap Dorjé, who bears the blue-black crown of Mikyö hidden on top of his head;[68] [19b] and the eleventh incarnation of Tai Situ Rinpoché, Pema Wangchok Gyalpo, who was extolled in the prophecies of Orgyen Dorjé as the third "bearer of the lotus tongue."

His students among the upholders of the Kagyü teachings also included the following: the tenth Tai Situ incarnation, Pema Kunzang Chökyi Gyalpo (whom Kongtrul Rinpoché extolled as "the second bearer of the lotus tongue"[69]); the ninth incarnation of Namdren Pawo Rinpoché, Tsuklak Nyimai Dé;[70] the great scholar Khenchen Karma Tashi Özer; Khenpo Karma Rinchen Dargyé; the Jedrung of Riwoché Monastery, Thrinlé Jampai Jungné; the exalted and sublime incarnation Ngawang Kunga Namgyal; Machen Rinpoché of the Taklung School; the regent of Zi, Jangchub Nyima; the two incarnations Je-ön Chöwang and Jé-ön Döndrup; Jé-ön Samphel;[71] the former and present Samten incarnations; the honorable Khamtrul;[72] the former and present incarnations of Zurmang

Monastery (Garwang, Tenga, Tertrul, and Trungpa *tulku*s);[73] and Dra Rampa Wangchuk.

The great upholders of the Sakya and Ngor traditions who were his students included the Pönlop of the house of Thartsé,[74] Jamyang Loter Wangpo, the foremost Sakya master who was both Kongtrul Rinpoché's teacher and student; the great abbot of the house of Khangsar in Ngor, Ngawang Sönam Gyaltsen;[75] the great abbot of the house of Phendé, Palden Lodrö Gyaltsen;[76] the Önpo of Dezhung, Nyendrak Lungrik Nyima;[77] and the master of teachings of Dzongsar Ngari, the vajra holder Kunga Jamyang.[78] [20a]

Kongtrul Rinpoché's students also included many major and minor upholders of the teachings of the Nyingma School of the secret mantra approach, including Gyatrul Rinpoché of the Palyul tradition, Karma Kunzang Sangngak Tendzin,[79] and the Dzakha Choktrul incarnation, Kunzang Namgyal;[80] these two were the foremost among those who were both Kongtrul Rinpoché's teachers and students. Other major Nyingma students of Kongtrul Rinpoché were the Fifth Dzogchen Rinpoché;[81] Kuzhap Gemang;[82] the former and present Lingtrul Rinpoché incarnations;[83] the Moktrul and Getrul incarnations of Kathok Monastery; the former and present Situ incarnations of Kathok Monastery; and the precious rebirth of the glorious Karma Gyurmé of Palyul.[84] In addition, Kongtrul Rinpoché taught the Lhatrul and Dzong-nang incarnations,[85] the Rabjam and Gyaltsap incarnations of Zhechen Monastery,[86] the greatly learned scholar, Mipham Jamyang Namgyal (from whom Kongtrul Rinpoché received explanatory oral transmissions for most of Mipham's own works);[87] the great scholar, Khenchen Lama Kunzang Sönam;[88] Rabjampa Geshé Norbu Tendzin;[89] the sun of the teachings of the Early Translation School, the Do Drupchen Choktrul incarnation, Jigmé Tenpai Gyaltsen;[90] Khenpo Könchok Özer of Dzogchen Monastery; Lama Sherab of Tsa-nyak; the lama Jangchub Sempa Lodrö Zangpo of Nyarong; Lama Dampa Pema; the Tsenri incarnation of Sa-ngen, Jangchub Chökyi Seng-gé (from whom Kongtrul Rinpoché received most of the cycles of Dechen Lingpa's teachings); Lama Gönpo Dorjé of Pheltsa (from whom Kongtrul Rinpoché received most of the cycles of Taksham's teachings); and the *tertön* Lerab Lingpa (from whom Kongtrul Rinpoché received most of that master's own *terma*s). The latter was unlike the usual kind of student, for the connection they shared, through their aspirations to carry out their extraordinary activities, was such that Kongtrul Rinpoché placed a great deal of trust in the *tertön*. [20b] Another such student was the Bönpo *tertön*, Tsewang Drakpa. As well, Kongtrul Rinpoché taught the sons of the great *tertön* Chokgyur Lingpa (1829-1870)—Tsewang Drakpa and Tsewang Norbu.

There were many great masters of the Gedenpa tradition[91] who studied with Kongtrul Rinpoché. These included the abbot of the Lower Tantric College in Lhasa, Geshé Yeshé Gongphel; the greatly learned Dongkam incarnation of Dragyap,[92] Ngawang Damchö Gyatso; the Thritrul incarnation named Punya;[93] and others.

Among his students were a number of great practitioners who were capable of ensuring benefit for themselves and others, including the lord among scholars, Khewang Lhaksam Tenpai Gyaltsen;[94] the vajra master Pema Norbu;[95] the vajra master Döndrup; the former Zhechen *tulku* Karma Ngédön Palzang; the translator of Tsawa, Rinchen Namgyal; the venerable Drupwang Tsoknyi[96] (from whom Kongtrul Rinpoché received the *sadhana* of enlightened mind, the secret instructions of the five stages, and other teachings of Ratna Lingpa); Adzom Drukpa Rinpoché;[97] the three incarnations of Kyodrak (Sal, Ten, and Drung); Kongtrul Rinpoché's grandnephews, the cousins Jamyang Namgyal Dorjé and Jamyang Lodrö Seng-gé; the vajra master Karma Tensal; Kongtrul Rinpoché's personal secretary, Jamyang Gelek; Jamyang Drakpa of Khargo;[98] and the two retreat graduates, Tsepak and Tsepal.

The foregoing are the most important among Kongtrul Rinpoché's students. Of all the countless learned scholars, realized and experienced meditators, and spiritual mentors, great and small throughout the three regions of Tibet—western Tibet, the central provinces of Ü and Tsang, and the eastern provinces of Dokham—[21a] there was none who was not Kongtrul Rinpoché's student. His students also included the regent of Tibet (the Achi Hotoktu incarnation of Radreng),[99] and the king, prince, and royal family of Dergé,[100] as well as other political figures—major and minor rulers, government ministers, generals, administrators, and others. There were also untold numbers of common folk who forged some spiritual connection with Kongtrul Rinpoché.

During his lifetime, Kongtrul Rinpoché participated in more than one hundred *drupchen*, *mendrup*, and *drupchö* rituals, at which time there were large public gatherings, so that overall he influenced hundreds of thousands in a solely positive way, through the empowerments and *samaya* substances he bestowed, so that they were as numerous as the grains of earth on a vast plain. In his later life, the renown and activities of my lord guru gradually spread, so that from Ü, Tsang, and the eastern Tibetan provinces (even as far as the borders with China and Mongolia), countless lamas, spiritual mentors, and ordinary men and women gathered like clouds massing to have their individual needs met with empowerments, formal permissions, instructions, oral transmissions, transmissions for the transference of consciousness, or even something as simple as an exorcism, a blessing with the hand, or an audience. These people, too, are included within the ranks of the students to be guided by my lord guru.

My lord guru was also highly motivated by a singular devotion to the activities of upholding, preserving, and spreading the teachings of the Sage as they are found in Tibet, the Land of Snows—particularly the eight great approaches of spiritual accomplishment—without any sectarian bias on his part. It was due to the power of that motivation that all schools—Sakya, Geluk, Kagyü, Nyingma, even Bönpo—regard him as one of their gurus, showing him the highest honors [21b] and relying on the nectar of his writings as the nourishment that brings liberation and well-being.

Even this much of a biography demonstrates that Kongtrul Rinpoché was a great master of the entire range of the teachings. Such holy and amazing stature as that of Kongtrul Rinpoché is something that has quite clearly not been found since in other great people of my own or other schools. This being the case, like bees being attracted to a fragrant lotus, the great figures of these schools were attracted to Kongtrul Rinpoché, to this powerful master of the enlightened minds of the vast array of learned and accomplished masters, solely intent on seeking him out with singular devotion. Thus, the great throne holder of Radreng, the Achi Hotoktu—the regent of Tibet, the Land of Snows, who holds his lofty position due to the order and prophecy of the Supreme Elders[101] that appointed him the temporal ruler—accepted Kongtrul Rinpoché as a guru. The great scholar Amchok Geshé of Amdo praised Kongtrul Rinpoché as being omniscient. The Mongolian scholar Sokpo Toyön Pandita[102]—who could have been Minister of the Interior to the Dalai Lama, but who shrugged off the wealth and power of rulership as one would spit saliva out of one's mouth—found that when he encountered the writings of Kongtrul Rinpoché, they captivated his mind, helpless to resist. In our present day, the Thirteenth Dalai Lama, Lobzang Thupten Gyatso[103]—the omniscient Vajradhara, the lord of victorious ones from the utterly positive realm to the west who is the master of the entire range of the Victorious One's teachings on the surface of the earth[104]— issued a proclamation in which he refers to "Kongtrul Yönten Gyatso Rinpoché, a guide who illuminates the teachings of the Victorious One, a holy master who is learned and accomplished, whose mindstream is imbued with the enlightened intent of the teachings without sectarian bias." [22a] In this proclamation, the Dalai Lama enjoined Kongtrul Rinpoché to further his activities for the welfare of the Land of Snows. In his precious edicts, he praised Kongtrul Rinpoché as "a great elder, an embodiment of Manjughosha," and prayed for the long life of Kongtrul Rinpoché and his patrons. Such facts call to mind the following words:

> If a person becomes endowed with enlightened qualities,
> others gather as a matter of course, without having to be gathered,
> just as bees swarm from a long distance
> to circle around a fragrant flower.[105]

In conclusion:

> You are the lamp that lights the three worlds,
> the culmination of the legacy of the omniscient lord of the
>   Buddhadharma.
> How can ordinary mortals comprehend what manifests clearly
> to the profound and lucid awareness of one who is entirely exalted?

> If the smallest ray of light—the tiniest fraction of your amazing deeds—
> can cause the night lily of my faith and inspiration
> to unfold its bloom, what need is there to speak
> of the entire moon of your life example, so vast and profound?

> You are the great mainstay of the world, extolled by the Victorious
>   One,[106]
> a regent of Padma, a learned and accomplished lord of the
>   Buddhadharma.
> Here I have described your final deeds in part,
> which your wise students have let fall from their lips.
> May the virtue of this ensure that we encounter you, O sublime and
>   glorious guru,
> in the pure realm for which you have departed;
> may the illumination of your speech banish the darkness in our minds,
> and may we attain enlightenment within the expanse of your intent,
> the state of equalness!

I had hoped to compose this account as a fitting conclusion to Kongtrul Rinpoché's lengthy autobiography. [22b] I received permission to do so from three masters—our holy spiritual mentor Tashi Özer, who was the foremost among the heart sons of my guru Vajradhara; the omniscient Pönlop,[107] who too is Vajradhara and a glorious protector of all the teachings; and Kathok Situ Mahapandita,[108] who mastered the five fields of knowledge. This was reinforced by the learned Tsering Tashi, who served Lord Khyentsé, and who impressed on me the necessity of writing this. As well, Sang-ngak Tendzin of Losal, who served as Kongtrul Rinpoché's attendant during audiences and ceremonies, told me, "You alone are qualified to undertake this task, so don't procrastinate." Although I did, in fact, let some time go by without doing anything about it, Lama Gönlu,[109] who served as vajra master at Kongtrul Rinpoché's hermitage, and numerous other interested parties urged me to write this. In response to their requests, I wrote this account, which I feel is just like a seed. It was written on an auspicious day close to the full moon of the fourth month in the Iron Ox Year [1901-1902], at Palpung Monastery, by me, Tashi Chöphel, a very ordinary person who was treated with enormous and extraordinary kindness by the great Jamgön Lama, who was Vajradhara.

Following this, my holy master's secretary, Tsering Döndrup, said, "It is truly wonderful that you have finished this. Now you should supplement it with any additional information that is appropriate." He also took responsibility for having the text published. The revision of the text was completed under auspicious circumstances at Alo Paljor Monastery. [23a]

May the virtue of this accomplishment serve as a cause for me and others to attain the state of the guru as one! May virtue and excellence flourish!

❀

Colophon by the Fifteenth Gyalwang Karmapa, Khakhyap Dorjé

Guru Vajradharaye [O guru who is Vajradhara!]
You whose name is the light from the orb of the sun in the stainless
    vault of space,
warming the lotus bud in my heart with its power
and causing it to bloom, unfolding its stamens of total peace—
O my venerable guru, again I recall your kindness.

Born of your sublime and profound awareness, your activity
is forever accomplished throughout a vast range of realms,
arising as a glorious setting for the spacious mandala
of the timeless awareness of an omniscient one.

These accounts, which give just a fraction of your life example,
shed light in the minds of those whose vision is limited.
May the virtue of publishing these be like soothing moonlight,
increasing the enjoyment of intelligent and fortunate people
and causing a soft rain from the potent clouds of nectar
to fall continually over the vast range of all beings,
alleviating all the torrid heat of our threefold suffering
and allowing the pleasure grove of enlightened experience to
     flourish!

These accounts of the life example of my venerable guru, who was the
protector Manjushri, have been included to adorn the great *Treasury of Precious Hidden Teachings*[110] by me, a servant who is called Khakhyap Dorjé.
Shriyantu![111]

ENDNOTES

1. An invocation in Sanskrit: "Homage to the all-knowing and all-seeing guru, Ocean
   of Qualities." The name *Guna Samudra* (Ocean of Qualities) in the opening invocation is the Sanskritized version of the Tibetan *Yönten Gyatso*, the shortened
   form of the name Kongtrul received when he took monastic ordination in the Kagyü
   School.
2. The ten powers are those of mastery over longevity, mind, material goods, karma,
   conscious rebirth, devoted interest, aspiration, miraculous powers, spiritual teachings, and timeless awareness. See *mDo kun las btus pa'i nang don rig pa'i tshig
   mdzod Mu tig phreng ba*, p. 780.
3. This is a collective term for the sambhogakaya and nirmanakaya manifestations of
   enlightened being.
4. A euphemistic way of referring to enlightened beings dying and taking rebirth in
   other circumstances in a conscious manner, all with the intention of benefiting
   others.
5. That is, Kongtrul.

6. That is to say, buddhahood with all its innate qualities being no longer present as latent potentials, but fully evident.

7. The image of clouds, laden with moisture, would be a particularly potent one in a dry land such as Tibet, as a symbol of richness and prosperity.

8. Mahayana Buddhist teachings maintain that four fully enlightened buddhas have already appeared in our present eon, Shakyamuni Buddha being the fourth. In all, more than one thousand buddhas will eventually appear. As the last in this series, Adhimukta will represent the culmination, with his qualities, activity, and influence equaling those of all the preceding buddhas combined.

9. The early Kadampa masters were regarded as paragons of impeccable adherence to ethical and spiritual values.

10. The Mahamudra teachings speak of four "yogas," or genuine states of being, that are signposts of progress on the path of spiritual development. These yogas are termed "one-pointedness," "simplicity" (literally, "freedom from elaboration"), "one taste," and "nonmeditation" (in the sense of one being beyond any formal structure of meditation technique). Each of these four is further subdivided into three phases of initial, intermediate, and supreme—for a total of twelve stages. Although Tashi Chöphel quotes Kongtrul as admitting to having reached the sixth of these twelve stages (that is, the supreme phase of simplicity), he seems to be attesting to his guru's realization being of the next stage, that of "one taste."

11. The Anuyoga teachings (in the Nyingma School) and those concerning the stage of completion for Anuttarayogatantra (in the Sarma Schools) discuss a subtler "body"—the vajra body—that coincides with the physical body, but consists of a network of channels, or pathways, along which subtle forms of energy pass. Through the use of physical postures, breathing exercises, and visualizations, the advanced yogic practitioner of the Vajrayana utilizes this subtle structure to accelerate his or her spiritual progress.

12. It is customary for Tibetan lamas, as a kind of benediction, to give those who seek audiences with them cords that have been blessed. Here, however, the implication is that Kongtrul was not impressed, but simply being polite and observing the niceties.

13. To receive leftovers from one's teacher's plate, especially from the teacher's own hands, is considered a great honor among Tibetans.

14. Puwo was a remote, sparsely-inhabited region in the far southeastern reaches of Tibet, near the border with the Indian state of Arunachal Pradesh.

15. The three repositories are those of the Sutras, or discourses of the Buddha; the Vinaya, or monastic codes; and the Abhidharma, or metaphysical teachings. The four classes of tantra—Kriya, Charya, Yoga, and Anuttarayoga—constitute the whole range of Vajrayana teachings from the point of view of the Sarma Schools, of which Tashi Chöphel was a proponent.

16. That is, benefiting others in his next rebirth; this idiom is an oblique reference to a master's impending death.

17. Kongtrul, in fact, confirms this in his comments on "Meditation" toward the end of his Autobiography.

18. When Khyungpo Naljor, the founder of the Shangpa Kagyü School for which Kongtrul had such affinity, was on the point of death, he told his students to pray to him in the buddha Amitabha's Realm of Bliss; see *Like An Illusion: Lives of the Shangpa Kagyu Masters*, p. 91.

19. That is, Jamyang Khyentsé Wangpo, whose *tertön* title was Pema Ösel Do-ngak Lingpa.

20. The Sakya School holds the distinction of transmitting the only lineage of Vajrakila that is not a *terma* lineage—the Khön tradition, named after Khön Nagendra Rakshita (also called Khön Luyi Wangpo), a member of King Trisong Detsen's court. It was Nagendra Rakshita who received the transmission from Guru Rinpoché, and from whom it passed down through the Khön clan, whose members have included the lineage masters of the Sakya School since its inception in the eleventh century to the present day.

21. Tsangnyön Heruka Rüpai Gyenchen (1452-1507) also authored the biographies of Marpa and Milarepa and the collected songs of Milarepa; he was a lineage holder who received the teachings known as the Rechung Nyengyü ("Oral Lineage of Rechungpa").

22. Also known as Thoyön Yeshé Döndrup Tenpai Gyaltsen. A Gelukpa master who lived from 1792 to 1855, Sokpo Thoyön Lama Döndrup Gyaltsen was also one of Jamyang Khyentsé Wangpo's teachers.

23. This commentary has been translated into English as *Mahāmudrā: The Quintessence of Mind and Meditation*.

24. This became one of the most widely practiced of Chokgyur Lingpa's Tersar cycles. Many empowerments are divided into two phases, the preliminary phase and the main empowerment, often given on consecutive days.

25. Sakya Pandita's discovery of an incomplete Sanskrit manuscript of *The Vajrakila Tantra*, at the hermitage of Sekzhing in the Shang Valley west of Lhasa, provided further proof of the authenticity of the tantras of the Nyingma School. This authenticity had been called into question since Sarma scholars such as Butön Rinchendrup began codifying the scriptures of the Kangyur and Tengyur collections. Kongtrul's masterful commentary to this tantra is found in Volume 3 of his collected works, *The Treasury of Extensive Teachings*.

26. That is, Jamyang Loter Wangpo, the Pönlop of Ngor Monastery.

27. This is probably Jamyang Lodrö Seng-gé, Kongtrul's grandnephew.

28. The monastic summer retreat is one of the "three bases of purification" in the Buddhist monastic code (the other two being the monthly ceremony to renew mo-

nastic vows and the ritual to determine infractions of the rules of conduct). The summer retreat begins on the sixteenth day of either the sixth or seventh month of the Tibetan calendar and lasts for three months, during which time the monastic community is cloistered in strict retreat and the participants devote themselves to study and spiritual practice.

29. That is, Tashi Özer, whose Sanskritized name would have been Mangala Rasmi.

30. Because the Tibetan year "overlaps" the Western year by at least one and a half months, Kongtrul's death would have occurred sometime in January of 1900.

31. Tibetan lamas often bless their students by placing their malas on the students' heads.

32. A common Tibetan metaphor, borrowed from the Indian tradition, compares the Buddhist teachings to an oasis-like lake, and beings to swans that are attracted to that lake. As Herbert V. Guenther notes (*Looking Deeper: A Swan's Questions and Answers*, p. ix), for Western audiences "swan" is a more appropriate way to translate the Tibetan term (*ngang pa*) than the more literal and accurate "goose."

33. This is to be seen as an expression of Tashi Chöphel's longing and despair, rather than implying any criticism of his master.

34. That is, Tashi Özer.

35. That is, Pönlop Rinpoché Jamyang Loter Wangpo ("Pönlop Vajradhara") and Khenchen Chöjé Tashi Özer ("Khen Lama").

36. A reference to gods and other nonhuman beings.

37. It was this master who performed the transference of consciousness for Kongtrul's grandnephew Jamyang Namgyal Dorjé when the young man passed away.

38. These rituals are designed to free a deceased individual's mindstream of any possible impediments or obstacles to the attainment of enlightenment.

39. There are many accounts, up to recent times, of certain organs remaining intact when a highly realized individual's remains are cremated; the eyes, tongue, and heart (corresponding to form, speech, and mind) are often mentioned.

40. The idiom "treasury of space" is a common allusion in Buddhist texts. It refers to the activity of the mythical bodhisattva Samantabhadra, who through the power of his meditative absorption could fill the vast expanse of *shunyata* (the emptiness that is the true nature of phenomena) with an enormous array of offerings.

41. That is, statues to represent form; texts to represent speech; and vajras, or perhaps small replicas of stupas, to represent mind.

42. That is, Tashi Özer.

43. This is a ceremony, at the conclusion of a ritual, to infuse the representations on the shrine with the blessings and presence of the deity on which the ritual focused.

44. These are the Jowo Shakyamuni statue in the Jokhang (the main temple of Lhasa) and the Jowo Mikyö Dorjé state of the Buddha in the nearby Ramoché Temple.

The original statues were held to have been brought to Tibet by his Chinese and Nepalese queens, as part of their dowries, but by Kongtrul's time both had been destroyed or confiscated by Dzungar invaders in the early eighteenth century, and the statues housed in the temples were replacements. See *The Power Places of Central Tibet: The Pilgrim's Guide*, pp. 45-46 and 59, and *Tibet Handbook*, pp. 84-85 and 92.

45. This refers to the custom of painting the faces of statues with a "wash" of gold paint; this would need to be renewed due to wear and age, and it was considered very meritorious to sponsor such restoration work.

46. That is, representations of the principles of enlightened form, speech, and mind— usually a statue, text, and small stupa, respectively.

47. This would have been the Thirteenth Dalai Lama, Thupten Gyatso, who lived from 1876 to 1933.

48. There are eight main styles of stupas, commemorating eight major events in the Buddha's life. The most common form is the stupa of enlightenment, commemorating Shakyamuni's attainment of buddhahood under the bodhi tree. The stupa of the descent from the gods' realm commemorates the occasion upon which the Buddha, having left the human realm to give teachings to the rebirth of his mother in a realm of the gods, descended to earth again on a miraculous staircase. For more information on these eight styles, see *Principles of Tibetan Art*, vol. 2, pp. 81-97.

49. This would have been the son of Chimé Takpai Dorjé.

50. Teachings that are "earth *terma*s" may be contained in chests or caskets, which once discovered must be opened by the *tertön* in a specific manner in order to reveal their contents properly.

51. That is, Kongtrul Rinpoché.

52. That is, the Buddha Shakyamuni.

53. In Buddhism, a "central country" is defined either geographically or spiritually. In the former sense, the "Vajra Seat" is modern-day Bodh Gaya in India, the site on which Shakyamuni attained buddhahood and thus the most holy site in Buddhism, which defines India as the "central country." Spiritually speaking, a central country is one in which the Buddhist teachings are studied and practiced. See *The Words of My Perfect Teacher*, pp. 22-23.

54. This is the Sanskritized version of Tashi Özer's name.

55. This lama had been one of Jamyang Khyentsé Wangpo's attendants.

56. This would be the fourth month of the Iron Rat Year, the year following Kongtrul's demise, corresponding to late June or early July of 1900.

57. That is, Jamyang Loter Wangpo.

58. "New Temple of the Classes of Tantra"; commonly referred to as Lhasar Temple.

59. I have not been able to ascertain whether this account was ever published. It was common for the writings of a master's main student to be included in the master's

collected writings (especially in cases where the subject matter was directly relevant to that collection). There are several works in Kongtrul's collected writings that were either authored or completed by Nesar Tashi Chöphel, but the account of the tomb does not appear in the table of contents to the twenty-volume edition of Kongtrul's works published by Ngodup in 1976 in Paro, Bhutan.

60. A Sanskrit name, the Tibetan equivalent of which would be *Tséchö*, probably short for *Tsering Chödrön*. It is interesting that Kongtrul makes no mention of this woman in his autobiography. According to the late Sakya scholar, the Third Dezhung Rinpoché, Kunga Tenpai Nyima (1906-1986), and the Sixteenth Chagdud Tulku, Pema Gargyi Wangchuk (b. 1930), Kongtrul had a spiritual consort (Tib. *sangyum*). These masters felt that this consort's role was like that of a muse, inspiring and enriching Kongtrul's spiritual development without their relationship ever being of an overtly physical nature. Nevertheless, for Kongtrul (as a fully ordained monk) to associate even socially with a woman was something that scandalized members of his retinue, who tried to prevent the woman from having private audiences with their master. This is only one example of the way in which spiritual masters can find themselves at the mercy of those around them! It is possible that Ayurdharma was this consort.

61. In his autobiography, Kongtrul refers to this master simply as Gyurmé Tendzin.

62. These would be, for example, demonstrations of how *torma*s or other offerings were to be prepared, how chants were to be performed, and so forth.

63. That is, Kongtrul had formulated these aspirations in former lifetimes; it was Khyentsé who, in this lifetime, awakened this potential in Kongtrul and helped him to fulfill his destiny.

64. Tashi Chöphel is implying that it was Khyentsé Rinpoché who, having already gained realization himself, had been "born before" and could then help the potential in Kongtrul to "hatch."

65. This is a reference to the rituals and practices that Kongtrul often performed on Khyentsé's behalf.

66. The image of a lotus opening to the sun's light and warmth is a common metaphor for a master's blessings opening and maturing the mind of a student.

67. That is, Kongtrul's.

68. This is a reference to the Vajra Crown of the Karmapas, the original of which is said to be invisible to ordinary eyes (and thus "hidden on top of his head") and to have been presented by *dakini*s to the Eighth Karmapa, Mikyö Dorjé. A physical crown was made and has been handed down through the lines of incarnations since that time, to be used in the famed ritual in which the current Karmapa dons the crown to transmit its blessings to those who witness the ceremony.

69. That is, the second Tai Situ incarnation whom Kongtrul met in his lifetime, the first being his root guru, Situ Pema Nyinjé Wangpo. Kongtrul lived to see a third

incarnation, the Eleventh Situ Pema Wangchok Gyalpo, who was born in 1886 after the untimely death of the Tenth Situ.

70. This was the Ninth Pawo Rinpoché (d. 1911) of Nenang Monastery, who was also known as Tsuklak Nyinjé; the title "Namdren" means "(spiritual) guide." Nenang, near the Karmapa's seat of Tsurphu in central Tibet west of Lhasa, was founded in 1333 by the First Zhamar, Tokden Drakpa Seng-gé (1283-1349) and became the seat of the Pawo incarnations, beginning with the First Pawo, Chöwang Lhundrup (1440-1503).

71. The honorific title *Jé-ön* indicates that the original incarnation in the series had been a blood relation of the Gyalwang Karmapa at that time, not necessarily that the incarnations mentioned were related to the current Karmapa. (RT)

72. This could be a reference to either the fifth Khamtrul incarnation of the Drukpa Kagyü School, Drubgyü Nyima (1781-1847), or the sixth, Mipham Tenpai Nyima (1849-1907).

73. The Zurmang Trungpa incarnations mentioned were the ninth, Karma Tenphel, and the tenth, Chökyi Nyima. The Eleventh Zurmang Trungpa, Chögyam Trungpa Rinpoché (1939-1987) journeyed to the western hemisphere and founded the Vajradhatu network of Buddhist centers, now maintained by his eldest son, Sakyong Mipham Rinpoché. Another of Trungpa Rinpoché's sons is the current Zurmang Tenga incarnation. The Twelfth Zurmang Trungpa incarnation has been recognized in eastern Tibet and is being educated at Palpung Monastery.

74. The abbatial throne of the Sakya monastery of Ngor Evam Chöden was held by members of four aristocratic houses in rotation. Each generation, these four houses—of Thartsé, Phendé, Luding, and Khangsar—produced a Khenpo, or Khenchen (abbot) and a Zhabdrung (regent). Other offices, such as that of Pönlop, might also be held, as in the case of the Thartsé Pönlop, Jamyang Loter Wangpo.

75. Khangsar Khenchen Ngawang Sönam Gyaltsen (c. 1835-c. 1895) was the fifty-fifth grand abbot of Ngor Monastery.

76. Palden Lodrö Gyaltsen, also known as Palden Lodrö Drakpa, was the fifty-sixth grand abbot of Ngor Monastery.

77. This is most probably the Second Dezhung Lungrik Tulku, Lungrik Nyima (c. 1840-1898). After fleeing Tibet in 1958 during the Communist military occupation, the Third Dezhung Lungrik Tulku, Kunga Tenpai Nyima (1906-1987) lived for many years in Seattle, Washington, having emigrated there in 1960. In 1986 he went to Nepal, where he founded Tharlam Monastery in memory of his principal guru, Gatön Ngawang Lekpa (1867-1941), and where his own incarnation, the Fourth Dezhung Lungrik Tulku, Ngawang Kunga Thekchen Chökyi Nyima (b. 1991), is currently being educated.

78. Kunga Jamyang was one of Jamyang Loter Wangpo's gurus.

79. This Gyatrul incarnation, also known as Do-ngak Tendzin (1830-1892), was the

seventh throne holder of the Palyul tradition of the Nyingma School; see *A Garland of Immortal Wish-fulfilling Trees: The Palyul Tradition of Nyingmapa*, pp. 91-99. The current Gyatrul incarnation (b. 1923) lives and teaches in the United States.

80. This was the second Dzakha Choktrul incarnation.

81. The fifth incarnation of Dzogchen Monastery was Thupten Chökyi Dorjé (1872-1935); the current incarnation, the Seventh Dzogchen Rinpoché, Jigmé Losel Wangpo (b.1964) is the head of the new Dzogchen Monastery founded near Bangalore in south India.

82. Gemang was a branch of Dzogchen Monastery. "Kuzhap Gemang" may be a reference to Gemang Orgyen Tendzin, who was also a student of Mipham Namgyal Gyatso.

83. The Lingtrul incarnations are associated with Kathok Monastery. The two referred to by Tashi Chöphel would presumably be the Second Lingtrul, Könchok Gyeypai Lodrö (1773-1838), and the Third Lingtrul, Lobzang Lungtok Tendzin Thrinlé (1850-1902). The current Lingtrul Rinpoché lives and teaches in North America.

84. Karma Gyurmé Ngédön Tendzin (1794-1851) was the first throne holder of Darthang Do-ngak Shedrup Dargyeling, a branch of Palyul Monastery founded in the Golok region of northeastern Tibet.

85. Lhatrul Pema Garwang Tendzin (1852-1935) was a major figure in the establishment of Darthang Monastery. The First Dzong-nang Rinpoché, Kunzang Gyurmé, lived during the late nineteenth and early twentieth centuries; he became the administrator of Palyul Monastery on the death of his teacher, Do-ngak Chökyi Nyima (1854-1906). The Second Dzong-nang Tulku, Jampal Dorjé, was born in 1936; after fleeing to India and Nepal, he founded centers in those countries and then moved to Taiwan, where he founded a center in Taipei before his death in 1987.

86. The First Zhechen Rabjam incarnation, Tenpai Gyaltsen (1654-1709), studied with the Fifth Dalai Lama and with Dzogchen Pema Rigdzin (1625-1697), who founded Dzogchen Monastery, one of the most important Nyingma monasteries in eastern Tibet, in 1684 or 1685 and was the first in the succession of Dzogchen Rinpoché incarnations. It was the Second Zhechen Rabjam, Gyurmé Kunzang Namgyal (1713-1769), who founded the monastery of Zhechen Tennyi Dargyeling in 1735. The Fourth Zhechen Rabjam, Garwang Chökyi Gyaltsen (c. 1810-1863), and the Fifth Zhechen Rabjam, Pema Thekchok Tenpai Gyaltsen (1864-1909), both lived during Kongtrul's lifetime and had opportunity to study with him. As the title *Gyaltsap* ("regent") implies, the Zhechen Gyaltsap incarnations served as regents between the Rabjam incarnations; spanning Kongtrul's lifetime are those of the Third Zhechen Gyaltsap, Orgyen Rangjung Dorjé Tsewang Druppa Tsal (d. c. 1870), and the Fourth Zhechen Gyaltsap, the great scholar and writer Gyurmé

Pema Namgyal (1871-1926), a student of Mipham Jamyang Namgyal and a teacher of Kongtrul's rebirth, Palpung Kongtrul Khyentsé Özer (1904-1953).

87. Mipham Jamyang Namgyal is another name for the great Nyingma scholar Jamgön Ju Mipham Namgyal Gyatso (1846-1912).

88. Kunzang Sönam was also known as Rangshar Khenpo.

89. Geshé Norbu Tendzin (b. 1835), also known as Tsokshul Lama, was a scholar from the region of Minyak in the far southeast of Tibet.

90. The First Do Drupchen was Jigmé Thrinlé Özer (1745-1821), a student of Rigdzin Jigmé Lingpa. The Second Do Drupchen, Jigmé Phuntsok Jungné (1824-1863), and the Third Do Drupchen, Jigmé Tenpai Nyima (1865-1926), were contemporaries of Kongtrul. The Third Do Drupchen is here referred to as Jigmé Tenpai Gyaltsen, but the accolade "sun of the teachings" (Tib. *tenpai nyima*) may be a reference to his name. The present incarnation, the Fourth Do Drupchen, Jigmé Thrinlé Palbar (b. 1927), resides at his center in Gangtok, Sikkim.

91. A variation on the name Gandenpa; another name for the Gelukpa School of Tibetan Buddhism.

92. The Gelukpa monastery of Dragyap Tashi Chödzong, over a hundred kilometers southwest of Dergé, was founded in 1621 by the First Dragyap Kyabgön, Kachu Drakpa Gyatso (1572-1638/9), and a branch monastery was established in 1640, making this area a strong Gelukpa presence in eastern Tibet. The present Dragyap Kyabgön, Loden Sherab (b. 1939), lives and teaches in Germany.

93. Not identified; the Tibetan equivalent of the Sanskrit name *Punya* ("merit") is Sönam.

94. Lhaksam Tenpai Gyaltsen was a khenpo of Palpung Monastery.

95. This is not a reference to the Lama Pema Norbu who graduated from Kongtrul's retreat center, but to the second Pema Norbu incarnation of the Palyul tradition, Pema Kunzang Tendzin Norbu, who lived from 1887 to 1932. The third and present Pema Norbu incarnation, Penor Rinpoché Thupten Lekshé Chökyi Drayang (b. 1932), lives and teaches at the monastery of Thekchok Namdrol Shedrup Dargyeling, which he founded in 1963 near Mysore, India. See *A Garland of Immortal Wish-fulfilling Trees: The Palyul Tradition of Nyingmapa*, pp. 107-115 and 121-130.

96. This was the first Drupwang Tsoknyi incarnation, Pema Drimé Özer, who was born in 1828 in the Nangchen region northwest of Dergé. He was recognized as a rebirth of Milarepa's student Rechungpa Dorjé Drakpa (1085-1161) and the great *tertön* Ratna Lingpa (1403-1479), and was a master of the Karma Kagyü School and the Six Yogas of Naropa in particular. The present incarnation, the Third Drupwang Tsoknyi Rinpoché, was born in Nepal in 1966, a descendant of Chokgyur Lingpa and son of Tulku Urgyen Rinpoché (1920-1996). He lives in Nepal and teaches at centers around the world.

97. Adzom Drukpa Drodul Pawo Dorjé (1842-1924) was recognized as a rebirth of Pema Karpo (1527-1592), the great scholar and fourth Drukchen incarnation of the Drukpa Kagyü School. Adzom Drukpa was a principal student of Kongtrul and Jamyang Khyentsé Wangpo; a major modern lineage of the Heart Drop teachings of the Dzogchen system was transmitted from Khyentsé through Adzom Drukpa to the late Dilgo Khyentsé Rinpoché.

98. Khargo was a monastery of the Drigung Kagyü School in eastern Tibet.

99. Radreng Monastery, located more than one hundred kilometers northeast of Lhasa, was originally founded by Atisha's student Dromtön Gyalwa Jungné (1004/5-1062) in 1056 as the center of the Kadampa School that he established. Radreng became a Gelukpa institution following the visit of Tsongkhapa Lobzang Drakpa (1357-1419), the founder of the "new Kadampa," or Gelukpa, School. From the time of the Seventh Dalai Lama, Kalzang Gyatso (1708-1757), the abbots of Radreng were candidates for the regency during the Dalai Lamas' minority. Achi Hotoktu is a Mongolian title meaning "Gracious and Exalted One"; a number of such titles taken from the Mongolian language were conferred by the Dalai Lamas on high-ranking *tulku*s in the Gelukpa School. The third Achi Hotoktu of Radreng, Ngawang Yeshé Tsulthrim Gyaltsen (1816-1863), was the abbot of that institution and served as regent during the minority of the Eleventh Dalai Lama, Khedrup Gyatso (1838-1855/6). He then retired back to Radreng, only to be summoned again to Lhasa upon the premature death of the Eleventh Dalai Lama. When Kongtrul met him in Lhasa in 1858, Achi Hotoktu was serving as regent for the infant Twelfth Dalai Lama, Thrinlé Gyatso (1856-1875), a position he held until his death in 1863.

100. The forty-third generation of the royal house of Dergé was Tsewang Dorjé Rigdzin, who was born in 1786. His father, Sawang Kundrup Dega Zangpo (b. 1768), died young in 1790 and his mother the queen, Tsewang Lhamo, served as regent until 1798, when she was forced to relinquish her authority to the government ministers, who ruled until Tsewang Dorjé Rigdzin assumed the throne in 1804. After ensuring the succession (he had three sons and one daughter), he renounced his throne and became a monk in 1826. His son, Damtsik Dorjé, succeeded him as king (the forty-fourth generation of the house of Dergé) and died before the forces of Nyarong Gönpo Namgyal conquered Dergé in 1863. Damtsik Dorjé's widow, Chöying Zangmo, and her son, Chimé Takpai Dorjé (the heir apparent to the throne of Dergé), were held hostage by the Nyarong forces until their release by the central Tibetan forces under the leadership of Phulungwa Tsewang Dorjé in 1865.

101. A reference to the line of Dalai Lamas, who from the time of the seventh, Kalzang Gyatso (1708-1757), considered the abbots of Radreng Monastery as candidates for the regency of Tibet during the minorities of the Dalai Lamas.

102. That is, Sokpo Thoyön Yeshé Döndrup Tenpai Gyaltsen (1792-1855).

103. Like his predecessor the great Fifth Dalai Lama, Lobzang Thupten Gyatso is remembered for his ecumenical outlook.

104. A reference to the Dalai Lamas as incarnations of Avalokiteshvara, the bodhisattva of compassion, in human form. The "utterly positive" realm of Sukhavati, identified with the western direction, is the realm associated with Avalokiteshvara.

105. I have not determined the source of this obviously well-known quotation.

106. This is a reference to the Buddha's prophecies in sutras such as *The Discourse on the Most Majestic State of Meditative Absorption*, to which Kongtrul alludes in his account of his previous lifetimes.

107. That is, Ngor Pönlop Jamyang Loter Wangpo.

108. That is, the Third Kathok Situ, Chökyi Gyatso (1880-1923/5).

109. In the eastern provinces of Tibet, personal names are often abbreviated or changed with suffixes that are signs of affection. A great master may be known to his close students by such a fond nickname. "Gönlu" would be derived from the proper name Gönpo. See *Among Tibetan Texts: History and Literature of the Himalayan Plateau*, pp. 276-277, n. 38.

110. Tashi Chöphel's account was included in one of the concluding volumes of *The Treasury of Precious Hidden Teachings* by its editor, the Fifteenth Karmapa.

111. A traditional benediction in Sanskrit: "May there be glory!"

THE MIRAGE OF NECTAR

A fragmentary account of the past lives
of Pema Gargyi Wangchuk Thrinlé Drodul Tsal,
a mere reflection of a renunciant,
who has only three ideas in mind[1]

BY JAMGÖN KONGTRUL LODRÖ THAYÉ
(1813-1900)

INTRODUCTION

[1b]   With great devotion, I pay homage to the venerable Pema Nyinjé
           Wangpo, who is Vajradhara.[2]

[2a]   You have emerged victorious in battle with the misleading
           perceptions of confused mind
        and have seen, without confusion, the way of abiding that is
           dharmakaya in all its nakedness,
[2b]   discovering the sublime state in which realization is simultaneous
           with freedom.
        Precious masters of the Kagyü School, grant me your blessings!

[3a]   Those who are born with potential and perfect this by applying
           themselves with diligence
        achieve the authentic qualities of the paths and levels of realization,

and so, through their sublime powers, can perceive the state of those
   to be guided.
Then even the sketchiest account of their lives will guide many
   beings.

But ordinary peole, who minds are obscured even to themselves,
   have no such qualities, due to the eight worldly concerns.
Nevertheless, they pretend to have them and rely on the support of
   others to brag about themselves.
They carry a heavy burden—that of contradicting the teachings

In degenerating times, when the force of wrong views is on the rise,
   some holy masters,
on the strength of their compassion, see that the minds of fools
need something that is provisionally meaningful and, so as to dispel
   even a bit of their complex confusion, speak about what would
   better be left hidden.

Even those who, as human beings, do have the qualities of a guru, should
not speak about themselves unless the occasion calls for it. Even the great
children of the Victorious One,[4] who abide on high levels of realization, did
not display their timeless awareness, meditative absorption, aspirations, or
miraculous powers to ordinary people unless the Tathagata[5] permitted it. [3b]
Vajradhara has commanded that the signs of success one achieves in the two
stages[6] of the Vajrayana path are to be kept even more secret and private. So
those who have insight into the true nature of phenomena reveal such things
only to a small degree and then only in order to guide those who are fortunate
enough to be guided. For those who are still on the path of application,[7] or
some lesser stage, to discuss such topics is contradictory to the *samaya* commitment to refrain from broadcasting secrets.[8] If people who have such commitments have no qualities, but pretend to have them—speaking about the
visions of gods and demons they have experienced, or sublime states of insight, or signs of successful practice achieved through the use of ritual substances or mantras—they violate their vows in a fundamental way. They deny
themselves the opportunity to gain spiritual attainments, and instead must suffer the limitless torments of the hot hell realms.
   It would seem, then, that those who understand the effects of karma would

not speak of such things, even if their lives were to depend on it. Even though more ordinary people have no such vows to impair, the act of lying itself constitutes an implicitly negative action, something shunned by the world at large (including the gods), for it means that one must suffer the torments of lower states of rebirth.

There are some who—due to a meritorious predisposition ripening from their past lifetimes, but fueled by a negative demonic force that goads them on—are able for a time to beguile people of limited merit and little good fortune with false words, and so gain for themselves food, clothing, and so forth. But eventually the liars' secret flaws are exposed and it becomes plainly evident that they have brought ruination on themselves and all connected to them, in this and future lifetimes. To say nothing of such cases—of pretending that something is so when it is not, [4a] or of having something one doesn't have—it would seem that there is a need to determine when it is timely to discuss even things that are true.

Since someone like me—a very ordinary person who has not even truly begun to follow the path of accumulation—has none of the qualities of a spiritually advanced being that would be worthy of concealment, any "secrecy" is already a moot point, like speaking of wealth being hidden in a pauper's house. While some stroke of luck may account for some minor good omens or some hazy dreams, these do not constitute signs of success on the spiritual path—or anything good or bad at all, for that matter—and so to maintain secrecy about such things doesn't give me any hope of gaining spiritual attainments thereby, while to talk about them doesn't cause me any apprehension of losing what I have gained. Although it might be claimed that I am the rebirth of someone, or an emanation, from my own perspective there is no point in discussing former lifetimes. I find that I can't call to mind even what I have wished for and done in this lifetime, for whatever I have done or said each day fades from my memory. So much for any hope of recalling past lifetimes! Although I may be able to recall certain things, it seems to me that I am lacking in any memory of some lifetime as a great being, someone whose life example is that of a spiritually advanced and holy person.

I am reminded of what is often said: "As to what you have done in the past, look at your present embodiment. As to what will happen to you in the future, your present actions dictate that. Your karma follows you as your shadow follows your body." This being so, I must have reinforced some fundamentally virtuous qualities for many lifetimes in the past, [4b] for I have gained a very pure human existence filled with spiritual pursuits. But my mind remains obsessed solely with the projections of my afflictive emotions. So if I were to assess myself by deducing from this fact, I would have to conclude that my nature is such that my mind has passed through the three realms of samsara and continues to wander endlessly in that cycle.

However, I have been encouraged by the assurances (which have not been kept private, but are now well known and much discussed) that I am in fact an emanation of great spiritual beings. These assurances constitute the individual intentions of my glorious gurus, whose vision due to their spiritual practice and timeless awareness makes them infallible. In addition, I have been assured by signs and prophecies from Orgyen, the second Buddha,[9] and others of the Three Roots. Because of this, most people, whether of high station or low, consider me a holy person, seeing in me an opportunity for them to increase their merit. Those who take me to be their guru, because of the vast scope of their pure perception, place great hopes in me, regarding what is only provisionally true to be definitively so.

In particular, I have forged good connections in past lifetimes with major spiritual figures and other great beings. Due to the momentum of their motivation and aspirations, I have been able to receive help from many great and famous masters in this life, principally Situ Rinpoché and the other major figures of the Karma Kagyü and Drukpa Kagyü Schools. [5a] They have conferred on me ripening empowerments and liberating teachings of the Vajrayana approach, mainstream traditions of teaching, and even instruction in secular fields of knowledge.

In the first place, then, it would be unfitting for me to downplay the proclamations of my venerable gurus, who have taken me under their care due to their unconditional compassion. And if I take what they have said as true in the sense of indicating my potential, their vajra words cannot possibly be untrustworthy, so the auspicious circumstances are in place for this potential to become a reality in the future. Secondly, should devoted people have faith in me, there is always the case of the dog's tooth that produced relics,[10] so if they pray to me with the conviction that I am an emanation of such holy beings, they will be cared for in all their lifetimes by those holy beings. Thirdly, if these major spiritual figures were, due to happenstance, to rely on someone very ordinary as a guru—someone without any characteristics or qualities that could be determined directly, or at least by inference—this would be a case of their exemplary lives being lived at odds with the Buddhadharma.[11]

Therefore, the following discussion is intended to render some service to these great people. I am concerned with three topics—my lifetimes as holy masters in the past; the prophecies concerning my present lifetime; and the ways in which I have, in some small measure, gained enough attainment to reveal profound *terma*s, or hidden teachings.

LIVES AS HOLY MASTERS IN THE PAST

[5b]
Concerning the first topic, throughout time without beginning, we all have been subject to the projections of our confusion, due to the moment-by-moment concepts based on our dualistic perceptions. We have taken rebirth in countless embodiments in all the states throughout the three realms. We have reinforced the karma produced by our afflictive emotionality on an inconceivable scale. We have been constantly buffeted by the waves of the three kinds of suffering, on the great ocean that is the endless state of samsara, and even now we have not yet begun to follow the spiritual path. So if I am honest with myself, how could I entertain hopes of being a rebirth or incarnation of some exalted or holy being? If wise people are unable to examine something and ascertain it through the power of direct and authentic reasoning, then for an ordinary man to misrepresent himself as a guru, pretending to be something he is not, or to have something he doesn't have, is for him deliberately to sow the seeds for a hellish rebirth. How could any right-thinking person do such a thing?

However, my glorious gurus, with their insight due to timeless awareness, and other great and authentic masters, have issued pronouncements that are not just attempts to buck me up or flatter me. In particular, there are prophecies concerning events that are concealed from ordinary view in the *terma*s left by the second Buddha, Padmakara,[12] which everyone, high and low, accepts as authoritative. It is on the basis of these sources that I set down my account, albeit incomplete.

In this regard, both Vajradhara Pema Nyinjé Wangpo [6a] and the Fourteenth Gyalwang Karmapa, Thekchok Dorjé, have said that I am an emanation of Minling Terchen. You can determine this from the prayer for my long life written by the former and the supplication to my former rebirths authored by the latter. And that great scholar, Dabzang Tulku, examined this point in his meditations and saw it clearly to be so.

The omniscient and all-seeing Jamyang Khyentsé Wangpo saw, during his meditations, that I had been Ananda, Bairotsana, Lumé, Zurchen, and Sherab Özer, a *tertön* from Thrango. In a dream, he saw that I had been Müchen Sang-gyé Rinchen and Bayo Chözang.[13] He also said that he clearly remembered me being Kunga Döndrup of Nyemdo. Whether due to some pure vision he experienced or some other reason, he didn't say, but he stated that he was forever convinced that I had been the venerable Taranatha and Tselé Natsok Rangdrol. The great *tertön* Chokgyur Lingpa saw continual signs and indications of my being an emanation of Bairotsana and also experienced clear impressions that I had been Payo Chökyi Lodrö.[14]

Nevertheless, the utterances of these holy masters have three ramifications—the underlying intent, their purpose, and my personal objections.

Underlying Intent

As to the intention underlying these pronouncements, let me quote from *The Ornament of the Class of Discourses*:
[6b]

> Suchness itself is no different for anyone,
> but for those who are pure
> there is the very state of having reached suchness.
> Therefore, all beings have that as their very essence.[15]

And *The Highest Continuum* states:

> Because the *kaya* of perfect buddhahood is pervasive,
> because of the undifferentiated state of suchness,
> and because of their inborn family trait, all embodied beings
> are forever endowed with the very essence of buddhahood.[16]

As these and other sources reveal in detail, from the primordial protector[17] on high to the lowest form of life, *sugatagarbha*—the "buddha nature"—abides within the mindstreams of all, with no hierarchy of greater or lesser, better or worse, more or less. So my masters would not be telling an unsubstantiated lie even if they were to say that I was Vairochana, let alone Bairotsana.[18] In another sense, it is as the *dakini* of enlightened awareness Yeshé Tsogyal said:

All in the future who will be devoted to the *terma* teachings
are nowadays seeing the face of the Guru and praying to him.
Since you all have such karma, feel joyful!
These words of mine are rarer than precious gold.

Given that she said this, there would be nothing amiss in considering me simply to be a suitable recipient—that when Guru Rinpoché and the great translator Bairotsana were in Tibet, I attained a human rebirth and forged some slight connection through meeting them, and that it is due to their innate compassion that I have again attained a state of freedom and opportunity[19] at present, have encountered the general and specific teachings of the Vajrayana approach so easily, [7a] and have been infused with the blessings of these holy masters.

PURPOSE

The purpose of such pronouncements is as stated in *The Ornament of the Class of Discourses*:

> At any given point in time,
> countless beings who have been reborn as humans
> are attaining perfect buddhahood.
> Therefore, do not indulge in feeling discouraged.[20]

They serve, then, to dispel the discouragement I have felt, and to arouse in me a strong sense of inspiration to accomplish something of benefit for myself and others. These pronouncements mean that if I have some slight qualities due to hearing, contemplating, and meditating on the Buddhist teachings, this will ensure some legacy that will promote those teachings. If others whose lot is equal to mine serve someone reputed to be the rebirth or incarnation of some holy being with faith and devotion, this ensures them a positive connection and will diminish the obstacles that hinder them. It is also said:

> Just as wounds are held to have "matured" once they have been drained,
> and foods once they have been enjoyed,
> so it can be shown that, with this working basis,[21] maturation comes

with the pacification of dualistic extremes and the experience of suchness.²²

Thus, due to the potential of even such positive habit patterns, it is conceivable that in the future I can act in ways that will fulfill the intentions of my holy masters.

PERSONAL OBJECTIONS

Regarding my personal objections, how could someone such as I—a completely ordinary person, mired in the swamp of his afflictive emotions—ever be the rebirth or emanation of such holy beings? [7b] Even in my dreams, I have no hope of even being blessed by them. However, as I said before, I will not treat these vajra words, with their respective purposes, in a disparaging manner, but will present them, if only in a rough and concise manner.

The great translator Bairotsana was someone whose enlightened intent was equal to that of Orgyen Guru Rinpoché. In that very lifetime, he attained the *vajrakaya* of the rainbow body, awakening to enlightenment in the youthful vase body.²³ He is united, in the single taste of enlightened intent, with the sovereign lord Vairochana; yet, until the realms of ordinary beings have been emptied, Bairotsana's emanations, guiding beings in whatever way is necessary under any circumstances, will never come to a halt. As *The Ornament of the Class of Discourses* states:

> Due to the sublime diligence of children of the Victorious One,
> if ordinary beings bring the accumulations to complete maturity,²⁴
> in order that even one other being's mind becomes positive,
> these children will not despair, though it takes a thousand eons.²⁵
>
> .   .   .   .
>
> In the midst of sublime gatherings, they reveal in its entirety
> a manifold display of countless states of meditative absorption,
> continually engaged for the sake of ordinary beings
> through emanations of artistry and rebirth, and sublime emanations.²⁶

Thus, we can be certain that it is in the very nature of buddhas that they reveal countless emanations—of artistry and rebirth, emanations and further emanations—simultaneously. As it is also said:

> Just as the sun sends forth infinite rays of light in all directions
>   effortlessly,
> [8a]   their manifold illumination ripening crops completely,
>   so the "suns" who embody truth, with their infinite "light"—the
>   dharma that brings total peace—
>   bring ordinary beings in all directions to maturity.[27]

And so, with awakening to manifest enlightenment[28] taking place on the majestic level of the primordial protector, emanations occur to guide those who are to be guided—one emanation giving rise to many, many resolving into one, and so forth—such that the ordinary minds of mere mortals can't fathom them. This is why there have been many famous emanations of Bairotsana appearing at the same time, or coming during the beginning, middle, and later stages of a single human generation. There have been many such cases, and even though these are difficult for a mind concerned with its immediate perceptions to comprehend, those who do grasp the implications of these inconceivable life examples of the bodhisattvas are moved to a sense of wonder. You should understand these to be the circumstances underlying the accounts that follow. To give one example, the *tertön* Sherab Özer came first, followed within about two generations by the incarnation of his enlightened form, Natsok Rangdrol; the incarnation of his enlightened speech, Terdak Lingpa; and the incarnation of his enlightened mind, Pema Dechen Lingpa—all of whom appeared within a single generation, with the latter two coming toward the end of the former's lifetime.[29] The succession of these four incarnations would seem to have been [8b] many variations from a single basis.

Of these, Sherab Özer Drodul Lingpa[30] is said to have emanated from the heart center of the spiritual hero Thöpai Dumbu Tsal, who lived in Shantipuri and who, in turn, was clearly an emanated manifestation of the great translator Bairotsana, who completely accomplished the fruition state.

The succession of rebirths in this case is said to have been as follows:

- Vairochana (the source from which the succeeding emanations and incarnations emerged)
- Vajradharma

- Ananda
- King Jah (or Indrabhuti)
- Thönmi Sambhota[31]
- Bairotsana
- Tsami Sang-gyé Drak
- the translator Rinchen Zangpo
- Ngok Loden Sherab
- Ja Dulwa Dzinpa
- Khedrup Khyungpo Naljor
- Zhang Tsöndrü Drakpa
- Palchen Chöyé
- Rokdolpa Sherab Gyatso
- Yakdé Panchen and
- Panchen Bumthrak Sumpa.

In the case of Minling Terchen, there are fourteen renowned rebirths in succession, which are generally considered to be the most important ones. The list of these successive prior lives is found in Minling Terchen's own *terma*s and the account of his personal impressions as recorded by Gyalsé Pema Gyurmé Gyatso.[32] Up to and including Ananda, they are as in the preceding case. The rest are listed as follows:

- Indrabhuti the Great
- the Buddhist king Suchandrabhadra
- King Jah (also known as Lungten Dorjé)
- Shantigarbha
- Thönmi Sambhota [9a]
- *Mahasiddha* Krishnacharya
- the monk Purna of Gyalmorong[33]
- the great translator Bairotsana
- Zurchen Shakya Jungné
- Dra-ngön Wangchuk Bar
- Rongzom Chökyi Zangpo
- Khedrup Khyungpo Naljor
- Tanak Bönpo Lhabum (also known as Guru Nöntsé)
- Tulku Rashak Chenpo
- Druptop Ngödrup
- Zhikpo Nyima Seng-gé

- Tenpa Zhungdzin
- Geshé Nyamdrowa
- Guru Jodar
- Yeshé Khyungdrak
- Sakya Panchen
- Longchen Rabjam
- Üpa Sang-gyé Bum
- Yakdé Panchen
- Dorjé Lingpa
- Kunkyong Lingpa
- Bodong Panchen Choklé Namgyal
- Draktokpa Sönam Zangpo
- Sokdokpa Lodrö Gyaltsen
- the venerable Taranatha
- Tulku Chokden Gönpo
- Sinpo Chökyi Gocha and
- Orgyen Terdak Lingpa.

The successive prior lives of Tselé[34] parallel these to some extent, although they include some other individuals. In particular, his actual predecessor was Tsungmé Dorjé,[35] who was a student of Tselé Orgyen Tendzin[36] and the founder of the monastic seat of Tselé.[37]

The successive incarnations of Pema Dechen Lingpa[38] are, in general, the same as the preceding, [9b] with a few additional figures (for example, Latön Namkha Rinchen[39]). In addition, the actual former rebirth of this master is said to have been that of Bubor Tashi Gyatso, the last of the "thirteen gurus in the line of succession of Kathok Monastery."[40]

The successive prior lives of the "venerable one of Jonang," beginning from the initial arousal of bodhichitta, continued through many rebirths and incarnations, of whom the foremost are known as the "thirteen incarnations." In the holy country of India, there were the following:

- *Mahasiddha* Krishnacharya and
- Ratan Bhahula.

Then, in Tibet:

- Rongzom Chökyi Zangpo
- Barompa Darma Wangchuk
- Avadhutipa (a student of Sakya Drakpa Gyaltsen)

- Zhangtön Drukdra Gyaltsen
- Nyö Sang-gyé Rinchen
- Nyö Sanghabhadra
- Jamyang Chöjé Tashi Palden
- Chökyi Nyinjé (a great Sri Lankan scholar) and
- the venerable Kunga Drolchok.

Then again in India, there was

- Gajé Sakyong.

And finally, there was

- the venerable and omniscient Taranatha.

Other than the preceding lists, there are no other famous figures, in either the old or the new schools of Tibetan Buddhism, that need to be mentioned. And of the prior lives of Minling Terchen, I have not located any accounts of both Tenpa Zhungdzin and Geshé Nyamdrowa. As for the "Guru Jodar" referred to in this list, another name of the *tertön* Guru Jotsé was Jowo Tsewang Darpa, [10a] so I feel that these are, in fact, one and the same.[41]

FORMER LIVES OF DRODUL SHERAB ÖZER AND MINLING TERCHEN: THE EARLY SCHOOL

Vairochana

The ground from which all these emanations emerge is Vairochana. While all buddhas are awakened within the state of equalness that is dharmakaya, the aspect of Vairochana known as "Glacial Lake of Timeless Awareness"[42] pertains to the fivefold certainty of the sambhogakaya,[43] within the Pinnacle Pure Realm of Dense Array. Among the incalculable array—of Vairochana's pure realms and enlightened embodiments—that manifests are the aspects of Vairochana abiding in the pinnacle pure realms that are found within the realm of form in this long-suffering world.[44] Concerning these, one tantra states:

> In the pleasant pinnacle pure realm,
> abiding above the pure realms of the gods,
> the completely awakened buddha awakened to buddhahood.
> An emanation awakened to buddhahood here.

A similar passage is found in *The Journey to Sri Lanka*.[45] The Madhyamika scholar Chöshé[46] explains that these citations refer to a special kind of nirmanakaya, classified as an aspect of the sambhogakaya that manifests within the experience of bodhisattvas who are on the path of seeing or higher.[47] These nirmanakaya embodiments, emanating on such a vast scale and transmitting teachings in the midst of these great and powerful beings, are in actuality expressions of the greater principle, that of the buddha Vairochana. But such a revelation of multiple forms is entirely acceptable, given the source from which these forms emanate.

How is this so? According to the tradition of the Early Translation School, dharmakaya abides as the nature of phenomena—the "inner" aspect of the lucidity of being.[48] It is this that expresses itself, as an "outward" aspect of that lucidity, as the field of what are, in fact, being's own manifestations. This field constitutes the manifest aspect of timeless awareness enjoying its own manifestations [10b]—an immeasurable range of enlightened embodiments and aspects of that awareness. The natural manifestation of this is that selfsame sambhogakaya teacher, Vairochana, the Glacial Lake of Timeless Awareness. It is this manifestation that is the "transitional manifestation,"[49] appearing as a fivefold array of pure realms in the perceptions of those who are to be guided and whose perceptions are (to some extent, at least) pure—that is, the powerful beings who are on the tenth level of realization. There are naturally occurring emanations, and from these derive the nirmanakaya manifestations that guide beings, revealing themselves on an inconceivable scale and in harmony with the circumstances of those who are to be guided.[50] (The intent underlying this explanation is identical to the preceding.)[51]

Vajradharma (or Vajrapani)

It is said in *The Guhyasamaja Tantra* that the tantras were entrusted to Vajradharma. This is explained as being the name by which Vajrapani was known when being entrusted with the tantras and empowered.

Vajrapani, the Lord of Secrets, is described in the glorious *Kalachakra Tantra* as the natural expression that unites, in this single form, the vajra faculty of hearing found in all *sugatas*.[52] *The Sphere of Timeless Awareness* states:

> In order to preserve the integrity of all views,
> there is engagement in a multiplicity of forms.

> Some appear as vajra holders,
> some in the forms of buddhas,
> some in the forms of *herukas*,
> some as *tathagatas*,
> some in the forms of bodhisattvas,
> and some like *shravakas*.
> Some are explaining teachings, O delightful lotus.
> Some seem to be reading texts.

[11a]   Some compose tantras and treatises
> and some uphold these.
> There is much to say about this, but what is the need?
> The one revealing this is the majestic Vajrapani.[53]

As this citation indicates, Vajrapani is the one upholding the limitless teachings of the *sugatas*. In the approach of Atiyoga this is Vajrasattva; in that of Anuyoga it is Kunjara, the most majestic among the masters of awareness;[54] and in that of the Mahayoga approach it is Vajradharma. In the Hevajra cycle it is Vajragarbha, while the one who codified the Kalachakra cycle was Suchandrabhadra.[55] In these and other ways, a single state of timeless awareness transforms into a manifold display. In the ultimate sense, as the glorious *Tantra of the Attainment of Secrets* states:

> There is no one else
> who codifies this.
> I alone have spoken it.
> The author of this tantra is the vajra of enlightened mind.

Thus, it is explained that although the Lord of Secrets reveals himself in the form of one codifying the teachings, there is nothing to be pointed to that is separate from the vajra of the enlightened mind of the buddhas. Parallel statements are found in *The Hevajra Tantra* and other texts.

Ananda (c. sixth century B.C.E.)

An emanation of the Lord of Secrets, Ananda was born into the Shakya clan and received the full ordination of a Buddhist monk. He served as the principal attendant to the Lord of the Shakyas,[56] who proclaimed him to have the most excellent retention of the teachings he heard. After the Buddha had passed into nirvana, [11b] Ananda became an *arhat*, codifying the classes of the discourses, or sutras, and serving as the second of the Buddha's seven successors.[57] In these capacities, he is honored as "the great *shravaka* master" who is comparable to the Buddha himself.

King Indrabhuti

This king ruled the realm of Oddiyana in western India during the Buddha's lifetime. Hearing the name of the Blessed One, the king paid homage to him with faith and devotion and offered a mental prayer, whereupon the Blessed One actually came to him. Emanating as the mandala of Akshobhya Vajra from the Guhyasamaja cycle, the Buddha conferred this empowerment on the king. In response to Indrabhuti's request for a method that would allow him to incorporate sensory pleasure into his spiritual path without having to abandon it, the Buddha revealed *The Guhyasamaja Tantra* and guided the king with his instruction. The king, on his part, thoroughly mastered the meaning of these teachings and undertook a vast number of elaborate activities, so that he and his retinue attained the level of *vidyadhara*s.

King Suchandrabhadra (c. sixth century B.C.E.)

The Buddhist king Suchandrabhadra was born the heir of King Suryaprabha of Shambhala.[58] When he was ninety-nine years old, Suchandrabhadra journeyed by miraculous means, accompanied by an enormous retinue, to the Shridhanyakataka stupa in the south of India, where the Blessed One was seated on a lion throne. The king requested that the Buddha open up the "precious treasure trove of the buddhas" [12a] by elucidating the vajra words of all the tantras in their entirety. Thereupon, the Buddha emanated as two mandalas—that of the basic space of phenomena, known as the "Powerful Lord of Enlightened Speech," below and, above that, the glorious mandala of the constellations. He then revealed the source tantra of the glorious Kalachakra cycle in twelve thousand stanzas. The Buddha also taught the source tantras of other cycles to the respective individuals requesting these teachings.

King Suchandrabhadra composed commentaries on all the tantras, and in particular a commentary in sixty thousand stanzas on the Kalachakra source tantra. He conferred the empowerment on his fortunate subjects who lived in some nine hundred and sixty million cities, and explained the tantra to them. In the pleasure grove of Malaya to the south of his capital city of Kalapa, the king erected enormous structures—the complete mandalas of enlightened form, speech, and mind from the Kalachakra cycle. Installing his son, Devendra, on the lion throne and empowering him to succeed him as the spiritual teacher of the kingdom, King Suchandrabhadra manifested as a sambhogakaya embodiment.

King Jah

In such sources as *The Discourse of United Intent,* the Buddha prophesies the coming of a "King Jah," eight (in some sources, twelve) years after the Buddha's passing into nirvana. This accords with a king of Sahora named Indrabhuti (that is to say, the "middle" Indrabhuti[59]), who was also known by the title of King Jah. While he was engaged in practicing the yogas of the lower classes of tantra, the king dreamed of seven remarkable omens. In connection with these dreams, [12b] there fell a rain of tantric texts of the Mahayoga class.[60] Putting these teachings into practice, King Jah came to understand the meaning of these tantras. However, in order to refute the idea that one could begin haphazardly, without a spiritual master, he sent an invitation to Kukuraja, a master who was guided by Vajrasattva, and studied all the tantras with him. King Jah meditated according to the system of the Vajradhatu mandala and attained the level of a *vidyadhara*, accompanied by a retinue of thousands.

Aryadeva (c. third century C.E.)[61]

The master Aryadeva was the son of King Panchashriga of Sri Lanka. He received his monastic ordination from the abbot Hemadeva and became very learned in the Tripitaka, the "three repositories" of the teachings. Later, he studied under Nagarjuna and gained many spiritual attainments. Nagarjuna entrusted Aryadeva with the ultimate teachings concerning the very essence of being. Aryadeva defeated a brahmin in debate, a teacher later known as Vira.[62] Aryadeva founded many religious institutions and helped Buddhism to flourish through his extensive teachings. He is thus enumerated as one of the "six ornaments of the world."[63]

Mahasiddha Krishnacharya[64]

Krishnacharya's king prophesied that he would gain spiritual attainment and awaken to buddhahood. He was taken under the care of the *mahasiddha* Jalandharipa[65] and so gained spiritual attainments. He spread the teachings of the Vajrayana in general, and most especially caused the lineage for the practice of Chakrasamvara to flourish. In accord with prophesies he received from his chosen deity, he composed the Six Works of Krishna and became renowned as the great innovator of an entire spiritual tradition.[66] Following him, [13a] there also appeared one called Krishnacharya the Younger, who was blessed by this master.

Shantigarbha (c. eighth century C.E.)

Shantigarbha was one of the eight great *vidyadhara*s in the mainstream transmission of the Early Translation School; he received the transmission of the practice known as *The Wrathful Mantra Curse*. It is said that Shantigarbha came to Tibet when the ground of Samyé Monastery was being tamed.[67] He attained the sublime state embodied in the great and glorious deity Black Mahabala.[68]

Thönmi Sambhota (sixth-seventh centuries C.E.)

An emanation of Manjushri, Thönmi Sambhota served under King Songtsen Gampo as minister for domestic affairs. He journeyed to India and studied under scholars there, training in Sanskrit and other secular fields of knowledge. He was responsible for first creating a script for the Tibetan alphabet and formalizing the rules of Tibetan grammar and pronunciation. Thus, it would seem that no one has done anything kinder or more marvelous for Tibet.

Bairotsana the Translator (c. 750-835)[69]

There are several differing accounts of the life of the great translator Bairotsana, who was an emanation;[70] accounts are found in *The Great Mask*, *The Record of Padma*, and *The History of the Oral Lineage of the Vajra Bridge*.[71] But since *The Great Mask* is said to have been spoken by Bairotsana himself, we must take it as authoritative. It recounts the following details:

Bairotsana was born at the confluence of the Nyang and Tsang Rivers. His father was Pagor Dorjé Gyalpo and his mother was called Drönkyi. They named their son Genjak Thangta. His paternal uncle was Pagor Hedö, and it is said that when Genjak Thangta's father passed away, [13b] his uncle looked after him. When he reached the age of eight, the boy displayed signs of his marvelous nature—riding on sunbeams, knowing some three hundred and sixty languages without having studied, and so forth.

When King Trisong Detsen was recruiting translators to translate the Buddhist teachings, Guru Rinpoché spoke to him about Bairotsana (as a rebirth of Ananda), Ka, and Chok.[72] In accord with the Guru's prophecies, the king summoned them to his presence, where they studied Sanskrit and other languages. Genjak Thangta received monastic ordination from the great abbot Shantirakshita, being one of the "seven chosen men" (the first Tibetans to be ordained), and he took the name Vairochanarakshita.[73]

When Bairotsana was fifteen, the king heard of a spiritual teaching that existed in India, concerning the transcendence of causality. He sent Bairotsana and Tsang-ngön Lekdrup[74] to search for it. They reached India after undergoing sixteen major life-threatening hardships. Searching for someone who was both learned and accomplished in the teachings of the pith instructions, they were told by all that the master Shri Simha,[75] who was living at the temple of Dhahena, combined these qualities of erudition and spiritual accomplishment. They sought out this master through various means, and when they reached him they were aided by a yogini whom they met fetching water. They met the master and offered to him a mandala of gold.[76] They requested that he grant them the Atiyoga teachings—the effortless means to awaken to buddhahood in this very lifetime.

Prior to that, [14a] there had been many omens that these teachings on the effortless approach would be taken away to Tibet, and so a law had been enacted that prevented anyone from transmitting these pith instructions. The extraordinary tantras and pith instructions resided in the memories of scholars and accomplished masters. The more ordinary classes of tantras, as well as the pith instructions associated with these, were sealed in the earth beneath Bodh Gaya by order of the scholars and rulers.

Shri Simha explained to Bairotsana that their lives were in danger unless they maintained extreme secrecy. And so, by day Bairotsana studied teachings concerning causality with other scholars, while by night Shri Simha—after taking precautions and ensuring circumstances so that others would have no knowledge—conferred on him the successive transmissions of the Categories of Mind, Expanse, and Direct Transmission.[77] Bairotsana also met the embodiment of Garab Dorjé's timeless awareness[78] and from him received the ultimate lineage of the six million four hundred thousand verses of the Dzogchen tantras, so that Bairotsana gained freedom at the moment he gained realization.[79]

He then achieved the power of fleetness of foot[80] and returned to Tibet, where he gave the teachings on causality publicly by day, while transmitting the Dzogchen teachings to the king in a private by night. Bairotsana produced the "five earlier translations" of the Category of Mind.[81] Due to the jealous machinations of the Indians who had lost these teachings to Tibet, as well as the intrigues of one of the Tibetan queens and the ministers who were opposed to Buddhism, Bairotsana was forced into exile, going to Gyalmo Tsawarong. [14b] There he taught Yudra Nyingpo at Drakla Gönpo Monastery and ripened and liberated many others. At Taktsékhar in Tsawarong, he taught the Dzogchen cycles to Sangtön Yeshé Lama, and he transmitted *The Vajra Bridge* to Sang-gyé Gönpo at Drakmar Dzong in Tongkhungrong by whispering the words into his ears.

When Bairotsana could return to central Tibet, he met with the great scholar Vimalamitra. The king of Tibet and his court of ministers and subjects and their retinues all paid him incredible honors, praising him with great devotion in recognition of his qualities. He taught the Dzogchen approach to Nyak Jnanakumara[82] and Princess Tsulthrim Drönma of Li. These two occasions, together with the three previous ones,[83] are known as the five stages of Bairotsana's teachings.

He served as the master editor of all the translations of Buddhist teachings, but he alone actually translated the Dzogchen teachings. During this period, many translators convened and worked on projects. The Sanskrit manuscript of *The Great Treasury of Analytical Explanations*[84] proved extremely difficult to translate, so it was divided into sections and assigned to different people to translate. It is said that while Bairotsana could translate his section, the others could not translate theirs, and so the project was abandoned.

Finally, Bairotsana conferred many words of advice and final admonitions on those in his retinue and went to a mountaintop in Drakyang Dzong, where he passed away in a sphere of light. Nowadays, one can still visit the cave in which Bairotsana passed into a body of light.[85] [15a] *The Great Mask* states that he accompanied Princess Tsulthrim Drönma to her home country of Li and spent a long time in meditation, after which he, as the emanation, was reabsorbed into the heart center of Vairochana. His life example, in short, was an incredible one.

Here in the land of Tibet, many emanations of the great translator Bairotsana have appeared—spiritual mentors who are learned, venerable, and spiritually accomplished, and especially *vidyadharas* who have been *tertöns*. The benefit they have brought to beings, acting in secret, has been limitless. All of them are emanations of timeless awareness. These are not ordinary individuals who take birth one after the other, in a succession of bodies resulting from karma and habitual patterns, but rather appear like the image of the moon being reflected in limitless vessels of water.

I have no confidence that I personally should be part of such a limitless process. Nonetheless, my guru,[86] with his flawless eye of timeless awareness, has repeatedly and quite specifically attested to me that one of my former incarnations was as Lumé Tsulthrim Sherab.

Lumé Tsulthrim Sherab (late tenth-early eleventh centuries C.E.)

Once the evil king Langdarma had persecuted the Buddhist teachings, there were no monastic communities. Ten men from the central provinces of Ü and Tsang heard that the line of oral transmission for abbots and preceptors had not been broken in eastern Tibet. They went to Kham province, where they received the full monastic ordination from Lachen Gongpa Rabsel and trained under him, becoming learned in the mainstream traditions of the general teachings [15b] and the practical application of the ethical codes. They also received much other spiritual advice.[87] Their abbot, Gongpa Rabsel, gave them individual responsibilities, telling them (among other things) that Lumé, being the most venerable, should act as their leader. At Yarlokha, Gongpa Rabsel requested that Lumé officiate as a priest; taking off his ceremonial hat he said, "Wear this and hold me in your memory, never forgetting me." With that, he placed it on Lumé's head.

The ten then turned their eyes toward Samyé and journeyed there, where they were welcomed by the elder of that institution. He asked them, "Who is your leader?," and they replied that Lumé was. The elder offered him the keys to the central temple[88] and other buildings, but Lumé remarked, "I have been appointed their abbot, and it would be wrong for the abbot to be burdened by contaminated or misappropriated offerings." Lumé accepted only a modest degree of recognition. Later on he oversaw the collection of many materials, which he used to thoroughly renovate the central temple. He also built many religious centers, including that of Lamo Chak De'u.[89]

Lumé Tsulthrim Sherab also established lineages through his students, so that following his time the land was filled with centers founded by his students as well as by Lumé himself. To these centers were brought the volumes of translated scriptures—the Buddha's words and the commentaries on these— that the lay masters and their students had concealed and kept in the past.[90] Lumé attracted many faithful students who gathered around him and took or- dination, so that many monastic communities flourished. Among his students were those known as the "four pillars," the "eight crossbeams," [16a] the "thirty- two ridge poles," and the "countless rafters."[91] He thus established the roots for the later spread of the ethical codes.[92] It is said that, following his passing into nirvana, Lumé Tsulthrim Sherab's remains did not corrupt, and were en- tombed at Chörten Öchen.

FORMER LIVES OF DRODUL SHERAB ÖZER: THE LATER SCHOOLS

The life examples of the learned and accomplished masters from the newer tantric schools of Tibetan Buddhism who were former incarnations of Drodul Sherab Özer are well-known. I will simply mention a few by name.

Rinchen Zangpo (958-1055)

After the Buddhist tradition had declined in Tibet and misinterpretations of the tantras were widespread, the ruler Lha Lama Yeshé Ö[93] wished to revivify the teachings and so dispatched the great translator Rinchen Zangpo to India. Rinchen Zangpo studied with many learned and spiritu- ally accomplished gurus, becoming himself a consummate scholar. He translated texts from the dialectical approach and from all four classes of tantra.[94] In particular, through his translations and explanations he was responsible for codifying the cycles of the Yogatantra class and that of Guhyasamaja.

Rinchen Zangpo refuted the misinterpretations of tantra and halted the untimely practice of the techniques of "union and release."[95] In taming a goatherd who had been endowed with magical powers by an evil *naga* named Lu Kargyal,[96] Rinchen Zangpo suppressed all the perversions of Buddhism

and ushered in the later spread of the teachings.[97] Later in his life, he practiced at three retreat centers in succession and passed away in a sphere of
light to the realm of Khechara; countless amazing omens were seen on that
occasion, and in the wake of that passing he left three pearl-colored relics,
[16b] but after some time even these rose into the sky with the sound of
thunder.

Ngok Lotsawa Loden Sherab (1059-1109)

Tenpai Nyima Loden Sherab, the translator of the Ngok clan, is famed as
having been prophesied by the Victorious One.[98] He was the nephew of Ngok
Lekpai Sherab, a student of the Noble Lord,[99] and developed his intellect to a
consummate degree. Loden Sherab stayed for some seventeen years in Kash-
mir, where he studied the sutras and tantras on a vast scale.

He was responsible for many translations, which became models for their
accuracy and fine quality. He founded many study centers and is famed for
having taught some twenty-three thousand students, including the ones known
as the "four eldest sons."[100] The "eight great lions"[101] and others appeared in
succession at his monastic seat of Sangphu.[102] The line of monastic succession
in upper Ling also developed after Loden Sherab, and Sangphu became renowned as the fountainhead of scholastic institutions.[103]

Ja Dulwa Dzinpa Tsöndrü Bar (1091-1166)

Tsöndrü Bar, a master of the Buddhist ethical codes who came from Ja, received his monastic vows from Dré Shebar,[104] taking the full ordination. He
studied the Vinaya literature with Sok Tsulthrim Lama, and following that
master's death he trained under Gyadul and Matso as secondary tutors,[105] becoming very learned. There was a saying that "the ethical codes are synony-
mous with Ja." He also studied the Middle Way philosophy and valid cognition
with Zhangyeng,[106] and the precepts of the Kadampa School with the translator Zangkar Lotsawa and the great Tölungpa.[107] Following this, Tsöndrü Bar
established the study center of Zulpur. [17a]

Pehar[108] emanated as a young monk and served him as an attendant. Other
than once wearing his robes with the rough side outward,[109] Pehar never saw
Tsöndrü Bar go against the ethical codes and so came to have faith in him and
vowed to aid those studying the *Commentary of Ja*.[110] After directing his com-

munity for nine years, Tsöndrü Bar pursued his spiritual practice. He had seventy-six students who were in their own right able to benefit beings.

Khedrup Khyungpo Naljor (978/990-1127)

The "learned and accomplished yogin" Khyungpo[111] first became learned in the Bön faith of his forefathers. He had some seven hundred students. Although he beheld many chosen deities in visions, this did not touch his heart, so he studied the instructions of the Dzogchen and Mahamudra systems.[112] Still he was not satisfied, and so he journeyed three times to the holy country of India, where he trained under one hundred and fifty learned and accomplished masters, studying the teachings of the sutras and tantras in their entirety.

Khyungpo Naljor received his ordination as a novice monk from the "middle" teacher named Vajrasana.[113] In particular, he was taken under the care of Niguma and Sukhasiddhi,[114] *dakinis* who had actually encountered Vajradhara and attained such realization that their very bodies were expressions of timeless awareness. From them he learned the "five golden teachings."[115]

In Tibet, Khyungpo Naljor received the full monastic ordination from Langri Thangpa.[116] He received the teachings on the white and blue-black forms of the Six-Armed Mahakala from the victorious Maitripa and the *mahasiddha* Rahula.[117] He displayed incredible signs of his attainments, such as actually manifesting the deities of the five classes of tantra in his five chakras.[118] [17b] He brought some one hundred and eighty thousand students to states of spiritual maturity, foremost among them the "five earlier sons" and the "one later son"—Mokchokpa Rinchen Tsöndrü—on whom he conferred a one-to-one transmission.[119]

Khyungpo Naljor is famed for having lived to the age of one hundred and fifty, and his lineage of "seven precious jewels" (in both its earlier and later stages) consisted of a succession of bodhisattvas in their final incarnation, while his spiritual lineage spread throughout the world—the holders of this line being known as the Shangpa Kagyü.[120]

Tsami Lotsawa Sang-gyé Drak (late eleventh-mid twelfth centuries C.E.)

Sang-gyé Drak, the translator of Tsami,[121] was born in the region of Ga in Minyak. At an early age he went to India, where he studied with Kalachakrapada, Abhayagupta, and many other learned and accomplished masters. He mastered the philosophical tenets of his own school and those of others, and so became famous throughout India, for everyone considered him an authority who had no rival. All the scholars looked to him as the arbiter to answer their questions and give them advice, and as the source of their pith instructions.

He received the name Sang-gyé Drak upon taking the full ordination of a monk. He upheld the treasury of the limitless classes of tantra and achieved the most sublime spiritual attainment, becoming a *vidyadhara* with power over longevity. He is famed as having had realization even higher than that of his teacher Abhayagupta. Sang-gyé Drak served as an abbot at Bodh Gaya and Nalanda, treating his Tibetan students with special kindness [18a] and teaching his own major commentary on the Kalachakra cycle.

In short, the sole Tibetan to teach Buddhism at Bodh Gaya in the holy country of India was Sang-gyé Drak, this master whose life example is so incredible.

Zhang Tsöndrü Drakpa (1123-1193)

Tsöndrü Drakpa of Zhang felt his spiritual inclinations for the Buddhist teachings awaken at an early age, and studied and trained extensively. He received instruction from four gurus whom he considered his principal teachers—Öngom Tsulthrim Nyingpo (a nephew of Dakpo Rinpoché), Palchen Galo, Mal Yerpawa, and Bairowa of Ngulchu—and completed his training.[122] In particular, he gained the ultimate experience of timeless awareness from Öngom, reaching the level of a great *siddha.*

Tsöndrü Drakpa brought enormous benefit to others. In the perceptions of extraordinary individuals, he did such things as manifesting eight forms of deities, or the Eight Manifestations, in eight places in his body. More ordinary people saw him engaged many times in conduct their ordinary minds couldn't accept, but which was an expression of his spiritual attainment. He oversaw construction of large stupas at Gungthang Temple.[123] His students, the "four named Ö"[124] among them, continued to help others on a vast scale. The succession of those holding his monastic seat, beginning with the incomparable Shakya Yeshé, became famed as the Tsalpa Kagyü School.

Rokdolpa Marzhurwa Sherab Gyatso (1059-1131)

Among the students of Potowa (who was in turn a student of Dromtön [18b] and one of the "three brothers"[125]), Sherab Gyatso held the lineage of the mainstream sources of the Kadampa School. He also studied the ethical codes with Gyadul[126] and directed a community of over a thousand monks. He was also the author of *The Blue Repository*, the text dealing with the stages on the paths of the three spiritual models, written according to the oral teachings of Potowa.[127]

Palchen Chöyé, or Chökyi Yeshé (twelfth century C.E.)

The great and glorious Chöyé was one of the three students of the Drigung Kyoppa hierarch Jigten Sumgön (1143-1219), who were known by the abbreviated title "the three *siddhas* Nyö, Gar, and Chö."[128] Initially, he spent a long time serving that lord of dharma as an attendant. To enrich his meditative experience and realization, Palchen Chöyé went to Tsaritra,[129] where he engaged in all the conduct of a tantric practitioner, awakening many special qualities in himself. He also authored many treatises, such as his *Fourfold Jewels*. He became famed as "Naktsangwa of Drigung."

Yakdé Panchen (1299-1378)

The great scholar Yakdé studied with more than a hundred gurus, including Lodrö Tsungmé of Sangphu, Rigdzin Kumaradza, Yungtönpa, and the two masters Zhu and Dol.[130] His wisdom embraced all the teachings on sutra and tantra in the old and new schools of Tibetan Buddhism. Being endowed with sublime states of perception, Yakdé Panchen was able to benefit others on a vast scale. He founded Ewam Monastery[131] and had many students, such as Ritröpa Gönpo Yeshé,[132] who in their turn carried out enlightened activities.

Panchen Bumthrak Sumpa (1432-1504?)

There seem to have been at least two different masters named Pandita Bumthrak Sumpa, one earlier than the other, but the one meant in this context is almost certainly the one who went to Bodong É.[133] [19a] I have not seen a detailed life story for this master.

FORMER LIVES OF MINLING TERCHEN

Zurchen Shakya Jungné (1002-1062)

Among the former incarnations of Minling Terchen, Zurchen Shakya Jungné received intimate spiritual advice from many learned and accomplished masters, including Nyang Yeshé Jungné and Rok Shakya Jungné.[134] He mastered this advice in his personal experience. He was a learned and enlightened master of all the philosophical schools of the sutras and the various classes of tantra. He taught his students the sutras and *The Web of Magic*.[135]

Devoting himself to his spiritual practice, Shakya Jungné gained accomplishments that made him indistinguishable from the "great and glorious deity."[136] To benefit others, he used his miraculous powers to erect a statue of this deity, Samyak, in the lower Shang Valley, following which he himself dissolved into a sphere of light that was absorbed into the deity's heart center.

Among his students was a group of five that included the "four summits" and Tsekok, and more than a hundred great meditators who all were able to show direct signs of their spiritual attainments. During the later spread of the teachings, it was Shakya Jungné who laid the foundation for the continuation of the Early Translation School. He was the first of the three masters referred to collectively as "the ancestors of the Zur clan."[137]

Drapa Ngönshé Wangchuk Bar (1012-1090)

Drapa Ngönshé was born in the region of Dra.[138] Being very learned in the higher metaphysical teachings, he experienced sublime states of supernormal perception. The name he received with his monastic ordination was Wangchuk Bar. Drapa Ngönshé brought forth *terma*s from their places of concealment—teachings on the cycles of Red Jambhala and Zhanglön,[139] and the four medical tantras.[140]

Supported by his spiritual attainment associated with the deity Jambhala, [19b] Drapa Ngönshé founded many centers, the religious community of Drathang foremost among these.[141] He became famed as a great professor, serving as the head of the monastic communities of both Drathang and Samyé.

Rongzom Mahapandita Chökyi Zangpo (eleventh century C.E.)

Rongzom Chökyi Zangpo was a scholar who was indisputably an incarnation, someone who was praised and honored by all the learned masters who were his contemporaries. He studied with many great Indian scholars and translated many tantras. His translations were of such fine quality that great scholars praised them as models for translators of the new schools.

He mastered so many sutras, tantras, and commentarial treatises that it was impossible for there to be anything he didn't know. He authored countless treatises of profound import that are nevertheless accessible, such as his pith instructions based on the three higher trainings.[142]

When Rongzom met with Lord Atisha, the latter remarked, "This is nothing less than the Indian master Krishnacharya passing from that life into this one. How could I ever be equal to discussing the Buddhadharma with him?" This brought Rongzom indisputable renown.

He could demonstrate sublime states of supernormal perception and signs of his spiritual accomplishment, so that anyone could perceive them. Rongzom Chökyi Zangpo lived to the age of one hundred and nineteen. Through his children, he initiated a lineage of masters who were accomplished in the teachings and practice of Vajrakila. Among his students were seventeen great translators, thirty-five *siddha*s, one hundred and eighty masterful yogins, and five hundred who were worthy of sitting under a ceremonial parasol.[143] [20a]

Bönpo Lhabum (b. 1136)

The Bön master Lhabum[144] was born at Tanak in the province of Tsang, and brought forth many *termas*—Buddhist, Bönpo, medical, and astrological teachings—from their place of concealment in the Dungpor Cliff of Tanak. For the most part, however, these teachings have not survived. Among the Bönpos, however, Lhabum is renowned as Guru Nöntsé, and his practice concerning the stages of development and completion for *The Sun of Innate Compassion*, a mother tantra, is still extant nowadays.[145]

Tulku Rashak Chenpo

The incarnate master Rashak Chenpo[146] was born on Yamdrok Plateau;[147] he was an emanation, at one and the same time, of Bairotsana and Drokmi Palgyi Yeshé.[148] From an early age he became proficient in "ransom rituals"[149] and the science of medicine. He developed into a great tantric yogin who realized the state of a deathless *vidyadhara*. Rashak Chenpo revealed a large number of *terma*s from the cliff of Paro Chal concerning Mamo Gangshar, the Bönpo teachings, ransom rituals, medical diagnosis, and other topics.

Druptop Ngödrup (twelfth century C.E.)

The accomplished master Ngödrup was born in the province of Tsang. His lifestyle was that of a lay "vajra holder," or tantric master. He accomplished the power to extend his life and lived for more than three hundred years. It was from this master that Lord Nyang received the transmission of the *kama* teachings of the Eight Commands called *The Narrow Passage to the Fortress*.[150] Druptop Ngödrup was constantly engaged in enlightened activities—for example, he revealed *The Last Testament of the King*[151] from its place of concealment in the Rasa Thrulnang Temple.[152]

Zhikpo Nyima Seng-gé

Zhikpo Nyima Seng-gé was a *siddha* in the lineage of the Zhijé system of Dampa.[153] It would seem that he also authored many treatises about these teachings.
[20b]

Guru Jotsé (thirteenth century C.E.)

Guru Jotsé revealed *terma* teachings and vast amounts of articles, and his relics and *terma* articles are still, it appears, benefiting beings nowadays.[154]

Yeshé Khyungdrak

Yeshé Khyungdrak revealed a minor *terma*, concerning the gaining of power over one's perceptions through the use of *sal* tree resin and honey, but I have not seen any more detailed accounts of his life beyond this.

Sakya Pandita (1182-1251) and Longchen Rabjam (1308-1364)

The biographies of these masters are so well-known that I will not discuss them here.[155]

Üpa Sang-gyé Bum (thirteenth-fourteenth centuries C.E.)

Sang-gyé Bum, who was from the central province of Ü, studied with two masters of Narthang—Rigpai Raldri and Jamyang Raldri—and became learned himself. Acting on the orders of these two masters, Sang-gyé Bum joined with Losel Jangchub Yeshé, the translator Sönam Özer, and Gyangro Jangchub Bum to gather all the texts then extant from the Kangyur and Tengyur collections and issue a fine new edition.[156] This was housed in the Jam Temple and copies became widely disseminated. The lineage of the oral transmission of this edition was, it seems, due entirely to the kindness of Losel.[157]

Dorjé Lingpa (1346-1405)

There was a prophecy concerning "five sovereign *tertön*s surrounded by a retinue of a hundred minor ones." Dorjé Lingpa was the third of these five.[158] It is said that his predilections, from his former lifetime as Bairotsana, gave him knowledge of three hundred and sixty languages and scripts. [21a] His wisdom unfolded as he received many spiritual teachings of the sutra and tantra traditions from both the old and new schools of Tibetan Buddhism.

When he was fifteen, Dorjé Lingpa opened the "treasure doorway"[159] in the cliff of Moshar in the lower Ching Valley. On that occasion, he entered a very spacious meditation cave in which Guru Rinpoché actually came to him and, after setting up the mandala and empowerment articles, conferred empowerment on him. Guru Rinpoché granted him the oral transmission for the scrolls,[160] reading from the beginning of each. Dorjé Lingpa received some forty-three major *terma*s and one hundred and eight minor, or secondary, ones—including four "regent" images, four volumes of teachings on the guru principle, one hundred scrolls, four vases of longevity, and a reliquary as an article of *samaya*,[161] all given to Dorjé Lingpa by the Guru with his own hands. When Dorjé Lingpa was revealing these *terma*s, Guru Rinpoché, Yeshé Tsogyal, and Bairotsana actually came to him, blessed him, and showed him incredible displays of their miraculous powers. These events are clearly set forth in his biography and *terma* teachings.

Kunkyong Lingpa (fifteenth century C.E.)[162]

Kunkyong Lingpa was the immediate rebirth of Dorjé Lingpa.[163] In the lower part of Zabbulung Valley in the Shang region, before a large crowd of people he flew like a bird to the sheer face of the cliff of Dorjé Kyé and brought forth a large number of *terma*s from the meditation caves. The guardian deities of the *terma*s—the Guardian Goddess of Mantra, the Oath-Bound One, and others[164]—emanated as women, Indian yogis, monkeys, people of the border tribes, and so forth and went among the crowd, serving him by handing out the *terma* articles. Thereupon, Kunkyong Lingpa's fame spread everywhere and his activities were extensive in guiding those to be guided. His sublime psychic powers were unhindered, [21b] and it seems that holy masters of all schools of thought, without any sectarian bias, came to receive whatever teachings and holy substances they could from him.

Bodongpa Panchen Jigdral Choklé Namgyal (1376-1451)

The wisdom of the great scholar of Bodong, Jigdral Choklé Namgyal, embraced all subjects without bias, and he had the power of total recall. He attained the state of a *mahasiddha* and had supernormal powers of perception and other miraculous powers. Blessed by Vajrasattva, Vajravarahi, Sarasvati, and other deities,[165] Bodong Panchen composed his great collected works, The Compendium of Suchness,[166] in one hundred and twelve volumes—the same number as the major and minor marks of a buddha's perfect form.[167] The centers that he founded throughout his life came to produce many learned and accomplished masters.

Draktokpa Sönam Zangpo (fourteenth century C.E.)

Sönam Zangpo of Draktok was a holder of the glorious Sakyapa lineage and someone who reached a consummate level of erudition, venerability, and nobility of character.

Sokdokpa Lodrö Gyaltsen (1552-1624)

The wisdom and realization of Lodrö Gyaltsen flourished, and when Tibet was threatened by armies on her borders, his power allowed him to repel these forces, so he became famed as Sokdokpa—"He who repelled the Mongols." He also engaged in wide-ranging activities in support of the Early Translation School of the Nyingma.[168]

Chokden Gönpo (1497-1557)

Chokden Gönpo was a rebirth of Kunkyong Lingpa and his life story consisted of countless marvels. Pema Lingpa cared for him with great affection. The chieftain of Gungthang Plateau in Ngari studied at his feet, as did most of the rulers of the provinces of Ü and Tsang. Chokden Gönpo's activities, both spiritual and political, were very extensive. To give an example, when he began a ritual in Lhasa to repel an invading army, the *torma* miraculously burst into flames and leaped into the air.[169] [22a] He is to be identified as the "Do-ngak Lingpa" prophesied in *The Record of Padma*, but due to some very basic circumstances going awry, it seems that he not only could not reveal any *termas*, but died due to some unfortunate and quite superficial cause.[170] A line of his successive incarnations appears to have continued until the present day, while the basis on which these emanations take place[171] is said to be that of Chökyi Gocha—a *vidyadhara* from the race of *rakshasa* demons who was taken under Guru Rinpoché's care on Zangdok Palri—manifesting as these successive incarnations.

Orgyen Terdak Lingpa (1646-1714)

Orgyen Terdak Lingpa was also known as Pema Garwang Gyurmé Dorjé. He was born into the clan of Nyö, in which an uninterrupted succession of vajra holders appeared. His noble father was Sangdak Thrinlé Lhundrup.[172] Terdak Lingpa studied with more that thirty tutors, including the great Fifth Dalai Lama, and from these masters he received the general range of *kama* and *terma* teachings of both the old and new schools of Tibetan Buddhism; in particular, he underwent various hardships to receive some very fragile transmissions. He pursued his meditation and spiritual practice to such a consummate limit that his realization flourished in conjunction with the four levels of empowerment[173] and he reached an advanced state of accomplishment.

At Sha-uk Takpo, Terdak Lingpa brought forth some five *terma* cycles—the most important being The Gathering of Sugatas[174]—and practiced them in the proper manner. Due to both his own wishes and the encouragement of others, he revivified the spiritual teachings of some minor lineages—including the Jonang, Shangpa, Zhijé, Chö, Bodong, and others.[175] In particular, with regard to the Early Translation School [22b] he composed many excellent works, the like of which had never been seen before, concerning the *sadhana* practices, mandalas, and teaching manuals for the *kama* tradition—primarily those of *The Web of Magic, The Discourse of United Intent,* and the Category of Mind[176]—and the *terma* tradition, including the former and later cycles of the older *terma*s and his own newer *terma*s. Terdak Lingpa taught on a vast scale, giving ripening empowerments and liberating teachings. He also founded the great monastic center of Orgyen Mindroling, which became a major well-spring of the theory and practice of the Early Translation School.

In such ways, Terdak Lingpa's activities in spreading the teachings—through his teachings, practice, and spiritual projects—were unparalleled. As for his students and the custodians of his teachings, these included most of the great gurus famed throughout the Land of Snows, the holders of the teachings of the Nyingma tradition in eastern Tibet, and the masters living in the main monastic seats. He had so many fine students that it would seem that, of all the authentic and venerable lineages of the Early Translation School—both its *kama* and *terma* traditions—there were none that did not stem from this master.

The protector Maitreya prophesied to Terdak Lingpa that immediately following that lifetime he would awaken to buddhahood in a pure realm as Pemé Gyenpa Namrol Thayé. On a more general note, it is clearly attested to in prophetic *terma*s that Terdak Lingpa was Bairotsana himself, and would be the final buddha of the one thousand to appear in this eon—the buddha Abhimukta, or Vairochana. He was, therefore, the incredible emanation of a powerful being with mastery of the tenth level of realization.[177] [23a]

FORMER LIVES OF JONANG JETSÜN TARANATHA

The thirteen successive prior lives of the venerable one of Jonang are widely renowned. I have already discussed the first of these—the great *mahasiddha* Krishnacharya. The second was a great lord among *siddha*s named Ratan Bhahula, who was the son of a king in the holy country of India.[178] The third rebirth was Rongzom the translator, Chökyi Zangpo, who has also been discussed earlier. The fourth was Barompa Darma Wangchuk;[179] he was a heart son of the incomparable physician of Dakpo[180] and the founder of one of the four major lineages of the Kagyü School. Fifth in the succession was Avadhutipa, a lord among *siddha*s and a student of Drakpa Gyaltsen of the Sakya School.[181] The sixth rebirth was Drukdra Gyaltsen, the great "destroyer of illusion"—a master of the Zhang clan who had received a transmission of the practice of Vajrabhairava.[182] The seventh was Sang-gyé Rechen, also known as Gyalwa Lhanangpa, of the Nyö clan, who was a heart son of Drigung Kyoppa Jigten Sumgyi Gönpo.[183] The eighth was this master taking conscious rebirth in the Nyö clan as a great learned and accomplished master named Sanghabhadra.[184] The ninth rebirth was Jamyang Tashi Palden; he was a student of Jé Rinpoché Lobzang Drakpa, a master who could expound on a hundred scriptural sources, and the founder of the glorious monastery of Drepung.[185] The tenth was the scholar Chökyi Nyinjé, who was born in the land of Sri Lanka and journeyed to Tibet.[186]

The eleventh in the succession of rebirths [23b] was famed everywhere as the rebirth of Charyadharendra,[187] who had made a vow to protect all those who saw, heard, remembered, or touched him. He was the venerable Kunga Drolchok Losel Gyatsoi Dé, a great spiritual being of unparalleled learning and accomplishment, who founded the seat of glorious Jomonang.[188]

The twelfth rebirth, Prince Gajé Sakyong, was born the son of a king in the holy country of India; from an early age he showed himself to be a natural lord among yogins.[189] And the thirteenth rebirth was Jonang Jetsün Rinpoché.[190]

Taranatha (1575-1634)

In the distant past, the venerable and omniscient Taranatha[191] aroused the awakening attitude of bodhichitta in the presence of the buddha Vipashyin.[192] In the presence of our Teacher,[193] he sat in the center of five hundred bodhisattvas and his intelligence became exceedingly purified, so that he could take up the challenge of spreading the teachings concerning the definitive meaning in an unbiased manner. There then ensued various emanations to guide beings; in the present case, Taranatha is said to have had many emanations in other worlds as well as this land of Tibet; for example, the eight manifestations—including that of a universal monarch named Riwoi Tsémo—displayed in the presence of the buddha Chambhaka in the eastern pure realm called Nya-ngen-dral.

The actual source of his emanation as Taranatha was a *daka* of Oddiyana named Vishnurajaya, [24a] manifesting as a nirmanakaya. He was born in the family line of the translator Ra Lotsawa in the province of Tsang.[194] During his boyhood, once when he was very ill the *mahasiddha* Jvalanatha actually came from the holy country of India and removed this obstacle. At any early age, Taranatha experienced the awakening of his spiritual predisposition for the Mahayana and, in particular, the Vajrayana approach. Without anyone having taught him, he would describe many tantric deities and recite many *sadhanas* aloud.

He clearly recounted his former life as the venerable Kunga Drolchok, so he was invited to Jomonang. From his holy tutors he received the full monastic ordination and studied the sutras and tantras—both the words of the Buddha and the treatises commenting on them—and knew these works merely upon hearing them. He became unrivaled in the three pursuits of explaining the teachings, debating, and composing texts.

The master Padmakara introduced him to the mandala of the *herukas*, and Yeshé Tsogyal conferred a profound empowerment on him through symbolic gestures. On the basis of these experiences, a cache of *termas* fell to Taranatha— The Fourfold Garland, a major developmental account of the spiritual path as described in the cycle The Graded Path of Magical Illusion—but due to circumstances beyond his control, he was unable to receive this particular cache. He did, however, produce a large body of works concerning the vast collections of tantras; in each and every case, this enormous accomplishment in the service of the teachings of the profound and secret Vajrayana approach was better than a number of less definitive *termas*. Thus, Taranatha did experience some problems in discovering his *termas*. He developed his meditative absorption to a consummate degree [24b] by practicing the stages of development and completion for tantras of the Anuttarayoga class.

With Chöku Lhawang Drakpa,[195] Taranatha gained direct realization of Mahamudra—the unchanging unity of bliss and emptiness. From three masters, including Buddhaguhyanatha (an Indian master who was a student of the *mahasiddha* Shantigupta), he received the quintessential spiritual advice that allowed him to fathom the profundity of the enlightened intent that underlies the tantras. The glorious Heruka[196] conferred the treasury of secrets on him, while the Lord of Sages invested him as a lord of all the Buddhist teachings. The eight great bodhisattvas blessed him as a source of all the sutras and tantras without exception. And the venerable Tara continually revealed herself to Taranatha, uttering prophecies and transmitting her timeless awareness to him. He was blessed by the sixteen great "mainstays" of the Indian Buddhist tradition[197] and all the *siddhas* who were lords among yogins; every time he prayed to them Taranatha received instruction, either directly or indirectly. In Devikoti he was blessed by the *dakini* of enlightened awareness Niguma and received her permission to compose *The Vast Plain of Profound Meaning*, his teaching manual on her Six Yogas. He met with Indrabodhi in Oddiyana, with Padmakara on Zangdok Palri, and with the Kulika monarchs in Shambhala, receiving the nectar of their personal advice. Deities such as Kalachakra, Guhyasamaja, and Vajravarahi conferred [25a] the "empowerment of supreme rays of light" on Taranatha and encouraged him by praising his commentaries on the ultimate meaning of the tantras.[198]

He dispelled all the mistakes due to confusion concerning the extensive lineages of the Vajrayana tradition. He composed large numbers of treatises that promulgated any and all of the great mainstream traditions, ensuring that these were not lost. In this, he was comparable to Abhayagupta of India, for here in Tibet his kindness was like that of the shining sun, revivifying the Vajrayana teachings that were dying out. When Taranatha was giving teachings and empowerments, performing *ganachakra* feasts or consecration ceremonies, or on other such occasions, there were always such signs as rainbow lights, showers of blossoms,[199] symbolic songs of *dakinis*, and fragrant odors wafting about.

In general, Taranatha greatly promoted the Buddhist teachings and ensured enormous benefit for beings. In particular he restored the center of Takten Phuntsokling, both the structure and its interior appointments. He had many learned and accomplished students, including his two regents, both named Gyatso.[200] It would seem that all the great holders of the teachings who were his contemporaries came to study at his feet.

Finally, having completed his mission, Taranatha withdrew the display of his emanation with many marvelous signs. He said that in the future he would be reborn in Oddiyana as Viryaraja, in Vaidurya and Sukhavati as mighty bodhisattvas on the tenth level of realization, and in Droding as Sukhanatha, [25b] who would spread the teachings of the three approaches—*The Web of Magic, The Discourse of United Intent,* and the Category of Mind. He indicated that several incarnations and other manifestations of his blessings would appear here in Tibet, too. He no doubt fulfilled the prophecy that after three lifetimes he would awaken to buddhahood as the *tathagata* named Akashabindu in the world known as Prabhavati.

OTHER FORMER LIFETIMES

I have naturally written brief biographical accounts of the successive incarnations of these holy masters to inspire interested people. Now my omniscient and holy gurus have specifically told me—a very ordinary person who only aspires to have some connections with these three holy ones[201]—that I am the rebirth of others. Of these I have already discussed Lumé.[202]

Nyemdo Tamché Khyenpa Kunga Döndrup (b. 1268)

Kunga Döndrup, the omniscient one of Nyemdo, was born the youngest son of Rok Tamché Khyenpa Sönam Palwa. From his father and older brothers Kunga Döndrup received all the spiritual instructions for the tantras of the old and new schools, as well as the three cycles of the Zhijé teachings. He also relied on many other holy masters, including Karma Pakshi and Tarlo Drakpa,[203] becoming learned in the five fields of knowledge and all the sutras and tantras.

In particular, from the *mahasiddha* Orgyenpa he received on two occasions the Kalachakra cycle—the empowerments, the explanations of the tantras, and the pith instructions. He put into practice the Six Branches of Union and the teachings of three approaches—that of Zhijé, Mahamudra, and Dzogchen—applying himself until the practice truly sank home, [26a] and such realization arose in him that there was no longer any distinction between his formal practice and postmeditation awareness. He was graced with visions of many of his chosen deities.

Nyemdo Kunga Döndrup offered to Lord Rangjung Dorjé[204] the entire range of the four classes of tantras—primarily the empowerments, the explanations of the tantras, and the pith instructions for the Kalachakra cycle—as well as that of the Early Translation (or Nyingma) School, the Zhijé School, the Lamdré cycle, and the cycles of sutra teachings. During that time, Lord Rangjung Dorjé experienced many special pure visions.

In addition, Kunga Döndrup conferred teachings on a vast scale on many great learned and venerable masters and many leaders—principally the Kalachakra cycle. He would also appear to have authored several treatises.

Kazhipa Ratnabhadra (Rigpai Raldri)

Ratnabhadra, a master of four fields of study,[205] was also known as Rigpai Raldri. He served as tutor to the Sixth Lord Karmapa, Tongwa Dönden,[206] and so figures in the mainstream succession[207] of the Kagyü School. His life example can be understood clearly from the account composed by the Sixth Lord Karmapa himself, in a tabular format with one hundred and eight entries.

Ratnabhadra's former incarnation, Gendun Bum, was a student of the *mahasiddha* Karma Pakshi and also received the entire body of teachings of the Karmapas from the omniscient Rangjung Dorjé.

Payo Chökyi Lodrö (fourteenth-fifteenth centuries C.E.)

Chökyi Lodrö of Payo held the monastic seat of Payo in Kongpo and studied with the realized master Khachö Wangpo[208] and with Rolpai Dorjé.[209] When the *tertön* Sang-gyé Lingpa[210] was young, Chökyi Lodrö served as his guardian and guru. [26b] Later on, Chökyi Lodrö was identified in prophecies as the foremost of the "twenty-one vase holders" of The United Intent of the Gurus, and he carried out that responsibility accordingly.

It would seem that Payo Chökyi Zangpo was the immediate rebirth of this master Chökyi Lodrö. He became a student of the Third Zhamar, Chöpal Yeshé,[211] and directed the monastic centers of Payo and Taktsé. In later times, Goshri Döndrup Nyingpo,[212] tutor of the Eighth Zhamar,[213] was said to be a rebirth of Payo Chökyi Lodrö.

Müchen Sang-gyé Rinchen (1450-1524)

Müchen Sang-gyé Rinchen was born the nephew of Müchen Sempa Chenpo Könchok Gyaltsen.[214] He developed his character by training in the three levels of discipline[215] under such masters as Sempa Chenpo himself, the *mahasiddha* Könchok Lodrö, the omniscient Sönam Seng-gé, and Gyaltsap Kunga Wangchuk.[216] He studied and contemplated the sutras and tantras to a consummate degree, and received *The Direct Introduction to the Three Kayas* from Gyalwang Chödrak Gyatso.[217]

For a long time, Sang-gyé Rinchen served as director of the monastic center of Nalendra.[218] He also traveled to the seat of Ngor and served there, empowering Lord Lhachok Seng-gé as his successor.[219] Sang-gyé Rinchen engaged in spiritual practice and meritorious actions that were incredible. He was continually engaged in promulgating the Buddhist teachings, as indicated by the fact that he transmitted the "precious excellent speech"[220] alone some fifty-one times. [27a] Jampa Chö-ö,[221] a practitioner of the *nyung-né* fasting ritual who was constantly graced with visions of Avalokiteshvara, received assurance from that exalted deity that Lord Sang-gyé Rinchen was a bodhisattva on the tenth level of realization.

Sang-gyé Rinchen always displayed unhindered powers of supernormal perception, and it seems that on the two occasions when he conducted rituals to prepare medicinal pills, there were all kinds of incredible omens.

His students included all the holders of the teachings of the glorious Sakya School in the central and eastern provinces of Tibet, including the Eleventh Sakya Dakchen,[222] three of the throne holders of Ngor, and Doring Kunpangpa.[223] He also taught the directors of the monastic seats of Ngamring, Narthang, and Jonang, as well as the great scholar Nyukla Panchen, Karma Thrinlépa,[224] and others, so that Sang-gyé Rinchen's lineage of students included countless holders of the teachings. It appears that his later incarnation was Müchen Sang-gyé Gyaltsen.[225]

Tselé Khechok Pema Lekdrup Natsok Rangdrol (b. 1608)

Pema Lekdrup Natsok Rangdrol, the sublime scholar of Tselé, was recognized in prophecies as an emanation of the great translator Bairotsana. He was also reputed to be the rebirth of Tsungmé Tendzin Dorjé,[226] and so was invited to Thangdrok Dratsang, the monastic community founded by his former incarnation. He studied with many learned and accomplished teachers, including the great translator Gong-ra Lochen,[227] mastering the mainstream traditions and instructions of the sutras and tantras from the old and new schools. He was scrupulous in his conduct—rather than drink even consecrated alcohol during *ganachakra* feasts, he let nothing touch his lips except water infused with cane sugar. [27b]

In his later life, Natsok Rangdrol dwelled in such places as Palri Götsang and the cave of Deshek Tsé in the south, where he developed his realization of Mahamudra and Dzogchen to a consummate degree. His students seemed to have included Gampopa Zangpo Dorjé, Bamteng Chöjé Miphampa,[228] and Ta'u Pema Lodrö.

Pema Dechen Lingpa (1663-1713)

Pema Dechen Lingpa, also known as Rongtön Chaknachen, was a "mind emanation" of the great translator Bairotsana. He was born on the plateau of Serthar.[229] Initially he studied with Serpa Yeshé Gyaltsen and developed superb experiences and realization of Mahamudra. Pehar tried to create obstacles for him, but many *termas* and "sky teachings" came to him.[230] He met Rigdzin Longsal Nyingpo,[231] who treated him with all the affection of a father reuniting with his son. Longsal Nyingpo conferred his cycle The Intense Blazing of TimelessAwareness, focusing on the wrathful form of Guru Rinpoché, on Dechen Lingpa and encouraged him to practice this.

Upon practicing this, Dechen Lingpa was freed from his earlier obstacles and received the record and prophecies concerning his "earth *termas*." For example, at Murdo Cliff, he brought forth The Heart Drop of the Dakini, while at Tsenri he discovered The Wish-Fulfilling Gem: The United Commands. As part of his personal lot, The United Intent of the Dakinis was to be found at Riwo Pakzhal, but Dechen Lingpa was not able to receive this.

He accepted Longsal's appointment to be the latter's regent and preside over the monastic seat of Kathok, [28a] but perceived that there would be great discord with Longsal's relatives and others, so he bowed out and made his seat at Tsenri Nenang. The students who upheld his lineage included such remarkable individuals as Rigdzin Tsewang Norbu, and his son and other relatives.[232]

Dechen Lingpa's immediate rebirth was Ta'u Rokjé Lingpa. Following this, he was reborn as a Lama Sherab Yarphel, who lived at the hermitage of Zhechen Monastery; by the age of nineteen, this lama had completed one hundred million repetitions of the six-syllable mantra and was graced with a vision of Mahakarunika. He taught *The Discourse on the Perfection of Wisdom in Eight Thousand Stanzas* more than eleven hundred times and directly experienced realization of the perfection of wisdom, so that he destroyed the confusion that affects us in this life. Sherab Yarphel said that he clearly remembered his former lifetime as Rongtön Chaknachen, but it seems that those around him were unaware of who Rongtön had been, and so no one recognized the import of this statement. It seems that I was born in the year following Sherab Yarphel's death, so if this can be considered sufficient cause for my being simply a rebirth of that old lama, this provides some slight justification..

PROPHECIES CONCERNING MY PRESENT LIFETIME

Introductory Remarks

The second topic is that of prophecies concerning my present lifetime. Generally speaking, the prophecies made by the Victorious One include clear predictions, undisputed by anyone, of some masters from the Indian tradition (notably the "six ornaments") and, here in Tibet, the incomparable Dakpo Rinpoché and Dromtön. [28b] In *The Source Tantra of Manjushri*, the kings of Tibet are foretold in their proper succession, and the names of Ganden and Lobzang appear quite plainly.[233] But I have not seen any other clear predictions—even of great masters who were the founders of traditions—in the sutras and tantras extant nowadays in Tibet. Of course, something can always be made to fit the occasion—one's individual followers can find names in such sources that bear some similarity to one's own, or use the letters found in *The Source Tantra of Manjushri* as some sign—and there seem to be some cases in which people come up with lines that have all the earmarks of indigenous Tibetan verse, claiming that these are prophecies found in sutras or tantras that were never brought to Tibet.

But someone such as I cannot hope, even in his dreams, to have been prophesied by the Buddha. As for the prophecies found in *termas*, as I stated earlier, I feel that these were spoken for some reason, but I am not convinced that these are definitive statements and I certainly have absolutely no sense of self-importance because of them. My glorious and holy gurus, who have been kinder to me than the Buddha himself, have granted me such indications in order to inspire me to free myself from cyclic existence. To belittle their efforts would be in contradiction to any spiritual approach in general, but especially in the peerless Dakpo Kagyü tradition [29a] it is said that if your guru tells you that fire is water and water is fire, the auspicious connection is forged if you understand that to be vajra speech and do not entertain the slightest doubt or wrong view. So I shall respect their wishes.

Specific Citations

The Discourse on the Most Majestic State of Meditative Absorption states:

> "There will come one who holds sublime meditative absorption in
>   his hands,
> who will be like the protector Maitreya of boundless fame,
> and who will bring much benefit to beings."
> With these words I prophesy "Boundless Intelligence."[234]

And *The Discourse on the Symbolic Embodiment of the Timeless Aware-ness of Those Gone to Suchness* states:

> One gifted in such ways will guide you—Anantamati of superb
>   intelligence.
> This is the intention of many billions of buddhas throughout the ten
>   directions.
> His analyses of the methods found in hundreds of my discourses will
>   be amazing and beyond measure.
> Applying himself to these discourses, he will gain the power of total
>   recall.

Concerning the meaning of these passages, my lord guru Jamyang Khyentsé Wangpo said that while there had been many masters named Lodrö in both the Indian and Tibetan traditions of Buddhism, he had never seen one with the name Thayé added, not in any teaching of the *kama* or *terma* traditions, nor in any histories. "This shows an extremely close tie with your own name," he said, and there are many colophons to his works in which he states the same thing. [29b] In general, of the one thousand sons of the universal monarch Dhritarashtra who were prophesied to become the buddhas of this fortunate eon, the youngest was the youth Anantamati, who would become the buddha Abhimutki Rocha.[235] It would seem that the great translator Bairotsana was also a rebirth of this youth, so it would appear not to be entirely arbitrary merely to suggest that the name found in the earlier prophecy would show up in all circumstances while the activity of enlightenment was being under-taken.

The Exalted Discourse on the Journey to Sri Lanka states:

> In times following that,
> there will come a great hero—
> the guide named Intelligence,
> demonstrator of the five objects of knowledge.[236]

My precious lord said, "In this passage, if the phrase 'five objects of knowl-edge' only referred, for example, to the five fields of knowledge,[237] this would not be anything worthy of special mention in a prophecy, for these five are the universal wealth of all learned scholars in India and Tibet. Rather, because it refers to five great treasuries that didn't exist previously,[238] this again shows an extremely close tie." Although he himself subscribed to this reading, the speech of the Victorious One is called "ubiquitous"—it is very open to interpretation, so that one can apply it under any circumstances whatever. So there is no point to being malicious or narrow-minded and thinking, "This is not appropriate," or, "This is reasonable in other cases, but has been misappropriated in this case."

Moreover, *The Tantra of the "Kalpa" Fragment* from *The Magical Illusion* of the Early Translation School states:

[30a]
In the realm known as the Land of Snows,
the heart of the lotus will be held by Kunga,
Lodrö Thayé, and others,
who will cause the teachings to flourish.

In the prophecies of the great *tertön* Pema Lingpa,[239] one finds the following reference:

In the Iron Horse Year, border wars will encroach on Tibet.
My emanation—a fully ordained monk named Lodrö—
will appear in the eastern provinces, on the banks of a flowing
golden river.
Through the power of his aspirations he will reverse the troubled
times.
In the Iron Sheep Year, the sun of happiness will shine.

The circumstances in this and similar passages coincide with the occasion, during the Iron Horse Year [1870-1871], when I performed a *mendrup* ritual based on the Eight Commands cycle The Gathering of Sugatas, in Tashi Nyida Palphuk Cave on the second snow-capped range of Yulung Valley.

In Rinchen Lingpa's text *Great Perfection: Freeing All in One Stroke* there is the following reference:

In the future, in the final times when the oral transmission is waning,
if this teaching blessed by Vimalamitra is to be practiced,
it is possible, through the motivation of Bairotsana, that three will
come to explain it—

one older, one younger, one just a youth—and that it will spread to
some extent.

Thus, when my lord guru received the transmission of this profound teaching (the lineage of which had been lost), I was the first to receive it when he
began promulgating it, and he identified me as the "older" emanation of
Bairotsana.

There also seem to be a few scattered references in caches of *termas*
discovered in the past by such masters as Dorjé Lingpa and Duddul
Dorjé.[240] In particular, [30b] there is a text entitled *Personal Advice: The
Graded Path of the Heart Essence of Timeless Awareness*, which was revealed by my precious lord guru and Chokling together. In this text is the
following verse:

> At that point, the first fortunate one
> will be Zhiwai Lodrö,
> one blessed by the translator Bairotsana.
> He will codify the profound and vast words and meanings.

On the basis of that reference, they gave me detailed explanations on the
source text.[241] They also stated that I should write a commentary and so, in
accord with the permission they granted me by both direct and indirect means,
I wrote one.[242]

The Union of All the Dakinis' Secrets is a rediscovered *terma* cycle from
Jomo Menmo.[243] The prophetic record found in it states:

> Furthermore, when the times are worsening in central and eastern
>   Tibet,
> the latest rebirth of the monarch of the Buddhadharma
> will be blessed by you, Tsogyal.
> Difficult for anyone to find,
> he will be a *vidyadhara* who tames beings in unpredictable
>   ways—
> a spiritual being who appears as an illusion does.
> Appearing in the east of Dokham, he will encounter this teaching.
> Though he will be united with the timeless awareness of the great
>   translator,

he will seem as though separate—
a bodhisattva, the last in a bloodline of *tantrikas*,
entrusted with an inexhaustible treasury of intelligence.
Due to both our aspirations,
some fortunate ones will be purified of the impairment and breaking
     of their vows,
some will engage in the uncontrived conduct of a *tantrika*,
while some will discover supremely blissful timeless awareness.
A banquet of spiritual attainments will unfold.[244]
[31a]

The significance of this passage was borne out in the fact that I acted as the scribe who initially wrote down this cycle and was granted the ripening empowerment and liberating teachings in a single transmission.[245] Since then, I have practiced the stages of approach and accomplishment in retreat, performed fulfillment rituals, participated in intensive group rituals, and explained and promulgated these teachings to others.

In addition, in Khyentsé Rinpoché's other *termas* of enlightened intent, oral lineages, and rediscovered *termas*[246] there are references to the coming of those who are emanations of the twenty-five intimate students of Guru Rinpoché,[247] and wherever there was mention of Bairotsana, my guru identified this as a reference to me, and kindly granted me the ripening empowerments and liberating teachings for those cycles. In this, I feel that I have been extremely fortunate.

The prophetic record found in *Dispelling Obstacles on the Path*, a *sadhana* of enlightened mind discovered by Chokgyur Lingpa, makes the following prediction:

One named Lodrö, an emanation of Bairotsana,
will receive transmissions, and will teach and write on a vast scale.
This will serve to cure him of a disease caused by *nagas*.

This proved accurate, for although my teaching and writing activities were not much developed when this record was revealed, they have become so in later years, and this teaching turned out to be what cured me of a disease caused by demonic forces of the nether regions. As well, toward the end of the *sadhana* for the five Tsering sisters (who are the guardians of this cycle of teachings), one can find the following reference:

The one named Yungdrung, the latest rebirth of Bairotsana,
endowed with "Boundless Intelligence,"
will appear as a scion who will promote
the Buddhist teachings on the heart essence.

When I was very young, the abbot of Menri [31b] had named me Tendzin
Yungdrung [Immutable Upholder of the Teachings] and henceforth I was
known by that name until I went to Palpung Monastery. In a similar vein, in
The Garland of Crystals (which is the history of the *sadhana* of enlightened
mind called *The Wish-Fulfilling Gem*) there is the following passage:

From the west will come one with intelligence, the latest rebirth of
Bairotsana,
bearing the name Tendzin, who will promote the Victorious One's
teachings
and gain mastery over a treasury vast and profound.

As for the direction referred to, the place in which this cache of *terma* teachings was found was Lhundrup Teng in Dergé,[248] and the great *tertön* himself[249]
said that this was a reference to my place of birth, which is directly to the west
of that. But I have already expressed my opinion on the interpretation of names
and terms.

The following appears in the prophetic record from The Seven Profound
Cycles:

This deity Yamantaka is the perimeter wall that guards the teachings.
An emanation of Bairotsana, ordained in the Bird Year
and bearing the name Wang, will be learned in the five fields of
knowledge.
There is a strict injunction that he will encounter these teachings in
his forty-sixth year,
and he should practice them, in particular the *sadhana* of
Vajrapani,
which he should make the core of his practice until he is fifty.
Then the teachings will flourish in the region of Dokham.[250]

This was said to be a partial reference to my ordination name, Karma

Ngawang Yönten Gyatso, and my secret tantric name, part of which is Pema Garwang. [32a] Furthermore, the prophetic record of *The Three Categories of the Great Perfection* states:

> There will be an emanation of Bairotsana, named Lodrö.
> You will have a very authentic encounter with him.
>
> .   .   .   .
>
> A rebirth of Bairotsana, whose fate is interwoven with this,
> one named Lodrö—give this to him as its custodian.

Because of such references, the great *tertön* himself had me arrange all his newly discovered *terma*s in ritual format and said to me on many occasions, "You are responsible for any additional manuals that are required."[251]

The records[252] of The Intermediate Cycle of Conditioned Existence, revealed by the *vidyadhara* Kundrol Sangwa Tsal,[253] give an account of the origins of the Khyungpo bloodline,[254] following which it states:

> From this line—at the same time that this profound *terma*, like a key,
> appears on the surface of the earth—
> there will come an especially exalted spiritual being.
> He will be an emanation of the monk Ananda,
> someone whose oceanic intelligence
> will embrace the limitless range of the knowable.
> He will guide five hundred thousand beings
> and reveal the path to liberation for all who meet him.
> He will constantly act
> to prevent the border people from invading the center.

As well, it would seem that there are many other sources in which there is reference to my collaboration with Jamyang Khyentsé Wangpo in rendering service to the *kama* and *terma* traditions of the teachings.

HIDDEN TEACHINGS REVEALED IN THIS LIFETIME

The third topic concerns the ways in which I have, at least to some degree, received transmissions of profound *terma*s. [32b]

When I was fifteen I dreamed of meeting Guru Rinpoché and receiving his blessing. Following that, as time passed I had many memories that led to my writing *sadhana*s and other works. When I was staying at Zhechen Monastery it became imperative for me to write a ritual of fulfillment and ransom focusing on Shri Devi,[255] so I began a composition. At that point, even though it was springtime, the surrounding area was struck by bolts of lightning and quite a few other disturbing signs occurred. After finishing those works, I wrote a *sadhana* and various activity rituals for Vajradanda, as well as a cycle of texts for the practice of the "three wild *tsen* brothers."[256] I presented these to Öntrul Rinpoché for his inspection and he praised them, saying, "They are due to the excellent power of your pure vision, which has a panoramic quality." He requested the oral transmission from me and practiced these techniques a bit himself, whereupon he felt positive signs. He said, "The practice of Shri Devi is useful in cases of diseases affecting both people and cattle nowadays, while the cycle of Vajradanda has a profound influence that dispels the obscurations due to impairments of *samaya* connection in these times of spiritual degeneration." At that time I was focused entirely on my studies and training, so I put off all kinds of spiritual practice for the time being. In the region around Zhechen I could see clear signs of "doorways" to *terma*s, but I did nothing about this.

Following that I went to Palpung and received my monastic ordination. [33a] Once I had entered the Kagyü School, I placed great importance on the advice of my gurus and spiritual companions, and so became more and more attached to the methods of the new schools of Tibetan Buddhism, to the point where I felt quite uninterested in *terma*s of enlightened intent and other such teachings. A few people for whom I felt high regard criticized the texts I had written previously, so I threw the texts into a fire and wrote a prayer of aspiration in the form of a vow; this can be found in the collection of my miscellaneous writings. These events led gradually to disturbing signs in my dreams and I was seized by an extremely severe and undiagnosable illness in my thirtieth year. Every day I constantly felt sure that I was going to die.

During that time, one night—I couldn't tell whether I was awake or dreaming—I met the Guru and his consort, and after I had asked a few questions and received their answers, they insisted that I take rebirth again. I then found myself back in my own bed, and for several days I had fleeting impressions that I was in the intermediate state after death. Rejecting any minor palliatives that might have been available, I undertook to have representations of enlightened form, speech, and mind constructed—primarily a set of thirteen scroll paintings depicting The United Intent of the Gurus.[257] Once the illness had dissipated, I went to the hermitage to practice, and although my body was weakened from the illness affecting my subtle energy, [33b] I had excellent signs in my dreams. There were still upsets from time to time, however. Word came from my precious lord guru at Dzongsar that the ritual of fulfillment and ransom for Shri Devi was crucial for me, and I myself dreamed of one of my devoted students, Karma Nyima Özer, saying to me, "If you do not perform a ritual of fulfillment and ransom for Shri Devi, no matter what else you do it will be difficult to cure your illness." But I failed to carry out the ritual. My composition entitled *A Propitiatory Prayer to the Gracious Goddess* came to my mind and I wrote it down. That day there were excellent and auspicious signs—the sky was a deep blue with a lustrous ring of rainbow light. Once I had recited that prayer a few times I felt better.

Later on, when the *tertön* Kundrol Sangwa Tsal—who was more widely known by the name Tsewang Drakpa—came to that area, I asked Lord Khyentsé Rinpoché for his advice.

"Given that he is a visitor whose birthplace is the same as mine," I said, "what do you think it would be appropriate for me to do?"

Khyentsé Rinpoché replied, "He is an authentic *tertön*, but he is such an exceedingly rough character that he will never be more than mediocre. However, if you were to meet with him, it would heal impaired circumstances from your past." Nevertheless, at that time I did not meet with the *tertön*.

My thirty-seventh year was a very crucial one[258] and I was ill on several occasions. [34a] Still, I undertook many intensive practices on the stages of approach and accomplishment. In particular, when I was engaged in an intensive practice of The United Intent of the Gurus, I dreamed of meeting Guru Rinpoché and bowing to him with great respect. He gave me his blessing while saying a few mantra syllables and then said, "The obstacle to longevity that you faced this year has been dispelled. After a few years you will actually meet me and I can continue your training." Following that, it was in the year I turned forty that I first met the great *tertön* Chokgyur Lingpa, feeling like a son reuniting with his father. In time the *tertön* himself, having become indisputable and widely-known, gave me many prophetic accounts that came to him over the years, concerning the kinds of moral choices I should make. It was about this time that I began the work of compiling my *Treasury of Precious Hidden Teachings*, but I acted scrupulously in observance of the meaning found in these prophecies—that I would live my full measure of life if I performed *ganachakra* feasts on as large a scale as possible and did not pay attention to any negative gossip there might be about me.

In particular, when the doorway to the holy place of Dzongshö was first being opened, the all-seeing Jamyang Khyentsé Wangpo, the great *tertön* Chokling, and I had just completed a *drupchen* ritual focusing on the Eight Commands. In Tzitta Sangphuk Cave, these two great *tertön*s erected a high throne made of rocks, covered this with a mat and had me sit on it. [34b] Bestowing on me the representations of enlightened form, speech, and mind and a mandala offering of gold, they performed a ceremony for my longevity, insisting, "The name that Guru Rinpoché conferred on you is Orgyen Chimé Tennyi Yungdrung Lingpa.[259] You should use this name from now on and heal the impairments of circumstances in order for you to discover profound *terma*s."

Following that, just as he had indicated to the *tertön* Kundrol Sangwa Tsal, my all-seeing guru revealed the records of the *terma*s in the area of Modrak Cliff in Lhamdo and gave them to me. Many clear visions arose in my mind, and in accord with these, at Dechen Pemakö in Lhamdo Burmo, in my fifty-eighth year I brought *terma*s forth from their place of concealment, including The United Intent of the Three Roots, the exalted Ananda's teachings, and the undergarment of the master Humkara.[260]

Later on, I revealed the following *terma*s in succession from Kuchok Dechen-phuk Cave on the left hand slope of the canyon of Ata:
• relics from the seven previous buddhas
• a five-beaded mala of the five classes of Guru Thöthreng[261]
• a scroll of background teachings for The United Intent of the Three Roots
• an undergarment of the *dakini* Yeshé Tsogyal
• and from the seal of the *terma* cache, the white and red bodhichitta nectar of the Guru and his consort.

On this occasion, there was also a marvelous omen, [35a] for drops of nectar-like dew fell in great number from the dry cliff in which the *terma* cave was located.

There are eight major holy sites associated with the principle of guiding beings through enlightened activity; Pema Lhatsé is the sublime place associated with such guidance based on the principle of the lotus family, and Jetsün-phuk Cave is found in its central mountain. From this cave I have revealed images associated with four cycles of *guru sadhana* (the most special being the "regent" image of the Guru called Tashi Palbar); background teachings for the guru sadhana of The United Intent of the Three Roots; seven strands of Guru Rinpoché's hair, which are referred to as "The Three Roots in Their Entirety";[262] and the cycle entitled Jewel Motes.

From the cave of Maratika I have brought forth five pills made of the nectar that Amitayus conferred on Guru Rinpoché (and rolled by the Guru himself with his own hands); the teachings of the great abbot Bodhisattva;[263] a sash used by the Buddhist king Trisong Detsen; major relics of buddhas of the ten directions; a statue of Manjushri an inch high, which had been the focus of the great translator Bairotsana's personal practice; and the scroll containing the five sections of The Heart Drop of Bairotsana.

From Tashi Terdzong in Marong Drugu I brought forth a chest containing a tooth of the perfect Buddha and some of his blood, but a very key circumstance was missing and the guardians of the terma reclaimed it. But the cave also yielded background teachings on the dakini practice from The United Intent of the Three Roots; the sadhana of Chandali, the "swift-acting consort of longevity"; [35b] a single lock of Yeshé Tsogyal's hair, called "The Lady of Rainbow Light"; an undergarment of Princess Mandarava;[264] pills made from the bodhichitta nectar of the five classes of Thöthreng; and medicinal pills deriving from the eight Indian vidyadharas.

Ödzong on Crystal Cliff in Rongkha was the site of my discovery of scrolls dealing with sadhanas for Amitayus and Hayagriva, longevity pills from Mandarava, and a leavening culture[265] of powerful substances for the sadhana of Hayagriva called Vanquishing All Arrogant Ones.

In Tashi Tsekpai Dzong in Tsangrong, I discovered special substances sacred to the eight great bodhisattvas, as well as a scroll with their sadhanas. It would seem that these teachings are an auxiliary part of Supreme Compassion: Taking Ease in Mind Itself, which is a profound terma discovered by my lord guru, Pema Ösel Do-ngak Lingpa.[266]

In the secret cave of Tsogyal, which is in the cliff face of Tsadra Rinchen Drak, I revealed the guru sadhana entitled The Sphere of Light, one of the Seven Cycles of the Secret Drop. I also discovered a scroll of the dakini sadhana called The Ocean of Supreme Bliss, wrapped in the silken skirts of five authentic dakinis. As well, many special samaya substances fell into my hands, including "Massing Clouds of Blessings" (a samaya substance of the Guru), flesh from the brahmin Aryasiddhi, and longevity pills consecrated by thirteen deathless vidyadharas.

The first time I entered the holy site of Deshek Düpa in Dzongshö, [36a] a

sublime medicine came into my possession—a medicine that brought liberation on being tasted, which Guru Rinpoché has produced through a ritual involving a human corpse. I came by this substance in the cave of Hayagriva,
the site associated with the principle of enlightened speech. Over the years I
had clear impressions of other substances to be found there—for example,
substances blessed by the eight *vidyadhara*s—but because I initially did not
act on these impressions, the troubled times made it increasingly difficult to
reveal these.

On the basis of an omen in my dreams, I sought the help of Lerab Lingpa.
Lord Khyentsé Rinpoché issued an injunction to the guardians of *terma*s and
instructed Lerab Lingpa. Accordingly, Lerab Lingpa and I were together
able, in Pal De'u, to reveal individual *sadhana*s for the eight Indian
*vidyadhara*s and *samaya* substances that were associated with these practices. If my precious lord guru were to have revealed The United Commands
of the Three Roots, these *sadhana*s would have constituted an auxiliary part
of this cycle. The holy place associated with enlightened mind yielded robes
and special practice objects used by these eight masters, while in the place of
enlightened speech I discovered hair from the nine *mahasiddha*s of Tibet
who received transmissions. And Yangleshö, the holy place associated with
the eastern direction, was the site where I revealed images representative of
one hundred and eighty *vidyadhara*s, relic pills from seven hundred and eight
lifetimes,[267] and a *samaya* substance called "Wish-Fulfilling Magical Essence"—which embodied the quintessence of the three lineages[268] of The United
Intent of the Three Roots. There were other *terma*s that were destined to be my
discoveries, [36b] but the place and time did not allow these to come into my
hands.

At the Sky Fortress at Yelphuk Cave, the great *tertön* Chokgyur Lingpa
brought forth from their place of concealment a statue of Yang-gön called
"Blazing Fire" and a *sadhana* concerning the Six-Armed Mahakala; these he
bestowed on me.

From the hills called "The Three Brothers" in Tsiké Norbu, Chokling recovered a "regent" image of Guru Rinpoché, the profound teaching known as
The Sevenfold Gem, and the records of my own share of *terma*s. I was the one
who codified the prophetic account, setting it down in writing. When I met
with him, the *tertön* gave me his personal assurance that there were other such
transmissions he intended to confer on me, but he passed away and these never
came into my possession. The prophecy concerning me would seem to be the

passage found in the prophetic account associated with Chokling's cycle of teachings entitled Auspicious Interdependence:

> . . . a great translator, endowed with the eye of timeless awareness, whose greatness lies hidden on the slopes of the "gem."
> Do not waver from your task, but reveal this and explain it to all who have faith.

The secret cave of the Guru in the cliff of Tsadra Rinchen Drak yielded The Secret Drop: The Three Cycles of Chosen Deities, revealed by Chokling. This, too, fell to me as my lot.

It is my personal conceit that all of these *terma* caches, major and minor, are reliable and of authentic origin, unsullied by any confusion. This is based on my own pure visionary experiences and also the fact that the omniscient Jamyang Khyentsé Rinpoché had pure visionary experiences, [37a] in which he received prophecies to this effect from gurus and deities. Accordingly, he would join me in performing *ganachakra* feasts, fulfillment rituals, and any other ceremonies necessary to dispel potential problems at the outset. I showed all the *termas* that came to me to Lord Khyentsé Rinpoché for his opinion, and he would praise their quality and perform extensive investiture ceremonies and *ganachakra* feasts.

In particular, The United Intent of the Three Roots itself epitomized the vast and profound cycles of teaching of the Five Treasuries in their entirety, and even the symbolic script[269] was of many different kinds. To inspire confidence in this and banish any doubts, I took this cycle to show it to my precious lord guru. He set up a very high seat and had me sit on it, handing me a beribboned bamboo scepter. He described how in the past Chokgyur Lingpa had received the scroll of his *sadhana* of enlightened mind entitled *Dispelling Obstacles on the Path*, but had left it alone without doing anything about it until Khyentsé Rinpoché helped him codify it and it had become useful. Now, Khyentsé Rinpoché indicated, he would help me to codify this teaching of mine. Since the tenth day of the tenth month fell on that day, we performed a *ganachakra* feast. Following that, in time Khyentsé Rinpoché had two visions of the Guardian Goddess of Mantra loosening the seal on these teachings and telling him when it was time for the seal of secrecy to be removed. Such things became quite clear to him. [37b]

One such special event he described was as follows: On the evening of the twenty-ninth day of a month, he had a lucid vision of being in a vast, open area that he took to be in India. It was filled with grass huts and women wearing ornaments of conch shell. Approaching from a ravine, he saw many women offering him fish taken from a pond. He then immediately found himself at the hermitage of Palpung Monastery; there, too, there were only women. He entered the temple, to find a solid and impressive throne of stone, on which was a grass mat covered with the hide of a black antelope. He said that I, Guna Samudra, was seated on this.[270] At a certain point he saw me turning into a middle-aged guru with a slight beard, wearing a red "lotus hat" and a cloak, speaking a great deal in Sanskrit. Khyentsé Rinpoché could not understand him, so a woman acted as interpreter. It turned out that the guru was the *vidyadhara* Humkara. Hearing this and other things, Khyentsé Rinpoché supplicated him with faith and devotion, whereupon the guru conferred on him the fundamental empowerment of the four mainstream transmissions for *The Sublime Sadhana of the Masters of Awareness* from The United Intent of the Three Roots; he conferred this in its entirety, beginning with the ritual to prepare the site, as though bestowing oral transmission and instruction. It seemed to Khyentsé Rinpoché that the empowerment articles and mandala were hanging in space, while the guru carried out the stages of the empowerment ritual as he intoned the words of each stage. Khyentsé Rinpoché told me that the empowerment into wisdom and timeless awareness and the other stages were performed quite cursorily—for example, a real consort was not used.[271] [38a] He then told me that the entire meaning of the scroll was particularly clear in his mind, and he gave me a list of the categories of teachings from *The Sublime Sadhana of the Masters of Awareness.* These were to be included within the four sections—concerning the Three Roots and the protective deities—to be found in *The Treasure Trove of Oral Transmissions,* the most important of the Five Treasuries.[272] He observed that if the symbolic *dakini* script were translated to the fullest extent, the text would amount to what Sang-gyé Lingpa revealed as The United Intent of the Gurus, but that it would be best if the codified version were of intermediate length, based on a less extensive translation of the script. He had codified some six sections of teachings when several important premonitory circumstances[273] caused him to become ill. By the time he recovered the available time for codification had passed, and I understood that this was the limit of the share allowed by people's collective merit.

At that time, I myself was recalling what I had written in the past, and I dreamed of many gatherings of *dakini*s. At one point I dreamed that my lord guru was dictating the contents of a scroll while someone else wrote them down. I, too, was recalling many things, writing them down endlessly. Following that, I found myself leading a large group of people in a clockwise circumambulation of an enormous stupa. We made many circuits as I chanted the seven-branch prayer from *The Aspiration Prayer of Noble Conduct* to a melody; I dreamed that everyone joined in on the verse [38b] beginning "Through homage, . . . " At a certain point my body became like a huge mountain, with springs of water flowing from my four centers—the crown of the head, the throat, the heart, and the navel; the water from my navel center was mixed with a white substance like soft clay. In succession, I had clear impressions of numerous tantras, *sadhana*s, and pith instructions concerning the guru principle, as the vajra of enlightened form; the chosen deity principle, as the vajra of enlightened speech; the *dakini* principle, as the vajra of enlightened mind; and the principle that unites the Three Roots in their entirety, as the vajra of timeless awareness. Immediately upon waking from this dream, I had clear and spontaneous awareness of many lines of verse; but when I later tried to recall these in detail, they swirled around in my mind like dust motes in a sunbeam, so that I couldn't distinguish them separately. When I just thought of them in general, however, they seemed endless, and even after I had awakened I had the impression that I could call the majority of these verses to mind.

At dawn on the seventh day of the twelfth month, I had a lucid vision in which I found myself in a beautifully appointed temple. There I beheld what was in essence Guru Rinpoché and in form my precious lord guru, his body one of light, empty yet clearly apparent, its shape shifting in indistinct ways. I bowed to him in devotion and he led me in reciting the liturgies of refuge, bodhichitta, and the seven-branch prayer from *The Daily Practice of the Masters of Awareness.*[274] Khyentsé Rinpoché then performed the stages for developing the visualization of the deity and bringing down the blessings. Holding a ritual vase, he placed it on the crown of my head; for the secret empowerment, he bestowed on me the bodhichitta nectar [39a] that came from his union with a consort; while for the empowerment into wisdom and timeless awareness he conferred a consort on me. In each of these three cases he spoke a single mantra, not reciting any other words to bestow the empowerments. Khyentsé Rinpoché took a crystal out of his heart center and showed it to me, introducing me directly to the nature of mind with the words, "The original purity of all phenomena is profoundly lucid, like this crystal globe; the dynamic radiance of their spontaneous presence arises as anything and everything, like the light shining from this crystal." His form then vanished. He suddenly reappeared and instantly summoned the guardian deities of the *kama* and *terma* traditions. They seemed to me to be actually present, and Khyentsé Rinpoché issued an injunction and entrusted them with the teachings, bestowed formal permission on them, and gave them spiritual instruction. Following this I heard him recite many lines of verse, rather like a record of prophecies, whereupon I awoke from this meditative vision. When we had codified the activity ritual, we performed it once, and while singing the vajra song during the *ganachakra* feast I felt intensely blissful and warm as a great flow of blessing welled up in me.

When I offered the scrolls of the *guru sadhana* and *dakini* practices from *The Secret Sphere* to Khyentsé Rinpoché for his opinion, the precious lord codified them on his own. He also kept half of the different kinds of *samaya* substances.

Once I myself had codified *The Profound Path in Seven Chapters*, I dreamed that someone named Pema Rigdzin, who was dressed like Guru Padmasambhava, conferred the oral transmission on me three times. [39b]

In Dagam Wangphuk Cave, while having a pure vision, I received a cycle of teachings concerning the Seven-Line Prayer as an oral transmission. When I told my precious lord guru the circumstances of this transmission, Khyentsé Rinpoché gave me symbolic objects representing the five principles of unending adornment and paper on which to write. Responding to his request, I codified these teachings and together my lord and I performed the *ganachakra* feast focusing on the nirmanakaya form known as the Lake-Born Vajra.[275] Lord Khyentsé Rinpoché had some special visions: through a symbolic gesture, the *dakini* Dechen Gyalmo told him that this cycle had five basic sections, while there were two auxiliary sections still unaccounted for. Accordingly, he received the complete empowerments and oral transmissions from her.

Once, Khyentsé Rinpoché and I performed the *ganachakra* feast and fulfillment ritual from the Dorjé Drollö cycle revealed at Rongmé Karmo Taktsang. On that occasion my lord guru had a vision of two huge scorpions, one white and one black; he remarked that this was a sign of great portent.

I had clear signs that both Tsadra Rinchen Drak and the palace of Deshek Düpa in Dzongshö were to have been my personal sites for *terma* revelation, but this turned out not to be timely and so later on it was Chokling who received the plan of the sites and the injunction to open the doorway to them. This served as a circumstance for his revealing the records of the twenty-five major holy sites from the cliff of Padrak, and he came to open the area up. [40a]

In accord with the instructions of my venerable lord guru Khyentsé, I myself opened the doorways to three major sites—Dzongchen Khamphuk Cave, Wal De'u in Alo, and Pewar (a secondary site associated with Tsadra)—and made these plain to all.

As regards the activities arising out of these discoveries, the empowerments and oral transmissions for those teachings that I did codify were received by many great holders of the teachings, foremost among them the omniscient Gyalwang Karmapa, and so spread widely. As well, many have put these teachings into practice. Beings have benefited from the blessed substances that have increased and been used as leavening cultures, which I have used throughout the three regions of eastern, central, and southern Tibet. While I have spoken briefly of these *terma* cycles out of my conceit over what is merely my good fortune, in the case of *samaya* substances one must, in any event, count on these to bring benefit to beings.

As for *terma*s, due to circumstances of place and time and other interdependent factors it can be difficult for these to prove useful. In my own case, I have devoted great efforts to render what service I can to the indisputable older *terma*s revealed in the past, and so I have tended for the most part to leave aside my own and others' more recent *terma* discoveries. For as has been said:

If even some inappropriate form is inappropriate,
how much more so a teaching one doubts?
Better, then, to leave it alone, for there is no fault in that.
[40b]
In conclusion:

Wealth and fame are like a dream.
I have seen them to be hollow and illusory,
and so I have cast off any hope that I will leave my mark on the world
or any fear that I will not.
Therefore, this has not been to sing my own praises
or prove me greater than others.
I have written this brief account, feeling that there is no harm
in discussing something that is neither exaggerated nor
downplayed.

If people have faith in this, may it plant in them the seeds of
    enlightenment,
and may even those without faith not be hindered by it,
so that everyone who reads it may find meaning therein,
bringing to consummation the noble path of conduct
and reaching the level of "the unsurpassable principle of timeless
    awareness."[276]
Sarva dikshu kale mangalam svasti bhavantu[277]

Concluding Verses to the Palpung Edition of the Text[278]

This magical edition of an oceanic treasure trove of marvels—
the account of the successive lifetimes
of Jamgön Lama, the single eye of the world—
is a magnificent wish-fulfilling gem that yields the two kinds of
    benefit in abundance.

The sublime incarnation, Do-ngak Chökyi Nyima,[279]
and the great steward Tashi Tsephel and his brother
have published this as a banquet that will give purpose to those
    connected to it—
the lineage of this master's students, who uphold the Victorious
    One's teachings
in these snowy reaches.

Through their ever-devoted efforts, resulting from their utterly
    superb merit,
may the whole range of samsara and nirvana be illuminated by this
    brilliant orb,
and may its power serve as a cause for all beings,
equal to space in their extent, to attain omniscience.

[41a]

May the fortunate guests, who aspire to the state of this sublime
    guide—
one who saw the flaws of falling into the extremes of samsara or
    personal salvation—

be inspired to undertake the oceanic conduct of supreme enlightenment, which frees them of the many states of dualistic extremes.

These verses of aspiration were composed as a colophon by Gyalsé Jamyang Chökyi Nyima Lodrö Gyepai Dé.[280] May they serve as a cause for all beings— for him and all others so connected—to be taken always under the care of the incomparable and glorious guru!

Sarvada kalyanam bhavantu![281]

ENDNOTES

1. The corresponding term in Sanskrit is *bhusuku*, a compound term formed from Sanskrit verb roots, referring to someone whose behavior is "restricted to the activities of eating (*bhuj*), sleeping (*sup*), and pottering around (*kutim* gata)." (*The Way of the Bodhisattva*, p. 174). Were this text written by a student of Kongtrul rather than by the master himself, such a disparaging term would never be used. Here, it is an expression of the self-deprecation that is common in the works of Asian authors. In the tradition of literary style that the Tibetan schools of Buddhism inherited from their Indian forerunners, an introduction to an authentic commentary on the Buddha's words should include an expression of homage, a statement of the author's intent in composing the work, a formal expression of self-abasement (to lessen the author's pride in presuming to write the commentary), and some expression to then inspire the author and reader concerning the message found in the work.

2. Pema Nyinjé Wangpo (1774-1853) was the ninth Tai Situ incarnation of Palpung Monastery, whom Kongtrul first met in the tenth month of the Water Serpent Year (corresponding to late 1833 in the Western calendar), when Kongtrul was about twenty years old. The Situ incarnations constituted the principal incarnation lineage of the Kagyü School in eastern Tibet, and were successively the heads of Palpung Monastery, its most important (though not its largest) monastic center in the region. Situ Pema Nyinjé Wangpo became Kongtrul's primary guru within the Kagyü system he adopted when he was required to move from the Nyingma monastery of Zhechen to Palpung.

3. These are concerns regarding gain or loss, fame or ill repute, praise or blame, and happiness or unhappiness.

4. Bodhisattvas are children in the spiritual sense that they are still awakening to buddhahood, whereas a buddha has already realized this goal and so stands as a kind of spiritual parent figure.

5. That is, the Buddha, who in his teachings described circumstances under which the demonstration of miraculous powers was useful.

6. The two stages of Vajrayana meditation are those of development and completion; the latter is further divided into a structured and an unstructured phase. For a concise discussion of these stages by Kongtrul himself, see *Creation and Completion: Essential Points of Tantric Meditation.*

7. The path of application is the second of the five paths. It is the phase that links the initial path of accumulation with the third phase, the path of vision, which corresponds to the first of the ten levels of realization and involves the first stable degree of insight into the true nature of reality.

8. The Vajrayana concept of *samaya* (Tib. *damtsig*) commitment can be a complex one, involving many guidelines and principles. Kongtrul's very detailed treatment of these is found in *Buddhist Ethics*, pp. 215-306; the particular commitment he refers to here, the seventh of some fourteen fundamental downfalls, is described on page 261.

9. This epithet demonstrates how deeply conscious Tibetans are of the role played by the master Padmakara (the "Lotus-Born") in bringing the Vajrayana teachings to Tibet in the eighth century. They refer to him fondly as "Guru Rinpoché" ("Precious Spiritual Master"), or simply "Orgyen," a reference to the site of his miraculous birth.

10. A well-known story of an old woman who prayed with faith to a dog's tooth, convinced that it was one of the Buddha's teeth and thus a holy relic. Due to the power of her faith, the tooth in fact began to produce further relics. The story is related by Paltrul Rinpoché in *The Words of My Perfect Teacher*, pp. 173-174.

11. In a slightly oblique way, Kongtrul is arguing the following: These great masters, who confirmed him as an incarnation or emanation, also considered him one of their gurus and received transmissions and teachings from him. If he were entirely unworthy of such trust, they would on their part be mistaken and acting in error; since this cannot be so, he implies, their pronouncements concerning his status must be taken seriously.

12. Before he left Tibet in the eighth century, Padmakara, or Guru Rinpoché, concealed countless teachings as *termas*, or hidden treasure teachings, to be revealed at appropriate points in the future, when the need for such teachings is most urgent. For a detailed and informative discussion of such *terma* teachings, see *Hidden Teachings of Tibet.*

13. Bayo Chözang was a master who was both teacher and student to the *tertön* Sanggyé Lingpa (1340-1396).

14. The historical figures mentioned in the preceding paragraphs are discussed later on in Kongtrul's account.

15. *The Ornament of the Class of Discourses* (Skt. *Mahayana-sutralamkara*), Section

Ten, verse 36. This text is one of the Five Works of Maitreya that the future buddha Maitreya is held to have transmitted to the Indian Buddhist master Asanga. *Indian Buddhism*, p. 407, gives Asanga's dates as about 290 to 350. The Five Works of Maitreya are standard scriptural sources of Mahayana doctrine, often cited to support arguments or validate points an author is making. In twenty-one chapters, *The Ornament of the Class of Discourses* discusses various topics, of both provisional and definitive meaning, that are found in the Buddha's discourses.

16. *The Highest Continuum* (Skt. *Uttaratantra*), Section One, verse 27. This text is another of the Five Works of Maitreya, and perhaps the single most important source concerning the "buddha nature." It lays out the view found in the group of the Buddha's discourses known as the "*tathagatagarbha* sutras," which discuss the "buddha nature" innate in all beings.

17. An epithet for the buddha epitomizing dharmakaya, the ultimate state of buddhahood, "primordial" in the sense that it is beyond any time frame of past, present, or future, being "ever-present." In the Nyingma School, this term refers to the buddha Samantabhadra; in the Sarma Schools, to Vajradhara.

18. The Sanskrit term Vairochana is used in this translation to refer to the sambhogakaya buddha, while the Tibetanized version of this name, Bairotsana, refers to the Tibetan translator, who took his name from the fact that he was considered an historical emanation of that buddha.

19. A euphemistic way of referring to the human state of rebirth, which represents freedom from other, less fortunate states, while providing opportunity for spiritual progress.

20. *The Ornament of the Class of Discourses*, Section Eleven, verse 12.

21. That is, the human state of rebirth, as the ideal working basis for spiritual growth.

22. *The Ornament of the Class of Discourses*, Section Nine, verse 12.

23. In the Sanskrit compound term *vajrakaya*, the term *vajra* connotes some seven qualities (invulnerability, indestructibility, authenticity, incorruptibility, stability, unobstructedness, and invincibility) (*Buddhahood Without Meditation*, p. 33), while the term *kaya* (literally, "body") refers to a stratum of being that constitutes "the gathering and amassing . . . of all aspects of pristine awareness and positive qualities" (Ibid., p. 119). The term "rainbow body" refers to an advanced level of spiritual accomplishment, at which point one's physical body is transformed into a form of light at death. The term "youthful vase body" is unique to the Dzogchen, or Great Perfection, system. To use the singular language of that approach, the youthful vase body represents the culmination of a process of spiritual development.

24. That is, reinforce their spiritual merit and deepen their insight to the utmost.

25. *The Ornament of the Class of Discourses*, Section Nine, verse 19.

26. Idem. This citation refers to the fact that the nirmanakayas (physical expressions

of enlightened being) manifest in a variety of ways. "Sublime emanations" are nirmanakaya manifestations such as the Buddha Shakyamuni.

27. Ibid., Section Ten, verse 53.

28. The Tibetan idiom refers to the manifestation of infinite enlightened qualities that is consequent on awakening to buddhahood.

29. Sherab Özer, the original source of the incarnations mentioned in this case, lived from 1518 to 1584. Tselé Natsok Rangdrol, the incarnation of Sherab Özer's form, was born in 1608. The other two of Sherab Özer's incarnations were the speech incarnation, Terdak Lingpa Gyurmé Dorjé (i.e., Minling Terchen, 1646-1714), and the mind incarnation, Pema Dechen Lingpa (1663-1713). It is relatively common for great masters to have more than one incarnation following their deaths. There were at least five incarnations of Kongtrul himself—representing his form, speech, mind, qualities, and activities—all of whom were born in the early years of the twentieth century (and so were contemporaries). Kongtrul's guru, Jamyang Khyentsé Wangpo, is credited with having produced eight incarnations in the years following his death in 1892.

30. Sherab Özer, whose *tertön* name was Drodul Lingpa, revealed the cycle The Sphere of Freedom: Naturally Free Intent, sections of which are contained in Kongtrul's collection, *The Treasury of Precious Hidden Teachings.*

31. In this account, Kongtrul consistently uses the less usual spelling "Thumi"; I have adopted the more usual spelling, which Kongtrul himself employs in his autobiography.

32. Gyalsé Pema Gyurmé Gyatso (1686-1717) was one of the sons and spiritual successors of Terdak Lingpa Gyurmé Dorjé, the founder of Mindroling Monastery.

33. Gyalmorong was a semi-autonomous region more than a hundred kilometers to the east of Dergé, with its own distinct language.

34. That is, Tselé Natsok Rangdrol (b. 1608), the above-mentioned form incarnation of Sherab Özer.

35. The incarnation preceding that of Tselé Natsok Rangdrol, the Nyingma master Tsungmé Tendzin Dorjé lived from 1535 to about 1605.

36. Tselé Orgyen Tendzin, also known as Tselé Sarma Densapa, lived in the sixteenth century.

37. According to *The Nyingma School of Tibetan Buddhism: Its Fundamentals and History* (Vol. 1, p. 788, n. 1055), Tselé Monastery was founded by Kunkhyen Chökyi Özer in Dakpo, a province in the southeast of Tibet where the Tsangpo River leaves Tibet and enters the Indian region of Assam as the Brahmaputra.

38. The above-mentioned mind incarnation of Sherab Özer.

39. *The Nyingma School of Tibetan Buddhism: Its Fundamentals and History* gives the title of this master as "Laptön" (vol. 1, p. 697) and identifies him as a student

of Khedrup Yeshé Gyaltsen. Dudjom Rinpoché lists Yeshé Gyaltsen as the last of the thirteen gurus of Kathok.

40. Bubor Tashi Gyatso does not appear in either of the two alternative lists of these thirteen gurus as given in *The Nyingma School of Tibetan Buddhism: Its Fundamentals and History* (Vol. 2, p. 171, citing Jamyang Khyentsé Wangpo and Gönpo Wang-gyal).

41. Guru Jotsé appears in the verse summary given by Kongtrul in his autobiography, in which he lists the *tertön*s whose revelations are included in his *Treasury of Precious Hidden Teachings*. Guru Jotsé's revelation is a technique for "ransoming" someone's life force, and is included in the section on more mundane activities.

42. According to Longchen Rabjam's *A Treasure Trove of Scriptural Transmission*, p. 418, this aspect of the buddha Vairochana is the "dharmakaya aspect of sambhogakaya." In Mahayana mythology, Vairochana holds some twenty-one universes (our own among them) in the palms of his hands; see *Myriad Worlds: Buddhist Cosmology in Abhidharma, Kālacakra and Dzog-chen*, pp. 51 and 103, and *Buddhist Cosmology: Philosophy and Origins*, pp. 143-157.

43. The sambhogakaya dimension of buddhahood is characterized by five constants. According to *Bod rgya tshig mdzod chen mo*, p. 656, these are: certainty of environment, in that the sambhogakaya abides solely within the pinnacle pure realm of dense array; certainty of embodiment, in that the sambhogakaya is adorned with major and minor marks of perfect form; certainty of retinue, in that this is composed solely of bodhisattvas on the three highest of the ten levels of realization; certainty of teaching, in that this is solely of the Mahayana approach; and certainty of occasion, in that this situation pertains "until cyclic existence becomes naught." There are several levels of interpretation concerning this fivefold certainty; see, for example, *A Treasure Trove of Scriptural Transmission*, p. 418, where this theme is treated from a Dzogchen perspective.

44. The term "Pinnacle Pure Realm of Dense Array" (Skt. *Akanishtha Ghanavyuha*; Tib. *Ogmin Tukpo Köpa*) refers to "the density of positive qualities that are spontaneously present within the ground of being" (*Buddhahood Without Meditation*, p. 125). As Kongtrul notes, however, the term applies not only to a realm of pure being that transcends the cycle of ordinary, conditioned existence (Skt. *samsara*), but in other contexts to the highest stages of the so-called realm of form within cyclic existence; see *Buddhist Philosophy in Theory and Practice*, p. 48. The term "long-suffering world" refers to our universe, described as a "three-thousand-fold universe"—that is, composed of a billion world systems similar to our own; see *Myriad Worlds: Buddhist Cosmology in Abhidharma, Kālacakra and Dzog-chen*, p. 104.

45. *The Journey to Sri Lanka* (Skt. *Lankavatara Sutra*) is one of the most important

Mahayana sutras; it became a major source for the Chittamatra (Mind Only) School of Buddhist philosophy and the theme of the three *kayas* of buddhahood. In the first chapter of his *Treasury of Philosophical Schools* (Tib. *Druptha Dzö*), Longchen Rabjam gives the citation from this sutra to which Kongtrul alludes:

> In the pleasant pinnacle realm of Dense Array,
>
> where even the pure realms of the gods are left behind,
>
> the perfect Buddha awakened to buddhahood
>
> An emanation awakened to buddhahood here.

46. Not identified; a master named Chökyi Shenyen (1453-1540) was the thirteenth throne-holder of Ganden Monastery in central Tibet; another Chökyi Shenyen lived in the twelfth century.

47. The path of vision is the third of the five consecutive paths of the Mahayana approach, and corresponds to the first of the ten levels of realization.

48. Although the Dzogchen approach employs such terms as "inner lucidity" and "outer lucidity," the distinction is purely nominal and experientially, not ontologically, based.

49. The dharmakaya of buddhahood is formless and intangible, while the nirmanakaya manifestations are fully perceptible to the senses of ordinary beings. The sambhogakaya, on the other hand, is only perceptible to spiritually advanced beings (bodhisattvas who have attained one of the three highest of the ten levels of realization). In the context of one's ordinary experience, dharmakaya is correlated to one's mind, nirmanakaya to one's body, and sambhogakaya to one's speech, which is also termed "transitionally manifest," because speech is perceptible to the sense of hearing, but has no visible form or other sensory quality.

50. Naturally occurring emanations are those that are only perceptible to spiritually advanced beings, while nirmanakaya manifestations that guide beings can be perceived by ordinary beings, who can develop relationships with these nirmanakayas as teachers and so progress spiritually.

51. That is, to the foregoing summary of the explanation followed by the Sarma Schools of the Tibetan Buddhist tradition, as distinct from this view of the Nyingma School. In his writings, Kongtrul often gives more than one perspective on an issue—a reflection of his *rimé* philosophy.

52. This characterization is a reference to Vajrapani's aforementioned role as the one initially responsible for hearing and setting down the tantras.

53. *The Sphere of Timeless Awareness* (Skt. *Jnanabindu*) is one of the mother tantras of the Anuttarayoga class. It deals primarily with the principle of enlightened qualities. *Heruka*s are wrathful masculine forms of tantric deities; *shravaka*s are models of the ideals that characterize the basic Buddhist approach, or Hinayana.

54. Skt. *vidyadhara;* Tib. *rigdzin.* One who, through profound means of spiritual development, maintains (and thus "masters") the experience of the pure awareness that is the nature of mind.

55. These figures are held to be various forms of Vajrapani, manifesting under different circumstances but performing the same function, that of requesting, hearing, and codifying the teachings. Suchandrabhadra was the king of Shambhala, the ancient mythical kingdom that became associated with the Kalachakra cycle; the other figures are sambhogakaya forms.

56. An epithet of the Buddha Shakyamuni, who was born into the Shakya clan of ancient India.

57. The seven successors were the seven generations of masters who were the foremost upholders of the Buddha's exoteric teachings following his passing— Kashyapa, the Buddha's younger cousin Ananda, Shanavasin, Upagupta, Dhitika, Krishna, and Mahasudarshana. See *Taranatha's History of Buddhism in India*, pp. 20-75 and 355-361.

58. Shambhala is an ancient kingdom whose location and origins are shrouded in myth and mystery. Suchandrabhadra requested that the Buddha Shakyamuni teach *The Kalachakra Tantra* and then propagated these teachings in his kingdom.

59. There are historical references to as many as three kings named Indrabhuti, all of whom are connected with lineages of Vajrayana teachings. See *The Nyingma School of Tibetan Buddhism: Its Fundamentals and History*, vol. 1, pp. 458-462.

60. The Sarma Schools recognize three sections of tantras within the Anuttarayoga class (the highest of their four classes of tantras)—father tantra, mother tantra, and nondual tantra. The Nyingma School, which discusses six classes of tantra, refers to the three highest of these as the "three yogas"—Mahayoga, Anuyoga, and Atiyoga. The Atiyoga class contains the sources for the Dzogchen tradition.

61. This master of the Indian Buddhist tradition is not mentioned above in any of the lists of incarnations given by Kongtrul. Aryadeva's most important work, *The Four Hundred Verses*, is a supplement to his teacher Nagarjuna's *Source Verses on Wisdom*.

62. This master, also known as Ashvaghosha, was perhaps the greatest poet of the Indian Buddhist tradition. He lived in the first century and his most famous work is *The Acts of the Buddha*, a verse account of the Buddha Shakyamuni's life, which has been translated into English by E. H. Johnston.

63. The "six ornaments of the world" are masters of the Indian Buddhist tradition— Nagarjuna and his student Aryadeva (the two ornaments of the Madhyamaka, or Middle Way, philosophy), Asanga and his student and younger brother Vasubandhu (the two ornaments of the Abhidharma teachings), and Dignaga and Dharmakirti (the two ornaments of epistemology). See *Crystal Mirror*, Vol. 5, pp. 59-85 (where the classification differs slightly from the usual one given here).

64. For a very complete account of this *mahasiddha*'s life, see *Tāranātha's Life of Kṛṣṇācārya/Kāṇha*.

65. One of the famous group of eighty-four *mahasiddhas*, or tantric saints, of the

Indian Buddhist tradition, Jalandharipa (also known as Jalandhara, or Jalandhari) was an important figure in the lineage of *The Hevajra Tantra*. See *Buddha's Lions: The Lives of the Eighty-Four Siddhas*, pp. 161-162, and *Masters of Enchantment: The Lives and Legends of the Mahasiddhas*, pp. 139-141.

66. The Tengyur collection attributes over one hundred and fifty works to authors whose names are some derivative form of Krishnacharya. The "six works of Krishna" consist of commentaries on the two stages of Vajrayana meditation—three on the stage of development and three on the stage of completion. Krishnacharya was a major figure in the historical transmission of the teachings focusing on *The Chakrasamvara Tantra*, one of the main mother tantras of the Anuttarayoga class.

67. Samyé, the first Buddhist monastic complex in Tibet, was built in the late eighth century, after Guru Rinpoché, Padmakara, was invited from India to tame the harmful spirits on the area who were preventing the construction.

68. The deity Mahabala is central to the cycle of The Wrathful Mantra Curse (*Möpa Drak-ngak*) practice; this is one of the two worldly practices that constitute part of the Eight Commands cycle of the Nyingma School. Guru Rinpoché received each of these eight practices from a specific Indian Buddhist master; it was Shantigarbha who imparted the practice of The Wrathful Mantra Curse to him.

69. For further material on Bairotsana, see "The Life and Teachings of Vairocana." Bairotsana's dates are Hanson-Barber's estimate (pp. 42-43).

70. In recognition of their genius in translating texts with accuracy and insight, the great translators who flourished during the early period of the introduction of Buddhism into Tibet were considered to be nirmanakaya emanations of buddhas, using their specific skills with language to benefit beings.

71. *The Great Mask* (Tib. *Drabak Chenmo*) is the extensive biography of Bairotsana, compiled by his student Yudra Nyingpo. *The Record of Padma* is an extensive biography of Padmakara, a *terma* revealed by Orgyen Lingpa in the fourteenth century, translated into English as *The Life and Liberation of Padmasambhava*; a number of chapters in this hidden treasure text are devoted to the life and works of Bairotsana. The Vajra Bridge is a Nyingma system of practice associated with the Category of Expanse (Tib. *Longdé*) of the Atiyoga class.

72. Bairotsana was considered part of a succession of incarnations that had included the Buddha Shakyamuni's cousin and attendant Ananda. Kawa Paltsek and Chokro Luyi Gyaltsen were two of the foremost Tibetan translators active during the same era as Bairotsana.

73. He was thus called Bairotsana (or simply "Bairo") due to the Tibetan pronunciation of "Vairochana." I have preserved the Tibetan pronunciation in order to distinguish this historical Tibetan figure from the sambhogakaya buddha Vairochana (particularly since Bairotsana is considered to have been an emanation of Vairochana, a further source of possible confusion).

74. According to *The Record of Padma*, Tsang-ngön Lekdrup was the son of Telen, the king of the south-central Tibetan province of Tsang, and was noted for his meditative accomplishments. See *The Life and Liberation of Padmasambhava*, p. 443, and the seventy-second chapter of *Padma bka'i thang yig*, p. 418.

75. Shri Simha (also known as Shri Singha or Shri Sengha) was an early master of the Dzogchen lineage. His guru was Manjushrimitra, the principal student of the first human Dzogchen master Garab Dorjé. Born in China, Shri Simha journeyed to India, where he met his guru and in turn transmitted the Dzogchen teachings to Padmakara, Vimalamitra, and Jnanasutra.

76. In this context, a "mandala offering" is a traditional ritual for presenting a formal request for spiritual teachings. As a liturgy is chanted, piles of grain are placed in a particular arrangement on a plate (usually of some precious or semiprecious metal) as a symbolic depiction of the entire universe. This offering is usually accompanied by an offering of gold or some other precious substance.

77. Tib. *Semdé*, *Longdé*, and *Men-ngakdé*. These are the three categories into which the Indian master Manjushrimitra divided the Atiyoga, or Dzogchen, teachings. Shri Simha further divided the Category of Direct Transmission into four cycles—outer, inner, secret, and most secret (or unsurpassable).

78. Garab Dorjé was the first human master of the Dzogchen transmission, having received the teachings from the dharmakaya buddha Samantabhadra through the sambhogakaya buddha Vajrasattva. The term "embodiment of timeless awareness" refers to the situation in which a highly realized individual's awareness is accessible to others of similar realization, and is perceived by them in an idealized form that can communicate teachings to them; though accounts of individuals meeting such embodiments closely resemble visionary states, they are considered a distinct process.

79. That is, the realization was simultaneous with the freedom being brought about, rather than any gap or linear process being necessary.

80. This is one of the so-called ordinary *siddhi*s, or spiritual attainments, one which allows the adept to traverse long distances with often astonishing rapidity.

81. These are five major sources for the Category of Mind in the Dzogchen approach—*Harbinger of Awareness* (Tib. *Rigpai Khujuk*), *Stirring of Supreme Dynamic Energy* (Tib. *Tsalchen Trukpa*), *Soaring of the Great Garuda* (Tib. *Khyungchen Dingwa*), *Smelting Gold from Ore* (Tib. *Dola Serzhun*, translated into English as *Primordial Experience*), and *Supreme Space: The Victory Banner That Never Falls* (Tib. *Minuppai Gyaltsen Namkha Ché*). These five texts are contained in the Atiyoga section (Volume 1) of *The Collected Tantras of the Nyingma Tradition*.

82. Jnanakumara of the Nyak clan was one of Guru Rinpoché's twenty-five intimate students in the eighth century.

83. That is, the previous occasions on which Bairotsana taught Yudra Nyingpo, Sangtön Yeshé Lama, and Sang-gyé Gönpo.

84. Skt. *Mahavibhasha*. Historically, this text was the major source of the Vaibhashika, or "Analytical," philosophy of early Indian Buddhism. It constitutes a survey of, and commentary on, the Abhidharma of the Sarvastivada School. Although the translation into Tibetan was never completed, there exists a Chinese translation.

85. This term refers to changes in the physical remains following the death of a spiritually advanced Dzogchen practitioner. In the most advanced cases, the body simply dissolves into light once the consciousness has left it.

86. Here Kongtrul is referring to Jamyang Khyentsé Wangpo; he has already noted Khyentsé's visions and other insights regarding Kongtrul's former lifetimes.

87. Langdarma, the younger brother of the Buddhist king Ralpachen, is notorious in Tibetan history for his persecution of Buddhism. During his brief reign of five years or so, Langdarma managed to destroy much of the Buddhist tradition in the central provinces. Over the next century, many teachers went to the outlying Tibetan provinces of the west and east, among them Lachen Gongpa Rabsel (953-1035), who had been born in the Penyul region northeast of Lhasa. For many years following King Langdarma's assassination in 841, lineages of teachings were reintroduced from these areas into central Tibet. Of the group known as the "ten men," five were from the central province of Ü—Lumé Tsulthrim Sherab, Dring Yeshé Yönten, Rakshi Tsulthrim Jungné, Ba Tsulthrim Lodrö, and Sumpa Yeshé Lodrö. Three were from the south-central province of Tsang—Lotön Dorjé Wangchuk, Tsongtsün Sherab Seng-gé, and Bodongpa Upadekar. Two individuals—the Orgyé brothers—were from Ngari province in western Tibet. These ten were key figures in the reintroduction of the lineage of monastic ordination and discipline.

88. The large central temple of the monastic complex at Samyé; for an excellent floor plan of the various levels, see *Tibet Handbook*, p. 176.

89. Lamo Monastery, some fifty kilometers northeast of Lhasa, was founded in 1109 by Lumé on his return to central Tibet.

90. These texts were concealed during the years of persecution by Langdarma, thus avoiding their being confiscated and destroyed. A similar phenomenon took place during the purges of the Cultural Revolution in the 1960s; in more recent times, texts and sacred objects long feared lost have begun to resurface.

91. The analogy here is that of the major elements in the construction of a house.

92. Following the destruction of the monastic structure in central Tibet by King Langdarma, the lineages of transmission for these teachings and ordination reentered the central provinces from outlying areas to both the east and west. According to E. Gene Smith (*Among Tibetan Texts: History and Literature of the*

Himalayan Plateau, p. 337, nn. 876 and 877), it was the Kashmiri scholar Shakyashribhadra who, in the twelfth century, reintroduced the lineage of ordination that became known as the "upper tradition," so called due to the higher elevation of the western provinces. This lineage was adopted by the Sarma Schools—the Sakya, Kagyü, and Geluk. To the east, in 974, Lachen Gongpa Rabsel received monastic ordination from three monks who had fled from central Tibet and a Chinese monk who made up the requisite number for conferring ordination. This lineage, maintained in the Nyingma School, became known as the "lower tradition," due to the lower elevation of the eastern provinces.

93. The ruler of Ngari who invited Atisha to Tibet in the eleventh century; his title, Lha Lama, indicates that he was both a temporal ruler and an ordained monk.

94. The term "dialectical approach" refers to the approach based on the teachings found in the sutras, which emphasizes the use of logic and reasoning, in contrast to the tantric approach, which is based more on direct experience. The Sarma Schools generally recognize four classes of tantras; the Nyingma, six.

95. These terms refer to two aspects of Vajrayana practice—sexual activity as a means of spiritual advancement, and the exercise of power to prevent others from causing harm by terminating their lives in such a way as to ensure their spiritual advancement. These techniques bear nothing in common to the playing out of ordinary sexual desire or aggression, but as Kongtrul notes, they are highly susceptible to misinterpretation and abuse. On the subject of the misinterpretation of the tantras by Westerners, Guenther notes, in *The Tantric View of Life*, pp. 1-2, "Either the literature was said to reflect a sad state of intellectual and moral degeneration, or it was believed to contain the keys to a world of power and sex, the two basic notions that haunt all those who are lacking in one or the other and especially those lacking in both. Although the degeneration theory has been largely abandoned, the assumption that power and sex are the primary concern of Tantrism is still widespread, for it is easier, and possibly more lucrative, to perpetuate ignorance than to gain and disseminate knowledge. The fact that in the Western world the word Tantra is almost exclusively used with reference to a power- and sex-inflated esoteric teaching and not at all in its broader connotation of 'expanded treatise,' is highly illuminating as far as Western thinking is concerned, but it does not throw any light on what Tantra means in itself." It is clear from Kongtrul's comments that such misunderstanding was a perennial problem among Tibetans, as well.

96. E. Gene Smith (*Among Tibetan Texts: History and Literature of the Himalayan Plateau*, p. 329, n. 805) suggests that "[t]his personage is probably to be identified with Gshen chen Klu dga' (996-1035), whose rediscovery of the Bon po *abhidharma* text, the *Srid pa'i mdzod phug*, in 1017 at 'Grig mtshams mtha' dkar marks the beginning of the later spread (*phyi dar*) of Bon. . . . Sa skya Pandita, in the *Sdom*

gsum rab dbye (chapter 3, lines 462-68), refers to him as Sangs rgyas skar rgyal and does not specifically name him a Bon po. He criticizes him as a person possessed by a malevolent *klu* [*naga*] spirit who adulterated (*log par 'chos*) genuine teachings." Elsewhere, in a section titled "The Origins of the Ris med Tradition" (Ibid., pp. 237-238), Smith notes, "The roots of eclecticism and tolerance are sunk as deep into the soil of Tibetan tradition as those of sectarianism and bigotry. From the very beginning, when Bon and Buddhism fought for the faith and patronage of Tibetan nomads and peasants, there have been those who would erect a barrier between the two so great that it could not be crossed. Yet there have also been those who viewed the two as kindred traditions that shared common cultural content and that probably sprang from a single source. In western Tibet (*Stod*) [Rinchen Zangpo's homeland] intolerance often predominated. The literature of the eleventh and twelfth centuries [Rinchen Zangpo's era] is filled with the struggles of Bon and Buddhism; we read of contests to the death between such figures as Lo chen Rin chen bzang po (958-1055) and Klu skar rgyal, between Mi la ras pa and Na ro bon chung. The pattern in the south (Lho brag and Lho kha) and east (Khams and A mdo), on the other hand, seems to have been one of good-natured synthesis, or at least mutual tolerance. In the central and western areas (Dbus and Gtsang), the puritanical intellectuals of the New Tantric transmissions composed polemics against the followers of the Old Tantras, the Rnying ma pa." [All bracketed comments mine.] In this present case, Kongtrul seems to be avoiding identifying Lu Kargyal with any specific school; instead he vilifies him ("goatherd") as someone whose power, obtained from the machinations of an evil spirit, caused him to pervert the teachings. Rinchen Zangpo's taming of Lu Kargyal is thus symbolic of the former's role as one who revivified the teachings and corrected errors of the past.

97. The development of Buddhism in Tibet is divided by native historians into two phases. The early spread of the teachings includes the first introduction of Buddhism during the reign of King Songtsen Gampo, its real flourishing during the reign of King Trisong Detsen (ruled 756-797), and the standardization of translation from Sanskrit into Tibetan during the of King Ralpachen (ruled 814-836/8). This early phase ends with the persecution that began when Ralpachen's younger brother Langdarma succeeded to the throne. The beginning of the later spread of the teachings is calculated in several ways. The Zhalu master Butön Rinchendrup (1290-1364) determined it to be fifty-three years before the introduction, in 1027, of the system of the sexagesimal cycle; it was in this year (i.e., 974) that Lachen Gongpa Rabsel (953-1035) received his full monastic ordination. Dromtön Gyalwai Jungné (1004/1005-1064) felt that the later spread began forty-eight years before the introduction of this system (i.e., in 979), when Lumé Sherab Tsulthrim and the rest of the "ten men" received their ordination from Lachen Gongpa Rabsel. Al-

ternatively, the later spread of the teachings is said to begin with the career of the Sakya master Rinchen Zangpo as a translator of Vajrayana texts from Sanskrit into Tibetan. Finally, some consider the later spread to have begun from the point that Yeshé Ö (the "royal monk" of the Gugé Purang dynasty of Ngari province in western Tibet, who lived from 947 to 1024) invited three Indian masters of the monastic tradition to revivify that tradition in his region. See *Bod rgya tshig mdzod chen mo*, p. 1127.

98. An epithet of the Buddha.

99. An epithet for Atisha.

100. Not identified. The Tibetan Buddhist Resource Center website lists five main students of Loden Sherab—Lodrö Jungné, Chökyi Lama, Rinchen Drak, Rinchen Namkha Dorjé, and Sherab Bar.

101. According to *mDo kun las btus pa'i nang don rig pa'i tshig mdzod Mu tig phreng ba*, p. 608, the "eight great lions" are eight students of Chapa Chökyi Seng-gé (1109-1169), the sixth abbot of Sangphu Monastery.

102. Sangphu Netok, in the hills about forty kilometers south of Lhasa, was founded in 1073 by Ngok Loden and his nephew, Ngok Lekpai Sherab—two translators who studied with the Indian master Atisha. Sangphu was originally a Kadampa institution, but by the thirteenth century it had a mixture of Sakya and Geluk colleges. The Sakya master Yakdé Panchen's meditation cave is nearby.

103. The Tibetan system of *shedras*, or monastic colleges, dates back to the early Kadampa School and its emphasis on methodical study of the traditional sources of the Buddhist teachings.

104. This would be Sherab Bar, one of the main students of Ngok Lotsawa Loden Sherab.

105. Sok Tsulthrim Lama, Gya Duldzin Wangchuk Tsulthrim, and Matso Jangchub Dorjé were all masters of the "lower tradition" of the monastic ordination lineage.

106. Courses of study in the monastic colleges of Tibet—which developed into the elaborate systems for the conferral of degrees such as *geshé* and *khenpo*—have tended historically to focus on certain main topics drawn from the sutras and commentaries. Five fields of study were considered particularly important; (1) the Prajnaparamita (Perfection of Wisdom) emphasizes study of such works as Maitreya's *Ornament of Manifest Realization* (Skt. *Abhisamayalamkara*), which explains the means by which a practitioner progresses through stages and levels on the path to enlightenment; (2) the Madhyamaka philosophy presents a systematic discussion of emptiness as the nature of reality, based primarily on the works of Nagarjuna and Chandrakirti of the Indian Buddhist tradition; (3) Pramana (epistemology) deals with standards of valid cognition through direct experience and correct inference; (4) Abhidharma consists of commentaries that elabo-

rate on the Buddha's original teachings, providing the basis for wisdom to develop through study, contemplation, and meditation; (5) Vinaya concerns various codes of morality and conduct.

107. The Kadampa School based its approach to the study of the Buddhist teachings on Atisha's works, supplemented by texts that became known as the Six Mainstream Sources of the Kadampa. Of these six, two are intended to inspire faith—*The Garland of Rebirths* (Skt. *Jatakamala*) compiled by Aryasura (which contains accounts of the Buddha's former lifetimes told as moral parables), and *The Aphorisms* of Dharmatrata (Skt. *Udanavarga*; similar in content to *The Dhammapada*, the Pali compendium of the Theravada Schools of Buddhism). Two texts deal with states of meditative absorption—*Stages of the Bodhisattva* (Skt. *Bodhisattvabhumi*) by Asanga and *The Ornament of the Class of Discourses* (Skt. *Mahayanasutralamkara*) by Maitreya. Two sources, both by Shantideva, treat the principle of conduct—*Engaging in the Conduct of a Bodhisattva* (Skt. *Bodhicharyavatara*) and *The Compendium of Training* (Skt. *Shikshasamucchaya*). In his autobiography, Kongtrul discusses the nature of the Kadampa teachings in more detail, from the point of view of a threefold division: mainstream sources; spiritual advice, which focuses on the system of *lojong* (mental training); and pith instructions, which include Vajrayana meditation techniques. Zangkar Lotsawa Pakpa Sherab (eleventh century) was one of the group of later translators whose work fueled the later spread of the teachings in Tibet. Tölungpa Rinchen Nyingpo (1032-1116) was a master of Yangpachen, a Kadampa monastery in central Tibet.

108. During the time he spent in Tibet, a great deal of Guru Rinpoché's attention was devoted to taming the indigenous spirits of the region and harnessing their energies to be used in the service of the Buddhist teachings. Pehar, a so-called *gyalpo*, or king demon, was one of the most powerful of these spirits. Pehar is credited with emanating in human forms to interact with, and influence the affairs of, human beings, much in the same way that Madame Pélé is said to do by many in Hawai'i.

109. This is a very minor infraction of the monastic code.

110. A commentary on the monastic code written by Ja Dulwa Dzinpa Tsöndrü Bar.

111. For further information on Khyungpo Naljor, see *Like An Illusion: Lives of the Shangpa Kagyu Masters*, pp. 44-92.

112. The Great Perfection, or Dzogchen, system of meditation is taught in the Nyingma School of Buddhism, and in the indigenous Tibetan tradition of Bön. The Mahamudra teachings are primarily transmitted in the Sarma Schools. Both systems deal with meditation leading to a direct experience of the nature of mind.

113. Vajrasana, an Indian scholar and master of the tenth and eleventh centuries, was a student of Maitripa. Maitripa and Vajrasana were two of the one hundred and fifty Indian masters with whom Khyungpo Naljor was said to have studied. If

this Vajrasana was the "middle" one, there were apparently at least three masters with the name Vajrasana, which is also the ancient Indian name for modern-day Bodh Gaya, the site of the Buddha's enlightenment. A monastic university was located there until its destruction during a Muslim invasion of the late twelfth to early thirteenth centuries; these masters may have taken their names from the fact that they studied or taught there.

114. Niguma and Sukhasiddhi were women in ancient India (c. ninth-tenth centuries) whose spiritual development culminated in them becoming quasi-divine "dakinis of timeless awareness." For their life stories, see *Like An Illusion: Lives of the Shangpa Kagyu Masters*, pp. 34-43. There is some confusion as to Niguma's relationship to the Indian master Naropa (1012/1016-1100). Riggs, citing Kalu Rinpoché in *Luminous Mind: The Way of the Buddha*, p. 213, describes her as the daughter of the brahmin Shantasamnaha and the sister of the great Indian master Naropa (*Like An Illusion: Lives of the Shangpa Kagyu Masters*, p. 35). Guenther, in *The Life and Teachings of Naropa* (p. xii, n. 1) cites Roerich, *The Blue Annals* (p. 730), as calling Niguma the sister of Naropa (she is also called that elsewhere in *The Blue Annals*, pp. 641 and 728). But Guenther also notes (Idem) that the Gelukpa scholar and historian Thukan Chökyi Nyima (1737-1802) refers to her as Naropa's wife; and Guenther states that Naropa's father was named Shantivarman and that, prior to becoming a Buddhist scholar and master, Naropa was party to an arranged marriage: " . . . in A.D. 1032 he was forced to marry. His wife came from a cultured brahmin family. The marriage lasted for eight years, then it was dissolved by mutual consent. His wife seems to have gone by her caste name Ni-gu-ma, and according to the widely practised habit of calling a female with whom one has any relation 'sister' she became known as 'the sister of Naropa.' She engaged in literary activities and her works, which show a marked affinity to those of Naropa, are preserved in the Tibetan bsTan 'gyur under her name Ni-gu-ma." (pp. xi-xii). The Tibetan term (*lcam*) used to describe Niguma's relationship to Naropa is ambiguous and can be interpreted as either "sister" or "nobleman's wife."

115. The five golden teachings of the Shangpa Kagyü School are described in terms of an analogy to a verdant tree: (1) the Six Yogas of Niguma (Tib. *Nigu Chödruk*) as the root, (2) the Amulet Mahamudra (Tib. *Chakchen Ga'u-ma*) teachings as the trunk, (3) the Three Methods of Carrying on the Path (Tib. *Lamkhyer Namsum*) as the branches, (4) the white and red forms of the goddess Khechari (Tib. *Khachö Kar-mar*) as the flowers, and (5) the Unerring Deathless State (Tib. *Chimé Chukmé*) as the fruition.

116. Langri Thangpa Dorjé Seng-gé (1054-1123) was a master of the early Kadampa School. He studied with Potowa Rinchen Sal, a student of Dromtön Gyalwai Jungné, who in turn had been Atisha's principal Tibetan student. Langri Thangpa

founded the monastery of Langri Thang (or Langthang), from which he took his name, in 1093.

117. These two number among the *mahasiddha*s of Buddhist India; Rahula is counted as one of the Eighty-Four *Mahasiddhas*. For traditional accounts of Maitripa, see *Taranatha's History of Buddhism in India*, pp. 304-305 and 310; *Masters of Mahamudra: Songs and Histories of the Eighty-Four Buddhist Siddhas*, p. 52 passim; and (for the account of Maitripa teaching Khyungpo Naljor) *Like An Illusion: Lives of the Shangpa Kagyu Masters*, pp. 58-61 and 68. For those of Rahula, see *Buddha's Lions: The Lives of the Eighty-Four Siddhas*, pp. 163-165; *Masters of Mahamudra: Songs and Histories of the Eighty-Four Buddhist Siddhas*, pp. 252-255; and (for the account of Rahula teaching Khyungpo Naljor) *Like An Illusion: Lives of the Shangpa Kagyu Masters*, pp. 71-74.

118. The Shangpa Kagyü cycle of The Deities of the Five Classes of Tantra includes the mandalas of Guhyasamaja, Mahamaya, Hevajra, Chakrasamvara, and Vajrabhairava (associated with the chakras of the crown of the head, throat, heart, navel, and genital region, respectively).

119. The five students who studied with Khyungpo Naljor earlier in his life were Me'u Tönpa, Yorpo Gyamoché, Ngultön Riwang, Könchok Khar, and Zhangom Chökyi Seng-gé; the one "son" who studied with him later on was Mokchokpa Rinchen Tsöndrü (1110-1170), who became the one to pass on the mainstream Shangpa Kagyü lineage that has continued to the present day. See *Like An Illusion: Lives of the Shangpa Kagyu Masters*, pp. 87-88.

120. The name "Shangpa" derives from one of Khyungpo Naljor's epithets—Lama Shangpa, "the lama from Shang," a reference to the monastery he founded in the Shang Valley, which is more than two hundred kilometers west of Lhasa and leads northward off the central valley of the Tsangpo (Brahmaputra) River. Shang Monastery became Khyungpo Naljor's principal seat in his later life, and he died there in 1127. The Shangpa Kagyü was originally a vibrant and independent school in its own right, but with the shifting tides of Tibetan religious and political history it has largely been absorbed into other, more mainstream schools, primarily the Gelukpa and Karma Kagyü. Kongtrul was particularly impressed with the Shangpa Kagyü teachings and was instrumental in codifying the teachings for posterity in his *Treasury of Spiritual Advice*. The Shangpa Kagyü has nonetheless remained a viable transmission to the present day; the last lineage holder was Kalu Rinpoché (1905-1989), who passed the transmission on to his principal student, the Second Bokar Rinpoché, Karma Ngédön Chökyi Lodrö, from western Tibet. Bokar Rinpoché, who lives and teaches at his monastery in Mirik, West Bengal, India, is the current holder of the Shangpa lineage and is directing the education of Kalu Rinpoché's rebirth, who was born in 1990.

121. Sang-gyé Drak is undoubtedly the Tsami Lotsawa from the Minyak region named

Möndrup Sherab, who worked with the Indian master Abhayadattashri to translate into Tibetan the collection of the inspired songs of the Eighty-Four *Mahasiddhas* of Buddhist India, compiled by Viraprakasha, and a commentary on these songs that was largely written by Abhayadattashri himself. Dowman suggests strong evidence for identifying Abhayadattashri with the Indian master and scholar Abhayakaragupta, and Möndrup Sherab (who is also known as "Tsami Lotsawa of Minyak") with Tsami Lotsawa Sang-gyé Drak; see *Masters of Mahamudra: Songs and Histories of the Eighty-Four Buddhist Siddhas*, pp. 384-388. Further evidence for this identification is found in Kongtrul's comment that Tsami Lotsawa studied with an Indian master named Abhayagupta.

122. As his title Öngom suggests, Tsulthrim Nyingpo was the nephew (*ön*) of Milarepa's principal student Gampopa Sönam Rinchen (called "Dakpo Rinpoché" after his home region of Dakpo in southeastern Tibet), who was himself one of Zhang Tsöndrü Drakpa's gurus. Gampopa installed his nephew Tsulthrim Nyingpo in 1150 as the second abbot of Daklha Gampo Monastery, and Tsulthrim Nyingpo performed the funeral rites for his famous uncle and oversaw construction of the tomb when the latter died in 1153; see also *The Life of Gampopa, The Incomparable Dharma Lord of Tibet*, p. 114. Palchen Galo (b. twelfth century), known as Ga Lotsawa Zhönnu Pal, was also the guru of Pamodrupa Dorjé Gyalpo (1110-1170), who was a student of Gampopa.

123. Gungthang Temple was built at the mouth of the Chongyé Valley, the ancestral seat of the ancient Tibetan kings in the Yarlung region of central Tibet, south of the Tsangpo River. There is a network of large stupas, called "vases," throughout the region, due to its historical importance. See "Yarlung: The Heart of Tibet" in *The Power Places of Central Tibet: The Pilgrim's Guide*, pp. 171-195.

124. Three of these four students were the Tsalpa Kagyü masters Kharakpa Dulwa Ö (b. twelfth century), Namkha Ö (1133-1199), and Lharipa Namkha Ö (b. twelfth century).

125. The "three brothers" (Tib. *kumché sum*) were the three main students of Dromtön Gyalwai Jungné (1004/1005-1064)—Potowa (or Putowa, or Butowa) Rinchen Sal (1027-1105), Chen-ngawa Tsulthrim Bar (1038-1103), and Puchungwa Zhönnu Gyaltsen (1031-1106).

126. This is the same master, Gya Duldzin Wangchuk Tsulthrim, with whom Ja Dulwa Dzinpa Tsöndrü Bar studied.

127. The three spiritual models were defined by the Indian master Atisha in verses 2-5 of his *Lamp for the Path to Enlightenment*. The lesser model is that of spiritual practitioners who are seeking to better their lot in the world and ensure themselves a fortunate rebirth (this is not seen as "wrong" so much as pathetically inadequate); the intermediate model is that of those who are seeking personal

salvation from suffering and liberation from the cycle of conditioned existence; the superior model is that of those who seek liberation and enlightenment for all beings (the bodhisattva model). This schema came to be adopted by all schools of Tibetan Buddhism as one of the most popular ways of presenting the teachings.

128. In this abbreviated reference, "Nyö" stands for Gyalwa Lhanangpa (1164-1224) of the Nyö clan (also known as Nyö Sang-gyé Rinchen, whose biography is given elsewhere in this book), "Gar" for Dampa Shakya Pal (1192-1254) of the Gar clan, and "Chö" for Palchen Chökyi Yeshé.

129. The holy site of Tsaritra is in southeastern Tibet, on the border with the Indian province of Arunachal Pradesh. It has long been a place of pilgrimage, famed for its spiritual energy and blessings.

130. Lodrö Tsungmé (late thirteenth-early fourteenth centuries) was a master of the famous eclectic center of Sangphu Netok. Rigdzin Kumaradza (1266-1343) was a Nyingma master and the principal teacher of Longchenpa (to whom he imparted the Dzogchen lineage), as well as one of the teachers of the Third Karmapa Rangjung Dorjé (1284-1339). Yungtönpa Dorjé Palwa (1284-1365) was a Nyingma teacher famed for his mastery of the Mahayoga approach. One of Yakdé Panchen's teachers was the First Zhamar Rinpoché of the Karma Kagyü School, Drakpa Seng-gé (1283-1349). "Dol" is a reference to the Jonang master Dolpopa Sherab Gyaltsen.

131. This was the Sakya monastery of Ewam Gönpa, in the Maldro Gungkar district, about seventy kilometers northeast of Lhasa on the banks of the Kyichu River; Yakdé Panchen founded it in 1358.

132. Ritröpa Gönpo Yeshé (b. fourteenth century) was a Sakya master of Jangkar Monastery in Metö.

133. Not identified positively. The epithet "Bodong Érphepa" may be a title, or simply descriptive. Established in 1049, the monastery of Bodong É was located north of Sakya, near the south bank of the Tsangpo River, in the southern central province of Tsang. Among its more famous masters was Bodong Panchen Choklé Namgyal (1376-1451), who composed over one hundred volumes of writings on an encyclopedic range of subjects; among his main students was a master named Panchen Jampa Lingpa Sönam Namgyal (1401-1475). There was a master of the Sakya School named Panchen Bumtrak Sumpa, who was born in 1432 and died in 1504; his main monastery was Jayul Gönpa, originally a Kadampa institution in central Tibet.

134. Nyang Yeshé Jungné was a Nyingma master in the lineage of the *kama* teachings. Shakya Jungné of the Rok clan was a teacher of Mahayoga.

135. The *Web of Magic* is another name for the tantra called *The Heart Essence of Secrets* (Skt. *Guhyagarbha*); this is the principal text of the Mahayoga class of the Nyingma teachings.

136. In this context, an epithet of the deity Samyak; of the five deities that are the central focus of the cycles known as the Eight Commands, Samyak is the deity embodying the principle of enlightened mind.

137. These three masters are: Zurchen (or Zurpoché) Shakya Jungné, who laid the foundation for the later spread of the Nyingma teachings, concomitant with the introduction of the teachings of the Sarma Schools from India; his nephew, Zurchung Sherab Drakpa, also known as Deshek Gyawo (1014-1074); and Zurchung's son, Dropukpa Shakya Seng-gé (1074-1134). The three masters of the Zur clan, together with Padmakara's student Nyak Jnanakumara (eighth century) and Nupchen Sang-gyé Yeshé (ninth century), were key figures in the lineages of the teachings of Mahayoga, Anuyoga, and the Category of Mind of Atiyoga; see *The Tantric Tradition of the Nyingmapa*, pp. 20 and 153. While the monastic establishment suffered enormously under King Langdarma's persecution, Nupchen Sang-gyé Yeshé was able to awe the king with his miraculous powers, and so is credited with having saved the lay practitioners of tantra from the worst of the king's excesses.

138. Dra is a region on the south bank of the Tsangpo River, downriver from the confluence of the Tsangpo and Kyichu. For more information on Drapa Ngönshé's life, see *The Rise of Esoteric Buddhism in Tibet*, pp. 92-96.

139. Jambhala is a deity of wealth, whose practice confers prosperity on the practitioner; Zhanglön is a guardian deity.

140. These four texts are the basis of the Tibetan Buddhist medical system—the basic tantra, the explanatory tantra, tantra of pith instructions, and the later tantra.

141. Drathang Monastery was located in Dranang, on the south bank of the Tsangpo River, about seventy-five kilometers from the confluence of the Tsangpo and the Kyichu (which flows down from the north, and on which Lhasa is situated). According to *The Power Places of Central Tibet: The Pilgrim's Guide*, p. 158, Drathang was one of four temples built by Lumé Tsulthrim Sherab, but its founding is usually ascribed (in 1081) to Drapa Ngönshé, who made it his principal seat a century after Lumé's time.

142. These three are the higher trainings in discipline, mind (that is, meditative absorption), and wisdom.

143. The parasol is a symbol of authority and respect adopted by Tibetans from Indian culture, where its function as a protection from the heat of the sun was seen by Buddhists as a metaphor for the protection that spiritual development gave against the heat of the passions. See *Buddhist Symbols in Tibetan Culture*, pp. 19-20.

144. A master named Lhabum, born in the twelfth century, was the elder brother of Tsangpa Gyaré Yeshé Dorjé (1161-1211), the first Drukchen incarnation of the Drukpa Kagyü lineage. I have not been able to determine if this was Bönpo Lhabum.

145. According to *The Philosophical View of the Great Perfection in the Tibetan Bon Religion*, p. 66, n. 205 and p. 278, in this tantra revealed by Bönpo Lhabum, or Guru Nöntsé, "the origin of the phenomenal world is . . . presented from an esoteric perspective recalling Great Perfection tenets."

146. Several of the *terma* discoveries of Tulku Rashak Chenpo (whose personal name was Sönam Dorjé and whose *tertön* title was Raksha Tertön) are included in Kongtrul's *Treasury of Precious Hidden Teachings*.

147. The Yamdrok Plateau is a region south of the confluence of the Tsangpo and Kyichu Rivers, in which there is a large sacred lake.

148. Bairotsana the translator has been discussed elsewhere. Drokmi Palgyi Yeshé was another of the group of twenty-five intimate students of Guru Rinpoché. He, like his future incarnation Rashak Chenpo, was born in the Yamdrok region. He received the transmission for the cycle known as The Imprecations of the Mamos (*Mamo Bötong*), and this connection is echoed in Rashak Chenpo's revelation of the Mamo Gangshar *terma*.

149. According to the *Bod rgya tshig mdzod chen mo* (p. 1387), these are rituals involving articles that are substitute offerings or gifts. These are of two kinds— in their higher sense, they are rituals to make offerings to deities, while in a more mundane context they are rituals to placate demonic or hindering forces.

150. "Lord Nyang" is Nyang-ral Nyima Özer (1136-1204), the first of the five "kingly *tertöns*" prophesied by Guru Rinpoché. The others were Guru Chökyi Wangchuk (1212-1270); Dorjé Lingpa (1346-1405); Orgyen Pema Lingpa (1450-1521); and Pema Ösel Do-ngak Lingpa, or Jamyang Khyentsé Wangpo (1820-1892). Most cycles of the Eight Commands are *terma* teachings.

151. This is a text concerning the ancient history of Tibet, attributed to King Songtsen Gampo. The king is held to have concealed it in the main temple of Lhasa. Guru Rinpoché discovered it, showed it to Songtsen Gampo's descendant, King Trisong Detsen, and then concealed it again. Finally, Druptop Ngödrup revealed the text. See *Hidden Teachings of Tibet*, pp. 250-251, n. 202.

152. Rasa Thrulnang is the ancient name of the main temple in Lhasa, now commonly called the Jokhang. During the time the original structure was being built (it was completed in 647, during the reign of King Songtsen Gampo), the king's capital was called "Rasa" because goats (Tib. *ra*) were employed to move earth (Tib. *sa*) to a site that was under water in order to create dry ground for building. After King Songtsen Gampo's time (born 569; reigned 582-650), Rasa became known as Lhasa (Place of the Gods), and the temple became known as the Jokhang (Temple of the Lord). This name refers to the main statue of the Buddha in the temple, Jowo Shakyamuni. See *The Power Places of Central Tibet: The Pilgrim's Guide*, pp. 41-48 and *Tibet Handbook*, pp. 78-92.

153. Zhikpo Nyima Seng-gé was also a student of Jikten Gönpo (1143-1217), founder

of the Drigung Kagyü School. The Zhijé (Pacification of Suffering) system of practice was codified in the twelfth century by the Indian Buddhist master Dampa, also known as Phadampa Sang-gyé, a brahmin from south India. He journeyed on five occasions to Tibet, where he taught this system based on the teachings of the Prajnaparamita (Perfection of Wisdom) Sutras. The system takes its name from a famous line in the Tibetan translations of the Heart Sutra, in which the mantra of Prajnaparamita is referred to as "the mantra that pacifies all suffering." Phadampa Sang-gyé's student Sönam Lama was the teacher of the famous Tibetan woman master Machik Labkyi Drönma, who incorporated the Pacification teachings into her system of practice, which became known as Chö ("Severance"). The Chö teachings and practices—the only case, until recent times, of an indigenous Tibetan system of practice that spread back to India—became very popular, spreading rapidly throughout all the other schools of the Tibetan tradition.

154. A *terma* revealed by Guru Jotsé is contained in the section of *The Treasury of Precious Hidden Teachings* that deals with exorcisms and rituals to ransom someone's life force from demonic forces. According to *The Power Places of Central Tibet: The Pilgrim's Guide*, p. 145, Guru Jotsé was a rebirth of the Tibetan king Senalek (who was King Trisong Detsen's youngest son and ruled from about 880 to 914), and the discovery of the *terma* took place in a cave blessed by Guru Rinpoché at Drakmar Zangyak Namkha Dzong on the "Five-Peaked Mountain" in central Tibet, between the Kyichu and Tsangpo Rivers.

155. There is a brief account of Sakya Pandita's life in *Luminous Lives: The Story of the Early Masters of the Lam 'bras Tradition in Tibet*, pp. 159-169; see also *Ordinary Wisdom: Sakya Pandita's Treasury of Good Advice*, pp. 1-4. For versions of the life of Longchen Rabjam in English, see *Masters of Meditation and Miracles: The Longchen Nyingthig Lineage of Tibetan Buddhism*, pp. 109-117, and *The Nyingma School of Tibetan Buddhism: Its Fundamentals and History*, vol. 1, pp. 575-596.

156. This "Old Narthang" edition of the Kangyur and Tengyur was the first recorded attempt to develop a definitive collection of the Tibetan translations of the Buddha's words and their commentaries. It consisted of handcopied manuscripts; woodblock editions, including the "new Narthang" woodblock edition, did not appear until the fifteenth century. See *The Blue Annals*, pp. 336-339, and "A Brief History of the Tibetan bKa' 'gyur."

157. For Tibetan Buddhism, one of the crucial elements in the viable transmission of teachings is the "oral transmission" (Tib. *lung*), in which someone who holds this aspect of the lineage reads a text aloud (often at high speed) in the presence of those receiving the transmission. The emphasis is not on the listener compre-

hending the content of the text at the time of the transmission, but the blessing inherent in hearing the text read aloud.

158. See *The Rise of Esoteric Buddhism in Tibet*, pp. 139-143.

159. For information on the discovery of *terma*, see *Hidden Teachings of Tibet*, pp. 77-91 and 137-141.

160. A reference to the yellow paper on which a *terma* is written in symbolic script, which can only be decoded by the *tertön* whose destiny it is to reveal that *terma*.

161. An article or substance that has been blessed by a great master and serves as a focus for spiritual practice.

162. If Kunkyong Lingpa was the immediate rebirth of Dorjé Lingpa, he would have been born in the next few years after that master's passing in 1405; Kongtrul notes below that Chokden Gönpo, who was born in 1497, was the rebirth of Kunkyong Lingpa.

163. This implies that the rebirth took place almost immediately after the passing of the former incarnation, without any significant period of time or other rebirth intervening. To add to the complexity of the situation, Kunkyong Lingpa was also one of the alternate names by which Dorjé Lingpa was known.

164. The Guardian Goddess of Mantra is also known as Ekajati; the Oath-Bound One is Vajrasadhu (Tib. *Dorjé Lekpa*). These are two of the most important protective deities associated with the Dzogchen teachings.

165. Vajrasattva is a sambhogakaya buddha, the central focus of the mandala of the five "buddha families," and associated with the principle of purification. Vajravarahi is a feminine deity of the Anuttarayoga class, the highest of the four classes of tantra recognized by the Sarma Schools. Sarasvati is a feminine deity whose practice brings the practitioner wisdom; she also inspires those involved in the arts, in the manner of a muse.

166. Tib. *Denyi Düpa*. Published in 137 volumes as *Encyclopedia Tibetica* (New Delhi: Tibet House, 1969-1981).

167. Thirty-two major and eighty minor marks of physical perfection adorn the sambhogakaya forms and those of the "sublime nirmanakayas"—that is, perfectly enlightened buddhas in human form, such as Shakyamuni. These marks are mentioned in *The Ornament of Manifest Realization* (Section Eight, verse 12), one of the Five Works of Maitreya.

168. Among other works, Sokdokpa Lodrö Gyaltsen authored a defense of the Nyingma system against its critics, which he wrote in 1604.

169. The *torma* is a ritual article made of dough, serving as the focus for meditation during a ritual such as this one. The invasion referred to would presumably have taken place in the decades preceding Chokden Gönpo's death in 1557. This was the period during which the Rinpung princes held political power in the central

provinces, after wresting it from their Phamo Druppa masters and before they were replaced by the Tsang princes in 1565. This was an interim era of lay rule, following the Sakya and Phamo Druppa governments and prior to the rise of the Dalai Lamas and the centralization of authority in a Gelukpa religious oligarchy in Lhasa. As Stein notes (*Tibetan Civilization*, p. 81), "There were many wars. The monks of Drépung attacked the 'people of the camps' (*sgar-pa*), i.e. the Karma-pa military camps, in 1546. The reason was that in 1537 the fifth Red Hat [that is, the Fifth Zhamar Rinpoché of the Kagyü School, Könchok Yenlak (1525-1583)] had formed an alliance with Drigung and the governor of Tsang, designed to suppress the Geluk-pas and their best patrons, the princes of Ganden. The uncertain fate of these temporary alliances and local struggles was to be decided by a fresh Mongol irruption onto the political and military scene." [Bracketed comments mine.] Chokden Gönpo's efforts to save Lhasa from an invasion would have been part of the larger mosaic of political instability during these years.

170. The ability of a *tertön* to be successful, in revealing the *terma*s that are his or her lot in a particular lifetime, is subject to any number of circumstances. Particularly in the case of so-called earth *terma*s (which are texts or other physical objects concealed in the earth), if these circumstances are not in place, the *tertön* may not be capable of revealing the *terma*s and may die prematurely.

171. This idiom refers to a source from which specific emanations emerge at any given point. These are ahistorical figures such as sambhogakaya buddhas or (as in the case of Chökyi Gocha) a being in a naturally manifest nirmanakaya pure realm (the Copper-Colored Mountain, the nirmanakaya pure realm of Guru Rinpoché).

172. Sangdak Thrinlé Lhundrup (1611-1662) was the son and principal student of Khedrup Do-ngak Tendzin (1576-1628), a holder of the mainstream Dzogchen lineage of the Heart Drop, or Nyingtik, teachings. He received these teachings from his father, as well as transmissions of the *kama* and *terma* teachings, and studied with many other Nyingma gurus. Thrinlé Lhundrup also studied with Sarma masters, including the Third Pawo Rinpoché of the Kagyü School, Tsuklak Gyatso (1567-1630/3), from whom he received his novice vows. Sangdak Thrinlé Lhundrup was renowned as a master of Dzogchen and a major figure in that lineage.

173. The usual progression of realization as it applies to the four levels of empowerment is as follows: the vase empowerment leads to realization of the unity of form and emptiness; the secret empowerment leads to realization of the unity of lucidity and emptiness; the empowerment of wisdom and timeless awareness leads to realization of the unity of bliss and emptiness; and the fourth, or word, empowerment leads to realization of the unity of awareness and emptiness.

174. A cycle focusing on the Eight Commands.

175. Most of these lineages are described elsewhere in the text or endnotes. The Bodongpa lineage focused on *The Kalachakra Tantra* and the advanced yogic practices (known as the Six Branches of Union) that are associated with that cycle; see *Among Tibetan Texts: History and Literature of the Himalayan Plateau*, pp. 179-181.

176. This is a concise way of referring to the Mahayoga, Anuyoga, and Atiyoga approaches.

177. The Mahayana teachings describe ten levels of realization as part of the bodhisattva's path to enlightenment; the eleventh level is that of buddhahood.

178. Kunga Drolchok compiled a series of eleven short biographies, collectively titled *Well-Spoken Words: A Garland of Successive Rebirths*. These are accounts of his former lifetimes, based on his personal recollections or drawn from the writings of other masters. The third account in this series is entitled "The Account of Ratan Bhahula." It concerns a *siddha*, or accomplished master, of India named Kanipa, who was a student of the *siddha* Jalandhari (one of the famed Eighty-Four *Mahasiddha*s of India. Kanipa displeased Jalandhari, who cursed him and caused him to be reborn as a prince named Ratan Parkhi. When Ratan Parkhi assumed the throne of his father's kingdom, he recalled his former lifetime as Kanipa, and in retaliation began oppressing spiritual practitioners in his kingdom, making them perform menial labor for him. A master named Goraksha confronted Ratan Parkhi, who repented and showed honor to the spiritual people he had formerly harmed. He gained attainment himself as a *siddha*, and Goraksha named him Ratan Bhahula.

179. According to "The Account of Barompa Darma Wangchuk," the fifth account in Kunga Drolchok's *Well-Spoken Words*, Barompa Darma Wangchuk (1127-1199/ 1200) was born in the Penyul region north of Lhasa. At the age of seven, he encountered a woman who was a student of the Kagyü master Gampopa (1079-1153), the foremost student of Milarepa; she told him that he shared a strong karmic connection with Gampopa. He was ordained by the abbot Darma Seng-gé and the preceptor Wangchuk Zhönnu, from whom he received the elements of his ordination name, Darma Wangchuk. He studied with masters from the Kadampa School of Tibetan Buddhism, as well as Darma Seng-gé, before searching out Gampopa and studying meditation under his guidance. It was Gampopa who identified Darma Wangchuk to be a rebirth of the Indian master Krishnacharya. Darma Wangchuk also studied with Jigten Gönpo (1143-1217), another of Gampopa's students, and founded the monastery of Barom. Of the four major branches of the Kagyü School founded by Gampopa's main students, the Barom Kagyü subschool was founded by Darma Wangchuk, the Drigung Kagyü by Jigten Gönpo.

180. An epithet of Gampopa, whose home region was Dakpo and who was a physician before he embraced the religious life.

181. According to "The Biography of Avadhuti Özer Pal" (which is the sixth account in Kunga Drolchok's *Well-Spoken Words*, Avadhuti Özer Pal was a practitioner of yoga who was afflicted with a form of leprosy and lived a simple lifestyle. He studied with Latöpa Könchok Khar (a student of the great Khyungpo Naljor (978/990-1127), founder of the Shangpa Kagyü lineage) and with Jetsün Drakpa Gyaltsen, one of the "five founding fathers" of the Sakya School, who lived from 1147 to 1216.

182. According to "The Account of Zhang Drukdra Gyaltsen," the seventh account in Kunga Drolchok's *Well-Spoken Words*, the Indian *mahasiddha* Krishnacharya took conscious rebirth as Drukdra Gyaltsen of the ancient Zhang clan of Tibet, whose members included many great masters in several lineages of the Tibetan Buddhist tradition. He received his name Drukdra (Thunder) from the fact that there was thunder and lightning in the sky at the moment of his birth. He was trained by his father, a lay Vajrayana teacher, in the practice of Yamantaka, the wrathful form of Manjushri. He married and became in turn a lay Vajrayana master with great spiritual power to exorcise demons.

183. The Nyö clan is an ancient Tibetan family line that produced a number of great masters. Sang-gyé Rechen, who was also known as Gyalwa Lhanangpa, lived from 1164 to 1224. According to "The Account of the Great One of the Nyö Clan, Gyalwa Lhanangpa" (which is Kunga Drolchok's eighth account in his *Well-Spoken Words*), Sang-gyé Rinchen, who was recognized in his lifetime as an emanation of the Indian Buddhist master Krishnacharya, belonged to this ancient clan of Nyö. His father, a learned lay master of the tantric teachings, educated the precocious boy in his family's traditions, and Sang-gyé Rinchen was himself teaching by the age of six. He originally intended to follow his clan's tradition by journeying to India and training as a translator of Buddhist texts, but met Jigten Gönpo, the founder of the Drigung Kagyü School, whose own master was Gampopa's student Pamodrupa Dorjé Gyalpo (1110-1170). Sang-gyé Rinchen received monastic ordination and studied the Buddhist monastic codes before moving to Drigung, where he was trained in that school's tradition of Mahamudra by Jigten Gönpo and so gained authentic realization. Jigten Gönpo affirmed that Sang-gyé Rinchen was his equal in qualities and realization.

184. According to "The Account of the Omniscient Sanghabhadra," the ninth account in Kunga Drolchok's *Well-Spoken Words*, Sanghabhadra was the conscious rebirth of Nyö Sang-gyé Rinchen. He was born in the late thirteenth century, close by Lhalung Monastery in the southern Tibetan province of Lhodrak, near the border with Bhutan. He proved to be an excellent scholar, particularly skilled in languages and scripts, and various arts and sciences, such as painting, sculpture,

astrology, and medicine. He journeyed to Narthang Monastery in the southern central province of Tsang, where he received his novice vows. Following the death of its charismatic abbot Rigpai Raldri in the thirteenth century, dissension in the monastic community led to the expulsion of a master named Khepa Chitön. Sanghabhadra followed this master to Sakya, where his fellow students included the future Jonang master Dolpopa Sherab Gyaltsen. Sanghabhadra became very learned in both the sutras and tantras, and at the age of twenty-three received full monastic ordination at the Kadampa seat of Yalung Gönsar. He studied further with his maternal uncle, Sang-gyé Pal, and then undertook seven years of intensive retreat on the deity Vajrapani. He then pursued a career as a teacher who focused on the Kadampa system of teachings. He died at the cave of Karla Phukchen, one of his favorite retreat sites, in 1359.

185. Tashi Palden (1379-1449) was a student of Tsongkhapa Lobzang Drakpa (1357-1419), founder of the Gelukpa School of Tibetan Buddhism. According to "The Account of Jamyang Tashi Palden," the tenth account in Kunga Drolchok's *Well-Spoken Words*, Tashi Palden was born in the region of Samyé Monastery in central Tibet. He received his novice vows at Tsethang (on the opposite bank of the Tsangpo River from Samyé Monastery) and embarked on an intensive course of study. He then received the full monastic ordination from Tsongkhapa and that master's students, Drakpa Gyaltsen (1374-1434/6) and Gyaltsap Jé Darma Rinchen (1364-1432, the second throne holder of Ganden Monastery). In 1416, Tashi Palden founded the Gelukpa monastery of Drepung near Lhasa, which by the time of the great Fifth Dalai Lama (1617-1682) had become a major seat of spiritual and political power in Tibet. He was famous for his mastery of the Buddhist teachings, many volumes of which he had committed to memory.

186. According to "The Account of the Scholar Chökyi Nyinjé," the eleventh account in Kunga Drolchok's *Well-Spoken Words*, Chökyi Nyinjé was born into a family of brahmins on the island of Singhala (modern Sri Lanka). He received full monastic ordination from a scholar of his own clan, Naraditya, who had studied with the Indian master Vanaratna (1384-1468), whom Naraditya had met in the central Indian province of Kalinga. (Vanaratna later journeyed through Bhutan to Tibet, where he received the *terma* cycle The Lotus Teaching on Longevity (Tib. *Pema Tséthri*) in a vision.) Chökyi Nyinjé practiced on "the sublime mountain on which the Buddha had planted his footprints"—undoubtedly the peak of Sri Pada (also called Adam's Peak) in southwestern Sri Lanka, holy to Buddhists, Hindus, Christians, and Muslims alike. Following a prophecy from his chosen deity, he journeyed to Wu Ta'i Shan, the "five-peaked mountain" in China that is sacred to Manjushri, and then to central Tibet, where he studied with several masters, including Ngawang Drakpa (1418-1496), the twelfth throne holder of the Taklung Kagyü School; the Seventh Karmapa, Chödrak Gyatso

(1454-1506); and the Sakya master Dorjé Denpa Kunga Namgyal (1432-1496), who founded the monastery of Gongkar in 1464. Chökyi Nyinjé's travels then took him to Kathmandu (where he studied the Chakrasamvara cycle with the Nepalese scholar Jipasyena and left the monastic life to follow the path of a tantric yogi) and on to India (where he visited Bodh Gaya). He then embarked on the return journey to his homeland, was shipwrecked and suffered temporarily from amnesia, but finally returned to Sri Lanka.

187. "Powerful Upholder of Conduct"; an epithet of the *mahasiddha* Krishnacharya.

188. Kunga Drolchok Losel Gyatsoi Dé, or Kunga Drolchok (1507-1565/6), was a master of the Jonang School of Tibetan Buddhism. This school developed from the "qualified emptiness" (*zhentong*) interpretation elaborated by Yumowa Mikyö Dorjé in the eleventh century. The school took its name from its main monastery, founded by Kunpang Tukjé Tsöndrü (1243-1313) on the ridge of Jomonang near Zhigatsé in the southern central Tibetan province of Tsang. Its doctrines were further developed by Kunpang's student, Dolpopa Sherab Gyaltsen (1292-1361), and Taranatha (who was also known as Jonang Jetsün, "the venerable one of Jonang"). Kunga Drolchok's immediate rebirth in Tibet was as Taranatha.

189. Not identified; presumably an Indian king (Tib. *sakyong*) named Rama (the Sanskrit equivalent of the Tibetan *Gajé*). Taranatha authored a work known as *The Account of Prince Rama*, which discusses this previous incarnation of his. Kongtrul's list makes it seem as though the rebirth of this king occurred between the times of Kunga Drolchok and Taranatha. However, the former died in 1565 or 1566, and Taranatha was born in 1575, so the inclusion of King Rama may, in fact, be a reference to an earlier (perhaps much earlier) incarnation. Alternatively, Gajé Sakyong and Taranatha may have been an example of a not-uncommon phenomenon—that of "parallel incarnations" living at the same time.

190. An epithet of Taranatha.

191. Taranatha (1575-1634) of the Jonang School was the immediate rebirth of Kunga Drolchok. Among his teachers was Kunga Gyaltsen, who had received Kunga Drolchok's lineage of the Jonang teachings.

192. The Vinaya teachings speak of seven buddhas who have already appeared in this world—Vipashyin, Shikhin, Vishvabhu, Krakucchanda, Kanakamuni, Kashyapa, and Shakyamuni. According to the Mahayana teachings, some one thousand and two buddhas will eventually have appeared during this eon; the Buddha Shakyamuni is held to have been the fourth, so that Vipashyin, Shikhin, and Vishvabhu appeared at the end of the previous eon.

193. An epithet for the Lord Buddha Shakyamuni.

194. Ra Lotsawa (b. 1016) was a Nyingma master who specialized in the practice of Yamantaka, the wrathful form of Manjushri. See *The Blue Annals*, pp. 374-380.

195. Chöku Lhawang Drakpa was a sixteenth-century Jonang master who received teachings from Taranatha's former incarnation, Kunga Drolchok, and then in turn passed these on to Taranatha.

196. As a proper name, Heruka is used by the Sarma Schools to refer to the deity Chakrasamvara.

197. I have not located a list of these sixteen masters; presumably they would include the aforementioned "six ornaments" and the "two excellent ones"—Gunaprabha (who was Vasubandhu's student) and Shakyaprabha, who were both commentators on the monastic codes.

198. Such visions, in which one receives permission or encouragement from one of one's chosen deities, constitute one of the highest standards of authenticity for one's writings.

199. According to the *Bod rgya tshig mdzod chen mo*, this idiom is a reference to mythical accounts of the gods casting flowers down onto the earth to celebrate auspicious events, but is to be taken here to refer to a rainfall of large droplets of water that form designs like lotus petals when they strike the earth.

200. These are two seventeenth-century two Jonang masters, Kunga Rinchen Gyatso and Yeshé Gyatso, who both bore the title of Gyaltsap ("regent") under Taranatha.

201. That is, Drodul Sherab Özer, Minling Terchen, and Jonang Jetsün Taranatha.

202. That is, Lumé Tsulthrim Sherab.

203. Karma Pakshi (1204-1283) was the Second Gyalwang Karmapa; "Tarlo Drakpa" is possibly a reference to the thirteenth-century Kalachakra master Tarpa Lotsawa Nyima Gyaltsen.

204. The Third Gyalwang Karmapa (1284-1339).

205. The Tibetan title Kazhipa refers to a scholar who has passed rigorous examinations in four disciplines—the Madhyamaka philosophy, the Prajnaparamita literature, the Vinaya, and the Abhidharma. Kazhipa Ratnabhadra was also known as Sok-ön Kazhipa.

206. The Sixth Gyalwang Karmapa lived from 1416 to 1453. See *The History of the Sixteen Karmapas of Tibet*, pp. 79-81.

207. Literally, "golden garland." This refers to the primary line of succession through which the key teachings of a given school have been transmitted.

208. Khachö Wangpo (1350-1405) was the Second Zhamar Rinpoché of the Karma Kagyü School.

209. The Fourth Gyalwang Karmapa (1340-1383). See *The History of the Sixteen Karmapas of Tibet*, pp. 61-68.

210. Sang-gyé Lingpa (1340-1396) is particularly known for his discovery of the cycle The United Intent of the Gurus.

211. The Third Zhamar incarnation of the Karma Kagyü School, who lived from 1406 to 1452.

212. Born in 1664, Goshri Karma Döndrup Nyingpo was a student of the Eleventh Gyalwang Karmapa, Yeshé Dorjé (1675-1702).

213. The Eighth Zhamar Rinpoché was Palchen Chökyi Döndrup (1695-1732).

214. Müchen Sempa Chenpo (1388-1469) was the second grand abbot of Ngor Ewam Chokden Monastery in the hills southwest of the town of Zhigatsé in Tsang. Ngor Monastery was the main seat of the Ngor subschool of the Sakyapa, and was founded in 1429 by Müchen Sempa Chenpo's guru, Ngorchen Kunga Zangpo (1382-1444/56), who served as the first grand abbot. Müchen Sempa Chenpo's nephew, Müchen Sang-gyé Rinchen, eventually succeeded to the throne of Ngor, becoming the eighth in the line of grand abbots.

215. These are the vows and disciplines of the Hinayana, Mahayana, and Vajrayana approaches. The Hinayana discipline is found in the "Individual Liberation" system—the ordinations of the laity, novices, and monks and nuns; that of the Mahayana is expressed in the bodhisattva vow; and that of the Vajrayana lies in the *samaya* commitments one undertakes in receiving tantric empowerments and teachings. The model of the "threefold vajra holder"—a master who upholds the full ordination of a monk or nun, as well as the bodhisattva vow and Vajrayana *samaya*—was based on the writings of Atisha, especially his *Lamp for the Path to Enlightenment*.

216. Könchok Lodrö (b. 1428), Sönam Seng-gé (1429-1489), and Gyaltsap Kunga Wangchuk (1424-1478) were all students of both Ngorchen Kunga Zangpo and Müchen Sempa Chenpo Könchok Gyaltsen. Also known as Gorampa, Sönam Seng-gé was one of the Sakya School's most original and controversial authors, particularly in the fields of epistemology and Madhyamaka philosophy; Gyaltsap Kunga Wangchuk (1424-1478) was the fourth grand abbot of Ngor Monastery.

217. The Seventh Gyalwang Karmapa Chödrak Gyatso (1454-1506). See *The History of the Sixteen Karmapas of Tibet*, pp. 83-87.

218. Pal Nalendra Monastery, founded in 1435 by the Sakya scholar Rongtön Chenpo Mawai Seng-gé (1367-1449), was located about thirty kilometers north of Lhasa. It became an important center of study and training in the Sakya School.

219. Lhachok Seng-gé (1468-1535) succeeded Müchen Sang-gyé Rinchen as the ninth grand abbot of Ngor.

220. Tib. *Sung-rap Rinpoché*. An epithet for the Lamdré teachings of the Sakya School, which present a systematic approach to the various levels of the Buddhist teachings and focus on *The Hevajra Tantra*.

221. Jampa Chö-ö (fifteenth century) was one of Müchen Sang-gyé Rinchen's gurus.

222. The Eleventh Dakchen Rinpoché was Ngawang Drakpa Gyaltsen (late fifteenth–mid sixteenth centuries) of the Phuntsok Phodrang house of Sakya. The current Dakchen Rinpoché, Jigdral Ngawang Kunga Sönam (b. 1929), lives in Seattle, Washington, where he directs the center of Sakya Monastery.

223. The three Ngor throne holders were likely the two preceding Sang-gyé Rinchen in the abbatial succession—the sixth, the famous Gorampa Sönam Seng-gé (1429-1489), and the seventh, Könchok Phelwa (1445-1514)—and the one following him—the ninth grand abbot, Lhachok Seng-gé (1468-1535. It is also possible that Sang-gyé Rinchen taught the famous Ngorchen Könchok Lhundrup (1497-1557), who became the tenth grand abbot of Ngor. Doring Kunpangpa Kunzang Chökyi Nyima (1449-1524) was a Sakya master of the lineage of Lamdré transmission.

224. I am assuming that "Ngomring" in the text is an alternative spelling of Ngamring, a Sakya monastery founded in the thirteenth century between two headwaters of the Tsangpo River in western Tsang. The Narthang abbot taught by Müchen Sang-gyé Rinchen may have been Drakpa Sherab (b. 1424), who became the twentieth grand abbot of Narthang after 1486, and the fifteenth-century Jonang master Namkha Chökyong may also have studied with Müchen Sang-gyé Rinchen. Nyukla Panchen Ngawang Drakpa (1458-1515) was a Kagyü master and author of the biography of his contemporary, the "mad saint of Ü," Ü-nyön Kunga Zangpo (1458-1532). Karma Thrinlépa (1456-1539) was also a student of the Seventh Gyalwang Karmapa, Chödrak Gyatso (1454-1506), and Thrulzhik Sang-gyé Samdrup, from whom Karma Thrinlépa received the transmission of teachings that focus on the *doha*s, or mystical songs, of the Indian *mahasiddha* Saraha; see *The Royal Song of Saraha*, pp. 3-20, and *Ecstatic Spontaneity: Saraha's Three Cycles of Doha*, pp. 3-15.

225. Müchen Sang-gyé Gyaltsen (1542-1618) was a Sakya master who studied with the Twenty-Sixth Sakya Thrichen, Drakpa Lodrö (1563-1617).

226. Tsungmé Tendzin Dorjé (1535-1605?) was a Nyingma master.

227. Gong-ra Lochen Zhenpen Dorjé (1594-1654) was a Nyingma master who codified the largest of the Eight Commands cycles, The Gathering of Sugatas, discovered by Nyang-ral Nyima Özer (1136-1204).

228. Gampopa Zangpo Dorjé was born in 1636; Bamteng Chöjé Miphampa, or Karma Mipham Gönpo, was a Karma Kagyü master.

229. A region of Golok Province in far northeastern Tibet, Serthar is the birthplace of the present Do Drupchen Rinpoché of the Nyingma School (b. 1924), and the main seat of Khenchen Jigmé Phuntsok Jungné (b. 1933), one of the greatest living scholars of the Nyingmapa.

230. "Sky teachings" (Tib. *nam-chö*) is a term for a particular way in which *terma* are revealed, in a manner similar to a vision.

231. Rigdzin Longsal Nyingpo (1625-1692) was a *tertön* who was instrumental in the founding of the important Nyingma monastery of Kathok in eastern Tibet.

232. Rigdzin Tsewang Norbu (1698-1755) was a Nyingma master of Kathok Monastery. Dechen Lingpa's son was Pema Wang-gyal (late seventeenth-early eighteenth centuries)

233. These are considered to be prophecies of Tsongkhapa Lobzang Drakpa (1357-1419) and the monastery of Ganden Namgyaling, northeast of Lhasa, which he founded in 1409, becoming its first throne holder until his death in 1419. Ganden was the first of the three large Gelukpa monasteries—Ganden, Drepung, and Sera—founded between 1409 and 1419, which came to be the focus of political power for the government of the Dalai Lamas. The government became known by the title "Ganden Phodrang," after the residence of that name built around 1530 by the Second Dalai Lama, Gendun Gyatso (1476-1542), on the grounds of Drepung Monastery in Lhasa.

234. This is one of the most common names (Lodrö Thayé) by which Kongtrul is known, and is part of the name he was given when he took the bodhisattva ordination from his guru, Situ Pema Nyinjé Wangpo, in 1839.

235. According to *The Discourse of the Fortunate Eon*, the buddhas who will all attain enlightenment during this eon were contemporaries in a former eon, a group of young princes who aroused the aspiration to attain buddhahood in the presence of a buddha known in Tibetan as Nüden Dorjé. This buddha prophesied their future enlightenment. The Sanskrit name Anantamati is the equivalent of Kongtrul's Tibetan name Lodrö Thayé.

236. This passage is found in the final section of *The Journey to Sri Lanka*; see Suzuki's rendering (*The Laṅkāvatāra Sūtra: A Mahāyāna Text*, p. 287, verse 803): "After the golden age there will appear a leader by the name of Mati [Intelligence], who is a great hero (*mahavira*) well acquainted with the five forms of knowledge." [bracketed comment mine]

237. These five traditional fields of knowledge are the arts, medicine, grammar (particularly the study of Sanskrit), logic, and the Buddhist teachings. One who has mastered these was considered worthy of the title "Great Scholar" (Skt. *Mahapandita*; Tib. *Panchen*).

238. This is another of Jamyang Khyentsé Wangpo's statements concerning the Five Treasuries that he had predicted Kongtrul would compile.

239. Pema Lingpa (1450-1521) was the third of the five "kingly *tertöns*" prophesied by Guru Rinpoché.

240. The *tertön* Duddul Dorjé (1615-1672) was a student of the famous *tertön* Jatsön Nyingpo (1585-1646) and a teacher of both Longsal Nyingpo and the first Dzogchen Rinpoché, Pema Rigdzin (1625-1697). In 1684/5, Pema Rigdzin founded the Nyingma monastery of Dzogchen in eastern Tibet, on the advice of the "Great Fifth" Dalai Lama, Ngawang Lobzang Gyatso (1617-1682).

241. For Jamyang Khyentsé Wangpo and Chokgyur Lingpa, this reference was proof that Kongtrul had been prophesied by Guru Rinpoché to be the custodian of this *terma*.

242. Kongtrul's commentary on this *terma*, *The Illumination of Timeless Awareness*,

together with the source verses, has been largely translated into English by Erik Pema Kunsang as *The Light of Wisdom*; three volumes have already appeared, with a fourth under preparation.

243. As well as being the consort of the *tertön* Guru Chökyi Wangchuk, Jomo Menmo (1248-1283) was one of the very few women who were *tertöns* in their own right; see *The Nyingma School of Tibetan Buddhism: Its Fundamentals and History*, vol. 1, pp. 771-774. A rediscovered *terma* (Tib. *yang-ter*) is one that is discovered and then, for any number of reasons, concealed again, to be rediscovered at a more appropriate time. The Union of All the Dakinis' Secrets was originally discovered by Jomo Menmo, reconcealed and then rediscovered by Jamyang Khyentsé Wangpo.

244. The speaker here is Guru Rinpoché, addressing Yeshé Tsogyal as he prophesies future events.

245. It was often the case that people would receive the empowerment at one point and only at a later point (if ever) receive the teaching based on the empowerment.

246. These are three of seven kinds of transmission that Jamyang Khyentsé Wangpo received during his lifetime. See *The Nyingma School of Tibetan Buddhism: Its Fundamentals and History*, vol. 1, pp. 855-858; *The Rise of Esoteric Buddhism in Tibet*, pp. 205-209; and *Hidden Teachings of Tibet* (esp. pp. 77-93, 137-144, and 164-166).

247. Tib. *Jé-bang nyer-nga* (literally, "the twenty-five—the Tibetan king and his subjects"). A term referring to King Trisong Detsen and the other Tibetans who formed this group of twenty-five. Authentic *tertöns* are considered to be emanations of one or another of these twenty-five original students who were present when Guru Rinpoché or Yeshé Tsogyal concealed *termas* in the eighth century.

248. Also known as Dergé Gönchen, the "great monastery of Dergé" founded by Thangtong Gyalpo in 1448.

249. The Wish-Fulfilling Gem is a *terma* cycle revealed by Drimé Kunga (late fourteenth century) that was concealed again, to be rediscovered by Jamyang Khyentsé Wangpo in the mid-eighteenth century; thus, the "great *tertön*" referred to here would seem to be Khyentsé. Kongtrul's birthplace in Rongyap was to the west of Lhundrup Teng, where the *terma* was discovered.

250. Dokham is a term for the eastern provinces of the greater Tibetan region, including both Amdo (Do) and Kham.

251. Many of the more recent *terma* discoveries (dating roughly from the mid-eighteenth century) are referred to in Tibetan as Tersar—literally, "new hidden treasure teachings." The "great *tertön*" here is Chokgyur Lingpa, whose *termas* are collectively termed the Chokling Tersar. Often a *terma* in the form in which it was revealed would need to be edited further in order to be used as a ritual, and

require supplementary liturgies or instruction manuals. All this would tend to be the responsibility of the custodian of the *terma* cycle, rather than the *tertön*.

252. The first step in a *tertön*'s discovery of a cycle of *terma* is a vision in which Guru Rinpoché appears to the *tertön* and confers the "records"—basically a list of the components of that cycle, to ensure that the cycle is discovered in its entirety.

253. Kundrol Sangwa Tsal was another name for the Bönpo tertön Tsewang Drakpa, which whom Kongtrul was associated in his later life.

254. The clan to which Kongtrul's real father, Khyungpo Lama Yungdrung Tendzin, belonged.

255. Tib. *Palden Lhamo*. One of the most important wrathful feminine protective deities.

256. Vajradanda and the "three *tsen* brothers" are guardian deities; the former is an expression of timeless awareness, while the latter are worldly spirits tamed by Guru Rinpoché and bound to the service of the Buddhist teachings. *Tsen*s are fierce nonhuman spirits, usually depicted as warriors in full battle armor, mounted on horseback.

257. Representations of form are statues and paintings; those of speech, scriptures; and those of mind, vajras, bells, stupas, and so forth. The act of commissioning the production or construction of any of these representations is held to be very meritorious and a way of counteracting the effects of negative karma.

258. Tibetan astrology is based in part on a cycle of twelve years, named after animals (as in the Chinese systems). Every time the animal of one's birth year comes around again, the year is a crucial one, during which events of great significance for the rest of one's life occur, for better or worse. Many practitioners choose to spend their crucial years in retreat, or at least engage in as much spiritual practice as possible. Tibetans feel that the third time the animal sign comes around is the most crucial point in a man's life, while for a woman it is the second time.

259. This name was conferred on Kongtrul by his two gurus in 1867, when he was 55 by Tibetan reckoning.

260. Humkara was one of a group of eight Indian *vidyadhara*s who were teachers of Padmakara. Each master conferred on him one of the transmissions that he synthesized into the Eight Commands format of practice. Humkara conferred the transmission of Samyak, the deity embodying the principle of enlightened mind, on Padmakara.

261. These are forms of Guru Rinpoché functioning as chosen deities (Tib. *yidam*).

262. The implication is that even a few strands of Guru Rinpoché's hair are so sacred that they are equivalent to the presence of all the Three Roots of Vajrayana Buddhism.

263. "The great abbot Bodhisattva" (Tib. *Khenchen Bodhisato*) is an epithet of the Indian master Shantirakshita, who was invited to Tibet by King Trisong Detsen

in the eighth century and who was instrumental in persuading the king to invite Guru Rinpoché to Tibet.

264. For information on the life of Mandarava, Padmakara's main Indian consort, see *The Lives and Liberation of Princess Mandarava.*

265. A leavening culture is a mixture of blessed substances, used generation after generation to impart blessings to new preparations of spiritual "medicine," analogous to the way in which a yogurt or sourdough culture is used.

266. This is Jamyang Khyentsé Wangpo's *tertön* title.

267. Possibly a reference to the previous lifetimes of these masters.

268. This is likely a reference to the three lineages of the Dzogchen tradition—that of mind-to-mind transmission of victorious ones, the transmission through symbols by *vidyadhara*s, and the oral transmission of human individuals.

269. *Terma*s are written down in symbolic script that only a qualified *tertön* (and often only the *tertön* whose destiny it is to reveal a specific *terma*) can decipher.

270. *Guna Samudra* (Ocean of Enlightened Qualities) is the Sanskrit equivalent of the Tibetan *Yönten Gyatso*, the main component in Kongtrul's ordination name.

271. The third of the four levels of empowerment is intended to arouse an experience of the unity of bliss and emptiness in the recipient. It has long been customary for the presiding master simply to display a card bearing a stylized depiction of an idealized feminine consort (given that the vast majority of recipients in Tibet were male) as a symbol of this unity. In the more distant past, it was at least occasionally the case that an actual woman would participate, with ritual sexual union being employed as the stimulus to arouse this experience.

272. Khyentsé Rinpoché is referring to *The Treasury of Precious Hidden Teachings* by an alternative title; Kongtrul's *terma* cycle, The United Intent of the Three Roots, is included in the collection.

273. When one is in strict retreat or otherwise engaged in intensive spiritual endeavors, interruptions from others can be particularly disruptive. Before such interruptions take place, there can be signs of their imminent occurrence that cause obstacles or upset to one's health or state of mind.

274. This is part of Kongtrul's *terma* cycle The United Intent of the Three Roots, which is included in *The Treasury of Precious Hidden Teachings.*

275. This is part of The Heart Drop of the Immortal Lake-Born One, a cycle revealed as a visionary transmission to Jamyang Khyentsé Wangpo and included in The Treasury of Precious Hidden Teachings, immediately before Kongtrul's cycle The United Intent of the Three Roots. Kongtrul was also responsible for helping to codify and supplement Khyentsé's visionary cycle.

276. The Tibetan term *yeshé lama* refers to the sixteenth and highest level of realization described in the Dzogchen teachings.

277. A benediction in Sanskrit that means, "In all directions and times, may everything be auspicious and excellent!"

278. Such verses are typically composed by those who sponsor the carving of the woodblocks for a text. As in the present case, they are usually written in a highly ornate style that owes much to the Tibetan interpretation of the Indian poetic form known as *kavya*, in which each line is dense with meaning and allusion. Such verses are thus difficult to translate gracefully into English; I have simply tried to present the meaning, without being able to do justice to the rhythms and structure of the original.

279. This is probably the third throne holder of the Nyingma monastery of Darthang, more than two hundred kilometers northeast of Dergé in the southern reaches of Golok Province. Do-ngak Chökyi Nyima (1854-1906) was a holder of the lineage of the Sky Teachings.

280. This is another name for Kongtrul's student Nesar Tashi Chöphel, who also edited Kongtrul's Autobiography and authored *The Marvelous Gem-Like Vision*, the account of Kongtrul's final days and the subsequent funeral observances that is included in this volume.

281. A benediction in Sanskrit that means, "May there be good fortune in every way!"

Bibliography

WORKS IN ENGLISH

Abhayadatta. *Buddha's Lions: The Lives of the Eighty-Four Siddhas.* Trans. James B. Robinson. Berkeley: Dharma Publishing, 1979.

Aryasura. *Once the Buddha Was a Monkey: Ārya Śūra's Jātakamālā.* Trans. Peter Khroche. Chicago: University of Chicago Press, 1989.

_____. *The Gātakamālā, or Garland of Birth-Stories by Aryasûra.* Trans. J. S. Speyer. Delhi: Motilal Banarsidass Publishers, 1990.

_____. *Stories of the Buddha, being Selections from the Jātaka.* Trans. and ed. Caroline A. F. Rhys Davids. New York: Dover Publications, 1989.

Ashvaghosha. *The Buddhacarita; or, Acts of the Buddha.* Complete Sanskrit text with English translation by E. H. Johnston. Delhi: Motilal Banarsidass, 1972.

Bryant, Barry. *The Wheel of Time Sand Mandala: Visual Scripture of Tibetan Buddhism.* San Francisco: Harper Collins, 1995.

Cabezón, José Ignacio and Roger R. Jackson, ed. *Tibetan Literature: Studies in Genre.* Ithaca, NY: Snow Lion Publications, 1996.

Carrasco, Pedro. *Land and Polity in Tibet.* Seattle: University of Washington Press, 1959.

Cornu, Philippe. *Tibetan Astrology.* Trans. Hamish Gregor. Boston: Shambhala, 1997.

Dagyab Rinpoche. *Buddhist Symbols in Tibetan Culture.* Boston: Wisdom Publications, 1995.

Dargyay, Eva M. *The Rise of Esoteric Buddhism in Tibet.* New York: Samuel Weiser, Inc., 1978.

Dash, Narendra Kumar. *A Survey on Sanskrit Grammar in Tibetan Language.* Delhi: Agam Kala Prakashan, 1993.

Dharma Publishing Staff, trans. *The Fortunate Aeon.* 4 vols. Berkeley: Dharma Publishing, 1986.

Dilgo Khyentse Rinpoché. *Enlightened Courage: An Explanation of Atisha's*

Seven Point Mind Training. Trans. Padmakara Translation Group. Ithaca, NY: Snow Lion Publications, 1993.

Dooboom Tulku, ed. *Buddhist Translations: Problems and Perspectives.* New Delhi: Manohar, 1995.

Dorje, Gyurme. *Tibet Handbook.* 2nd ed. Bath, U.K.: Footprint Handbooks, 1999.

Douglas, Nik and White, Meryl. *Karmapa: The Black Hat Lama of Tibet.* London: Luzac and Company, Ltd., 1976.

Dowman, Keith. *Masters of Enchantment: The Lives and Legends of the Mahasiddhas.* Rochester, Vermont: Inner Traditions International, Inc., 1988.

_____. *Masters of Mahamudra: Songs and Histories of the Eighty-Four Buddhist Siddhas.* Albany, NY: State University of New York Press, 1985.

_____. *The Power Places of Central Tibet: The Pilgrim's Guide.* London and New York: Routledge and Kegan Paul, 1988.

Dudjom Lingpa. *Buddhahood Without Meditation.* 2nd ed. Trans. Richard Barron and Susanne Fairclough. Junction City, CA: Padma Publishing, 2001.

Dudjom Rinpoche, Jikdrel Yeshe Dorje. *The Nyingma School of Tibetan Buddhism: Its Fundamentals and History.* 2 vols. Trans. Gyurme Dorjé and Matthew Kapstein. Boston: Wisdom Publications, 1991.

Edou, Jérôme, trans. and commentary. *Machig Labdrön and the Foundations of Chöd.* Ithaca, NY: Snow Lion Publications, 1996.

Gampopa Sönam Rinchen. *The Jewel Ornament of Liberation.* Trans. H. V. Guenther. Boulder: Shambhala, 1971.

_____. *The Jewel Ornament of Liberation.* Trans. Khenpo Konchog Gyaltsen. Ithaca, NY: Snow Lion Publications, 1998.

Gega Lama. *Principles of Tibetan Art: Illustrations and explanations of Buddhist iconography and iconometry according to the Karma Gadri school.* 2 vols. Trans. Richard Barron. Antwerp: Karma Sonam Gyamtso Ling, 1985.

Guenther, Herbert V. *Buddhist Philosophy in Theory and Practice.* Boulder, CO: Shambhala, 1976.

_____. *Ecstatic Spontaneity: Saraha's Three Cycles of Dohā.* Berkeley: Asian Humanities Press, 1993.

_____. *The Royal Song of Saraha.* Seattle: University of Washington Press, 1969.

_____. *Looking Deeper: A Swan's Questions & Answers.* Porthill, ID: Timeless Books, 1983.

_____. *The Tantric View of Life.* Boulder, CO: Shambhala, 1976.

Gyalwa Jangchub and Namkhai Nyingpo. *Sky Dancer: The Secret Life and Songs of the Lady Yeshe Tsogyel.* Trans. Keith Dowman. London: Routledge and Kegan Paul, 1984.

_____. *Mother of Knowledge: The Enlightenment of Ye-shes mTsho-rgyal.* Trans. Tarthang Tulku; ed. Jane Wilhelms. Berkeley: Dharma Publishing, 1983.

_____. *Lady of the Lotus-Born: The Life and Enlightenment of Yeshé Tsogyal.* Trans. Padmakara Translation Group. Boston: Shambhala, 1999.

Haksar, A. N. D. *Daṇḍin: Tales of the Ten Princes.* New Delhi: Penguin Books India, 1995.

Hanson-Barber, A. W. "The Life and Teachings of Vairocana." Ph.D. diss., University of Wisconsin, 1984.

Harding, Sarah (trans.). *Creation and Completion: Essential Points of Tantric Meditation.* Boston: Wisdom Publications, 1996.

_____. *Machik's Complete Expanation: Clarifying the Meaning of Chöd.* Ithaca, NY: Snow Lion Publications, 2003.

Harrison, Paul. "A Brief History of the Tibetan bKa' 'gyur." In José Ignacio Cabezón and Roger R. Jackson, ed. *Tibetan Literature: Studies in Genre.* Ithaca, NY: Snow Lion Publications, 1996.

Hookham, S. K. *The Buddha Within.* Albany, NY: State University of New York Press, 1991.

Jamgön Kongtrul Lodrö Thayé. *Buddhist Ethics.* Trans. International Translation Committee of Kunkhyab Chöling. Ithaca, NY: Snow Lion Publications, 1998.

_____. *Jamgon Kongtrul's Retreat Manual.* Trans. Ngawang Zangpo. Ithaca, NY: Snow Lion Publications, 1994.

_____. *Myriad Worlds: Buddhist Cosmology in Abhidharma, Kâlacakra and Dzog-chen.* Trans. International Translation Committee of Kunkhyab Chöling. Ithaca, NY: Snow Lion Publications, 1995.

Jinpa, Thupten and Jas Elsner, trans. *Songs of Spiritual Experience: Tibetan Buddhist Poems of Insight and Awakening.* Boston: Shambhala, 2000.

Jonang Târanâtha. *The Seven Instruction Lineages.* Trans. and ed. David Templeman. Dharamsala: Library of Tibetan Works and Archives, 1983.

Kalu Rinpoché. *The Chariot for Traveling the Path to Freedom: The Life Story of Kalu Rinpoché.* Trans. Kenneth I. McLeod. San Francisco: Kagyu Dharma, 1985.

_____. *Luminous Mind: The Way of the Buddha.* An Anthology of Teachings Compiled Under the Direction of Lama Denis Töndrup. Translated from the French by Maria Montenegro. Boston: Wisdom Publications, 1997.

Kolmaš, Josef. *A Genealogy of the Kings of Dergé: sDe-dge'i rgyal-rabs (Tibetan Text Edited with Historical Introduction)*. Prague: Publishing House of the Czechoslo-vak Academy of Sciences, 1968.

Lha btsun Rin chen rnam rgyal. *The Life and Teachings of Naropa*. Trans. and commentary Herbert V. Guenther. Boston: Shambhala, 1986.

Longchen Rabjam. *The Exposition of the Quintessential Meaning of the Three Categories*. Trans. and ed. Padma Translation Committee. Junction City, CA: Padma Publishing, 1988.

_____. *The Precious Treasury of the Basic Space of Phenomena*. Trans. and ed. Padma Translation Committee. Junction City, CA: Padma Publishing, 2001.

_____. *The Precious Treasury of the Way of Abiding*. Trans. and ed. Padma Translation Committee. Junction City, CA: Padma Publishing, 1998.

_____. *A Treasure Trove of Scriptural Transmission*. Trans. and ed. Padma Translation Committee. Junction City, CA: Padma Publishing, 2001.

Maitreya. *The Changeless Nature*. 2d. ed. Trans. Ken and Katia Holmes. Eskdalemuir, Scotland: Karma Drubgyud Darjay Ling, 1982.

_____. *The Uttaratantra of Maitreya*. Trans. E. Obermiller. Bibliotheca Indo-Buddhica No. 79. Delhi: Sri Satguru Publications, 1991.

Michael, Franz. *Rule by Incarnation: Tibetan Buddhism and Its Role in Society and State*. Boulder, CO: Westview Press, 1982.

Milarepa (Lhatsün Rinchen Namgyal, ed.) (Lama Kunga Rinpoche and Brian Cutillo, trans.) *Drinking the Mountain Stream*. New York: Lotsawa, 1978.

Milarepa (Lhatsün Rinchen Namgyal, ed.) (Lama Kunga Rinpoche and Brian Cutillo, trans.) *Miraculous Journey*. Novato, CA: Lotsawa, 1986.

Mullin, Glenn H. *The Fourteen Dalai Lamas: A Sacred Legacy of Reincarnation*. Santa Fe, NM: Clear Light Publishers, 2001.

Nālanda Translation Committee, trans. *The Rain of Wisdom*. Boulder, CO: Shambhala, 1980.

Namgyal, Dakpo Tashi. *Mahāmudrā: The Quintessence of Mind and Meditation*. Trans. Lobsang P. Lhalungpa. Boston: Shambhala, 1986.

Namgyal, Dakpo Tashi. *Teachings of Tibetan Yoga*. Trans. Garma C. C. Chang. New Hyde Park, NY: University Books, 1963.

Nam-mkha'i snying po. *Mother of Knowledge: The Enlightenment of Ye-shes mTsho-rgyal*. Trans. Tarthang Tulku. Berkeley, CA: Dharma Publishing, 1983.

Nobel, J. *The Foundations of Indian Poetry and their Historical Development*. Calcutta Oriental Series, No. 16, E. 9. Calcutta: Calcutta Oriental Press, 1925.

Padmakara. *The Lives and Liberation of Princess Mandarava*. Trans. Lama Chonam and Sangye Khandro. Boston: Wisdom Publications, 1998.

Paltrul Rinpoché. *The Words of My Perfect Teacher.* Trans. Padmakara Translation Group. The Sacred Literature Series. San Francisco: Harper Collins, 1994.

Ricard, Matthieu. *Journey to Enlightenment: The Life and World of Khyentse Rinpoché, Spiritual Teacher from Tibet.* New York: Aperture, 1996.

Richardson, Hugh E. *Tibet and Its History.* Boston: Shambhala, 1984.

Riggs, Nicole, trans. *Like An Illusion: Lives of the Shangpa Kagyu Masters.* Eugene, Oregon: Dharma Cloud Press, 2001.

Rigzin, Tsepak. *Tibetan-English Dictionary of Buddhist Terminology.* Dharamsala: Library of Tibetan Works and Archives, 1986.

Roerich, George N., trans. *The Blue Annals.* Delhi: Motilal Banarsidass, 1979.

Rossi, Donatella. *The Philosophical View of the Great Perfection in the Tibetan Bon Religion.* Ithaca, NY: Snow Lion Publications, 1999.

Sadakata, Akira. *Buddhist Cosmology: Philosophy and Origins.* Trans. Gaynor Sekimori. Tokyo: Kôsei Publishing Co., 1997.

Sakya Pandita. *Ordinary Wisdom: Sakya Pandita's Treasury of Good Advice.* Trans. John T. Davenport. Boston: Wisdom Publications, 2000.

Shantideva. *The Way of the Bodhisattva.* Trans. Padmakara Translation Group. Boston: Shambhala, 1997.

Smith, E. Gene. *Among Tibetan Texts: History and Literature of the Himalayan Plateau.* Boston: Wisdom Publications, 2001.

Snellgrove, David and Hugh Richardson. *A Cultural History of Tibet.* Boston: Shambhala, 1986.

Sogyal Rinpoche. *The Tibetan Book of Living and Dying.* San Francisco: Harper Collins Publishers (*rev. ed.*), 2002.

Sonam Rinchen, Geshe. *Atisha's Lamp for the Path to Enlightenment.* Trans. and ed. Ruth Sonam. Ithaca, NY: Snow Lion Publications, 1997.

Stearns, Cyrus. *Luminous Lives: The Story of the Early Masters of the Lam 'bras Tradition in Tibet.* Boston: Wisdom Publications, 2001.

_____. *The Buddha from Dolpo: A Study of the Life and Thought of the Tibetan Master Dolpopa Sherab Gyaltsen.* Albany, NY: State University of New York Press, 1999.

Stein, R. A. *Tibetan Civilization.* Stanford, CA: Stanford University Press, 1972.

Stewart, Jampa Mackenzie, trans. *The Life of Gampopa, The Incomparable Dharma Lord of Tibet.* Ithaca, NY: Snow Lion Publications, 1995.

Suzuki, Daisetz Teitaro. *The Laṅkāvatāra Sūtra: A Mahāyāna Text.* Buddhist Tradition Series, v. 40. Delhi: Motilal Banarsidass Publishers, 1999.

Taranatha. *Tāranātha's History of Buddhism in India.* Trans. Lama Chimpa and Alaka Chattopadhyaya. Calcutta: K.P. Bagchi and Company, 1980.

Taranatha. *Tāranātha's Life of Kṛṣṇācārya/Kāṇha*. Trans. David Templeman. Dharamsala: Library of Tibetan Works and Archives, 1989.

Tarthang Tulku, ed. *A History of the Buddhist Dharma*. (Crystal Mirror Series, vol. 5) Berkeley: Dharma Publishing, 1977.

_____, ed. *Masters of the Nyingma Lineage.* (Crystal Mirror Series, vol. 11) Berkeley: Dharma Publishing, 1995.

_____, ed. *Survey of Buddhist History.* (Crystal Mirror Series, vol. 7) Berkeley: Dharma Publishing, 1984.

_____, ed. *The Three Jewels and History of Dharma Transmission.* (Crystal Mirror Series, vol. 6) Berkeley: Dharma Publishing, 1984.

Tenzin Gyatso, The Dalai Lama. *The Kalacakra Tantra: Rite of Initiation.* Trans. and ed. Jeffrey Hopkins. London: Wisdom Publications, 1985.

Thinley, Karma. *The History of the Sixteen Karmapas of Tibet.* Boulder, CO: Prajña Press, 1980.

Thondup, Tulku. *Buddhist Civilization in Tibet.* New York and London: Routledge and Kegan Paul, 1987.

_____. *Hidden Teachings of Tibet.* London: Wisdom Publications, 1986.

_____. *Masters of Meditation and Miracles: The Longchen Nyingthig Lineage of Tibetan Buddhism.* Ed. Harold Talbott. Boston: Shambhala, 1996.

_____. *The Tantric Tradition of the Nyingmapa.* Marion, MA: Buddhayana, 1984.

Tobgyal, Orgyen. *The Life and Teaching of Chokgyur Lingpa.* Trans. Tulku Jigmey and Erik Pema Kunsang. Kathmandu: Rangjung Yeshé, 1988.

Tripathi, Jayashankar. *Daṇḍin.* Trans. Deepali Bhanot. Makers of Indian Literature Series. New Delhi: Sahitya Akademi, 1996.

Trungpa, Chögyam. *Born in Tibet.* Boston: Shambhala, 1985.

Tsang Nyön Heruka. *The Life of Marpa the Translator.* Trans. Nālanda Translation Committee. Boulder, CO: Prajñā Press, 1982.

_____. *The Life of Milarepa.* Trans. Lobsang P. Lhalungpa. Boulder, CO: Prajñâ Press, 1982.

_____. *The Hundred Thousand Songs of Milarepa.* 2 vols. Trans. Garma C. C. Chang. Boston and Shaftesbury: Shambhala, 1989.

Tsering, Tashi. "Ñag-roṇ mgon-po rnam-rgyal: A 19th Century Khams-pa Warrior." In Barbara Nimri Aziz and Matthew Kapstein, ed. *Soundings in Tibetan Civilization,* New Delhi: Manohar, 1985.

Tsering Lama Jampal Zangpo. *A Garland of Immortal Wish-fulfilling Trees: The Palyul Tradition of Nyingmapa.* Trans. Sangye Khandro. Ithaca, NY: Snow Lion Publications, 1988.

Tsogyal, Yeshé *The Life and Liberation of Padmasambhava.* 2 vols. Trans. Kenneth Douglas and Gwendolyn Bays. Berkeley: Dharma Publishing, 1978.

Tsonawa, Lobsang N., trans. *Indian Buddhist Pandits from "The Jewel Garland of Buddhist History"* Dharamsala: Library of Tibetan Works and Archives, 1985.

Tucci, Giuseppe. *Tibetan Painted Scrolls.* 3 vols. Rome: Libreria dello Stato, 1949.

Wangchuk Dorjé, The Ninth Karmapa. *The Mahāmudrā Eliminating the Darkness of Ignorance.* Commentary by Khyentsé Rinpoché, trans. Alexander Berzin. Dharamsala: Library of Tibetan Works and Archives, 1978.

_____. *Mahāmudrā, The Ocean of Definitive Meaning.* Trans. Elizabeth M. Callahan. Seattle: Nithartha International, 2001.

_____. *Pointing out the Dharmakaya.* Commentary by Khenchen Thrangu Rinpoché; trans. Lama Yeshé Gyamtso. In *Shenpen Ösel,* vol. 4, no. 3 (December 2000). Seattle, WA: Kagyu Shenpen Ösel Chöling, 2000.

Warder, A. K. *Indian Buddhism.* Delhi: Motilal Banarsidass, 1980.

Wayman, Alex, trans. *Yoga of the Guhyasamājatantra: The Arcane Lore of Forty Verses.* New York: Samuel Weiser, Inc., 1980.

Yeshe De Project. *Ancient Tibet: Research Materials from the YesheDe Project.* Berkeley: Dharma Publishing, 1986.

Zangpo, Ngawang, trans. and commentary. *Guru Rinpoché: His Life and Times.* Ithaca, NY and Boulder, CO: Snow Lion Publications, 2002.

WORKS IN TIBETAN

Alak Zengkar Rinpoché, et al. *Bod rgya tshig mdzod chen mo.* Beijing: People's Press, 1996. 2 vols. (A very well-researched modern dictionary, with entries in Tibetan and definitions in Tibetan and Chinese.)

Kun dga' grol mchog, rJe btsun. *sKye ba'i rabs kyi phreng ba Legs par brjod pa'i gtam.* In *The Autobiographies of Jo-nan Kun-dga-grol-mchog and his previous embodiments.* New Delhi: Tibet House, 1982. (A series of eleven biographical accounts of Kunga Drolchok's former lifetimes.)

Kong sprul bLo gros mtha' yas. *rGya chen bka' mdzod: A Collection of the Writings of 'Jam-mgon Koo-sprul bLo-gros mtha'-yas.* Reproduced from a set of prints of the Dpal-spuos xylographic blocks at the order of the Ven. Dingo Chhentse Rinpoché. 20 volumes. Paro: Ngodrup, 1976. (The collected works of Kongtrul not included in any of the other Treasuries, plus the *Treasury of the Knowable* (*Shes bya mdzod*), which comprises the last four volumes.)

Kong sprul bLo gros mtha' yas, et al. *Kong sprul Yon tan rgya mtsho'i rnam thar.* Chengdu: Sichuan People's Press (*Si khron mi rigs dpe skrun khang*), 1997. (Contains the typeset Tibetan text of Kongtrul's account of his past lives; his autobiography; Nesar Karma Tashi Chöphel's account of Kongtrul's final days and the funeral observances; and Tashi Chöphel's index to Kongtrul's collected works.)

_____. *'Du shes gsum ldan spong ba pa'i gzugs brnyan Padma gar gyi dbang phyug phrin las 'gro 'dul rtsal gyi rtogs pa brjod pa'i dum bu sMrig rgyu'i bdud rtsi* (Kongtrul's accounts of his past lives, translated here as *The Mirage of Nectar*). Bir, India: Tibetan Khampa Industrial Society, 1973.

_____. *Phyogs med ris med kyi bstan pa la 'dun shing dge sbyong gi gzugs brnyan 'chang ba bLo gros mtha' yas kyi sde'i byung ba brjod pa Nor bu sna tshogs mdog can* (Kongtrul's Autobiography, translated here as *A Gem of Many Colors*). Bir, India: Kandro, 1973.

_____. (ed.) *Rin chen gter mdzod chen mo* (*The Great Treasury of Hidden Teachings*). A Reproduction of the Stod-lun mTshur-phu redaction of 'Jam-mgon Kon-sprul's great work on the unity of the gter-ma traditions of Tibet. With supplemental texts from the Dpal-spuns redaction and other manuscripts. Reproduced at the order of the Ven. Dingo Chhentse Rinpoché under the esteemed patronage of H.M. Ashé Kesang, Queen Mother of Bhutan, and H.R.H. Ashé Phuntso Choedron, Senior Royal Grandmother. 111 volumes. Paro: Ngodrup and Sherab Drimay, 1976-1980.

_____. *Theg pa'i sgo kun las btus pa gsung rab rin po chei mdzod bslab pa gsum legs par ston pa'i bstan bcos Shes bya kun khyab* (*Shes bya mdzod*) Beijing: People's Press (*Mi rigs dpe skrun khang*), 3 vols., 1982.

_____. *Zab mo'i gter dang gter ston grub thob ji ltar byon pa'i lo rgyus mdor bsdus bkod pa Rin chen bai dūrya'i phreng ba* (popularly known as the *gTer ston rgya rtsa*) (Volume 1, pp. 291-759 of the *Rin chen gter mdzod* collection.)

bKra shis chos 'phel, gNas gsar. *rJe kun gzigs 'Jam mgon Ngag gi dbang phyug Yon tan rgya mtsho'i zhabs kyi 'das rjes kyi rnam par thar pa Ngo mtshar nor bu'i snang ba* (the account of Kongtrul's final days and the funeral observances, translated here as *The Marvelous Gem-Like Vision*). Bir, India: Kandro, 1973.

_____. *rGyal bas lung bstan shing rta chen po 'Jam mgon bla ma thams cad mkhyen gzigs Karma Ngag dbang Yon tan rgya mtsho bLo gro mtha' yas pa'i sde'i zhabs kyi gsung 'bum rin po che rGya chen bka' mdzod kyi dkar chag mdor bsdus Zab rgyas rgya mtsho'i mtha' yas la 'jug pa'i gru bo.* Vol. 16 (Ma), pp. 525-611, *rGya* chen bka' mdzod: A Collection of the Writings of 'Jam-mgon Koo-sprul bLo-gros *mtha 'yas.* Paro, Bhutan: Ngodup, 1976. (Index to Kongtrul's collected writings.)

mKha' khyab rdo rje, Karma pa XVth. *sNga 'gyur zab mo Rin chen gter gyi mdzod chen mo'i dkar cag Nor bu'i bang mdzod.* Index to *The Precious Treasury of Hidden Teachings.* (Vol. 111 of the *Rin chen gter mdzod* collection)

bDud 'joms Rin po che 'Jigs bral ye shes rdo rje, ed. *Gangs can bstan pa'i phyi mo snga 'gyur pa'i chos mdzod ring brgyud ma nyams bka' ma'i gzhung (rÑio ma bka' ma rgyas pa).* A collection of teachings and initiations of the rÑio-ma-pa tradition passed through continuous and unbroken oral lineages from the ancient masters in 58 vol. Kalimpong, West Bengal: Dupjung Lama, 1982-1987.

Phur bu tshe ring. *mDo kun las btus pa'i nang don rig pa'i tshig mdzod Mu tig phreng ba.* Lhasa: Bod ljongs mi dmangs dpe skrun khang, 1994.

Mi nyag mgon po. *Gangs can mkhas dbang rim byon gyi rnam thar mdor bsdus.* Beijing: Krung go'i bod kyi shes rig dpe skrun khang, 1996.

Nang don rig pa'i ming tshig bod dbyin shan sbyar. n.p., n.d.

bLa brang skal bzang. *Bod kyi sprul sku'i rnam bshad.* n.p., 1997.

Ringu Tulku, Dr. (Karma Tsultrim Gyurme Thinley). *Rimay Philosophy of Kongtrul:* A Study on the Buddhist Sects of Tibet Based on the Works of Kongtrul Yonten *Gyatsho.* Gangtok, Sikkim: Sikkim National Press, 1985 (Tibetan text of Ringu Tulku's doctoral thesis.)

Tshe dbang rdo rje rig 'dzin. *dPal sa skyong sDe dge chos kyi rgyal po rim byon gyi rnam thar dGe legs nor bu'i phreng ba 'dod dgu rab 'phel (sDe dge rgyal rabs).* Chengdu: Sichuan People's Press, 1990.

Thub bstan chos dar, Mi nyag. *rNying ma rgyud 'bum gyi dkar chag gSal ba'i me long.* Beijing: Mi rigs dpe skrun khang, 2000.

Ye shes mtsho rgyal. *Padma bka'i thang yig (U rgyan gu ru padma 'byung gnas kyi skyes rabs rnam par thar pa rgyas par bkod pa padma bka'i thang yig).* Chengdu: Si khron mi rigs dpe skrun khang, 1987 (The text of *The Record of Padma).*

gYu sgra sNying po, et al. *Bai ro'i rnam thar 'Dra 'bag chen mo (rJe btsun thams cad mkhyen pa Bai ro tsa na'i rnam thar 'dra 'bag chen mo)* Chengdu: Si khron mi rigs dpe skrun khang, 1995 (The text of *The Great Mask).*

WORKS BY KONGTRUL IN ENGLISH TRANSLATION

Note: This is not intended to be an exhaustive overview of Kongtrul's works in English, but a listing of translations that are published and widely available. Versions of many of Kongtrul's liturgies, prayers, and other practice-oriented materials have been printed by various Buddhist centers in English-speaking countries, but I have made no attempt to catalog these.

Dargyay, Eva M. *The Rise of Esoteric Buddhism in Tibet.* New York: Samuel Weiser, Inc., 1978. (Contains excepts from Kongtrul's account of the lives of the *tertöns,* Zab mo'i gter dang gter ston grub thob ji ltar byon pa'i lo rgyus mdor bsdus *bkod pa Rin chen bai ḍūrya'i phreng ba,* from vol. 1 of the *Rin chen gter mdzod*)

Fuchs, Rosemarie, trans. *Buddha Nature: The Mahayana Uttaratantra Shastra with Commentary.* Ithaca, NY: Snow Lion Publications, 2000. (A translation of the source text, the *Uttataratantra* of Asanga, and the commentary by Kongtrul (*Theg pa chen po rgyud bla ma'i bstan bcos snying po'i don mngon sum lam* gyi bshad pa srol dang sbyar ba'i rnam par 'grel ba phyir mi ldog pa seng ge'i *nga ro*)).

Garry, Ron, trans. *The Teacher-Student Relationship.* Ithaca, NY: Snow Lion Publications, 1977. (A translation, with commentary, of the first part of the fifth section of Kongtrul's *Shes bya mdzod* (*Treasury of the Knowable*)).

Hanson, Judith, trans. *The Torch of Certainty.* Boulder: Shambhala, 1977. (A translation, with commentary, of *Phyag chen sngon 'gro bzhi sbyor dang dngos gzhi'i khrid rim mdor bsdus Nges don sgron me,* in volume 8, pp. 3-123 of the *rGya chen bka' mdzod: A Collection of the Writings of 'Jam-mgon Koo-sprul bLo-gros mtha'yas*).

Harding, Sarah, trans. *Creation and Completion: Essential Points of Tantric Meditation.* Boston: Wisdom Publications, 1996. (A translation, with commentary, of *Lam zhugs kyi gang zag las dang po pa la phan pa'i bskyed rdzogs kyi gnad bsdus*).

International Translation Committee, trans. *Buddhist Ethics.* Ithaca, NY: Snow Lion Publications, 1998. (A translation, with commentary, of the fifth section of Kongtrul's *Shes bya mdzod* (*Treasury of the Knowable*)).

_____. *Myriad Worlds: Buddhist Cosmology in Abhidharma, Kâlacakra, and Dzog-chen.* Ithaca, NY: Snow Lion Publications, 1995. (A translation, with commentary, of the first section of Kongtrul's *Shes bya mdzod* (*Treasury of the Knowable*)).

Khenchen Thrangu. *The Practice of Tranquillity and Insight: A Guide to Tibetan*

Buddhist Meditation. Trans. Peter Roberts. Boston: Shambhala, 1993 ("A commentary on the eighth chapter of the *Treasury of Knowledge* by Jamgön Kongtrül").

Khenpo Tsultrim Gyamtso Rinpoche. *Ascertaining Certainty About the View.* Trans. and ed. Michele Martin. Auckland: Zhyisil Chokyi Ghatsal Publications (Prajna Editions), 2002 ("Chapter Seven, Section Three from the *Treasury of Knowledge*).

Kongtrul, The Third Jamgön. *Cloudless Sky.* Boulder: Shambhala, 1992. (A translation, with commentary, of Kongtrul's *Vajra Song,* which was included in the Tibetan collection translated as *The Rain of Wisdom,* pp. 81-90).

Kunsang, Erik Pema, trans. *The Light of Wisdom.* Boston: Shambhala, 1995 (Vol. 1); Boudhanath, Hong Kong and Esby: Rangjung Yeshe Publications, 1998 (Vol. 2) and 2001 (Vol. 4) (A translation of most of Kongtrul's *Lam rim ye shes snying po'i 'grel pa Ye shes snang ba rab tu rgyas pa,* a commentary on *Zhal gdams lam rim ye shes snying po* by Padmakara, a *terma* revealed by 'Jam dbyangs mkhyen brtse'i dbang po and mChog gyur bde chen gling pa).

McLeod, Ken, trans. *The Great Path of Awakening, An Easily Accessible Introduction* for Ordinary People: A Commentary on the Mahayana Teaching of the Seven *Points of Mind Training.* Boston and London: Shambhala, 2000. (A translation, with commentary, of Kongtrul's *Theg pa chen po blo sbyong don bdun ma'i khrid yig blo dman 'jug bder bkod pa Byang chub gzhung lam*).

Zangpo, Ngawang, trans. *Enthronement: The Recognition of the Reincarnate Masters of Tibet and the Himalayas.* Ithaca, NY: Snow Lion Publications, 1997. (A translation, with commentary, of *Byams mgon mchog gi sprul pa'i sku seng ge'i khrir phebs pa'i maṇḍala rgyas bshad Ngo mtshar sgo brgya 'byed pa'i dga' ston,* volume 9 (Ta), pp. 121-178 of the *rGya chen bka' mdzod: A Collection of the Writings of 'Jam-mgon Koṅ-sprul bLo-gros mtha 'yas*).

_____. *Jamgon Kongtrul's Retreat Manual.* Ithaca, NY: Snow Lion Publications, 1994. (A translation, with commentary, of *dPal spungs yang khrod kun bzang bde chen 'od gsal gling gi sgrub ra rnams kyi kun spyod bca' khrims blang do rab gsal Phan bde'i 'byung gnas,* volume 11, pp. 257-320 of the *rGya chen bka' mdzod: A Collection of the Writings of 'Jam-mgon Koṅ-sprul bLo-gros mtha 'yas*).

_____. *Sacred Ground: Jamgon Kongtrul on "Pilgrimage and Sacred Geography".* Ithaca, NY: Snow Lion Publications, 2001. (A translation, with commentary, of *Thugs kyi gnas mchog chen po de wi ko ṭi rtsa 'dra rin chen brag gi rtogs pa brjod pa Yid kyi rgya mtsho'i rol mo,* volume 11, pp. 477-546 of the *rGya chen* bka' mdzod: A Collection of the Writings of 'Jam-mgon Koṅ-sprul bLo-gros *mtha 'yas*).

Appendix

Tables of Contents to Collections
Compiled by Jamgön Kongtrul
(Traditions or masters are shown in parentheses.)

TANTRIC TREASURY OF THE KAGYÜ SCHOOL
(Kagyü Ngakdzö)
(8-volume edition published in Paro, Bhutan: Lama Ngodrub and Sherab Drimey, 1982)

XVI. Sankshipta-kula Manjushri (*Manjushri-nama-samgiti*)

XVII. Rakta Yamari (Red Yamantaka) five deity mandala   5

XVIII. Vajrabhairava nine deity mandala

XIX. General Texts for Marpa Kagyü rituals (*ganachakra* ritual,
     retreat manual, consecration ritual, empowerment instructions)

XX. Four-armed Mahakala   6

XXI. Shridevi Dhumavati

XXII. Tashi Tseringma five deity mandala

XXIII. Supplemental volumes on Vajrapani   7-8
     (added by Dilgo Khyentsé Rinpoché)

TREASURY OF SPIRITUAL ADVICE
(Dam-ngak Dzö)
(18-volume edition published in Paro, Bhutan:
Lama Ngodrup and Sherab Drimey, 1979-1981)

VOLUME

I. Nyingma   1

    A. Mahayoga

    B. Anuyoga

    C. Atiyoga

        1. Category of Mind (*Semdé*)

        2. Category of Expanse (*Longdé*)

        3. Category of Direct Transmission (*Men-ngakdé*)   2

        4. Supplementary material

            a. *Trilogy on Natural Freedom* by Longchenpa

            b. *Gurupuja* to Nyingtik lineage

            c. Protective deity - Ekajati

II. Kadampa   3

    A. Source texts - Stages on the Path (*lamrim*)

    B. Advice - Mental training (*lojong*)   3-4

    C. Pith instructions - Shodasha-bindu *sadhana*

    D. Supplementary material

        1. Four deities of the Kadampa - Shakyamuni, Avalokiteshvara, Green Tara, Achala

        2. Gelukpa *lamrim* material

        3. Madhyamaka and *Zhentong* instructions

        4. *Gurupuja* to Atisha and Kadampa lineage

        5. Protective deites - White Jambhala and Kartari-dhara Mahakala

III. Sakya   5

    A. Lamdré source texts

    B. Empowerments - Hevajra

    C. Instructions

        1. Extensive, direct, and very direct lineages

        2. Instruction manuals - Dombhi Heruka, Padmavajra,   6
Krishnapada, Uchita, Nagarjuna, Indrabhuti, etc.

        3. *Parting from the Four Attachments* (*Zhenpa Zhidral*)

TREASURY OF PRECIOUS HIDDEN TEACHINGS
(Rinchen Terdzö)
(111-volume edition published in Paro, Bhutan:
Ngodrup and Sherab Drimay, 1976-1980)

"Under the category of hidden treasures, previously nothing very extensive that stands on its own came to light under this heading. Since the great Vajradhara, the sovereign lord Jamgön

[Kongtrul] was not able to receive the entire cycle of Chokling's revealed treasure The Three Categories of the Great Perfection, for the time being these have not been included in this collection. Should the transmission of the ripening empowerments and liberating teachings for this *terma* be received, or should any other such *terma* with authentic origins be revealed, these are to be included at this point. Such was his advice allowing for such an eventuality." (from the index by the Fifteenth Karmapa Khakhyap Dorjé)

TREASURY OF EXTENSIVE TEACHINGS
(Gyachen Kadzö)
(20-volume edition published in Paro, Bhutan: Ngodrup, 1976)

	VOLUME
Eulogies	1
*Guruyoga*s - Karmapa	
Guru empowerments and *sadhana*s (Marpa and Milarepa)	
Guru puja - Dzogchen Nyingtik lineage	
Prayers	2
*Guruyoga*s	
Guru puja - Eight Lineages of Accomplishment	
Nyingma *sadhana*s - Samyak Heruka	
Nyingma *Kama sadhana*s	3
Vajrakila Tantra commentary	
Khön Tradition of Vajrakila	
Ningma Kama sadhana*s (cont'd.)*	4
Nyingma Terma sadhana*s*	
Nyingma Terma sadhana*s (cont'd.)*	5
Sarma *sadhana*s	6
Sutra-oriented practices (cont'd.)	7
Instruction manuals	8
Nyingma materials	
Instruction manuals (cont'd.)	9
Advice and answers to students' questions	
Commentaries	
Personal advice	
Vajra songs	10
Personal advice (cont'd.)	

Letters
Indices and inventories

TREASURY OF THE KNOWABLE
(Shéja Dzö)

TABLE OF CONTENTS

This outline has been adapted from E. Gene Smith's Introduction to *Kongtrul's Encyclopedia of Indo-Tibetan Culture*, edited by Prof. Dr. Lokesh Chandra, published by the International Academy of Indian Culture (New Delhi, 1970).

(C) Anuttarayoga

(D) Kalachakra

    ii. Nyingma schools

    iii. Miscellaneous traditions

3. Eight practice lineages

    a. Nyingma

    b. Kadampa

    c. Sakya

    d. Marpa Kagyü

    e. Shangpa Kagyü

    f. Zhijé and Chö

    g. Kalachakra - Six Branches of Union

    h. Stages of Approach and Accomplishment for the Three Vajras

    i. Minor schools

4. Secular fields of study

    a. Sanskrit grammar

    b. Epistemology

    c. Fine arts

    d. Medicine

    e. Astrology

    f. Poetics

    g. Metrics

    h. Synonymy

    i. Miscellaneous

V. The Higher Training in Discipline

1. Characteristics of teacher and student

2. Individual Liberation (*Pratimoksha*) vows

3. Bodhisattva vows

4. Vajrayana samaya

VI. The Process of Study

1. Mundane scholasticism

2. Hinayana and Mahayana tenets

3. Madhyamaka tenets

4. Vajrayana tenets

VII. The Higher Training in Wisdom

1. Definition of the evaluation process

2. Classification of provisional and definitive teachings

3. Ascertainment of correct view

4. Four contemplations to turn the mind toward spiritual practice

VIII. The Higher Training in Meditative Absorption

1. Calm abiding (*shamatha*) and profound insight (*vipashyana*)

2. Stages of meditation in the dialectical approach

3. Stages of meditation in the Vajrayana

4. Stages of meditation in the Dzogchen approach

IX. The Spiritual Paths and Levels

1. Paths and levels of the dialectical approach

2. Paths and levels of the Vajrayana

3. Enhancements to spiritual progress

4. Paths and levels of the Mahayoga, Anuyoga, and Atiyoga
approaches

X. The Fruition State

1. Interpretation of the dialectical approach

2. Mundane attainments in the Vajrayana

3. Vajrayana interpretation

4. Atiyoga interpretation

Tables of Contents to Collections
Compiled by Jamyang Khyentsé Wangpo and Jamyang Loter Wangpo

COMPENDIUM OF ALL SADHANAS
(Druptap Kuntü)
(14-volume Dergé edition published in Dehradun (U.P.):
G. T. K. Lodoy, N. Gyaltsen and N. Lungtok, 1970)

VOLUME

I. Three "White Deities" (Tsarpa)   1
   1. White Amitayus (Mitrayogi)
   2. White Chintamanichakra Tara (Tsarpa)
   3. White Sarasvati (Mahapandita Samantashri)
II. *Sadhana*s for the attainment of immortality
   1. Commentary on longevity practices
      (by Jamgön Kongtrul Lodrö Tayé)
   2. Amitayus (Tsarpa, from Machik Druppai Gyalmo)
   3. Amitayus (Sakya, from Machik Druppai Gyalmo)
   4. Nirmanakaya Amitayus (Sakya)
   5. Nirmanakaya Amitayus (Gyalwang Taklungpa)
   6. White Amitayus (Rechungpa, from Machik Druppai Gyalmo)
   7. Amitayus (seven-day practice format) (Rongtön)
   8. Nine deity mandala of Amitayus (Sakya)
   9. Kaurava longevity *sadhana*
  10. Kaurava protective mantra practice
  11. Kaurava longevity *sadhana* (Drigung Kagyü pure vision
      transmission)
  12. Amitayus-Hayagriva (Thangtong Gyalpo)
  13. Direct transmission longevity *sadhana* (combines *kama*, *terma*, and
      daknang)
  14. Nine deity mandala of Ushnishavijaya
  15. Mahamayuri longevity *sadhana*
  16. Amara Vajradevi
  17. Ritual for burning hair and nails
  18. Ritual for cheating death based on *Bhadracharya-pranidhana-raja*
  19. Ritual for consecrating images based on White Tara

5. Eleven-headed Avalokiteshvara five-dakini *sadhana* (Bhikshuni Shri)
6. Eleven-headed Avalokiteshvara fasting ritual (Bhikshuni Shri)
7. Concise seven-point mandala offering
8. Mahayana *poshadha* ceremony to receive and renew vows
9. Mahakarunika Amogapasha
10. Mahakarunika Amogapasha with *poshadha* ceremony

VI. Guhyapati Vajrapani

1. Nilambharadhara Vajrapani (sutra)
2. Nilambharadhara Vajrapani (Drozang)
3. Mahachakra Vajrapani (Gelukpa)
4. Bhutadamara Vajrapani
5. Ucharya Vajrapani
6. Chanda Vajrapani (Rechungpa)
7. Vajrapani three deity *sadhana* (Drupchen Lekyi Dorjé)
8. Prayer invoking Trikula-natha

VII. Tara

1. White Chintamanichakra Tara
2. White Chintamanichakra Tara (history and activity rituals)
3. Prayer to White Tara (direct lineage)
4. White Tara (Mahapandita Shakya Shri)
5. White Chintamanichakra Tara (extraordinary version)
6. Shrabanadevi (dream divination)
7. Tara (dream divination) (Acharya Chandramitra)
8. Rebirth divination (Buddha Churuka)
9. Divashanata-ratrikruddha Tara
10. Sarvatrasahara Tara (Atisha)
11. Twenty-one Taras (Atisha)
12. Four-mandala Tara ritual (Sakya)
13. Four-mandala Tara ritual (Atisha)
14. Green Tara (Kashmiri Pandita Shakya Shri)
15. Invocation prayer to Tara

VIII. Anuttarayoga deities   4

1. Hevajra (Sakya, from Acharya Prahevajra)
2. Kalachakra (Kalachakrapada)
3. Chakrasamvara (Sakya, from Acharya Prahevajra)
4. Chakrasamvara
5. Chakrasamvara confession ritual

6. Naro Khechari (Sakya)

7. Indrabhuti Khechari (Sakya)

8. Maitri Khechari (Sakya)

9. Varahi (Chal tradition)

10. Red Wrathful Vajravarahi (Mahasiddha Shridhara)

11. Krodhikali (Phadampa Sang-gyé)

12. Mahamaya (Mahasiddha Shantigupta)

13. Guhyasamaja Akshobhya (Lilavajra)

14. Guhyasamaja Manjuvajra (from *Druptap Gyatso* collection)

15. Rakta Yamari (Red Yamantaka) (Virupa)

16. Vajrabhairava (Ra Lotsawa)

17. Chittavikshamana Mahakarunika (Mitrayogi)

18, Mahakarunika Jinasagara five deity mandala (Kagyü)

19. White Tara (Kagyü, from Ngok and Atisha)

20. White Chintamanichakra Tara (Kagyü)

21. Chintamanichakra Tara longevity *sadhana* (Atisha)

22. Tarayogini (Shantigupta)

23. Shadanga Tara (Nagarjuna)

24. Twenty-one Taras (Suryagupta)

25. Eulogy to Twenty-one Taras (Suryagupta)

26. Tara for release from prison (one of Twenty-one Taras)

27. Mangala-siddhartha Tara (Acharya Chandragomin)

IX. Nirmanakaya forms of Tathagathas   5

1. Trisamaya-vyuha-raja Bhagavat (from *Druptap Gyatso* collection)

2. Munindra with sixteen Sthavira (Atisha)

3. Munindra with sixteen Sthavira ritual

4. Munindra Pratityasamutpada-hridaya protection ritual (Virupa)

5. Munindra (Chimtön)

6. Sutra recitation instructions

7. Bhaishajyaguru seven-buddha mandala (Shantirakshita)

8. Bhaishajyaguru sutra ritual

9. Bhaishajyaguru eight-buddha ritual

10. Bhaishajyaguru sutra ritual supplement

11. Amitabha (sutra ritual)

12. Amitabha (tantra ritual)

13. Akshobhya purification ritual (Atisha)

14. Akshobhya pacification ritual (Atisha)

15. Nagendra-raja (Atisha)
16. Nagendra-raja rain ritual
17. Nagendra-raja treasure vase ritual (Nagarjuna)

X. Four Deities (Kadampa)
  1. Four Deities *sadhana* (Kadampa)
  2. Four Deities ritual (Kadampa)

XI. Six Deities (Vajrasana)
  1. Six Doctrines of Vajrasana
  2. Marichi *sadhana*
  3. Marichi *upadesha*
  4. Blue Achala

XII. Three Secret *Sadhana* Cycles (Shangpa Kagyü)

XIII. Deities from *Kalachakra Tantra*
  1. Vajravega
  2. White Vishvamatri
  3. Vajra Garuda

XIV. Three Deities from *Vajrapanjara Tantra*   6
  1. Bhutadamara Vajrapani
    A. Bhutadamara Vajrapani *sadhana*
    B. Bhutadamara Vajrapani eulogy
    C. Bhutadamara Vajrapani *homa* (fire ritual)
  2. White Prajnaparamita
    A. White Prajnaparamita *sadhana*
    B. Ekakasharimata Prajnaparamita Sutra
  3. Pratisara

XV. Deities of Purification
  1. Vajrasattva Heruka (Sakya)
  2. Vajrasattva (from *Guhyasamaja Tantra*) (Marpa Kagyü)
  3. Samayavajra (Sakya)
  4. Samayavajra
  5. Vajradaka *homa* ritual
  6. Vajradaka ritual
  7. Samayavajra confession ritual
  8. Bodhisattva vow renewal ritual
  9. Akashagarbha *sadhana*
  10. *Pratimoksha* vow renewal ritual
  11. Grahamatrika *sadhana*

8. Maitreya eulogy
9. Maitreya eulogy
10. White Sarasvati (Mahapandita Chandrakumara)

XIX. Remedial Deities

1. Yamantaka
2. Vajrapani (Gyalwa Yazangpa)
3. Chanda Vajrapani five-garuda mandala (Chöwang)
4. Red Hayagriva (Drupgyal)
5. Hayagriva four deity *shvana* mandala (Atisha)
6. Hayagriva secret *sadhana* (Kyergangpa - Shangpa Kagyü)
7. Black Hayagriva *sadhana* (Chandradvaja)
8. Black Hayagriva averting ritual (Chandradvaja)
9. Peaceful Guru Guhyasamaja (Chöwang)   8
10. Acharya Padmakara guru *sadhana* (Tsarpa)
11. Acharya Padma supplication
12. Red Guru Drakpo (Nyang Nyima Özer)
13. Shabala Garuda
14. Shabala Garuda (from *Kalachakra Tantra*)
15. Shabala Garuda amulet (from *Kalachakra Tantra*)
16. Black Garuda (Sakya)
17. Black Garuda (from *Kalachakra Tantra*)
18. Black Garuda (Rechungpa)
19. Red Garuda
20. Simhamukha (Sakya)
21. Simhamukha (Gongkar)
22. Blue Simhamukha three deity mandala
23. Simhamukha five-family mandala
24. Simhamukha averting ritual
25. Simhamukha (Bari Lotsawa)
26. Red Simhamukha (Mahapandita Vanaratna)
27. Ushnisha Sitatapatra
28. Ushnisha Sitatapatra protective ritual
29. Ushnisha Sitatapatra averting ritual (Chak)
30. Krodhiraja Ushnishajvala (Atisha)
31. Dvajagra-keyura
32. Bhanasani averting ritual

XX. Deities of Wealth
1. Kurukulle (Sakya)
2. Kurukulle five deity mandala (Dombhi Heruka)
3. Red Ganapati (Sakya)
4. Red Kamaraja (Sakya)
5. Three deities of power—Kurukulle, Red Vasudhara, and Tinumadevi (Nyen Lotsawa)
6. Tinumadevi
7. Red Tara (Sakya)
8. Vaishravana   9
9. Vaishravana nine deity mandala (from Drozang tradition of Vajrapani)
10. White Vaishravana (Atisha)
11. Yellow Jambhala (from *Guhyasamaja Tantra*)
12. Yellow Jambhala (from *Druptap Gyatsa* collection)
13. Red Jambhala (Sakya)
14. Red Jambhala (Drapa Ngönshé *terma*)
15. Green Jambhala (from *Kalachakra Tantra*)
16. Black Jambhala (Mahapandita Shakyashri)
17. Black Jambhala (from *Druptap Gyatsa* collection)
18. Yellow Vasudhara (from *Vajrapanjara Tantra*) (Pandita Jamari)
19. Jambhala and consort nine deity mandala
20. Yaksha mandala
21. White Ganapati (Atisha)
22. Ganapati four deity mandala (Atisha)
23. Danda three deity mandala (Sakya)

XXI. Guardian Deities
1. Hevajra self-visualization
2. Hevajra body mandala (Lamdré)
3. Hevajra offering ceremony
4. Consecration ritual - environment and offerings
5. Confession
6. Mahayana aspiration prayer

XXII. Guardian Deities - Natha (masculine)
1. Panjara-natha three- and eight deity mandalas
2. Four-faced Mahakala (Tathagatarakshita)
3. White Four-faced Mahakala

24. General longevity ritual
25. Alchemical ritual

XXVI. Miscellaneous   11

   1. Ushnisha Sitatapatra amulet
   2. Kshitigarbha and *tenma* goddesses
   3. General collection of activity rituals
   4. Instructions on subtle energy (Jahabhira)
   5. Concise *homa* rituals (Sakya)
   6. *Upadesha* from *Throphu Gyatsa* collection
   7. *Upadesha* from Taklung Kagyü
   8. Eight songs and four sealed practices (Khyungpo Naljor)
   9. White Vaishravana
  10. White Chintamani Mahakala (Shangpa Kagyü)
  11. White Chintamani Mahakala prosperity ritual
  12. Tashi Tseringma five deity mandala
  13. Prayers of dedication, aspiration, and benediction
  14. Index to *The Compendium of All Sadhanas*

XXVII. Supplementary material   12

   1. One Hundred Teachings of Bari Lotsawa (*Bari Gyatsa*) collection
     A. Indian sources
     B. Individual *sadhana*s
     C. Individual formal permission rituals
     D. Lineage prayer
     E. Introductory remarks for empowerments and formal permissions
   2. *Sadhana* of seven successive buddhas
   3. Munindra and eight great bodhisattvas
   4. Eight great bodhisattvas ritual
   5. Praise of Shakyamuni
   6. Praise of Munindra and eight great bodhisattvas
   7. Praises of the eight great bodhisattvas
   8. *Sadhana*s for four Anuttarayoga deities (Drigung Kagyü)
   9. Completion stages for four Anuttarayoga deities (Drigung Kagyü)
  10. Blessing for collected mantras of Guhyasamaja cycle
  11. Blessing for collected mantras of Vajrabhairava cycle
  12. Blessing for collected mantras of Chakrasamvara cycle
  13. Blessing for collected mantras of Vajrayogini cycle

14. Ritual of three longevity deities—Amitayus, White Tara, Ushnisha-vijaya
15. *Guruyoga* of three longevity deities
16. Amitayus sutra
17. Formal permission for three longevity deities
18. White Chakrasamvara (Mahapandita Shakya Shri)
19. Index of deity practices in *Druptap Gyatsa* collection
20. Formal permission for Trikula-natha   13
21. Twenty-one Taras *sadhana*
22. Shabari three-family mandala (Ségyü)
23. Mahaheruka (Acharya Humkara)
24. Samyak Heruka
25. Samyak Heruka (Khön)
26. Vajrakila cycle (Khön)
27. Vajrakila daily practice (Chokgyur Lingpa)
28. Offering ritual for mundane protectors
29. Prayers to lineages of *terma* cycles
30. *Spontaneous Fulfillment of Wishes*, prayer to Orgyen Rinpoché
31. Tenth-day ritual of Guru Guhyasamaja
32. Offering ritual of Red Guru Drakpo (Nyang Nyima Özer)
33. Khorwa Dongtruk (Guru Chöwang)
34. Ritual to consecrate vases associated with five buddha families
35. Hayagriva activity rituals (Guru Tseten Gyaltsen)
36. Amulet to avert negativity
37. Devi Mahalakshmi
38. Danda three deity mandala
39. Shramana Devi
40. Pratisara protection amulet
41. Daily prayers and practices
42. Concise daily prayers and practices
43. Explanation of consecration ritual
44. Mahakarunika practices—Tsembupa, Bhikshuni Shri, Chandradvaja, Kyergangpa, Songtsen Gampo
45. Longevity *sadhana* (Thangtong Gyalpo)
46. Longevity empowerment (Drupchen Lekyi Dorjé)
47. Amitayus empowerment (Taklung Kagyü)
48. Sarvavid consecration ritual

49. Amulet to protect communities
50. One Hundred Teachings of Narthang (*Narthang Gyatsa*) collection
    A. Deity descriptions
    B. Individual *sadhana* and formal permission rituals
XXVIII. Eighty-Four *Mahasiddha*s   14
    1. Histories of the Eighty-Four *Mahasiddha*s
    2. Songs of the Eighty-Four *Mahasiddha*s
    3. Commentary on the songs of the Eighty-Four *Mahasiddha*s
    4. Blessing rituals for the Eighty-Four *Mahasiddha*s (Drukpa Kagyü)
    5. Formal permission rituals for the Eighty-Four *Mahasiddha*s
       (Sakya)
XXIX. *Dharmapala*s
    1. Panjara-natha (Thangtong Gyalpo)
    2. Black Brahmana-rupa-dhara Mahakala (Thangtong Gyalpo)
    3. Bhagavan Mahakala mounted on a tiger
    4. Red Danda Mahakala offering ritual
    5. Shridevi Dhumavati (Ngok)
    6. Vajraprakashit Devi
    7. Putra Mingsing (Ngor)
    8. Chitipati amulet
    9. Chitipati retreat manual
    10. Gönpo Nyingzhuk (Kyishöpa)
    11. Parvati Rajni retreat manual (Gelukpa)
    12. Parvati Rajni offering ritual
    13. Red Sokdak
    14. White Jambhala five deity prosperity ritual (Atisha)
    15. Red Jambhala prosperity ritual
    16. Prayers of dedication, aspiration, and benediction

COMPENDIUM OF ALL CLASSES OF TANTRA
(Gyüdé Kuntü)
(30-volume Dergé edition published in Delhi: N. Lungtok
and N. Gyaltsen, 1970)

VOLUME

I. Kriyatantra   1
   1. Trikula-natha (Manjushri, Avalokiteshvara, and Vajrapani)
   2. Shakyamuni five deity mandala (from *Trisamaya-vyuha*)
   3. Bhaisajyaguru forty-seven deity mandala
   4. Vimalarasmi six deity mandala
   5. Pancharakshadevi fifty-six deity mandala
   6. Grahamatrika Mahavidya fourteen deity mandala
   7. Sitatapatra seventeen deity mandala
   8. Sitatapatra twenty-seven deity mandala
   9. Vimaloshnisha five deity mandala   2
   10. Amitayus

      A. Amitayus nine deity mandala (Acharya Jetari)
      B. Dundubhisvara Amitayus five deity mandala
   11. Dundubhisvara Amitayus seventeen deity mandala
   12. Amogapasha basic sixteen deity mandala
   13. Eleven-faced Avalokiteshvara thirty-seven deity mandala
       (Nagarjuna)
   14. Vajra Akshobhya nine deity mandala
   15. Nirmanakaya Akshobhya nine deity mandala (Atisha)
   16. White Vajravidarana nineteen deity mandala (Acharya Sawari)
   17. Wrathful Black Vajravidarana ninety-seven and ninety-nine deity
       mandalas (Nur)
   18. Blue Vajravidarana fifteen deity mandala (Drukpa Kagyü)
II. Charyatantras   3
    1. Abhisambodhi-karunodgata Vairochana one hundred and
       twenty-two deity mandala
    2. Manjushri Arapachana five deity mandala
    3. Supplemental rituals for the "Two Vimala" mandalas
III. Yogatantras   4
     1. Vajradhatu one thousand and thirty-seven deity mandala
     2. Trailokya-vijaya one thousand and thirty-seven deity mandala

3. Chakrasamvara sixty-two deity mandala (Luhipa)   11
4. Chakrasamvara sixty-two deity mandala (Krishnacharin)
5. Chakrasamvara five deity mandala (Ghantapada)
6. Chakrasamvara inner body mandala (Ghantapada)   12
7. Chakrasamvara thirteen deity mandala (Maitripada)
8. Chakrasamvara five deity mandala (Karma Kagyü)
9. Vajravarahi five deity mandala (Karma Kagyü)
10. Vajrayogini thirty-seven deity mandala (Ra Lotsawa)
11. Vajrayogini Naro Khechari mandala
12. Chakrasamvara sixty-two deity mandala (Vajrapani)   13
13. Chakrasamvara sixty-two deity mandala (Abhayakaragupta)
14. Chakrasamvara thirteen deity mandala (from *Mahasamvarodaya
    Tantra*)
15. Chakrasamvara sixty-two deity mandala (from *Vajradaka Tantra*)
16. Dhutaguna Chakrasamvara thirteen deity mandala (Acharya
    Kambalapada)
17. Shatchakravarti Chakrasamvara seventy-one deity mandala
    (from *Abhidhana*)
18. Manjuvajra Vagishvara Chakrasamvara twenty-five deity mandala
    (from *Abhidhanottara*)   14
19. Kharamukha Chakrasamvara thirty-seven deity mandala
20. Lakshabhuja Raudra Chakrasamvara sixty-two deity mandala
    (from *Abhidhanottara*)
21. Vajrasattva Krodha Chakrasamvara fifty-one deity mandala
    (from *Abhidhanottara*)
22. *Dakarnava-mahayogini-tantra* fifteen-hundred deity mandala
23. Vajravarahi seventeen deity mandala (Abhayakirti)   15
24. Mahavarahmukhi thirty-seven deity mandala
    (from *Dakarnava-mahayogini-tantra*)
25. Varahi nineteen- and twenty-one deity mandala (Shantigupta)
26. Samyak Heruka nine deity mandala (Sakya Khön)
27. Buddhakapala thirty-five deity mandala (Ngok)
28. Mahamaya five deity mandala (Ngok)
29. Catuhpitha ninety-seven and seventy-seven deity mandalas (Ngok)
30. Catuhpitha thirteen deity mandala (Ngok)
31. Mahakarunika Jinasagara nine deity mandala (Karma Kagyü)   16
32. Mahakarunika Jinasagara five deity mandala (Mitrayogi)

Mahakala